ARTHUR MILLER

ARTHUR MILLER

COLLECTED PLAYS 1987–2004
WITH STAGE AND RADIO PLAYS
OF THE 1930s & 40s

Tony Kushner, *editor*

THE LIBRARY OF AMERICA

The following are published by arrangement with Viking, a member of
Penguin Group (USA), LLC, a division of Penguin Random House
Company: *The Ride Down Mt. Morgan* copyright © 1991, 1999 by Arthur
Miller and Inge Morath as Trustee. *The Last Yankee* copyright © 1993 by
Arthur Miller and Inge Morath as Trustee. *Broken Glass* copyright © 1994 by
Arthur Miller and Inge Morath as Trustee, © 2009 by The Arthur Miller
2004 Literary and Dramatic Property Trust. *Mr. Peters' Connections* copyright
© 1999, 2000 by Arthur Miller, © 2009 by The Arthur Miller 2004 Literary
and Dramatic Property Trust. *Resurrection Blues* copyright © 2006 by The
Arthur Miller 2004 Literary and Dramatic Property Trust.
Finishing the Picture copyright © 2009 by The Arthur Miller 2004
Literary and Dramatic Property Trust. "About Theatre Language"
copyright © 1994 by Arthur Miller. "Preface" copyright © 1999 by
Arthur Miller and Inge Morath as Trustee. All rights reserved.

The following are published by arrangement with The Arthur Miller 2004
Literary and Dramatic Property Trust: *The Golden Years* copyright © 1943,
1989 by Arthur Miller and Inge Morath as Trustee. *The Ryan Interview, or
How It Was Around Here* copyright © 1995 by Arthur Miller and Inge Morath
as Trustee. *The Grass Still Grows, The Half-Bridge, Captain Paul, Buffalo Bill
Disremembers, The Battle of the Ovens, Thunder from the Mountains, Glider
Doctor, Mare Island and Back* copyright © 2015 by The Arthur Miller 2004
Literary and Dramatic Property Trust. All rights reserved.

The following are published by arrangement with Grove Atlantic, Inc.:
I Can't Remember Anything copyright © 1986 by Arthur Miller. *Clara*
copyright © 1986 by Arthur Miller. *Almost Everybody Wins* copyright © 1995
by Arthur Miller and Inge Morath as Trustee. "On Screenwriting and
Language" copyright © 1990 by Arthur Miller. "Author's Note" copyright
© 1995 by Arthur Miller and Inge Morath as Trustee. All rights reserved.

This paper meets the requirements of
ANSI/NISO z39.48–1992 (Permanence of Paper).

Distributed to the trade in the United States
by Penguin Random House Inc.
and in Canada by Penguin Random House Canada Ltd.

Library of Congress Control Number: 2014946641
ISBN 978–1–59853–353–8

First Printing
The Library of America—261

Manufactured in the United States of America

Contents

DANGER: MEMORY!

I CAN'T REMEMBER
ANYTHING

CHARACTERS

LEO
LEONORA

The time is now.

LEO'*s living room–kitchen in a nondescript little wooden house on a country back road. A woodburning stove near a handmade plywood dining and drawing table; some canvas folding chairs, one of them repaired with needle and thread; a wicker chair; a couple of short benches; a well-worn modern chair and a lumpy couch—in short, a bachelor's heaven. A couple of fine, dusty landscapes on one wall as well as tacked-up photos and a few drunken line drawings of dead friends.*

At the big table LEO *is carefully lettering with a marker pen on a piece of cardboard, a newspaper open at his elbow. There are a few patches on his denim shirt and his pants are almost nothing but patches. They are his resistance to commercialism in the last quarter of the twentieth century. He has a stubborn little face.*

LEONORA *enters through the front door; she is a large woman who opens her long, many-colored woolen shawl and shakes it out as she sits in a chair not far from him, giving a little cough and swallowing a few times and catching her breath. Now she turns to him. Her speech is New England with a European aristocratic coloration of which, however, she is not aware.*

LEONORA: Well. You might at least look up.
LEO: I saw you.
LEONORA: Well, that's a greeting, isn't it. "I saw you."
LEO: I've got chicken again.
LEONORA: I don't care, everything tastes the same to me anyway. May I have my colored water?
LEO: It's over there.
LEONORA: Thank you. (*She goes, pours some bourbon, holds up the glass, adds a bit more.*)
LEO: You always have to pour it twice.

3

LEONORA: Because I have to see whether it's enough or too much.

LEO: But it's never too much, it's always too little.

LEONORA (*taking a pitcher and holding it in her hand*): May I have some water?

LEO: There's some in there.

LEONORA: I see that. May I have it?

LEO: You certainly may. (*Finishes his drawing, inspects it, sets it aside. Takes a pencil and starts on a crossword puzzle.*) I see you bashed in your new car.

LEONORA: It's what I said the last time; they are placing these light poles too close to the road.

LEO: The light poles are the same distance they have always been.

LEONORA: Well, they're not, but there's no use arguing about it.

LEO: Maybe you ought to forget about driving under certain conditions.

LEONORA (*sits some distance from him, facing front*): There's simply no use talking to you.

LEO: Not about the distance of light poles to the road there isn't.

LEONORA (*takes a thin package out of her enormous bag*): I got this in the mail this morning; it's from Lawrence.

LEO: It might be one thing if you could be sure to kill yourself. But you're liable to end up crippled or blind or killing somebody else, then what?

LEONORA: Oh, what's the use? (*Sips; a deep relaxing sigh, then . . .*)

LEO: Where is Lawrence?

LEONORA (*glancing at the package*): In Sri Lanka, apparently.

LEO: Is he still in that monastery or whatever the hell it is?

LEONORA: It's not a monastery, it's one of those retreats, I think.—But I can never finish reading one of his letters. He just goes on and on and on until I fall asleep. Do you have a knife?

LEO: On the table.

(*She gets up, goes to table, picks up knife, starts cutting package open, indicates whiskey bottle.*)

LEONORA: You know you're almost out.

LEO: I know, but I couldn't get to town today. Isn't there enough for you?

LEONORA: What about you?

LEO: I haven't touched whiskey in at least a year, since I got my arthritis. Haven't you noticed?

LEONORA: I was just trying to be polite.

LEO: That bottle was full day before yesterday . . . just to remind you.

LEONORA: You've had guests?

LEO (*pointedly*): No, just you.

LEONORA: Well, what's the difference?

LEO: By the way, if you come in here one night and I'm dead, I want you to call Yale–New Haven Hospital and not this . . . whatever you call him . . . mortician what's-his-name in town.

LEONORA: What good is a hospital if you're dead, for God's sake?

LEO: I just finished making arrangements for them to take my organs.

LEONORA: Really!

LEO: For research. So call Yale–New Haven. This mortician here used to have a Nixon bumper sticker.

LEONORA: What do they expect to find from *your* organs?

LEO: Why?—My organs aren't good enough?

LEONORA: But I should imagine they would want people with some interesting disease. All you've got is arthritis. Aside from that, you'll probably die in perfect health.

LEO: Well, I might get something.

LEONORA: Where, for heaven's sake? You never go anywhere but the post office or the grocery store.

LEO: I go to the gas station.

LEONORA: The gas station! What do you expect to pick up at the gas station?

LEO: I don't know. Gas disease.

LEONORA (*laughing*): Gas disease!

LEO: This is another one of those conversations.

LEONORA: Well, I certainly didn't start it.

LEO (*showing her his newly drawn sign in block letters*): This is Yale–New Haven, see? I'm going to tack this number over the phone.

LEONORA: But I'll certainly be dead before you.

LEO: In case you're not dead and you walk in and there I am with my eyes crossed and my tongue hanging out.

LEONORA (*grimacing*): Oh, stop that, for God's sake.

LEO: Well, that's how you look when you have a stroke. (*Returns to his newspaper. Pause.*)

LEONORA: There's nothing in the paper, is there?

LEO: Yes, a few things.

LEONORA: Well, don't tell it to me, it's all too horrible.

LEO: I wasn't going to tell it to you. (*Pause.*) You want rice?

LEONORA: I hate rice.

(*He returns to his paper.*)

Why are you being so difficult, Leo?

LEO: Me? I'm the one who invited you to have rice, for Christ's sake.

LEONORA: I can't for the life of me figure out why I haven't died.

LEO: Well, maybe it'll come to you.

LEONORA: I used to believe, as a girl—I mean, we were taught to believe—that everything has its purpose. You know what I'm referring to.

LEO: My mother was the only atheist in Youngstown, Ohio; she never talked about things having purposes.

LEONORA: Well, in New England you tended to believe those things!—But what purpose have I got? I am totally useless, to myself, my children, my grandchildren, and the one or two people I suppose I can call my friends who aren't dead . . .

LEO: Then why don't you stop being useless?

LEONORA: How can I stop being useless, for God's sake? If a person is useless, she is *useless*.

LEO: Then do something.—Why don't you take up the piano again?

LEONORA: The piano!

LEO: Oh, come on now, for Christ's sake, you used to play Mozart and Chopin and all that stuff. You can't tell me you don't remember playing the piano, Leonora.

LEONORA (*without admission or denial*): I don't know where I'd ever begin a thing like that.

LEO: Well, the accordion, then.

LEONORA: *What?* I certainly never in my life played the *accordion*.

LEO: Except with thirty or forty people dancing on the grass, and everybody pissed to the gills, and Frederick banging on a soup pot, and a big salami tied between his legs.

LEONORA: Really? (*A sudden laugh.*) A salami?

LEO: Sure, and a pair of oranges. Waving it around at the women.

LEONORA (*stares*): Sometimes . . . I *think* I remember something, but then I wonder if I just imagined it. My whole life often seems imaginary. It's very strange.

LEO: I know something you could kill time with.

LEONORA: There is nothing. I don't even have the concentration to read anymore. Sometimes I wonder if *I'm* imaginary.

LEO: Why don't you try to get people to donate their organs to Yale–New Haven? You could just sit at home with the phone book and make calls.

LEONORA: You mean I'm to telephone perfect strangers and ask them for their organs?

LEO: Well, it's important; they really need organs.

LEONORA: Where do you *get* these ideas?

LEO: I tell you, I just wish I had your health.

LEONORA: Something's burning.

LEO: Christ, it's the rice! (*Struggles to get up.*)

LEONORA: May I . . . ?

LEO (*waving at her*): Yes! Take it off the stove!
(*She hurries to a point, returns with a pot into which she is looking.*)

LEONORA: It looks terrible. You can't eat this.

LEO: Well, I was just using it up. I have salad, it'll be enough.

LEONORA: You only have one plate out.

LEO: Oh? I must have got distracted. I think somebody phoned when I was setting the table.—Who the hell was that, now . . . ?

LEONORA: Perhaps you don't want me to dinner.

LEO: Oh, get a plate, will you? They're right up there in the cabinet.

LEONORA: Good heavens, after all these years I know where the plates are. (*She goes, brings down a plate, knife and fork, and napkin.*)

LEO: I'm having some bread; *you* don't want any, though.

LEONORA: Bread! I haven't eaten bread in a decade.

LEO: You ate some last week . . . that that girl brought me from the nature store.

LEONORA (*stops moving*): I can't remember anything.

LEO: Well, you did. You ate three slices.

LEONORA: I can't have eaten three slices of *bread*.

LEO: You did, though.

LEONORA: I simply cannot remember anything at all.

> (*They are seated at their plates facing each other, and he has served the chicken and they eat. He picks up his pencil and enters a word in the puzzle as he eats.*)

Oh! Do you mean that young girl with the braids?

LEO (*preoccupied*): Uh-huh.

LEONORA: The one with the lisp.—She's quite pretty.

LEO: Oh, she's some doll.

LEONORA: "Doll!"—I will never understand your attraction for these women when you really don't like women at all.

LEO: I like women. I just don't like dumb women.

LEONORA: Oh, is she clever?

LEO: She's writing a master's thesis on Recurrence. That's a mathematical principle.

LEONORA (*doesn't know what to say*): Well!

LEO: Yes. But you couldn't understand anything like that.— You can talk to that girl about something.

LEONORA: I don't recall you being so intellectually particular in the old days.

LEO: I used to drink more in the old days.

LEONORA: Oh, I see; and now that you can't drink you discuss mathematics.

LEO: Who was the President of France when the War started?

LEONORA: Good God, how should I know?

LEO: Well, you were living there then, weren't you?

LEONORA: Yes, but nobody *ever* knows who the President of France is.

LEO: Well, you wouldn't have known anyway.

LEONORA (*slamming her fork down*): I would certainly have known if it was of any importance.

LEO: No you wouldn't.

LEONORA (*throws her napkin straight at him, speechless with anger. Pause. He goes on with the crossword*): May I have my napkin?

LEO (*returning the napkin to her*): I think it begins with a P.

LEONORA: I hate crossword puzzles. They do nothing but add triviality to the boredom of existence.—"President of France"! Before the War no one *cared* who the President was. It's not like being the President of the United States.

LEO: Everybody knows that, for Christ's sake.

LEONORA: You don't. You don't know anything about France.

LEO: Could it be Poincaire?

LEONORA: "Pwancare"! It's Poincaré.

LEO: Well, Pwancaray.

LEONORA: I believe Poincaré was Prime Minister at some point, but not President. Why do you ask me questions like that? I can't remember anything political. (*Making a face.*) Will they take out your brain too?

LEO: I guess so. For sweetbreads.

LEONORA (*screwing up her face*): Why do you *say* things like that!

LEO: And my liver with onions.

(*She laughs painfully, and then they both eat in silence.*)

LEONORA: This is really quite good. Is that thyme?

LEO: Rosemary.

LEONORA: I mean rosemary. God, I simply can't keep anything straight.

LEO: You used to use a lot of rosemary.

LEONORA: Did I?

LEO: On gigot. You had a wonderful touch with any kind of lamb, you always had it nice and pink, with just enough well-done at the ends; and the best bread I think I ever ate.

LEONORA: Really!

LEO: You don't remember Frederick holding the bread to his chest, and that way he had of pulling the knife across it, and handing it out piece by piece to people at the table?

(*Slight pause.*)

LEONORA: Well, what difference does it make?

LEO: I don't know, it's just a damn shame to forget all that. Your lamb always had absolutely clear pink juice, like rosé wine. And the way you did the string beans, just exactly medium hard. Those were some great dinners.

LEONORA: Were they?

LEO: Yes.

LEONORA: Well, I'm glad you enjoyed them. To me—when I do think of anything like that—it's like some page in a book I once read. Don't you often forget what you've read in a book? What earthly difference does it make?

LEO: But it's not a book, it's your life, kiddo.

LEONORA: Yes, well . . . so what? Look at these millions of people starving to death all over the place, does anyone remember them? Why should I remember myself any more than I remember them?

LEO: Well, it's not the same.

LEONORA: Naturally. That's because you come from central Ohio.

LEO: What the hell's that got to do with it?

LEONORA: In central Ohio everything always turns out for the best.

LEO: Youngstown doesn't, for your information, happen to be in central Ohio.

LEONORA: Well, it might as well be.

LEO: Well, I have work to do tonight.

LEONORA: I won't stay, I'll just sit here for a bit and look out the window. Is that all right?

LEO: Sure. (*Gets with difficulty to his feet, picks up plates . . .*)

LEONORA: Here, let me . . .

LEO (*a command*): I'll do it! (*He shuffles to the sink as she sits staring front.*) What'd Lawrence send?

LEONORA: Oh! (*She had forgotten and reaches to the table and the package, from which she takes a record.*)

LEO: Another record? Oh, Christ.

LEONORA (*uncertain*): He never sent me a record before.

LEO: Sure he did, about three years ago, that goddam Indian music, it was horrible.

LEONORA: Yes, I remember now . . . It was wonderful for a certain mood.

LEO: Sounded like a bunch of cats locked in a toilet.

LEONORA: What do you know about music, for heaven's sake? (*She finds a note with the record.*) I don't have my glasses. (*Hands him the note.*)

LEO (*reads*): "Dear Mother. This one is quite different. Let me know how you like it. My group has been invited to play in New Delhi, isn't that terrific? Love, Lawrence."

LEONORA: Well!—That's short and sweet, isn't it? After three years, did you say?

LEO: Wait, there's a P.S. "P.S. Moira and I have decided to separate, you'll be glad to hear."

LEONORA: Moira? Who is Moira? (*She stares ahead tensely, struggling to remember.*)

LEO: Sounds like somebody he married.

(*He hands back the note. Her eyes moisten with tears which she blinks away, looking at the record.*)

I hope you're not going to play that here.

LEONORA (*an outcry*): I have no intention of playing it here . . . or anywhere, since my machine has been broken for at least five or six years!—When did it all begin getting so vile, do you know?

(*He sits at table again and picks up a pencil, poring over some diagrams.*)

Are you working at something?

LEO: I promised my friend Bokum I would check out some of his calculations that he made for the new bridge in town.

LEONORA: I didn't even know there was an *old* bridge.

LEO: Across the river; you drive over it half a dozen times a week.

LEONORA: Oh, that one!—Strange, I never think of that as a bridge.

LEO: What do you think of it as?

LEONORA: I don't know . . . just the road. Are you going to rebuild it?

LEO: I'm not doing anything, just checking out Bokum's numbers. (*Opening a file folder.*) But everything keeps slipping out of my head. I could do this stuff in twenty minutes and now I can't calculate worth a damn.

LEONORA: Well, now you know what I mean . . .

LEO: That was one thing I admired about Frederick, he never once slowed down mentally.

LEONORA: Didn't he?

LEO: For Christ's sake, you remember whether he slowed down mentally, don't you?

LEONORA: Well, I'm sorry if it irritates you!

LEO: It doesn't "irritate" me, I just don't think you ought to be forgetting that, that's all.—The man was sharp as a tack to his last minute!

LEONORA: You know, I could criticize you too, if I wished to.

LEO: Well, go ahead!

LEONORA: I wouldn't bother. (*Pause.*) By the way, I am never going back to your dentist.

LEO: Neither am I. I'm sorry I recommended him.

LEONORA: What gets into you? You are forever sending me to doctors and dentists who are completely incompetent. That man nearly killed me with his drill. Why do you do that?

LEO: I don't know, he seemed okay for a while there.

LEONORA: It was the same thing with that awful plumber. And that idiotic man who fixed the roof and left me in a downpour. I think there's something the matter with you; you get these infatuations with an individual and just when you've got everybody going to them you stop going.

LEO: He just seemed like a nice guy; I don't know.

LEONORA: He seriously wanted to pull out all my teeth.

LEO: Did he? Son of a bitch.

LEONORA: Well, he actually pulled all yours, didn't he? (*She silently swallows a drink.*)

LEO: Well . . . not *all*.

LEONORA: But all the front ones.

LEO: He didn't like my gums.

LEONORA: And you allowed him to pull out all your front teeth?

LEO (*defensively angry*): Well, he seemed okay! I liked him!

LEONORA: Yes, you certainly did. (*She looks at her glass.*) May I have another?

(*He nods, studying his puzzle. She goes and pours.*)

All it is is a little color for conviviality. (*She returns to her chair, sits.*) I saw the most beautiful young deer today. Near the waterfall, so she couldn't hear me until my car was right next to her. She turned to me and there was such a look of surprise! I felt ashamed. Imagine how frightening we must be to them! And how we must stink, when they feed on nothing but grass and green things. And we full of dead chickens and rotting cow meat . . .

(*She drinks. He does his puzzle.*)

LEO: You know it's Frederick's birthday tomorrow.

LEONORA (*with a faint guilt in her eye*): Tomorrow?

(*He gives her an impatient, nearly angry look.*)

Why do you look at me like that? I simply didn't think of it. (*With defiance.*) I never think of anything. I just drive around the countryside and look at the trees, I don't see what's wrong with that. I love the trees; they are strong and proud and they live a long time, and I love them very much. (*She is filling up, takes a breath to suppress her feelings.*) Everything is so awful, Leo; really and truly this is not the same country.

LEO: You don't have to convince me. I've been a Communist all my life and I still am, I don't care what they say.

LEONORA: I believe you really are, aren't you?—And why not?—You've always given everything you have away. It's your finest trait. But I think . . . were we in Russia once . . . ?

LEO: Sure you were, about twenty years ago . . .

LEONORA: All I remember is that it was all perfectly dreadful.

LEO: Well, you were rich.

LEONORA: Oh, by the way . . . (*Digging into her large bag, brings out a large handful of unopened envelopes and lays them on the table before him.*) The lawyers say I ought to give away a lot more, would you look at these? I've been meaning to bring them all week.

LEO: Jesus!—They've really got your name down. But I don't know anything about these organizations. Christ, here's the Baptist Mission to Pakistan.

LEONORA: Good God!—There's something there for African Relief, isn't there?

LEO: You sent them something last time, didn't you?

LEONORA: But there are so many of those children. Would five thousand seem too much? I'd like it to matter.

LEO: If that's what you want, go ahead.

LEONORA: Except that I read that some of the money never gets there; it's stolen, they say.

LEO: I don't know what to tell you.

LEONORA: How terrible it is . . . In the old days I never once thought of someone stealing money we donated to . . . like the Spanish Republicans, for instance. Did you?

LEO: Well, people believed in something those days.

LEONORA: But what do they have to *believe*?—It's just common decency. Or is that a stupid thing to say? Tell me honestly—wasn't there something more precious about human life before . . . let's say . . . before the War?

LEO: Maybe. Although not in Ohio. I mean my father died drunk in the entrance of a coal mine—the other guys just forgot he was in there and they come back next morning and he'd froze to death, just croaked.

LEONORA: Why do you use that *language*?

LEO: It'll be dark in a few minutes, you're going to have to drive that car.

LEONORA: I'm perfectly fine. May I have what's left?

LEO: Well . . . if that's what you want, sure.

(*He watches her, not approvingly, as she pours the whiskey and water.*)

LEONORA (*sitting*): Have you ever seen that raccoon again?

LEO: Which raccoon?

LEONORA: The one who stole your hamburgers off the outdoor griddle.

LEO (*laughs*): Oh, him! Yeah, he comes by occasionally.— Although not for a couple of weeks now.

LEONORA: I will never forget your description of how he tossed the hot hamburger from one paw to another to cool it off.

LEO (*chuckling*): Oh, yeah . . .

(*Mimes tossing a hot hamburger from hand to hand. She guffaws.*)

LEONORA (*through her laughter*): And how did you describe him?—Like a chef in a fur coat?

LEO: Well, he looked . . . kind of annoyed, y'know? Like a French chef. Haven't seen him around for quite a while, though. Probably got shot by now.

(*Pause. She sips, staring out the window.*)

LEONORA: Why don't they leave those poor animals alone?

LEO: Well, for one thing, the deer are ruining the apple trees.

LEONORA: Well, maybe that is what they're supposed to be doing. Would you like to be shot because you ate something?

(*He works his crossword puzzle. She sips, stares out the window.*)

LEO: It's your birthday too, of course.

(*She glances at him. He returns to his puzzle.*)

Happy birthday.

(*She stares front, a certain distress in her eyes.*)

I guess there's no reason not to tell you . . . I still miss him. He was the greatest man I ever met in my life.

LEONORA: Was he?

LEO: Yes, he was. It's over ten years and I don't think a day goes by that I don't hear his laugh or that nasal voice. God, he had common sense.

LEONORA (*after a long sip, and an inhale*): He shouldn't have died first, Leo.

LEO: I know. (*Pause.*) Listen: just in case you come in here some night and find me dead, I think he'd have wanted you to . . . live. I'm sure of that, kiddo. (*Pause.*)

LEONORA: We were married just a month over forty-five years; that's a very long time, Leo.

LEO: But even so . . .

LEONORA: One can't just skip off and start over again.

LEO: You're twelve years older than me and you've got more life in you than I have. Chrissake, you hardly look sixty-five, if that; you might have ten years to go yet . . .

LEONORA: Oh, God help me.

LEO: How about taking a trip somewhere, maybe find somebody to go along with you?

LEONORA: Everybody is dead, don't you realize that? Everybody except you.

LEO: It doesn't seem possible . . . All those hundreds of people that used to be at your parties . . . Three days later there'd still be people sleeping it off in the flower beds or out in the cars.

LEONORA: All dead.

LEO: Well, they can't *all* be . . .

LEONORA: . . . For God's sake, Leo, the last party must have been at least fifteen years ago! There's something the matter with you. You are not growing old, or something.

LEO: How about Asia? You've never been to Asia.

LEONORA: You're getting worse than I am. When Frederick did that Ganges bridge, and we were six months with the Maharajah . . . ?

LEO: Maybe you could visit him?

LEONORA: Good heavens, he was nearly seventy twenty years ago . . . Anyway, I hated it there; all that bowing and scraping, and those poor elephants. And everyone telling you nothing but lies.—And besides, those people were Frederick's friends, not mine. All our friends were.

LEO: Even so, Frederick was absolutely nuts about you, Leonora, you can't ever forget that.

LEONORA: Of course. I'm not talking about *that*. (*Pause. A smile grows on her face.*) The very first time we met . . .

LEO: . . . On a train, wasn't it?

LEONORA: Of course . . . to California for one of his bridges there. And he found my mother alone in the dining car and said, "Your daughter has the finest backside I have ever seen."

LEO: Ha! She wasn't scandalized?

LEONORA: Why? It's a complimentary thing to say, isn't it? Besides, she was still headmistress of the Boston College for Women.

LEO: So?

LEONORA: Well, she had plenty of means of comparison. (*Laughs her high, hawking laugh.*)

LEO: See now?—You remembered all that.

LEONORA (*a tension rises in her, which she suppresses*): Well, that was so long ago it hardly matters. (*Nearly blushing.*) I want to ask you something personal, may I?

(*He turns to her, waiting.*)

Well, may I?

LEO: What?

LEONORA: Why do you pretend that you aren't discouraged?

LEO (*surprised by this*): . . . Well, I'm not as down on everything as *you* are, but . . .

LEONORA (*her anxiety intensifying*): But why can't you just admit that it's all nothing? You *know* it's nothing, Leo.

LEO (*stalling*): What's nothing?

LEONORA: Why, our lives, the whole damned thing.—That's what is so irritating, you simply refuse to . . . to . . . (*A new idea.*) I mean you go on and on reading that stupid newspaper with the same vileness every day, the same brutality, the same lies . . .

LEO: Well, I like to know what's happening.

LEONORA: But nothing is "happening"! Excepting that it keeps getting worse and more brutal and more vile . . .

LEO: What the hell are you getting so angry about if I read a newspaper?

LEONORA: Because after thirty or forty or whatever goddamned awful number of years it is, you are still a sort of *strangeness* to me. I ought to know you by now, oughtn't I? Well, I don't. I don't know you, Leo!

(*He is mystified but impressed with the depth of her feeling, and wondering what she is trying to say to him. He watches her profile.*)

LEO: Well, what would you like to know?

LEONORA: Every evening I feel this same condescension from you, when you know perfectly well that it is all continually getting worse.

LEO: Listen, I'm depressed too . . .

LEONORA: No, you are not depressed, you just try to *sound* depressed. But in the back of your mind you are still secretly expecting heaven-knows-what incredible improvement just over the horizon.

LEO: I still don't understand what you're trying to . . .

LEONORA: This country is being ruined by greed and mendacity and narrow-minded ignorance, and you go right on thinking there is hope somewhere. And yet you really don't, do you?—but you refuse to admit that you have lost your hope. That's exactly right, yes—it's this goddamned hopefulness when there is no hope—that is why you are so frustrating to sit with!

LEO (*he lets her steam for a minute*): The trouble is you don't understand science.

LEONORA: Science! I am asking you for your truthful opinion about your *life*! What has that to do with science, for God's sake?

LEO: Well, I don't think I'm as important as *you* think *you* are.

LEONORA (*caught by a suggestion now*): Ah. That's interesting.

LEO: I never accomplished anything much except . . .

LEONORA: Why?—You helped Frederick immensely for . . . more than twenty years, wasn't it? And before that you taught so many students . . .

LEO: Well, the thing is, I figure I've done what I could do, more or less, and now I'm going back to being a chemical; all we are is a lot of talking nitrogen, you know . . .

LEONORA (*outraged, and laughing*): Talking nitrogen!

LEO: And phosphorus and some other elements . . . about two dollars' worth if you discount inflation. So if you're wondering why you're alive . . . maybe it's because you *are*, that's all, and that's the whole goddam reason. Maybe you're so nervous because you keep looking for some other reason and there isn't any. (*Pause.*)

LEONORA: It's not that, Leo.

LEO: I know.

LEONORA: What do you know?

LEO: Frederick was your life, and now there's nothing.

LEONORA (*with a wild, furious grin*): So if I told you how unimportant I think I am, I might disappear in thin air, like a speck of dust on the nose of a mouse.

LEO: Okay, well . . . I've got to work.

LEONORA: I don't even remember why we started talking about this.

LEO: That's better than me—I don't even remember what we were talking about.

LEONORA (*laughs, throwing her head back, deep prolonged laughter filled with pain*): . . . Oh, dear, dear . . .

LEO: I've got to get this done. (*He bends over his papers.*)

LEONORA (*looking at the record in her hand*): Could I play just one minute of it? My machine's really broken.

LEO: Okay, a minute, but that's all.

LEONORA (*puts record on the turntable*): Am I wrong? Didn't you and I dance once?

LEO: Once?

LEONORA: More?

LEO (*shaking his head as though all they did was dance*): Phew!—Okay, forget it.

LEONORA: Oh, of course!

LEO: Christ, there must have been a couple hundred nights when I'd come over and just the three of us would play records, and Frederick and I would take turns dancing with you 'cause you'd never get tired . . . and drink a dozen bottles of wine . . . and he had that fantastic French corkscrew . . .

LEONORA (*as she lowers the tone arm on the record . . .*): I think I still have that corkscrew . . .

    (*Music: A samba beat, but with wild, lacy arpeggios and a driving underbeat.*)

LEO (*They both listen for a moment. He is pleasantly surprised*): Chrissake, that's nothing but a samba.

(*She listens.*)

Isn't it? (*He moves his shoulders to the beat.*) Sure, it's just a plain old-fashion' samba.

(*She begins to move to it. She is remarkably nimble, taking little expert steps . . . and her sensuality provokes and embarrasses him, making him laugh tightly . . .*)

You dancing, for Christ's sake?

(*She lets herself into the dance fully now, and he lets his laughter flower, and, laughing, he struggles to his feet and, unable to move more than an inch at a time, he swings his shoulders instead, clapping his gnarled hands. And she faces him tauntingly, reddening with shyness and her flaunting emotions; one moment bent over and backing nearly into him, the next, thumbing her nose at him, and as the music explodes to its crescendo she falls into a chair, breathless, and he collapses into another and they both sit there laughing, trying to breathe. The music ends.*)

LEO: Well, that's sure as hell not Indian music. Maybe he decided to stop wasting his time and start playing human music.

LEONORA: He does what is in him to do. Just like you. And everyone else. Until it all comes to an end. . . . Well, thank you for dinner . . .

(*She stands, a bit unsteadily; he turns back to his calculating.*)

Shall I come by for breakfast?

(*He doesn't reply, staring at the paper.*)

Is something wrong?

LEO: I just can't calculate. Phew, this is the worst yet. I used to be able to do these logarithms a-b-c and now . . . it all keeps getting stuck. (*Struggling to his feet.*) I think I'll go to bed and get up early. Stay and watch the tube if you like.

LEONORA (*still a bit breathless, throwing her shawl over her shoulders*): Good night, Leo.

LEO: Maybe stay.

LEONORA: Don't be silly, I only have to drive a few hundred yards.

LEO: Well, suit yourself. Be sure you turn your headlights on, it's pitch out there. I don't think there's a moon.

LEONORA: Isn't that the moon?

LEO: That's my outside lamp, for Christ's sake. Listen, maybe better stay here, but I've got to go to sleep and get up with a clear head; I promised Bokum I'd have it tomorrow.

LEONORA: No-no, I'm going.

LEO: Then go, will you? Good night.

LEONORA: Thanks for remembering . . . our birthday. (*She starts for the door.*)

LEO: Leonora?

　(*She halts.*)

We could have a lot more interesting conversations if you'd stop saying you can't remember anything.

LEONORA: Or if you could occasionally learn to accept bad news?

LEO (*waving her off, going toward his bedroom*): Call me when you get home.

LEONORA: It doesn't matter. Good night.

　(*He shuffles out as she goes to the door. Once he is gone, she halts. Then goes back to the table and picks up the cardboard sign he had printed with the hospital's number and holds it at arm's length to read it. Puts it down, staring at the air, then goes out. He reappears, shirt off, suspenders hanging down, his nightgown trailing from his hand. Goes to the door and opens it as a motor starts. Headlights cross the window and flash upon him in the doorway and vanish as the car speeds up the road. He leans far out the doorway to watch it going away.*

　He closes the door, slips the nightgown over his head, sits down painfully, manages to get out of his trousers, then stands and goes to the phone, addressing it.)

LEO: Well, come on, will you?—I've got to go to sleep!

　(*Phone remaining silent, he goes to table, takes the cardboard sign and with a couple of pushpins fastens it to the wall over the phone. It reads, "Yale–N. Haven 771-8515." The phone rings.*)

LEO (*into phone*): Okay. Yeah, good night, good night. (*Hangs up and, shuffling to his bedroom, with his pants trailing from his hand, he shakes his head . . .*) Jesus . . . !

CURTAIN

DANGER: MEMORY!

CLARA

CHARACTERS

Clara Kroll
Albert Kroll
Detective Lieutenant Fine
Tierney

Living room of CLARA KROLL*'s apartment-office. All the action is confined to a small lighted area downstage. Beyond it are suggestions of the room, which in a few feet are swiftly lost in the surrounding darkness.*

A couple of MEN *are heard quietly talking in what is probably an adjoining room, then silence.*

A MAN *is lying on the floor with one arm resting over his eyes. He is in a suit and topcoat and his overturned hat lies nearby. He is* ALBERT KROLL.

DETECTIVE LIEUTENANT FINE *enters from the darkness carrying a file drawer, which he sets on a small table beside a chair, and sits.*

The reflection of a camera flash illuminates the darkness for a second.

Once settled in his chair, FINE *glances down at* KROLL, *then pulls a folder from the file and opens it, removing letter after letter, which he quickly scans. Again little bursts of quiet conversation from the adjoining room, and silence.*

A loud saxophone—John Coltrane—splits the air. FINE *turns in his chair and shouts upstage.*

FINE: Hey! Who's doing that! Shut that off! (*Record stops.*) Tierney? Is that you?
> (*Out of the darkness upstage,* TIERNEY, *a young cop, enters, record envelopes under his arm.*)
TIERNEY: Sorry, Lieutenant. I happened to touch the button on the turntable.
FINE: I want Douglas to dust that record for prints, they may have been playing it.

23

TIERNEY: It's okay, I didn't touch the record.—She must have been in the Peace Corps, there's a citation on her office wall.

FINE (*returning to the file*): I know.

TIERNEY (*starting upstage*): By the way, who's going to feed the budgie in the kitchen?

(FINE *looks up at him.*)

That bird in the cage.

FINE: You want it?

TIERNEY: I mean it's going to die.

FINE: It's okay, steal it.

(TIERNEY *turns to leave.*)

But nobody has to feed those phonograph records.

(*A flashbulb in the dimness far upstage.*)

TIERNEY: I'm lookin', that's all . . . She had quite a collection here.

FINE: Right.

(TIERNEY *exits.* FINE *scans letter after letter. It is not getting him anywhere. He sits back in the chair, staring ahead.* KROLL *moves his arm.* FINE *turns, looks down at him.*)

How are you coming, Mr. Kroll?

(KROLL *is silent.*)

You hearing me now?

(KROLL *manages to get up on his elbows.*)

Feeling any better?

(EFFECT: *Upstage in darkness an exploding flash illuminates for a subliminal instant in the air over the two men a color photo of the bloodied body of a partially stripped woman.*)

KROLL: I can't understand why I didn't think of it: she may be gone skiing somewhere.

FINE (*A pause. And with a gesture toward upstage . . .*): You've seen her, haven't you?

(*Now* KROLL *sits up completely, staring.*)

You know who I am now.

KROLL: The Lieutenant.

(EFFECT: *A color photo of a bloody, wounded hand appears overhead, lasting a millisecond or so.*)

Why am I seeing these pictures?

FINE: They're photographing the body. Polaroids.

KROLL: Ah! . . . But why would they be coming through to

me?—Oh, it's because there's no rubber in the camera, is that it?

(FINE *is silent.*)

. . . Except . . . No, that's not right. (*Confused, brows knitted, he stares for a moment.*) Well, one thing anyway—when she gets a look at these shots she'll know what I've been talking about . . . Setting up an office in a neighborhood like this. They always smell of cats.

FINE (*not urgently*): Mr. Kroll, you told me you had a look at her when you walked in, didn't you?

KROLL: That's what I'm talking about. But she has that . . . kind of dedication, you just can't budge her. (*Suddenly laughs.*) "Rubber in the camera!"—Jesus, what an idea! Boy . . . ! (*Shakes his head as he laughs and rubs his forehead.*) Don't mind me, I'll be all right.

FINE: Don't rush; shock can be funny; I've got to wait for the Medical Examiner anyway. Wouldn't you feel better in a chair?

KROLL: In a minute; I don't want heights just yet.

FINE: Take your time. (*Starts to read a letter . . .*)

KROLL: Time did you say?

FINE: One-o-five.

KROLL (*smiles*): . . . Don't you ever look at your watch?

FINE: Don't have to. You know who I am now?

KROLL: Oh, sure. Sorry I mixed you up with Bert, but you're almost the spitting image, even the way you sit with your legs crossed. And the same kind of attitude.

FINE: Well, there are only so many types, you know.

KROLL: Bert and I. I'm going back a ways now, but we were so damned close for years and years. One morning, out of the blue . . . this was after I'd been doing all his landscaping for at least ten years . . . and never a contract—a handshake and that's that. And I show up on this particular Monday morning with my crew and my tractors and he comes out and says, "What're you doing, Albert?" And I says, "We're going to start the grading . . ."—he'd put up these twenty, thirty houses, y'see . . . and he says, "I got somebody else, Albert, I'm sorry." And that was that! (*Laughs.*) Completely out of the blue! Man was practically my best friend. (*Laughs, shakes his head.*)

FINE (*after a pause*): What's the point of that story, Mr. Kroll?

KROLL: . . . I don't know, I guess I'm just talking, it's that you just can't ever let yourself rely on anything staying the way it is . . .

> (*He suddenly cries out in paroxysms of horror and clamps his hands over his eyes, and continues crying out with great heaves of breath.* FINE *does not move, watching him as gradually his cries weaken and he goes silent.*)

FINE: It's up to you, but in my experience it's generally better to talk about it. What you can't chase you'd better face or it'll start chasing you, know what I mean? I'd appreciate if we could talk right now, because whoever did this has a big headstart on me and I would like very much to catch up with him.

KROLL: I think she was robbed once before . . .

FINE: No robbery this time . . .

KROLL: No. I remember now, that's right.

FINE: There are two cups on the stove with teabags, and the kettle is melted. There was a fight but no sign of forced entry, and there's still over a hundred dollars in her pocketbook, and the TV and the rest all untouched. It was somebody she was making tea for . . . You with me?

KROLL: Huh?—Yes, making tea for.—Have I called my wife?

FINE: Not to my knowledge. Would you like me to?

KROLL: Oh, no! No, please, I'll . . . I'll do it. (*Takes a breath, looking around.*) Go ahead, I can talk. Someone she was making tea for.

FINE: You're clear about what's happened, right?

KROLL: It . . . starts to slip away now and then, but, yes, I . . .

FINE: Try to hold on to it; Clara's been attacked and murdered.

KROLL: I've no idea. (*Shaking his head.*) Funny, I was in the middle of a zoning board meeting . . . last night, I guess —yeah, last night. And I got this sudden feeling of . . . I felt lonely for her. So I called here when I got home and there was no answer. And this morning Saint Francis hadn't heard from her either.

FINE: She on the staff there? (*Stands, bends over to touch his shoes.*)

KROLL (*nods*): Not that we've been in touch that often but, you know, with this kind of a neighborhood I decided to come down . . . Bad back?

FINE (*straightening up*): Nothing, just psychosomatic. I've been trying to decide whether to retire. My body seems to be voting.

KROLL: What'll you do?

FINE: What they all do—sit looking at the ocean somewhere, wondering where my life went.—What was her idea moving into an area like this, do you know?

KROLL: Oh, it goes back a long way with her; she was hardly fifteen, sixteen when she got this job going into back alleys in Poughkeepsie all hours of the night; teaching these women how to take care of children, nutrition, so on. Just never knew what fear was.

FINE: I notice there's only one lock on the door.

KROLL: I'm surprised there's that one! Even as a child, this great big dog came charging down the street, snarling, snapping, people running into their houses, they thought he was rabid maybe, and there's Clara playing in the front yard with her doll and just holds out her hand . . . (*he holds out his hand*) . . . and that dog stopped in his tracks, quieted right down and just sat.

FINE: Huh! (*Shakes his head.*)

> (CLARA *enters out of the darkness holding up a birdcage and extending one finger, crosses and vanishes.*)

Incidentally, her bird is here. You want it?

KROLL: Ah . . . I don't think so. Maybe we could get somebody to . . . ?

FINE: One of the cops wants it.

KROLL: Good. Same thing with that bird . . . always had to have a bird; and lets them out and holds out her finger and they come right back and she pops them into the cage. I don't know where she gets that from . . . You say I haven't called my wife.

FINE: You've been lying there since I came in. How do you feel, you think you could answer a few questions?

KROLL: I simply can't believe it. She loves everybody.

FINE (*glancing about*): It has that atmosphere. She never seems to have been married, is that right?

KROLL: Married? No. (*Seems to change his mind.*) Ah . . . no.

FINE: Something you want to say . . . ?

KROLL: No—no . . . I thought I heard voices.

FINE: There's a man dusting for fingerprints. You're clear now about who I am and where you are, right?

KROLL: . . . And your name again? I'm sorry . . .

FINE: That's all right. Lew Fine.

KROLL: Oh, that's why!—My friend was Bert Fine.

FINE: How old was Clara, by the way?

KROLL: She's . . . let's see . . .

FINE: Was.

KROLL: What?

FINE: She was.

KROLL: Oh. Yes. God. (*Slight pause.*) Twenty-eight last July.

(CLARA *enters, closing the door of a cage in which there is now a bird; she pauses behind* KROLL, *and a look of intense love passes over a sublime smile on her face and she moves away in the darkness.*)

FINE: Look, Mr. Kroll, if I'm going to get anywhere . . .

KROLL: No—no, please—I'm with you. It's just so unreal to me that I . . .

FINE: I understand, but every minute counts in a thing like this. Now, what can you tell me about Clara? For instance, these files don't indicate any female patients . . .

KROLL: Oh, well, she was mainly interested in prisoner rehabilitation.

FINE: Ah.

KROLL: She worked for three years in Botsford Penitentiary . . . and also Mount Carmel.

FINE: Ah, good—that's good information. And then I suppose she worked with these men after they got out.

KROLL: Oh, yes, helped a lot of them. Had wonderful letters from them. They idolized her.

FINE: I can imagine. You sound very proud of her.

KROLL: Oh, I guess so, I just . . . you just can't help worrying about her, that's all.

FINE: Well, you had reason. Did you kill your daughter, Mister Kroll?

KROLL (*instantly*): What!

FINE: I just wanted you to notice how clean and direct that answer was. Can you feel it? There was no flypaper on that answer. Sorry if I shocked you, but why don't you try to give me clean, direct answers like that, huh?

KROLL: I'm not trying to . . .

FINE: I realize you're all upset . . .

KROLL: Good God, I have to call my wife! Why wouldn't I be upset!

FINE: Okay, okay . . .

KROLL (*almost embarrassed*): It's amazing. The way you say okay, okay . . . that's exactly like Bert.

FINE: Well, there are just so many human types, you know.

KROLL: . . . I just thought of something to ask you, but I'm embarrassed to.

FINE: Go ahead.

KROLL: Well . . . no . . .

FINE: Come on, let's get to know each other.

KROLL: Do you have all your toes?

FINE (*silent for a moment*): No.

(KROLL *stares at the floor, shakes his head, lost.*)

Does that depress you?

KROLL: Is it the left foot?

FINE: What's so amazing? After all, we've got interchangeable kidneys, hearts, and a coupla ten years from now we'll all be working for two or three big corporations . . . so your friend and I have missing toes, so what? I don't think I'm anything special, you think you're something special?

KROLL: I can't believe this is happening.

FINE: Why?—He probably lost them in the War, right?

KROLL: That's right. France.

FINE: Well, you realize the number of men lost toes on their left foot in all the wars?

KROLL: . . . You just made me realize something.—I never thought of it this way, but for two or three years before we broke up, he was really turning into a first-class son of a bitch.

FINE (*laughs happily*): Well, you've learned *something* tonight, anyway.

KROLL: Oh, yeah . . . He really started cheating his suppliers and nobody could collect on him without threatening to go to court. (*Laughs.*) I should be glad to have gotten rid of him instead of . . . !

FINE: . . . You've got a real sentimental streak, don't you?

KROLL: Well . . . you like to give people the benefit of the doubt. I mean, by the same token, Bert could turn around and be, you know—warmhearted and generous, and— God!—intelligent . . . ?

FINE: Yeah, and then slit you right up the belly.

KROLL (*looking out, aware* . . .): You know?—In the old days I can't remember people being this complicated.

FINE: Why complicated?

KROLL: You mean . . . ?

FINE: Sure, nothing's changed. I'd like to get back to your daughter, can we?

KROLL: You have children?

FINE (*his smile vanishing*): One . . .

KROLL: . . . Didn't kill himself, did he?

FINE (*nods*): Mmhm.

> (KROLL *presses his fingers to his eyes.*)

Nothing to be depressed about; a good number of them did that to themselves during Vietnam, probably hundreds. Our statistics probably crossed, your friend and I, it's bound to happen somewhere on the graph. Same as your daughter, probably. Nine times out of ten she'd have been perfectly okay down here, but she might've said the wrong thing to the wrong guy at the wrong minute, and—(*A gesture.*) We're all one step away from a statistic, Albert.—What do you say we get back to it? Why don't you get up . . . Come on, fella . . . sit in a chair . . .

> (*He takes command, lifts* ALBERT *into a chair.*)

Did you ever meet any of her friends, or associates, anybody she knew?

KROLL (*frightened now*): Well, let me think.

FINE: This is what I'm referring to, Albert . . . Do you really have to cloud up like this before you answer that question? Did you ever meet any of her friends?

KROLL: Well, I'm trying to remember!

FINE: Okay, okay.

> (KROLL *reacts.*)

But I said *"any"*! Just in general . . . *a* friend?

KROLL: Well, yes, of course.

FINE: Albert, it's this simple, you are all I've got. If you're not going to level with me, I am out of business. What is it, you afraid of something embarrassing?

KROLL: No—no. I . . . I just . . . (*Breaks off.*)

FINE: What's the problem? You want to find this man, don't you?

KROLL: I heard something drop on piano keys before.

FINE: Yes, I heard it. Probably Douglas; he's dusting for prints.

KROLL: But I don't think Clara had a piano.

FINE (*slight pause*): This is her apartment, isn't it?

KROLL: . . . It seems like it.

FINE: I'm not following you.

KROLL: I'm just wondering, maybe I should wait before I answer any more questions.

FINE: Wait for what?

KROLL: Ah . . . (*Looks confused.*)

FINE: Oh. You mean it might all go 'way.

KROLL: Well, not "go away" exactly, but . . .

FINE: . . . But not be so definite.

KROLL: To be honest . . . I . . . still (*he is groping for the thought*) don't see the necessity. I mean she is not the type of girl who . . . I can't explain what I mean. I mean there was no *necessity* for this.

FINE: I understand.

KROLL (*relieved*): Do you?

FINE: But it's Clara. Why else would you be here, why would you have passed out cold? I think you probably forgot there's a piano here.

KROLL: But everybody loved Clara!

FINE: Except one.

KROLL: Just one in the whole city.

FINE: That's all you need; one makes it a necessity.

KROLL: You know, I do . . . recall now . . . I played on that piano one evening.

FINE: Of course.—Tell me, when you say you did meet friends of hers, how'd that come about?—She ever bring them home?

KROLL: Yes, home. In fact, this last Christmas. A fellow—I'm not trying to hide anything from you . . .

FINE: Good. Was this an associate? A patient?

KROLL: Well, he'd been in prison, but he was out a number of years.

FINE: And . . . what kind of relationship . . . acquaintance or what?

KROLL (*slight pause*): No, I guess it was more than that.
(*A long pause.*)

FINE: Yes?

(KROLL *gives him a veiled look, then looks at the floor.*)
What had he been convicted of, do you know?

KROLL: Murder.

FINE: Who did he murder, did they say?

KROLL (*feeling shame*): A girlfriend.

FINE: Served ten years or something?

KROLL: Something like that, I don't recall.

FINE: What was his name?

KROLL: . . . I'll have to think for a minute.

FINE: Go ahead. (*He resumes going through a file. Then . . .*)
She worked at Botsford, you say?

KROLL: Yes.

FINE: She in that riot they had there last summer?

KROLL: Oh, they held her hostage, had a knife to her jugular.
(*A laugh.*) And when it was over, she went right back in.

FINE: Guess you couldn't talk to her, huh?

KROLL: What can you say?

FINE: Yeah—specially when deep down you were proud of her
doing that, right?

KROLL: Well, in a way . . .

FINE: Sure.

(CLARA *is entering with the birdcage, waggling her finger
at the bird.*)

KROLL: What's the use? She'd always give you the same answer
. . . "If my work requires me to be in a place . . ." (*Continues mouthing the words as . . .*)

CLARA: ". . . people somehow know it and they never hassle
me."

KROLL (*simultaneously*): "Never hassle me."

(*She moves into darkness.—Now he sits staring at the air;*
FINE *keeps going through the file.*)

FINE: You're trying to remember that name, right?

KROLL: Name?—Oh, yes, yes. It'll come to me.

FINE: You're in the landscaping business?

KROLL: Not for some years now; my legs, I couldn't take it
anymore.

FINE: Oh, you actually did the work?

KROLL: Oh, sure, I did a lot of digging in my time. But pick and shovel gets you in the knees, finally.

FINE: Retired now?

KROLL: No, I'm with Ruggieri Industries.

FINE (*brows knitting*): Ruggieri. Ruggieri Construction?

KROLL: Road building, bridges, heavy stuff. New England.

FINE: Down here too, aren't they?

KROLL: That's Patsy, the brother.

FINE: Right. He had a little trouble there for a while.

KROLL: Ya.

FINE: Right. You're not an easy man to put together, are you? What do you do for Ruggieri?

KROLL: General factotum; I hold down the central office in Poughkeepsie. I'm with Charley, not Patsy.

FINE: Patsy went away for a while, didn't he?

KROLL: But they're completely separate organizations. Charley's never had any trouble.—I mean there's no . . . hit involved here if that's what you . . .

FINE: Uh-huh.—What do you say we really concentrate on this man's name who she brought home? Would your wife remember . . . ?

KROLL: No—no, don't . . . I'll call her if I can't remember . . . I know I'll get it, though.

FINE: Call her yourself if you like.

KROLL (*quickly*): No, I'll do it in a while, if I . . . if I . . . Let's see now . . . (*He seems pressed.*)

FINE: Why'n't we try to reconstruct it.—You live where, in the town, out in the country?

KROLL: In the country. I used to have my nursery next to the house.

FINE: What sort of fella? Jewish, Irish, Italian . . . ?

KROLL (*a slight hesitation*): . . . Hispanic.

FINE: Oh. José? Pablo? Federico? Luis?

KROLL: No.

FINE: Short? Tall?

KROLL: Medium.

FINE: She drive him up?

KROLL: Yeah, they rented a car.

FINE: And what happened, she pulled up in the driveway and got out . . . and did you come out to meet them?

KROLL: I was out; I was on the tractor plowing snow.

FINE: And what?—She kiss you? Shake hands?

KROLL: . . . No. She kissed me.

FINE: And said, "Daddy . . ."? Call you Daddy or Pop?

KROLL: No, Daddy.

FINE: "I want you to meet . . ."? Who?

> (KROLL *touches forehead, shaking his head slightly.*)
>
> You know about mental blocks, don't you?—You've been to college, haven't you?

KROLL: No, just high school.

FINE: You seem like a college man.

KROLL: No, I went right to work.

FINE: Generally—you probably know—we block things we're ashamed to remember.

KROLL: I know.

FINE: Things that make us feel guilty, you know what I mean?

KROLL: It'll come to me, I'm still kind of . . . (*Covers his eyes with his fingers.*)

FINE: This animal is digging deeper and deeper into the haystack as we sit here, Albert.

KROLL: I'm trying. I want to help you, it's just hard to keep . . .

FINE: I understand. (*Slight pause.*) They stayed the night?

KROLL: Yes.

FINE: And?

> (KROLL *silent.*)
>
> Why'n't you try to relax and let it come? What do you say?
>
> (KROLL *looks at him, silent.*)
>
> They sleep in the same room?

KROLL: Yes.

FINE (*a synthetic smile*): You could have just told me that, couldn't you?

KROLL: Well, I have. (*Looks down.*)

FINE: But I'm pulling one tooth after another; why string this out? (*A glow of light opens over their heads.*) What do you want me to make out of this, Albert? Are you with me or we going for a walk on flypaper?

> ("LUIS" *appears overhead and quickly fades out.*)

KROLL: Luis.

FINE: Good man. Luis what?

KROLL: But why did I see it . . . like on a screen?

FINE: Maybe the shock . . . Okay now, let's go for the second name. This helps a lot, Albert. Tell me, if you don't mind— how'd you feel about them sleeping together in the house? And, incidentally, how would he have been dressed? Wind- breaker? Regular jacket and overcoat . . . ?

KROLL: Windbreaker. Plaid. Like a short mackinaw.

FINE: Good. And you understand if any of these questions are sensitive, it's only to help bring back . . .

KROLL: I understand.

FINE: Where is your wife all this time? She come out to the car?

KROLL (*visualizing*): No, she was in the kitchen cooking dinner.

FINE: So the three of you went inside, right? And Clara says, "Mother? I'd like you to meet Luis . . ." She must have said his second name right then, didn't she?

(KROLL *knits his brows, trying* . . .)

Okay—how'd your wife react to him? Or wasn't he the first ex-inmate Clara had brought home?

KROLL: No, he was the first.

FINE: And she probably surmised a relationship going on, huh?—What's your wife's name, incidentally?

KROLL: Jean. She did, yes.

FINE: How'd that hit her—this Puerto Rican in a windbreaker?

KROLL: Jean was a Rockette.

FINE: Excuse me?

KROLL: She'd been dancing in Broadway shows for years when we met—they're accustomed to associating with all kinds of people in show business.

FINE (*skeptically*): Right.

KROLL: . . . I may as well tell you—I had a black company during the war. I spent three years with those men.

FINE: Uh-huh.

KROLL: Although tell you the truth, every once in a while I just about give up on those people, but all I'm saying is . . . you know.

FINE: No. What are you saying?

KROLL: Well, that . . . I've had more than the usual amount of experience with them.

FINE: Tell me: you and Jean—you knew he'd been in prison for murdering his girlfriend?

KROLL: Well, no, they only told about that after dinner.

FINE: I'm curious how that happened to come up.

KROLL: Clara brought it up herself. She was specially proud of his adjustment.

FINE: And you? Can I ask how you felt about that?

    (KROLL *silent.*)

Did you believe it?

    (KROLL *looks at him.*)

    . . . The adjustment? . . . I'm just trying to bring back some of your feelings, you see? I mean when she said, "Luis was in prison, Daddy. He murdered his girlfriend." What'd that do to you?

KROLL: I . . .

    (CLARA *enters, sits facing* KROLL's *profile. She now wears outdoor country clothes, big sweater, slacks.*)

    . . . felt proud.

FINE: Uh-huh, why?

KROLL: . . . Well, that she was doing some good in the world.

FINE: Right. What good do you mean?

KROLL: Well . . . working with men like that.

FINE: One of whom probably murdered her.

KROLL: Well, yes, but . . . (*Breaks off.*)

FINE: Yes?

    (KROLL *gropes for a word.*)

I'm wondering, Albert—are you guilty because you didn't put your foot down right then and there?

KROLL (*toughening*): I said I was proud of her.

FINE: I'm going to be blunt with you, Albert . . . You mean you're standing there saying good night—is that correct?—while she climbs the stairs to her girlhood room with this convicted killer, and you're full of happiness?

KROLL: I didn't say that . . .

FINE: Then what are you saying? You're not furious and you're not happy. What are you? . . . Forgive me, I'm only trying to help you, but you're blocking this off and I think that's why you can't tell me his name—because you refuse to remember what you were feeling.

KROLL: It's a long time ago . . .

FINE: Two months? But okay, let's relax it, let's just let it come. I'm sorry if I seem like I'm leaning on you, Albert . . .

KROLL: That's okay . . . I'm trying my best . . .

FINE: I figure we're both on the same side, right?

KROLL (*after a pause*): Excuse me saying it, but I would have thought, being Jewish, that you'd have more understanding . . . of this kind of situation. I mean, you're suddenly faced with an underprivileged man like that, you just naturally feel . . .

FINE: Yes, I know what you mean. I used to. I used to have a lot of understanding. But I gave up on it.

KROLL: I see.

FINE: I couldn't deny it; I finally had to face it—I have my limitations; Jewish or not Jewish, I think a man who cuts off a woman's head is a criminal. And if he's been discriminated against and had a bad upbringing, I can only tell you that most of the Puerto Rican people don't become criminals and they have the same background. I used to have a lot of questions about life, but in these last years I'm down to two—what did the guy do, and can I prove it? Whether his mother left him in the same shitty diaper for weeks at a time is not our problem. You agree or not?

KROLL (*pause*): I don't know how to explain . . .

FINE: But you agree with what I just said.

KROLL: Of course, but . . .

FINE: But what, Albert?

KROLL: I can't explain it.

(FINE *goes motionless and light dulls on him.* CLARA *moves now.*)

CLARA: He has two things that are a lot like you, Daddy. He's soft and he's strong. And he's overcome so much that we can't even imagine. But it's made him deeper, you see? It's made him love life more . . .

KROLL: I don't understand enough about the mind, darling. How a man can ever kill a woman.

CLARA: But you've killed.

KROLL: In a war. That's a different thing.

CLARA: But you understand rage. You weren't firing from a distance or dropping bombs from a plane . . .

KROLL: But they'd jumped us, Clara. I was fast asleep in the tent and suddenly they were all over me like roaches.

CLARA: You felt that same uncontrollable rage, though . . .

KROLL: It's not the same . . .

CLARA: Yes, it is.—When you grabbed that Japanese and bent him over your knees till you broke his back . . . that was the strength of rage.

KROLL: But this man, with a woman . . .

CLARA: It was his illusion that he was defending his life . . . He'll never have that illusion again, Papa.

KROLL: . . . You know me, darling—I'm always ready to believe the best of anybody . . .

CLARA: I know. But you still don't understand it.

KROLL: No. Before we go to bed, dear . . . unless you don't want any comments . . .

CLARA: Of course I do . . . from you, always.

KROLL: I got the feeling at dinner that you're like a medal he's wearing on his chest. You're like an accomplishment for him.

CLARA: That doesn't have to be a bad thing.

KROLL: No. But is it you he's in love with or the accomplishment? You understand what I mean?

CLARA (*lowered eyes*): Nothing is settled, Papa.

KROLL: God bless you, Clara.

    (*She walks into darkness.* FINE *moves.*)

FINE: Where would that be, some island?

    (KROLL *looks at him, uncomprehending.*)

    That fight in the tent.

KROLL: Oh! Yes, the Philippines. Was I talking? . . . (*Breaks off, points at* FINE. *And still confused about it* . . .) Of course I was, I'm sorry.

FINE (*skeptically*): And you had no rifle? No sidearms?

KROLL: We were all asleep. And then I had to load men into a truck and get them to the aid tent, and I felt this wetness . . . (*a laugh*) . . . and I look down and my whole insides are falling out; I had to drive with one hand! (*Laughs, and holds his belly with his left hand as he mimes steering with the right.*) But I wonder if I should ever have told her that story.

FINE: Made you into a hero.

KROLL: In a way. (*He stares.*)

FINE (*slight pause*): Why, is it a phony story?

KROLL: Heh? No.

FINE (*a moment of hesitation*): You know, Albert, a wound that deep up the belly will stay with a man right into the grave.

KROLL: I know.

FINE: You got a wound like that?

> (KROLL, *surprised to be asked, pulls up his shirt and* FINE *looks.* KROLL *puts his shirt back into his trousers.*)

My God.

KROLL: Listen, you won't call my wife, will you? Promise me that.

FINE: How can I promise you? I have to know who he . . .

KROLL: I know it'll come to me, just give me a few minutes. It would be so much worse, a strange voice on the phone . . . You're right, though, I guess I am a little ashamed of one thing. I didn't tell Clara how strongly I felt about this man.

FINE: Of course . . .

KROLL: But by the same token, you see . . . (*a private matter which he hates to speak of*) . . . she was always a serious girl. Never dressed up for boys the way they do . . .

FINE: There'd never been boyfriends?

KROLL: A few, not many. And now she was looking so excited, and all flushed—you know, when she talked about this fellow. I'd never seen that side of her . . .

FINE: So you didn't have the heart to.

KROLL: Yes.

FINE: But Jean knew right away he was dangerous.

KROLL: Pretty much, yes.

FINE: Well, I can see why that's going to be a tough phone call to make.

KROLL: Terrible.

FINE: You mean you actively encouraged Clara.

KROLL: Not *encouraged* . . .

FINE (*impatiently*): Come on, Albert, what's holding you up? I'm not laying judgment on anybody, I just want . . .

KROLL: . . . It's about a year ago now . . . I came down to the city to buy some music . . .

FINE: Records.

KROLL: No. I sing. Churches, even a couple of synagogues. I was a professional after the War, sang in eight musicals, it's how I met Jean.

FINE (*laughs eagerly*): You are something to piece together . . . !

KROLL: I'm not complicated. Anyway, I . . .

FINE: You say synagogues—you're not Jewish, are you?

KROLL: Catholic. But I enjoy the liturgical music.—Where was I? Oh, yes, I had dinner here that evening.—I forgot why I'm telling you this.

FINE: That you're ashamed you didn't put your foot down.

KROLL: Oh. (*Stops.*) I keep feeling I'm falling asleep.

FINE: Well, shocks are funny.—You had dinner here one night.

KROLL: Yes. She had a friend of hers, a social psychologist from Bellevue, I think.

FINE: Man? Woman?

KROLL: Woman.

FINE: Yes?

KROLL: . . . She was a bit older, I think, maybe thirty-five, even forty . . . Not that this necessarily means . . .

FINE: I've been through all the mutations and permutations; I don't make judgments; just try to tell what happened. What happened?

KROLL: Well, it'd gotten late and Clara accompanied her downstairs to her car . . . And after five, ten minutes I started to wonder and went over there to the window and she was . . . standing next to the car talking. (*Sighs.*) And this woman stuck her head out the window. (*Stops.*)

FINE: They kissed?

KROLL: Yes.

FINE: This is what I mean—now you're giving me the story. So in other words . . .

KROLL: I'm not necessarily implying . . .

FINE: What you're telling me, Albert, is that it was such a relief to see her involved with a man . . . even a Puerto Rican murderer wearing a mackinaw, that you . . .

KROLL: I think so . . .

FINE: That's perfectly understandable. You wouldn't recall this woman's name.

KROLL: Her name?

("ELEANOR BALLEN" *flashes overhead.*)

Eleanor Ballen.

FINE: Now we're moving!

KROLL: I can't understand why I am seeing it like on a screen . . .

FINE (*making a note*): You are breaking through, you're a hell of a guy . . .

KROLL: He worked at an airport.

FINE: Luis?—which airport?

KROLL: I reached into the car to help with her bag and he took it from me and laughed and said he knew all about handling bags . . . and it came out. But I don't know if he mentioned which one.

FINE: That's all right, keep going.—How about Mercado? Sender? (*To both,* KROLL *gives a negative gesture, staring at his blank memory.*)

Let me come at it from a different angle. And try to relax, we're gaining on it.—Am I wrong? I get an impression that you wouldn't want to blame a minority for this . . . on some kind of political grounds?

KROLL: It's not exactly political, but . . . as chairman of the zoning board I've been under terrific pressure to either raise the acreage requirement or lower it. You have to have two and a half acres now . . .

FINE: To build a house.

KROLL: Yes. A lot of them want to raise it to three and even four, and some want to reduce it to one or even less.

FINE: So it's a race problem.

KROLL: Not just race, it's to keep out less affluent families or let them in.

FINE: And where are you on this?

KROLL: We've got to let them in. I don't know what else to support. Or you end up with two societies. In fact, we could easily get sued by the federal government for housing discrimination if we go to four acres. But the feeling runs very hot on both sides . . .

FINE: I can imagine. How hot?

KROLL: Well, for a while there the sheriff told us to move our dining room table away from the picture window. And I've had five or six mailboxes stolen or knocked over, and found a dead rat in the front seat of my car. Some of them get to sounding really crazy.

FINE: You think they could be involved in this?

KROLL: No—no, I can't believe that.

FINE: In other words, if it turned out to be a Puerto Rican, it would be pretty embarrassing for you up there . . . after all you tried to do for them.

> (KROLL *simply turns up his palms and shakes his head at the thought of it.*)

What about Menendez? Carillo? Lostados . . . ?

> (KROLL *indicates "No" and covers his eyes in despair.*)

What is it?

> (KROLL *shakes his head. Then he stares straight ahead at* FINE.)

Yes?

KROLL: What time is it now?

FINE: One-o-five.

KROLL (*a pause*): You said that before.

FINE: Make it later, then. Look at yours.

KROLL: I seem to have lost my glasses. (*Searches his pockets.*)

FINE: Albert, listen.

> (KROLL *goes still.*)

You listening?

> (KROLL *nods.*)

You're still guilty about that name, aren't you?

> (KROLL *looks out front.*)

I feel for you. You didn't level with Jean about this lady friend; you didn't put your foot down when you know you never believed that this man was adjusted; and you've gone public in favor of these people coming into the community when you know they're liable to do anything comes into their heads. They are dirty and not responsible and they're going to lower the value of your property, turn the whole area into a slum. You're tied up about this name . . . correct me . . . because you can't stop telling your lies. You're not protecting a name, are you? You'd like this man caught and killed, right? It's not him, it's your lies you can't let go of. It's ten, twenty, thirty years of shit you told your daughter, to the point where she sacrificed her life, for what?—To uphold what you don't believe in yourself.

KROLL: And what do you believe in?

FINE: Me? Greed. Greed and race. Believe it or not, I have never taken an illegitimate nickel, but if you ask what I trust to run the world, it's greed—and that secret little tingle you get when your own kind comes out ahead. The black for the black, and the white for the white. Gentile for Gentile and the Jew for the Jew. Greed and race, Albert, and you'll never go wrong. And, believe me, if you could admit the truth here, I'd have that name in one minute flat.

KROLL: The truth . . .

FINE (*slowly*): You don't owe those people anything. Not then, and especially not now. (*Pause.*)

KROLL: But your boy . . .

FINE: My boy was shot dead by propaganda that he had some kind of debt to pay. I failed him; I failed to simplify the way it was simplified for me. I took the sergeant's exam three times; I know I got perfect grades three times, but I was one of the kikes, and they finally gave me my stripes out of sheer embarrassment. I was on a par with an Arab bucking for sergeant in the Israeli police department. But it's nothing to be sad about, right? Unless you're going to be way up there looking down at the rest of us down here. But you're working for Ruggieri, you're not way up there, are you?—Not when you're holding down that office for Charley Ruggieri; right? Albert? . . . Albert?

KROLL (*with great difficulty*): That's right.

FINE: I mean the payoffs on those tunnels and highways and bridges—right? You carry the bag, or what? Well, it's none of my business, but in that office you've gotta be one of us, Albert; so how about that name? Clara's gone, kid, there's no reason to carry this on anymore—you're one of us. You admit that to yourself and I'll bet that name comes popping right out.

KROLL: As a matter of fact . . . I don't know what the hell I'm trying to . . . to . . .

FINE: Sure! Get it out, come on—what were you going to say?—And I know how this hurts, kid, but let me tell you a quick one. That day in 1945, remember?—when they first showed those pictures of the piles of bones? Remember that? The bulldozers pushing them into those trenches, those arms and legs sticking up? That's the day I was born again, Albert, and I've never let myself forget it.—"Do it to them before they can do it to you. Period." Now you were saying . . . ?

KROLL (*fear, suddenly*): Sometimes Charley . . . (*Breaks off.*)
. . . I don't know why I'm saying this . . .

FINE: Don't hold it, Albert, come on now . . . it's the goods
. . . What! Talk to me! Charley Ruggieri?

KROLL (*nods*): Sometimes . . . he goes half crazy trying to
figure what to do with himself. He gave his daughter a
Miami hotel for her birthday, and a helicopter to his son and
two Arabian horses. He flies his jet to London to get some
ties. And then the plastic bags.

FINE: What?

KROLL (*with increasing difficulty, but grinning, still amazed*):
Gets people together and sit around with plastic bags on
their heads till they get high. From the carbon dioxide.
Come as close as you can to . . .

FINE: And women?

KROLL: . . . Yes.

FINE: You?

KROLL: A couple times, but I stopped . . .

FINE: Brings on one hell of an erection, doesn't it? Practically
rigor mortis.

KROLL: Yes.

FINE (*rapidly, with a driving, contemptuous assurance*): Velaz-
quez? Zuela? Ricon?
(*Negative nods from* KROLL.)
Martinez, Mercado . . .
(*Officer* TIERNEY *enters carrying a record in a cover.*)

TIERNEY: This is him, I think; you want it?

FINE (*takes record, looks at cover*): This yours?

KROLL: Oh, long ago, yes. (*Reaches out and is given the cover.
Smiles faintly, shakes his head.*) Huh! Yes. (*Hands it back to*
FINE.) A choral group I had for a while. Many years ago.

FINE (*stares at the record in his hands*): The haircuts in those
days! . . . Could I hear it?
(KROLL *shrugs, but seems curious too.*)

TIERNEY: Couple of good numbers on it.

FINE (*hesitates, looks at* KROLL, *who seems to be embarrassed*):
Go ahead.
(*Hands the record to* TIERNEY, *who exits with it.*)
Maybe it'll relax you a little; get a new slant, you never know.

Got to wait for the Medical Examiner anyway. Can I ask your permission to take a nip of that Scotch over there?

KROLL: Oh, that's okay.

(FINE *goes to bottle, pours. Pause.*)

That record has got to be at least twenty-five . . .

(*A chorus singing "Shenandoah."* KROLL's *voice, young and strong, solos in the foreground.*

TIERNEY *enters a moment after* KROLL *is heard and indicates* KROLL *to* FINE *as the soloist.*)

(*Hearing his own voice*): Good Lord.

(KROLL *is listening, staring front.* CLARA *enters, a very young girl now, ribbon in her hair. After a moment . . .*)

CLARA: Mama said to ask you.

KROLL: No—no, it's nothing for you to hear; maybe when you're older.

CLARA: But I want to. Please tell. Daddy? Please!

KROLL (*for a moment he listens to the music which continues behind him*): When the war began they needed officers so bad they took you without a college degree. When I got my commission at Benning they sent me over to Mississippi . . . a camp a few miles out of Biloxi.—God, just listen to that! (*He stares for a moment.*) Most of the officers were Southerners and I could hardly understand . . . (*Smiles.*) . . . you know—what they were saying; or else they were college guys from the North and they'd be discussing all these books I never heard of, so I understood what they were saying but not what they were talking about. (*A soft laugh.*) So it ended up where I'm practically eating by myself. (*His eyes begin to see, his smile goes.*) The Army was still completely segregated then, and one day the Colonel—who was from Alabama, I think—comes into the mess and asks for a volunteer to take command of a black company in a new transport battalion—you know, truck drivers and laborers. And of course—nobody wanted a black company. But Grandpa'd always had Negro people working in the nursery and, you know—I'd been around them all my life and always got along with them, and I thought . . . maybe with them I'd have somebody to talk to, so I raised my hand. (*His breathing begins to deepen, his voice on the record strong and young, singing through the air.*) In a couple of months we had a pretty sharp battalion—later in the Pacific MacArthur gave us three citations. But at this time—it was a brutal hot July day and eight or nine of my boys asked if they could go into Biloxi for the afternoon, just to get a beer and walk around. (*Sighs.*) A couple of hours later I get this call that some kind of lynch mob is chasing them through Biloxi and I better come quick. I run into the Colonel's office, but he refused to have anything to do with it. So I said, "Look, I've got hardly any rank, nobody's going to listen to me." But he just walked away. So I strapped on a sidearm and grabbed a jeep and driver from the pool, and we zam down the highway with his foot to the floor, and Biloxi . . . is a madhouse, clumps of people running up and down yelling to each other, people racing around corners with clubs and guns, or down on their hands and knees searching under the porches. Finally I find out a couple of the boys had insulted some white women on the street, and they're going to lynch the whole lot of them. You just couldn't talk to those people, and suddenly I hear this unbelievable roar coming up the avenue and here comes a mob with half a dozen of my guys, some of them already had ropes around their necks. I tried to push through to them, but I couldn't and they're going to hang them then and there. So I jumped up onto the hood of the jeep and took out my .45 and fired it into the air. And they turned around, looking up at me, and I . . . I . . . I didn't know what I was doing by this time, it was like some dream . . . and I yell out . . . (*roars*) . . . "I am an officer of the United States Army! Now you untie my men and hand them over to me right now!" (*He glances about before him, almost panting for breath.*) All you could hear was the panting, people trying to catch their breaths. So I called to them, to the boys—"Leroy! Richards! Haley! . . ." And . . . my God, I couldn't believe it . . . one by one they let them out of the crowd. Nobody touched them, and three or four got into the jeep and the rest lay down flat on the hood and some stood on the bumpers and we drove down Main Street and out of the town.—Seems two of them had stopped at a store and seen these great big ladies' hats in the window, and started laughing. Never seen hats like that and it was funny to them, so they fell all over themselves and just then these two women come out of the store and thought they were laughing at *them*. And that's how it started.

CLARA: Oh, Papa . . .

KROLL (*out of his double awareness*): Oh, no. No. No, honey . . . I just didn't have time to think! It was nothing!

CLARA (*kissing his hand*): Papa!

KROLL: No, Clara!—Before I knew it, I was standing there with this gun in my hand . . .

CLARA (*standing*): Oh, my dear Papa . . . !

> (*She is moving backward toward the darkness and he is trying to follow . . .*)

KROLL: Oh, be careful, darling . . . Oh, my wonderful Clara. (*Straightening, joyfully declaring.*) I am so proud of you! (*As she vanishes, his terrified, protesting outcry . . .*) Clara!

> (*A doorbell.*)

FINE (*to* TIERNEY): Medical Examiner.

> (TIERNEY *hurries out.*)
>
> ("HERNANDEZ" *suddenly blazes up in the air above and vanishes.*)

KROLL: Hernandez.

FINE: What!

KROLL: Luis Hernandez. Worked at Kennedy. For Pan American.

> (FINE *instantly rushes out.* TIERNEY *appears, carrying the bird in its cage; he pauses for an instant to take in* KROLL, *then goes into the darkness. From the darkness quiet greetings to the doctor—*"Come on in, Doctor, how're you doing?" *etc. The choral recording stops abruptly, the needle lifted off.* KROLL *stares into space, standing erect and calm now.*)

CURTAIN

THE GOLDEN YEARS

A New World Tragedy

CHARACTERS

MONTEZUMA
GUATEMOTZIN
CUITLAHUA
CAGAMA
ASTRONOMER
TALUA
PARACH
BOY SACRIFICE
JUDGE
TAPAIA
TECUICHPO
COURIER
MESA
FR. OLMEDO
ORDAZ
CORTEZ
MARINA
LEON
MONTEJO
OLID
ARBENGA
ALVARADO
XICOTENGA
QUAUHOPOCA
NARVAEZ

What if the glory of escutcheoned doors.
And buildings that a haughtier age designed,
The pacing to and fro on polished floors
Amid great chambers and long galleries,
    lined
With famous portraits of our ancestors;
What if those things the greatest of mankind
Consider most to magnify, or to bless,
But take our greatness with our bitterness?

Rough men-at-arms, cross-gartered to the knees
Or shod in iron, climbed the narrow stairs,
And certain men-at-arms there were
Whose images, in the Great Memory stored,
Come with loud cry and panting breast
To break upon a sleeper's rest
While their great wooden dice beat on the board.

I have loved you better than my soul for all my words . . .

William Butler Yeats

THE AZTEC NAMES

Since the Conquistador could not read Aztec symbols, he wrote as he heard. The names are therefore in a nearly phonetic form.

Montezuma .... (Just as it spells)
Guatemotzin .... (Gwa-te-mótzin)
Cuitlahua .... (Cwit-lá-ooah)
Tecuichpo .... (Tek-whisch-pó. The 'i*ch*' as in the German 'Rei*ch*')
Xicotenga .... (Shi-ko-ténga, the '*sh*' is hard)
The god Quetzalcoatl .... (Kwetzal-kwatl)
The god Huitzilopochtli ..... (Whitzl-pochtli: the '*ch*' again as in 'Rei*ch*')
The commander, Quauhopoca (Kwaw-cowa-páwka)

ACT ONE

A night in Autumn, 1519.

Tenochtitlan (now Mexico City), Capital of the Aztec Empire.

This is the Mountain House of MONTEZUMA, *King of the Aztec Nation, Emperor of the World. Over the left half of the stage the open sky is seen. A night sky thick with stars. The roof covers only the right half. On a medium level, at its centre is the large throne, built square and low with a high slanting back, and carved with the jagged Aztec design. Up above it two torch lamps burn. In the background the faint outline of mountain peaks at the edge of the sky.*

On the rise, the room is lighted only by the torches and the greenish glare of the moon. MONTEZUMA *sits deep in the throne, flanked on a lower level by his council, the Lords* GUATEMOTZIN, *a man of twenty-four and built lithely for war;* CUITLAHUA, *about forty and of slower movement;* CAGAMA, *solid, stocky, about forty-five.* MONTEZUMA, *standing, is watching the* ASTRONOMER *who, charts in hand, is rapidly calculating the stars which he looks up to frequently. On this lowest level, but at the far right,* TAPAIA *stands watching* MONTEZUMA *for the slightest command. Beside the* AS-TRONOMER, TALUA, *a boy, stands studying the stars and comparing them with a stone-covered book he holds open in his arms.*

There is no movement, but the ASTRONOMER *for a moment, the Lords and the King watching him as though waiting for him to say something.* MONTEZUMA *glances at the moon, rises slowly, and walks left and stops when he is abreast of the* ASTRONOMER *but above him.*

All men—deep sonorous chant in background.

MONTEZUMA (*looking up*): My star seems bleeding.
ASTRONOMER (*intent on charts*): The sun is on it, my Lord, from around the world.

MONTEZUMA (*pause. To* ASTRONOMER): When will you be finished with your charts and numbers?

ASTRONOMER: A moment more.

(MONTEZUMA *looks at the sky. Pause.*)

GUATEMOTZIN (*nervously takes a few steps*): The air . . . the air is growing heavier, Uncle. How much longer before the moon dies?

(ASTRONOMER *lifts hand for silence.* GUATEMOTZIN *feels the air.*)

The air seems to be filling with water.

CUITLAHUA: No wind is a good sign. The flame of the sacrifice may easily rise to the moon.

GUATEMOTZIN: Is this the way the world ends? Not with battles, but waiting like old men? Uncle, what are your thoughts now?

MONTEZUMA: My life and the meaning of it . . . when will you speak?

ASTRONOMER: The calculations are done, my Lord.

(*All come toward him anxiously—humming stops.*)

Look there, the Eastern Star . . .

MONTEZUMA: To the point, how long have we . . . ?

ASTRONOMER: Depending on that star, my Lord. It is dropping fast, and when it falls behind the horizon, the speckled moon will ride into eclipse and . . .

CUITLAHUA (*points up*): What's that!

ASTRONOMER: There it is, my Lord, the black tip of the shadow . . .

MONTEZUMA: I see it now . . .

(*Distant single drum beat.*)

ASTRONOMER: It will move across the moon, and if your sacrificial fire does not burn it off, the world is dead this quarter hour.

MONTEZUMA: A quarter hour?

ASTRONOMER: She's black within a quarter, my Lord, no longer.

MONTEZUMA (*slight pause. Nervously*): Perhaps an error . . . ?

ASTRONOMER: Impossible. You see, the earth turns on this orbit I have drawn. (*Shows him chart.*) . . . and when the sun revolves . . .

MONTEZUMA: Enough, enough. (*Comes away from him towards centre.*) Tapaia. Bring the sacrifice to me. (*Pause.*) Is my judge dead yet?

TAPAIA: He is being taken to the block now my Lord.

MONTEZUMA: Bring him here . . . hurry. And remember, they must keep an eye on the high road. I am expecting a courier.

(TAPAIA *bows . . . starts out.*)

CUITLAHUA: Tapaia, wait a moment.

(TAPAIA *stops.*)

(*To* MONTEZUMA.) My lord, I think it would be wise for you to send a proclamation to the people.

MONTEZUMA: The people? What can I say to the people?

CUITLAHUA: This year was filled with terrors for them, and now the moon,—your word might calm their hearts . . .

MONTEZUMA: Their hearts must not be calmed. They must be terrified tonight, and we, we must be wondrous and search-ing, not calm. The meanings in this moon we will not read at our ease, but suffering! The sacrifice, Tapaia, hurry.

(*Exit* TAPAIA.)

CUITLAHUA (*as* MONTEZUMA *goes up a level*): You are strange tonight, my Lord.

MONTEZUMA: I am all questions, Cuitlahua. (*Looks upward.*)

(*Drum stops.*)

CUITLAHUA: And I.

CAGAMA (*anxious, nervous*): When you brothers speak to-gether, I hear. But it's another language, secret between you. Am I dull, my Lord? I am not afraid to die.

(*Silence. No answer.*)

When there was a war to fight, I fought. A kingdom to knock down, I was ready with the blow . . . I am not afraid now. I have lived honorably.

(*No answer.*)

Montezuma, you are wiser, closer to the gods than I. Tell me why I should be afraid. What do you see that I am blind to? The Spaniards, my Lord? If you've proof now that they're gods I'll be happy to join you in welcoming them . . .

CUITLAHUA: Cagama . . .

CAGAMA: No, let me speak if my lord will let me. The time is very short. Montezuma, I am rich and if the Spaniards are proven gods, I'll give them my wealth with all my heart. But I cannot be expected to exult. Not when I know the towns they've wrecked, the countryside they've burned, the black destruction they bring wherever they march. And you've done nothing to stop them, my Lord. I confess, they are nearing the city and my mind is uneasy . . . What do you see in the moon, my Lord? Montezuma, I will not be arrogant! What do you see that I cannot!

MONTEZUMA: I see only what any man might who will open eyes. I tremble under this menacing sky, remembering the hostile shudderings of the earth this year. How the lakes overflowed. Why? . . . without reason; how lightning would strike silently, thunderless; and the stars that fell in the afternoon,—what were the gods striving to tell us? Are we so strong, so proud and tall that when volcanoes fill the air with fiery stones and comets fall like rain we may go our ways indifferent, saying it will be well, we are too great to fall? And now the moon, the moon is shrouding over while striding inward from the East a band of white-faced strangers, unknown to mankind, from out of the sunrise they come calling *my* name. And what am I advised? What wisdom do we draw from such miracles? Pray God for the moon, you say!—we must not die! Slaughter the Spaniards, they've come to conquer! I say the world is agonized, profligate with signs that point to some cancer in the heart of the state: the gods roar warnings in our ears that something must be changed and we're blind and deaf to the signs!

GUATEMOTZIN: But the signs meant the ending of the world.

MONTEZUMA: And more, Guatemotzin—more a thousand-fold than the ending of the world!

(*Sounds—enter* PARACH *and* BOY SACRIFICE.)

PARACH: My Lord, our offering to the Gods approaches your Majesty.

MONTEZUMA: May the weight of your step on my threshold bring a blessing to this house.

BOY SACRIFICE: My Lord, my great King!

MONTEZUMA: How beautiful you've grown.

PARACH: He must be on the mountain soon.

MONTEZUMA: I want him here a moment. (*To* BOY. *Smiling.*) You shall hear strange questions in this room. Listen and carry them to heaven in the flame; and I pray you, beg the gods to send us an answer. Roses . . . (*Touches* BOY

SACRIFICE.) You're lovely as the flowers you wear . . . (*To Lords.*) A god to walk with the gods. (*To* BOY SACRIFICE.) Are you sad tonight?

BOY SACRIFICE: It has been such a happy year for me, great King.

MONTEZUMA: And you'll not forget how you drank of oldest wine? How you fed on succulent meat? And the concubines we lay at your side on the couch of down, and the perfumed air, you'll not forget?

BOY SACRIFICE: Oh, my Lord, in the flame, in the wind, in the clouds beyond the sun, I will remember this holy year!

PARACH: His pyre is ready, the wood is dry. We stand talking, talking, the moon withers . . .

MONTEZUMA: He will carry a question to the gods.

PARACH: Questions? A priest answers questions. Only a priest . . .

(*Sound of chains. Enter fettered* JUDGE *with* TAPAIA.)

JUDGE: Why am I dragged here from the block?

PARACH: Now the Emperor even confers with criminals!

MONTEZUMA: Tapaia bring the courier to me as soon as he arrives.

(TAPAIA *disappears.*)

Old friend . . .

JUDGE: A judge may claim the privilege of death.

MONTEZUMA: I do not take you from the block to spare you. Nor am I sad that you die a criminal.

JUDGE: I *will* die, Montezuma.

MONTEZUMA: So will all of us perhaps.

JUDGE: But the world will *live* if the flame goes high. And I must not be here when tomorrow comes. I'll kill myself!

MONTEZUMA (*slight pause*): I must know why you're afraid to live. You took a bribe, a rich man, a rich and honoured man—a bribe that would not buy him a sandal for his foot. Why? What calamity is wracking my world that my greatest judge must debase himself?

JUDGE: Let me die . . .

MONTEZUMA: What is your secret? In all our history, no judge has ever been corrupt. We have no penalty in law for such a crime. How is it possible! Speak!

(JUDGE *pauses. He cannot bear to look at the King.*)

JUDGE: I have only horrors to tell you, my Lord, let me go!

MONTEZUMA: I have seen horrors this year. I can bear another!

JUDGE: My Lord, you fought your last war a year ago. When that war finished, I looked out on the world. There is hardly a rise of ground left for you to conquer, Montezuma.

MONTEZUMA: Aye, all horizons are garrisoned.

JUDGE: Then where is the further glory? What step can you take but downward?

GUATEMOTZIN: The man is mad, my Lord! Take him away!

MONTEZUMA: No. Let him speak!

JUDGE: Then I saw the waters rising. I saw the silent lightning, and the comets falling. I could not sleep, what did they mean? I walked the streets of your cities, listened to the people, the potter, the jeweller, the monger, and the fisherman. "The price is high," they said, "I am a poor man." "Crops are good," they say, "but I starve for food." "I had a son, they took him for the wars." Whispering, the cities of empire sullen, whispering: "Montezuma? He lives like a god and we suffer." "How long? How long? How long? How long?"

GUATEMOTZIN: Stop it!

JUDGE: Would the gods I could! But between the lips of both oceans the empire is cracking!

(*The Lords are furious.*)

GUATEMOTZIN: Insolent man!

MONTEZUMA: Leave him! (*Quiet.*) He sees it too.

CAGAMA (*astounded*): Sees what my lord?

MONTEZUMA: The empire is cracking, Cagama.

(*Pause.*)

The gods are loitering here, let the truth confront them. (*To the* JUDGE.) And you thought, how the situation might be saved?

JUDGE: I did, until that dawn three months ago, when the Spaniards landed on the Eastern coast.

MONTEZUMA (*to* BOY): Hear it, Holy Boy, hear it now! (*To* JUDGE.) And what did you think then?

JUDGE: You wove the tapestry of Mexico but now the threads run out.

GUATEMOTZIN: How can you listen to him Uncle?

MONTEZUMA (*rapidly*): You've seen it from below; what will

mend the cracking? How would you mend the state if you were king?

GUATEMOTZIN: Troops made it and troops will mend it! The whip will shut their mouths!

MONTEZUMA: Aye, and for how long, how long, Guatemotzin?

GUATEMOTZIN: Until they whisper again, then whip again!

MONTEZUMA: And if it only cracks wider still?

(*Pause.*)

JUDGE: Now you are wise! You have reached the hour where force no more will rule the state . . .

MONTEZUMA: Yes . . .

JUDGE: And force will not bind up its rotting limbs.

MONTEZUMA: Hear it. (*To* BOY.) Holy Boy, hear it, a question for the gods!—This is the horror I see rising on the state, the question that the writhing universe has thrown up in my brain;—how shall I rule if not with the sword!

JUDGE: Die with me now, Montezuma!

MONTEZUMA: Die!

JUDGE: Now, at the zenith of your glory, die as you lived; Emperor of the World, or you'll crumble furious in storms.

CAGAMA: He dare not . . . !

GUATEMOTZIN and LORDS: Kill him! Kill the madman!

JUDGE (*to Lords*): You are the madmen! Fools! Mad with power and the riches you hold! Your day is over. The people are reaching for arms! Him they'll follow, but where? Can he lead them to conquer the oceans? If you love this King let him die in glory!

MONTEZUMA: Enough!

JUDGE: My Lord . . . !

MONTEZUMA: I would die with you now for I see the same horror. But I'll not believe that all I've built, my golden cities, my roads, my gardens, aqueducts and spires, my state, my Aztec state unparalleled on earth before—I'll not believe they rose out of the earth for spiders to devour.

JUDGE: Everything dies!

MONTEZUMA: Not this! This will end only with the world! There must be a way to govern that does not end in ruins!

JUDGE: But if you can't rule by force can you rule without it? Therefore the thing is finished!

CAGAMA: I don't understand! My lord, are we all mad? How can you govern except by force?

ASTRONOMER: My lord, the shadow is moving quickly!

(*All look up at the moon.*)

MONTEZUMA (*still looking up. It is quiet*): Parach, will the sacrificial flame soar so high?

PARACH: Emperor, what is turning in your mind? How can you rule without force?

MONTEZUMA: Parach, will the world go on?

PARACH: I pray for a tall flame.

MONTEZUMA: Then I bid you, Holy Boy, tell this to the gods in heaven. I, Montezuma, made this nation in the way I knew—and war was enough for a king to know. But what the sword has won the sword alone cannot keep safe. But I am not sad; I know that my thoughts come to me from heaven, although I do not always understand them. But I have imagined rivers of flowing brass where swords and shields have melted, and I often think of times before our fathers, and their fathers before them—when the world was young and a man-god lived on this ground we love, and he ruled here with a soft voice and never touched weapons. You know his name, Holy Boy, our Quetzalcoatl god, gentle Lord of the moving wind, the white god who walked into the sunrise and with his going, murder burst on the world, and war. But he promised to return one day . . .

GUATEMOTZIN: These Spaniards are murdering . . . !

MONTEZUMA: "I will return!" he said, "and the Golden Years will shine again from my outstretched hands."

GUATEMOTZIN: How could *they* be . . . ?

MONTEZUMA (*to* BOY SACRIFICE): The Spaniards are white, and they came from the sunrise! It's true they've come calling commands, ruthless; but I've not stopped them and I will not raise a hand until I know; are they God's children, or mortal strangers coming for conquest? Go now; beg the spirits, send this King a sign to go by; in the trees, in the sky, brand them with a name! Are they men or gods? They're close now. If I must kill again, it must be soon. Take him Parach, take him to the mountain top. And may the flame of your strong body burn us onward to a stronger year! Farewell, Holy Boy.

BOY SACRIFICE: I will ask the spirits to send my Lords a sign; farewell.

ASTRONOMER: The time is short, my Lord!

MONTEZUMA: Hurry, Parach, and let the flame climb heavenward from his burning heart!

(PARACH *and the* BOY *go out. There is a pause.*)

CAGAMA: I understand nothing . . .

GUATEMOTZIN: My Lord . . . is war . . . my life and all I've learned and worshipped . . . suddenly to be despised?

MONTEZUMA: Try to understand . . . and you, Cagama . . . (*Breaks off angrily.*) I am not mad; a better time has never been for gods to return . . . Brother, my Lords, does not one prince tremble with me! The gods may have returned!

CUITLAHUA: I am ready to believe.

MONTEZUMA (*eagerly*): You have received a sign Cuitlahua?

CAGAMA: My lord, I see only *your* eyes. All my cities and I will travel by the clear conviction of those stars.

MONTEZUMA: That is good. And you, Guatemotzin, your cities?

GUATEMOTZIN: If there is a sign . . . then I'll bow to Spaniards. But how a peaceful god can sack your towns . . .

CUITLAHUA: But the people resist, they must be put aside . . .

GUATEMOTZIN: Put aside, and raped! Uncle, I know I am too young to understand, but if they're men, we're opening the gates to conquerors, and . . .

MONTEZUMA: *Four hundred* conquerors. I can muster eighty thousand troops this hour. Be sure of it, Guatemotzin, if they're men they'll die as all my enemies have died!

(*Enter* TAPAIA, *hurrying.*)

TAPAIA: The courier is in sight, my Lord, coming down the high road from the East.

ASTRONOMER: The moon is almost covered! The stars are fading!

MONTEZUMA: Hurry, bring him to me!

(*Exit* TAPAIA. *A man laughs quietly.*)

(*Startled.*) Ah!

(*Man laughs again.*)

I had forgotten you.

JUDGE: But death forgets no one, my Lord.

MONTEZUMA: Spare me your wisdom. Go—take him!—Go,

and be a good example for the country; die bravely, as befits one of Montezuma's judges.

JUDGE: I will die with my memories of Aztec hands building a world. The stones now are dropping from the walls . . . I see dust rising . . .

(*Enter* TECUICHPO.)

TECUICHPO: Don't let him say any more Father!

MONTEZUMA: Tecuichpo.

TECUICHPO: Take him away!

JUDGE: I pray the Montezuma king will not outlive his honour.

MONTEZUMA: Take him.

(*Exit* JUDGE.)

TECUICHPO: There is some spirit here; making us mad Father . . . I must not keep it from you—I have prayed in the Temple . . . it came upon me suddenly to pray . . . that they will come here to us.

GUATEMOTZIN: You prayed in the Temple for Spaniards?

TECUICHPO: It was like a great hand on my back, pressing me upward . . .

GUATEMOTZIN: She has prayed for your death, Uncle!

TECUICHPO: No. Not death, Guatemotzin! . . . for the coming-to-life of my dreams!

MONTEZUMA: You dreamed . . . ?

GUATEMOTZIN: They've poisoned the air we breathe!

MONTEZUMA: Tell me what you dreamed!

TECUICHPO: A thousand dreams, father, since the hour they touched the coast they have walked into my nights; brightly, brightly father, like the sun on wet rock, and I must see them now, how they move, and how they talk . . . I want to touch their eyes . . . !

GUATEMOTZIN: And if it's conquerors you've prayed for!

MONTEZUMA: What did they say, did they speak?

TECUICHPO: Like rivers, with the voices of rivers . . . last night they gave me a white swan . . . (*recalling*) and it died in my hands . . . I had—

MONTEZUMA: A swan died . . . ?

TECUICHPO (*seeing their fright*): What does that mean? Oh, Father, I can't have prayed for conquerors! Guatemotzin, there *will* be a wedding in the Spring! (*Sees they draw from her.*)

Why do you turn from me? Then attack with your armies; I
don't want them here—who will forgive my wicked heart!

(*A slight pause.* MONTEZUMA *turns to* CUITLAHUA, *won-deringly.*)

MONTEZUMA: I have never known such a dream . . . a white
swan, and it died . . .

(*Sudden booming of drums in distance.*)

ASTRONOMER: The stars are gone!

GUATEMOTZIN: The drums!

TAPAIA: Here is the courier from the coast, my Lord.

(*As they all start towards the open sky, enter* TAPAIA *support-ing* COURIER. MONTEZUMA *rushes to him.*)

MONTEZUMA: Speak. Have you seen the Spaniards!

COURIER: A great battle is preparing, my Lord. In Tlascalla,
fifty thousand troops are facing the Spaniards!

CAGAMA (*joyously*): *Fifty thousand*! Tlascalla is standing up to
them!

MONTEZUMA: You left before the battle started?

GUATEMOTZIN: Tlascalla will wipe them out!

MONTEZUMA (*to* COURIER): But you saw no fighting?

COURIER: No, my Lord. But I thought you should see this
before the moon goes dark . . . I stole it from their camp
as you commanded . . . (*He hands* MONTEZUMA *a cloth-covered object.*)

MONTEZUMA: This . . . this is . . .

(MONTEZUMA *uncovers it in silence but for the rising
drumbeats in the distance. All eyes glued to it . . . as the
cloth falls from it, the drums suddenly get louder and . . .*)

COURIER: His helmet, my Lord. Cortez wore it on his head.

ASTRONOMER: Montezuma . . . the moon is black!

MONTEZUMA: Tapaia, the torch! (*Still eyeing the helmet.*) Now
we'll know what they are . . .

CAGAMA: What does it mean . . . ?

TECUICHPO: Look at all the people on the mountain!

MONTEZUMA: On the head of the Quetzalcoatl god who
stands in the Temple is the metal helmet he left behind,
when he departed into the sun . . .

CUITLAHUA: Compare them!

ASTRONOMER: A falling star! Signal the mountain, Montezuma! Burn the Holy Boy!

MONTEZUMA: My Lords . . . if the moon returns and lights up the world again we'll go to the Temple, compare this with the headpiece of the god, and if they match!—The gods have come; we . . .

TECUICHPO: Oh, Father, I'm afraid now!

GUATEMOTZIN: And if they do not match!

ASTRONOMER (*frenzied*): They're waiting for the signal! My lord, the torch . . .

MONTEZUMA: Signal the mountain to start the sacrifice!

(*An Aztec horn is blown which echoes through the atmosphere.*)

GUATEMOTZIN: My Lord, if they are not at all the same!

TECUICHPO: The sky is lower!

CUITLAHUA: They're lighting the pyre!

MONTEZUMA: Pray God to return us the world; we attack tomorrow if they're not the same. And the waiting's done, and we'll drive the Spaniard back to the sea!

(*The sky reflects a rising fire.*)

CUITLAHUA: The flame! Look, the mountain is burning!

GUATEMOTZIN: The smoke leaps to heaven!

(*The drumming becomes louder.*)

CUITLAHUA: It's reaching for the shadow! Like morning!

TECUICHPO: The sky is closer! The world is burning!

CUITLAHUA: The flame is red! The boy is burning now, my Lord!

GUATEMOTZIN: Look at the mountain, bright as the sunrise!

(*Pause.*)

CAGAMA: Why doesn't it move?

TECUICHPO: The shadow's not moving from the moon . . . oh, my wicked heart!

ASTRONOMER: The world is standing still! It is the end!

(*The wind rises suddenly during the invocation. There is humming behind his invocation.*)

MONTEZUMA (*calls up to the heavens*):

I call to the lightning!
Strike out of slumber!
Crack open the tomb!
I call to the stars;
Light on the world again!

Thunder in the clouds again!
On mountains we burn, burning the beautiful,
I call to all gods, and the god of all;
Return us the light,
Resurrect the shrouded moon! . . .

ASTRONOMER (*hushed*): My Lord . . . the wind!

MONTEZUMA (*feeling it*): Wind?

CUITLAHUA (*alarmed*): . . . Suddenly . . .

GUATEMOTZIN (*opening his palm to it*): . . . Feel it . . . how swift . . .

ASTRONOMER (*fearful*): My Lord, the moon is not moving . . .
(*Pause.*)

CAGAMA (*the fright grows*): It's flattening out . . .

GUATEMOTZIN: The people are running away!

CUITLAHUA: Brother, the flame's blowing out!

MONTEZUMA: No!

ASTRONOMER: My Lord, the end!!

MONTEZUMA (*rushes out to the sky, throws his arms out, and roars . . .*): Stop the wind! STOP THE WIND!

CUITLAHUA: It's out! The fire is out!!

(*They stand fixed, staring at the black sky,* MONTEZUMA'*s hands rigid over his head. A long silence when the faintest greenish light sprays the sky and their faces.* MONTEZUMA'*s arms come down slowly to his sides. The others survey the sky, mystified.*)

(*Softly, struck.*) The flame did not rise.

CAGAMA: How can it be . . . ?

TECUICHPO: The stars . . . !

GUATEMOTZIN (*facing the moon*): The moon is shining again . . . why . . . how . . . ?

(GUATEMOTZIN *turns to* MONTEZUMA *with the others.* MONTEZUMA *turns slowly from the moon to the helmet which gleams brightly in the moonlight. They follow his eyes. He goes softly, lifts it as though it were alive. All are entranced by it. He turns it over in his hands again, then raises his eyes to them. They return the look wide-eyed and transfixed with fearful wonder as the light fades into complete darkness.*)

SCENE 2

All men required.

The gloomy interior of a deserted temple several days' march from the capital. Night. As the light goes up MESA, *a young fellow, not armoured, approaches clutching his arm . . . followed by* FR. OLMEDO *supporting* ORDAZ, *a giant man who is gulping down air . . .*

MESA: It's broke, my arm—it's broken! (*Looks around.*) Where are we? What is this place?

FR. OLMEDO: Lie down here, Ordaz . . .

ORDAZ (*almost weeping, flaying his arms about . . .*): The horses! The devil damned horses did it!

FR. OLMEDO: There will be other battles, Diego. Mary watches over us . . .

MESA (*clutching his arm*): My arm, Padre!

> (*As* FR. OLMEDO *goes to him, enter* CAPTAINS *and a few* SOLDIERS *limping, holding an arm, etc. . . . and one frantically searching himself as though he'd lost something. All talk breathlessly and vociferously at once, followed a moment later by* CORTEZ *and* MARINA *who is patting his neck with a cloth. As their words become distinguishable and they enter the lighted area . . .*)

LEON (*to* MONTEJO): Where in hell were the cannon, Montejo?

MONTEJO: Where they should've been!—I couldn't fire into Spaniards, could I? . . .

OLID: You should've shot them off in the air! . . .

> (MARINA *nurses* CORTEZ *who sits.*)

ARBENGA: They were all loaded . . . !

OLID (*to* ARBENGA): Shut your mouth, Arbenga!

MESA (*to* OLID): There was no time for cannon . . . !

LEON (*to* MESA): Damned Italian blunderer!

MESA: Damn yourself . . .

ORDAZ (*from the floor. To* LEON): Don't curse the cannoniers, you puppy!

LEON (*turns on him*): I spit on cannoniers!

ORDAZ: And I spit on your stinkin' horses!

LEON: The horses saved our lives!

ORDAZ: The foot-soldier saved your lives! Montejo, what did the horses do but box us in so we couldn't fire a cannon without hitting our own people?

LEON: You can't gallop a horse on those rocks!

ORDAZ: Then why in Lucifer's hell didn't you get out of the way!?

OLID: That's easy to say!

ORDAZ: Ship your cows back to Cuba, for Jesus' sake; every time I lift a sword there's a horse's ass in my face!

CORTEZ: Señores! (*Quiet.*) There is still work to be done. Leon, be so good as to see that the horses are watered.

LEON: Hernando, you're bleeding . . .

CORTEZ: A flesh wound in the neck. And I couldn't find my helmet. Go, Leon. Montejo . . .

LEON: I'll find some water for you . . .

CORTEZ: Do as I say. See to the horses.

LEON: Aye . . . take care of him, Marina. (*Exit* LEON.)

CORTEZ: Montejo, see your cannon are kept loaded . . .

MONTEJO: It was impossible to fire, Hernando . . .

CORTEZ: I know, I know. Go on . . . what are you searching for?

MONTEJO: My purse . . . it's been stolen by the infidel.

CORTEZ (*wry smile*): Maybe that's why the cannon didn't go off.

(*The men laugh.*)

MONTEJO: You mustn't say that, Hernando . . .

CORTEZ (*suddenly angering but restraining himself*): I am saying, Montejo!—The cannon fell asleep like drunkards clutching a purse!

MONTEJO: I am ready to weep, Hernando . . .

CORTEZ: Be ready to fight, Señor, and we'll live longer! Now see to your cannon.

(*Pause.* MONTEJO *goes out, ashamed.*)

CORTEZ: Pedro, will you . . . ? (*Looks around near him.*) Pedro . . . where is Alvarado! (*Stands quickly.*)

OLID: He must be with the men . . .

CORTEZ: Is he hurt, did you see him?

OLID: No, but . . .

CORTEZ: Find him, Olid . . . go and find Alvarado . . . Pedro . . . go with him . . . find Pedro . . .

FR. OLMEDO: I'm sure he's safe . . .

CORTEZ: How you all love to *talk*! Go and find Alvarado!!

> (FR. OLMEDO *hurries out,* OLID *more leisurely . . . after a few steps, he turns.*)

OLID (*softly*): It was a blunder, Hernando.

CORTEZ: Señor de Olid, I appreciate your learning, but will you spare me strategy and find Alvarado?

OLID (*bows with a touch of sarcasm*): I spare you strategy. (*He goes out.*)

CORTEZ (*calling after* OLID): And see to the wounded! Ordaz, can you walk?

ORDAZ: I'm tired, Hernando.

CORTEZ: Follow him? He'll stir up trouble again I think.

ORDAZ (*rises with difficulty*): Ahh . . . (*He's almost weeping.*) I hate that man. Despise him!

CORTEZ: But will you go and follow him?

ORDAZ: You're different, Hernando. You're a horseman but a foot-soldier is not dirt to you. I tell you the foot-soldier is the heart of this army!

CORTEZ: I know, Diego, follow him.

ORDAZ (*starts and stops*): What will be the end of it, Hernando. We can't fight another such battle.

CORTEZ: God is with us, Captain.

ORDAZ: Aye . . . Find a way, Hernando, I'm an old man, but I'm not meant to die here. We'll not die here, Hernando!

CORTEZ: We'll live to be Kings, Diego.

ORDAZ (*smiles sadly*): How sweet you are . . . Christ will speak to you . . . (*Rushes to him weeping, kisses his cheek, embraces him.*) Think, Hernando, think . . . we must not die here! (*To* MESA.) Come with me, Mesa.

MESA: My arm . . .

ORDAZ: Let him think . . . come on.

> (MESA *does not move.*)

Italian!

MESA: I'm coming.

ORDAZ (*assuringly*): Don't worry for Alvarado . . . and think, Hernando, there must be a way out of this . . . I'll follow Señor de Olid the intellectual . . .

> (*Some mocking laughter.*)

>> (ORDAZ *hurries out with* MESA *behind him.* MARINA *is*

alone with CORTEZ, *standing behind him patting his neck
with the cloth. He is seated. He stretches out his right leg and
squeezes the muscle of his thigh, staring straight ahead. She
comes around, kneels before him and massages his thigh, he
tightens with the pain. She stops then continues more softly.*)

CORTEZ: What is this building?

MARINA: A temple. They deserted it when we came.

CORTEZ (*looks about*): You're weeping, Marina.

MARINA: No.

CORTEZ: Why?

MARINA (*slight pause*): I thought you would die. They aimed
for you . . . all of them . . . for your face!

CORTEZ: They know me now. (*Pause.*) You're not weeping for
me, Marina.

MARINA: Who then?

CORTEZ: The enemy.

MARINA: The enemy are people too.

CORTEZ (*looks at her, lifts her chin*): Your eyes are so dark now.
You used to smile always.

MARINA (*she gets up*): Tell me, Hernando, how long must you
go on killing?

CORTEZ: Sometimes men must kill to bring a blessing.

MARINA: Never, Hernando, never.

CORTEZ: You're so foolish . . . this is war . . .

MARINA: But I didn't come with you to fight wars . . .

CORTEZ: How else can we make them Christians?

MARINA: As you told me Christ made Christians.

CORTEZ (*smiles*): Yes, but, these people are not . . .

MARINA: They are not animals! They are not to be burned as
you've burned them, stabbed as you've stabbed them . . .
Hernando, ten thousand childen are fatherless since you
marched from the coast!

CORTEZ: Stop it!

MARINA: Turn back!

CORTEZ: Eh? Marina, what did you say? (*He rises.*)

MARINA: Turn back to the coast. I'll lead you as I led you
here . . .

CORTEZ: I don't want you to utter those words again, Marina.

MARINA: You can't . . .

CORTEZ (*flares up*): Never again!! Never.

(*She lowers her eyes. He strides from her, turns to her . . . almost appealing.*)

What can I do? Would you have me go out to them without arms, without . . .

MARINA: Without arms, without blood . . . I would walk with a cross before you. I would speak to them, "People, good people, hear the voice of the True God!" They would listen . . .

CORTEZ: How pure you are . . . They would never listen. They would wipe us out . . .

MARINA: Then we would die, and God would remember us. Hernando, I walked alone out of the forest to meet you. I was the first,—why?—to kill? I had enough of killing; my father died in battle, I was sold to another who died in war, captured again in war . . . over the face of Mexico I ran before the storm,—peace was the star I sought, and peace was the word you gave me. Peace on earth, you said, and I believed it. The white sails of your ships, full in the wind,— I knew at the sight of them heaving on the waves—this was clean, and I walked on the beach to touch you, to believe in you, and now, I'm killing with you . . . killing my people.

CORTEZ: When you stood that day on the sunlit deck, the holy water still wet on your cheeks, what did I say to you? Marina, we will tear this people from the claws of antichrist and Jesus will reign in Mexico and blood and stone will not stop us!

MARINA: But what has killing brought you? Here you are; Hernando—you have less than four hundred men now and out there fifty thousand people are gathering to fight again! What force will save you now!

CORTEZ (*desperately*): My sword and Christ will save us now!

MARINA: Go back, Hernando . . . !

CORTEZ: Enough!!

(*He raises his hand as though to strike her. She springs away as though he'd done it before. We hear* ALVARADO *call* "HERNANDO" *off stage. Enter* ALVARADO *hurrying, leading a struggling Indian girl by a rope tied around her waist . . .*)
(*With deep joy.*) Pedro! Are you hurt!

ALVARADO: Only my heart! Hernando . . . look. (*Indicates the girl.*) Every time we capture women what happens to mine? I go to sleep and by morning, psst! . . . Some bastard's son is riding her under my nose. So this time I resolved,—Alvarado, find thee a rope. Result? I'll tie this one to my leg and sleep in peace.

(*Laughter.*)

(*Sound of grumbling men coming closer and entering. All turn towards doorway except* MARINA *who crosses to girl and talks to her quietly.*)

(*Confidentially.*) Hernando . . . there's going to be trouble.

CORTEZ: What trouble?

ALVARADO: The men say the Tlascallans are bringing up more troops . . .

CORTEZ: Who told them that?

ALVARADO: Some of them want to retreat . . .

CORTEZ: Who's spreading this?

ALVARADO: I think it's Cristobal de Olid.

CORTEZ: Ah? And what do they want me to do?

ALVARADO: I don't know, but speak to them, they only need your word . . .

(MARINA *comes quickly from girl.*)

MARINA: Alvarado . . . this girl is twelve years old.

ALVARADO: I know, but she seems . . .

MARINA: Hernando, she's a child!

CORTEZ (*hearing men entering*): Shut up . . . !

(*Enter Captains* ORDAZ, MONTEJO, LEON *and* FR. OLMEDO. *These come forward silently and flank* CORTEZ, *turning to watch the* SOLDIERS *come in.*)

Come in, good soldiers! Let the wounded sit! Well now . . . what can I do for you, dear friends?

(*The* SOLDIERS *enter the lighted area, sullen, those behind growling, etc. They halt. The officers flanking* CORTEZ *are facing the men, whose ranks seem to reach far back into the shadows. All of those visible are bandaged on some part of their bodies.*)

CORTEZ (*he inspects each face, identifying them. He turns and looks over his officers. To the men*): Speak. What is it? (*Silence. To his officers.*) One of my officers then? (*They don't speak. To the men.*) Señores, I am ashamed of you. What brings you here?

ARBENGA (*steps forward, doffs his cap*): Señor Cortez, we . . .

CORTEZ: Arbenga.

ARBENGA: Yes, Captain, I'm no trouble-maker. But . . . we've fought . . . like Spaniards. And, what have we got for it?

CORTEZ: Before the mason finishes the house he cannot sleep in it.

ARBENGA (*looks at him blankly*): Yes. (*Nods. Turns to men.*) Alfredo . . .

> (ALFREDO *tries to edge back into the crowd.* ARBENGA *grabs his wrist and drags him forward.*)

Tell him what you told me!

ALFREDO (*frightened, dumb*): I only . . .

ARBENGA (*yells*): Tell him!! Won't one of you tell him? (ARBENGA *turns to all of them appealingly to say something, but they're cold. He turns quickly to Captain de Olid.*) Captain Olid.

> (OLID *draws away from him.*)

CORTEZ: Ah?! (*To* OLID.) Can *you* explain, Cristobal de Olid?

OLID: I? Why do you ask me? I have nothing to do with this!

CORTEZ: Come, Cristobal, speak up for this rebellion!

OLID: Arbenga!—Have I spoken to you of rebellion?

ARBENGA (*looks at* OLID, *pause*): No, Captain de Olid. (*To* CORTEZ.) Señor, I am a simple man. I know only what I see. I came from Cuba for gold. I was prepared to fight for it. And we fought,—aye, Señor,—how did we fight, ten thousand upon thousand of heathen and we slew them all. And some of us died, and tonight not one of us is without a wound.

CORTEZ: Aye; when there is war there are wounds, you speak truly.

ARBENGA (*points outside*): If you will look, Señor, more than fifty thousand Tlascallans are gathering out there on the plain below.

CORTEZ (*simply*): I have seen them.

ARBENGA: Aye, and there are three hundred and eighty-five Spaniards alive tonight?

> (*Silence.*)

We can't hold them off again. I beg you, Captain, let us not die among the heathen: let us go back to the coast.

CORTEZ: And then, what?

ARBENGA (*hesitates*): We wish to return to Cuba.

CORTEZ: Cuba? (*Angering.*) I never heard of gold in Cuba.

VOICE I (*from among the men far back*): But who's rich from the gold in Mexico!

VOICES: Aye!

CORTEZ (*straining over the heads of the men. Pointing*): *You* will be rich! (*Some laughter.*) Hey? Do you think you stand in a barren forest here? This is the gateway to an empire and we've got our toe in the crack! (*Walks up a level.*) Climb the trees and look to the Western hills where Montezuma sits! Gold you say?—The very sky glares yellow over that golden city! Spit on Cuba, spit on it, I say!

(*Dead silence. No response.*)

ALVARADO (*yelling at them*): You frogs! (*Dashes up and down before them.*) You bloody whoreson cowards!

CORTEZ: Pedro!!

ALVARADO (*waving his sword*): By God's blood I swear I'll . . . !

CORTEZ: Put away your sword, Alvarado!

(ALVARADO *subsides, turns, spits towards* OLID, *and walks glaring at him.*)

(*To men*): Think. Where are you running? Cuba?—The lazy air and the day sleeping on your shoulders; the bloodless women smiling for your purse . . . is this for Spaniards? And did you forget the fleet? Remember, Señores, we scuttled the fleet in Vera Cruz harbour when we came. Every ship but one lies at the bottom. Have you forgotten how we stood on the shore and cried, "sink the fleet, we'll fight this land until we're kings in it!" *There* were Spaniards!

VOICE 2 (*holds up his bandaged arms and rushes forward*): I'm wounds and scabs from head to foot! I can't lift a sword.

SOLDIERS (*roar*): He's right! Back to Cuba! Back to Cuba.

CORTEZ (*roaring back*): Do I not bleed!! In the neck? Here . . . in both legs!?

(*Silence.*)

What did you expect if not bleeding? Did you come to play with flowers? Did I tell you Montezuma would hand you his head on a dish, or did I say we'd kill for it! What did I tell you and what did you come for! Answer me that!!

(*Pause.*)

OLID: May I answer that, Hernando?

(CORTEZ *doesn't turn around for a moment. Then slowly he turns and moves toward him.*)

CORTEZ: You have something to say now, Captain de Olid?

OLID: Aye, Captain Cortez, I have something to say.

(*The captains move toward him threateningly. He quickly starts to speak.*)

Señores. Captain Cortez forgets one very important fact. We shipped on this expedition not to conquer Mexico at all.

SOLDIERS: He's right . . . he's telling truth!

OLID: On the contrary, we had explicit orders from Señor Velasquez, Governor of Cuba, to scour the coast for trade and were forbidden to march inland!

CAPTAINS: Stop it . . . that's enough! (*Etc. . . .*)

SOLDIERS: Let him speak! Go on!

OLID: But what happened! Certain officers among us became —how shall I say—ambitious. And the night before we sailed, decided in secret, mind you, that we were going on this suicidal expedition to conquer Mexico!

(*Shouts for and against.*)

Finally! Finally, I say! When the plot leaked out to the Governor's ear, Cortez pulled anchor and sailed that night before the Governor could stop him! In short, those of you who love your country will decide to return to it because we sailed on a stolen fleet; under the law, we are bandits and are therefore cursed by God!

(*The* SOLDIERS' *shouts of approval are loudest.* CORTEZ *draws his sword, leaps to the platform and jabs it down into the crowd. Sudden silence.*)

CORTEZ: What are you—peasants! I picked no farmers for the fleet! I took hidalgos, Spaniards, conquistadors, fighters with blood to give!!

VOICE 2: Back to Cuba!

MEN: Cuba! Cuba! (*Etc.*)

CORTEZ: All right, you pigs, you stupid oxen, you bungling bottom-lice! Back to Cuba, come on!

(*The men cheer.*)

(*Mocking them.*) Aye! Hurrah! Hurrah!

(*Quiet.*)

But of course, brave Señores, valiant conquistadors, the moment we set foot on Cuban soil we'll hang for high treason!

(*Silence.*)

What . . . no cheers? Why not? Cuba? Come on, to Cuba! You think the flags will fly when you reach Santiago! Governor Velasquez will crush you like rats! To him you're thieves, mockers of his authority, stinking scum of the earth!

SOLDIER (*from deep back*): Make way! Make way!

(*The crowd opens up and a Spanish soldier comes rushing through.*)

CORTEZ: Well?

SOLDIER: Captain, their King wants an audience with you at once.

CORTEZ: What! (*Comes down quickly.*)

SOLDIER: King Xicotenga, the King of this country, he's waiting beyond the lines.

CORTEZ: Marina, what would this mean?

MARINA: This is how they bring an ultimatum.

CORTEZ: Go and tell him to come here. And keep a clear eye on their troops.

SOLDIER: Aye, Captain.

CORTEZ: Hurry!

(SOLDIER *exits.*)

(CORTEZ *jumps up to the level.*) To your positions now. If we must fight, fight we will and like Christians and Spaniards. Do I hear your answer?

(*Men pause. They start to turn, obeying, but sullenly.*)

Wait, señores!

(*They stop.*)

I promise you I will try to avoid a battle. But it may be we will have to fight . . . Do you hear? Señores!

(*Silence.*)

Then remember this, we have come so far and vanquished forty thousand at a time not because of strength or swordplay. Divinity, Señores, the unconquerable Spanish name, the gods in our speech, in our prancing horse, in the wild glare of our armour—these are what we've ridden on, and conquered on. But let them once see us turn our backs, and we will fight as armoured *men*, not gods but *men*, and we are done!

(*Pause.*)

So, we are Christians and conquistadors, from this night on we fling across these purple hills a voice of terror as a *god* would fling—aye, gods in iron with thunder beating out— attack if we must, and to victory! To your posts, Señores. Those who are not badly injured remain here. Adios!

(*The men go out.*)

Leon, go outside and mount your horse. Wait until the King comes in—then, give her the whip and gallop right past this

doorway. Do it every few minutes and plenty of noise mind.
You understand?

LEON (*smiles*): Aye.

CORTEZ (*as* LEON *goes*): At full gallop!

LEON (*smiles again*): She'll sound like thunder. (*Exit* LEON *at a lope.*)

CORTEZ (*to the* CAPTAINS *and remaining men*): Remember we are a victorious army treating indignantly for peace. We are deeply offended that they dared attack us. The face is determined, the bearing, proud,—erect, Montejo. This time, when I touch my breastplate, so (*he does so*), everyone cries out in anger.

ALVARADO: *And* half-draw our swords.

CORTEZ: That's good. And half-draw the sword. (*To* SOLDIER 2.) You bring me the King . . . alone!

SOLDIER 2: Yes, sir. (*Exit* SOLDIER.)

ALVARADO: I think our bandages should come off, Hernando.

CORTEZ: Yes, yes. Off with them. Quickly.

MESA: My arm'll bleed.

CORTEZ: Take it off, Mesa!
    (*As they take off their visible bandages.*)
Erect now! (*He inspects them.*) Gonzalo, no stick.

GONZALO: My knee . . .

CORTEZ: Gonzalo!
    (*Kicks the stick from under him and shoves it aside as the* SOLDIER *enters.*)
No stick.
    (*The men chuckle.*)

SOLDIER 2: The King, Señor.

CORTEZ (*looks at all the men*): Marina, stay here beside me. Alvarado, here on my left. (*A final inspection.*) Now bring him in.
    (*Enter King* XICOTENGA. *He is in his prime, tall, proud, lithe. He comes part way in. Runs his eyes along the soldiers. Comes further in, warily, but unafraid, inspects the Captains, his eyes stop at* CORTEZ.)

XICOTENGA: You are Hernando Cortez?

CORTEZ: And you, Your Majesty, the renowned Xicotenga. I regret the state of my accommodation for you.

XICOTENGA: It was more comfortable before we stripped it bare.

CORTEZ: An unnecessary precaution, your Majesty, we will not be with you long.

XICOTENGA: I have come to tell you that. You will depart my territory this hour.

CORTEZ (*pause, smiles*): Surely you are not serious, my lord.

XICOTENGA (*motions outside*): I have sixty thousand troops in the valley.

CORTEZ: And I have a hundred thousand outside that doorway.

XICOTENGA: A pity they refused to fight with you today.

CORTEZ: Oh, they did not refuse, Señor, I simply dislike slaughter. But perhaps you would like to meet . . . say a thousand of them.

XICOTENGA (*smiling*): I would be honoured.

> (*Fierce gallop of hooves past the doorway.* XICOTENGA *starts, then quickly composes himself. During the noise* CORTEZ *shouts something to* ALVARADO. *As it dies down,* ALVARADO *stands looking incredulously at* CORTEZ.)

CORTEZ: Go, Captain, bring in the soldiers.

> (ALVARADO *goes out.*)
>
> (*Comes very close to the King, talks into his face, but still smiling.*) You realize of course, that your people are still alive because I preferred not to kill them yet.

XICOTENGA: I . . .

CORTEZ: But you must realize that!

XICOTENGA: I will wipe you out in an hour.

CORTEZ: You truly believe that . . . ? (*He looks straight into his eyes for a moment, then smiles.*) Are you aware that I am in your country only because it lies on the road to Montezuma?

XICOTENGA: What do you want with the Aztec?

CORTEZ: I want to conquer him.

XICOTENGA (*amused*): *You* will conquer Montezuma?

CORTEZ: I never lie, Señor.

XICOTENGA: You are his enemy and he lets you come so far? He would crush you with the rise of his smallest finger!

CORTEZ: In a word, Señor, Montezuma is afraid of Spaniards. He dares not attack us!

XICOTENGA (*he slowly looks about at the officers and men, then back to* CORTEZ): In one hour, I attack. My people despise you. They'll not rest until every one of you is dead. One hour, Cortez; farewell.

(*He turns. As he starts to walk the hooves gallop past the doorway violently. He stops and wheels around as* CORTEZ *touches his breast-plate and all half-draw their swords, clinking.*)

MARINA: Hernando!

CORTEZ: You've angered the monsters, Señor!

XICOTENGA: You would not dare harm my person . . .

CORTEZ: A Christian wants to harm no one! (*To* ALVARADO *who comes in carrying a cannon ball.*) Ah, Pedro, put it here. This, Señor, is called a cannon ball.

   (ALVARADO *puts down the ball, the King staring at it . . .* CORTEZ *pats it . . .* ALVARADO *takes position at entrance.*)

A thousand fighters sleep in here, waiting for my command. I have a hundred like this. At a word they will dig a hole in the ground the size of a tree, or tear a cloud and bring rain,—or break the back of a nation. Shall I awaken them Señor,—or may I pass through to Montezuma?

XICOTENGA (*eyes wide, he turns from the ball*): I will attack . . .
   (*Galloping of the horse outside. Involuntarily he wheels around towards the doorway.*)

CORTEZ: Do I pass or do I not!

XICOTENGA (*quickly turns back to him . . . frantically*): I will attack!

CORTEZ: Wake up a thousand troops and by the one god Jesus Christ,—let them speak! Alvarado—the signal.

   (ALVARADO *raises his arm. Cannons boom close by.* XICOTENGA *claps his hands over his ears and sinks down in obeisance.*)

XICOTENGA: Tonatiuh! Tonatiuh! (*Breaks off into incoherent mumble.*)

CORTEZ: What is he saying?

MARINA (*tears in her eyes*): He is calling you . . . the sun.

CORTEZ (*smiles. Bends and lifts him to his feet*): Lift up your eyes, foolish King.
   (*The King does.*)
Do you understand?

XICOTENGA: Have mercy on me . . . whatever I possess is yours . . . take whatever you need . . .

CORTEZ: Send your troops away.

XICOTENGA: Let me give you some . . .

CORTEZ: I? What use have I for troops?

XICOTENGA: Do me the honour, I beg you, take ten thousand, they will fight with you . . .

CORTEZ: But they would be afraid of Montezuma . . .

XICOTENGA (*pause*): No . . . with you, they would battle even the Aztec. They would be honoured . . . I beg you . . .

CORTEZ: Well . . . they'll probably be an encumbrance, but if they would enjoy the fight, I'll accept . . . say . . . two thousand five hundred men.

XICOTENGA: From my heart, deep thanks. Now, will you let me go and explain to my people . . .

CORTEZ: You are free to move as you please. You will return here in the morning.

XICOTENGA: I will bring you ten loads of fine things to eat.

CORTEZ: Good night, Your Majesty.

XICOTENGA (*a smile dawns on his face*): When Montezuma hears of this, he'll not smile.

CORTEZ: No, he'll not smile.

XICOTENGA (*going*): It will be . . . a great year in Mexico.

CORTEZ: Aye, a great one.

(XICOTENGA *stands smiling at the thought of it, bows and moves out facing* CORTEZ . . .)

(*When* XICOTENGA *is at the door,* CORTEZ *shouts suddenly.*) But if there is treachery, Señor, the ground will open under you!

XICOTENGA: Believe it, there is honour still among mankind.

(*He bows and goes out. Everyone peers out after him to make sure he's gone, then all rush at* CORTEZ *roaring, congratulating him, slapping him on the back, etc. except* MARINA *who stands aside watching unhappily.*)

ALVARADO: Gods! That's what we'll be!—The Sun, by Jesus!

(*All roar laughing.*)

CORTEZ (*jubilant*): And see that we act like gods! From to-night, the Spaniard is God in Mexico! Now, go out to your men, explain what has happened, but!—No drinking! We are austere. And in the morning, we march westward with legions behind us! The road is clear to Montezuma! Until dawn, Señores.

ALL (*going*): Good night, sleep well, thank God . . . (*etc.*)

CORTEZ: Sleep well. And thank you. Good night. (*To* OLID.) Oh, Cristobal. It was a blunder, Cristobal . . . eh?

OLID (*going*): You're a very lucky man, Hernando Cortez.

CORTEZ: Yes. And you are not. Good night.

ALVARADO (*indicates the departed* OLID, *and with infinite pleasure*): How bitter is the gall! Lucifer himself never fell so hard and so fast as Cristobal de Olid! Sleep well, Hernando!

(*Both laugh as he turns to go.*)

Hey!

(*Searching around him wildly.*)

CORTEZ: What?

ALVARADO: My girl! . . .

CORTEZ: Even with a rope tied round your ankle, Pedro!

ALVARADO (*rushing about*): Who did it! . . . (*To* MARINA.) Did you see her!

CORTEZ: Look in your pocket!

ALVARADO: My death! What was her name! (*Rushes out.*)

CORTEZ (*laughs until he turns and sees* MARINA *who is alone with him*): He'll discover some day that you're the culprit and it will not go well with you.

MARINA: A beast should sleep with cows not children. He always finds a child.

CORTEZ: Ahh . . . I'm tired, Marina. Help me out of this . . . (*off with his breastplate.*) What do you suppose Montezuma looks like?

MARINA: A man. Like you.

CORTEZ: Handsome?

MARINA: So they say. (*She goes and spreads out a blanket.*)

CORTEZ: And will *he* believe that Gods are walking in his state?

MARINA: I pray he does not.

CORTEZ (*lying down*): Why?

MARINA: Hernando, how will you ever break a lie when it's grown so large?

CORTEZ: When we've conquered, only the truth will reign. Believe in me, Marina!

MARINA: Tell me this, I know the others, but you—was it God or gold that brought you here to Mexico? Look in my eyes, Hernando!

CORTEZ (*pause*): Aye, there's gold in it, and a good many things that an empire's made of . . . but by my conscience, Marina, the Christ is in it too, and as deep, I think, as any other thing.

(*He has her hand, pulls on it, she resists.*)

Believe it, Marina, I swear it to you! Come, here beside me.

(*She lies down beside him, and he leans over, kisses her. Softly.*)
We'll live in golden palaces, and drink from golden cups,
and you shall be a golden queen, rubies in your hair, and
from o'er the sea the Kings of the world will come to do
obeisance at your feet . . . Marina, . . . you're weeping
again. I love you child . . . look at me. Why are your eyes
so dead to me. I love you, believe it . . . stop crying! . . .
Stop it! You'll not leave me! Marina, I need you! Smile to
me! Marina, you can't go away . . . I need you, Marina.
Smile to me! There—that's better.

(*She smiles slowly, the tears in her eyes. He laughs suddenly,
and buries his face in her breasts . . . as the lights dim out.*)
Oh, my dear woman, you will thank Cortez all the days of
your royal life!

SCENE 3

*In the tower of the great Temple in Tenochtitlan, the tall figures
of the two chief gods face each other: the peaceful* QUETZALCOATL
on the left and HUITZILOPOCHTLI, *the God of War on the right.
Before the latter, stirring a steaming cauldron which is set on a
tripod, is* PARACH.

PARACH (*alone*):
Stir, stir in thy bed of evening clouds,
Descend, descend, O Huitzilopochtli God of War,
O Battlemaker, possess again the King's faint heart,
Strike from his arms the chains of peace
That are breaking his honour as a bone.
O Lord of War, the Emperor is beguiled
By a vision that corrupts his powers.
Descend, Thunderer, burst upon the earth
Brilliant in arms! Walk again thy restless form
Into the living flesh of the Montezuma King!
Stir and descend, stir and descend . . .
(*He recedes from the God and approaches* QUETZALCOATL
on the left. To QUETZALCOATL.)

I pray you, Lord of the Wind, forgive me, Quetzalcoatl.
You blew down the flame and returned the moon
And I know it; And I know your power; I confess
I have not led the King to favour you these years
But I will change and feed you flowers once again
Abandon your revenge, O Peaceful Heart,
He is coming now to compare the Spaniard's helmet
With yours, and when he sees how unlike they are
Trick him no more, and let him destroy the Spaniard.
I will honour you again, I will not forget you
In the Years to come. . . .

> (*Enter* MONTEZUMA, GUATEMOTZIN, CAGAMA, *and* CUIT-
> LAHUA. MONTEZUMA *carries the helmet.* PARACH *bows.*
> *They stand centre, looking up at* QUETZALCOATL.)

Welcome my Lords to the Great Temple of Tenochtitlan.

MONTEZUMA (*he stands a little ahead of them, without turning
from the God*): What is your prayer, my Lords?

> (*Pause.*)

CUITLAHUA: It will come to be.

GUATEMOTZIN: It will never be.

> (*Slight pause.*)

MONTEZUMA: And Cagama?

CAGAMA: My mind is filled with garrisons and marching men.
But compare the helmets. I should like to see.

> (PARACH *mounts the* QUETZALCOATL *God.*)

MONTEZUMA: O Evening Star, if I beguile myself now, instruct
me . . . let this other world begin tonight, or send me
warring on the earth again! Descend, Parach, and bring me
the helmet of the God.

> (*The Lords watch with breathless attention as* PARACH *re-
> moves the God's helmet. He descends, hands it to* MONTE-
> ZUMA *who compares it with the Spanish helmet and his
> hands suddenly fly up and the helmets bound down the stone
> steps. He stands as though frozen, hands in air. Below, after
> a silence,* PARACH *picks both of them from the floor, Lords
> look at them and turn startled as* MONTEZUMA *slowly de-
> scends. As he nears the bottom . . .*)

(*Softly.*) Parach? Are they not the same? Cortez's helmet and
our loving God's?

PARACH (*blankly, dazed*): A god returns, but in other ways
. . . a god . . . a god returns but surely not like this. (*He
walks into the shadows mumbling.*)

MONTEZUMA (*pause. With his eyes on the helmet*): Leave me
now, my lords. Go to the treasury. Take two loads of gold.
Precious stones. Assemble an embassy. Go to Cortez; in my
name . . . welcome him to Mexico.

(*They don't move.*)

Shall I do battle with stars because a history is written and I
am at the end of it?

(*Silence.*)

Welcome them now . . . I'll remain in fasting here for two
days until they arrive. I'll be sure then, I will plunge into my
soul, I'll not let them into the city until I'm sure . . . Send
heralds through the empire; proclaim a state of prayer. Go,
my lords—I will speak with the gods tonight.

GUATEMOTZIN: The people will see danger . . .

MONTEZUMA: Then tell them that I will never betray them to
mortal man, but neither will I by impious haste unloose on
them the anger of heaven.

(*Pause.*)

CUITLAHUA: May the gods bless your fast, my Lord.

MONTEZUMA: And your journey to the Spaniard. Farewell.

(*They bow and all go out, right.*)

(*Alone in the Temple, he stands between the gods. Turns from*
HUITZILOPOCHTLI *to* QUETZALCOATL.) Great God Quetzalcoatl, I am not afraid. Though you come burning cities
and mocking my name, I pray your return. Aye, though I
must walk from the throne and treasured gold, from an
empire of cities into the desert, though the price of your
returning is an impoverishment to this robe on my back, I
would be ready. But even as I scented every wisp of wind
for signs, the final augury I knew would come not from
without, but from within my heart, and search it now,
there is no singing here. Why, am I not struck dead with
such doubting in my breast? Perhaps this is but a metal
that by some dark coincidence matches your very own? O
Tranquil God, do I mock myself! The Spaniard bleeds and
dies,—when did a god die? And they were seen eating

maize! And yet, what army of men could endure what they endure and live? And yet, they . . . and yet, and yet, and yet! I cannot yield an empire for a turning in bronze! I'll not give away a people to conquerors! Plant a word in my heart! Speak now in thunder, call through the lightning. (*Shouts.*) It is time for a word! O Eastern Star, oh God of the gentle heart, in what darkness shall I seek for thy word . . . ! (*Slow curtain as he speaks.*)

ACT TWO

The sunlit rooftop of the temple. TALUA *alone, looking excitedly off into the distance, the history under his arm. Enter* MONTEZUMA *and* LORDS *and* TECUICHPO. *All dressed magnificently. The King wears golden sandals, a brightly striped toga, from his shoulders hangs a great chain of gold, fabulously engraved, his golden crown, the shape of the pontifical tiara flashing the light.* PARACH *stands beside him. As they enter,* TALUA, *unable to restrain himself.*

TALUA (*pointing out*): They're turning down the avenue, my Lord!—coming this way!

TECUICHPO: Look Father how their metal throws back the sun!

MONTEZUMA: How cautiously they move.

TALUA: And those marvellous animals? See!—sparks, their feet are filled with sparks! My Lord, a boy told me the brown ones can talk!

PARACH: Be quiet Talua.

CUITLAHUA: That must be Cortez on the white one.

CAGAMA: His back is like a spear!

MONTEZUMA: You're certain, Guatemotzin, all the garrisons are prepared?

GUATEMOTZIN: We could attack this moment!

MONTEZUMA (*pause*): Cagama, your people are ready?

CAGAMA: We could cut them down like grain, my lord.

GUATEMOTZIN: Uncle, I beg you, let me bring two thousand down the causeway from Chapultepec, five thousand over the lake from Coyoacan and we've got them in between!

MONTEZUMA (*pause. He moves nervously*): I'll meet him . . . we have nothing to lose.

GUATEMOTZIN: But you sat two days before the gods and no word came. Look, here come the Tlascallan marching with the Spaniards! We fought them a hundred years and now they walk into the city! You cannot permit this, Uncle!

MONTEZUMA (*more uncertain*): Cuitlahua, you have men at the drawbridges.

CUITLAHUA: No one can leave the city now.

GUATEMOTZIN: My lord, look how silently the people wait in the doorways. They would bless you to let them fight!

PARACH (*looking out*): Look there! Those must be their priests. They bring a new god, not ours!

GUATEMOTZIN: Uncle, give me the golden word and I'll slaughter them where they stand!

MONTEZUMA: I cannot attack before I know.

CAGAMA: They're cut off, we've got them . . . !

MONTEZUMA: I'll hear no more! Wolves could take them now and hungry coyotes might find some honour in it! But (*touches prophecy in* TALUA's *hand*) we have our God's prophecy, my Lords, his promise of peace and wisdom on the throne of the world. You will not smash that down before I know the word the Spaniard brings!

TECUICHPO: Father, they're stopping. A woman is with them! Look!—she's dark!

GUATEMOTZIN (*all looking out, he explodes*): Oh, if it's all a mirage of words!—my Lord, who will have tears to weep for you!

MONTEZUMA: Guatemotzin, I'll not hear this again; I need no custodian for my honour. I will fight when time is for fighting.

TECUICHPO: A few of them are coming this way . . .

MONTEZUMA (*glances below*): Come—we greet the Spaniard not with the grinding teeth of barbarians, but with the confidence and smiles of our great inheritance. My Lords, we shall descend to greet them . . . let them know our race!

(*Exit all but* TAPAIA.)

TAPAIA:

From the cloudless heights he descends . . .

From the black holes of the earth they climb . . .

To touch hands on a path of flowers.

(*Enter the Aztec company from the left, descending the bottom steps of the Temple and turning into the court, then from the right, the Spaniards, the path of flowers connecting both parties.*

CORTEZ *flanked by* FR. OLMEDO *and* MARINA, *followed by* ALVARADO, ORDAZ, MONTEJO, DE LEON *and* DE OLID. *Part way down the flower path they stop. They all bow.*

CORTEZ *comes forward with* FR. OLMEDO *and* MARINA.
CORTEZ *makes a sweeping bow before* MONTEZUMA, *stands erect.* MONTEZUMA, *with simple ease, goes to him, stands a moment looking at his face, and from his shoulders he takes off the golden chain, holds it out.*
CORTEZ *takes it, puts it on.*)

MONTEZUMA: I welcome you to Mexico.

CORTEZ: Your Highness, in the name of the one God, the Son, and the Holy Ghost . . . creator of the turning heavens and maker of man, by the hand of my most Catholic master Charles, I bring you greetings and most fervent wishes for your health and boundless prosperity. A token of our friendship, my Lord.

(FR. OLMEDO *takes out a large string of glass beads.*)

. . . From my brothers and myself, these imperishable beads!
(CORTEZ *takes the beads and starts to put them over* MONTEZUMA'*s head.* MONTEZUMA *starts back.* MARINA *takes the necklace quickly and holds it out by her fingertips.* MONTEZUMA *takes it, puts it on.*)

MONTEZUMA (*fingering the beads*): I have never seen such stones . . . what are they?

CORTEZ: Glass, your Majesty. Sand, water and sun. They are imperishable.

MONTEZUMA: And . . . where does your . . . your world . . . lie?

CORTEZ: Far to the east and beyond the sea, my lord.

MONTEZUMA (*indicating officers*): And these are your brothers?

CORTEZ: Brothers, your Majesty, under our Lord Jesus Christ.

MONTEZUMA (*to* MARINA): But the woman is one of my subjects, are you not?

MARINA: I am a Christian, great Lord. I have always dreamed of seeing you . . .

CORTEZ: Marina has guided our journey, your Majesty. She is the first of your Christian subjects—the first to see the light of the one true God.

MONTEZUMA (*pause*): You have splendid eyes, Cortez.

CORTEZ: My Lord, they but reflect the Majesty of so magnificent a prince.

MONTEZUMA (*pause*): Tell me, Cortez . . . why have you come to Mexico?

CORTEZ (*pause*): Your Excellency, the question reveals a largeness of mind.

MONTEZUMA: The matter has occupied my thoughts. Why are you here?

CORTEZ: Let me be candid. My God and divine Master was heavy of heart that so magnificent an empire as your own should dwell without the blessings of our Lord, Jesus Christ. And nothing would suffice but I must carry the word of God to your Majesty and your people. For this purpose I have Padre Olmedo here—my holy man—and his brothers, who live only for the hour when they may bring you to baptism and open the gates of heaven to your princely soul. For this, my lord, I am here in Mexico. I bring you your own true God.

MONTEZUMA (*looks from* CORTEZ *to the officers, to* FR. OLMEDO, *nods*): I should like to speak with your holy priest.

FR. OLMEDO: I am honoured, your Majesty.

MONTEZUMA (*smiling*): As for myself, you have doubtless heard wild tales of my opulence, how I dwell in golden palaces and feed emeralds to birds, and other such nonsense . . .

MARINA (*laughs*): We were taught that your eyes are made of gold.

MONTEZUMA: Only my eyes? I am usually gold from head to foot!

(*They laugh.*)

No, as you see, I am flesh and blood, and my city is stone and wood.

CORTEZ: But a marvellous one, my lord. When we topped the final mountain peak and saw this city on the lake below, we felt we had truly climbed into the clouds and some holy vision sparkled before our eyes.

MONTEZUMA (*flattered and happy*): It is no vision, but I do think you will find it as beautiful as I do . . .

CORTEZ: I am most anxious to see it all, your Majesty. In Cempoala they said one could buy everything in the world in your market-place.

MONTEZUMA: Ah . . . the market-place! (*Glances smiling at his Lords.*) There is a sight for your King to see. It will be open tomorrow . . . I shall send you guides to lead you. Go with your Spaniards, see the thousands of canoes glancing in and out of the canals bearing the wealth and cargo of my state. And be at ease with the people, walk with the crowds in the pleasure of the abundance that flows up from my market-place. And be sure to look in on the artists. You will find the crouching potters and jewellers from Cholula, the goldsmiths from Azcapozalco, the hunters from Xilotepec, and the painters are sometimes there from Tezcuco. Every art and article of my people will lie open to your eyes. Tapestries are sold, and cotton—spun and in bales, dresses for women, and coverlets too, and in cages are animals of every kind and colour, wild and tame,—Cortez, I—I wish I could take you by the hand and show you my city!

CORTEZ: Your Majesty, I shall remember this hour forever . . .

MONTEZUMA: I think we shall have happy days, Cortez. And soon you must tell me of *your* world? We shall . . . (*laughs*) . . . exchange wonders.

MARINA: They bring a gentle God, my Lord . . . the greatest wonder.

MONTEZUMA: But now . . . you must need rest . . . My steward will show you to my old palace.

CORTEZ: Most generous, Montezuma.

MONTEZUMA: I have but one request. Your Tlascallan allies . . .

CORTEZ: Not allies, your Excellency,—followers. They will all be Christians soon.

MONTEZUMA: Nevertheless they cannot be quartered in the city.

CORTEZ (*smiling, but stubbornly*): It will be hard to give them that news, my Lord . . .

MONTEZUMA: I regret the necessity. We have been at war with Tlascalla this sheaf of years, and my people despise them. Send them to the outskirts.

MARINA: That would be best, Hernando.

CORTEZ (*slight pause*): As you wish, my lord.

MONTEZUMA: I shall be pleased to receive you tonight. And bring the holy man with you . . .

FR. OLMEDO (*obsequiously. Holds his crucifix*): Will it please your Majesty to receive this into your hand?

MONTEZUMA: What is it?

MARINA: The crucifix—sign of Jesus Christ . . . it will help you to understand, great Lord.

(MONTEZUMA *looks at it carefully, then reaches out and takes it.*)

FR. OLMEDO: My Lord, you hold in your hand the key to the riddle of the Universe . . .

CORTEZ (*jubilantly*): Your Majesty, no traveller in any age was ever blessed with such a journey's end . . . ! I embrace you in . . .

(*He suddenly goes to embrace* MONTEZUMA, *who quickly cries out and steps back in horror as* GUATEMOTZIN *and* CAGAMA *push* CORTEZ *away. Two Spaniards rush in and there is a scuffle for a moment.*)

(*To* ALVARADO, *who is violently pushing* GUATEMOTZIN *away from him.*) Pedro, stop!

(*Silence. Both sides stare shocked at each other.*)

MONTEZUMA: . . . I am never touched.

CORTEZ (*relaxes*): Oh, my lord, I meant only to embrace you in friendship—a thousand, thousand pardons. I beg you, forgive me!

(MONTEZUMA *is at a loss for what to say.*)

Farewell, your Majesty . . . until tonight.

(*He waits for some word, but there is none. He bows, the Spaniards bow, back out along the path, turn and go out into the roadway and disappear.* TAPAIA *bows to* MONTEZUMA *and follows them. The Lord and the King watch the empty entrance way in silence.*)

TECUICHPO (*frightened*): Father . . . how fierce their eyes became!

MONTEZUMA: The key to the riddle of the Universe!

(MONTEZUMA *looks at the crucifix in his hand, the Lords look at it.* MONTEZUMA *turns towards the stairs, consternation on his face, and as he mounts the stairs with* GUATEMOTZIN . . .)

GUATEMOTZIN (*noticing something out beyond the wall*): Uncle . . . look . . . The city . . . the city is empty!

MONTEZUMA: . . . Where are the people? Where are *my* people? (*Astonished.*) (*He turns quickly to the crucifix in his hand; as though it held the reason for the empty city; and he quickly goes up, turning it in his hand.*)

(*The stage darkens.*)

SCENE 2

About two weeks later on the rooftop of the Temple. This is the highest point in the city,—a flat platform ending on the right in the top few steps of the stairway up the side of the building, and on the left leading into the entrance of the Temple Tower. Overhead a clear sunlit sky.

Discovered are CAGAMA, CUITLAHUA, *and* PARACH *intently looking down the stairway at something far below. Silence a moment, then all turn about as* MONTEZUMA *hurries from the tower with* GUATEMOTZIN.

MONTEZUMA: How do you interrupt me at prayer?

GUATEMOTZIN: My Lord, Cortez is climbing up with his troops . . .

MONTEZUMA: Troops? He said nothing about bringing troops.

GUATEMOTZIN: Will you come and see for yourself, my Lord.
(*Leads the King to the platform's edge and points below.*)

PARACH: They'll curse us all with their impudence.

GUATEMOTZIN: Do you see them, my Lord? Two weeks and they walk the city like masters.

CAGAMA: I think it is time they understood their welcome is ended . . .

MONTEZUMA (*hesitates, then returns from the edge*): They must not be antagonized. They understand they are to leave soon. He asked to visit me here.

CUITLAHUA (*indicating below*): But what does this mean? Troops . . .

(*As he speaks,* TECUICHPO *enters from around the front of the tower, and gradually makes her way to the edge.*)

MONTEZUMA (*impatiently*): What do you think it means, brother? Is the city to be attacked now by such a brigade?

GUATEMOTZIN: But how do we know . . . ?

MONTEZUMA: You are too quick to distrust them! I have not yet heard all Cortez has to say. (*Turns to* PARACH.) He's come to see the statues of our sacred Gods.

PARACH (*astounded*): You'll bring them *into* the temple . . . ?

MONTEZUMA: Jesus Christ is not a stranger there I think.

PARACH: How can you say such . . . ?

MONTEZUMA: Listen when Cortez speaks; you might be wiser
now. Christ like Quetzalcoatl walked the earth as a man, he
cured the sick and like the white god He promised to return
one day . . .

PARACH: I see it in your eyes; you're turning from our gods!

MONTEZUMA: Or searching for them?

PARACH: In Cortez?

MONTEZUMA: Perhaps. There is a hint of God in Hernando
Cortez's eyes, something I feel we must touch and if we do,
it will lift us up. (*To* LORDS.) I also see the danger, but . . .
be patient. Come, Parach.

> (*He goes into the temple tower,* PARACH *follows him, shaking
his head.*)

CUITLAHUA (*reverently*): How his thoughts fly heavenward. A
priest-king!

GUATEMOTZIN: Aye, but if they're mocking him—(*Turns suddenly and shakes his fist towards those below* . . .)

CUITLAHUA (*looking down*): Who are those two coming up?

TECUICHPO: The tall one is Alvarado.

GUATEMOTZIN: Your eyes are uncommonly sharp, Tecuichpo.

TECUICHPO (*smiling*): Alvarado is an uncommon Captain.

GUATEMOTZIN (*turns full to her*): Indeed, my love.

TECUICHPO: Yes, and if my lords would leave me to greet
him . . .

GUATEMOTZIN: Alone?

TECUICHPO: Oh, he'll not harm me if I let him talk. (*Smiles.*)
The Captain loves to talk.

GUATEMOTZIN: Have you spoken to him before?

TECUICHPO: Last week when father took me to visit them. Alvarado is quite human.

GUATEMOTZIN: Well!

TECUICHPO: . . . But not Cortez. Cortez never talks about
himself.

CUITLAHUA: Let her talk to him, Guatemotzin.

GUATEMOTZIN: But alone?

TECUICHPO: Please, Guatemotzin, leave me with him. Sometimes a woman . . . can see in the dark.

> (*She looks up at him into his eyes. He lifts her hand and
kisses it.*)

Hurry. They're coming.

(*All the* LORDS *hurry into the tower. Above, she strolls a little to the left, smoothing her gown. Enter* ALVARADO *and* LEON. *Her back is turned to them.*)

ALVARADO (*puffing, happily surprised on seeing her alone. Bows*): Ah, Princess!

TECUICHPO (*turns suddenly as though surprised*): Oh!

ALVARADO: I am only Captain Alvarado.

TECUICHPO: It is a long climb from below.

ALVARADO: Depending on who is at the top, Princess. I may say you are even more lovely by day than by night.

TECUICHPO: Thank you, Captain. And is this Captain Sandoval?

LEON: De Leon, Princess. (*To* ALVARADO.) We have a message to deliver.

ALVARADO: Let me deliver it alone, Leon.

LEON: But . . .

ALVARADO: By your love for me, Leon.

LEON: I know, but . . . Princess, will you tell your father . . .

ALVARADO: Gonzalo! (*Turns slowly to her, bows.*) Excellent lady, we bear a communication from our beloved Cortez, Señor Hernando Cortez. He desires to inform his Majesty, the Emperor, that he has come for an audience. Will my lady be so kind as to notify her father?

TECUICHPO: Your words fall like feathers through the air.

ALVARADO: You may trust the Princess to deliver the message.

LEON: But Hernando is waiting . . .

ALVARADO: Señor?

LEON (*shakes his head*): Oh, Pedro, Pedro . . . (*He turns and goes down the stairs.*)

ALVARADO: My comrade has no poetry.

TECUICHPO: But he knows his duty.

ALVARADO: But I love to talk to you. I am so far from home, gentle lady. Have you ever been far from home?

TECUICHPO: No, but I should like to see your country.

ALVARADO: Spain would kneel at your feet. I am famous in Spain, you know.

TECUICHPO: Are you? And is Cortez more famous?

ALVARADO: Well . . . yes. He is famous too, but my father was Commendador—a Lord as you say.

TECUICHPO (*trying the word*): Commendador.

ALVARADO: Say it again, please?

TECUICHPO: Commendador.

ALVARADO: Your lips *embrace* a Spanish word!—Say my name.

TECUICHPO: Alvarado.

ALVARADO: Princess . . . your voice is the sound of Spain. (*Moves closer.*) Have you ever heard how I swam three miles in full armour?

TECUICHPO: You must be very strong.

ALVARADO: I broke a crocodile's jaw with this arm. Feel it.

TECUICHPO (*touches his forearm*): Like iron, Captain.

ALVARADO (*looks in her eyes*): You . . . have never heard of the crocodile?

TECUICHPO: I . . . I'll tell my father you've come . . . (*She draws from him.*)

ALVARADO (*takes her arm*): . . . Say my name again. I have not heard a woman say it in so long.

TECUICHPO: Alvarado.

ALVARADO: Your voice . . . is Christian.

TECUICHPO: And I?

ALVARADO: You are the most beautiful woman I have ever seen.

TECUICHPO (*pause*): And . . . what are you?

ALVARADO: I? (*Pause.*) I am a man. A Christian man.

TECUICHPO: Is that more than a man?

ALVARADO: Is a man more than an animal? It is a man with God in him.

TECUICHPO (*pause*): I'll give my father your message.

(*She starts left, he snatches her hand.*)

ALVARADO: Gentle girl . . . will we meet alone again?

TECUICHPO (*smiles, frightened*): We may, Captain . . . Alvarado.

ALVARADO: Oh, my heart!

(*He tries to embrace her, she pushes him away.*)

TECUICHPO (*a hushed shout*): Please! . . .

(*Enter* CORTEZ *and other Captains up the stairs.*)

CORTEZ: Pedro!

(ALVARADO *breaks from her.*)

(*Bowing.*) My deepest apologies, Princess.

(*She turns about and rushes inside.*)

(CORTEZ *goes to* ALVARADO.)

(*Hushed*): Are you mad? Are you *mad*? This is a temple! A holy place!

ALVARADO: I have been eating too much meat.

CORTEZ: Am I announced or is your brain altogether addled?

ALVARADO (*a little dazed*): She's gone to tell him now. Oh, Hernando, what a jewel to pin a sheet with!

CORTEZ: You'd better see to your duty, Captain. Come here, Señores.

(*Captains gather round him.*)

(*To* ALVARADO.) Now do as I tell you, Alvarado. (*Motions below.*) Burn that scene into your eyes. I want the exact position of every drawbridge on every causeway . . . throw her out of your mind.

ALVARADO: I'll have it, I'll have it.

CORTEZ: Remember, you'll draw a map of it when we're back in quarters. You, Señores, form a circle around Pedro, but at ease. The King is very suspicious. (*To* ALVARADO.) Precise now, Pedro. We may live or die by this. The drawbridges are the windpipes of this city. See you know where they are—exactly.

ALVARADO: I will, Hernando.

CORTEZ: Marina, tie up my sandal?

(*She bends to it.*)

Spread out now, Señores. At your ease.

ALVARADO: A crucifix on this height could be seen for miles around.

MONTEJO: A fairy white city in the heart of heathendom. It never seemed so white from below.

CORTEZ (*restlessly glancing at the tower doorway*): Why does he keep us waiting like this?

FR. OLMEDO: Hernando, I am beginning to think we're moving too fast.

CORTEZ: Too slow, Padre. We're here two weeks with nothing accomplished.

(MARINA *finishes with his sandal, he walks away.*)

. . . nothing . . .

MARINA: You're too impatient, Hernando. We've made friends with him . . .

CORTEZ: I did not leave Spain to make friends with Montezuma. What does he mean by this?

MONTEJO: Another polite hint to go home, I think.

CORTEZ: Treachery, he's famous for it.

MARINA: It's a grave decision for him to make. Unbelievers are never allowed here in the temple.

CORTEZ: I am tired of hearing what is allowed and what is not allowed!

FR. OLMEDO (*softer*): Hernando, be reasonable. Is it good judgement to insist on converting such a heathen in sixteen days?

CORTEZ: Is it better judgement, Pedro, to wait until his weathercock brain decides we're devils come to destroy his Gods?

FR. OLMEDO: Your fancy is running away with you.

CORTEZ: Fancy! Is it my fancy, or have we been served inedible food these last three days? Have the servants been rude or have they not? Montezuma is turning against us, Padre. Believe it.

ORDAZ: Aye.

MARINA: I don't believe it.

LEON: You don't believe anything.

MARINA: And you don't understand these people. They live to brood. And if we're being told to leave now, we deserve no better.

CORTEZ: And what does that mean?

MARINA: He gives you a palace to live in, the finest to eat, and drink, servants, women—kings could ask no more, and what do you do? You curse him for a heathen . . .

CORTEZ (*ignoring her*): Montejo, go down and tell them to keep a sharp eye up here.

(MONTEJO *goes down.*)

MARINA: Hernando, you must change your ways or . . .

FR. OLMEDO: I say we go down.

CORTEZ: We are going inside, Padre.

FR. OLMEDO: Zeal is warping your judgement, Hernando.

CORTEZ: Zeal, zeal! (*Strides about.*)

FR. OLMEDO: A superstition as black as his is not thrown off in two weeks.

CORTEZ: I've seen it thrown off in an hour!

FR. OLMEDO: By threats! With a knife held over them!

ORDAZ: He's had time enough to understand Christ. Too much.

MARINA (*to* ORDAZ): *You* have blood in your eyes, Ordaz.

FR. OLMEDO: Hernando, for the sake of his soul, stop forcing Christ on him.

CORTEZ (*wheels about*): Understand me, Padre. We are not safe in Mexico until Montezuma is Christian.

FR. OLMEDO: But so quickly! The man is not a peasant . . .

CORTEZ (*out of patience*): Padre. I beg of you understand me. It is no longer a question of Montezuma's soul. He must brood no longer under the claws of that priest of his, or he'll hatch a vulture to devour my heart . . . if he's not doing it already.

FR. OLMEDO: I can only tell him the truths . . .

CORTEZ: You can bring him faster to baptism.

FR. OLMEDO: In time . . .

CORTEZ: There *is* no time! On the day you are Montezuma's confessor, Mexico is ours, and not until then.

FR. OLMEDO (*sighs*): I'll try my best.

CORTEZ: More, Olmedo, you will save his soul today or we are parted from ours tomorrow!

FR. OLMEDO: Trust me, Hernando.

CORTEZ: I do, but remember this as you love your life; we are no Gods,—he'll know it soon, and when he does he'd better be a Christian convert or we'll be walking with the Holy Ghost. (*Cocks his ear towards the doorway.*) (*Low to* AL-VARADO.) Take care, Pedro, he's coming. Remember, Señores, at ease.

(*Enter* MONTEZUMA, *plus* GUATEMOTZIN, CAGAMA, CUITLA-HUA *and* TECUICHPO. *All bow, saying, "My Lord . . . Majesty . . ." etc.*)

MONTEZUMA: I hope you are not weary climbing so high.

CORTEZ: Spaniards are never weary, my lord.

MONTEZUMA (*pause. He turns to* ALVARADO): Are you Alvarado?

ALVARADO: Captain Pedro de Alvarado, your Majesty.

MONTEZUMA (*looks closely a moment, turns to* CORTEZ): I have glad news for you, Cortez. My priest will permit you to see the Gods.

CORTEZ: I am most grateful, my Lord. I would hardly know how to excuse myself to my master if I failed to see them.

MONTEZUMA: Then you are leaving us soon?

CORTEZ (*slight pause*): Quite soon, your Majesty.

MONTEZUMA: But not today.

CORTEZ: Oh no, my Lord.

MONTEZUMA: Because I have so much to ask you.

CORTEZ: I enjoy a question, my Lord.

MONTEZUMA: But tell me, what will you say of my city when you see your Lord?

CORTEZ: Why . . . I will describe its beauties, and its . . .

MONTEZUMA: But what *exactly*? Sometimes, Cortez, I fear you are more polite than enthusiastic.

CORTEZ: An injustice, my Lord. As I have said before, there are great cities in my country—Burgos, Medellin, Madrid, Seville, —names that bring most graceful towers to my sight. But this, your Majesty, is to Seville as a full-bodied woman to a scrawny maid. This . . .

MONTEZUMA: No, you must make a picture for his mind. Here . . . (*Takes* CORTEZ *to the right upstage corner.*) Tell your King . . . say . . . say . . . Montezuma's city is a woman and she floats, white and clean, on the rippling waterface, bathing her sides on an inland sea.

> (*As he speaks,* ALVARADO, *who is downstage, motions for the* CAPTAINS *to shield his back, and takes out a piece of paper and sketches what he sees below, at a furious pace.*)

. . . and her hair is forty fountains that wave with the sunlit breeze. And tell him of the palace with the sweetwood ceilings and the cedar walls. And the aviary too where the birds are kept . . . tell him of the birds. And the hospital there where the sick are tended, and the avenue, Cortez, where forty men may walk abreast . . . and the House of Wild Animals . . . tell him what you see.

> (GUATEMOTZIN *appears out of the shadow downstage of the tower. He watches* ALVARADO.)

CORTEZ: My Lord, I will tell him that Montezuma's city surpasses Rome, and Rome as I have told you, is the seat and glory of the world.

> (GUATEMOTZIN *springs forward, snatches* ALVARADO'*s paper.*)

ALVARADO (*as the paper is snatched from him*): Hey . . . !

> (*He goes for* GUATEMOTZIN *as* MONTEZUMA *and* CORTEZ *rush downstage.*)

CORTEZ: Pedro . . . !

ALVARADO (*trying to wrest the paper from* GUATEMOTZIN): Give me that paper . . . !

MONTEZUMA: What has happened . . . !

CORTEZ: Let him go, you fool! Did you hear me, Alvarado?

> (*They break apart.* GUATEMOTZIN *examines map. Enter* CAGAMA *and* CUITLAHUA *and* TECUICHPO *quickly.*)

MONTEZUMA (*glancing at* ALVARADO): What is that, Guatemotzin?

CORTEZ: Pedro, what did you do . . . ?

GUATEMOTZIN: The captain is an artist, my Lord. Look.
(*Hands map to* MONTEZUMA. MONTEZUMA *examines it,
his face hardens, he seems to expand.*)

CORTEZ: What is it, my Lord?

GUATEMOTZIN (*to* LORDS): This one draws a map and he dares
ask what . . . !

CORTEZ: A map! Captain, did you draw a map?

ALVARADO: It's a lie, I never . . . !

CORTEZ: There must be an error . . .

MONTEZUMA (*restraining himself by laughing*): Many, yes . . .
I looked upon a man and saw a God, and you took a King
for a fool!

CORTEZ: Let me explain . . . !

MONTEZUMA: Explain, explain! Or do Christians save an emperor's soul with a military map!

CORTEZ: I ordered no map drawn so it is not a map!

MONTEZUMA: What is it then—the plan of that other world
you brought me from the sun? Why have you come to Mexico, Cortez?

CORTEZ: Well, my lord, since I am convicted as a villain there
is nothing more to say . . . (*Angry.*) But I would never
have believed that the Aztec state could see danger in three
hundred and fifty mortal men!

MONTEZUMA: Danger? I see no danger; only mockery,—but it
ends now! What do you want in Mexico?

CORTEZ: Want? I want another heaven here, I want a way of
life in Mexico that Jesus Christ will bring, I want a country
where men will live not in revolt against a righteous king
but as brothers on the earth,—aye, my Lord, I want nothing
here but the brotherhood of man, and I crossed the sea to
lay it in your hand!
(*Enter* TAPAIA.)

TAPAIA (*breathless*): My lord . . . !

MONTEZUMA: What is it?

TAPAIA: A courier from the coast: a new army . . . a thousand
Spaniards have landed!

(*The Spaniards freeze.*)

The commander says he'll arrest Cortez on sight as a rebel to his own King!

(MONTEZUMA *turns to* CORTEZ, *his eyes moist.*)

CORTEZ: Pay them no attention, my Lord . . .

MONTEZUMA: Oh, we are diseased . . .

CORTEZ: I will attend to them, they're bandits, the lowest of the low, they . . .

MONTEZUMA: "My lord, I want another heaven here . . ."

CORTEZ: They have no right to come here . . . !

MONTEZUMA: "Men will live as brothers on the earth . . ."

CORTEZ: They're traitors, they . . . !

MONTEZUMA: Traitors? Out of that other heaven? *I* have traitors, *I* have mortal enemies, but I rule by force and not the brotherhood of man!

CORTEZ: Let me . . . !

MONTEZUMA: Leave me! The map is drawn and Christian curses Christian . . . and man is still man! (*He turns and starts into the temple.*)

CORTEZ (*threateningly*): You misunderstand me, Montezuma.
    (MONTEZUMA *turns about slowly.*)
    I cannot leave Mexico until you are Christian.
    (*Pause.*)

MONTEZUMA (*points out around the horizon*): There are twenty-two cities around this lake and eighty thousand troops who would bless me to end this in blood! Begone!

CORTEZ: I will not leave your soul for the fires of Hell! Be Christian or by the wrath of Jesus Christ, I'll crash the heavens down upon your head!

MONTEZUMA: You leave the city by tomorrow sunset, and in three days if there is a Spaniard left on the soil of my Empire, he'll die on it!

CORTEZ: Emperor, I pity your soul!

MONTEZUMA: Out of my sight!!—a *man* I can kill!
    (CORTEZ *turns and goes down followed by all the Spaniards and* MARINA. MONTEZUMA *and the* LORDS *quickly to the ledge and look down.*)

CAGAMA (*undertone*): Pull the drawbridges . . . ! Cut them off!

GUATEMOTZIN: Fall on them now . . . let me signal the garrisons . . . !

MONTEZUMA: We will not attack until tomorrow sunset . . .

CUITLAHUA: They'll never go without a struggle! They never will!

MONTEZUMA: I promised peace until tomorrow . . .

CAGAMA: But *they* promised nothing!

MONTEZUMA: Let them go!

GUATEMOTZIN: We could bury them in arrows now!

CUITLAHUA: The armies are ready, why should we wait!

MONTEZUMA: You're changed, brother!

CUITLAHUA: Yes, I stand with Cagama and Guatemotzin.

MONTEZUMA (*walks from them, shaking*): Stand? Against what do you stand?

CUITLAHUA: . . . against nothing, my Lord.

MONTEZUMA: Then you stand for the standing's sake! (*Almost weeping.*) I saw another world . . . a world where every door stood wide unbolted in the night, where the single ear of corn grew heavy as a child, and all the brass of war, swords and shields, were melted into rivers and the silver sea . . . into the sunrise . . . Let them walk away. I cannot bring my hand to kill them yet. (*He looks at each one, then testingly.*) Good day, my Lords.

  (*They don't stir.*)

  (*With a note of command and warning.*) Good day, my lords!

  (*Slight pause, then they bow stiffly and start to go.*)

  (*Stronger.*) He will suffer who lifts an arrow before I command.

  (*The LORDS are immobile, silent.*)

  I say they are not molested, my lords!

  (*They avoid his eyes.*)

  Am I unworthy of an answer!!

  (*Slight pause.*)

GUATEMOTZIN: Your honour and your state will be defended.

  (MONTEZUMA *searches their eyes. Nods.*)

MONTEZUMA: Leave me.

LORDS: My Lord, great Lord!

  (*They bow and go down the steps. He is alone with* TECUICHPO.)

MONTEZUMA (*stands quietly a moment*): Was ever such a fool as Montezuma? Such a proud and pompous fool to sit

private among clouds while down below the charts are
drawn to loot him while he prays!

TECUICHPO (*goes close to him*): Father . . .

MONTEZUMA: Oh, my child, my child, it was so clear, so clear
in my eyes . . . ! (*He clasps her face and weeps, his tears
buried in her hair.*)

    (*Slow curtain.*)

ACT THREE

SCENE I

The Spanish quarters in the old palace. At the left is a large wooden cross standing at the wall, a low table with papers on it and a candle.

It is a few hours before dawn. The Captains are scattered all over the floor, asleep in their armour. CORTEZ *is slowly and silently pacing back and forth deep in thought. He stops at the table, looks at the papers and starts for the men as though to wake them but changes his mind. As he is resuming his pacing, he stops as though at a noise and* MARINA *hurries in and goes directly to him.*

They speak hushed.

MARINA: Hernando!

CORTEZ: Where have you been . . . !

MARINA: You've got to leave.

CORTEZ: Why? Where were you!

MARINA: When we were coming back from the Temple I heard a man in the street saying "Guatemotzin will attend to them before long." I followed him . . . Hernando, the priests are telling the people that a flood will come if you aren't killed at once. The Lords have broken with the King, and they're getting ready to attack you . . . !

CORTEZ: When?

MARINA: There'll be an uprising if you're not away tomorrow! Go now . . . !

CORTEZ: Ssh! (*He quickly goes to* ALVARADO *and prods him with his toe.*) Up! Up!—Wake up, Pedro.

ALVARADO (*violently lashing out flies up to a sitting position*): Take it out! Take it out, you . . . ! Oh . . .

MONTEJO: Heh? What? What?

LEON (*jumping up*): What's happened?

CORTEZ: Wake up! Wake up! (*He goes to the table and examines the papers.*)

ORDAZ: It's the middle of the night.

OLID: Who made that noise?

ALVARADO: I dreamed I walked up to Panfilo Narvaez and his thousand men and broke his neck in my hand.

LEON: Where were you all night, Marina?

CORTEZ (*for quiet*): All right, all right! Quiet.

ORDAZ (*scratching*): Fah! I'm lousy as the King of France—

LEON: Some day you should take a bath, Ordaz.

ORDAZ: Aye, and you . . . !

CORTEZ: Señores! Please.

ORDAZ: A foot-soldier doesn't travel on his ass so that he can afford to drain away his strength in hot water . . . !!

CORTEZ: Gentlemen! Marina says they will attack us tomorrow! (*Slight pause.*)

OLID: Who? Who will attack?

CORTEZ: The Lords have broken with Montezuma!

MONTEJO: Then we must leave. . . !

OLID: What are we waiting for?

ALVARADO: Shut up . . . !

CORTEZ: Will you let me talk or must we die like idiots! (*Silence. Goes to the table, lifts a paper.*) I have two letters. Aztec troops attacked our garrison on the coast yesterday, and killed Captain Escalanto.

MONTEJO: It's started . . . !

ALVARADO: I told you Montezuma is treacherous!

ORDAZ: What happened . . . !

CORTEZ: I don't know if the King ordered that attack, but this I do know, our subject towns are mumbling revolution against us, or they couldn't have persuaded a man to attack the coast garrison. Now here's another note—from the prodigy of the good governor of Cuba,—Captain Panfilo Narvaez. I read: "You are outlaws, my dear Cortez, and I am in Mexico to bring you to justice. Either you forfeit to me all properties, and claims you have stolen, or you pay the fine in blood."

ALVARADO: Who in hell is Narvaez to tell us . . . !

CORTEZ: Who is he? He is fourteen ships, a hundred and fifty arquebussiers, over nine hundred men, heavy guns, a thousand Cubans, eighty horses and enough ammunition to blow Madrid to the stars.

OLID: Plus the law, Hernando, which is not on our side.

ALVARADO: What law? What are you gibbering about?

OLID: Simply that we are disowned by his Majesty's officer, the governor of Cuba! (*To* CORTEZ.) Now: if you had a document from Charles . . .

ORDAZ: A fart on documents! We're here, and we bled to get here, and if stiff-necked Narvaez wants to root us out let them come and do it!

OLID: Oh, he's coming, Ordaz, and with more logic than you have . . .

ORDAZ: A fart on logic! I have too many wounds to be read out of Mexico! What's the word, Hernando?

CORTEZ: The word? We must go out and pound that bastard into submission whatever his force. Narvaez must be stopped.

MONTEJO: But we can't kill Spaniards. The Aztec would see!

ORDAZ: Let them! Once we've got Narvaez, we . . .

OLID: Yes, we're out of the city and there'll be war getting back in!

MONTEJO: We'll never get in again!

CORTEZ: Unless!

MONTEJO: Heh?

CORTEZ: . . . unless we hold in our hands before we leave, such a precious thing as no Aztec will dare injure us for fear of injuring it!

(*Dead silence.*)

Yes, Señores, we can't remain here, or go away until we take Montezuma prisoner.

(*Silence.*)

MARINA: Prisoner . . . !

MONTEJO: Are you mad?

CORTEZ: It must be done!

ORDAZ (*to* CORTEZ): I'm with you, Hernando!

MARINA: The whole country would fall on you!!

ALVARADO (*to men*): How can you hesitate!

OLID: They'll wipe us out!

MONTEJO: Listen to her, she knows these people! Marina . . . !

MARINA: Hernando, you'll never . . . !

MONTEJO (*to* MARINA, *desperate*): They'd let us out peacefully, Marina, wouldn't they?

CORTEZ: Nonsense!

MARINA: Nobody would harm you if you left.

MONTEJO: There!

ORDAZ (*to* MONTEJO): Just because you're loaded with gold, Montejo—is no reason to deny others the opportunity.

MARINA (*to* ORDAZ): But, Señor, Montezuma is . . . a God would not dare touch him . . . ! Hernando, what will you do if he won't . . . if he refuses to . . . (*Breaks off seeing their faces.*)

CORTEZ: He would be worthless, dead.

MARINA: I don't care what he would be worth, you . . . you would never kill him?

(*Silence. Beginning to plead.*)

He'll be Christian one day . . . I know . . . he will . . . (*Silence.*) Hernando, you would never kill a King!

CORTEZ: No more words. We must decide, Señores.

MARINA: I don't understand, what will you decide?

CORTEZ: That's enough, Marina!

MARINA: But he'll be Christian if you let him . . . !

CORTEZ: Shut your mouth!

(*Makes to strike, she recoils.*)

MONTEJO (*nervously*): I don't see it. That's all, I don't see it.

LEON: I think perhaps . . .

MONTEJO: She says they'll let us out and we ought to go! It would be another matter if, for instance . . . (*Sound.*) What are you doing removing the cross?

(CORTEZ *is moving the cross out of the niche in the wall. They come up slowly one by one behind him,* MARINA *with them.*)

CORTEZ: When Taurez, the carpenter, carved out the altar here, he found a door behind the plaster. I shall open it, Señores, but as you love me, keep secret what you see.

(*He pushes open a stone door in the wall. They peer inside, blocking* MARINA'S *view. One comes away with an audible gasp, another jumps to fill his place.*)

LEON: El Dorado . . . !

MONTEJO: There must be a million pesos worth . . . !

MARINA: What is it, let me see! (*She is blocked.*)

ORDAZ: All the gold in the world! (*To* MONTEJO.) Well, Montejo, are you still rich enough?

(MARINA *is looking in, carefully.*)

MONTEJO: It must be one . . . no three billion pesos worth! Let me feel it in my hands!

(*He starts to go into the compartment as* MARINA *turns about quickly, and bars the way with her body.*)

MARINA: No! What have you done?

MONTEJO: Out of my way . . . !

MARINA: It is a tomb! (*Silence.*)

CORTEZ: What is happening to you, Marina?

MARINA: These things are never touched . . .

CORTEZ (*angering*): But what is becoming of you!

MARINA: This is sacred, Hernando, the heritage of all the Aztec kings, their crowns, their clothes are buried here.

CORTEZ: There's more in there, more than all the Kings of Europe own!

MARINA: The vilest thief would never dare to violate . . . !

MONTEJO: We're going in, Hernando!

VOICES: We'll have it . . . ! Tell her to get away! (*Etc.*)

CORTEZ (*goes to her with an embrace*): Marina, why do you . . .

MARINA (*repelling him*): No. This can never belong to you. In there . . . is Mexico.

CORTEZ: Let them go in.

MARINA (*slight pause*): Hernando—will you desecrate a tomb?

CORTEZ: Leave!

(MARINA *looks at him for a moment, then goes. He strides to her and swings her about.*)

Where are you going?

MARINA: I'll tell him, I'll break the lie to the King . . . !

(CORTEZ *slaps her across the face.*)

Hernando . . .

(*She half stumbles away from him. He snatches at her, she tries to go on.*)

CORTEZ: Where!! (*Grabs her arm. Into her face.*) Where are you going!! Where! Where! (*He hits her to the floor.*) We have two hours until dawn, Señores. Rest till sunbreak; I will send word to Montezuma that I am visiting; while I am talking to him Avila has twenty five men sauntering into the palace in twos and threes. Leon sees that the remainder of the army is in the courtyard and surrounding the palace in the streets. As soon as we take him, I leave to deal with Narvaez and . . .

MONTEJO: We'll die at it, I know we'll die!

CORTEZ (*shout*): We'll take him!—and without a blow . . . I know that man.

SCENE 2

Next morning in the throne room. MONTEZUMA, *with* QUAUHO-POCA, *commander of the Tuxpan garrison. At his feet is a round leather box.*

MONTEZUMA: I still see no excuse, Commander. You had no order from me to kill Spaniards.

QUAUHOPOCA: I never dreamed Cuitlahua would issue a command without your consent.

MONTEZUMA: You were not trained to take commands from my brother.

QUAUHOPOCA: The word was on all lips that you were moving to war.

MONTEZUMA: Do you command my Tuxpan garrison by rumour now? (*Noticing the box.*) What is in this box?

QUAUHOPOCA: The head of the Spaniard, Juan de Escalante, my lord.

MONTEZUMA (*his eyes fastened to the box*): Let me see.

QUAUHOPOCA (*opening the box*): He branded the faces of women . . . (*Begins to lift the head out.*)

MONTEZUMA (*turns his eyes*): Take it away.

QUAUHOPOCA: You never used to quail at dead things.

MONTEZUMA: Take it out of the city, and don't offer it to any God,—they're leaving today . . . you should never, never have done it!

(*Enter* TAPAIA.)

TAPAIA: Your daughter has come, my Lord.

MONTEZUMA (*not listening*): Very good, Tapaia.

TAPAIA: There is something I cannot understand, my Lord.

MONTEZUMA: Yes?

TAPAIA: A great many Spaniards have been seen coming into the palace.

MONTEZUMA: Naturally, Cortez is coming to say farewell.

TAPAIA (*resolutely*): A guard should be here with you . . .

MONTEZUMA: I am not at war. Let Tecuichpo enter.

(TAPAIA *bows and goes out.*)

(*To* QUAUHOPOCA.) Wait outside, Commander.

    (QUAUHOPOCA *picks up box.*)

I am expecting Cortez. If he wishes to question you, answer him and only with the truth.

QUAUHOPOCA: I had never expected I should be accounting to a Spaniard for my actions.

MONTEZUMA: You will do as I say, Commander.

QUAUHOPOCA: To the last of my days.

    (*Enter* TECUICHPO.)

Princess . . . (*Exit* QUAUHOPOCA.)

MONTEZUMA: He has grown very insolent.

TECUICHPO: You summoned me, my Lord?

MONTEZUMA: Come here, daughter. (*Embraces.*) You know, that Cuitlahua, Guatemotzin and Cagama have not attended me since yesterday.

TECUICHPO: Yes, father. Old Tapaia told me.

MONTEZUMA (*pause*): Guatemotzin left no word with you where he might be found?

TECUICHPO (*sadly*): No, I have not seen him since he left yesterday.

MONTEZUMA: You would not tell me an untruth?

TECUICHPO: He left me no word, father. Why do you not send a call out for him?

MONTEZUMA: I have sent out more than a call. If he is found he is under arrest.

TECUICHPO: Arrest . . . !

MONTEZUMA: Guatemotzin is a traitor. And my brother and Cagama too,—all traitors!

TECUICHPO: But they mean only to defend you . . .

MONTEZUMA: I am still able to decide when I need protection and when obedience. Guatemotzin is rousing the people against my laws and will suffer for it.

TECUICHPO: How will he suffer, father?

MONTEZUMA: You are about to weep.

TECUICHPO: Yes, I am about to weep.

    (*Pause.*)

MONTEZUMA: Your tears will not help him. I have borne the last of his disobedience.

TECUICHPO: You will not harm Guatemotzin, Father.

MONTEZUMA: You may go.

TECUICHPO (*a frantic cry*): You must not harm him, Father.

MONTEZUMA: Leave me!

TECUICHPO (*weeping as she shouts*): Always a reason to pardon the Spaniard;—pardon their sacrilege, pardon their murders, pardon their fingers that creep for my body, but the anger is quick for the princes who worship you . . . !

MONTEZUMA: Traitors who mock me . . . !

TECUICHPO: Go then,—find Guatemotzin, run him down like a thief for the love that he bears you,—but seek for no mourners when your blood runs out!

MONTEZUMA: Daughter . . . !

TECUICHPO: Has your skin turned white that you persecute friends and honour your enemies?

  (*She rushes from the room as he reaches out for her.*)

MONTEZUMA: Tecuichpo! (*He stands still facing the doorway, then covers his eyes.*) My child.

  (*Enter* TAPAIA. *Stands a moment.*)

TAPAIA: My Lord?

  (MONTEZUMA *is silent.*)

  Cortez is here.

  (*No response.*)

  My Lord, will you look down into the courtyard?

  (MONTEZUMA *mechanically turns and goes towards the window.*)

  There are seventy of them. They have no baggage for travelling.

MONTEZUMA (*turns angrily*): How dare he mobilize such numbers inside the city! Call him here!

TAPAIA: Would it not be wise to remove your daughter from the palace my Lord?—in case of violence in the streets . . .

MONTEZUMA: There will be no disturbance, Tapaia.

TAPAIA: The people are angry my Lord, and now with these Spanish soldiers . . .

MONTEZUMA: Very well. Take her to the Temple.

TAPAIA: And let me summon you a guard, my Lord?

MONTEZUMA (*annoyed*): Have you lost your senses? Who ever dared touch me? Go; I'll see the Spaniard.

TAPAIA: At once, my lord. (*Exit* TAPAIA.)

  (MONTEZUMA *looks slowly at the courtyard, then goes to the throne and sits on it slowly, perturbation on his face.*)

(*Pause. Enter* CORTEZ, MARINA, ALVARADO, ORDAZ, LEON *and* MONTEJO. *All bow saying "My lord, Majesty," etc. All men needed.*)

MONTEZUMA: I am honoured, Captain, but I gave no permission for such a massing of men before the palace!

CORTEZ: I regret that I found it necessary to bring so many soldiers for my protection.

MONTEZUMA: Protection?

CORTEZ: Your Majesty. From the very first instant of my entrance into Tenochtitlan I ordered my Captains to do all in their power to help and serve you,—but you have done exactly the opposite for us.

MONTEZUMA: The opposite? I have done everything . . .

CORTEZ (*louder, fiercer*): I am astonished, your Majesty, astonished, that after declaring yourself my friend you should stoop so low as to order your garrison at Tuxpan to take arms against my Spaniards.

MONTEZUMA: I never gave that order . . .

CORTEZ: You murdered my brother!

MONTEZUMA: It is not true! You're mistaken . . . !

CORTEZ: Juan de Escalante dead is no mistake, Montezuma! I demand that those responsible be apprehended and severely chastised.

MONTEZUMA (*pause*): As for chastising my officers, Cortez, I am the one to decide that. And as for my ordering the slaying of your captain, you must accept my word I was ignorant of the order.

CORTEZ: I do accept your word, but I will only be convinced when you bring the guilty parties from the coast for my questioning.

MONTEZUMA: I am happy to give you that opportunity now. Will one of you go into the outer room and call Commander Quauhopoca?

CORTEZ: What does this mean?

MONTEZUMA: He is the commander of my Tuxpan Garrison.

CORTEZ (*waves his hand impatiently*): I have no interest in seeing him now.

MONTEZUMA: But surely you want the truth?

CORTEZ (*stands boiling with rage. With an angry jerk of his hand, his teeth clenched, he glances at* LEON): Bring him in then Leon.

MONTEZUMA: You will *call* him in.

    (*Exit* LEON.)

I am afraid, Captain Cortez, that you have given ear to the tales of my enemies.

CORTEZ: I give ear to no tales, I know truth from falsehood . . .

    (*Enter* QUAUHOPOCA *erect as always, proud to the set of his lips.*)

MONTEZUMA: Commander, this is Captain Hernando Cortez.

    (COMMANDER *bows stiffly.*)

Captain, is there something you would like to ask him?

CORTEZ (*swaggers up to* QUAUHOPOCA, *speaks two inches away from his eyes*): So this is the man who murdered Juan de Escalante?

QUAUHOPOCA: I murdered no one. Your man was killed in battle.

CORTEZ: But you attacked, did you not!

QUAUHOPOCA: I am not spoken to in such a fashion.

CORTEZ (*shouting*): By my beard but you will be!

MONTEZUMA: He will not! He is not to be shouted at, Cortez. He is . . .

CORTEZ (*overriding*): Did you attack my garrison at Villa Rica?

QUAUHOPOCA: I attacked your garrison and your man was killed.

CORTEZ: From whom did you receive the command to march?

QUAUHOPOCA: From my Lord Cuitlahua, the Emperor's brother.

CORTEZ (*bursting*): But you knew, of course, that Cuitlahua could give no command without the Emperor's consent?

QUAUHOPOCA: This time the order was without his consent.

CORTEZ: Am I to believe that you, a garrison commander, will move your troops without knowing first whether your Emperor approves?

QUAUHOPOCA: What you believe is of no interest to me!

MONTEZUMA: Quauhopoca, you must answer the Captain.

QUAUHOPOCA: I have given him the truth, my Lord, but I do not think he will be satisfied with it.

CORTEZ: No, not with your kind of truth. You tell me you killed Escalante on Cuitlahua's orders. Will you tell me which sovereign you serve?

QUAUHOPOCA: What other sovereign could I serve, but Montezuma?

CORTEZ (*suddenly*): Your Majesty, I must speak with you alone.

MONTEZUMA: Wait outside, Quauhopoca.

(QUAUHOPOCA *bows and exits.*)

CORTEZ: Do you not have a guard for him?

MONTEZUMA: My soldiers need no guards to detain them. So you see, Captain, you were too hasty in putting the crime on me.

CORTEZ: I see nothing of the sort.

MONTEZUMA: You heard the Commander . . .

CORTEZ (*venomous crescendo*): I heard the Commander, and I heard too that your army is running wild killing Spaniards, knowing only the authority of their own beastly lust! Do you expect me to depart when there is such disorder in the country? Do you think me blind not to know that your own nobility is holding secret consultations seeking my annihilation?

MONTEZUMA: There are troops out at this moment to arrest my rebellious lords. You will not shout at me, Captain.

CORTEZ (*pause. He walks from him, the blood pounding in his head. His hand is on his sword, his jaw out-thrust*): My dear Majesty, it is apparent to me, despite my fervent wish, that you have not the slightest intention of giving *my* sovereign the satisfaction of a fair hearing!

MONTEZUMA: Fair! Why, Cortez . . .

CORTEZ (*shouts*): I see it!!

MONTEZUMA (*with the shout; the impact of unreasonable, relentless force hits him. He scans the captains*): What is the point of this? What do you want here? Cortez, what do you want?

CORTEZ: Your Majesty, I do not wish to begin a war over this matter, and it would grieve me if I had to destroy this lovely city; which I assure you, I could do at a moment's notice. But your conduct has been such that I no longer feel my soldiers are safe while you are left to your own devices unsupervised by Spaniards. Therefore, your Majesty, I am willing to forgive your crimes against me and your treachery a thousand times manifested, only if silently, and without raising any disturbance, you will come with us to our quarters where you will be served and honoured as you are here . . .

(MONTEZUMA *emits an inarticulate sound.*)

. . . but cry out and you will die!

MONTEZUMA (*slowly, as though pressing his fears behind him, he rises from the throne*): I am not the person to whom such an order can be given.

ALVARADO: You're wasting words on this son of a bitch! Seize him, and if he resists, swords in his guts!

(*All whip out their swords.*)

MONTEZUMA (*the clang on the metal forces him back a step*): You dare not . . .

(CORTEZ *points his sword at* MONTEZUMA*'s heart and begins to advance.*)

MARINA (*rushes to* MONTEZUMA): Go with them! They will treat you with honour! They'll kill you, otherwise, they will, I know it!

MONTEZUMA: You dare not do it! I am Montezuma . . . do you hear me, I am the Emperor! . . .

CORTEZ (*prods him up against the wall*): Lower your voice, Señor! You will not go as prisoner, but as the Emperor changing his residence from one palace to another. (*Pause.*) Well? What is your decision?

MONTEZUMA: They will come from Cholula, out of Xilotepec, from the corners of Empire destroying the world, they'll tear out your hearts!

CORTEZ: Out with the word, Montezuma!—or I will murder you myself!

MONTEZUMA (*his hands raised, the sword at his heart, he searches the helmetted faces around him. His voice choked with hatred, sadness and the humiliation of his hour*): I will go with you.

CORTEZ (*thrusts sword back in scabbard. Makes to embrace* MONTEZUMA): Majesty!

(MONTEJO *runs out.*)

MONTEZUMA: Do not touch me.

CORTEZ: We must be friendly now, my lord. It was all God's will.

(MONTEZUMA *looks senselessly at* CORTEZ.)

(*To* ALVARADO.) Pedro, I leave for Narvaez.

ALVARADO: With victory, Hernando.

CORTEZ: And those of you that remain, remember, Captain Alvarado's word is my word, and he who disobeys it will answer to me! (*To* MONTEZUMA.) You will be given every courtesy and if there is one thing wanting I will appreciate your reporting it to me when I return. However, should you be tempted to join in any movement to incite rebellion; you will be the first to fall by my sword. I repeat, the slightest suspicion of treachery will push a swordspoint through your heart!

(MONTEJO *approaches with chains and manacles.*)

MONTEZUMA (*dumbly*): Chains? There must be no chains.

CORTEZ: Only until . . .

MONTEZUMA: I cannot have chains on my body.

CORTEZ: They will be removed in a little while when you go to our quarters. Come, Señores, you that are coming. Marina?

MARINA: Why must you chain him, Hernando?

CORTEZ: Marina, there is no time for this.

> (MARINA *goes to* MONTEZUMA, *curtsies low; goes out without raising her eyes.*)

SEVERAL: God bless you, Hernando! Farewell . . . (*Etc.*)

CORTEZ (*to* ALVARADO): Pedro? (*Silence.*) The arm is strong, but the touch is light. Farewell . . . Montezuma.

> (*Exit* CORTEZ, LEON, SANDOVAL. *Silence.* MONTEZUMA *stares blankly at them.*)

ALVARADO: The irons, Montejo.

> (*As they take the chains out of the bag,* ORDAZ *goes to* MONTEZUMA, *lifts the gold chain he wears from his neck. And while the ankles and wrists of the king are being shackled . . .*)

ORDAZ: I will take your necklace, sir, or it might get stolen. How beautiful! You know, if your people had the sense for religion that they have for fashioning gold, your country would be the first in the world . . .

MONTEZUMA (*with a roar, he flings his half-chained arms in the air*): My Lords!! Guatemotzin!! Oh, my country, forgive me . . . !!

ALVARADO: Stop his mouth!

> (*They do so.*)

That's better. Now the chains. Hands and feet my boys.

> (MONTEZUMA *weeps.*)

SCENE 3

The boom of the cannon from close by. The curtain rises on the Spanish quarters. On the left the large cross is pushed aside; the door of the concealed room open, and near its entrance is a great ornamented case overflowing with the treasure,—heirlooms and gold pieces of art of all kinds. Strewn about the floor are cloths, feathers, etc., ripped off the objects leaving only the gold.

CAPTAIN DE OLID *is at this work; digging about in the case, fetching up a piece, ripping off all non-gold, and giving the remainder to* MESA; *who stands over a cauldron and dumps in the booty.*

ARBENGA *is busy with a long-handled mould which he dips into the cauldron, fills, lifts out, dips into a bucket of cold water, and opens over a neat pile of gold bars on the floor near Centre. They are working feverishly when stage lights up, as though impelled by the cannon outside and the noises of war. There is no sound from them until* ARBENGA, *after adding a bar to the growing pile.*

ARBENGA: At last, his Royal Majesty, the King of Spain has his name stamped on Montezuma's gold. (*Chuckles, counts bars.*) Uno, dos, tres, quatro, cinco . . .

OLID: Arbenga!

ARBENGA: I'm only counting, Captain. I love it.

OLID: You'll wear them down with all your counting. Get back inside and fetch out more gold to be melted down.
    (ARBENGA *returns to his work.*)

MESA (*stirring the cauldron*): But we're dying of thirst. Oh, if gold could turn to water for one minute.

OLID: You'll have water enough as soon as we get out of here. Now Mesa, we melt gold—as much gold as we can.

MESA (*lifts ladle high, pours molten gold before his tongue*): By the Good Mary, I'm dry enough to drink it down.

ARBENGA: And when we're back in Castile you can show them how to piss pesos!
    (*They laugh as* CORTEZ, ALVARADO, MONTEJO, ORDAZ, LEON *quickly enter.*)

OLID: Señores! Hernando, you've returned, thank God.

CORTEZ (*goes straight to gold pile*): Is this all?

OLID: The cauldron took time to heat.

CORTEZ: Keep at it a little longer. But hurry, Olid. (*Notices gold pitcher on floor.*) What is this pitcher?

OLID: I am keeping that out.

CORTEZ: Everything goes in . . . Everything.

OLID (*grabs it from him*): No! It is too beautiful, Hernando.

CORTEZ (*slight pause*): Oh, very well. How much longer can the south wall hold them off, Ordaz?

ORDAZ: Maybe . . . twenty minutes, twenty five.

CORTEZ: And the west section, Montejo?

MONTEJO: I'll hold it.

CORTEZ: What is your opinion, Alvarado?

ALVARADO: We'll hold them off if they're not reinforced again.

(*Agreement—pause.*)

CORTEZ: Leon, bring Montezuma here.

LEON: He refuses to move.

CORTEZ: Refuses! Then drag him by the ears! Now! We must crack this siege!

(*Exit* LEON.)

(*Directed at* ALVARADO, *with anger.*) The King is changed since I left, Pedro, we must talk now. (*Turns to Captains.*) To your posts, Señores! And Montejo, tell Sandoval that his corner gun is firing too high. Go, Señores, the siege is broken in twenty minutes and we are out of here.

(*Exit* MONTEJO *and* ORDAZ.)

Well, Pedro, I am ready to listen. What started this uprising?

ALVARADO: Treachery, it was all treachery, Hernando.

CORTEZ: But the reason?—and I tell you it had better be good!

(*Off the thundering step of a hurrying man. Enter Señor Panfilo Narvaez, fat, a patch over his right eye, a spade in his hand.*)

NARVAEZ: I'll not suffer this a moment longer!

CORTEZ: To your post, Narvaez!

NARVAEZ: To treat me like a groom! I, Panfilo de Narvaez, they force me to dog for water! The Governor will hear of it, Cortez, I warn you!

CORTEZ: Señor Narvaez, if I have to listen to another outburst from your Excellency, I'll rip out your left eye as I did your right!

NARVAEZ: Ha! So this is how you subdued this country! (*Mimicking.*) Montezuma is my vassal!—Oho! A Spaniard can go from one end of the country to the other without a sword!—Oho! They'll break through your devil-damned walls in a moment!

CORTEZ (*whips out sword*): Señor?

NARVAEZ (*backing away*): His Majesty will hear of this! He'll . . . what's this? My God, Cortez . . . !

CORTEZ: Yes, Panfilo . . . there's enough gold on this floor to buy every pig in Europe to stuff your fat gut with.

(NARVAEZ *laughs greedily.*)

Get back to your post now!

(*Exit* NARVAEZ.)

ALVARADO: There goes the devil's ass.

CORTEZ: Well, I'm waiting—what started it, Pedro?

ALVARADO: Everything was all right till the day before yesterday when we burned that bastard Quauhopoca before the palace.

CORTEZ: I hope Montezuma had approved the death sentence.

ALVARADO: Oh, he did, yes. The people were disturbed by the burning, but I paid little attention to that because we were holding Montezuma. Well, yesterday I'm petitioned to allow one of their religious festivals in the Temple court. I give them permission providing there was to be no human sacrificing and no arms carried. They agree. Then I find out that all the heads of the noble families are to take part; and they are going to carry concealed arms, and it is not to be a religious celebration at all, but a signal for an uprising. I wait until they are all assembled last night, let them begin the dancing and the music, and then we fell on them leaving not one of them alive. In one hour the city is in revolt, and we are under siege. There is the truth, Hernando, by my honour!

CORTEZ: I heard it another way, Pedro. (*Silence.*) You never received information about a signal for insurrection.

ALVARADO: Hernando! They carried arms!

CORTEZ: Then show me those arms! (*Roars.*) By Blessed Mary, where are they?

(ALVARADO *is silent.*)

I'll wager though you can show me the gold trinkets you robbed from the bodies after the slaughter. You looted their best men before their eyes, and now we're bleeding.

ALVARADO: Very well . . . if you call me liar . . .

CORTEZ: You're a fool, Pedro. You've conducted yourself like a madman!

(*Enter* MONTEZUMA *brought in by* LEON *and soldiers.*)

MONTEZUMA (*off*): I do not want to see him. His voice still wracks in my ears!

CORTEZ: Is this the value of your pledge?—to besiege my Spaniards as soon as I turn my back?

MONTEZUMA: I would have been honoured to have led the attack.

CORTEZ: You wretched dog of a King! . . .

MONTEZUMA (*sees the gold processing*): What is this?—(*He looks from the case to the cauldron to bars; and goes to* OLID, *grasping his wrist.*) Spaniard, you mistake your eyes . . . This is not gold you rip apart. This is Mexico you plunder here, not gold. (*Lifts out bracelet.*) Look, what will this bring?—but an Emperor wore it on his arm . . . and here, a feather-weight of gold, but lines of Aztec Kings were nourished from this cup . . . my father's sceptre! Don't, don't throw that in . . . !

(*Sound: a loud hiss.*)

Cortez . . . you are melting down a history, are you wise enough for that! Man!—we are nothing but these dead bars . . . is this your Christian art I failed to understand? (*He cries out—scuffle.*)

CORTEZ: Stop him!

MONTEZUMA: Let me burn with the rest!

CORTEZ: Keep him tied up and hurry . . . on with the work quickly! Melt down as much as you can.

(*Enter* ORDAZ *running.*)

ORDAZ: They've fired the sheds on our side of the east wall.

CORTEZ: Montezuma, it is within my power to blow up your city and leave it in ashes . . .

MONTEZUMA: You will die in those ashes . . . !

CORTEZ: Señor, be assured that before I do, not a stone will be left standing in Tenochtitlan. I will call off the fighting if you will speak to your people now, and tell them to open a path for us out of the city.

MONTEZUMA: You had not reckoned with such bravery in Aztecs, did you, Cortez?

CORTEZ: I did not reckon with such treachery!

MONTEZUMA: Bravery, captain, say it! Say it, Spaniard!

CORTEZ: Yes . . . they are very brave.

MONTEZUMA: Then they are not fool enough to hear Montezuma again.

CORTEZ: They still respect you, they'll listen.

MONTEZUMA: May the Gods forbid it.

CORTEZ (*shouting*): I'll smash every building into dust! I'll destroy their city forever!

MONTEZUMA: I believe you! I will go, I will go to my people. For the sake of the living who are about to die, and the dead whom I betrayed. For love of a city unparalleled on earth before, I go to my city, and if you live to see your King again, tell him how you beguiled an Emperor, but do not omit how you bent your knee before his betters, the people of his state.

> (*Turns quickly, goes out, followed by soldiers, and as* CORTEZ *follows* . . .)

CORTEZ: Olid, haste, haste, Olid . . . melt everything. (*Exit* CORTEZ.)

> (*They continue with the gold-melting at an even faster pace as* . . . *the light fades.*)

SCENE 4

The roof of the great temple moments later. The booming of cannon and sounds of war seem to come from the streets below.

Curtain up on the rooftop empty. The sky overhead is grey with approaching rain.

MONTEZUMA *enters followed by* CORTEZ, ORDAZ, ALVARADO, MONTEJO *and* SOLDIERS. *From the group a* DRUMMER *steps out to the ledge and beats out an insistent roll while a* SOLDIER *appears next to him holding high a white banner. Gradual silence below.* DRUMMER *stops.* MONTEZUMA *steps from the group to go to the ledge, and it is perceived that* MONTEZUMA *has a short-sword at his back. He turns to* CORTEZ.

CORTEZ: Raise the banner. Let them see the sign.

> (*Drum begins again, reaches crescendo, hushed silence below.*)
> Your Majesty, speak to the people!

MONTEZUMA: With your sword in my back, Conquistador?

CORTEZ: In case there is still treachery in you. Speak to them!

MONTEZUMA: My people, it is late for Montezuma to be

coming from his house with words for his countrymen. But I see in your eyes a question: What does Montezuma have in his heart that he speaks now? What more will he take from us, this King who holds council with murderers?—I want nothing from you; I speak not to be obeyed, but to plead with you. I come no more the golden Montezuma on his royal way, I am but an Aztec man who would preserve his countrymen from further butchery . . .

GUATEMOTZIN (*from below*): You led us to butchery, Montezuma!—you!

(*Shouts of assent.*)

MONTEZUMA: Guatemotzin, I hear your voice, and I am grateful. (*Pause.*) It is better that I lose your love than I should hear you weep for me and forfeit up your spirit. And I speak to you, Guatemotzin, and you, Cuitlahua, my brother who stands with arrows, and you, Cagama, and to all the rest— noble men who could not bide with vassalage, and you, Tenochtitlan, my fearless city, hear me. You have met the conqueror with thunder on his tongue, and you have conquered him. You, the mixer of lime, the breaker of stone, the scribe, the hawker of wares, you have conquered the conqueror, who came to enslave you.

CUITLAHUA: The Spaniards continue to fight! They will not be conquered, until we kill them all!

MONTEZUMA: They continue to fight because they cannot bear to die unless the city be buried with them! (*Pause.*) Believe me, my country, I ask no mercy for them. But if this war goes on there will be no stick of wood unburned in Tenochtitlan, and no family spared. You have been valiant, —generations shall sing of your valour, but is it valour now or folly to destroy what is yours uncontested and safe? (*Pause.*) I ask you then, I, Montezuma, the king without right to ask of you the dust of your feet!—We must not live out our lives among ashes! People of Tenochtitlan . . . lay down your arms!

(*Silence below.*)

GUATEMOTZIN (*a furious shout*): O base man!!

MONTEZUMA (*raises his arms*): Guatemotzin, let the Spaniards depart.

GUATEMOTZIN: Base Aztec.

(*Great cry of anger from below.*)

CAGAMA: Woman!

CUITLAHUA: Coward!

CAGAMA: The white men have made you a woman!

(*A roar of anger below—flights of arrows.*)

MONTEZUMA (*raises arms quickly, as though to ward off a blow*):
No, brother . . . !

(*Scream of terror.*)

No!!

CORTEZ: Shield his body!

(*Before the Spaniards can shield him,* MONTEZUMA *is struck
and falls into a Captain's arms.*)

He's hit! Carry him inside, Alvarado!—Hurry! The rest follow me.

(*Disappears unsheathing his sword.* ALVARADO *lifts* MONTE-
ZUMA *to take him inside the temple.*)

ALVARADO: Your Majesty? I will find someone to come and
tend your wounds.

(ALVARADO *sets* MONTEZUMA *down, goes toward the stairway. Silence—left, out of the shadows,* TALUA, TAPAIA *and*
TECUICHPO *furtively appear.* ALVARADO *stops a distance
from the princess. All stand awaiting his move. Presently,*
ALVARADO *bows.*)

TECUICHPO (*running forward*): Father! Father!

ALVARADO: Princess.

MONTEZUMA: Tecuichpo! . . . Captain . . .

ALVARADO: She is safe, Señor. (*To her.*) While I am gone, be
kind to your lovely face. (*Snatches her to him and kisses her
roughly.*) Buenas Noches, Señorita . . . I will dream of
you. (*He runs up the stairs and disappears.*)

TECUICHPO (*tears streaming*): Oh Father . . .

MONTEZUMA: Where have you been, Tecuichpo?

TECUICHPO: Hidden here in the Temple. I will find medicines.

MONTEZUMA (*takes her hand*): No. Stay.

TAPAIA: You bleed, my lord, let me find surgeons.

MONTEZUMA: I am beyond surgeons, old man. Tapaia, you
must take her to safety . . .

TECUICHPO: Where? Where shall we go?

MONTEZUMA: To Guatemotzin's city.

(*She weeps.*)

Aye, we have come the full circle.

TECUICHPO: Let me stay with you, Father . . .

MONTEZUMA: No, no . . . take her, Tapaia, and when the Spring is come to Mexico again, let there be a great wedding. And in the day of that glory, let not the halls of Guatemotzin's house hear my name.

FR. OLMEDO: Let me touch your head with holy water . . .

MONTEZUMA: Oh, false, false priest. Take your holy water, Cortez, and drown your sins; I am not so fallen that a serpent can bring me into grace.

(FR. OLMEDO *rises slowly.*)

CORTEZ: For the last time, I beseech you renounce your idols and open your way into heaven.

MONTEZUMA: And you Captain? Will you go to heaven?

CORTEZ: When I have made my last confession.

MONTEZUMA: If there is a God who will forgive you your sins, Hernando Cortez, you betray me again, for your God is bloodier than mine. There could have been a time when I would be Christian. I believe it so. But now, I tell you with my remaining breath; Jesus Christ may be good above all gods; but Christians are debased below all men.

CORTEZ: Señor . . . with all my heart I beg you . . . ! Live . . . and when I return . . .

MONTEZUMA: . . . Your very steps will dig your grave and we will rot together in the gentle earth, for when my people struck me, I was oppression in their eyes. Look on me, Conquistador; in my unmourned face see your face, and in my destiny, the destiny of all oppression that dares to dig its heel in the living heart of Mexico.

(CORTEZ *starts to speak as* MONTEJO *dashes in.*)

Farewell, my daughter.

(*They embrace.*)

TECUICHPO: Farewell, Father.

TAPAIA: Farewell . . . my world—come, child.

(*Takes* TECUICHPO'*s arm and they go.*)

MONTEZUMA: And you, Talua? Will you not leave me?—

(TALUA *stands silent, as though he will never go.*)

Go then, and bring me the written history—

(TALUA *bends and kisses his hand, rises and goes out through shadows on left, through which* TECUICHPO *and* TAPAIA *have just gone.*

Enter CORTEZ, MARINA, FR. OLMEDO, *carrying a crucifix, and soldiers. They enter from right quickly.* MARINA *kneels on his right side,* FR. OLMEDO *on the left,* CORTEZ *at his feet; stands and looks at him a moment.*)

MARINA: See, he bleeds . . . find water . . . (*Starts to minister to him.*)

MONTEZUMA: Leave me . . .

CORTEZ: Let Marina bind your wounds, my Lord.

MONTEZUMA (*tears away a bandage*): No! Away with the medicines. Leave me!

CORTEZ: I have come so that you may be baptized in the name of Jesus Christ.

MONTEZUMA: Is my blood not enough but I must also render up my soul? You'll not have it, you'll not have it from me, though it wander lost to the end of time betrayed at every turning of the wind.

MONTEJO: They're digging under the barricades with their fingers,—we can't hold . . . !

CORTEZ: Then we break for the open streets! (*Draws sword.*) Come!

(*He hurries up the stairs and out; sword in hand; followed by* FR. OLMEDO. MARINA *halts as she sees* TALUA *coming out of the shadows, the prophecy under his arm. She watches as* TALUA *slips to his knees beside the King.*)

TALUA: My lord . . . The history . . .

MONTEZUMA (*long pause*): Talua . . .

TALUA: I write of this year?

(MARINA *appears from the shadows, listens.*)

MONTEZUMA: Write the truth, yes.

TALUA: What is the truth my lord.

MONTEZUMA (*pause*): Let the history tell how an emperor died in search of the golden years. And by no hand but his own. For while his eyes were searching heaven for meanings and signs, a sword was pointing at his breast, and as it caught the light with such brilliant glare, it seemed to hold the sanction of the sun, and he dared not turn the killing blade away. And when the sun was set, and the light was gone, the emperor felt for the face of the god but the steel stood turning in his heart.

(MARINA *rushes down to him, weeping.*)

MARINA: My Lord, what have I done! (*She falls to her knees beside him.*)

TALUA: He's dying, Marina.

MARINA: Why does he smile?

MONTEZUMA: Talua . . . read to me again . . . how the god shall return . . .

TALUA (*opens the stone book*): "From out of the place where the sun comes up, warming the ocean sea . . ."

(*A terrific booming of cannon very close by.* TALUA *is frozen.* MARINA *starts towards the stairs when her eye is caught by a helmet on the floor. She picks it up, looks tearfully at* MONTEZUMA, *and goes up the stairs as . . .*)

"From out of the place where the sun comes up, warming the ocean sea, there shall come again the departed one, and with him, shining brightly from his hand, a year has come. The first of a sheaf of The Golden Years . . ." (*As he reads . . . Cannon.*)

(*Slow curtain.*)

ALMOST EVERYBODY WINS

A Screenplay

CHARACTERS

Angela Crispini
Tom O'Toole
Connie
John Callaghan
Judge Harry Marks
Felix
Jerry
Amy
Robie
Sonny
Montana
Bellanca
Judge
Defense Attorney
Father Mancini
Dr. Levy
Mrs. Hearst
Jean
Interviewer
Lobby-man
Guards, Cops

Exterior: Day

*We are introduced to Minorville—at least to its surface aspects—
through the window of a moving car. It is a New England city of
perhaps 100,000 in the fall of the year. The white colonial church
speaks of order and goodness, and the surrounding Victorian
houses seem untouched by our century. Peaceful scenes flow past—
the neat schoolyard and kids playing; the firehouse with gleaming
machines within or being polished out front, and so on. Now a
different aspect—rows of rents, two or three-storey wooden buildings with outside stairways; decayed stores and a few loungers out
on the streets; and a bridge across a river from which we see both
the lovely tree-lined shores and one or two immense abandoned
mills with hundreds of windows, many of them smashed. And
now Main Street with some ambitiously modern storefronts
alongside the undistinguished and corny and decayed.*

Few shoppers are out at mid-morning.

*We move in a nondescript, working-class neighborhood and come
to a stop before a house.* TOM O'TOOLE *leaves the car and com-
pares the house number with one he has jotted on a slip of paper,
rings the bell, waits, looking up and down the quiet street. He is
in his forties, dressed in a small-town way, in a knee-length re-
versible and porkpie hat.*

*He rings again, looking up at the windows; looks at his watch, shakes
his head in anger at himself as well as the human race for this waste
of his time, starts back to his car in a beginning temper . . .*

ANGELA, *heels rapping, comes running up the street to him, already waving. She is chronologically over the hill, perhaps, but
only chronologically. A low-cut dress, makeup too heavy for the*

morning, high heels, and an incongruous attaché case in one hand and a fresh newspaper in the other. She is breathless.

ANGELA: You're right on time! Hi!
(*She holds out her hand, he shakes it, somewhat thrown off.*)
You're even handsomer than your pictures, aren't you. But I'd know you in a minute. Can we go?—Sorry, but I had to run around and pick up my *New York Times* . . . they only get three a day in this whole town! (*Indicates car.*) Okay?

TOM (*recovering from this barrage*): I think you must've misunderstood, Mrs. Crispini. I only agreed to talk about the case with you today . . .

ANGELA: Oh my God . . . ! But I already told him you're coming! What happened? I sent you the transcript . . .

TOM: I mailed it back to you, I read it. But I told you when you called . . . I'd be glad to talk about it and be of any help I can but I don't know if I want to start a whole new case . . .

ANGELA: I didn't sleep all night just thinkin' about him meetin' you today . . . 'cause he gets so discouraged, you know?

TOM: Well, I'm sorry if I . . .

ANGELA (*a new idea*): Listen—Let me show you something upstairs . . . (*Tugging his sleeve.*) Two minutes! Just to show you what I think of you!—and not just lately!
(*Before he can demur she is rattling up the stoop and into the house and he follows, intrigued but not unworried.*)

Interior: ANGELA*'s apartment—Day*

The room is a mess, an amazing profusion of bras, underwear, skirts, blouses, shoes—she has probably tried on her whole stock and dropped it on the run before meeting him.

She is just slipping a cassette into her VCR.

ANGELA: You probably won't even remember this . . . the day you got the reversal on the baby Schmidlap case?
(*TV screen:* TOM, PROSECUTOR CALLAGHAN—*Courthouse steps. A TV news* INTERVIEWER *has a mike up to* TOM*'s face. He is glancing with highly pleasurable irony toward State's*

Prosecutor CALLAGHAN, *who stands there trying not to explode.*)

INTERVIEWER: How do you feel about this victory, Mr. O'Toole?

TOM: Frankly, superb; but of course, getting reversals of a prosecutor's case is not all that unusual—I mean in this particular jurisdiction.

INTERVIEWER: And you, Mr. Callaghan?

CALLAGHAN (*a rather preppy type, but tough and intelligent and nattily dressed; about forty, probably reddish, nicely barbered hair*): I intend to try the defendant again and you can be sure he will be convicted again, and of course the public will pay the costs again. I regret very much that we have come to where so-called private investigators can shoot down the verdicts of faithful, hard-working juries and make a travesty of our whole system of justice!

(ANGELA *shuts off the machine.*)

TOM (*immensely excited—flattered*): What're you doing with that?

ANGELA: Can I tell you in the car? Felix is really expecting us!

(*He opens his mouth to resist again, but the will to do so has weakened before her insistence and the simple fact that she has opened the door and is standing there winsomely—and wittily—asking . . .*)

Please?

Interior: TOM*'s car—Day*

The car is several years old and has never been washed.

ANGELA: Can I call you Tom?

TOM: Sure!

ANGELA: Then you can stop calling me Mrs. Crispini.

(*He drives through town, heading for the interstate. She takes out a cigarette, holds it for a moment, then returns it to the pack.*)

Anyway, I'm really a Finn. (*Slight pause.*) Which is not the same as a Swede. 'Cause you might hear people calling me "the Swede." (*Slight pause.*) Not that I was ever in Finland.

(TOM *simply nods and grunts, glancing at her in fascination and puzzlement.*)

I just can't believe I'm actually sitting next to you! I mean, to me,—reading about you the last few years, and seeing you on TV fighting for people like that . . . (*Turning to him, confessionally.*) . . . I might as well say it—to me, if there is such a thing as hope for the world, a man like you is it.

TOM (*embarrassed laugh*): Wish I could say the same— Incidentally, what's your connection with this case?

ANGELA: In a few words? (*She is thoughtful for a moment, rapt, eagerly tense, trying to formulate a complicated thought . . . then gives up . . .*) We'll have to sit down; . . . I mean it's very complicated . . . (*She draws a cigarette out and holds it, puts it between her lips, then returns it to the pack.*)

TOM: Don't you ever light them?

ANGELA: I'm bustin' my nuts trying to quit. So I go through the motions. Everything in the world is suggestion, you know—like one step away from a dream.

TOM (*mystified, yet drawn on*): It sure feels like it sometimes.

ANGELA: Like I had this doctor telling me I had a cancer.

TOM: You're kiddin'.

ANGELA: But I don't.

TOM (*impressed*): How do you know?

ANGELA: Because. From the day I made up my mind, the pains stopped.

TOM: No kiddin'!

ANGELA: But of course I completely gave up alcohol. And sex.

TOM: No kiddin'!!

ANGELA: You don't think it's possible?

TOM: Listen, the way you look I'd have to doubt it, but . . . I know it's *possible.*

ANGELA (*eyes him with surprise*): Can I ask what you mean by that?

TOM: What I said.

ANGELA: But why sex?

TOM (*blushing, but something about her liberates his feelings*): I don't know . . . the usual, I guess—sooner or later Mother Nature starts to let you down.

ANGELA: Really. At your age. It's purified me completely, I never felt . . . you know . . . this clean.

TOM: Well, that's good. I have sort of mixed feelings about it myself.
> (*He ducks to look up at a gate guard, who recognizes him and waves him through.*)

Interior: Visitors' room, Penitentiary—Soon after

TOM *and* ANGELA *are seating themselves in two adjoining chairs that face a long table, dividing the room. The guard gives her a lusty glance and a super-appreciative gesture to* TOM, *who seems a bit embarrassed by it, but proud, too, of his implicit distinction. Guard leaves.*

ANGELA: Boy, you are great-looking! (*Now intimately.*) It's so important you came—see, his appeal comes up on Thursday . . .

TOM: On what grounds?

ANGELA: Well, we're claiming his lawyer was incompetent, see.

TOM: That's not very good grounds.

ANGELA (*searching in her attaché case*): I know—so if we lose the appeal, it's very important he should feel something else is being done, y'see?

TOM: Hold it, will you? I'd have to study the case a lot more before I commit myself . . .

ANGELA: I want to show you what he looked like when they arrested him. You're not going to believe this. (*She searches in her attaché case.*)

TOM: Y'know, I still don't dig your connection—did you say you didn't know him before the murder . . . ?

ANGELA: Oh no, I never knew Felix till the trial. But Abe had been my doctor.

TOM: Abe . . . oh, you mean the man who was killed.

ANGELA: Dr. Daniels. Didn't I mention that? He'd been a very wonderful friend to me. So I started attending the trial.

TOM: Oh! Well, now I understand.

ANGELA: It got me so upset I couldn't sleep. I mean, to listen to that Callaghan going on day after day about absolutely zero . . . he had no evidence!

TOM: I may as well tell you; John Callaghan is the one big reason

I even returned your call. You know, he's tried to get my investigator's license revoked, damn near put me out of business.

ANGELA: Please don't talk to me about John Callaghan because I get so upset I can't . . . (*She realizes she has a newspaper clipping in her hand.*) Oh . . . here's Felix. When they arrested him. Look at that man.

(TOM *takes the clipping.*)

(*Close-up: Photo of* FELIX. *He is a conventionally dapper man in his late thirties, successful, topcoat over his arm, hat in hand.*)

Interior: Visitors' room—Same time

Guard enters first, followed by FELIX. TOM *and* ANGELA *stand.* FELIX *now has a head of straggly white hair, a long white beard and haunted, frightened eyes, and stands a bit bent. He seems a recluse living under a rock. Guard leaves.* ANGELA *approaches* FELIX *delicately, unsure whether he even recognizes her.* TOM *is immediately quite moved, but not swept away.*

ANGELA: Hello, dear . . . It's Angela. You remember.

FELIX: . . . You came back?

ANGELA: I always come back, dear! I brought Mr. O'Toole, *Tom* O'Toole, remember?—On TV when he got the reversal on the Baby Schmidlap case?

(FELIX *stares at* TOM, *undecided.*)

TOM: Whyn't we sit down, Mr. Epstein?

(*As they do—*ANGELA *nurses* FELIX *into a chair.*)

ANGELA: You don't look like you're eating, Felix.

FELIX (*to* ANGELA): Terrible class of people in here.

ANGELA: But you have to eat.

FELIX: They cook everything in antiseptic.

(TOM *clears his throat.*)

TOM (*taking charge*): If you don't mind, Felix; I understand you live in Boston—how'd you come to be all the way down in Minorville the night your uncle was killed?

FELIX (*stares*): For the thousandth time—I wanted to talk to him about putting up for a mortgage on my shopping mall, which I was building in the River Basin area up there.

TOM: But why that night in particular?—a weekend and all?

FELIX (*against a threatening upsurge of anger against himself*): Because my ex-girlfriend, Martha Solomon lives in Minorville and she agreed to have dinner on Saturday night—is that some kind of crime that we might get together again?

TOM: But there's no mention of your date in the transcript . . .

(*Suddenly* FELIX's *sleepiness is gone and he is crying out.*)

FELIX: Because my lawyer was such a big shot intellectual schmuck who wouldn't be bothered to call her in! That man destroyed me! Lunchtime he's reading poetry instead of thinking! And twenty-five thousand dollars he took for that!

ANGELA: Ssh! Everything's going to change now, dear.

TOM (*lets him subside*): Felix, can you tell me . . . what's the first notification you had of your uncle being murdered?

FELIX: I read it in the paper—he's cut up like a chicken in his living room. I nearly fainted!

TOM: And what next?

FELIX: . . . Two days later a couple of Boston detectives come into my office—"Can we look at your comb?" "My comb? Sure." I take it out of my pocket. They leave, and next day, I am under arrest. I have to tell you, Mr. O'Toole, this woman has been wonderful, but I am not in this world any more—I am walking around, but I'm dead. I'm not crazy yet, you understand, but I'm . . . I . . .

(*He weeps softly.* ANGELA *gives* TOM *a "you-see-how-innocent-he-is" look, but* TOM *resists sentiment.*)

TOM: I'd like you to listen.—Felix?

ANGELA: Felix, listen to him, dear, he's wonderful.

TOM: In your uncle's house that night, can you remember?—did you comb your hair?

FELIX: I've been over that a thousand times . . . I'm talking to him about investing a hundred thousand dollars, how do I come to start combing my hair?

TOM: How about in the bathroom? You'd just had dinner with your date, right? Didn't you have to go to the bathroom?

FELIX: Say, now . . . That's right, I remember there were gold faucets.

TOM: And you used to be a pretty neat dresser, right?—wouldn't you have combed your hair in there?

FELIX: But they found the broken tooth of my comb in the living room, it was right next to the bodies.

TOM: Not according to their first report. Only days later, on a second search, they miraculously find the tooth of your comb on the carpet next to where the bodies were.

FELIX: You mean it was moved there?

ANGELA (*points at* TOM. *To* FELIX): What'd I tell you!

TOM (*abruptly*): Well, it was nice meeting you, Felix—I'll be thinking about it and if I come up with any ideas I'll be in touch with Mrs. Crispini. Take care now . . .

> (*He turns to* ANGELA, *but she is gone from her chair; he looks around and sees her standing by a window, gets up and goes to her. A remarkably intense look is upon her; she seems elevated, a seer and at the same time somehow sensually charged up. She turns to him and whispers.*)

ANGELA: My God! Your face . . . you suddenly looked like the sun shooting out lights . . . You've got to take this case, you were born for this!

TOM (*put off and drawn in as well by her strange intensity*): Let me think about it. I don't know . . .

Interior: Courtroom—Day

It is all from TOM's *viewpoint: he is seated at the back of the courtroom, observing as the* DEFENSE ATTORNEY *is concluding his appeal to the Bench, while* PROSECUTOR CALLAGHAN *waits his turn. Chief of Detectives* BELLANCA *looks on from* CALLAGHAN's *side.*

ANGELA *sits in another part of the room, attaché case on her lap, pad and pencil at the ready.*

DEFENSE ATTORNEY: It comes down, Your Honor, to the perfectly obvious fact that Felix Epstein did not have competent counsel, and we appeal to the court for a new trial.

JUDGE: Mr. Callaghan?

CALLAGHAN: Your Honor, defendant's counsel was very successful in numerous other cases; he is a well-known attorney with a reputable law firm. Epstein was convicted of a bloody and brutal murder; there is not the slightest doubt about his guilt . . .

(ANGELA *violently shakes her head, "No!"*)

. . . the evidence is damning and complete. This appeal has absolutely no basis in fact; the State asks that it be denied.

(TOM *observes that* CALLAGHAN *has shot a glance toward* ANGELA, *but its meaning is not clear to him—does he know her or is it simply that he suddenly noticed a strange woman in the empty courtroom?*)

JUDGE (*turns down to the* DEFENSE ATTORNEY): Defendant's appeal for a new trial is denied.

Interior: Courthouse corridor—Later

TOM *and* ANGELA *are about to turn a corner in the corridor when they nearly run into* CALLAGHAN, *who engraves a wide grin onto his face. He seems not to have noticed* ANGELA *at all . . . he keeps moving.*

CALLAGHAN: O'Toole!—what brings you here!—I haven't seen any cameras.

TOM (*with a wry grin holds up a finger*): Wait!

(*They both are angrily intense and affect to laugh—* CALLAGHAN *throws an unreadably blind glance at* ANGELA *as he turns and walks away.*)

Exterior: ANGELA*'s block—Night*

Her street. Wooden three-storey "rents"—not a slum, but working-class definitely. TOM*'s car pulls up before her house, in which no lights shine.*

Interior: TOM*'s car—Same time*

She is opening her door; he is looking ahead; she lingers.

ANGELA: So where would you say we are?—Could I ask you up for a minute?

TOM: I've got a court appearance first thing in the morning, I better hit the pike.

ANGELA: . . . I'm really scared what Felix might do when he hears the appeal's been turned down.—And incidentally, he's not poor, you know, you'd get paid.

TOM: That'd be nice, how about you?

ANGELA: Me!

TOM: I'm sorry, kid, but I still don't dig your connection— what's this all about?

ANGELA: Look, I can't talk here. (*With a mixture of seductiveness and some unexplained fear she grips his arm, smiling wittily . . .*) Come up, will you? I get so little chance to talk to anyone who isn't stepping on his own fingers . . . I mean, Christ, you look like a *man*!

TOM (*laughs, flattered*): Hey, gimme a break, will ya?

ANGELA: Please!

TOM (*serious now*): I don't understand why they would want to frame Felix. Do you?

ANGELA: They're watching.

TOM (*juices flow*): Who's watching?

ANGELA: On the corner. Cops.

> (*He turns to look up the street, then down the other direction.*) They just pulled out.
>
> (*Her fear is so palpable that as she gets out of the car he gets out, too, and they head to her door.*)

TOM: You sure? I didn't see anybody.

> (*With hand shaking, she works her key nervously in the lock. He helps insert the key with a steady hand.*)

Interior: ANGELA's *apartment—Moments later*

The living room is practically bare with no personality of the owner. Everything is neat as if the room is never used.

ANGELA: Lock the door, will ya?

> (TOM *does—three locks and a safety chain.*)
> (ANGELA *calls from the bedroom.*) Come on in.

Interior: Bedroom—Same time

TOM *enters the bedroom; this time he has a moment to examine it. It is a crowded, intensely lived-in, cavelike room. He observes* ANGELA *neatening up, scooping up the debris of underwear, bras, stockings, skirts, blouses, shoes that are scattered everywhere.*

ANGELA: Be with you in a second . . . would you like some vitamins?

TOM: Use your phone?

ANGELA: Sure!

> (*She swings the door of the bathroom open and goes in, closing it behind her. He picks up the phone beside her bed and dials.*)

TOM: Me, Connie. I'll be leavin' in a couple of minutes. No-no, I'm stayin' out of it.—I don't know, I suppose Epstein could've done it, but I have to admit there is a slightly putrid smell about it.—Well, John Callaghan was the prosecutor, need I say more? Fifteen years ago I'd have gone after it, but I'm tired, kid.—Now? I'm waitin' for the woman to come out of the bathroom so I can give her my opinion, why?—I said I'm not gettin' into it, what do you want, a signed contract!! Why should I be mad . . . Do I sound mad? (*He hangs up, furious, but it quickly subsides. He is sitting in a boudoir-type armchair. Looks about the room—the rumpled bed, covered with a satin throw, worn carpet, Grand Rapids Baroque plastic-tufted head-board . . . and finally he spots a surprising shelf of books, walks over to inspect the titles. And under it, a kind of drape which is partly open, revealing, once he gently moves it completely aside, an oak double-drawer filing cabinet. A heavy padlock has been affixed to the drawers. He lets the drape fall closed again.*)

> (ANGELA *enters.*)

ANGELA: Well! This is better!

> (*She is in a very nearly transparent negligee, which forces him instinctively to glance down and away.*)

TOM (*with nearly a snigger of laughter*): Boy, that's quite a little outfit there.

ANGELA (*stretching onto the bed*): Like some herb tea?

TOM: No, I'm fine. Now listen . . . (*As much to ward off her incitation as anything else, he sits on the edge of the chair, looking very businesslike.*)

ANGELA (*openly stretching the moment*): What's this case you're on?

TOM: Nothing important. I work for insurance companies occasionally, pick up some easy bread.

ANGELA: That must be very interesting.

TOM: Molto boring. I run checks on executives they're thinking of promoting. This one's gonna be made Vice-President of a ball-bearin' company and they want to know if he's gay.

ANGELA: Jeeze, they still doin' that?

TOM: Well, you can't have a homosexual Vice-President of a ball-bearin' company. (*Shifts, about to rise.*) Maybe, I'll see you around—go into this further sometime.

ANGELA: There's a lot bigger case here than meets the eye, Tom.

TOM (*already loath to lose contact, equivocally*): Maybe you better not tell me.

ANGELA: I guess so, if you're staying out of it . . . You're breaking my heart, y'know.

TOM: Tell you the truth, it's got that old familiar stink, but I really can't see myself goin' up against the system again. I just don't have it any more.

ANGELA: Can I tell you the reason I called you?—Because the man who does this case is going to need a pair of brass balls, which I happen to know is what you've got.

TOM (*flattered*): I know, kid, but the time comes when you realize the public has to love corruption or you wouldn't have crooked judges fallin' out of the trees every ten minutes, and they wouldn't be electing unscrupulous meatheads like John Callaghan to run the criminal justice system . . .

ANGELA: You're a thrill just to listen to. I mean you're the only one who can talk about something else besides money and pussy.

TOM: Well, I couldn't resist my curiosity, bein' it's a John Callaghan case, but let me maul it over some more. (*Stands. Holds out his hand.*) Take care, and it was terrific meetin' you . . .

ANGELA: I know the murderer.

TOM (*it stops him cold, but he tries to remain cool and skeptically apart*): Yeah?

    (*The issue is her credibility and she stares him right in the eye.*)

That raises a number of questions, doesn't it.

ANGELA: Oh, the cops know who it is. In fact, they had him and let him go.

TOM: You knew this when they were trying Felix?

ANGELA: There was no way I could say anything.

TOM (*postponing*): . . . Right. But now?

ANGELA: I'm ready to talk. But there's a couple of things I still need to prove; that's why I need you. Felix is the tip of the iceberg, this case goes to the top of the criminal justice system. (*Pats her mattress as she stretches out on the bed.*) God, I'm exhausted . . . could you sit just a minute before you go?

(*He sits beside her on the bed.*)

You mind if I touch your hand?

TOM: Don't try to crank me up, kid, you'll only get tired.

ANGELA: I talk better when I'm touching . . . According to that interview you got nuns in the family?

TOM: A sister and two brothers priests. But it never rubbed off.

ANGELA: I'm more into it since my cancer scare—I have a friend, Father Mancini at Saint Jude's?

TOM: Don't know him.

(*Her sensuality toward him is becoming unabashed, and he sees it plainly and is aroused.*)

ANGELA: When I told him my feelings about you,—the kind of fighter you are—he said, "God places certain people on the earth to fight for truth and justice." He thinks you're one. And I'm another. You mind if I kiss you?

(*Before he can react she is drawing him down and kissing him . . . rather chastely, temptingly.*)

You could wrap up the case in a month—I know what to look for and where to look.

(*Her hand moves down his body; he is exploding with surprise.*)

Hey!—what's this about Mother Nature lettin' you down!

(*He is on her with ravishing happiness.*)

Interior: TOM*'s bathroom—Night*

He is just slipping on his pyjama top and stares at himself in the mirror—he admires himself as though he has just discovered his attractiveness.

But as he turns to go out his eyes show his mystification and guilt. He opens the door and goes into his bedroom where his lover CON-NIE *is sitting up in bed. A high-school teacher, she is correcting a small pile of papers resting on the blanket beside her.*

CONNIE: She sounds ditsy to me.

TOM: I would prefer librarians, but they rarely know where the bodies are buried.

CONNIE: But you don't even know who she is or her connection to the case.

TOM (*picking up one of the papers*): I've got a gut feeling, that's all. There's a quagmire under this thing a mile deep.—What's this word supposed to be?

CONNIE (*a glance at the paper he is pointing to*): "Apparently."

TOM: "A-p-o-r-o-n-d-l-y?"

CONNIE: It's creative spelling. But he's captain of the swimming team.

TOM: He'd better be. I don't know how you can go on trying to teach anything to these clucks.

CONNIE: I concentrate on the good ones—(*Shyly, but determined to underline this.*) We've all got to accentuate the positive, don't we?—I mean, that's life.

TOM: Right. (*Takes a book off the nightstand, opens it. Embarrassed.*) I can't always do what I'd like to, Connie.

CONNIE: I know. (*Puts down her papers.*) I'm here when you're ready.

    (*He touches her hand thankfully, full of conflict.*)

    —I thought you weren't going to take on any more long criminal cases.

TOM: Connie . . . the woman claims Callaghan convicted an innocent man—

CONNIE: But if she knows the murderer why doesn't she just come out and tell you?

TOM: Darlin', please, the woman is scared, that's understandable . . .

CONNIE (*affecting amusement*): She really got you going, didn't she . . .

TOM: What are you talking about . . . ?

CONNIE: Good night, dear.

    (*She turns on her side, closes her eyes. He stares ahead in turmoil, mystified. Phone rings. Shocked, he picks it up as* CONNIE *half rises.*)

TOM (*into phone*): Yeah? . . . Oh, hya!

   (*She witnesses the excitement flaring in his face.*)

   Now? I'm an hour away, I'm in bed! . . . Well, good, I'm glad you feel that way about it . . . Right, talk to you in the morning. 'Night. (*He hangs up. He sees the anxiety and incipient jealousy in* CONNIE*'s face; his only hope is to ignore it.*)

Exterior: Country road—Day

His car proceeding slowly on a narrow dirt road. It stops as a motorcyclist comes zooming out of the brush beside the road—this is JERRY, *but* TOM *barely gets a glimpse of his face before he disappears up the road.* TOM *gets out and turns to look down a dirt driveway leading to a gloomy, small house, surrounded by trees and brush. He starts up the driveway. A shot. He halts. Second shot. He steps behind a tree and looks.*

TOM*'s point of view: In front of the house, a stringy young woman, wearing jeans and a bandanna and a man's coat is just lowering a shotgun, which is pointed off camera, not at* TOM.

Exterior: AMY*'s house—Same time*

TOM *steps from behind the tree . . .*

TOM: Excuse me . . .

   (AMY *screams in shock, drops the gun, paralyzed. He approaches her. She is drug-pale.*)

   Sorry about that.

AMY: There's a woodchuck. He's always . . . like comin' around.

TOM: No kiddin'. I guess you must be Amy, right?

AMY: Why? Who . . . ?

TOM: I'm Mr. O'Toole. Friend of Angela? Remember Angela? She talked to you this morning on the phone. Said I was coming.

   (AMY *simply waits expectantly.*)

Could we go in and sit down for a minute? I'm not the police, I'm a private investigator. I'm looking into the Dr.
Daniels murder, you remember that?—Abe Daniels?

(*She turns and walks up to the house, he following; she is escaping as unnoticeably as she can.*)

(*Walking behind her*): Angela says you were very helpful
during the trial and I was wondering if I could talk about a
few . . .

(*She opens a screendoor and a frightened chicken flies right
out past her head, but she seems not to notice.*)

Interior: AMY's *house—Same time*

TOM *follows* AMY *into the living room, a mess: broken couch, a
sleeping dog, and half a dozen chickens strolling about. She
doesn't sit, but stands like one of the chickens, staring at nothing.*

TOM *reaches down into a bare clay pot and pulls out . . . an egg!*

AMY *glances at it.*

AMY: That's an egg.

TOM (*at least this is some progress*): Right!

AMY: Jerry doesn't live here any more.

TOM (*gently replacing the egg*): Which Jerry is that, dear?

AMY: The one who killed that Dr. Daniels . . .

(*Straight-faced,* TOM *lets a beat pass.*)

TOM: I wonder if you could help me out, Amy. See I'm comin'
in a little late and there's some things I'm not clear on . . .
Like to sit down?

(*He draws a chair closer for her and she sits, looking at him
with some surprise at his kindness.*)

You know, don't you, that there's a man in prison for killing
Dr. Daniels.

AMY: Oh no, he didn't do it, Jerry did it.

TOM: Gee whiz, that's what Angela's been tellin' me. But I'm
glad to hear it from another person . . . Incidentally, how
do you come to know Angela?

AMY: Angela? . . . Bimini.

TOM: Bimini . . . you mean down the Caribbean?

(AMY's *expression changes—she seems to relate momentarily.*)

AMY: I told all this to the cops, though . . . And then Jerry went down.

TOM: Jerry went where, dear?

AMY: To the cops. He was all covered with blood.

TOM: And what did the cops do?

AMY: They sent him here to go to sleep.

TOM: He told the cops he'd killed Dr. Daniels?

AMY: He was going crazy about it, so I said you better get it off your mind 'cause he's so religious; he's raised Catholic, you know.

TOM: Where is Jerry now, dear, do you know?

AMY: He might be in the cemetery, but I don't think he's dead.

TOM: . . . Why do you think he's in the cemetery if he's not dead, dear?

(*Sleep threatens to overcome her then and there . . . she goes to the couch.*)

Amy?

AMY: Well, praying there to Major McCall.

TOM (*it is getting more and more weird*): Praying to Major McCall?

AMY: . . . Or to his church, maybe—you know, the mill.

TOM: And where would that be located, darlin'?

AMY: Like by the Winslow Bridge . . . or ah . . . Yeah, where you come down to the river . . . You know . . . that mill . . . (*She breathes deeply, falls fast asleep.*)

Exterior: Cemetery—Dusk

TOM *moves, glancing about at the grave-markers and monuments. His eye is caught by a base with the monument broken off and removed. He touches the broken cement which once joined the two. He reads the inscription. Close-up:*

> MAJOR JEROME SETH MCCALL
> POET AND SOLDIER
> HIS LIFE FOR THE NATION
> *1825–1862*

Now he sees, on the ground at the foot of the monument's base, what look like burned bones in a little pile. The grass around the pile is blackened. He stands and walks toward his car nearby.

Exterior: TOM*'s car—Day*

TOM *is on a road above the river when he sees a motorcycle approaching; the rider—this will turn out to be* JERRY*—has both arms raised in the air and is facing up to the sky as though imploring heaven.*

TOM *quickly pulls over to stick out his head, and watch the man who disappears around a turn. Then he drives on. In a moment he stops the car, seeing . . .*

Exterior: Abandoned mill—River—Day

It is a large New England mill, long since abandoned, beside the river. The Winslow Bridge, as AMY *had specified, is in the near distance.*

Exterior: Abandoned mill—Day

TOM *is approaching the mill fairly cautiously. Notes the broken window panes, the weeds around the front door. Opens it and walks in.*

Interior: Abandoned mill—Day

An immense space, a shambles of old broken machinery. The light from the windows is sepulchral; as TOM*'s eyes adjust he sees an object standing against a wall, goes to it.*

The statue of a Civil War major, sword in scabbard, proudly moustached, one foot forward—the conventional Civil War monument. It has been placed on a rough base, a wooden box. A few candles stand before it.

He moves about and sees a rumpled cot, a dented kerosene stove with a pot on it and a few cans of beans nearby.

Now he sees a live lamb in a makeshift pen.

He walks to a wide loading door on the water side of the building, looks out on a boat-landing ramp or pier.

He turns now to return to the door through which he entered, and practically walks into ANGELA. *She is dressed now in a navy-blue straight-cut suit, carrying a rather sedate leather handbag.*

TOM: Jesus!—Boy, you scared me! Whatcha doin' here?
> (*She stares at him, strangely, without immediately answering. Her eyes seem to see inward, rather than out. She seems somehow different than before—stands with a certain elegance, almost aloof, her vocal tone deeper in the throat and cultivated, although the grammar is not quite perfect.*)

ANGELA: Why didn't you tell me you were coming here?

TOM (*mystified, searching her odd look*): Well, Amy said he might be here . . .

ANGELA: "What Amy said" is hardly consequential.

TOM (*absolutely baffled*): Hey, look, I'm only . . .

ANGELA (*with haughty command*): We're going to have to discuss this if you intend to continue.
> (*Mystified,* TOM *decides to let this pass for the moment, and points to the Major's statue and the penned lamb.*)

TOM: What's this about, do you know?
> (ANGELA *glances down at the sacrifice; there is some loaded quality to her simple reply.*)

ANGELA: It's his religion.

TOM: Jerry?
> (*She looks up at the Civil War soldier's statue, and it seems to touch her with some reverential feeling . . . which she instantly dispels.*)

ANGELA (*factually*): He believes the Major is God and that he's His son.
> (*As she says this* TOM *detects the barest suggestion that she may share this belief, and is even feeling out his reaction.*)

TOM: Well, he's got a right, I guess.—Is this a one-man religion or . . . ?

ANGELA: Oh, there was a group once, but . . . they're practically all gone off now. You know.

TOM (*a stab*): Were you in it?

ANGELA (*rather quickly*): No, but . . . (*She looks up at the Major. And now defensively . . .*) Our Father's house has many mansions, you know.

> (*He doesn't reply, trying to fathom her, for she has a different tonality than earlier, a certain command.*)

But listen, I want you to tell me before you decide to take off after somebody again, you understand?

TOM: Hey, hold it now . . .

ANGELA: Well you want to know what's involved, don't you?—before you get hurt or something?

TOM: Kid, if I'm doing the investigation I make those decisions, not you.

ANGELA (*flaring up incredibly fast*): Don't you understand *anything*?

> (*She hesitates a moment, then turns and starts away. He lunges out and stops her.*)

TOM (*friendly, but decisive*): You want to tell me what's going down here, Angela, or should I go home now and stay there?

ANGELA (*her brows knit*): Why are you calling me that kind of name?

TOM: What name you want me to call you?

ANGELA (*with a nuance of haughtiness*): Why Renata, of course.
> (*She walks away. Dumbstruck, he stares after her.*)

Interior: TOM*'s bathroom—Day*

He is drying off after a shower. Through the half-open door he sees CONNIE *entering the bedroom with fresh sheets. Wrapping the towel around him he goes halfway toward her.*

TOM: Incidentally, I've just about decided to cut out of that Abe Daniels case.

CONNIE: Boy, that's good news. I thought she sounded off the wall from day one.

TOM: Well, some of her information *has* checked out, but . . . she's just too complicated. It's like chasing feathers in a tornado. I'm telling her this morning. (*Pats her cheek gently.*) I feel better already.

Interior: Coffee shop—Next day

Close shot: A woman's beautiful legs folding one over the other. Pulling back, we see TOM *trying not to stare at the woman at a nearby table in a coffee shop where he sits at the counter having his cup. He pays and walks into the street.*

The madness of his awakened sexuality is bubbling in him and wherever he turns he can see only temptation. In the street, the shop windows, stepping down from a halted bus, getting into cars, their photos on magazines at the newsstand—the bodies of women assault him like a naked army.

Suddenly he sees her waiting for a light to change . . . ANGELA *standing there, available, his own if he wants her. His brain shatters and as she steps off the curb to cross the avenue he rushes and calls after her . . .*

TOM: Ang . . . (*Breaks off—remembering.*) Renata! Hey!
    (*She doesn't turn around. Now he is a few feet behind her . . .*)
  Renata?
    (*She still doesn't turn around.*)
  Angela?
    (*Now she turns.*)
ANGELA (*immensely happy to see him*): Hello! Where you been, why haven't you rung me?
TOM: Listen, what am I supposed to call you—Renata or Angela?
ANGELA (*mystified*): Renata? What do you mean?
TOM: Well, the other day in that place by the river . . .
ANGELA: . . . Oh God. Did I do a number or something?
    (*She breaks off, the blood draining out of her face, and he grips her arm.*)
  Get me home, will you?
    (*Alarmed, he helps her to walk.*)

Interior: TOM*'s car—Day*

ANGELA *is deeply upset, staring ahead. The car is parked in a lot behind the courthouse.*

TOM: Listen . . . I was coming over to tell you that I'm pullin' out of the case.
> (*She turns to him, incredulous, deeply shocked and lost. But his indecision begins returning as he realizes her need.*)

Let's face it, kid, I'm not getting the story from you.

ANGELA (*bravely, letting him feel her hurt, she gives him a wounded smile*): Okay, Tom. (*Gives his arm a pat.*) I know when I lose. But I'm not giving up on Felix. Can you get me home?

TOM (*takes her hand; his look has become desperate*): I don't think I want to lose you.

ANGELA (*a witty grin and toss of her head*): Then don't.

TOM (*delaying the end . . .*): Frankly, I've had the thought that . . . I'd really love to take a shot at shaking up the prosecutor.

ANGELA (*an electric reaction—excited but tinged with alarm*): Callaghan?

TOM (*sensing more than mere curiosity*): . . . You know him?

ANGELA (*evading, but expertly*): Well . . . you know, like everybody.

TOM: I'd love to put the fear of God in that college boy. Just to see what drops out. You never know, y'know?

ANGELA: Do I love brass balls! (*She grasps his face and plants a deep kiss on his mouth.*)

TOM: I love you, Angela. (*Quickly grips his head.*) Now what the hell'd I say that for!

ANGELA (*moved*): Oh, you're dear! Let's go home!

TOM: Yes, mam!
> (*He starts to drive. As she lifts an arm to straighten her hair he sees the edge of bandage around her wrist.*)

What's that?

ANGELA (*there is some conflict*): . . . I . . . had an accident yesterday.

TOM: When?

ANGELA (*she hesitates: he sees this: then she decides to let him know*): A guy came up behind me and threw me against a car.

TOM: What!! Why?

(*Their eyes meet.*)

ANGELA: A cop, I think. Out of uniform.

(*His face hardens in fury.*)

Interior: CALLAGHAN*'s office—Next day*

TOM, BELLANCA, CALLAGHAN. BELLANCA, *Chief of Detectives, is in full stride. This is* JOHN CALLAGHAN*'s courthouse office;* BELLANCA *is both subservient and contemptuous of his classy, alcoholic superior. Toward* TOM *he is openly sarcastic.*

BELLANCA: I mean, John, you can't seriously be asking us to listen to his crap! I know the woman he's been talking to—Angela Crispini, and she's as crazy as a worn-out whore can get!

TOM: Bellanca, I made up my mind at breakfast that I'm not gonna get mad all day . . .

BELLANCA: Oh, give us a break, O'Toole—who gives a shit if you get mad?

TOM (*turning to* CALLAGHAN): I came to tell you that I have been retained on the Epstein case, to find new evidence that will get him a retrial. I am asking for cooperation from the relevant personnel. I am not on a vendetta. I pounded a Chicago beat for a lotta years . . .

BELLANCA (*to* CALLAGHAN): Till they threw him out, I heard.

TOM (*still to* CALLAGHAN): There is no question in my mind that Felix Epstein is innocent and I want him out of jail.

BELLANCA: You finished?

TOM: Bellanca, you got the wrong man and the smart thing would be to face it now.

BELLANCA (*furious, he stands; to* CALLAGHAN): The woman who is feedin' him this garbage is an alcoholic and a hooker for twenty years! (*Counts on his fingers.*) The Ramada Inn, the Hilton, Looie's 48 Club, Ritchy's Truck Stop—you name it she's hooked there, and he's taking her word against ours! (*To* TOM.) Felix Epstein killed his uncle, period!

(BELLANCA *shoulders his way to the door and goes out.* TOM *seems slightly shaken, but is still furious.*)

CALLAGHAN (*barely concealing his gladdened heart*): Okay . . . this department will not obstruct any legitimate investigation of the Epstein case.

TOM: I will want to look at evidence.

CALLAGHAN: If we've got it you can see it.

TOM: Right. (*He stands, goes to the door.*)

CALLAGHAN: O'Toole?

(TOM *turns.*)

You will never get Epstein—A. B: this is the biggest mistake of your life. See you around.

(TOM, *filled with anger and uncertainty, leaves fast.*)

Interior: ANGELA*'s bedroom—Evening*

TOM *is just entering the room.* ANGELA *is sitting up in bed in a negligee, busily writing in a notepad. Beside her, a file folder lies open, filled with newsclips, jottings, etc. . . .*

ANGELA: Be right with you. I know a wonderful pasta joint, you like ziti?

TOM: Couple of things we got to discuss, Angela, before we go out—I really have to.

(ANGELA, *stuffing notebook in folder, gets off bed, crossing room.*)

ANGELA: God, you're a great-looking man.

(*He watches her as she puts the folder into a file, which she shuts, snaps the large padlock, and closes the drape over it.*)

TOM (*intent on clarification*): Angela, I been going over in my mind . . .

ANGELA: You're my first since I gave up on it and I can't get it out of *my* mind.

TOM: Well, I can't tell you what it's meant to me.

ANGELA: Why not tell me? Please, Tom. (*She snuggles to him, anticipating.*) Let's just talk; not about the case . . . just anything. You reading anything lately? I'm just finishing the biography of Joan Crawford by her daughter. Did you read that?

TOM (*with a grin*): I'm not too big on trash.

ANGELA: Well some trash is interesting but I thought it was uncalled for . . . I mean, her own *daughter*. My father raped me, but I'm not writing books about him.

TOM: Really raped you?

ANGELA: For years. By the same token, though, with people like him it wasn't, you know, all that unusual with a daughter. But it sure did *me* in.

(TOM *stares at her for a moment. Then remembers his point.*)

TOM: This is important, kid, so let's . . .

ANGELA: It's not important a woman was raped?

TOM (*openly impatient*): Now listen, Angela, it's out in the open now that I'm on the case . . . I don't want to make a fool of myself—I have to know what your involvement is, okay?

(*He notes an inexplicable sort of tension coming over her, an* internalized *quality walled off from him.*)

ANGELA (*strained, highly anxious*): I told you. Abe Daniels was my *doctor* . . . (*Her breathing is deeper, flooding with some anxiety, she is clenching and unclenching her hands.*)

TOM: And Felix?—you really never knew him before the trial?

ANGELA (*angrily offended*): I don't understand, you mean I can't be upset by an innocent man bein' put away?

TOM: Sure you can, but I am layin' my whole reputation on the line here! The least you can do is level with me . . . ! I mean . . . (*He breaks off, aware now of her transformation.*)

ANGELA (*she stands; voice like gravel, her whole aspect is transforming into a crude streetwalker*): Caman, will ya, why don't you just come out with it . . . !

(TOM *looks up at her, startled.* ANGELA *is strangely freed, one hip thrown out, arms akimbo, mouth distorted into a tough sneer.*)

What you really mean is where does a fuckin' whore come off trying to . . .

TOM: Now wait, I did not call you a . . . (*He catches himself.*)

ANGELA: Go on, you're full of shit—you know I been a hooker.

TOM: Angela, I—

ANGELA: Screw this "Angela"! What's this "Angela"? (*Cupping her breasts to thrust them forward, she mimics him.*) Grab onto this you jerked-off choirboy . . . come on, get your finger out of your yum-yum and try some of this!

TOM (*holding his head*): Holy God.

ANGELA: Go on, you don't kid me . . . (*She turns, trying to force his hand onto her buttocks.*) Grab hold, you fucking milk-face, you think you're better than anybody else?

TOM: Angela, Jesus . . . !

(*A struggle; he forces her onto the bed. She screams and tries to fight him off, loses her wind, gasping, as he stands up. Watching him . . . pushing his hand off.*)

ANGELA (*she is clearly transported to another time and place, and he is a total stranger to her*): Well, if you can't get it up get goin'. I've got a line into the street tonight. Tip the hat-check girl—if you can part with a dollar. And the name is Leontine in case you want to ask for me next time.

(ANGELA *has gradually lost an inner pressure and seems to fall asleep.* TOM *goes and bends over her, moved and mystified. Draws a blanket over her. Then he straightens up and peers into the air and leaves the room.*)

Interior. Living room—Same time

TOM *is undoing the locks of the living-room door when she calls from the bedroom.*

ANGELA (*awakening*): Tom?! . . . Tom, please don't leave! Let me explain . . . !

(*Slowly,* TOM *walks back to the bedroom.*)

Interior: Bedroom—Same time

ANGELA *is sitting on the bed.* TOM *seats himself in a chair facing her, waiting.*

ANGELA *in shame lowers her eyes contritely and speaks in a whisper. Her secret is out.*

ANGELA: I'm sorry, Tom, I should have leveled with you, but I wasn't sure you'd understand.

(*He waits.*)

(*Taking a breath.*) I'm a . . . I mean I have like schizo tendencies, Tom. I . . . like break up.

TOM: Are you under psychiatric care?

ANGELA: I used to be. Abe sent me to this Dr. Levy. But I haven't had episodes in about three years. I'm just under a lot of stress right now, see. But it doesn't mean I don't tell you the truth, you understand?

TOM: It's just that the way you suddenly come at me just now. And over at Jerry's place.

ANGELA (*a clear flowering of anxious uncertainty*): Jerry's place?

TOM: You said your name was Renata. You don't remember that *at all*?

ANGELA: In a way, but it's . . . What else?

TOM: That I must never go tracking anybody without your permission . . .

ANGELA: Tracking who? Who was I talking about?

(TOM *is amazed.*)

TOM: This Jerry who everybody says killed Daniels.

ANGELA (*trying to penetrate the fog, alarmed*): Jerry?

TOM: We'll have to clarify this. I can't be asking anybody's permission to follow my leads.

ANGELA: But that's impossible!

TOM: It's the way it's gotta be.

ANGELA (*as certain as she is, it seems suddenly distant to her . . .*): But Jerry . . . died.

TOM: Died!

ANGELA (*grips her head for a moment, trying to clear her mind*): Couple of months ago . . . in Georgia, or Alabama someplace . . . Amy told me. He'd get loaded and ride his bike with his arms . . . (*She starts lifting her arms.*)

TOM (*flinging his arms into the air*): Up in the air.

ANGELA: How'd *you* know?

TOM: I saw him do it on the road near his church.

ANGELA: But it's impossible . . .

(*She presses her hands to her temples, alarm in her face. And now he is scared for his own sanity.*)

TOM: I saw a man on a bike doin' that!—Look, you could have misunderstood Amy; she's so drugged-up it's hard to make out what she's saying—or maybe he did get hurt down there and recovered now.

(ANGELA *lies down on the bed, deeply worried and exhausted.*)
You want to go to sleep?

ANGELA: Please sit here.

> (*She pats the bed; he moves from the chair to sit beside her. An intimacy of tone now.*)

TOM: I don't mean to be leanin' on you, honey, but I'm goin' up against the whole power structure on this one and I hate to do that blind on one side . . .

> (ANGELA *is visibly filling with emotion as she looks at him; now lays a hand on his, she lifts it reverently to her mouth, kisses it, sets it back and chastely removes her hand from it. He smiles, embarrassed and moved. Now, after a clear hesitation, he takes her hand and kisses it. Tears burst into her eyes.*)

ANGELA: Tom?

TOM (*he has crossed one bridge now*): Yes.

ANGELA: I used to be with Abe.

TOM: *Abe Daniels*? I thought he was such a pillar.

> (ANGELA *is staring straight up with this.*)

ANGELA: Abe saved me. He paid for Dr. Levy, my psychiatrist. I will always owe Abe. (*That was said like a vow, solemnly.*)

TOM (*deeply stirred*): He sounds great. Must've been some shock then, heh.

ANGELA: Butchered. And the killer practically advertising himself and they go and put Felix away . . . I can't stand it! . . . Listen, I want to talk to you for days, but I have to feel we're friends . . .

TOM: I've never known anybody it was so hard to get a fix on.

ANGELA (*feeling slightly released, smiling*): Well, I've got a lot of sides . . . But that makes it more interesting, doesn't it?

> (*As though unable to hold back any longer, she suddenly comes up off her pillow and, grasping his face, kisses him on the mouth with a strangely determined desperation.*)

Oh, Tom, I need you . . . !

TOM: Honey, please . . . we've got to discuss the . . .

> (*She unzips his sports shirt . . .*)

(*Laughing now as the whirlpool takes him down*): Hey . . . hey! Wait! Hey!

> (*She lowers her open mouth onto his stomach and he laughs. She is mounting him like a rock in a torrent, triumphantly smiling down at him.*)

Oh, God, I'm flyin'!

ANGELA (*laughing in victory*): Fly, baby, fly!

Interior: Courthouse evidence-locker—Day

A nondescript storage room in the courthouse basement. TOM *is at a table sorting through a box of Abe Daniels' effects—bloodied clothing, etc. Finds a manila envelope, opens it and removes several photos which he shuffles until, coming on one, he stares at it.*

Close shot: Photo—Daniels' living room. Taken soon after the murder, it shows a blood-drenched carpet, blood over the wall behind it, furniture overturned, chaos. The photo becomes real.

Interior: Daniels' living room—Sometime later—Day

The room is now empty of furniture or carpet; sun is shining through barred windows. MRS. HEARST, *a real estate agent, is selling hard.*

MRS. HEARST: . . . And as you can see, it's a very well-protected house—the windows are barred on all floors, and you have a kennel out there for the dogs . . . (*she swings open the front door and points up at an overhead TV monitor*) and this camera tells you who's at the door before you open it.

TOM (*indicates a built-in screen near door*): Terrific . . . we're nuts on security.

MRS. HEARST: You have children, Mr. Franklin?

TOM (*continually taking in the place*): Seven. But only four are still home.

MRS. HEARST (*confidentially*): I think you could get a steal on this place . . . you know . . . after what happened . . .

TOM: I was thinkin' the same. (*He is examining the five locks on the front door.*) Five locks! Boy, he sure wasn't kiddin' about lockin' up . . .

MRS. HEARST: I know the estate would consider any reasonable offer . . .

TOM (*one final look around*): Think they'd take a million?

MRS. HEARST: Well . . . I could certainly enquire.

TOM: Please do. I've got to be running now . . . you have my card . . .

MRS. HEARST (*reading from the card in her hand*): That's the Franklin Periscope Company?

TOM: Correct—we service all the submarines. Talk to you soon. (*He walks out the front door.*)

Exterior: AMY*'s house—Later*

TOM *is moseying around the shabby place, but moving in the direction of the front porch—his eyes are roving everywhere for anything significant. The front yard is a cycle-nut's mess, plus a rusting old car or two. He climbs up on the front porch, knocks on screen door; no response. Looks in window.*

TOM (*calling*): Amy? You home? (*No reply. He comes down porch steps to return to his car, parked yards away, when he is startled by something inside one of the rusting car wrecks. He walks over.*)

   (AMY *is sitting on the broken back seat, which rests on the car's floor, dressed in jeans and a man's jacket, two or three illustrated magazines open around her. She has a bruised cheekbone. She is petting a hen on her lap.*)

Hiya, Amy.

AMY (*as though his appearance were perfectly ordinary*): Oh, hi.

TOM: Whatcha readin'?

AMY: About crocheting.

TOM (*enthusiastically*): No kiddin'! You do crocheting?

AMY (*warmed by his interest*): Maybe I'd take it up. 'Cause people would buy them.

TOM: Say, I'll bet!—Your friend Jerry wouldn't be around, would he? I'd like to meet him.

AMY: He died, you know.

TOM: So I hear. But he's back ain't he?

AMY: Yeah, he's over at Robie's . . . I'm wondering if I ate today.

TOM: . . . Tell ya . . . I was about to go get myself a big pizza; would you two like to join me?

AMY (*her tongue running over her lip*): I guess so; we could go over and get him.

TOM: That's just what I was thinkin'!—What happened to your eye?

AMY: Oh . . .

(*With a denigrating wave of her hand she hungrily starts for his car across the yard's debris, but he watches her with marked curiosity as they make their way . . .*)

Exterior: Car—Day

AMY *is just pointing out* ROBIE*'s to* TOM, *and he sees* . . .

Exterior: ROBIE*'s shop and abandoned mill—Day*

TOM*'s point of view. The two places are not far apart on the river.*

Exterior: ROBIE*'s tractor shop—Day*

A chaotic scene; "Robie's" sells new and used and unusable tractors which stand scattered across a large field in front of his steel shed. Intermixed are auto wrecks and motorcycle remains, alongside new tractors in crates.

The immense sliding doors of the shed are always open; amid the chaos inside are parts bins and a new tractor or two being assembled, or a snow plow or mower being set up for delivery to a customer. But not yet a sign of a human.

TOM *is moving amid the stuff looking around for somebody.* AMY, *meanwhile, has found a litter of kittens under a machine and is sprawled on the ground trying to entice them out so she can pet them.*

TOM *comes to what appears to be an eight-by-twelve office and looks in through the doorway, finding rotund, seventy-three-year-old* ROBIE *scraping bread dough into two trays before a filthy-looking oven. Beside the oven is a cot with a feather blanket in disarray and a not too clean pillow. Against the walls are file cabinets, a rolltop desk permanently decked with invoices and odd tractor parts and next to it an old refrigerator and stove with a stew cooking on it.*

As TOM *arrives in the doorway he sees* ROBIE *with a knife making a mark on the dough with a certain intensity, closing his eyes as though in prayer.*

Close shot: Bread and knife: The knife is making the mark of an inverted cross in the dough.

ROBIE *gingerly removes two finished loaves out of the oven—each similarly marked—and brushing away some urgent mail, he sets the loaves on his desk. Now he puts the two trays of fresh dough into the oven.*

TOM: Excuse me.
> (ROBIE, *snapping his finger against the crusts, he listens for the sound, paying no attention to* TOM.)

That sure smells good.
ROBIE (*wryly—he has a pipe in his mouth*): Well, buy yourself a tractor and I might throw in a loaf.
TOM: Could I buy one of *them*?
ROBIE: Oh no. They're not for sale, they're just for—you know—just us.
TOM: —I'm lookin' for Jerry, wouldn't be around, would he?
ROBIE: They're all out there someplace. Sonny?
> (TOM *turns to face* SONNY, *who is bald, about six foot seven and keeps shifting his weight from one foot to the other and is carrying a large transmission main gear. He stammers.*)

SONNY: Pa, do-do-do we get one of these o-o-off a John D-D-Deere 941?
ROBIE: You can't be carryin' that with your hernia.
SONNY: It's okay—I been prayin' over it. Don't hurt at all now.
ROBIE: We'll be prayin' over you if you keep liftin'. (*Taking the gear from him.*) He's looking for Jerry.
SONNY: Sure, here's Jerry.
> (TOM *follows* SONNY *into the tangle of machinery, tractors up on blocks, rubbish . . .* SONNY *stops, once surrounded*

with machines, takes a folded-up magazine out of his hip pocket, and with a shy smile . . .)

Would you like to re-re-read so-so-something in-in-interesting about G-God?

(TOM *takes the magazine, unfolds it. "SATAN'S WORD" in large letters decorates the cover over the same sign of the inverted cross as was cut into the bread.*)

(*Voice over*): It'll d-d-do you a lot of g-g-good.

(KENNY MONTANA *appears, a fierce-looking monster, maybe three hundred pounds, a heavy breather with a black fedora, black moustache, and the look of a Sumo wrestler. He doesn't speak often, but stares a lot instead, and without expression.*

He appears from around a machine so that TOM *suddenly finds himself face-to-face with him and his cryptic silence.* SONNY *moves off and* TOM *gladly follows him, with* MONTANA *bringing up the rear, breathing.*

They discover JERRY; *he is in a corner of the shop working on his motorcycle. Like the other two men he has a forest simplicity in his gaze. He also has a ten-inch hunting knife sticking up out of his riding boot and is a long-time addict of most of the known drugs but is for the moment clear-eyed, with a searching look and a certain mystifying depth.*

SONNY, *by far the most sociable of the three, shifting from foot to foot, gestures awkwardly toward* JERRY.)

TOM: Hiya, I'm Tom O'Toole, friend of Angela? Angela Crispini?

(JERRY *has turned from his bike but with only the mildest curiosity . . . or is it suspicion? The moment is saved by the arrival of* AMY *who is cradling two kittens in her arms, followed by the mother cat.*)

AMY: I'm hungry.

(*As* TOM *speaks now,* JERRY *stares quizzically into his eyes as though sensing some vaguely palpable center of gravity there . . .* (*every happening* means *something, if only one knew*).)

TOM (*taking the plunge*): Glad a meet you, Jerry . . . Tell ya, I happen to be in the cemetery the other day and I seen those burned bones layin' there; I'm very interested in that—is that a sacrifice or . . . Watch it!!

(*The mother cat has dislodged a truck driveshaft which was leaning against the wall behind* JERRY. *This six-foot tube of heavy steel begins toppling onto him.* TOM, *with an automatic reaction, violently pushes* JERRY *out of its way as it bounces on the cement floor with a resonating clang.*

In the excitement AMY *dropped the kittens, and now the cat is carrying one of them away in her mouth.*

For a moment AMY, SONNY, MONTANA *and* JERRY *stare at the cat moving away—they seem to feel some* meaning *in its action. Now* JERRY *turns to* TOM *as though seeing him in an aura. But his intensity could be hostility . . .)*

. . . Sorry to push you, but . . .

JERRY (*a knowing, excited little grin*): You *felt* that comin', didn't you.

TOM: Well no, I saw the cat rub on it . . .

MONTANA: You the cops?

JERRY: No, he's famous. I seen you once on the TV.

TOM: Right. I'm trying to help Angela, kind of, you know?

(JERRY, *as susceptible as anyone else to notoriety, turns and walks out into the field and halts, looking up at the sky.* SONNY *and* MONTANA *remain behind in the shop staring off at unpredictable* JERRY *with some expectancy.*)

AMY (*calling to* JERRY *a bit more desperately*): He wants to buy a pizza! Okay?

(TOM *goes out into the field to* JERRY. *His instinct is not to speak yet, but physically to communicate with him and hopefully to draw him out that way.*

JERRY *sits now on a piece of machinery in the field; the long knife in his boot is prominent.*)

JERRY: Trouble with Angela is she can't communicate.

(AMY *enters the shot, sits on the grass with one of the kittens.*)

She can't unload.

TOM (*as naively as he is able*): You think that's what she wants to do?

JERRY: It's what everybody wants to do—tell it, get rid of it, put it behind you. The Major could help but she won't let him.

(SONNY *and* MONTANA *move into the shot, their arrival creates the feeling of a séance as they intently listen.*)

AMY: He was almost a priest.

TOM (*alerted*): Say that's right; you're Catholic, aren't you?

JERRY: I wasn't normal enough for the priesthood—kept tryin' to get out over the wall to find girls. But I saw Jesus once. But he never come back. But the Major's *there*, man, he's *there*. But Angela's got nobody. So she keeps goin' off that way.

AMY: Can't we eat?

TOM: Goin' off how, Jerry?

JERRY: —Changin' herself into this one and that one. You've seen her do that, haven't you? But that's nothin' but psychic possession, that's never going to get her clear.

TOM: Clear of what, Jerry? I'm really trying to help her, see— what do you think is grabbing her?

JERRY (*stares into* TOM*'s eyes a long moment*): You been to seminary, haven't you.

TOM: Funny you ask that—No. But I've got two brothers in the church, and my sister's a nun.

JERRY: I knew it. (*Shakes his head in wonder—a glimmer of warmth now.*) Can always tell.

(*His perceptiveness shown, he gets up, walks a couple of yards;* TOM *follows, but when* SONNY *and* MONTANA *start to follow,* JERRY *turns to them sharply, but as much plea as command . . .*)

I'm *talkin'* to this man!

(*They halt obediently.* JERRY *turns his back on them, sits on one heel and slips the knife out of his boot.* TOM *kneebends to be on his level.*)

Major give me this. People don't believe it, but he did. Read that?

TOM (*reads inscription on knife*): "Grand Army of the Republic." Huh! And he give you this?

JERRY: It was his battle knife from the Civil War. One night I come and it was layin' there right at his feet on top of his grave, shining in the moonlight. You believe it?

TOM: Why not?

(AMY *moves into the shot.* JERRY *never takes his fascinated eyes from* TOM.)

AMY: Don't I ever get to eat today! I'm hungry!

TOM: Come on, what you say? It's my treat.

JERRY: I'd like to talk to you . . . I never met one before.

TOM: One what?

JERRY: Meet you at the diner.

(JERRY *walks away,* AMY *trailing behind, and* TOM *starts toward his car, excitement in his eyes.*)

Interior: Diner—Later

TOM, AMY, JERRY. AMY *is gorging the last of a large pizza.*

JERRY (*gently stroking her hand, straightening her hair*): She backfired once and never been the same. I'm trying to straighten myself out, see, but I'm . . . I'm kind of loaded up all the time . . .

TOM: I'm reading you, Jerry . . .

JERRY: I know. I knew it soon as you looked at me. But it's . . . (*sighs, shaking his head* . . .) so hard.

TOM (*lets a moment pass*): I know; but that shows you're not an animal, doesn't it—I mean there's lots that wouldn't be bothered at all.

(*This stab leaves* JERRY *staring ahead. After a moment* . . .)

JERRY: I think sometimes I died and came back, but I didn't . . . like get here yet.

TOM: I know the feeling. Some things can pull you down and under if you don't unload.

JERRY: I can't hardly breathe sometimes.

AMY: . . . There's somebody else involved, see.

TOM: Well . . . that makes it tougher.

(TOM *watches* JERRY*'s reaction to this revelation; but he calmly stands, lifts* AMY *to her feet with a magisterial touch.* TOM *hurriedly writes on a napkin, his excitement difficult to hold down. He stuffs the napkin into* JERRY*'s shirt pocket.*)

That's my home and office number . . . day or night, you hear? I'll be by again in a day or two, okay?

(JERRY *looks up at him helplessly.* AMY *chews deliciously.* TOM *stands, tucking a bill under the ketchup bottle.*)

Guess I don't have to tell you, Jerry—there's no power in the world strong enough to break a man's grip on his own throat.

(JERRY *looks at him with recognition.*)

But you know who *can*, don't you.

(JERRY *stares ahead at the challenge.*)

See ya.

Interior: DR. LEVY*'s office—Day*

LEVY, *fortyish, hip, sits behind his desk facing* TOM *who is seated with his coat in his lap.*

LEVY: . . . No-no, not schizophrenia—Mrs. Crispini has a multiple personality. That's quite different.

TOM: I can't thank you enough for seeing me, Doctor—I'll be very quick. The big question for me is whether to believe her. I mean, coming on like that with these different personalities . . .

LEVY: A fear reaction—when she's frightened enough she changes her identity. It's something we all do but not to such an extreme degree.

TOM: In other words, I've got to look at her more as . . . really normal.

LEVY: Was there something specific?

TOM: You knew Dr. Abe Daniels, I understand.

LEVY: Many years. Wonderful human being.

TOM: She claims to have been Dr. Daniels' girl, and for a long time—is that credible to you?

LEVY (*he seems uncomfortable, almost apprehensive*): Well . . .

TOM: . . . Unless that gets into your medical relationship—I know she used to be your patient couple of years ago.

LEVY: I really shouldn't say any more. (*A glance at his watch.*) Afraid I'm out of time . . .

(*Stands—*TOM *does too.*)

I can understand your dilemma; she can be very contradictory . . .

(*Going to the door together . . .*)

TOM: Doctor, every time we talk I end up one foot's wet and the other one's dry!

(*Laughs; they find themselves face-to-face, nodding in agreement . . .*)

. . . That woman's a real piece of work, you know? I mean she's an *original*!

(*They are chuckling into each other's face; it is a sudden, unforeseen communion, in effect they are celebrating her somehow . . . (and as this happens* TOM *knows that* LEVY *has been her lover). A shy softness descends on* LEVY*'s face as he speaks.*)

LEVY: Mrs. Crispini is one of those great levelers—the kind of woman who can put the peasant and the king on exactly the same level.

TOM: Right!

> (LEVY *continues, but now a certain unresolved confusion of his own is entering into him.*)

LEVY: They can distort a man's vision . . . they can blind you, destroy your basic common sense . . .

> (*They exchange a shared enthralled look—only for an instant, but it is enough for* TOM *to sense* LEVY'*s connection to* ANGELA.)

TOM (*his gaze has a knowingness now*): Gotcha . . . Thanks again, Doctor. This's been very helpful.

Exterior: LEVY'*s street—Day*

TOM *is starting to drive away from* LEVY'*s office—which is actually in a large Victorian house on a quiet residential street. Suddenly he notices* ANGELA *who is emerging from a cab in front of the house. He sees her go in. A look of quandary suffuses his face.*

Exterior: Day

Skeet discs are being shattered against the sky with blasts of a shotgun. Backing, we find the shooter to be retired judge HARRY MARKS, *a man in his late sixties. Former criminal lawyer, he has now turned rosy and wise, chews an unlighted cigar; lot of vanity here but also sentiment, when affordable.*

Behind him is his great house, lawns, and TOM *standing to one side admiring his accuracy.* MARKS *finishes the load, offers the gun to* TOM.

MARKS: Want to try it?

TOM: Why embarrass myself?—

> (*They walk toward the house.*)

Listen, Judge, don't be shy about throwin' me out if I'm taking too much time . . .

MARKS: Cut it out, Tom—I owe you my son's life; for you I have time. What's it about, this Crispini woman again?

TOM: I wanted to run some more stuff past you.

MARKS: Baby, I'm wondering if the time has come to ask you the obligatory question.

TOM (*embarrassed*): Well . . . the answer is yes—But it's nothing—you know—serious.

(*They enter the house.*)

Interior: JUDGE MARKS' *study—Day*

MARKS *sits before a desk, on which are photos of himself with Ed Sullivan, Eisenhower, Stevenson, Reagan, etc. . . .*

MARKS: For a romantic like you all sex is serious. Watch out! Just because you're screwing don't start believing everything she tells you.

TOM: Oh, no, I'm not . . .

MARKS: Strong sex always ends up the captain of the ship, and this captain sounds crazy to me. Now let's talk practical. I would think twice before going ahead with this case.

TOM: You serious?

MARKS: . . . This is our third discussion, Tom, and I still don't know why she got so interested in saving this Epstein fellow—

TOM (*abashed*): Look, that's all I've been trying to get out of her, but she . . .

MARKS: Tom, if she won't come clean you have got to get up and walk. This is basic.

TOM (*holding his head*): Harry, you're killing me . . . !

MARKS: All this time and you have nothing tangible about her connection! You're walking on bubbles!

TOM: Yes. I'm ashamed of myself—I guess I've been letting my dingus do my thinking.—Judge, I can't thank you enough. This is why I love to run things past you, you cut right to the gut of it.

MARKS: Callaghan'll eat you alive if you don't button this down tight . . . and I mean *tight*!

TOM: I'm absolutely clear now—she comes clean or I'm out. I can't thank you enough. (*He starts to leave.*)

MARKS: Incidentally . . . I've read the transcript of Epstein's trial. She's quite right to be upset—All they proved in court was that he was in the doctor's house, but not that he killed anybody.

TOM (*his fears gone, depression over, he is almost shouting with revived indignation*): See?—this is what I mean! Callaghan did it again!

MARKS: But you've got to nail that woman! *Evidence*, not bubbles!—*where is she coming from!*

TOM: Right!! (*Pointing at* MARKS.) Bless every breath you take, Judge. (*He stomps out full of juice.*)

Interior: TOM*'s bedroom—Night*

CONNIE *is sleeping on her back;* TOM, *on his side, facing away from her. Her eyes open; she is mourning her life. He stirs.* CONNIE *half turns to him. He turns onto his back and they are staring at one another. His hand appears and cups her face. She is surprised, hardly dares smile; he raises up and kisses her. An awareness of his potency creeps into her eyes. He slides onto her and she almost laughs with astonished pleasure. He starts making love and they are both experiencing renewed hope for themselves. As climax approaches . . .*

The phone rings . . . CONNIE *pulls* TOM *into her even deeper.*

The phone rings again . . .

CONNIE *holds him tighter—willing them to an orgasm.*

The phone rings again . . .

ANGELA *will not give up—*

and neither will CONNIE.

Interior: TOM*'s kitchen—Early morning*

In pyjamas and robe, TOM *is staring out at the first morning light in the sky. His face is filled with bewilderment, but he has been quickened, trying to figure himself out.* CONNIE *appears in frame beside him, in a trim suit, dressed for school, reading her watch, picking up her briefcase . . .*

CONNIE: Sorry I have to run; why don't you make yourself an omelette?

TOM: Not hungry. (*Kisses her.*) Bye.

CONNIE: . . . Can't you smile? You're really very different since you got on this case.

TOM (*he glances up at her with a troubled, slightly shamed smile*): Well I'm frustrated. But the psychiatrist says she could be tellin' the truth. And he used to treat her.

CONNIE: But how do you know she's not makin' it with him?

TOM (*astounded, gulping*): Now where do you come up with an idea like that?

CONNIE: Why not? From the way it sounds, it's her way of sayin' hello.

TOM: I can't stop now!—This Jerry character practically confessed to me . . .

CONNIE: But he's an addict and he's crazy!

TOM (*menaced, he flies up*): I tell you there's something here and she knows what it is.—And just incidentally, there's still an innocent man in jail!

CONNIE: There always is.

TOM: Well there is, goddammit!—whether she's crazy or not!

Interior: Spaghetti joint—Day

TOM *and* ANGELA *are finishing dishes of spaghetti. She eats sensuously. He watches her intently, but covers up with a good imitation of ease.*

TOM: You eat everything like it's ice cream.

ANGELA (*indicating his half-full dish*): Aren't you going to have it?

TOM: Not hungry.
    (*She takes his dish and digs in.*)

ANGELA: Eating spaghetti is the second best thing in life. (*Grinning.*) You still don't trust me, do you.

TOM (*trying to laugh*): For God's sake, Angela, I've laid my whole professional life in your hands, and now I don't trust you?

ANGELA: I don't understand it, there's something changed . . .

TOM: All right, I'm going to admit something—I been to see this Dr. Levy, the psychiatrist you used to go to?

ANGELA (*cryptically*): What for?

TOM: Well, to be honest, I wanted his opinion about how . . . how much to believe . . . of what you been telling me.

ANGELA (*on the verge of high resentment*): You don't say! And what's his opinion?

TOM: He thinks you're absolutely believable.

ANGELA (*surprise in her face*): Really!—How is old Levy? I should go see him again, I haven't been there in so long . . .

TOM (*eyes flattening at this lie*): Angela, listen . . . I happen to have seen you going into his office yesterday. I mean I have to say it.

(*She stands, gathers up her purse and coat, and starts to leave.*)

Now wait a minute! Angela! I didn't mean . . .

ANGELA (*furious*): I had to tell him! I didn't see any reason to mention it to you, but I had to!

TOM: Tell him what?

ANGELA (*tears forming*): About us. You've changed my life, Tom—I hadn't had anybody in nearly six months. I just had to tell somebody, it made me so happy.

(*Weeping she races into the street.* TOM *follows.*)

Exterior: Street—Same time

ANGELA *hurries down the street and stops suddenly.*

ANGELA: There's got to be trust!

TOM: Angela, listen to me . . .

ANGELA (*tough again*): . . . And anyway, O'Toole, without me, you're nowhere on this case.

TOM: I didn't say . . .

ANGELA: I haven't even begun; Jerry and Amy are nobody

compared to who I could . . . (*Turning on him.*) Look if you don't want to go on okay, but there's an innocent man in jail! . . . or did I make that up, too?
(TOM *stands there—conflicting emotions pulling at him.*)

Interior: ANGELA's *bedroom—Night*

They are in bed.

ANGELA: You like me a little?
TOM: A little? (*Rolls onto his back, a depth of feeling in his eyes.*) This is the most unexpected thing ever happened to me.
(*She watches him—a mixture of happiness with apprehension.*)
Can't you still trust me? Can't you tell me the story? I'm at the end of my rope, kid, I really am.
(*A last hesitation, and then . . .*)
ANGELA: Jerry was a runner. He ran drugs for Abe.
TOM: Dr. Abe Daniels was in *drugs*?
ANGELA: He was the main man between here and Boston.
TOM: . . . Boy, I'm really out of it—that never crossed my mind.—But why didn't they arrest Jerry with all that blood on him?
ANGELA: He knows all the connections, and he's crazy enough to start talking.
TOM: Connections to . . . ?
ANGELA: Drugs and the police, the Detective Squad, Bellanca . . . Jerry's a timebomb on a motorcycle.
TOM: How come they didn't just waste him?
ANGELA: Maybe they will.
TOM: You mean if he keeps talking to me.
ANGELA (*nods*): And . . . those bulls working over in the shop with him. They're all disciples, you know.
TOM: Why'd Jerry do it to Daniels, Angela?
ANGELA (*shaking her head with remorse*): Oh, he'd built up this crazy idea—he really believed it—that Daniels had promised to build him a church for his new religion. And when he refused he went berserk. He'll do anything, you know.
TOM: And Callaghan was onto all this when he prosecuted Felix?

(*She barely nods, openly afraid.*)

He turned it all into a family fight between relatives.

(*She confirms with a glance.*)

Well . . . it all suddenly makes sense. And I can see why you always seem so terrified.—You are, aren't you.

(*Her helplessness moves him. He turns and glances over at a table on which several framed pictures stand. Picks up one of them, looks at it.*)

(*Close shot:* ANGELA *on motor boat: She is in a bikini—a gangster type in sunglasses behind her—posing spread out on an open deck.*)

Is this Bimini?

(ANGELA *nods, her eyes full of calculations.*)

Amy says now and then she and you would donkey the stuff up from there.

ANGELA: I stopped two years ago. I just couldn't stand the tension any more.

(*She genuinely weeps for a ruined life. He holds her close.*)

TOM: The cops must know about that, don't they?

(*She nods.*)

So how do you come to be beatin' on them with this case now?

(*His logic makes her turn her face to him—an imminent outrage in her eyes.*)

I have to ask, kid, I'm going up against some heavy hitters and I don't dig this!

ANGELA: Because I know how innocent Felix is and I can't bear it!

(*Open disbelief descends on his face and he makes no attempt to conceal it.*)

TOM: I gotta be gettin' home.

ANGELA: I have to tell you something.

(*He slips out of bed and begins to dress, and his failure to get excited by some new revelation enrages and alarms her.*)

I am trying to tell you something!

(*Resolutely deadpan, he simply sits on a chair facing the bed, leaving a space between them.*)

I used to be with John Callaghan.

TOM (*this seems total madness*): We're talkin' about the prosecutor now.

(*She barely nods; it is a confession with suffering attached. —He is straightfaced, but doubt is in his tone.*)

You were banging the prosecutor?

ANGELA: He set up an apartment over at Wyndham Place. He nearly left his wife.

TOM (*is this possible or complete insanity?*): No kiddin'.

ANGELA: The best two years of my life. Until he began rigging the case against Felix—then I just couldn't stand it any more.

(*She notes his less than utter rapture at this news.*)

But he suffered torments over having to do this—he goes to retreats, you know, in a monastery.

TOM: I must have missed his spiritual side—why'd he have to do it?

ANGELA: A man as important as Abe Daniels chopped up like that . . . they had to nail it to somebody, and Jerry was absolutely out—Jerry could bomb the whole police department plus both parties in this town in the bargain. This case goes to the top of the mountain, Tom, the *top*. That's why I'm scared.

(*She gets up, moves now with a verve and energy, acting out the story.* TOM *watches mesmerized, trying to pierce the truth of this outrageous, yet somehow circumstantially, convincing story.*)

We'd go out to John's place on the beach and sit staring at the fire . . . tears were pouring down his cheeks, it was killing him. I pleaded with him, "You could end up President of the United States," I said, "you could be anything, but you cannot do this to an innocent man!" . . . But Bellanca handed him the proof against Felix—that stupid comb, and the jury believed it. And it was all lies.

(*A beat.*)

TOM: I'm going to ask you a question, Angela. It's very important.

(*Intensification of alertness shows in her eyes.*)

How well have you known Jerry?

ANGELA: Pretty well.

(*He gets the message which, again, has a double edge, hurting him and offering the possibility of hard information.*)

TOM: I got a gut feeling he'd like to confess to me. Would you help me with him? He seems to still like you.

(*She seems to struggle a bit with her breathing, in a high conflict which she strives to conceal.*)

ANGELA: Why would he confess?

TOM: I guess the same reason he ran to the cops after he killed Daniels—he's afraid of God.—I don't want to scare him off with a wrong move, so I thought the three of us might sit down; him, you and I . . .

ANGELA (*at this, her vocal register thins, rising higher*): You'd better be very careful with Jerry . . . (*She begins moving about. She is nearly struggling to breathe. Can she fear* JERRY'*s confessing?*) He can be very tricky, you know . . .

TOM: Oh, I know . . .

ANGELA: Don't say you know, you don't know!

(*Her swift slash of anger astonishes him. She is beginning to gasp now.*)

TOM: Okay. But if we could get him to unload in front of a lawyer, we've nailed the case . . .

ANGELA (*a deepening heaving of breath begins*): Yeah, but I can't imagine him . . .

TOM: But it's worth a big try, Ange, it's the whole ballgame, and I really think you owe it to . . . What's the matter?

(*She is nearly gasping for breath, and it stops him—she starts to lie down weakly on the bed, curling up in a defensive fetal position, and he starts to touch her hand . . .*)

Angela?

(*With a child-like cry she throws off his hand and quickly scampers into a corner, whimpering, hands raised protectively before her face. He is afraid to move and frighten her further . . .*)

ANGELA (*truly, a child's voice*): Please don't! Don't! Angie be good now!

TOM (*flabbergasted . . .*): Okay. Can I help you to bed?

(*Still whimpering, she allows him to approach and to pick her up in his arms, but suspicion is still at the edges of her eyes. He lays her down on the bed and she quickly looks sleepy, and curls up again.*)

All right, Angie . . . you try to sleep now, heh?—like a good little girl?

(*Her eyes flutter and close. He covers her with a blanket.*)

(*Stalemated, he stands thinking for a moment. He picks a polaroid photo of her off the table, and pockets it. Now her photo on the boat in Bimini catches his eye and he picks it up to study the gangster in it, blocking off her face with his*

*hand. A sliver of paper sticking out under the photo's edge
interests him; he draws out from behind the photo a newspaper photo of a man—*JOHN CALLAGHAN. *Glancing at her
on the bed, he slips it into his pocket and leaves.*)

Interior: Apartment-house lobby—Next day

It is a fairly posh lobby. TOM *enters from the street to face the
uniformed* LOBBY-MAN.

TOM: Super around?

LOBBY-MAN: That door there. But there's no vacancies.

TOM (*taking bill out of his wallet*): Say, maybe you could help
me, I'm trying to check something for Aetna Insurance, you
ever see this woman? (*He slips the bill to the man as he holds*
ANGELA'*s polaroid photo up to him.*)

LOBBY-MAN (*a puzzled look at the photo . . . then . . .*): Oh
. . . sure, that's Mrs. Crispini—Angela. Couple years ago,
Apartment 6C.

TOM: Jeeze, thanks a whole lot. Tell me—she live there alone,
or what?

LOBBY-MAN (*careful now . . .*): Well . . . you know . . .

TOM (*producing the newspaper photo of* CALLAGHAN *from a
pocket . . .*): This man ever come by?

LOBBY-MAN (*studies photo; uncertain*): Well . . . (*Decides.*)
No. (*But on the other hand . . .*) Wait a minute. (*Studies it
again; shakes his head.*) I really don't know. Maybe.—Lot of
people coming in and out of here . . .

TOM (*nods, stashes both photos*): Thanks. Take care of yourself.
(*He hurries out to the street, elated—*ANGELA *is legit!*)

Interior: Church—Day

TOM *is seated midway back in the nearly empty church, observing
as, at the altar,* FATHER MANCINI *is giving* ANGELA *the wafer
and blessing. (A previous communicant is just departing.)*

The intense, silent exchange of intimate feeling between her and the fascinated young priest, as she opens her mouth with uplifted eyes locked on his gaze, are a shock to TOM. *And as she approaches him now there is a mixture of amazement and disgust on his face.*

Cut to:

Interior: Vestry room—Day

TOM, MANCINI. *Throughout this scene* TOM *is intrigued by the idea that she has seduced this priest. They are entering the room . . .*

MANCINI (*putting away his vestments*): Thank you so much for coming today. Angela's spoken so often about you that I thought we should meet.

TOM: She's talked about you, too, Father—I think you're her favorite fella in the whole world right now.

MANCINI: Not quite—I think you are. (*With a professional chuckle he sits on a window seat, thinking out his next words; he has a naive, sensuous face, rampant with idealism.*) She's terribly worried, you know, that you may break off your commitment to the Epstein case.

TOM: Father, a lot depends on whether she can get herself to tell me where she's comin' from; why is she in this case, do you know?

MANCINI (*surprised*): But it's obvious—she is a profoundly idealistic woman!

TOM: But Father, why is it like pulling teeth to get the simplest facts out of her? She's driving me crazy with this cat-and-mouse . . .

MANCINI: Mr. O'Toole, please—let me say only one thing to you—You are her lifeline now.

   (TOM *is flattered, but baffled by this.*)
I'm not sure you realize that . . .

   (*Camera emphasizes his spiritual sensuality here—perhaps stained glass rises behind him and he stands in a halo of light and his transfixed eyes almost convince* TOM *of the incredible fact behind his emotion . . .*)
She is a woman who has sinned; but somehow she challenges

us—you must have felt that challenge, haven't you?—the challenge to live life, to care, to live up to our claims to responsibility and love of humanity; for her, to think is not sufficient—we must act, we must perform deeds in the world . . . ! This woman is the very spirit of *love*!

(*During this speech, intercut* TOM*'s face, with his shocked realization that* MANCINI *is probably her lover. Moreover, he is saying what* TOM *himself has been feeling about* ANGELA. *In* MANCINI*'s mid-flight, slowly fade to:*)

Interior: TOM*'s car—Sundown*

TOM *is just pulling up in front of* ANGELA*'s house.*

ANGELA (*starting to open the car door*): Comin' up, aren't you?

TOM: Close the door a second.

(*She does. He lays a paternal hand on hers. His inner exhaustion is beginning to show.*)

I got a call this morning from one of the guards at the Penitentiary, a friend of mine. About Felix. Seems he is going through the bottom . . . he's suicidal.

ANGELA: But I just wrote him again . . .

TOM (*delicately*): The thing is, honey . . . I love bein' with you, but I—I think I better be spending my nights running down whatever I can find.

(ANGELA *is hurt and apparently angry.*)

ANGELA: Okay.

TOM: Well, you understand why I'm saying this, don't you?

ANGELA (*archly*): Y'know, incidentally, I went to Mary Immaculate High School which just happens to be the highest-rated school in the state . . .

TOM (*to head off an explosion*): Oh, now look . . .

ANGELA: Because sometimes you talk to me like my head's full of gravel.—Listen, you cutting out?

TOM: Angela . . .

ANGELA: Then cut! It's the story of my life! (*She pulls her door open and is getting out.*)

TOM (*angered*): Dammit, I didn't mean it that way . . . ! (*She being out of his reach, he opens his door and starts to get out.*)

Exterior: Street—Same time

TOM *has practically emerged into the side of a squad car, which has glided to a halt next to his, and he is looking into the face of* BELLANCA, *in the passenger seat beside a cop driver.*

BELLANCA *wears a supercilious grin, glances similarly to* AN-GELA, *then signals to the cop driver and rides off down the street. When* TOM *turns back to* ANGELA . . .

Close-up: ANGELA. *She is suppressing great, trembling fear, staring down the street at the departing detective.*

TOM *enters shot. She looks up at him and swallows. Without waiting for him she hurries up her stoop, and he follows.*

Interior: ANGELA*'s apartment—Moments later*

They are just entering. She turns the three locks on the door, fixes the chain in place and hurries through the unused living room to the bedroom. TOM *follows.*

Interior: Bedroom—Same time

In silence, she gets out of her coat, hangs it in closet, finally sits on bed and stares. TOM, *still in coat and hat, sits, waiting for her to speak.*

ANGELA: Bellanca was following us.
TOM: I don't know—maybe he just happened to come by.
    (*She looks at him with a certain mystified suspicion.*)
    Just trying to keep it real, kid. (*He breaks off, to avoid alienating her.*)
ANGELA (*a plea, as well as fear—anger*): They've got a squad car parked on each corner some nights!
TOM: I never saw one, but I . . . (*Skeptically, tired of pretending.*) I wouldn't put it past them.
ANGELA (*weak with fear, she lies back*): Come over here.
    (*He comes and sits on the bed beside her and she takes his hand.*)

On the street today . . . it's practically every time I go out now . . . right on Crowley Square, they pull up beside me and ride along slowly while I'm walking.

TOM: Why?

(*She suddenly pulls him down to her.*)

ANGELA: Hold me.

(*He wraps her in his arms, only half-willingly, still in his coat.*)

TOM: Angela . . . darlin'! Why don't you let me help you!

ANGELA: Oh, God, I worship you!

(*Weeping, she buries her face in him; his frustration mounts. Now she lies on her back, staring up.*)

They're trying to scare you away.

TOM (*separating from her*): That's good, I like makin' them nervous—Now look dear . . .

(*He sets himself for some difficult news, as she lies there looking up at him with her clear need. He holds out a hand to her, palm down, smiling—she senses a farewell and shows surprise . . .*)

I am not going to let Felix burn out up there, honey. (*Pause.*) Be well. (*He moves to the door.*)

ANGELA: I have letters . . . from him.

(*He turns back to her at the door.*)

TOM: Who's that, dear?

ANGELA (*calming now, the struggle past*): John.

TOM: Callaghan?

(*She nods. A little tension laugh escapes him.*)

Like . . . what do you mean? Love letters or something?

ANGELA (*nods. Then . . .*): And about the case . . . One of them.

TOM (*still with a shred of skepticism*): Actually . . . referring to it?

ANGELA (*a longish pause*): Yes.

TOM: My God, Angela . . .

ANGELA: . . . Asking me not to let the case get between us. Because of what he had to do.

(*He looks past her face to the padlocked cabinet.*)

TOM: If you got something like that—you know that wraps it all up, don't you?

ANGELA: I can't bear to do that to him, it would destroy him . . .

TOM: He is the chief law enforcement officer of this county and he knowingly rigs a murder case? He's *gotta* be destroyed.

ANGELA: I can't do that! . . . He's the love of my life.
    (TOM *stares at her.*)

TOM: What the hell is going down here, are you using *me* or something? What've I been doing, standing in for John Callaghan? Answer me, dammit!

ANGELA: No, I'm through pleading for . . . for some respect, for Christ's sake!

TOM: *You* pleading! You pleading! I been on my knees since I walked into this! But listen . . . you got something to tell me, give me a ring. I'm hittin' the pike.
    (*He resolutely starts out. She is trying to restrain herself, then can't any more . . .*)

ANGELA: When you get downstairs, see if there isn't a squad car parked on both corners of this block!

TOM: What squad cars, what are you talking about?

ANGELA: I wrote John last week that I would call you off the case if he would reinvestigate it himself. Next thing I know, there's two cars parked almost every night, one on each corner. Just sitting there.

TOM: And he's still the love of your life?
    (*The contradiction sends her jumping angrily off the bed and she picks up a shoe and throws it.*)

ANGELA: All right, just get out. Get out!!

TOM: In other words—is this it?—you wanted me to investigate just enough to get Felix out—but not enough to implicate anybody you don't want to hurt. Is that the story? In other words, you are trying to get me to protect the bastards who put him in there! Well no wonder you're nervous—
    (*He pushes both his arms back and forth in opposite directions. She is bending over, rocking in frustration.*)
You been trying to go north and south and powder your nose all at the same time! (*Laughing viciously.*) Well it can't be done, baby—not with me!
    (*As he turns to go she straightens up from her crouch and with a cry from her belly . . .*)

ANGELA: HELP ME!

TOM: You read me one sentence in a letter from Callaghan—or even just show me his signature on one, okay? Do that, and I'm your man. Otherwise, *I am out!*
    (*Clutching her hair, breathing hard, she sits at the edge of*

*the bed with clenched jaws, face raised as she struggles with
herself. He stands there watching her, refusing to crumble
before her need, struggling to keep from rushing in again to
assuage her pain . . . waiting for her, in effect, to break.)*

Interior: Prisoners' visiting room—Day

FELIX *is just being led in by the guard.*

TOM: Andy? Give us a minute, will ya?
    (*Guard releases* FELIX *and waits by the door.* FELIX *stands
    on the other side of dividing counter, suspiciously glancing
    at* TOM, *and not without hostility.*)
Now look, Felix, I hope you're not gettin' too discouraged,
'cause I'm gaining on it every day now. It won't be long, you
are definitely going to walk out of here, you understand?
    (*No response.*)
You don't know me, Felix; I have my minuses, but I never
let go. Understand me? Never. So I want you to start eating,
you hear? And focus your thinking on . . .
    (FELIX *turns and walks to the door . . .* TOM *feels humili-
    ated, and angry too . . .*)
I'll be back in a week or two, okay? I'm going to have
news . . . !
    (FELIX *moves through the door without turning back, the
    guard taking him from there. With a surge of peaking frus-
    tration and determination,* TOM *smashes his hat onto his
    head and storms out.*)

Interior: TOM*'s bedroom—Night*

TOM *and* CONNIE *asleep. Phone rings. She is awake at once and
immediately furious. She reaches over him to the phone.*

CONNIE (*into phone*): . . . Stop trying to destroy this man,
you phoney, you whore!
TOM: Connie! (*He grabs the phone from her. Into phone.*) Listen
    . . . now wait a minute, I'll come down. Yes, right away.

Okay, right, right. (*Hangs up. Without a word, gets out of bed and starts dressing.*)

CONNIE: I can't believe it.

TOM (*angrily and hurriedly throwing on clothes*): I wish you hadn't done that, Connie.

CONNIE: What is happening to you? Tom!

TOM (*white with indignation*): Don't you ever do that again.

CONNIE (*with a plea, now*): What's happening! I don't know you!

TOM: Ever!

> (*The flash of fury in his face silences her. There is a deranged look in his face now. He quickly turns and hurries out of the room.*)

Interior: McDonald's restaurant, hours later—Night

Except for the two of them and a guy mopping up the place is empty because it is three a.m. and raining outside. He is having a hard time keeping his eyes open, while she is fascinated with herself. Time in large quantities has apparently passed.

ANGELA: . . . So naturally, I got very confused about myself. That's what happens when your father rapes you . . . Am I boring you?

TOM: I didn't say you . . .

ANGELA: Well I beg your fucking pardon!

TOM: It's almost four o'clock in the morning, Angela; at this hour a nudey version of *Gone With the Wind* would put me to sleep.

ANGELA (*touching his hand invitingly*): Come, take me home . . .

TOM: No, tonight I want to talk sitting up.

> (*She indignantly turns away.*)

—I refuse to believe that for this rendering of your childhood you backed me out of my pyjamas tonight, I just refuse to believe it, kid.

ANGELA: You know what *I'm* beginning to believe? I'm beginning to believe that you are kind of stupid.

TOM: To coin a phrase, honey, by this time I am so confused I couldn't count to twenty-one without taking off my clothes. Did you or didn't you have something to tell me?

ANGELA: I was with John tonight.

TOM: John.—What are you talking about? . . . Callaghan? Angela? Talk to me . . . *Tonight?*

ANGELA: I love him, Tom. Oh, God, I love him!

TOM: . . . He was really there?

ANGELA (*erupts*): What do you mean, "really there"!

TOM: What did he want?

ANGELA: His letters back.

> (*It all seems to grind to a halt in* TOM. *He is getting silly with exhaustion.*)

TOM: And I suppose you gave them to him and unfortunately nobody can ever see them again.

ANGELA: No, I didn't give them.

TOM: So you burned them instead, out of bitter disappointment . . . anyway, they're not there any more.

ANGELA: They're there.

TOM: But?

ANGELA (*flaring up*): What am I, a gas station? I have to feel that we're . . . we're *together*, don't I?—you're asking me to bomb the love of my life!

> (*He is tempted, and afraid of giving way again.*)

TOM: All right, okay—I'll take you home, but I'm going to wait downstairs, and you bring me what you want me to see. (*Stands.*) Okay?

ANGELA: What are you, afraid of your virginity or something?

TOM: No, I'm afraid of wriggling on the hook again till my gills dry up. Ready?

ANGELA: In other words, you don't believe one word I've told you.

TOM: The man's dyin' up there, kid—you got something that can get him out?—give it to me.

> (*Lifts her to her feet.*)

Let's go before the sun comes up and blinds us.

ANGELA: I don't like your attitude.

TOM: Neither do I but it's all I got left.

Interior: TOM*'s car—Rain—Night*

TOM *is driving through the downpour.* ANGELA *is sitting stiffly, eyes front.*

Close shot: ANGELA: *The terror is rising in her eyes—the passing street lights flash across her breathless gaze.*

ANGELA: I must say, you know, that this kind of mistrust is very annoying.
> (*Close shot:* TOM: *He slowly turns to her as he hears the Renata tonality. This is bad news.*)
> (*She takes out a cigarette—and lights it.*)

Exterior: ANGELA's *street—Night*

The car pulls up to her house in the downpour.

Interior: Car—Same time

ANGELA *is sitting very rigidly, smoking "elegantly."* TOM *is disarmed, treats her with delicate care, for she is not "there."*

TOM: Here we are.
> (ANGELA *turns to him, the distant look in her eye. He now dares take her hands in his.*)
> Please, honey, don't be afraid. I'm with you all the way. (*But he sees she is not moving out.*) . . . Okay, I'll go up with you.
> (*He gets out, comes around the car as she is getting out—and notes how demurely she pulls down the hem of her skirt . . .*)

Interior: ANGELA's *room—Moments later*

ANGELA *stands there letting* TOM *help her out of her coat. He keeps his on. She stands in thought for a moment, then decides, goes to a book above the filing cabinet and takes a key stashed inside of it. She grasps the padlock . . .*

ANGELA: No, fuck it. I don't have to prove anything—you don't believe me? then go and crack the case by yourself!
TOM: I thought you cared so much about Felix.—Or is there *anything* in there!

ANGELA (*Eleanor Roosevelt*): You are terribly irritating to me!

TOM (*yelling straight to heaven*): What did I do to deserve this!

ANGELA: I must say, what astounds me is how you get to think you're such a high-grade cultured individual and such a great Catholic . . .

TOM: All right, Renata, forget the whole thing . . . !

ANGELA: But all you really are is gutteral!

TOM (*can't help laughing*): You're not even using that word right!

ANGELA: Your whole manner is gutteral because your whole background is gutteral!

TOM (*spreading out his arm*): Okay, Renata, pull out the nails, I want to come down!

ANGELA: *You* can call me Miss Sherwood—stupid bastard. (*She sits on the bed, her breath beginning to fail.*)

TOM: By this time Miss Renata Sherwood ought to know that respectable ladies like her don't call people stupid bastards.

(*She is dropping back slowly onto the pillow.*)

ANGELA: Which I would be delighted to do if these stupid bastards had the mental competence to understand any other kind of language, you dumb shit.

(ANGELA's *eyes are closing and she is breathing deeply. He looks down at her; the key is now becoming visible as her fingers begin to open. He reaches down . . . her fist instinctively clamps shut and she rolls over onto her stomach burying her hand beneath her.*)

Interior: Diner—Night

Filling up with self-contempt and remorse and guilt, TOM *stares at his cup. One or two night-owls sit grinding the night away nearby. He goes to a wall phone, dials.*

TOM: Sorry to wake you, Connie, but . . . please, let me talk for a second? I want to apologize. For everything. It all turned out nothing, and I'm a damned fool. Try to forgive me, will you? . . . Who? When! Jesus! (*Hangs up and rushes out.*)

Exterior: Abandoned mill, river—Night

Moving very fast, TOM*'s car pulls up a distance from the mill, he gets out and goes to a door which is standing ajar.*

TOM: Jerry? It's Tom, can I see you? (*No response. He enters the place. In the enormous space he can hardly make out anything definite.*) Jerry? (*He moves to the river side of the building, seeing a large loading door open to the river. He looks outside.*)

   (*At the very edge of the ramp* JERRY *is sitting on his motorcycle, its motor idling, front wheel an inch from the drop down.* TOM *approaches him cautiously, sensing a sort of rapture upon him.*) Hiya.

   (JERRY *seems not to have heard.*)
   Jerry?
   (JERRY *stirs out of his deep reverie.*)
   You called? I just got the message. (*Indicates ignition key.*) Want to shut it off? (TOM *turns the key.*)

JERRY: You believe He walked on the water?

TOM: I don't know how to believe it, kid, but I guess there's no way not to—for one of *us*, right?

   (JERRY *looks out on the dark river flowing by.*)

JERRY: You came just in time.

   (TOM *alerts to this suicide implication, glancing at the river and back to him. He waits, trying to read* JERRY *who, after a moment, dismounts and walks into the mill.*)

Interior: Mill—Night

As TOM *follows him in,* JERRY *pulls an electric switch; a ten-foot-high cross lights up, the Major's statue on an improvised box in front of it, and the sacrificial lamb standing in its pen. There are two or three planks on cement blocks as pews. The place, in contrast to the earlier visit, is immaculate.*

TOM: Man, what'd you do here! It's beautiful! You got yourself a church! People coming yet?

   (JERRY *sits, despair all over him.* TOM *sits near him, trying to decipher him.*)

JERRY: I am unclean.

TOM: Truthfully, kid . . . I been kind of wondering about that myself.

> (JERRY *looks at him.*)

You know the saying—coke is high and smack is higher but there's no high on God's earth like a true confession. I respect the agony, kid.

> (JERRY *stares ahead at* TOM*'s meaning, seems to expand toward some beckoning liberation.*)

Wanted to say this to you . . . I've talked over the situation with an old friend of mine—without mentioning names. Retired federal judge, used to be one of the great criminal lawyers, smart as a whip. If you'd give him an affidavit, Jer, that you tried to confess about Dr. Daniels to the cops that night but they threw you out on the street . . . he's sure the Feds would let you walk—for helpin' them clean out City Hall, y'know? Because the town's gotten horrendous, Jer . . . you know that.

> (JERRY *looks at him wide-eyed.*)

You got a whole life ahead of you, kid. You got something important to say to people! You're a man who *made it*! You understand me? *You made it, Jerry*! Now take what you made.

> (JERRY *slowly stands.* TOM *stands.* JERRY *turns to him and opens his arms and they embrace* . . .)

I'll stick with you, kid, I'll . . .

JERRY: Angie . . . know about this?

TOM: . . . Me coming here? No. Why?

JERRY (*shakes his head remorsefully, but he is excited by his coming rebirth . . . keeps holding onto* TOM*'s hand*): See, I kept trying to just talk to him about the new building for my church, but he wouldn't let me in, wouldn't even open the goddamned door. So . . . she . . . I . . . (*Breaks off.*)

TOM: I'm not readin' you, Jer . . .

JERRY: Well, he'd always open up for *her.*

> (*A stillness begins to flow over* TOM*'s face.*)

TOM: Angela . . . was with you?

JERRY: Just so he'd open up . . . see, I wasn't intending to do anything, I swear!

TOM: Right.—So what'd you do, wait in the bushes till he opened the door, . . . or what?

(JERRY *nods.*)

. . . She didn't go into the house with you, did she?

JERRY: I think so, I don't remember, I just lost my . . . [mind . . .]

TOM (*he can't bear any more*): Okay, let's go! I've got my car . . .

JERRY: No, I want my bike! (*As he backs for the open loading door and his bike, a lofted look on his face . . .*) Y'know? I'm already feeling good about this . . . I *feel* it . . . !

TOM: Oh, you're going to be a new man, Jerry! (TOM, *unable to continue, turns and hurries out the opposite direction—the front door.*)

Exterior: Car—Night

The moment TOM *is alone in his car he covers his face and loudly groans in open agony . . .*

The roar of the bike near him—he starts to drive with a cheerful wave to JERRY, *offscreen.*

Exterior: Highway—Night

TOM'*s car enters a highway with the bike following several lengths behind.*

Long shot through rear-view mirror of TOM'*s car: The bike's single lamp, following steadily. Now it gains on the car, the lamp enlarging in the mirror.*

Exterior: Highway—Same time

JERRY *has sped up alongside* TOM'*s window, and, keeping abreast, raises a victorious fist—as though they were now comrades—showing a look of high resolve and happy inner peace.*

TOM *returns the closed-fisted gesture, and* JERRY *drops back to follow the car again.*

Interior: TOM*'s car—Same time*

TOM *loses the happy victory grin, and his jaw sets to his formidable task, to get* JERRY*'s confession . . . and then to deal with* AN-GELA. *He glances up at the mirror and a new flare of anxiety leaps into his face.*

TOM*'s point of view: Its headlamp is following steadily, but now* JERRY*'s motorcycle speeds up and gains on the car.*

Exterior: Highway—Same time

JERRY, *once again alongside the car, turns to* TOM *with a victoriously raised fist; his expression seems inspired, "high," and he now roars past in a burst of speed and twenty yards ahead he lifts his hands off the handlebars as though letting a spirit guide him.*

Interior: TOM*'s car—Same time*

TOM*'s expression is changing from a comradely happiness and amusement to apprehension, and now horror . . .*

Exterior: Highway—Same time

The bike—or rather its headlight and red tail-light and a dimly-seen rider—is out of control and flying off the road . . . into a flaming crash.

Interior: TOM*'s kitchen—Day*

TOM *is in his overcoat and hat, and is removing the lid of a cookie jar and then a small pistol.* CONNIE *turns from the sink where she is doing the breakfast dishes as he slips the pistol into his pocket . . .*

TOM: I've got to finish it.
CONNIE: I know.

(*He starts out.*)
Just don't buy her nightmares.
TOM: There's still an innocent man in jail.
CONNIE (*absolutely barren of comment*): I know.
(*He leaves.*)

Exterior: Woods—Day

TOM *and* MARKS *are walking in silence;* TOM *is glancing at* MARKS, *awaiting his word. They come to a rough bench,* MARKS *sits, then* TOM.

TOM: I really hate taking up your time like this, Harry . . .
MARKS: Forget it; old guys have more time than anything else.—Now tell me the primary question.
TOM: Well . . . she's an accessory to a homicide, correct?
MARKS: Yes. But the witnesses are all kaput.
TOM: Right. But if I could get her to sign a statement that she saw Jerry killing Dr. Daniels—You suppose a deal could be cut?—in exchange for her testimony could Felix get a new trial?
MARKS: Listen . . . if she got Abe Daniels to open his door for that killer . . . that's serious business.—Why should she ask for trouble, coming out with that now?
TOM: She's got the monkey on her back. She's eyewitness proof that Felix is innocent. I think this could be what's been making her crazy.
MARKS: Yeah?
TOM: What don't you believe?
MARKS: Well . . . let's spitball. Supposing she did more than get Jerry into the house; what if she . . . helped him kill the doctor?
TOM: Wow.
MARKS: Who knows what could pop out of the underbrush—there's no end to a woman like this . . . Now listen to me, Tom: I've been traveling the world since my wife died . . . I've lectured in a number of countries on criminal law. Russia, Israel, England, France etcetera. They're all different—except for one thing—corruption. That's everywhere and forever. And kid, winning this case is not going to end it here.

TOM: But Felix is innocent, Harry; I can't get past that. What do you think, is there a possible deal so she doesn't go to jail if she unloads?

MARKS: You're really not going to give up on this . . .

TOM: . . . I can't. Listen . . . (*Grins in embarrassment.*) Can I beg you to give her half an hour? Just to see if there's some angle? I'm desperate for your impression, Harry, I really am.

MARKS: Half an hour. But make it clear to her that I am absolutely not getting involved in this!

TOM: Absolutely not—fantastic!

Interior: Seaside restaurant—Dusk

It is a fish restaurant, quite middle-class, almost empty now, out of season. A view of the ocean from the table. ANGELA *is digging into a lobster.* TOM *studies the drink in front of him.*

TOM: Angela . . .
    (*She glances up at him, with a butter-smudged smile.*)
    We are in a situation.

ANGELA: What situation?

TOM: I was with Jerry just before he died. (*Slight pause.*) He told me what went down the night he did it to Daniels. You're an accessory to a homicide.

ANGELA: I'd love a B-and-B.
    (*He summons a waiter.*)

TOM (*to waiter*): B-and-B for the lady.
    (*The waiter leaves. Another slight pause.*)
    This was what you were trying to cough up, wasn't it . . . from day one.

ANGELA: I'd love to go dancing, you want to?

TOM: Did you ever confess it to that priest?—No, huh?
    (*Her silence concedes this.*)
    Listen—I have a friend, a retired federal judge. Used to be one of the great criminal lawyers . . .
    (TOM *waits as the waiter sets a B-and-B in front of* ANGELA *and leaves.*)
    He'd be willing to see you, Ange.

ANGELA: Why should I see him?

TOM: You're eyewitness testimony that Jerry was at the scene a few minutes before he was running all over the neighborhood, covered with blood. It just about clears Felix.

ANGELA: And what happens to me?

TOM: That's why I think you ought to talk to the judge.

ANGELA: I want to go somewhere.

TOM: We are somewhere.

(ANGELA *moves to get up.*)

Please, Ange . . . it's not going to go 'way.

ANGELA (*with a brand new realization*): Why isn't it?

(*She sees* TOM*'s eyes—filled with pity for her, but also a certain* direction, *and she hears the fearful absence of a reply from him; he reaches toward her with a calming hand, and with new alarm and anger and confusion she flings him off and walks. He quickly leaps up and follows, worried and scared.*)

Exterior: Boardwalk—Same time

An all-but-deserted resort, with boarded-up rides and ice cream stands, a small Coney Island off-season. They are walking separately, not touching; she emotionally trying to escape, he persistently hanging on. They hear *a distant barking and halt, turned toward the sea.*

ANGELA: Dogs out there?—They sound hurt.

TOM: No, that's seals, I think. Talking to each other.

(*They sit on a bench, still not touching.*)

ANGELA (*a tense attempt at a grin*): You going to turn me in?

TOM: Angela, my evidence died on a motorcycle. How could I turn you in even if I wanted to?

ANGELA (*impatiently now*): What's happening, Tom?

TOM: I think if you dictated a deposition, stating that you got Abe to open the door for Jerry . . .

ANGELA: . . . I'd be accessory to a murder.

TOM: Not necessarily—I mean if Jerry forced you into doing it, it was under duress . . . or if he tricked you. See, this is why I want you to get with the judge.

ANGELA: And what do I do when the rest of it starts coming into it?

(TOM *goes silent, stalemated.*)

How does the great Dr. Daniels come to've known bums like Jerry and Montana? That has to go straight to the drugs, baby, and that means the cops come into it, right? And then Angela's floatin' out there, feeding those seals.

(TOM *concedes, lowers his eyes.*)

TOM: Why did you call me in on this case, Angela?

ANGELA: . . . To spring Felix. I thought maybe you could find some way . . .

TOM: . . . Without involving you.

(*She concedes in silence.*)

You couldn't bear carrying this any more, is that it?

(*She barely nods, eyes lowered.*)

Funny—I keep trying to figure what it is that always pulls me back to you.—It's your conscience. Which nobody is going to believe, but here it is.

(*This statement of his respect for her pushes a sob into* AN-GELA, *but it may also be guilt for lying to him. She suddenly strides away down the boardwalk, her conflict intolerable. He hurries after her.*)

Honey! Wait! Angela! Listen to me!

(*He catches up with her, and she is openly weeping.*)

ANGELA: Please don't turn me in!

(TOM, *wracked, folds her into his arms, but no reassurance comes to his lips.*)

Interior: Motel room—Night

TOM, ANGELA. *A "MOTEL" sign is blinking outside their window. They sit facing each other on two beds. They are still in their coats.*

She is staring, avoiding his eyes. For a long moment nothing is said.

ANGELA: The thing is . . . I don't know if I have enough control; if I ever got on a witness-stand God knows what I might start saying.

TOM: Like what, honey?

ANGELA: Well like . . . I might have made all that up about

Callaghan. (*She looks directly at him for the first time.*) . . . I mean I'm not absolutely sure.

TOM (*the question rises in his face—is she slyly using her illness to manipulate him? Or is she really trying to avoid a catastrophe for them both in a court?*): No kidding.

ANGELA: I don't know. I'm almost sure of it, but suddenly every once in a while I . . . (*She breaks off, staring.*)

TOM: But you remember going to the doctor's house that night with Jerry.

ANGELA (*she stares, trying to visualize, then . . .*): I'm not . . . I'm not sure. I'm not even sure Abe Daniels was into drugs.

TOM (*a new hardening, a skepticism, but he downs it*): No kidding.

ANGELA: I couldn't get up on a stand and face John Callaghan. I mean God knows, maybe all I ever did with him was shake hands once in the courthouse. How can I talk to this judge now, you see what I mean? I'm just not sure enough of anything.

(TOM *grabs her arm.*)

TOM: Honey, there's a few things I know independently of you.—I talked to Jerry myself.

ANGELA (*the faintest hardening*): Jerry was crazier than me. He was brain-damaged. You know, he tried to kill himself—

TOM: Because he'd murdered Daniels. (*Gripping her shoulders, his frustration boiling up in him.*) Hacked his head off, right? (*Shouting close at her.*) Chopped it off? Nearly cut his heart out of his chest?

(*She tries to draw away but he grips her.*)

Nobody dreamed *that*, kid.

(*She is trying to wrench free.*)

You saw it all, didn't you! Went inside with him, didn't you? Is that it?—You saw him cut his head off, is that what's driving you crazy?

(*She violently disengages and this makes him sense there is more that she knows, and he rushes to the door and yanks her back into the room.*)

What'd you, help hold him down, is that it? You held Daniels down for him? Angela!!

(*A most pleasurable, wild grin grows on her face.*)

What're you laughing at? (*Shaking her violently.*) Stop laughing at me!

ANGELA: You realize what you're saying to me? You hear your own words? (*Suddenly screaming into his face.*) I helped cut a man's head off? Do you hear your mouth!

  (*He is stunned by the sudden insanity of the idea, for her indignation is very real.*)

Maybe now you get the feeling—do you?—that everything is possible, and impossible at the same time, right? You feel it? This is what I live with.

  (*With an anguished laugh compounded of contempt and her feeling of loss, she walks out of the room.*

  Its door opens onto a parking space where his car stands. She walks past it.

  Alone for a moment, TOM *is at crisis: what to believe? He rushes out of the room.*)

Exterior: Boardwalk—Night

TOM, ANGELA. *She is walking without purpose or destination: her terror is that he may in the end turn her in. She hears him hurrying up to her from behind, and turns in absolute uncertainty to face him again.*

TOM: Okay! Honey, listen: I understand. Let me take you to the judge, see if he can come up with an idea. Just give it a try! (*He takes her hand, pleading.*) He's really one of the greats. I love you, darlin'; I can't help it, I always will.

  (*His unguarded confession seems to move her . . .*)

ANGELA: . . . If you let me see him alone . . .

TOM (*slightest tinge of suspicion over her relief and joy*): Of course, absolutely!

  (*He takes her hand to move her back to the car, but she turns him back to her. In her face is a sweep of an almost worshipful feeling for him, and a hope of her own resurrection. It is also her instinctive means of control. She grasps his hand and leads him quickly to the sand . . .*)

(*Laughing*): Wait! Listen . . . !

  (*She is pulling him down to the sand, unbuttoning his shirt, biting into his belly . . . a desperation in her fierce, cat-like love-making.*)

Interior: TOM'*s car—Later*

Driving, sexual contentment on his face, he glances over to her and worry moves into his eyes.

Shot widens to include her; her anxiety is back, but even more tensely as they near the destination.

He pats her thigh reassuringly.

Interior: JUDGE MARKS' *house—Later*

TOM *and* ANGELA *stand before the impressive door to* JUDGE MARKS' *study.* ANGELA *pats her hair, worriedly.*

ANGELA: How . . . how do I look?
TOM: Marvelous. Beautiful.
> (*The door opens. Shooting between* TOM'*s and* ANGELA'*s heads we see the surprised excitement on* MARKS' *face as he sees* ANGELA. *Whether it be the shock of her sexuality or her fable, as* TOM *has told it to him, his ageing face lights up with pleasure.*)
MARKS: Well! How do you do?
> (*They enter his study.*)
TOM: I'll take off now, Harry. Be in touch. And I don't have to say how thankful I am. 'Bye, Angela.
> (*She has been absorbing* MARKS' *personality, and for an instant doesn't register* TOM'*s farewell, then suddenly turns to him as to an afterthought.*)
ANGELA: Oh!—'Bye.
> (*He senses something like a dismissal, and goes to the door. There he turns for a last farewell.*)
TOM: Good night, Judge.
> (MARKS, *his eyes locked on* ANGELA, *waves him off.*)

Interior: Coffee shop—Next day

TOM *is nursing a cup, looking at his watch, jiggling a foot on the stool rung. He goes to the wall payphone and dials.*

TOM: Judge Marks' secretary, please. Hi, Jean!—it's me again, has he come in yet? (*As restrained as he can get.*) —Jean, dear, the housekeeper says he's at his office—you wouldn't be kidding ol' Tom, would you? (*Angering.*) Just tell me if he's there so I can stop wasting my time, darlin'. Okay, don't get mad, I believe you. (*He hangs up, mystified for a moment, then dials another number.*) Connie? Listen, did she call since I left? "She"? "She" is Angela Crispini! I think she's avoiding me for some reason; I can't figure it out!

Exterior: ANGELA*'s front door—Day*

TOM *is leaning on the buzzer. No answer. Goes around the house to try to see up into her apartment windows. His face is stuffed with mystification and alarm . . . and anger. And perfectly senselessly he yells up . . .*

TOM: Angela!!

Interior: MARKS*' outer office—Shortly after*

JEAN, JUDGE MARKS*' powerhouse secretary is just emerging through a closing door, and* TOM *stands to meet her.*

JEAN: Now listen, Tom, he simply can't be disturbed . . . he's in an important meeting in chambers.
TOM: Jean, please—I'm desperate to find out how it went with a woman I asked him to see.
JEAN: If it's the Epstein case . . .
TOM: That's it, yes . . .
JEAN: Well, he's on his way down from the prison.
TOM: Who's on his way?
JEAN: Felix Epstein. The judge is getting him a new trial. You'll have to excuse me . . .
> (*She goes back through the door she came out of.* TOM, *in near shock, lets out a victory laugh, claps his hands together and rushes off, astounding several passing lawyer types in the corridor.*)

Exterior: Courthouse—Day

At the peak of anxiety and happiness, TOM *is hurrying to a public phonebooth at the entrance of the courthouse. As he dials, a hostile cop walks by, giving him a dour look which* TOM *returns with a wink and a pistol-mime with his forefinger. Into phone . . .*

TOM: Connie! I did it! Epstein is out! The judge hasn't called, has he?—I don't know, the secretary says he's getting him a new trial . . . (*Seeing something off-camera.*) Hey! Call you back!

Exterior: Courthouse area—Day

TOM*'s viewpoint.* MARKS *is on the sidewalk below the courthouse steps, walking toward a limousine parked at the curb.*

Exterior: Courthouse area—Day

TOM *is rushing down the steps . . .*

TOM: Judge! Wait!

Exterior: Courthouse area—Day

TOM *rushes up to* MARKS, *who turns to him, but with an inexplicable air of reserve . . .*

TOM: My God, Harry—Jean just told me you got him out! She must really have impressed you, huh?—Angela?
MARKS: Remarkable woman.
      (MARKS *turns and moves to the limo whose driver is opening the door for him.* TOM, *mystified, follows him . . .*)
TOM: Harry . . . what's wrong? You mad at me or something?
MARKS: This is a very deep woman, a sensitive woman. You had no call being that rough on her.
TOM (*flummoxed*): Me! How was I rough?

MARKS: You either believe her or you don't, there's no need to be hounding her.

TOM: Harry, please! I was only trying to get her to tell what she knows. (*Flattering.*) But I knew she'd agree to testify the minute you got your hands on her!

MARKS (*stalwart protectiveness*): No, no! There's no need for her to enter the court.—Callaghan failed to reveal exculpatory evidence to the defense—it's a technicality, but enough to reverse.

(*Alarm springs onto* TOM's *face as* MARKS *starts to bend to get into the car.* TOM *dares to grasp his arm in his desperation.*)

TOM: Harry, please listen—there's a whole connection to the police that she knows about. The case is all about drugs and Callaghan and the police department—it goes to the top of the mountain!

MARKS: No-no, Epstein will be a free man and that's the end of it . . .

TOM: But she could expose the corruption of the whole state, she could hang them all out to dry!

MARKS: Now listen to me! The killer is dead. And the poor woman has been through enough! That's the end of it!

(MARKS *bends and enters the car and the chauffeur shuts the door behind him, and gets behind the wheel.* TOM *can't help one more try and bends to speak to the judge through the closed window . . .*)

TOM: Harry . . . I can't believe this!

(*He sees something within the car that splashes his face with astonishment.*

TOM's *point of view:* ANGELA *in the back seat is lifting a tentative finger of greeting to* TOM *as* MARKS *stares at her with stars in his eyes. The car pulls away.*)

Exterior: Limo back window—Same time

TOM's *viewpoint:* ANGELA *has turned around, and looking out the rear window of the limo at* TOM, *is lifting both hands and squinching up her shoulders, happily declaring her helplessness before her victory, as well as begging his understanding of her happy plight. She blows him a kiss. Two, in fact.*

Exterior: Street—Day

He is open-mouthed watching the car moving away.

Dissolve. Now a serio-comical kind of orchestration blots out the sound of the following: over the above a small crowd on courthouse steps: TV crews in action, interviewing FELIX, *who is now shaved and looking pretty good in a business suit, with a topcoat over his arm, and* ANGELA *beside him, looking terrific:*

FELIX: I owe everything to this wonderful woman! Thanks, Angela!

>*(And beside her stands* JUDGE MARKS *grasping her elbow as he speaks into an interviewer's microphone.*
>
>*While next to him stands* JOHN CALLAGHAN *manifestly agreeing with what he is telling the TV interviewer, namely . . .)*

MARKS: No-no, there are no hard feelings with my old friend John Callaghan. An honest mistake was made and it is now rectified. I must say, though, that only the noble efforts of this remarkable woman have righted this terrible injustice to an innocent man!

ANGELA *(smack into the lens)*: What can I say? I want to thank the judge and . . . I don't know, just to be able to look at this man (FELIX, *that is*), standing at last in the open sunshine like this, gives me such a feeling of happiness that I can only say thank you, thank you, thank you . . . !

>*(While she is thanking everybody, the music thunders out of her and the camera sweeps across the crowd in the midst of which in a*
>
>*Close shot:* TOM *and* CONNIE
>
>*we find the couple looking on, and in a momentary lull in the volume of the music . . .)*

CONNIE: It's really remarkable—everybody wins!

TOM *(with a deep, ironic nod)*: . . . Almost.

>*(Camera swiftly rises over the crowd, the courthouse, the town . . .)*

THE RIDE DOWN
MT. MORGAN

To Inge

CHARACTERS

LYMAN FELT
THEO FELT
LEAH FELT
BESSIE
FATHER
NURSE LOGAN
TOM WILSON

STAGING NOTE

Notwithstanding the present stage directions, the play may be performed in open space, with scenes separated by light and arrangements of furniture and props.

The play veers from the farcical to the tragic and back again and should be performed all-out in both directions as the situation demands, without attempting to mitigate the extremes.

ACT ONE

A hospital bed with LYMAN FELT *in it. He is a man in his fifties, but he is ordinarily so fit it is hard to tell exactly. Now his leg is in a cast, his arm as well, and he is deeply asleep.* NURSE LOGAN, *a black woman, is seated near the bed, leafing through a magazine under a lamp.*

LYMAN (*his eyes still shut*): Thank you, thank you all very much. Please be seated.

(NURSE *turns, looks toward him.*)

We have a lot of material . . . not material . . . yes, material . . . to cover this afternoon, so please take your seats and cross your legs. No-no . . . (*Laughs weakly.*) . . . Not cross your legs, just take your seats . . .

NURSE: That was a lot of surgery, Mr. Felt. You're supposed to be resting . . . Or you out?

LYMAN (*for a moment he sleeps, snores, then . . .*): Today I'd like you to consider life insurance from a different perspective. I want you to look at the whole economic system as one enormous tit.

NURSE: Well, now! (*Embarrassed laugh.*)

LYMAN: So the job of the individual is to get a good place in line for a suck. Which incidentally gives us the word "suck-cess." Or . . . or not. (*Snores deeply.*)

NURSE: You keep this up we're going to have to see about another shot. . . . (*Goes back to turning pages.*)

(FATHER *enters; wears a Panama hat, carries a cane, smokes a cigarette in a holder, drags a broad black cloth behind him. He comes and bends over* LYMAN *as though to kiss him . . .*

LYMAN *stiffens, utters a cry of mixed fear and hopeful surprise, his eyes still shut.*

FATHER *straightens up and shakes his head mournfully.*)

FATHER: Very bad for business.

(LYMAN *whimpers reassuringly.*)

What you need skates for, you fall down they laugh at you. Never talk business with women, God only makes them for one thing, obey God. Your teeth stick out, ears stick out,

205

everything stickin' out, I'm sorry to say you very stupid boy, big disappointment. (*Shaking his head he moves into darkness.*) Very bad for business.

LYMAN: I promise. Papa! (*Calling.*) I promise! (*He opens his eyes, gradually taking in the* NURSE.) You black?

NURSE: That's what they keep telling me.

LYMAN: You ah . . . RSP?

NURSE: RN? Yes.

LYMAN: Good for you. I've got a big training program for you guys, biggest in the industry, and first one to put you in sales. There's no election now, is there? Eisenhower or something?

NURSE: Eisenhower! He's long gone, long gone. And it's December.

LYMAN: Oh. 'Cause you're more likely to be talking to strangers election time. . . . Why can't I move, do you mind?

NURSE: You broke some bones. They say you went skiing down that Mount Morgan in a Porsche.

(*She chuckles. He squints, trying to orient himself.*)

LYMAN: What's that music? Sounds like Earl Hines.

NURSE: Music? There's no music.

LYMAN (*sings*): "I'm just breezin' along with the breeze . . ." Listen to that, will you? . . . that just beautiful? (*Whistles the tune for a moment, then falls fast asleep again. Wakes.*) Jimmy Baldwin once called me a nigger underneath. (*Chuckle.*) That's an honor. He liked couple of my stories, when I was still a writer. Long time ago. (*Slight pause.*) My wife used to ski like a Methodist—straight up . . . she used to say I skied like an Arab—pants kept falling down. No chairlifts in those days, y'know—used to climb back up the mountain on your skis. Herringbone. Women did it easier 'cause their knees opened wider. Get horny just watching them climb. What'd you say?

NURSE: I didn't.

LYMAN: Oh. And where is this I am?

NURSE: Clearhaven Memorial Hospital.

LYMAN (*as it is slowly penetrating*): Clearhaven?

NURSE: Your wife and daughter just arrived up from New York.

LYMAN (*attempting canniness, but still confused*): . . . From *New York*? Kinda looking woman, how old?

NURSE: Fifties, probably.

LYMAN (*alarm starts*): Who called them?

NURSE: What do you mean? Why not?

LYMAN: And where is this?

NURSE: Clearhaven.—I'm from Canada myself, I just started here. We've still got railroads in Canada.

LYMAN: Listen . . . I'm not feeling well. What are we talking about Canadian railroads for?

NURSE: No, I just mentioned it as there is a storm.

LYMAN: Now what . . . what . . . what was that about my wife from New York?

NURSE: She's here in the waiting room. And your daughter.

LYMAN (*peering intensely*): And this is *where*?

NURSE: I told you, Clearhaven Memorial.

LYMAN (*looks around warily*): You have a mirror?

NURSE: Mirror? Sure. (*Takes one out of her purse, goes to him.*) You don't look extra great, I can tell you that now.

LYMAN (*looks at himself, touches bandage in surprise*): Could you . . . touch me?

   (*She puts finger on his cheek. He lowers the mirror, looks at her, suddenly angry.*)

Who the hell called them, for God's sake?

NURSE: I'm new here! I'm sorry if I'm not satisfactory. (*Unnerved, she returns to her chair.*)

LYMAN (*high anxiety*): Who said you're not satisfactory? What's all this unnecessary . . . *verbiage*?—not verbiage, for Christ's sake, I meant . . . (*Panting.*) Listen, I absolutely can't see anyone and they have to go back to New York right away.

NURSE: But as long as you're awake . . .

LYMAN: Immediately! Get them out of here, okay? (*Stab of pain.*) Oh!—listen . . . there's nobody else, is there? To see me?

NURSE: Not that I noticed.

LYMAN: Please, quickly, go—I can't see anybody!

   (*Bewildered, she exits.*)

My God, how could I have done this!—Christ, I can just see them! . . . Oh how terrible! It can't happen, it mustn't happen! (*Slipping out from the rear of the cast, he moves into the clear—still in hospital gown, but not bandaged. The empty cast remains on the bed as it was. His eyes wide as he stares at his catastrophic vision . . .*) Oh, I can just see it . . .

Bessie is weeping, oh poor darling! But not Theo . . .
No, Theo is completely controlled, yes . . . controlled and
strong . . .

(*As he speaks the beds move away behind him, and a
chintz-covered wicker chair and couch, furniture of the hospital waiting room, truck on. Lights change to brighter,
more cheerful tone. His wife,* THEODORA, *and daughter,*
BESSIE, *are seated on the couch.*)

No—no, it mustn't happen . . . ! (*He is looking on in high
tension, but since he is invisible to the others he may move right
up to them, sit beside them, etc.*)

(THEODORA's *beaver coat is beside her;* BESSIE's *mod cloth
coat on her lap.* THEODORA *is sipping a cup of tea. She is an
idealistic, intellectually forceful woman turning sixty now,
physically strong, if somewhat stiff and ungainly.*

BESSIE, *after a moment, is suddenly swept by a fit of sobbing and covers her face.* THEODORA *grips her hand.*)

THEO: Darling, you must try not to.

BESSIE: I can't help it.

THEO: Of course you can. Try to think of all the happiness;
think of his laughter; Daddy loves life, he'll fight for it.

LYMAN (*looking on with intense admiration*): God, what a
woman!

BESSIE: . . . I guess I've just never had anything really bad
happen.

LYMAN: Oh, my dear Bessie!

THEO: But you'll see as you get older—everything ultimately
fits together . . . and for the good.

LYMAN (*with a mix of love and condescension toward her
naïveté*): Ah, bless her, what an American!

THEO: —Now come, Bessie.—Remember what a wonderful
time we had in Africa? Think of Africa.

BESSIE: What an amazing woman you are, Mother.

(NURSE LOGAN *enters.*)

NURSE: It'll still be a while before he can see anybody. There's
a good motel just up the highway; it's ski season but my
husband can probably get you in, he plows their driveway.

BESSIE: Do you know if he's out of danger?

NURSE: I think so but I'm sure the doctors will let you know.

(*Obviously changing subject.*) I can't believe you made it up from New York in this sleet.

THEO: One does what one has to.—I think I would like to lie down, would you call the motel? It was a terrible drive. . . .

NURSE: Sometimes I feel like going back to Canada—at least we had a railroad.

THEO: We'll have them again; things may take time in this country but in the end we get them done.

(NURSE *exits.*)

(*Turns to* BESSIE, *smiling painfully*): What was so funny?

BESSIE (*touching her mother's hand*): It's nothing . . .

THEO: Well, what was it?

BESSIE: Well, I mean . . . things really don't always get done in this country.

THEO (*disengaging her hand; she is hurt*): I think they do, ultimately. I've lived through changes that were inconceivable thirty years ago. (*Straining to laugh.*) I'm really not *that* naïve, Bessie.

BESSIE (*angering*): Well, don't be so upset, it's not important. (*Pause. To heal things . . .*) They certainly are very nice people around here, aren't they.

THEO: Oh yes. I've often been sorry you never knew small-town life, there *is* a goodness.

BESSIE: I'm wondering if we ought to call Grandma Esther.

THEO: If you like. (*Slight pause.*) She gets so impressively emotional, that's all.

BESSIE: Well I won't if it upsets you.

THEO: Oh, no, I have nothing against her anymore; she simply never liked me and I always knew it, that was all. But she loves you.

BESSIE: I know she's a superficial woman, but she can really be so funny and . . .

THEO: Funny, yes.

BESSIE: I've never understood why you feel she's cold.

THEO: I just don't like women who are forever seducing their sons.

LYMAN (*with mock-righteousness*): Right!

THEO: It's a miracle she didn't turn him into a homosexual.

LYMAN: Perfect!

THEO: I used to think it was because he didn't marry Jewish . . .

BESSIE: But she didn't either.

THEO: Yes, but what she does doesn't count. But she'd have disliked any woman he married. Go ahead, call her, she is his mother and she adores you.

> (LEAH *enters. She is about thirty; blondined hair, in an open raccoon coat, high heels.* NURSE *enters with her.*)

LYMAN (*on the instant she enters, he is terrified, claps hands over his eyes*): No, she mustn't! It can't happen! It mustn't! (*Unable to bear it he starts to flee, but stops as . . .*)

LEAH: After all the money we've put into this hospital it seems to me I ought to be able to speak to the chief nurse, for Christ's sake!

NURSE: I'm doing my best to get her for you . . . !

LEAH: Okay, I'll wait here.

> (NURSE *starts to go.*)

I'm only asking for a little information, dear!

> (NURSE *exits. Pause.* LEAH *sits, but quickly stands again and moves restlessly.* THEO *and* BESSIE *observe her indirectly, with polite curiosity. Now their eyes meet. She throws up her hands.*)

The same thing when I had my baby here, it was like pulling teeth to get them to tell me if it was a boy or a girl.

BESSIE: Is it an emergency?

LEAH: My husband; he cracked up the car on Mount Morgan. You?

BESSIE: My father. It was a car, too.

LYMAN: Oh dear God, not this way . . . please!

THEO: The roads are impossible.

LEAH: It's that damned Mount Morgan road—there've been half a dozen horrible crashes in the last couple of years. . . . I still can't believe it—the man driving on ice . . . and at night yet! It's incomprehensible! (*A sudden explosion*): Damn them, I have a right to know what's happening! (*She charges out.*)

BESSIE: Poor thing.

THEO: But she *knows* how busy they are . . .

> (*Silence now;* THEO *leans back, closing her eyes. Another sobbing fit threatens* BESSIE, *who downs it, covers her eyes. Then suddenly she breaks down and weeps.*)

Oh, Bessie, dear, try not to . . .

LYMAN (*staring front*): If I could only get myself over to the window . . . and out!

BESSIE (*shaking her head helplessly*): . . . I just love him so!

(LEAH *returns, more subdued now. She sits tiredly, closes her eyes. Pause. She gets up, goes to a window, looks out.*)

LEAH: Will you look at that moon? Everybody smashes up in the dark and now you could read a paper out there.

BESSIE: You live around here?

LEAH: Not far. We're on the lake.

BESSIE: It looks like such beautiful country.

LEAH: Oh yes. But I'll take New York anytime. (*A great sob bursts from her.*) I'm sorry.

(*She weeps helplessly into her handkerchief.* BESSIE *is affected and begins weeping, too.*)

THEO: Now really . . . ! (*Shakes* BESSIE's *arm.*) Stop this! (*She sees* LEAH's *indignant look.*) You still don't know how serious it is, do you? Why are you carrying on like this?

LEAH (*rather unwillingly*): You're probably right.

THEO (*exulting—to* BESSIE *as well*): Of course! I mean there's always time to despair, why should . . . ?

LEAH (*sharply*): I *said* you were right, I was agreeing with you!

(THEO *goes stiff, turns slightly away.*)

I'm sorry.

(*Short pause. The women cease moving, as* LYMAN *talks to himself.*)

LYMAN: What admirable women! What strong, definite characters. Luckily, I'm not here and it isn't happening, but if it were, I'm sure this is how they'd be with one another. (*Musing.*)— Now what would they say next?

BESSIE: You raise things on your place?

LEAH: We grow most of what we eat. We have sixty head of cattle. And we're starting to raise thoroughbreds now, in a small way.

BESSIE: Oh, I'd love that . . .

LEAH: I envy your calmness—both of you. Really, you've made me feel better. What part of New York are you in?

BESSIE: East Seventy-fourth Street.

LYMAN (*gripping his head*): Oh no! No-no . . . !

LEAH: Seventy-fourth, really? We often stay at the Carlyle. . . .

BESSIE: Oh, it's very near.

THEO: You sound like a New Yorker.

LEAH: I went to NYU School of Business for three years, and I really love the city, but I was raised here in Elmira and my business is here, so . . . (*She shrugs. Goes to the window again.*)

THEO: What sort of business do you have?

LEAH: Insurance.

LYMAN: No!—that's enough, stop it!

BESSIE: Oh, that's what Daddy does!

LYMAN (*hands clasped, facing heaven*): Oh don't, don't let it happen!

LEAH: Well, there's a million of us. You in it, too?

BESSIE: No, I'm at home . . . take care of my husband.

LEAH: I'm hoping to sell out, in maybe three-four years, get a place in New York and just paint morning to night the rest of my life.

BESSIE: Really?—my husband's a painter.

LEAH: Professionally or . . . ?

BESSIE: Oh yes. He's Harold Lamb.

LYMAN: No!—my God! (*He rushes out holding his head.*)

LEAH: Harold Lamb?

> (LYMAN *returns, unable not to witness this.* LEAH *has ceased all movement, staring at* BESSIE. *Now she turns to stare at* THEODORA.)

THEO: What is it?

LEAH: Your husband is really Harold Lamb?

BESSIE (*very pleased and proud*): You've heard of him?

LEAH (*to* THEO): You're not Mrs. Felt, are you?

THEO: Why, yes.

LEAH (*her puzzled look*): Then you . . . (*breaks off, then*): You're not here for Lyman, are you?

BESSIE: You know Daddy?

LEAH: But . . . (*Turning from one to the other*): . . . How'd they come to notify *you*?

THEO (*uncomprehending, but beginning to take affront*): What's that?

LEAH: Well . . . after so many years.

THEO: What do you mean?

LEAH: But it's over nine . . .

BESSIE: What is?

LEAH: Your divorce.

(THEO *and* BESSIE *are struck dumb. A silence.*)

You're Theodora Felt, right?

THEO: Who *are* you?

LEAH: I'm Leah. Leah Felt.

THEO (*a haughtiness begins*): Felt!

LEAH: Lyman is my husband.

THEO: Who *are* you? What are you talking about!

BESSIE (*intensely curious about* LEAH, *she angers at* THEO): Well, don't get so *angry*, for heaven's sake!

THEO: Be quiet!

LEAH (*seeing* THEO*'s genuineness*): Well, you're divorced, aren't you?

THEO: Divorced!—who the hell *are* you!

LEAH: I'm Lyman's wife.

(THEO *sees she is a serious woman; it silences her.*)

BESSIE: When . . . when did you . . . ? I mean . . .

THEO (*in motion again*): She's insane!—she's some kind of a nut!

LEAH (*to Bessie*): It'll be nine years in September.

THEO: Really. And who performed this . . . this *event*?

LEAH: The Elmira City Hall clerk, and then a rabbi the next day. My son's name is Benjamin, for his grandmother's father, and Alexander for Lyman's father—Benjamin Alexander Felt.

THEO (*with a weak attempt to sustain mockery*): Really!

LEAH: Yes. I'm terribly sorry if you didn't know.

THEO: Didn't know *what*? What are you *talking* about?

LEAH: We have been married over nine years, Mrs. Felt.

THEO: Have you! And I suppose you have some document . . . ?

LEAH: I have our marriage certificate, I guess . . .

THEO: You guess!

LEAH (*angrily*): Well I'm sure I do! And I know I have Lyman's will in our safe-deposit box . . .

THEO (*helplessly mocking*): And it names you as his wife!

LEAH: And Benjamin his son.

(THEO *is halted by her factuality.*)

. . . But I guess you have more or less the same . . . is that right?

(THEO *is still as a stone.*)

There was really no divorce?

BESSIE (*with a glance at her stricken mother . . . softly, almost apologetically*): . . . No.

LEAH: Well, I think we'd better . . . meet, or something. Mrs. Felt? I understand your feelings, but you'll just have to believe it, I guess: We have a terrible problem. Mrs. Felt?

THEO: It's impossible; nine years ago . . . (*To* BESSIE): That's when we all went to Africa.

BESSIE: Oh, right!—the safari!

THEO (*to* LEAH, *with a victorious, if nearly demented laugh*): We were never closer in our lives! We traveled through Kenya, Nigeria . . . (*As though this clinched everything*): . . . we even flew to Egypt!

(NURSE *enters. It instantly galvanizes all of them. She glances from one to the other.*)

NURSE: Doctor Lowry would like to see Mrs. Felt now.

(*For one instant no one moves—then both* THEO *and* LEAH *rise simultaneously. This actualization of* LEAH's *claims stiffens* THEO, *forcing her to start assertively toward the nurse—and she sways and starts to fall to the floor.*)

LEAH: Catch her!

BESSIE: Mother!

(NURSE *and* BESSIE *catch* THEO, *then lower her to the floor.* LEAH *becomes frantic through this collapse, rushing toward the periphery, yelling . . .*)

LEAH: Help here, someone's fainted! Where's a doctor, goddammit!

BLACKOUT

A couch and chair. LEAH *is seated facing* TOM WILSON, *a middle-aged but very fit lawyer who is reading a will, and sipping coffee. After a moment she gets up and moves to a point and stares, eyes filled with fear. Then dialing a phone, turns to him.*

LEAH: Sorry I'm not being much of a hostess. Sure you wouldn't like some toast?

TOM (*immersed*): Thanks. I'm just about done here.

LEAH (*dialing*): God, I dread it—my boy'll be home from

school any minute . . . (*To phone*): Put my brother on,
Tina. . . . Lou?—I don't know, they won't let me see him
yet. What'd Uniroyal say? *What?* Well, call L.A. this minute!
I want that business!—But we discussed all this yesterday!
Jet lag doesn't last this long. (*Hangs up.*) I don't know what
it is; there's no sense of continuity from one day to another
anymore.

(TOM *closes the file.*)

—I know you're her lawyer, but I'm not really asking advice,
am I?

TOM: I can discuss this. (*Returning her the file.*) The will does
recognize the boy as his son but you are not his wife.

LEAH (*lifting the file*): But this refers to me as his wife . . .

TOM: That's meaningless—he never divorced. However . . .
(*Breaks off, pressing his eyes.*) I'm just stunned, I can't absorb it.

LEAH: I'm still in midair someplace.

TOM: What'd you ask me? Oh yes—provided the legal wife
gets a minimum of one-third of the estate he can leave you
as much as he likes. So you're very well taken care of. (*Sighs.
Leans forward gripping his head.*) He actually flies a plane,
you say?

LEAH: Oh yes, soaring planes too. We own one.

TOM: You know, for years he never got off the ground unless it
was unavoidable.

LEAH: Oh, he's wonderful in the air. (*Pause.*) I'm not here. I'm
simply . . . not here. Can he be insane?

TOM: . . . May I ask you . . . ?

LEAH: Please. . . . Incidentally, have you known him long?

TOM: Sixteen, seventeen years. . . . When you decided to
marry, I assume he told you he'd gotten a divorce . . .

LEAH: Of course. We went to Reno together.

TOM: No kidding! And what happened?

LEAH: God, I'd forgotten all about this . . . (*Breaks off.*) How
could I have been so *stupid!*—You see, it was July, a hundred
and ten on the street, so he had me stay in the hotel with the
baby while he went to the court to pick up his divorce decree . . . (*She goes silent.*)

TOM: Yes?

LEAH (*shaking her head*): It's incredible . . . I was curious to
see what a decree looked like . . .

(LYMAN *enters, wearing short-sleeved summer shirt.*)

. . . no particular reason, but I'd never seen one . . .

LYMAN: I threw it away.

LEAH (*a surprised laugh*): Why!

LYMAN: I don't want to look back. Darling, I feel twenty-five! (*Laughs.*) You look stunned!

LEAH (*kisses him lightly*): I never really believed you'd do it, darling.

LYMAN: I know. It's a miracle. (*He draws her to him;* TOM *is a few feet away.*) I feel you flowing round me like I'm a rock in the river.—I have a car and driver downstairs; come to your wedding, Leah my darling!

LEAH: But can I tell you the wedding vow I wish we could make?—it's going to sound strange, but . . .

LYMAN: No!—say it!

LEAH: I'm embarrassed but I will: "Dearly beloved, I promise everything good, but I might have to lie to you sometime." Could one say that and still love someone? Because it's the truth . . . nobody knows what can happen, right?

LYMAN (*slight, amazed pause*): What balls you have to say that! Yes, it's the truth and I love you for it! (*He kisses her, then seems distracted.*)

LEAH: You seem drained—are you sorry you divorced her?

LYMAN: I'm . . . a little scared, that's all, but it's natural. Tell you what. I'm going to learn to fly a plane . . .

LEAH: But you hate flying!

LYMAN (*lifts her to her feet*): Yes. But no more fear. Ever! Of any kind!

(LYMAN *exits without lowering his arm. She turns to* TOM.)

LEAH: . . . And it was all lies! How is it possible! Why did he do it? What did he want?

TOM: Actually . . . (*Tries to recall.*) . . . You know . . . I think we did have a discussion about a divorce . . .

LEAH: You did? When?

TOM: About nine years ago . . . although at the time I didn't take it all that seriously. He suddenly popped into my office one day with this "research" he said he'd done . . .

(LYMAN *enters in a business suit.*)

LYMAN: . . . I've been looking into bigamy, Tom.

TOM (*laughs, surprised*): Bigamy!—what are you talking about?

LYMAN: There was a piece in the paper a few weeks ago. There's an enormous amount of bigamy in the United States now.

TOM: Oh? But what's the point . . . ?

LYMAN: I've been wondering—how about bigamy insurance? Might call it the Desertion Protection Plan.

TOM (*laughs*): It's a great name for a policy . . . but you're kidding.

LYMAN: I mean this. We could set the premiums very low, like a few cents a week. Be great, especially for minority women.

TOM: Say now!—(*Greatly admiring.*)—where the hell do you get these ideas!

LYMAN: I don't think they're ideas, I just try to put myself in other people's places. (*Laughs, enjoying his immodesty.*) It's what's made me what I am today! Incidentally, how frequently do they prosecute for bigamy anymore, you have any idea?

TOM: No. But it's a victimless crime so it can't be often.

LYMAN: That's my impression, too. Get somebody to research it, will you, I want to be sure.—I'll be in Elmira till Friday. (*Starts to leave but dawdles.*)

TOM: Why do I think you're depressed?

LYMAN: Slightly, maybe. (*The self-deprecating grin.*) I'm turning fifty-four this July.

TOM: Fifty's much tougher, I think.

LYMAN: My father died at fifty-three.

TOM: Well, you're over the hump. Anyway, you're in better shape than anybody I know.

LYMAN: Famous last words.

TOM: —Something wrong, Lyman?

LYMAN (*slight pause; he decides to tell*): I was having lunch today at the Four Seasons, and just as I'm getting up this woman—beautifully dressed, smile on her face—leans over me and says, "I hope you drop dead you son of a bitch." You know what she was talking about.

TOM: I can't believe that's still happening.

LYMAN: Oh, three or four times a year; they don't always come out with it but a lot of people still think I turned in my partner to keep myself out of jail.—Which maybe I did, but I don't think so; I think Raoul paid for his crookedness, period. (*Smiles.*) But I can't help it, I still love that little bastard. We had some great years building the firm.

TOM: Well, it's over the dam and out to sea.

LYMAN: I did the right thing; it's just the imputation of cowardice that . . . (*Breaks off.*) Well, fuck it, I've lived my life and I refuse to be ashamed of it! Talk to you soon. (*Stands, but hesitates to leave.*)

TOM: —Is there something else?

LYMAN: I don't think I have the balls. (*A pause.* LYMAN *stands perfectly still, controlled; then, facing his challenge, turns rather abruptly to* TOM.) It's funny about you, Tom—I've been a lot closer to other men, but there's nobody I trust like you. (*A grin.*) I guess you know I've cheated on Theodora, don't you.

TOM: Well, I've had my suspicions, yes—ever since I walked in on you humping that Pakistani typist on your desk.

LYMAN (*laughs*): "Humping"!—I love that Presbyterian jive of yours, haven't heard that in years.

TOM: Quaker.

LYMAN (*confessionally, quietly*): I don't want to be that way anymore. It's kind of ridiculous at my age, for one thing. (*With difficulty.*) I think I've fallen in love.

TOM: Oh, don't tell me!

LYMAN (*pointing at him and laughing*): Look at you! God, you really love Theodora, don't you!

TOM: Of course I do! You're not thinking of divorce, are you?

LYMAN: I don't know what I'm thinking. It's years since anything like this has happened to me. But I probably won't do anything . . . maybe I just wanted to say it out loud to somebody.

TOM: I have a feeling it'll pass.

LYMAN: I've been waiting for it to, but it keeps getting worse. —I've frankly never believed monogamous guys like you are honestly happy, but with her I can almost see it for myself. And that can't ever be with Theodora. With her I'll be on the run till I croak, and that's the truth.

TOM: You know she loves you deeply. Profoundly, Lyman.

LYMAN: Tom, I love her too, but our neuroses just don't match.

TOM: Frankly, I can't imagine you apart from each other—you seem so dependent.

LYMAN: I know. I've always relied on her sense of reality,

especially her insights into this country. But I just don't want to cheat anymore—it's gotten hateful to me, all deception has. It's become my Nazi, my worst horror—I want to wear my own face on my face every day till I die. Or do you think that kind of honesty is possible?

TOM: I don't have to tell you, the problem is not honesty but how much you hurt others with it.

LYMAN: Right. What about your religion? But there's no solution there either, I guess.

TOM: I somehow can't imagine you praying, Lyman.

(*Short pause.*)

LYMAN: Is there an answer?

TOM: I don't know, maybe all one can do is hope to end up with the right regrets.

LYMAN (*silent a moment*): You ever cheated, Tom?

TOM: No.

LYMAN: Honest to God?—I've seen you eye the girls around here.

TOM: It's the truth.

LYMAN: Is that the regret you end up with?

(TOM *laughs bashfully. Then* LYMAN *joins him. And suddenly,* LYMAN*'s suffering is on his face.*)

. . . Shit, that was cruel, Tom, forgive me, will you?— Dammit, why do I let myself get depressed? It's all pointless guilt, that's all! Here I start from nothing, create forty-two hundred jobs for people and raise over sixty ghetto blacks to office positions when that was not easy to do—I should be proud of myself, son of a bitch! And I am! I am! (*He bangs on the desk, then subsides, looks front and downward.*) I love your view. That red river of taillights gliding down Park Avenue on a winter's night—and all those silky white thighs crossing inside those heated limousines . . . Christ, can there be a sexier vision in the world? (*Turning back to* TOM.) I keep thinking of my father—how connected he was to his life; couldn't wait to open the store every morning and happily count the pickles, rearrange the olive barrels. People like that knew the main thing. Which is what? What's the main thing, do you know?

(TOM *is silent.*)

—Look, don't worry, I really can't imagine myself without Theodora, she's a great, great wife! . . . I love that woman! It's always good talking to you, Tom.

(*Starts to go; halts*): Maybe it's simply that if you try to live according to your real desires, you have to end up looking like a shit.

(*He exits.* LEAH *covers her face and there is a pause as* TOM *observes her.*)

TOM: I'm sorry.

LEAH: He had it all carefully worked out from the very beginning.

TOM: I'd say it was more like . . . a continuous improvisation.

LEAH: What's so bewildering is that he was the one who was pushing to get married, not me. It was the baby, you see— once I was pregnant he simply wouldn't listen to reason . . .

(LYMAN *hurries on in a winter overcoat, claps a hand over her mouth.*)

LYMAN: Don't tell me it's too late. (*Kisses her.*) Did you do it?

LEAH: I was just walking out the door for the hospital.

LYMAN: Oh, thank God.

(*Draws her to a seat, and pulls her down.*)

Please, dear, give me one full minute and then you can do as you like.

LEAH: Don't, Lyme, it's impossible. (*Obviously changing the subject—with pain.*) Listen, up here they're all saying Reagan's just about won it.

LYMAN: Well, he'll probably be good for business. The knuckleheads usually are.—You know if you do this it's going to change it between us.

LEAH: Darling, it comes down to being a single parent and I just don't want that.

LYMAN: I've already named him.

LEAH (*amused, touching his face*): How do you know it's a him?

LYMAN: I'm never wrong, I have a very intimate relationship with ladies' bellies. His name is Benjamin after my father, and Alexander after my mother's mother who I loved a lot. (*Grins at his own egoism.*) You can put in a middle name.

LEAH (*with an unhappy laugh*): Well thanks so much!

(*Tries to stand up but he holds her.*)

He asked me not to be late.

LYMAN: The Russians—this is an ancient custom—before an important parting, they sit for a moment in silence. Give Benjamin this moment.

LEAH: He is not Benjamin, now stop it!

LYMAN: Believe in your feelings, Leah, the rest is nonsense. What do you really and truly want?

(*Silence for a moment.*)

I would drive him to school in the mornings, take him to ballgames.

LEAH: Twice a month?

LYMAN: With the new office set up here, I could easily be with you more than half the time.

LEAH: And Theodora?

LYMAN: It's difficult to talk about her.

LEAH: With me, you mean.

LYMAN: I can't lie to myself, darling, she's been a tremendous wife. It would be too unjust.

LEAH: But keeping it secret—where does that leave me? It's hard enough to identify myself as it is. And I can't believe she won't find out sooner or later, and then what?

LYMAN: If I actually have to choose it'll be you. But she doesn't know a soul in this whole area, it'd be a million-to-one shot for her ever to find out. I'm practically with you half the time now, and it's been pretty good, hasn't it?

LEAH (*touching her belly*): . . . But what do we tell this . . . ?

LYMAN: . . . Benjamin.

LEAH: Oh stop calling him Benjamin! It's not even three weeks!

LYMAN: That's long enough to be Benjamin—he has a horoscope, stars and planets; he has a *future!*

LEAH: There's something . . . why do I feel we're circling around something? There's something I don't believe here —what is it?

LYMAN: Maybe that I'm this desperate. (*Kisses her belly.*)

LEAH: Are you?—I can't express it . . . there's just something about this baby that doesn't seem . . . I don't know— *inevitable.*

LYMAN: Darling, I haven't wanted anything this much since

my twenties, when I was struggling to be a poet and make
something of my own that would last.

LEAH: Really.

LYMAN: It's the truth.

LEAH: That's touching, Lyman. . . . I'm very moved. (*So it is
up in the air for the moment.*) But I can't, I won't, it's the
story of my life, I always end up with all the responsibility;
I'd have to be in total charge of your child and I know I'd
resent it finally—and maybe even you as well. You're putting
me back to being twelve or thirteen and my parents asking
me where to go on vacations, or what kind of car to buy or
what color drapes. I hate that position! One of the most
sensuous things about you was that I could lie back and let
you drive, and now you're putting me behind the wheel
again. It's just all wrong.

LYMAN: But when you're thirty-six I'll be sixty.

LEAH: Doesn't mean a thing to me.

LYMAN: Dummy, you're not listening; when you're forty-six
I'll be *seventy.*

LEAH: Well it's not eighty.—I've made up my mind, dear.

LYMAN: I thought if we lived together let's say ten years, you'd
still be in the prime, and pretty rich, and I'd . . .

LEAH: . . . Walk away into the sunset?

LYMAN: I'm trying to be as cruelly realistic as life, darling.
Have you ever loved a man the way you love me?

LEAH: No.

LYMAN: Well? That's the only reality.

LEAH: You can drive me to the hospital, if you like realism so
much.

(*She stands. He does.*)

You look so sad! You poor man. (*She kisses him; a silent
farewell is in this kiss; she gets her coat and turns to him.*) I
won't weaken on this, dear, so make up your mind.

LYMAN: We're going to lose each other if you do this. I feel it.

LEAH: Well, there's a very simple way not to lose me, dear, I
guess that's why they invented it.—Come, wait in the hospital if you want to. If not, I'll be back tomorrow.

(*She draws him on, but he halts.*)

LYMAN: Will you give me a week to tell her? It's still early for
you, isn't it?

LEAH: Tell her what?

LYMAN: . . . That I'm going to marry you.

TOM: I see.

(LYMAN *moves into darkness.*)

LEAH: I don't understand it; he'd had dozens of women, why did he pick me to be irreplaceable? (*Looks down at her watch, stares in silence.*) God!—how do I tell my boy?

TOM: He's nine now?

LEAH: And worships Lyman. Worships him.

TOM: I'd better get to the hospital. (*He moves to go, halts hesitantly.*) Don't answer this if you'd rather not, but you think you could ever take him back?

LEAH (*thinks for a moment*): How can you possibly ask me that? It's outrageous.

TOM: I'm terribly sorry. I apologize.

LEAH (*curiosity aroused*): Why?—would Theodora?

TOM: I've no idea.

LEAH: Why do you ask me?

TOM: I've a feeling it could be important.

LEAH: It's impossible. How could I trust him again? (*Slight pause.*) She struck me as a rather judgmental sort of woman. Is she?

TOM: Oh, she has a tender side too.—I guess she hasn't had time to think of the future, any more than you have.

LEAH (*slight pause*): —I could never take him back, but all this reminds me of an idea I used to have about him that . . . well, it'll sound mystical and silly . . .

TOM: Please. I'd love to understand him.

LEAH: Well . . . it's that he *wants* so much; like a kid at a fair; a jelly apple here, a cotton candy there, and then a ride on a loop-the-loop . . . and it never lets up in him; and sometimes it almost seemed as though he'd lived once before, another life that was completely deprived, and this time around he mustn't miss a single thing. And that's what's so attractive about him—to women, I mean—Lyman's mind is up your skirt but it's such a rare thing to be wanted like that—indifference is what most men feel now—I mean they have appetite but not hunger—and here is such a splendidly hungry man and it's simply . . . well . . . precious once you're past twenty-five. I tell you the truth, somewhere deep down I think I sensed something about him wasn't on the level, but . . . I guess I must have loved him so much that I . . . (*Breaks off.*) —But I mustn't talk this way; he's unforgivable! It's the rottenest thing I've ever heard of! The answer is no, absolutely not!

TOM (*nods, thinks, then*): Well, I'll be off. I hope it's not too difficult for you with the little boy. (*He exits.*)

BLACKOUT ON LEAH

LYMAN *is softly snoring; a troubled sleep, however—bad dreams.*

FATHER *appears; smoker's cough announces him in the surrounding dimness.*

FATHER: Stay off the roof—very bad for business the way you fucking all these girls up there. I'm ashamed in front of my brothers. (*Sits on bed.*) Why you talking so much to your mother?—she don't know nothing. She don't want to go Florida with me, she says one state is enough. Stupid woman. I thought a Jewish woman gonna be smart. You both a big disappointment to me. I'm telling you stay off the roof before you make disgrace for the business.

(TOM *enters with* NURSE. *She raises* LYMAN*'s eyelid.* FATHER *disappears, coughing.*)

NURSE: He still goes in and out but you can try him.

TOM: Lyman? Can you hear me?

(LYMAN *stops snoring but eyes remain shut.*)

It's Tom Wilson.

NURSE: Keep going, he shouldn't be staying under this much by now.

LYMAN (*opens his eyes*): *You* in the store?

TOM: It's the hospital.

LYMAN: Hospital? Oh Jesus, right, right . . . (*Trying to focus.*) Give me a second, a little mixed up. How'd you get here?

TOM: Theodora called me.

LYMAN: Theodora?

TOM: Your car is registered in the city so the state police called her.

LYMAN: I had some weird dream that she and Bessie . . . (*Breaks off.*) They're not here, are they?

NURSE: I told you your wife came . . .

TOM (*to* NURSE): Excuse us, please?

NURSE: But I told him. (*She exits.*)

TOM: They've met, Lyman.

LYMAN (*pause. He struggles to orient himself*): Theo . . . didn't collapse, did she?

TOM: Yes, but she's come around, she'll be all right.

LYMAN: I don't understand it, I think I dreamed the whole thing . . .

TOM: Well, that wouldn't be too difficult, it's all pretty inevitable.

LYMAN: Why're you sounding so brutal?

TOM: There's no time to fool around, you've got things to decide. It's all over television . . .

LYMAN: Oh, —Have you met her?—Leah? I'm finished.

TOM: We've had a talk. She's a considerable woman.

LYMAN (*gratefully*): Isn't she?—She's furious, too, huh?

TOM: Well, what do you expect?

LYMAN: See . . . I thought I'd somehow divorce Theo later. —But it sort of settled in where I had both of them. And after a while it didn't seem so godawful . . . What about Bessie?—

TOM: It's hit her pretty bad, I guess.

LYMAN: God, and poor little Benny! Jesus, if I could go through the ceiling and just disappear.

TOM: It's all over the television. I think you ought to issue a press statement to cut the whole thing short. As to your intentions.

LYMAN: What intentions? Just give each of them whatever they want. I'll probably go and live somewhere . . . maybe like Brazil or something . . .

TOM: You won't try to hold onto either of them.

LYMAN: Are you mad? They wouldn't have anything to do with me. My God . . . (*He turns away, tears in his eyes.*) How could I have destroyed everything like this!—my fucking character! (*Higher intensity*): Why did I drive into that storm!—I can't understand it! I had the room in the Howard Johnson's, I think I was even in bed . . .

TOM: Maybe it'll clear up. —Can you give Theo a few minutes? She wants to say goodbye.

LYMAN: How can I face her? Ask her to wait till tomorrow, maybe I'll feel a little better and . . .

(THEODORA *and* BESSIE *enter;* LYMAN *does not see them as they are above him.*)

TOM: They're here, Lyman.

(LYMAN *closes his eyes, breathing fast.* BESSIE, *holding* THE-ODORA *by the elbow, accompanies her to the bedside.*)

BESSIE (*whispering in some shock*): Look at his bandages! (*Turning away.*) Oh, Mother!

THEO: Stop that. (*Bending to* LYMAN.) Lyman? (*He can't get himself to speak.*) It's Theodora.

LYMAN (*opening his eyes*): Hi.

THEO: How are you feeling?

LYMAN: Not too bad now. I hope I make sense with all this painkiller. . . . Is that you, Bessie?

BESSIE: I'm only here because of Mother.

LYMAN: Oh. Okay. I'm sorry, Bess—I mean that my character's so bad. But I'm proud that you have enough strength to despise me.

BESSIE: But who wouldn't?

LYMAN: Good! (*His voice starts to break but he controls himself.*) That was well-spoken, sweety.

BESSIE (*with quick anger*): Don't call me that . . .

THEO (*to* BESSIE): Sshh! (*She has been observing him in silence.*) Lyman?—is it true?

(*He closes his eyes.*)

I have to hear it from you. Did you marry that woman?

(*Deep snores emerge from the head bandage.*)

(*more urgently*): Lyman?

BESSIE (*points*): He's not really sleeping!

THEO: Did you have a child with that woman? Lyman? I insist!!

(LYMAN *emerges from the upstage side of the bed, hands clapped to his ears, while the figure in the cast remains as it was. He is in a hospital gown, but unbandaged.*

Light change: an ethereal colorlessness now, air devoid of pigment.)

LYMAN (*agonized cry, ears still covered*): I hear you!

(THEO *continues to address the cast's bandaged head, and* BESSIE *is fixed on it as well, but her attitude has become formalized as she becomes a part of his vision—everything is now superemphatically threatening to him.*)

THEO: What in God's name have you done!

(*Almost writhing in conflict,* LYMAN *clears his throat. He remains a distance upstage of the bed.*)

BESSIE (*bent over the head of the cast*): Ssh! He's saying something!

LYMAN: I realize . . . how crazy it sounds, Theodora. . . . (*Breaks off.*)

THEO: Yes?

LYMAN: . . . I'm not really sure, but . . . I wonder if this crash . . . was maybe to sort of subconsciously . . . get you both to . . . meet one another, finally.

THEO (*with disgust*): Meet *her?*

LYMAN: I know it sounds absurd but . . .

THEO: Absurd!—it's disgusting! She's exactly the type who forgets to wash out her panties.

LYMAN (*wincing, but with a certain pleasurable recognition*): I *knew* you'd say that!—I admit it, though, there *is* a sloppy side to her . . .

THEO: She's the worst generation in our history—screw anybody in pants, then drop their litters like cats, and spout mystic credos on cosmic responsibility, ecology and human rights!

LYMAN: To my dying day I will stand amazed at your ability to speak in complete paragraphs!

THEO: I insist you explain this to me yourself. Lyman? Lyman!

(LEAH *enters.* THEO *reacts instantly.*)

There'll be no one in here but the family! (*To* BESSIE): Get the nurse!

LEAH (*despite* THEO, *approaches the cast, but with uncertainty about his reaction to her*): Lyman?

THEO (*to* TOM): Get her out of here!

(TOM *is immobile, and she goes to him furiously.*)

She does not belong here!

LEAH (*to the cast . . . with a certain warmth*): It's me, Lyme. Can you hear me?

THEO (*rushing threateningly toward* LEAH): Get out, get out, get out . . . !
> (*Just as she is about to lay hands on* LEAH, LYMAN *throws his arms up and cries out imploringly.*)

LYMAN: I want everybody to lie down!
> (*The three women instantly de-animate as though suddenly falling under the urgency of his control.* LYMAN *gestures, without actually touching them, and causes* LEAH *and* THEO *to lie on the bed.*)

LEAH (*as she lies down; voice soft, remote*): What am I going to tell Benny? Oh gee whiz, Lyman, why did you . . . ?

THEO (*lying down beside* LEAH): You have a bitter smell, you should use something.

LEAH: I have, but he likes it.

THEO: Blah. (*To* LYMAN): And what would you say if one of us took another man to bed and asked you to lie next to him?

LYMAN (*lifting off her glasses*): Oh, I'd kill him, dear; but you're a lady, Theodora; the delicate sculpture of your noble eye, your girlish faith in me and your disillusion; your idealism and your unadmitted greed for wealth; the awkward tenderness of your wooden fingers, your incurably Protestant cooking; your savoir-faire and your sexual inexperience; your sensible shoes and devoted motherhood, your intolerant former radicalism and stalwart love of country now—your Theodorism! Who can ever take your place!

LEAH (*laughing*): Why am I laughing!!

LYMAN: Because you're a fucking anarchist, my darling! (*He stretches out over both of them.*) Oh what pleasure, what intensity! Your countercurrents are like bare live wires! (*Kisses each in turn.*) I'd have no problem defending both of you to the death! Oh the double heat of two blessed wives—this is heaven! (*Rests his head on* LEAH *while holding* THEO*'s hand to his cheek.*)

LEAH: Listen, you've got to make up your mind about something.

LYMAN: I'm only delaying as long as possible, let's delay it all till we die! Delay, delay, how delicious, my loving Leah, is delay!

THEO (*sits up*): How you can still go on talking about love is beyond my understanding.

LYMAN: And still I love you, Theodora, although certain parts of your body fill me with *rage!*

THEO: So you simply got yourself some other parts instead.

(LEAH, *still lying on her back, raises one leg in air, and her skirt slides down exposing her thigh.*)

LYMAN (*replying to* THEODORA, *kissing* LEAH's *thigh*): That's the truth, yes—at least it was all flesh at first.

LEAH (*stretching out her arms and her body*): Oh how good that was! I'm still pulsing to the tips of my toes. (*Stands, comes up to him.*) You're really healthy, aren't you.

LYMAN (*wry attempt*): You mean for my age?—yes.

LEAH: I did *not* mean that!

(*He links arms and they walk; the others go dark while bright sunlight hits them.*)

LYMAN: My health is terrific; in fact, it keeps threatening my dignity.

(*They sit—as on a park bench.*)

LEAH: Why!

LYMAN: Well, how do I come to be lounging in a park with a girl, and on a working day! I really hadn't planned to do that this afternoon. Did you know I was going to?

LEAH: No . . . but I never do.

LYMAN: Really? But you seem so organized.

LEAH: In business; but not in pleasure.

LYMAN: What surprised me was the openness of your laughter with those heavy executives at the table.

LEAH: Well, your presentation was so funny. I'd heard you were a real brain, not a comic.

LYMAN: Well, insurance is basically comical, isn't it?—at least pathetic.

LEAH: Why?

LYMAN: You're buying immortality, aren't you?—reaching up out of the grave to pay the bills, remind people of your love? It's poetry. The soul was once immortal, now we've got an insurance policy.

LEAH: You sound pretty cynical about it.

LYMAN: Not at all—I started as a writer, nobody lusts after the immortal like a writer.

LEAH: How'd you get into insurance?

LYMAN: Pure accident. How'd you?

LEAH: My mother had died, my dad had his stroke, and insurance was something I could do from home. Dad knew a lot of people, being a doctor, so the thing just took off.

LYMAN: Don't take this wrong—but you know what I find terrifically sexy about you?

LEAH: What?

LYMAN: Your financial independence. Horrible, huh?

LEAH: Why? (*Wryly*—) Whatever helps, helps.

LYMAN: You don't sound married, are you?

LEAH: It's a hell of a time to ask!

(*They laugh, come closer.*)

I can't see myself getting married . . . not yet anyway.—Incidentally, have you been listening to me?

LYMAN: Yes, but my attention keeps wandering toward a warm and furry place . . .

(*She laughs, delighted.*)

It's funny; my generation got married to show its maturity, yours stays single for the same reason.

LEAH: That's good!

LYMAN: How happy I am! (*Sniffs his hands.* . . .) Sitting in Elmira in the sun with you, and your scent still on my hands! God!—all the different ways there are to try to be real!

LEAH: What do you mean by that?

LYMAN: I don't know the connection, but when I turned twenty I sold three poems to *The New Yorker* and a story to *Harper's*, and the first thing I bought was a successful blue suit to impress my father how real I was even though a writer. He ran an appetizer store on Fortieth Street and Ninth Avenue, Middle Eastern specialties . . . you know, olives, grape leaves . . . all kinds of wonderful-smelling realities. (*Grinning, near laughter.*) And he sees the suit and says, "How much you pay?" And I said, "Twenty-nine-fifty," thinking I'd got a terrific bargain. And he says, "Pray God keep an eye on you the rest of you life."

LEAH (*laughs*): That's awful!

LYMAN: No!—it spurred me on. (*Laughs.*) He had two pieces of wisdom—never trust anybody, and never forgive.—Funny, it's like magic, I simply can't trace how we got into that bed.

LEAH (*a glance at her watch*): I really have to get back to the office.—But is Lyman an Albanian name?

LYMAN: Lyman's the judge's name in Wooster, Mass., who gave my father his citizenship. Felt is short for Feltman, my mother's name because my father's was unpronounceable and they wanted a successful American for a son.

LEAH: Then your mother was Jewish.

LYMAN: And the source of all my conflicts. In the Jewish heart is a lawyer and a judge, in the Albanian a bandit defying the government with a knife.

LEAH: What a surprise you are! (*She stands, and he does.*)

LYMAN: Being so silly?

LEAH: Being so interesting, and in the insurance business.

LYMAN (*taking her hand*): When was the moment?—I'm just curious.

LEAH: I don't know . . . I guess at the conference table I suddenly thought, "He's basically talking to me." But then I figured, this is probably why he's such a great salesman, because everybody he talks to feels loved.

LYMAN: You know?—I've never before with a Jewish girl.

LEAH: Well, you're my first Albanian.

LYMAN: There's something venerable in your eyes. Not old— ancient. Like our peoples.

LEAH (*touches his cheek*): Take care, dear.

LYMAN (*as she passes before him to leave, he takes her hand*): Why do I feel I know nothing at all about you?

LEAH (*shrugs, smiles*): Maybe you weren't listening . . . which I don't mind if it's in a good cause.

LYMAN (*letting go her hand*): I walk in the valley of your thighs. (*She laughs, gives him a quick kiss.*)
    When you move away now, would you turn back to me for a moment?

LEAH (*amused*): Sure, why?

LYMAN (*half-kidding his romanticism*): I have to take a small commuter plane and if I die I want that vision as I go down—

LEAH (*backing away with a wave*): 'Bye, Lyman . . .

LYMAN: Can I ask who that fellow was banging on your apartment door?

LEAH (*caught off-guard*): Somebody I used to go with . . . he was angry, that's all.

LYMAN: Are you afraid of him?

LEAH (*shrugs in an accepted uncertainty*): See you, dear. (*She turns and walks a few yards, then halts and turns her head to look back at him over her shoulder.*)

LYMAN: Beautiful.

(*She exits.*)

(*Alone*): Miraculous. (*Thinks for a moment.*) Still . . . was it really all *that* great? (*A phone is lit up, he goes to it, picks it up, troubled.*) Theo?—hi, darling, I'm just about to take off. Oh, definitely, it has the makings of a much bigger operation; had a talk with Aetna's chief rep here, and she's agreed to take us on, so I'll probably be spending more time here. —Yes, a woman; she's got a great agency, I might try to buy into her.—Listen, dear, how about you flying up here and we rent a car and drive through the Cherry Valley—it's all bursting into bloom now!—Oh, I forgot; no-no, you'd better go to your meeting then, it's okay; no, it just suddenly hit me how quickly it's all going by and . . . You ever have the feeling that you never got to really *know* anybody?

(*She never has; he resents it, and a sharpness enters his voice.*) Well, yes, I do feel that sometimes, very much; I feel I'm going to vanish without a trace. (*Unhappily now, with hidden anger, the romance gone.*) Theo, dear, it's nothing against you, I only meant that with all the analysis and the novels and the Freuds we're still as opaque and unknowable as some line of statues in a church wall.

(*He hangs up. Now light strikes the cast on the bed. He moves to it and looks down at himself.* BESSIE, THEO *and* LEAH *are standing motionless around the bed and* TOM *is off to one side, observing.* LYMAN *slowly lifts his arms and raises his face like a supplicant.*)

We're all in a cave . . .

(*The three women now begin to move, ever so slightly at first; their heads turning as they appear to be searching for the sight of something far away or overhead or on the floor.*)

. . . where we entered to make love or money or fame. It's dark in here, as dark as sleep, and each one moves blindly, searching for another; to touch, hoping to touch and afraid; and hoping, and afraid.

(*As he speaks, the women and* TOM *move in criss-crossing, serpentine paths, just missing one another, spreading out further and further across the stage until one by one they disappear.* LYMAN *has moved above the bed where his cast lies.*)

So now . . . now that we're here . . . what are we going to say? (*He bends and enters his cast.*)

(*Light change: pigment and the air of the present reality return.*

TOM appears with the NURSE. They come to the cast and she examines LYMAN, bending close to his face exactly as she did at her first entrance at the beginning of the scene, lifting his eyelid, etc.)

NURSE: He still goes in and out but you can try him. Come dear, doctor doesn't want you staying under too long.

TOM: Lyman? Theo wants to come in to say goodbye.

(*THEO enters with BESSIE and comes to the bed.*)

THEO: Lyman? Did you marry that woman? I insist you explain this to me yourself! I insist!

(*LEAH enters. THEO reacts instantly.*)

I'll have no one but the family in this room!

(*LEAH proceeds anyway.*)

Get out, get out, get out! (*As she nears LEAH to strike her . . .*)

LYMAN (*an animal outcry from his very bowel. It stops THEO, and all turn to look at him as he lies there panting for breath. Now he turns to look at them all*): My God!—*again*?

THEO (*quietly to TOM, mystified*): What did he say?

BLACKOUT

ACT TWO

The hospital waiting room. TOM *seated with* THEODORA.

TOM: Really, Theo, I wish you'd let Bessie take you back to the city.

THEO: Please stop repeating that! (*Slight pause.*) I need to talk to him . . . I'll never see him again. I can't simply walk away. Is my head trembling?

TOM: A little, maybe. Should you let one of the doctors look at you?

THEO: I'll be all right, my family has a tendency to tremors, I've had it for years when I'm tense. What time is it?

TOM: Give them a few minutes more.—You seem pale.

THEO (*pressing fingers against her temples to steady herself*): When you spoke with this woman . . . was there any feeling about . . . what she has in mind?

TOM: She's as much in shock as you. The child was her main concern.

THEO: Really. Somehow I wouldn't have thought so.

TOM: Oh, I think he means everything to her.

THEO (*begrudgingly*): Well, that's nice. Messes like this are basically comical, aren't they—until you come to the children. I'm very worried about Bessie. She lies there staring at the ceiling. She can hardly talk without starting to weep. He's been her . . . her world. (*She begins to fill up.*) —You're right; I think I'll go. It just seemed unfinished, somehow . . . but maybe it's better to leave it this way . . . (*She starts for her bag, stops.*) I don't know what to do. One minute I could kill him, the next I wonder if some . . . aberration got into him . . .

(LEAH *enters. They did not expect to see each other. A momentary pause.* LEAH *sits.*)

LEAH: Good morning.

TOM: Good morning.

(*Awkward silence.*)

LEAH (*asking*): He's not in his room.

THEO (*as it is difficult for her to address* LEAH, *she turns to her only slowly*): They're treating his eye.

234

LEAH: His eye?

TOM: It's nothing serious, he tried to climb out his window during the night. Probably in his sleep. His eyelid was slightly scratched by a rhododendron.

THEO (*making a stab at communication*): He must not have realized he's on the ground floor.

(*Short pause.*)

LEAH: Hm! That's interesting, because a friend of ours, Ted Colby, called last night—he's commander of the state police here. They'd put up a wooden barrier across the Mount Morgan road when it got so icy; and he thinks Lyman moved the barrier aside.

TOM: How could they know it was him?

LEAH: There was only one set of tire tracks in the snow.

THEO: Oh my God.

LEAH: He's worried about him. They're good friends, they go hunting together.

THEO: Lyman hunts?

LEAH: Oh sure.

(THEO *shakes her head incredulously.*)

—But I can't imagine him in that kind of depression, can you?

TOM: Actually . . . yes, I think I can.

LEAH: Really. He's always seemed so . . . up with me, and happy.

(THEO *glances at her, irked, then away.* LEAH *glances at her watch.*)

I just have to settle some business with him for a few minutes, I won't be in your way.

THEO: *My* way? You're free to do anything you like, as far as I'm concerned.

LEAH (*slightly taken aback*): Yes . . . the same with me . . . in your case. (*A beat.*) —I mean as far as I'm concerned. (*The hostility turns her to look at her wristwatch again.*) I want to tell you . . . I almost feel worse for you, somehow, than for myself.

THEO (*gives a hard laugh*): Why! Do I seem *that* old?

(*The second rebuff stiffens* LEAH.)

I shouldn't have said that. I apologize. I'm exhausted.

LEAH (*letting it pass*): How is your daughter?—she still here?

THEO (*a hostile color despite everything*): In the motel. She's devastated.

TOM: Your boy taking it all right?

LEAH: No, it's wracked him, it's terrible. (*To* THEO): I thought Lyman might have some idea how to deal with him, the kid's always idolized him so. I'm really at my wits' end.

THEO (*bitterly angry, but contained*): We are his dust; we billow up behind his steps and settle again when he passes by. Billie Holiday . . . (*She touches her forehead.*) I can't recall when she died, it's quite a while, isn't it.

TOM: Billie Holiday? Why?

(TOM *and* LEAH *observe, puzzled, as* THEO *stares in silence. Then . . .*)

LEAH: Why don't I come back in a couple of hours—I've got a nine o'clock conference call and it's getting a bit late . . . (*She stands, goes to* THEO, *and, extending her hand*): Well, if we don't meet again . . .

THEO (*briefly touching her hand, hostility momentarily overcome*): . . . Do you understand this?

LEAH: It's baffling. He's raced the Mount Morgan road, he knows what it's like even in summer.

THEO: Raced? You mean cars?

LEAH: Sure. He has a Lotus and a Z. He had a Ferrari, but he totaled it.

(THEO *turns and stares at space.*)

I was thinking before . . .

THEO: He's always been terrified of speed; he never drives over sixty . . .

LEAH: . . . He reminds me of a frog . . .

THEO: A frog?

LEAH: . . . I mean you never know when you look at a frog whether it's the same one you just saw or a different one. (*To* TOM): When you talk to him—the television is hounding us; he really has to make a definite statement to stop all this stupid speculation.

THEO: What speculation?

LEAH: You've seen the *Daily News*, haven't you?

THEO: What!

LEAH: We're both on the front page with a headline . . .

TOM (*to* THEO, *placating*): It's unimportant . . .

THEO (*to* LEAH): What's the headline?

LEAH: "Who Gets Lyman?"

THEO: How dare they!

TOM: Don't be upset, I'll get a statement from him this morning . . .

LEAH: Goodbye, Mrs. . . . (*Stops herself; a short laugh.*) I was going to call you Mrs. Felt but . . . (*Correcting again.*) . . . Well you are, aren't you—I guess I'm the one who's not! I'll come by about ten or so. (*She exits.*)

THEO: She wants him back, doesn't she.

TOM: Why?

THEO (*gives a bitter little laugh*): Didn't you hear it?—she's the only one he was happy with!

TOM: Oh, I don't think she meant . . .

THEO (*fiercely*): That's *all* she meant; there's something vulgar about that woman.—I pity her, though—with such a young child. (*She fumes in silence.*) *Can* it have been suicide?

TOM: Frankly, in a way I'd almost hope so.

THEO: . . . It would indicate a moral conscience, is that what you mean?

TOM: Well, I'd hate to think all this duplicity meant nothing to him.

THEO: Unless his mind simply shattered. The Lyman I know could no more hunt animals and drive racing cars than . . .

TOM: I don't know, maybe he just wanted to change his life; do things he'd never done; be a completely different person . . .

THEO (*stares for a moment*): . . . Maybe not so different.

TOM: How do you mean?

THEO (*a long hesitation*): I don't know why I'm still trying to protect him—he tried to kill me once.

TOM: You're not serious.

> (LYMAN *appears in sunlight in swim trunks, inhaling deeply on a boat deck. She begins walking toward him.*)

THEO: Oh yes! I didn't know this woman existed then, but I see now it was just about the time they had either married or were on the verge. (*As she moves toward* LYMAN, *her coat slides off, revealing herself in a swimsuit.*) He seemed very strange, unreal. We'd gone for a two-day sail off Montauk . . .

> (LYMAN *is doing breathing exercises.*)

LYMAN: The morning mist rising from the sea is always like the first day of the world . . . the "oysterygods and the visigods . . ."

(THEO *enters into his acting area.*)

THEO (*Finnegans Wake*): Like some tea, dear?

LYMAN: Great!—yes! (*Kneels, tunes a radio; static as she makes tea.*) I'll get the weather. Is that a new suit?—it's sexy as hell.

THEO: Two years ago. You bought it for me in San Diego.

LYMAN (*mimes pistol to his head*): Bang.

ANNOUNCER (*voice over*): . . . Due to the unusually warm spring tides there've been several shark sightings off Montauk . . . one is reported to be twelve to fourteen feet long . . .

(*Heavy static intervenes;* LYMAN *mimes switching radio off.*)

LYMAN: Jesus.

THEO: Oh, that's ridiculous, it's only May! Watch the tea water, will you? I'm going in for a dip . . . (*She looks over into the ocean.*)

LYMAN: But the man said . . .

THEO: Nonsense. I've sailed around here since my childhood, and father did and grandfather—there are never sharks till July if at all, the water's much too cold. Come in with me?

LYMAN (*resentfully smiling*): I'm the Mediterranean type— we're unreliable and hate cold water. But go ahead, I'll wait here and admire you.

THEO: Darling, I'm allowed to say that sharks are impossible this time of year, aren't I?

LYMAN (*strained laugh at the outrageousness*): I know I shouldn't say this, Theo, but how you can hang onto your convictions in the face of a report like that . . . just seems . . . I don't know—fanatical.

THEO (*with a hard, determined laugh*): Now that is really uncalled for! You're just as stubborn as I am when you're committed to something.

LYMAN: Goddammit, you're right! And I love your convictions! You're just great, honey—(*swings an arm around her*)—go ahead, I'll keep an eye out.

THEO (*with loving laughter*): You simply can't stand me contradicting you, darling, but it's the best exercise for your character.

LYMAN (*laughs, with her, points front*): Right! And a miserable character it is. Into the ocean! (*He leaves her side, scans ocean.*)

THEO (*bends to dive*): On the mark . . . get set . . .

LYMAN (*points leftward*): What's that out there?

THEO: No, sharks always move, that's a log.

LYMAN: Okay, go ahead, jump in.

THEO: I'll run in! Wait, let me warm up. (*Backs up to make a run for it.*) Join me!—come on.

LYMAN: I can't dear, I fear death.

    (*She is behind him, running in place. His back is to her and his eye now catches sight of something toward the right-front; his mouth drops open, eyes staring in horror following the moving shark. She bends to start her run.*)

THEO: Okay, one . . . and a two . . . and a . . . three!

    (*She runs and as she comes abreast of him he suddenly reaches out and stops her at the edge.*)

LYMAN: Stop!

    (*He points front; she looks, horror rising in her face as their eyes follow the fish.*)

THEO: My God, the *size* of him! Ahhh . . . !

    (*She bursts into tears of released terror; he takes her into his arms.*)

LYMAN: Honey . . . when are you going to believe something I say!

THEO: Oh, I'm going to be sick . . . !

    (*About to vomit, she bends and rushes into darkness. Light goes out on* LYMAN *and up on* TOM *in the waiting room; he is staring ahead, listening. The light widens and finds* THEO *standing in her fur coat.*)

TOM: That sounds like he saved you.

THEO: Yes, I've always tried to think of it that way, too, but I have to face everything now—(*coming downstage; newly distressed by the memory*)—it was not quite the top of his voice. I mean it wasn't . . .

    (*Light flares up on* LYMAN *in trunks. At top voice and in horror, he shouts . . .*)

LYMAN: Stop!! (*He stands mesmerized looking at the shark below. Blackout on him.*)

THEO: . . . It was more like . . .

(*Light flares up on* LYMAN *again, and he merely semi-urgently—as he did in the scene—shouts . . .*)

LYMAN: Stop.

Blackout LYMAN

THEO: I tell you he was on the verge of letting me go.

TOM: You're angry now, Theo, and I don't think you really believe that. I mean how could you have gone on living with him?

THEO: Well, we did have two serious breakups and . . . months have gone by without—relations. (*An embarrassed, determined smile as she gradually becomes furious.*) No, dammit, I'm not going to evade that question.—How I've gone on? Maybe I'm corrupt, Tom. I wasn't, once, but who knows, now? He's rich, isn't he? And vastly respected, and what would I do with myself alone? Why does anybody stay together, once they've realized who they're with? (*Suddenly livid.*) What the hell am I hanging around here for? This is the stupidest thing I've ever done in my life! (*Indignantly grabs her bag.*)

TOM: You love him, Theo. (*Physically stops her.*) Please go home, will you? And give it a few weeks before you decide anything? (*A silence. Then she stifles a sob as he embraces her.*) I know how crazy this sounds, but part of him worships you. I'm sure of it.

THEO (*suddenly screams into his face*): I hate him.

(*I hate him! She is rigid, pale, and he grips her shoulders to steady her. A pause.*)

—I must lie down. I just have to know what happened, as long as I'm here. We'll probably go back to the city by noon.— Or maybe I'll just leave, I don't know. Call me if he wakes up soon. (*She passes her hand across her brow.*) I feel I look strange.

TOM: Just tired. Come, I'll find you a cab . . .

THEO: It's only a few blocks, I need the air. (*Starting off, turns back.*) How beautiful the country still is up here—it's kind of surprising that it hasn't been ruined! (*She exits.*)

(*Alone,* TOM *stands staring into space, arms folded, trying to figure an approach.*)

BLACKOUT

LYMAN's *room. He is deeply asleep, snoring placidly at first. Now he starts muttering.*

NURSE: Whyn't you take some time off? You do more work asleep than most of us does awake. You ought to come up fishing with us sometime, that'll slow you down.

(NURSE *goes out. Now there is a tensing up, he is groaning in his sleep.* LEAH *and* THEODORA *appear on either side of him, but on elevated platforms, like two stone deities; they are in kitchen aprons, wifely ribbons tying up their hair. But something menacing about their deathly stillness as the sepulchral dream-light finds them, motionless in this tableau. After a long moment they animate. As in life they are reserved, each measuring herself against the other.*

Notwithstanding the humor of some of their remarks, their manner of speaking is godlike, deathly.)

THEO: I wouldn't mind at all if you did some of the cooking, I'm not all that super.

LEAH (*generously*): I hear you make good desserts, though.

THEO: Apple cobbler, yes; gingerbread with whipped cream. (*Gaining confidence.*) And exceptional waffles for breakfast, with real maple syrup, although he's had to cut out the sausages.

LEAH: I can do potato pancakes and segadina goulash.

THEO (*disapproving*): And all that *paprika?*

LEAH: It has to be blended in, of course.

THEO (*at a loss, sensing a defeat*): Ah, blended in! I'm afraid I couldn't do something like that.

LEAH (*smiling, brutally pressing her advantage*): Oh yes, blended in and blended really *in!* And my gefilte fish is feather-light. (*Clapping her cupped palms together.*) I wet my hands and keep patting it and patting it till it shapes up just perfect!

THEO (*struggling with loss*): He does love my glazed ham. Yes!—and my boiled tongue. (*A sudden bright idea.*) Custard!

LEAH (*generously*): You can do all the custard and glazed ham and I'll do all the gefilte fish and goulash . . . *and* the blending in.

THEO: But may I do *some?* Once or twice a month, perhaps?

LEAH: Let's leave it up to him—some months you can do more . . .

THEO: Yes!—and some months you.

LEAH: 'Kay! Would you wash out my pants?

THEO: Certainly. As long as he tells me my lies.

LEAH: Good! Then you'll have your lies and I'll have mine!

LEAH and THEO: Hurrah for the menu!

LEAH (*filled with admiration*): You certainly have class!

> (LYMAN *chuckles in his sleep as they come together downstage of the cast and embrace each other warmly; and arm in arm walk upstage to his bed. Each kneebends on opposite sides of the bed, resting her chin on the mattress and staring at him from both sides. He changes . . .*
>
> *He begins to pant in anxiety, as though imprisoned by their threatening stares. Now each gently but surely grasps one of his hands and sucks on one of his fingers. He writhes in terror, gasping for breath and shouting incoherently. The women stand and go into darkness.*
>
> *A black cloth bundle, unobtrusive on the floor, stirs and he bends over the edge of the bed and looks down at it. From it a lighter flares, lighting a cigarette;* FATHER *sits up and coughs quietly, then inhales the cigarette.*)

FATHER: Stupid. Very bad for business.

> (LYMAN *slips out of the cast, picks up a broad-brimmed Panama hat from the floor and defiantly mimes urinating into it; then with a certain anticipation of violence offers it to* FATHER *who snatches it out of his hands angrily.*)

(*looking into the hat*): What you do here?

> (LYMAN, *defiance weakening, becomes intensely embarrassed and grips his crotch. Tries to get behind the bed, but* FATHER *stands and begins to stalk him, the broad black cloth trailing behind him.*
>
> *A rhythmic, profound sounding as from the center of the earth.*)

You piss in you father's hat, you son of a bitch? You Communist, something?

LYMAN: No-no, Pa!—pumpkin pie!

FATHER: Pumpkin pie? You think you gonna be an American? *You? American?* You make me laugh? (*Looks into his hat.*)

How I gonna tip my hat to the customers, full of piss? Very bad for business!

LYMAN (*hopefully enticing*): Fifty thousand dollars?

FATHER: And how you pay me back? More piss? (*Stands with the help of a walking stick, raises the cloth with both hands.*) All you can do?—Piss in your father's hat?! I catch you I show you something . . . !

> (*He tries to throw the black cloth over* LYMAN*'s head,* LYMAN *skitters away.*)

LYMAN: Don't, Pa, please . . . !

FATHER (*points with stick at* LYMAN*'s penis*): Why everything on you sticks out?

> (LYMAN *climbs into his cast with little frightened cries.* FA-THER *now starts viciously pounding the stick on the bed; with each blow a booming sound resonates as from deep in the earth* . . .)

Stay off the roof with those American girls! All whores, these American girls! Very bad for business!

> (LYMAN *is crying out in terror as the* NURSE *hurries in* . . . *and* FATHER *disappears into darkness* . . . *coughing, the black cloth trailing behind him.*)

Get off the roof, you got no respect, you stupid?

> (*Underground sound stops.* NURSE, *carrying a bowl of water and cloth, heads straight for the cast. She takes his hand, patting it as he whimpers.*)

NURSE: All right now, let's come back, come on, dear, come on back . . .

> (*He stops struggling and opens his eyes.*)

LYMAN: Wah. Oh. What dreams. God, how I'd like to be dead.

NURSE: Don't start feeling sorry for yourself; you know what they say—come down off the cross, they need the wood.

LYMAN: I'm suffocating, can't you open a window?

NURSE: Not anymore, I can't.

LYMAN: Huh?—Oh, listen, that's ridiculous, I wasn't trying to climb out, it was just those pills got me crazy . . .

NURSE: Well, maybe later. I got to wash you up now. Your lawyer's asking can he come in . . .

LYMAN: I thought he'd gone back to New York. I look terrible?

NURSE (*swabbing his face and hands*): You takin' it too hard. Be different if you deserted those women, but anybody can see how well taken care of they are . . .

LYMAN: Go on, you don't kid me, Logan—underneath all this cool you know you're shocked as hell.

NURSE: Go on, brush your teeth. (*As he does*): The last shock I had come off a short in my vacuum cleaner . . .

(*He laughs, then groans in pain.*)

One thing I *have* been wondering, though.

LYMAN: What've you been wondering?

NURSE: Whatever got into you to actually marry that woman?— man as smart as you?

LYMAN: Were you talking about ice before?

NURSE: Ice? Oh, you mean . . . ya, we go ice fishing on the lake, me and my husband and my boy.—You're remembering a lot better now.

LYMAN (*staring*): —I've never not been married, you know. I have a feeling it's going to be like suddenly your case has been dismissed and you don't have to be in court anymore.

NURSE: Don't you talk about those women; they don't look mean to me.

LYMAN: She had a fantastic smell; Leah smelled like a ripe, pink, slightly musty cantaloupe. I just never felt such jealousy, and I've known a lot of women. And her smile—when she showed her teeth her clothes seemed to drop off. We had some prehistoric kind of connection—I swear, if a hundred women walked past me on a sidewalk I could pick out the clack of her heels. I even loved lying in bed listening to the quiet splash of her bath water. And of course slipping into her soft cathedral . . .

NURSE: You have the dirtiest mind I ever seen on an educated man.

LYMAN: I couldn't lose her, Logan. I couldn't lose her. I could not lose her, and that's why I married her. And those are all good reasons, unless you're married already.

NURSE: I'll get your lawyer, okay?

(*He seems suddenly overcome, weeps.*)

Now don't you start that cryin' again . . .

LYMAN: It's just my children . . . you can't imagine how they respected me . . . (*Bracing himself.*) But nobody's any better, goddammit!

(TOM WILSON *enters.*)

TOM: May I come in?

LYMAN (*uncertainty, trying to read* TOM): Hi! I thought you'd gone back—something happen?

TOM: Can we talk?

(NURSE *exits.*)

LYMAN: If you can bear it. (*Grins.*) You despise me, Tom?

TOM: I'm still staggering, I don't know what I think.

LYMAN: Sure you do, but that's okay. (*His charming grin.*) What's up?

TOM: I've been discussing things with the women . . .

LYMAN: I can't bear talking about them—I thought I told you—or did I?—just give them what they want. Within reason, I mean.

TOM: That's the thing—I'm not sure they know what they want.

LYMAN: Go on—they want to kill me, don't they?

TOM: Oh, no doubt about *that*, but . . . I really believe Theo'd like to find a way to forgive you.

LYMAN: Oh no!—that's impossible!

TOM: She's a great spirit, Lyman.

LYMAN: . . . Not that great; I'd have to live on my knees the rest of my life.

TOM: Maybe not—if you were clear about yourselves and came to an understanding . . .

LYMAN: I'm pretty clear now—I'm a selfish son of a bitch. But I have loved the truth.

TOM: And what's the truth?

LYMAN: A man can be faithful to himself or to other people— but not to both. At least not happily. We all know this, but it's immoral to admit it—the first law of life is betrayal; why else did those rabbis pick Cain and Abel to open the Bible?

TOM: But the Bible doesn't end there, does it.

LYMAN: Jesus Christ? I can't worship self-denial; excuse me, but it's just not true for me. We're all ego, kid, ego plus an occasional prayer.

TOM: Then why'd you bother building one of the most socially responsible companies in America?

LYMAN: The truth? I did that twenty-five years ago, when I was still trying to deny my unrighteousness. But I don't deny anything anymore.—What should I say to them, Tom? What should I do?

TOM: Am I wrong?—you seem deeply depressed.

LYMAN: I dread seeing them again. Especially Bessie. I absolutely can't bear the thought of her . . . Advise me, tell me something.

TOM: Maybe you ought to give up trying to seem so strong. (*Slight pause.*)

LYMAN: What do you want me to say, I'm a loser?

TOM: Well? Right now—aren't you?

LYMAN: Well . . . no, goddammit. A loser has lived somebody else's life, I've lived my own; crappy as it may seem, it's mine. And I'm no worse than anybody else!—Now answer that, and don't kid me.

TOM: All right, I won't kid you; I think you've done these women terrible harm.

LYMAN: You do.

TOM: Theo especially. I think you've raked her soul. If you want to get off this dime you're on I'd begin by confronting that.

LYMAN: I've also given her an interesting life, a terrific daughter, and made her very rich. I mean, exactly what harm are you talking about?

TOM: Lyman, you deceived her . . .

LYMAN (*fury overtaking him*): But she couldn't have had all that if I hadn't deceived her!—you know as well as I that nobody could live with Theo for more than a month without some relief! I've suffered at least as much as she has in this fucking marriage!

TOM (*demurring*): Well . . .

LYMAN: . . . Now listen, you want the rock-bottom truth?—I curse the day I ever laid eyes on her and I don't *want* her forgiveness!

TOM: For Pete's sake don't get angry . . .

LYMAN: All right, I ever tell you how we met?—let's stop talking as though this marriage was made in heaven, for Christ's sake!—I was hitchhiking back from Cornell; nineteen innocent years of age; I'm standing beside the road with my suitcase, and I have to take a leak. So I leave the suitcase and go behind a bush. This minister sees the suitcase and stops, gives me a ride and I end up at an Audubon Society picnic where, lo and behold, I meet his daughter, Theodora.—Had I taken that suitcase with me behind the bush I'd never have met her! —And serious people still go around looking for the moral purpose of the universe.

TOM: Give or take a bad patch or two, you've had the best marriage of anyone I ever met.

LYMAN (*a sigh*): I know.—Look, we're all the same; a man is a fourteen-room house—in the bedroom he's asleep with his intelligent wife, in the living room he's rolling around with some bare-ass girl, in the library he's paying his taxes, in the yard he's raising tomatoes, and in the cellar he's making a bomb to blow it all up. And nobody's different . . . Except you, maybe. Are you?

TOM: I don't raise tomatoes . . . Listen, the TV is flogging the story and it's humiliating for the women; let's settle on a statement and be done with it. What do you want?

LYMAN: What I always wanted; both of them.

TOM: Be serious . . .

LYMAN: I know those women and they still love me! It's only what they think they're *supposed* to feel that's confusing them.—Do I sound crazy?

TOM: There's something else we have to discuss . . .

LYMAN: —What's Leah saying . . . anything?

TOM: She's stunned. But frankly, I'm not sure she's out of the question either . . . if that's the move you wanted to make.

LYMAN (*deeply touched*): What size these women have! I wish I was struck dead! (*Weeping threatens again.*) Oh Tom, I'm lost!

TOM: . . . I'm sorry, but there's one urgent thing. I got a call from Jeff Huddleston at six this morning. He heard it on the radio. He's going to insist you resign from the board.

LYMAN: Not on your life! I started that company and I'm keeping it! It's outrageous! Jeff Huddleston's got a woman stashed in Trump Tower and two in L.A.

TOM: *Huddleston?*

LYMAN: —He offered to loan me one once! Huddleston has more outside ass than a Nevada whorehouse!

TOM: But he doesn't marry them.

LYMAN: Right!—in other words, what I really violated was the law of hypocrisy.

TOM: Unfortunately, that's the one that operates.

LYMAN: Yes. Well not with me, kid—what I wish I do!

> (BESSIE *and* THEO *enter.* THEO *stands beside his bed staring at him without expression.* BESSIE *doesn't so much as look directly at him. After a long moment . . .*)

> (*Downing fear*): My God, Theo—thank you . . . I mean for coming. I didn't expect you . . .

> (*She sits down in a potent silence.* BESSIE *remains standing, fiercely aloof. He is openly and awkwardly ashamed . . .*)

> . . . Hi, Bessie.

BESSIE: I'm here for her sake, she wanted to say something to you. (*Hurrying her along.*) Mother?

> (*But* THEO *takes no notice, staring at* LYMAN *with a fixed, unreadable smile. After a long awkward moment . . .*)

LYMAN (*to fill the void*): How are you feeling today? I heard you were . . .

THEO (*dead flat; it cuts him off*): I won't be seeing you again, Lyman.

LYMAN: Yes, well . . . I guess there's no use apologizing, you know my character . . . I am sorry, though.

THEO: I can't leave my life lying all over the floor like this.

LYMAN: I'll talk about anything you like, Theo. Make it as tough as you want to.

THEO: I seem confused but I'm not; there's just so much that I . . . that I don't want bottled up in me anymore.

LYMAN: Sure, I understand.

THEO: —Do you remember that young English instructor whose wife had walked out on him—and his advice to you about sex?

LYMAN: An English instructor?

THEO: "Bend it in half," he said, "and tie a rubber band around it."

LYMAN (*laughing, but a little alarmed*): Oh sure, Jim Donaldson!

THEO: Everyone used to laugh at that.

LYMAN (*her smile is empty, his charm desperate*): Right! "Bend it in half and . . ." (*Continues a strained chuckling.*)

THEO (*cutting him off*): I *hated* you laughing at that; it showed a vulgar and disgusting side of you. I was ashamed . . . for you and for myself.

LYMAN (*brought up short*): I see. But that's so long ago, Theo . . .

THEO: I nearly ended it right then and there, but I thought I was too inexperienced to make a judgment on something like that. But I was right—you *were* a vulgar, unfeeling man, and you are still.

(*Anxiously,* LYMAN *glances over to* BESSIE *for help or explanation of this weirdness.*)

LYMAN: I see. Well, I guess our whole life was a mistake then. (*Angered but attempting charm.*) But I made a good living.

BESSIE: Please, Mother, let's go, he's mocking you, can't you hear it?

LYMAN (*flaring up*): Must I not defend myself? Am I supposed to lie agreeably and be destroyed? Please go ahead, Theo, I'm listening, I understand what you're saying, and it's okay, it's what you feel.

THEO (*seeming perfectly relaxed*): —What was the name of the river, about half an hour's walk past the Chemistry building?

LYMAN (*puzzled . . . is she mad?*): What river?

THEO: Where we went skinny-dipping with those geologists and their girls . . .

LYMAN (*at a loss for a moment, then*): Oh, you mean graduation night!

THEO: . . . The whole crowd swimming naked at the falls . . . and their girls all laughing in the darkness . . . ?

LYMAN (*starting to smile—uncomprehending*): Oh, sure . . . that was a great night!

THEO: I straddled you, and over your shoulder . . . did I dream this?—I recall a white wall of limestone, rising straight out of the river . . . ?

LYMAN: That's right, Devonian. It was full of fossils.

THEO: Yes! Beetle imprints, worm tracks, crustacea fifty million years old going straight up like a white temple wall . . . and we floating around below, like two frogs attached in the darkness . . . our wet eyelashes touching.

LYMAN: Yes.

THEO: It was very beautiful, that evening.

LYMAN: I'm glad you remember it that way.

THEO: You see, I am not at all a Puritan, it is simply a question of taste—that night was inspiring.

LYMAN: Well, I never had taste, we both know that. But I'm not going to lie to you, Theo—taste to me is what's left of life after people can't screw anymore.

THEO: You should have told me that thirty years ago.

LYMAN: I didn't know it thirty years ago.

THEO: And do you remember what you said as we floated there?

LYMAN (*hesitates*): Yes.

THEO: No you don't.

LYMAN: I said, "What could ever come between us?"

THEO (*in immense wonder and relief*): Yes. And did you mean that then? Or was I naïve to believe you? Please tell me the truth.

LYMAN (*affected*): Yes, I believed it.

THEO: When did you begin to fool me?

LYMAN: Please don't go on anymore . . .

THEO: I am trying to pinpoint when my life died. Just so I can know; that's not unreasonable, is it?

LYMAN: From my heart, Theo—I ask your pardon.

THEO: —When did Billie Holiday die?

LYMAN (*perplexed*): Billie Holiday?—oh, I don't know, ten-twelve years ago? Why?

(*She goes silent, stares into space. He is suddenly weeping at the sight of her suffering.*)

Oh, Theo, I'm so sorry . . .

(*She remains staring.*)

Why do you want to know about Billie . . . ?

BESSIE: All right, Mother, let's go, huh?

LYMAN: Bessie, I think it might be better if she talked it out . . .

BESSIE: No one is interested in what you think. (*To Theo*): I want you to come now!

LYMAN: Have mercy on her!

BESSIE: *You* talking mercy!?

LYMAN: For her, not me!—she loved me! Don't you hear what she's trying to say?

BESSIE: How can you listen to this shit!

LYMAN: How dare you! I gave you a damned fine life, Bessie!

BESSIE: You have nothing to say anymore, you are a nonsense!

THEO: Please, dear!—wait outside for a few minutes.

(BESSIE, *seeing her adamance, strides out.*)

You've torn out her heart.

(*He turns away trying not to weep.*)

Was there some pleasure in making a fool of me? What was behind this? Why couldn't you have told me about this woman?

LYMAN: I did try, many times, but . . . I guess it sounds crazy, but . . . I just couldn't bear to lose you.

THEO: But—(*with sudden, near-hysterical intensity*)—you were lying to me every day all these nine or ten years, and before that about other women, weren't you?—what would you possibly lose?

LYMAN (*determined not to flinch*): . . . Your happiness.

THEO: *My* happiness!

LYMAN: I love you.

THEO: You love me.

LYMAN (*daring to, after a hesitation*): Only the truth can help us, Theo—I think you were happier in those last years than ever in our marriage—you feel that, don't you?

(*She doesn't contradict.*)

And I think the reason is that I was never bored being with you.

THEO: You'd been bored with me?

LYMAN: Same as you'd been bored with me, dear . . . I'm talking about—you know—just normal marital boredom.

(*But she seems obtuse to this, so he tries to explain.*)

You know, like at dinner—when I'd repeat some story you'd heard a thousand times . . . ? Like my grandfather losing three fingers under the Ninth Avenue trolley . . . ?

THEO: But I loved that story! I was *never* bored with you . . . stupid as that was.

LYMAN (*now she just seems perverse*): Theo, you were bored—it's no sin! Same as I was when you'd start telling people for the ten thousandth time that—for instance . . . (*his charming laugh*) . . . as a minister's daughter you were not permitted to climb a tree and show off your panties?

THEO (*sternly resisting his charm*): But I think people are interested in a kind of society that has completely disappeared! That story has historical importance!

LYMAN (*the full agony*): But darling, that story is engraved in my flesh! . . . And I beg you, don't make this a moral dilemma. It is just common domestic tedium, dear, it is life, and there's no other woman I know who has the honesty and strength to accept it as life—if you wanted to!

THEO (*a pause; above her confusion, she is striving desperately to understand*): And why do you say I was happier in these last years?

LYMAN: Because you could see my contentment, and I was content . . .

THEO: Because she . . . ?

LYMAN: Because whenever you started with your panties again I could still find you lovable, knowing that that story was not going to be my entire fate till the day I died.

THEO: . . . Because she was waiting for you.

LYMAN: Right.

THEO: You were never bored with *her*?

LYMAN: Oh God yes! sometimes even more than with you.

THEO (*with quick intense hopeful curiosity*): Really! And what then?

LYMAN: Then I would thank my luck that I had you to come back to.—I know how hard this is to understand, Theo.

THEO: No-no . . . I guess I've always known it.

LYMAN: What.

THEO: You are some kind of . . . of giant clam.

LYMAN: Clam?

THEO: Waiting on the bottom for whatever happens to fall from the ocean into your mouth; you are simply a craving, and that craving you call love. You are a kind of monster, and I think you even know it, don't you. I can almost begin to pity you, Lyman. (*She turns to leave.*) I hope you make a good recovery. It's all very clear now, I'm glad I stayed.

LYMAN: It's amazing—the minute the mystery of life appears, you think everything's cleared up.

THEO: There's no mystery to me, you have never loved anyone!

LYMAN: Then explain to yourself how this worthless, loveless, treacherous clam could have single-handedly made two such different women happier than they'd ever been in their lives!

THEO: Really! (*Laughs ending in a near-scream*): Really and truly *happy*?!

LYMAN (*stepping out of the cast, outraged—she remaining fixed on the cast, of course*): . . . In fact, if I dared admit the whole idiotic truth, the only one who suffered these past nine years—was *me!*

(*An enormous echoing roar fills the theatre—the roar of a lion. Light rises on* BESSIE *looking front through field glasses; she is wearing shorts and pith helmet and khaki safari jacket.*)

THEO: *You suffering?*—oh dear God save us!

(*She is trying to sustain her bitter laughing and moves toward* BESSIE, *and as she enters* BESSIE's *area her laughter dies off and she takes a pith helmet out of a picnic basket and puts it on.* LYMAN, *at the same time, emerges from his cast and, remaining in his hospital gown, follows* THEO. *There is no dialogue break.*)

LYMAN: . . . What would you call it, then—having to look into your innocent, contented faces, when I knew the hollowness your happiness was based on? That isn't suffering? (*He takes his place beside the two women, looking in the same direction out front, shading his eyes. With no break in dialogue . . .*)

BESSIE (*looking through field glasses*): Good heavens, is he going to mount her *again?*

LYMAN: They don't call him king of the beasts for nothing, honey.

BESSIE: Poor thing, how patient she is.

THEO (*taking the glasses from her*): Oh come, dear, she's not *only* patient.

BESSIE (*spreading a tablecloth and picnic things on the ground*): But it's only once every half a year, isn't it?

LYMAN: Once that we *know* about.

THEO (*helping spread the picnic*): Oh no, they're marvelously loyal couples.

LYMAN: No, dear, they have harems—you're thinking of storks.

BESSIE (*offering an egg*): Daddy?

LYMAN (*sitting—happily eating*): I love you in those helmets, you look like two noble ladies on safari.

THEO (*stretching out on the ground*): The air here! The silence. These hills.

BESSIE: Thanks for bringing me, Daddy. I'm so sorry Harold had to do those lectures. I'll never forget this trip.—Why do you look sad?

LYMAN: Me? No.

THEO: It's just guilt.

LYMAN (*alarmed*): Guilt?

THEO: He's been away from the office for a whole week.

LYMAN (*relieved*): Oh.—Actually, though, why do we think of monogamy as a higher form of life?

THEO: Well, it implies an intensification of love.

LYMAN: How about that, Bess? You had a lot of boyfriends before Harold, didn't you?

BESSIE: Well . . . yes, I guess it is more intense with one.

LYMAN: But how does that make it a higher form?

THEO: Monogamy strengthens the family; random screwing undermines it.

LYMAN: But as one neurotic to another, what's so good about strengthening the family?

THEO: Well, for one thing it enhances liberty.

BESSIE (*puzzled*): Liberty? Really?

THEO: The family disciplines its members; when the family is weak the state has to move in; so the stronger the family the fewer the police. And that is why monogamy is a higher form.

LYMAN: Jesus, did you just make that up? (*To Bessie*): Isn't she marvelous? I'm giving her an A-plus!

THEO (*happily hurt*): Oh shut up.

LYMAN: But what about these Muslims? They're very big on stable families but a lot of them have two or three wives.

THEO: But only one is really the *wife*.

LYMAN: Not according to my father—they often had two main women, one to run the house and the other for the bed. But they were both serious wives.

THEO: Your father's sociology was on a par with his morals—nonexistent.

LYMAN (*laughs; to* BESSIE): Your mother is a classical woman, you know why?

BESSIE (*laughing delightedly*): Why?

LYMAN: Because she is always clear and consistent and . . .

THEO: . . . Rather boring.

(*He guffaws warmly, clapping his hands over his head in appreciation.*)

BESSIE: You are not boring! (*Rushing to embrace* THEO): Tell her she is not boring!

LYMAN (*embracing* THEO *with* BESSIE): Please no . . . I swear I didn't mean boring!

THEO (*tearfully hurt*): Well I'd rather be boring and clear than cute and stupid!

BESSIE: But I don't think he meant . . .

LYMAN: Who asked you to be cute?

THEO (*with a tortured look*): I wish I knew how to amuse you!

LYMAN: I swear to God I am not bored, Theo!—now please don't go on about it.

THEO: Your eyes have been glazed over since we stepped onto this wretched continent!

LYMAN (*guiltily stretching an awkward embrace toward her*): I *love* this trip, and being with both of you . . . ! Theo, please!—now you are making me guilty!

(*The lion's roar interrupts and they all look front in shock.*)

BESSIE: Is he heading here . . . ? Daddy!—he's trotting!

GUIDE'S VOICE (*off, on bullhorn*): You will have to come back to the car, everyone! At once!

LYMAN: Quick! (*He pushes both women off.*)

BESSIE (*on exiting*): Daddy, come . . . !

THEO (*sensing he is remaining behind*): Lyman . . . ?

LYMAN: Go! (*He pushes her off, but turns back himself.*)

GUIDE'S VOICE: Come back to the car at once, Mr. Felt!

(*Lion's roar—but closer now.* LYMAN *facing front and the lion, prepared to run for it but holding his ground.*)

Mr. Felt, get back to the car!

(*Another roar.*)

LYMAN (*eyes on the lion, shouting toward it with fear's exhilaration*): I *am* happy, yes! That I'm married to Theodora and have Bessie . . . yes, *and Leah, too!*

(*Another roar!*)

BESSIE (*from a distance*): Daddy, please come here!

LYMAN: And that I've made a mountain of money . . . yes, and have no pending lawsuits!

BESSIE (*from a distance*): Daddy . . . !

LYMAN (*flinging his words toward the approaching beast, but crouched and ready to flee*): . . . And that I don't sacrifice one day to things I don't believe in—and that includes monogamy, yes!—We love our lives, you goddam lion!—you and me both!

(*Wide-eyed, still crouched to run, he is watching the approaching lion—whose roar, as we now hear, has changed to a rather more relaxed guttural growling, much diminished; and* LYMAN *cautiously straightens up, and turns triumphantly toward the women offstage. And* BESSIE *flies out and throws her arms around him in ecstatic relief, kissing him.*)

BESSIE (*looking front*): Daddy, he turned back! What did you do that for!

(THEO *enters.*)

THEO: He turned back! (*To* LYMAN): How did you do that! (*To* BESSIE): Did you see how he stopped and looked at him and turned around? (*To* LYMAN): What happened?

LYMAN: I think . . . he sensed that I—darling, I think I've lost my guilt!

THEO: What!

LYMAN (*staring in wonder*): His roar hit my teeth like voltage and suddenly, it was so clear that . . . (*Turns to her.*) I've always been happy with you, Theo!—I just somehow couldn't accept it! It's a miracle—I'm a happy man and I am never going to apologize for it again!

THEO (*with tears of gratitude, clasping her hands together prayerfully*): Oh, Lyman! (*Rushing to kiss him*): Oh, darling!

LYMAN (*still riding his wave, holding out his hand to her*): What old good friends we are, Theo! Put her there!

(*She laughs and manfully shakes hands.*)

What a *person* you are, what a grave and beautiful face you have!

BESSIE: Oh, Daddy, that's so lovely!—you're just marvelous! (*She weeps.*)

LYMAN: How the hell are we still together—do you realize how she must love me to stand for my character? Well I love her too! I definitely worship this woman, Bessie!

THEO: Oh, this is what I always saw happening someday!—(*a sophisticated laugh*)—not with a lion, of course, but exactly this sudden flash of light . . . !

LYMAN: The whole future is clear to me now! We are not going to sidle shamefully into our late middle age, we're marching in heads up! I'm going to build a selfish little cottage in the Caribbean and we'll fill it up with all the thick English novels we never got to finish . . . plus Proust!—and I'll buy two mopeds with little baskets on the handlebars for the shopping trips . . .

THEO: I knew it, I knew it!

LYMAN: . . . And I'll spend every day with you—except maybe a week or two a month in the Elmira office!

BESSIE: How fantastic, Mother!

THEO: Thank you, lion! Thank you, Africa! (*Turning to him.*) Lyman?

LYMAN (*already mentally departing the scene*): . . . Huh? Yes!

THEO: I am all new!

> (*She throws her arms around him, burying her face in his neck. He looks front with an expression of deepening agony.*)

BESSIE: This has been the most fantastic two weeks of my life! I love you, Daddy!

> (*She rushes to him and with one arm he embraces her, the other around* THEO. *Tears are starting in his eyes.*)

Are you weeping?

LYMAN: Just amazement, honey . . . at my luck, I guess. Come, we'd better go back.

> (*Somberly he turns them upstage; lights are changing, growing dimmer, and they walk into darkness while he remains behind. Alone—in his hospital gown still—he slowly turns front; light spreads and reveals the* NURSE *sitting near the bed.*)

NURSE (*to the cast, exactly as earlier*): The only thing I don't understand is why you married that woman, a smart man like you.

> (LYMAN *stares ahead as* LEAH *appears, isolated in light; she is in her fur coat, exactly as in Act One when she was about to go for an abortion. The* NURSE *remains in the periphery, immobile.*)

LEAH: Yes, I suppose it could wait a week or so, but . . . really, Lyman, you know you're never going to leave her.

LYMAN: You cancel the operation, okay? And I'm telling her tomorrow.

LEAH: You're telling her what?

LYMAN (*almost holding his breath*): I will not rationalize you away. I have one life! I'm going to ask her for a divorce.

LEAH: My God, Lyman!

LYMAN (*pulling her into his arms*): Why are we so *connected?*— do you feel it?

LEAH: I don't understand it. I seem to have known you forever. But listen, I know your attachment to her . . .

LYMAN: I trust you . . . I'd like to tell you something. (*He takes a pause out of sheer caution.*) I had a son once, with a terrific girl I knew. A long time ago now.—I'm ashamed of this—I convinced her to have it. I was crazy about her. But I had to break it off or lose my marriage. It was torture.—About seventeen years later I am checking into Pan Am in Los Angeles, and I see this young guy in line in front of me. My spitting image. Unmistakable. When he laid his ticket on the counter the clerk said his name, sure enough—it was his mother's. We sat facing each other in the waiting area. I was paralyzed.

LEAH: Why couldn't you have introduced yourself!

LYMAN: Well, he was dressed kind of poor . . . and he had an unhappy look. He'd have to feel I'd betrayed him, I was sure he'd hate me . . . (*Pause; he kisses her hand.*) Please keep this baby. Will you? And stay home and cross your legs, you hear?—no dates.

LEAH: But stop worrying about another man, okay?—Please, I'm not really like that, if I'm committed.

LYMAN (*with mock anger squeezing her cheeks together*): A nunnery for you till I get back, you hear?

LEAH: This is serious?

LYMAN: This is serious. I'm asking her for a divorce.

LEAH: Suddenly . . . why am I not sure I want to be a mother!—Do I, you think?

LYMAN: Yes you do, I think!

> (*Kisses her. They laugh together. He turns to leave; she grasps his hands and presses them together between hers in a prayerful gesture; and facing heaven . . .*)

LEAH: Please! Some good luck! (*To* LYMAN *directly*): Why is everything so dangerous! (*She gives him a violent kiss.*)

BLACKOUT

THEO *appears walking; she is hiding something behind her back and smiling lovingly.* LYMAN *appears. He looks solemn, prepared for the showdown.*

LYMAN: Theo, dear . . . There's something I have to tell you . . .

THEO (*holding out a cashmere sweater*): Happy birthday!

LYMAN (*startled*): Hah? But it's not July, is it!

THEO: But it was so sinfully expensive I needed an excuse. (*Putting him into the sweater*): Here . . . straighten it. It's Italian. It's not too big, is it? (*Stepping back to admire.*) It's gorgeous, look in the mirror!

LYMAN: It's beautiful, thank you, dear. But listen, I really have something to . . .

THEO: My God, Lyman, you are simply magnificent! (*Linking arms with him and walking in her cumbersome way.*) I have another surprise—I got tickets for the Balanchine! And a table at Luigi's afterwards!

LYMAN (*grimly screwing up his courage—and beginning to resent her domination*): I have something to tell you, Theo, why do you make it so hard for me!

THEO: What.

(*He is paralyzed.*)

What is it? Has something happened? (*Alarmed now*): Lyman!—(*asking*)—you went for your checkup!

LYMAN (*about to explode*): God's sake, no, it's not that!

THEO: Why is your face so gray? Please, what is it, you look terrified!

(*He moves away from her and her awful caring, and halts facing front. She remains behind and calls to him from the distance.*)

—My cousin Wilbur's still at Mass. General, we can go up there together . . . ! Please, darling, don't worry about anything . . . ! What is it, can you tell me?

(*In total blockage—both in the past and present—he inhales deeply and lets out a gigantic long howl, arms raised, imploring heaven for relief. In effect, it blasts her out of his mind— she de-animates and goes dark, and he is alone again.*)

LYMAN (*to himself, facing front*): No guts. That's the whole story. No guts!

(*A hospital gurney rolls on.* LEAH *is lying on it. She raises up
on her elbows.*)

LEAH: You got here!

LYMAN (*grinning broadly*): Of course I got here!

LEAH: Have they shown him to you? He's a boy!—and you see
how he looks like you?

LYMAN: No, not me—like my father after a shave. (*Kisses her.*)
What an airy softness on your eyes; like God leaned down
and lightly kissed your breast.

LEAH: I was so hoping you'd come. (*Kisses his hand.*) Thank
you for him, darling. I love you. And I do understand why
you can't divorce her, and it's okay. Really. In fact, it's ironical, you make me understand what real commitment means.

LYMAN: I love you, Leah. You have a sublime gift of near-
ness . . .

LEAH: You'll still come and see us, won't you?—when you can?
(*He covers his face.*)

Don't feel bad, we could still have a good life! What can I
name him?

LYMAN (*lowering his hands, in the throes of loss*): I filled out the
form for you.

LEAH (*laughs*): *You* did?

LYMAN: I put down Benjamin, is that okay?

LEAH: If it's from you it's beautiful. What about a second
name?—I guess mine, huh?

LYMAN: I want to put down Felt—in fact, I did.

LEAH: Felt!—how will I explain that to him?

LYMAN (*hesitates . . . then, with a tense smile . . .*): I know
you owe me nothing, darling, but they tell me there's been a
man coming in to see you.

LEAH: A doctor; he stops by; I used to know him. But truthfully . . . I do feel more sure I'm going to end up married.
Maybe not, but definitely maybe—I mean someday.

LYMAN: With who?

LEAH: I don't know! When I came out of the anaesthetic, I
thought—maybe if I was married we could both be guilty,
and it would make it easier for you.

LYMAN: I'm not even going to try to understand that.

LEAH (*laughing, she suddenly weeps . . .*): Please go, dear, I can't bear this . . . Come later if you can or just write me—or call me up and make me laugh!

LYMAN: Oh, my darling, my darling . . . we've got to stay together!

LEAH (*angering*): But you can't!—why do you keep saying that!

LYMAN: What if I got you a loft downtown in the City, and I'd buy you out here and you can stay home with him and paint? What do you say? I'd set up a trust fund . . .

LEAH: Why don't we just play it by ear?

LYMAN: Meaning what?

LEAH: Come up when you can, and we'll meet in the City sometimes when I come down . . .

LYMAN: . . . My heart's going to die . . . you're drifting away!

LEAH (*direct and tough*): . . . But how can I commit myself and you just stop by now and then . . . I mean sooner or later won't that irritate me?—You poor man, you're so divided . . . or do you think you're too old?

(*Tremendously conflicted, he avoids her eyes. She strokes his face.*)

Well, don't get depressed; we are how we are. . . . Anyway, I'm not absolutely sure I should be married to anybody—I think I may still be too curious.

LYMAN: About men.

(*She nods, mystified. He is suddenly decisive.*)

Give me a month! By June first I either settle with Theo or I disappear, okay?

LEAH: You poor man. I wish I could help you, but I'm so mixed up myself . . .

LYMAN: I've lost my judgment, I'm out of sync with my age and I'm being foolish.

LEAH: But you are not old, you're a sensualist and romantic, and I think it's just marvelous!

LYMAN (*moving into a light as she is vanishing*): No! I know what's wrong with me—I could never stand still for death! Which you've got to do, by a certain age, or be ridiculous—you've got to stand there nobly and serene . . .

(LEAH *is gone now, he's alone.*)

. . . and let death run his tape out your arms and around your belly and up your crotch until he's got you fitted for that last black suit. And I can't, I won't! . . . So I'm left wrestling with this anachronistic energy which . . . (*as he enters the cast, crying out to the world* . . .) . . . God has charged me with and I will use it till the dirt is shoveled into my mouth! Life! Life! Fuck death and dying!

(*Light widens, finding* LEAH *in the present, dressed differently than in the previous—in her fur coat—standing near the bed with the* NURSE, *listening to his shouts.*)

NURSE: Don't be afraid, just wait a minute, he comes out of it. I'm sure he wants to see you.

LEAH (*moving tentatively to the cast*): Lyman?

(*He looks at her with cloudy recognition.*)

It's me, Leah.

(NURSE *exits.*)

LYMAN (*now fully aware of her*): Leah! (*Turning away from her*): Jesus, what have I done to you!—wait . . . (*a moment; he looks around.*) Was Theo here?

LEAH: I think she's gone, I just got here.

LYMAN: I don't know where the hell I am. . . . Oh, Leah, it's sitting on my chest like a bag of cement.

LEAH: What is?

LYMAN: My character.

LEAH: Yes, well . . . it's pretty bad.

LYMAN: And still, I swear, all I've ever done is try to be honest. (*Moved*): Thanks for coming.

LEAH: I only came about Benny, I don't know how to begin explaining this to him.

LYMAN (*about to weep again*): What balls you have to come here and talk so coolly, I really salute you.—What's he saying?

LEAH (*frustrated, turns away*): He's excited that he has a sister.

LYMAN (*painful admiration*): Oh that dear boy!

LEAH: He's very badly mixed up, Lyman; he's seen us all on TV and one of the other kids told him he has two mothers. He sweats in his sleep. He keeps asking me are you coming home again. It's twisting my heart. I'm terrified if this isn't settled right it could screw up the rest of his life. (*Tears start.*) You're his idol, Lyman!—his god!

LYMAN: Oh, the wreckage, the wreckage . . .

LEAH: Tell me the truth; it's okay if you don't, I just want to know—do you feel a responsibility or not?

LYMAN (*flaring up, scared as much as indignant*): How can you ask such a thing?

LEAH: Why! That's a reasonable question!

LYMAN: Now you listen—I know I'm wrong and I'm wrong and I'm wrong but I did not throw you both across my saddle to rape you in my tent! You knew I was married, and you tried to make me love you, so I'm not entirely . . .

LEAH: Lyman, if you're blaming me I'm going to sink through this floor!

LYMAN: I'm talking about truth not blame—this is not entirely a one-man disaster!

LEAH: It's amazing, the minute you talk about truth you always come out looking better than anybody else!

LYMAN: Now that's unfair!

LEAH (*slight pause*): I want to talk about Benny.

LYMAN: You could bring him tomorrow if you like. But go ahead, we can talk now.

(*A pause as she settles down.*)

LEAH (*with a flushed grin*): Incidentally . . . I'm just curious, how's everything with your wife?—they tell me you spent over an hour with her.

LYMAN: All she did was sit there telling me I'm a monster who never loved anybody.

LEAH (*with a hard grin*): And I suppose you reassured her otherwise.

LYMAN: Well, I did love her. Just as I loved you. The truth is the truth, kid.

LEAH: What a piece of work you are, Lyman, really—you go falling off a mountain and you still don't understand anything.

LYMAN: What should I understand?

LEAH: Never mind.

LYMAN: Well what?

LEAH (*with anxiety and anger*): It's no business of mine, but your hatred for that woman is monumental. I mean it's . . . it's *oceanic*.

LYMAN: What the hell are you going on about!

LEAH: Because it's unnerving to have to listen to this shit all over again!

LYMAN: What shit? What have I said!

LEAH: My dear man, in case it slipped your mind, when I was two months' pregnant we went to New York and you picked the Carlyle Hotel to stay at—four blocks from your house! "Loved her" . . . good G—!

(*A window begins to appear upstage with* THEO *seated in profile, reading a book. He is staring as he emerges from the cast, turning to look up at the window. . . .* LEAH *goes on with no pause.*)

What was all that about if it wasn't hatred!—And walking me past your front window with her sitting there . . . ? And— yes, my God I almost forgot—going in to see her yet? You had murder in you and you still do!—probably for me too!

LYMAN (*glancing up at* THEO *in the window*): But it didn't feel like murder at all. I was dancing the high wire on the edge of the world . . . finally risking everything to find myself! Strolling with you past my house, the spring breeze, the lingerie in the Madison Avenue shop windows, the swish of . . . wasn't it a taffeta skirt you wore? . . . and my new baby coiled in your belly?—I'd beaten guilt forever!

(*She is moving toward him, part of his recall.*)

. . . And how languorous you are, your pregnant glory bulging under the streetlamp!

(*She takes on the ease of that long-ago stroll, and . . .*)

LEAH: Is that her?

(LYMAN *looks up at* THEO *then at* LEAH, *inspired, alive.*)

LYMAN: Oh Leah darling, how sexy you look against tall buildings.

LEAH (*with a warm smile, taking his arm*): You're tense, aren't you.

LYMAN: Well, I lived here with her for so many years . . .

LEAH: Was she very upset when you told her?

LYMAN (*tragically; but hesitates*): . . . Yes, dear, she was.

LEAH: Well, maybe after the divorce she'll think of marrying again.

LYMAN (*with a glance to the window; loosening her grip on his arm*): I doubt it, somehow.

LEAH (*with an intrigued smile*): Mustn't we touch?

LYMAN (*quickly regaining her arm*): Of course!
    (*They start walking away.*)
LEAH: I'd love to meet her sometime . . . just as friends.
LYMAN: You might.
LEAH: You're still feeling guilty, aren't you.
LYMAN (*halts; a strange determination suddenly*): A little, yes.
    And I hate it.—Listen, I'd like to see if I can go in and say
    hello.
LEAH: Really! Would you like me to come?
LYMAN: Not just yet. Would you mind a lot? Tell me.
LEAH: No, go ahead. I kind of like it that you don't just drop
    people.
LYMAN: God, you have balls! I'll see you back at the hotel in
    twenty minutes, okay?
LEAH: Take your time! I'll play with all that gorgeous under-
    wear you bought. (*Touching her belly.*) I'm so contented,
    Lyman!
    (*She turns and walks toward the cast, which lights up. He re-
    mains below the window, staring at her departing figure.*)
LYMAN: Why is it, the happier she is the sadder I get? It's this
    damned *objectivity!*—Like God must feel when he looks at
    happy people—knowing what he knows about worms! (*Now
    he looks up at* THEO, *and his heart sinks.*) What have I done!
    Have I only doubled the distance that I stand from my life?
    (*Violent determination.*) Idiot!—love her! Now that she
    doesn't deprive you anymore let love flow to your wise and
    wonderful wife! (*He rushes toward* THEO, *but then turns
    away in terror, walking around in a circle and blowing out
    air and covering his face.*) To hell with this guilt!
    (*Now gritting his teeth he again hurries toward the window
    . . . which disappears, as she rises, startled.*)
THEO: Lyman!—you said Tuesday, didn't you?
    (*He takes her in his arms, kisses her with frantic passion. She
    is surprised and happy.*)
LYMAN: What a handsome lady! Theo, you are God's hand-
    writing.
THEO: Ralph Waldo Emerson.
LYMAN: Some day I'm going to swipe an image you never
    heard of! (*Laughing, in comradely style, embraces her closely as
    he takes her to a seat—turning on a certain excited intimacy*

here.) Listen, I hitched a ride down with this pilot in his new Cessna—I have meetings up there starting seven-thirty tomorrow but I just had to astonish you.

THEO: You flew in a small plane *at night?*

LYMAN: That whole fear was guilt, Theo—I thought I *deserved* to crash. But I deserve to live because I am not a bad guy and I love you.

THEO: Well, I'm floating away! When must you go back?

LYMAN: Now.

THEO (*near laughter at the absurdity*): Can't we even chat?

LYMAN: No. In fact, I'd better call that I'm on my way. (*Dials a phone.*)

THEO: I'll drive you to the airport.

LYMAN: No, he's picking me up at the Carlyle . . . Hello?
   (*Light opens on* LEAH, *holding a phone.*)

LEAH: Darling!

LYMAN: Be there in ten minutes.

LEAH (*puzzled*): Oh? Okay. Why are you calling?

LYMAN: Just to be sure you didn't forget me and took off.

LEAH: Your jealousy is so comforting!—You know, she made a very dignified picture, reading in the window—it was like an Edward Hopper, kind of haunted.

LYMAN: Yes. Well, I'm leaving right now. (*Hangs up.*)

THEO: You won't forget about dinner Thursday with Leona and Gilbert . . . he's gotten his hearing aid so it won't be so bad.

LYMAN (*with a certain solemnity, taking her hands*): —I just had to steal this extra look at one another . . . life's so stupidly short, Theo.

THEO (*happily*): Why is death always sitting on your shoulder, you've got more life in you than anybody! (*Ruffling his hair.*) In fact, you're kind of sparkly tonight.

LYMAN (*breathlessly*): —Listen, we have time to make love.

THEO (*with a surprised, delighted laugh*): I wish I knew what's come over you!

LYMAN: I'm alive, that's all!—I've got to have you! (*He starts to lead her.*) I keep forgetting what a sweet piece of ass my wife is.

THEO: Must be the new office in Elmira—beginnings are always exciting!

LYMAN (*turning her to him, he kisses her mouth*): Keep meaning to ask you—has there ever been a god who was guilty?

THEO: Gods are never guilty, that's why they're gods—except Jesus, of course.

LYMAN: It feels like the moon's in my belly and the sun's in my mouth and I'm shining down on the world. (*Laughs with a self-mocking charm.*) . . . A regular planetary flashlight! Come! (*And laughing in high tension takes her hand and moves her into darkness . . .*)

THEO: Oh, Lyman—how wonderfully, endlessly changing you are!

BLACKOUT

Light up on LEAH *in hospital room;* LYMAN *is returning to his cast.*

LEAH: So you bopped her that night.

LYMAN: What can I say?

LEAH: There's just no end to you, is there.—And when you came back to the hotel, didn't we . . . ?

LYMAN: I couldn't help myself. Maybe it was that you were practically around the corner, but she suddenly looked absolutely gorgeous! How can that be evil?

LEAH (*with a sigh*): —Listen, I have to talk business. I want the house transferred to my name immediately.

LYMAN: What are you saying? Leah . . . !

LEAH: I know how much feeling you put into it but I want the security for Benny's sake.

LYMAN: Leah, I beg you to wait with that . . .

LEAH: I will not wait with that! And I want my business returned to me.

LYMAN: That'll be complicated—it's many times bigger than when I took it over . . .

LEAH: I want it back! I would have expanded without you! I'm not going to be a *total* fool! I will sue you!

LYMAN (*with a very uncertain grin*): You'd really sue me?

LEAH (*searching in her pocketbook*): I'm not fooling around,

Lyman. You've hurt me very deeply . . . (*Breaks off, holding back tears. She takes out a sheet of paper.*)

LYMAN (*forced to turn from her*): Jesus, how I hate to see you cry.

LEAH: I have something I want you to sign.

LYMAN: To *sign*?

LEAH: It's a quit-claim on the house and my business. Will you read it?

LYMAN: You're not serious.

LEAH: I had Ted Lester draw it up. Here, read it.

LYMAN: I know what a quit-claim is, don't tell me to read a quit-claim. How can you do this?

LEAH: We aren't married and I don't want you making claims on me.

LYMAN: And . . . and what about Benny. You don't mean you're taking Benny from me . . .

LEAH: I . . .

LYMAN: I want you to bring him here tomorrow morning so I can talk to him.

LEAH: Just a minute . . .

LYMAN: No! You're going to bring him, Leah . . .

LEAH: Now you listen to me! I've been through this with Ted Lester and you haven't a legal leg to stand on. I will not allow you to see him until I know what you intend to say to him about all this.

LYMAN: I'll tell him the truth—I love him.

LEAH: You love him!

LYMAN (*threateningly*): I said I love him, Leah!

LEAH: But what is he going to make of that? That it's all right to deceive people you love?

LYMAN: Human beings can lose control when they fall in love, it won't hurt him to know that. You're overprotecting him.

LEAH: But how is he going to figure this out?—you love him and lied to him so terribly? He's all I have now, Lyman, I am not going to see him go crazy!

LYMAN: Now you stop that! I did a helluva lot more than lie to him . . .

LEAH (*outpouring*): You lied to him!—why don't you seem to register this? The whole thing was a lie!

LYMAN: I love that boy!

LEAH: . . . To buy him the pony, and teach him to ski, and take him up in the glider . . . you made him worship you —when you knew what you knew! That was cruelty!

LYMAN: All right, I won't argue. What do you think I should tell him?

LEAH: I think you have to say that you do love him but he mustn't follow your example because lying to people injures them. And you beg his pardon, and promise you'll never mislead him again.

LYMAN: I am not grinding myself up in front of my son's face! That is not education for him, kid, it's your revenge on me! If I can teach him anything now it's to have the guts to be true to himself! That's all that matters!

LEAH: Even if he has to betray the whole world to do it?

LYMAN (*in an agony*): Only the truth is sacred, Leah!—to hold back nothing!

LEAH: You must be crazy—you held back everything! You really don't know right from wrong, do you!

LYMAN: Jesus Christ, you sound like Theo!

LEAH: Well maybe it's what happens to people who marry you! Look—I don't think it's a good idea at the moment . . .

LYMAN: I have a right to see my son!

LEAH: I won't have him copying you, Lyman, it will destroy his life! (*She starts to leave.*)

LYMAN: I want Benny! I want Benny, Leah! You will bring me Benny!

(*Enter* BESSIE *alone. She is extremely tense and anxious.*)

BESSIE: Oh! I'm so glad you're still here. Listen . . .

LEAH: I was just going . . .

BESSIE: Please don't! She's had an attack of some kind—they're looking at her in a room down the hall.

LYMAN: My God, Bessie . . . what is it?

BESSIE: I really think it would help if she saw that you're to-gether . . .

LEAH: But we're not together.

BESSIE: Oh!—well, I'm not too sorry to hear that, I thought you were going to let him get away with it.

LYMAN: Well it isn't quite settled . . .

LEAH: Maybe it is, dear. (*To* BESSIE.) —What did you mean?— to see we're together?

BESSIE: She talks about taking him home with her.

LYMAN: No kidding!

BESSIE (*a quick hostile glance at him, then* . . .): She's a little delusionary.

LYMAN: Why must it be a delusion? Maybe Mother really wants me back . . .

BESSIE (*with a frustrated stamp of her foot*): I want her out of here and home!

LYMAN: What should I do, stick horns on my head and a tail on my ass? I am not a monster, Bessie! My God, where did all this cruelty come from!

LEAH: He wants her, you see . . .

LYMAN: I want you both!

BESSIE (*with a hysterical overtone, screaming*): Will you once in your life think of another human being. (*To* LEAH): Please!—would you come and tell her what you think of him?

(TOM *and* THEO *enter with the* NURSE; *he has her by the arm. She has a heightened,* seeing *air about her, a fixed dead smile, and her head trembles.*)

LYMAN: Theo!—come, sit her down, Tom!

LEAH (*to* BESSIE; *fearfully*): I really feel I ought to go . . .

THEO: Oh, I wish you could stay a few minutes! (*To* NURSE.) Please get a chair for Mrs. Felt.

(*The reference causes surprise in* BESSIE. LEAH *looks quickly to* BESSIE, *perplexed because this is the opposite of what* BESSIE *said* THEO *wished.* LYMAN *is immensely encouraged. The* NURSE, *as she goes out for the chair, glances about, perplexed.*)

Well! Here we are all together.

(*Slight pause.*)

TOM: She's had a little . . . incident, Lyman. (*To* BESSIE.) I've arranged for a plane; the three of us can go to the City together.

BESSIE: Oh, good.—We're ready to leave whenever you say, Mother.

LYMAN: Thanks, Theo . . . for coming.

THEO (*turns to him, smiling blankly*): Socialism is dead. (*A beat.*) And Christianity is finished, so . . . (*searches*) . . . there is really nothing left to . . . to . . . Except simplicity? To defend? (*She crosses her legs, and her coat falls partially open revealing a bare thigh.*)

BESSIE: Mother!—where's your skirt?

THEO: I'm comfortable, it's all right . . .

(NURSE *enters with a chair.*)

BESSIE: She must have left her skirt in the room she was just in—would you get it, please?

(NURSE, *perplexed again, exits.*)

THEO (*to* LEAH): I wish I hadn't carried on that way . . . I'm sorry. (*Turning to* LYMAN.) The surprise is what threw me. I was just totally unprepared. But I'm better now. (*To* LEAH.) I'm really much better . . . (*Breaks off.*) Do you see the *Village Voice* up here?

LEAH: Yes, occasionally.

THEO: There was a strange interview some years back with Isaac Bashevis Singer, the novelist? The interviewer was a woman whose husband had left her for another woman, and she couldn't understand why. And Singer said, "Maybe he liked her hole better." I was shocked at the time, really outraged—you know, that he'd gotten a Nobel; but now I think it was courageous to have said that, because it's probably true. Courage . . . courage is always the main thing! Everyone knows that, of course, but suddenly it is so . . . so *clear* . . .

(NURSE *enters, offers* THEO *the skirt.*)

NURSE: Can I help you on with it?

THEO (*takes the skirt, looks at it without recognition and drops it on the floor*): I can't remember if I called you Leah or Mrs. Felt.

LEAH: I'm not really Mrs. Felt.

THEO (*with a pleasant social smile*): Well, it doesn't really matter —I guess we're all sort of interchangeable anyway. Except for the children. (*Short pause.*) Your boy needs his father, I imagine.

LEAH: Well . . . yes, but . . .

THEO: Then he should be here with you, shouldn't he. (*To* LYMAN.) You can come up here whenever you want to . . . if that's what you'd like to do.

BESSIE (*to* TOM): She's really too ill for this.—Come, Mother, we're going . . .

THEO (*to* LYMAN): I can say "fuck," you know. I never cared for the word but I'm sure she has her limitations too. I can say "fuck me," "fuck you"; whatever.

(LYMAN *is silent in guilty anguish.*)

BESSIE (*to* LYMAN, *furiously*): Will you tell her to leave? Just out of respect, out of friendship!

LYMAN: Yes. (*Delicately.*) She's right, Theo, I think that would be the best . . .

THEO (*to* BESSIE): No, I can take better care of him at home. (*To* LEAH.) I really have nothing to do, and you're busy, I imagine . . .

BESSIE: Tom, will you . . . ?

TOM: Why don't we let her say what's on her mind?

THEO (*to* BESSIE): He had every right to resent me. What did I ever do but correct him? (*To* LEAH.) You don't correct him, do you. You like him as he is, even now, don't you. And that's the secret, isn't it. (*To* LYMAN.) Well I can do that. I don't need to correct you . . . or rather pretend to . . .

BESSIE: I can't bear this, Mother!

THEO (*calmly to* BESSIE): But Bessie dear I've always pretty well known what he was doing. I think I have, anyway; why have I tolerated it? (*Suddenly screams at the top of her lungs.*) Why have I tolerated it!

(*Silence. Fear in all of them.*)

BESSIE (*terrified for her mother*): Daddy, please . . . tell her . . . ?

LYMAN: But she's trying to tell the truth, darling.

LEAH (*suddenly filling up*): You poor woman! (*To him.*) What a bastard you are; one honest sentence from you and none of this would have happened, it's despicable! (*Appealing to* THEO.) I'm so sorry about it, Mrs. Felt . . .

THEO: No-no . . . he's absolutely right—he's always said it —it's life I can't bear! But you accept it, you trust it, and that's why you *should* win out . . .

LEAH: But it's not true—I never really trusted him! Not really! Not really *trusted*. To tell you the truth, I never wanted to marry anybody, I've never known one happy couple!—Listen, you mustn't blame yourself, the whole damned thing doesn't work, it never works . . . which I knew and went ahead and did it anyway and I'll never understand why!

LYMAN (*with bitter anger*): Because if you hadn't married me you wouldn't have kept Benny. Don't start being a dumbbell, Leah!

(*She can't find words.*)

You wouldn't have had Benny or this last nine years of your happiness. You've become the woman you always wanted to be, instead of . . . (*Catches himself.*) Well, what's the difference?

LEAH: No, don't stop—Instead of what? What did you save me from?

LYMAN (*accepting her challenge*): All right . . . from all those lonely postcoital showerbaths, and the pointless pillow talk and the boxes of heartless condoms beside your bed . . . !

LEAH (*speechless*): Well now!

LYMAN: I'm sick of this crap, Leah!—You got a little something out of this despicable treachery!

THEO: That's a terrible thing to say to the woman.

LYMAN: But the truth is terrible, isn't that what you've just finished saying? Are you still looking for your purity, Theo? You tolerated me because you loved me, and more than I deserved, but wasn't it also the good life I gave you. —Well what's wrong with that? Aren't women people? Don't people love power? I don't understand the disgrace!

BESSIE (*to both women*): Why are you still sitting here, don't you have any pride! (*To* LEAH.) This is disgusting!

LEAH: Will you please stop challenging everybody? I have business with him, so I have to talk to him!—I'll go out of my mind here! Am I being accused of something?

BESSIE: You shouldn't be in the same room with him!

LEAH (*rattled*): I just explained that, didn't I? *What the hell do you want?*

LYMAN (*his voice cracking with a sob*): She wants her father back!

BESSIE: You son of a bitch! (*Raises her fists, then weeps helplessly.*)

LYMAN: I love you, Bessie!—all of you! You are all magnificent!

BESSIE: You ought to be killed!

(*She bursts into tears. A helpless river of grief which now overflows to sweep up* LYMAN; *then* LEAH *is carried away by the wave of weeping. All strategies collapse as finally* THEO *is infected. The four of them are helplessly covering their faces.*

It is a veritable mass keening, a funerary explosion of grief, each for his or her own condition, for love's frustration and for the end of all their capacity to reason. TOM *has turned from them, head bent in prayer, hands clasped, eyes shut.*)

LYMAN: Theo, please!—put some clothes on! *(Turning for help to* TOM.*)* Tom, I can't bear her doing this . . . ! *(Breaks off.)* Are you praying, for Christ's sake?

TOM *(staring ahead, only glancing at them)*: There is no way to go forward. You must all stop loving him. You must, or he will destroy you. He is an endless string attached to nothing. —Theo needs help now, Lyman, and I don't want a conflict, so I don't see how I can go on representing you.

LYMAN: Why? Am I not worthy? Who is not an endless string? *(A shout, but with the strain of his loss, his inability to connect.)* Who is attached to something in this world now?—I am human, I am proud of it!—of the glory and the shit!

TOM: You must face it, Lyman, you moved that barrier . . .

LYMAN: That was not suicide—I am not a cop-out!

TOM: Why is it a cop-out to have a conscience? You were ashamed, weren't you? Why can't you acknowledge that? Isn't a conscience human? Your shame is the best part of you, for God's sake . . . ! *(Breaks off, giving it up.)* I'm ready to go, Theo.

LYMAN: Let her stay a while. *(To* THEO.*)* You want to stay, don't you?

BESSIE: Mother? *(She raises* THEO *to her feet. Her head is trembling. She turns to* LYMAN.*)*

LYMAN: You can't really leave me, Theo—you can't!

THEO: I'm afraid I have nothing . . . in me anymore, Lyman. *(*BESSIE *takes her by the arm to go.* LEAH *stands, as though to leave.)*

LYMAN: —Bessie? I'll see you again, won't I?—sometime? *(*BESSIE *is silent.)* Leah?—you can stay a little, can't you?

LEAH *(an evasive color)*: I have work in the office . . .

LYMAN *(with a scared laugh)*: You all pulling out?—what is this?

LEAH: I'll try to stop by tomorrow, if I can . . .

LYMAN *(in open terror at her cool tone)*: I want you to bring Benny.

LEAH: I can't, it's a schoolday . . .

LYMAN (*terrified*): You're not taking Benny from me?
  (*She can't answer.*)
  You bring Benny to me, Leah!
    (FATHER *appears, shaking out his black shroud. They are all moving to leave.*)

LEAH: Stop shouting!—I can't bring him!
    (FATHER *flaps out the shroud, which billows out before him.* LYMAN*'s fear rises.*)

LYMAN: Don't leave me like this, for Christ's sake!
    (*They continue moving; he is terrified.*)
  I said wait a minute . . . ! Don't leave me! Leah, Bessie
  . . . Theo, listen . . . !
    (*With a sudden movement,* FATHER *sweeps the black cloth billowing out over* LYMAN *on the bed, covering him completely. He shouts from underneath . . .*)
  No! Don't! Pa! Please! Don't do it!

LEAH: Stop this! Why are you yelling!

LYMAN (*thrashing around in terror*): Where's the light! Where
  is the fucking light!
    (*To* TOM *for help*): What is he doing?
    (LYMAN *flings off the shroud—all they see is that he has been thrashing about; and he lies there now panting for breath as* FATHER *walks into darkness trailing the shroud, muttering.*)
    (*Starting away swiftly*): I can't bear it anymore!

LYMAN (*with a look of amazement*): Wait! Wait, please . . . I
  remember what happened!—how I got on the mountain!
  (*As memory floods back.*) —I kept calling you from the Howard Johnson's—yes. To tell you I'd be staying over because
  of the storm . . . but the line was busy. So I went to bed,
  yes . . . But it was still busy . . . over an hour . . .
  more! And I . . . yes, I started to ask the operator to cut in
  as an emergency, but . . . (*Breaks off.*) I remembered you
  once said to me . . .

LEAH: I was talking to . . .

LYMAN (*in quick fury*): I'm telling you what *happened*!—let
  me finish!

LEAH: I was talking to my brother!

LYMAN: In Japan, for over an hour?

LEAH: He just got back on Monday.

LYMAN: Well it doesn't matter.

LEAH: It certainly does matter!

LYMAN: Leah, remember you once said . . . "I might lie to you," remember that? Way at the beginning? It seemed so wonderful then . . . that you could be so honest; but now, on my back in that room, I started to die.

LEAH (*outraged*): I said it was my brother!

LYMAN: You're not understanding me, I'm not blaming you. I got dressed and back in the car to . . . *feel something again.* 'Cause it had all died in me, Leah—this whole ten-year commute was just . . . ludicrous! I was a corpse buried in that room . . . (*Humiliated, and trying to smile, his eyes filling with tears.*) I know it was crazy but I thought if I walked in two, three in the morning out of a roaring blizzard like that . . . you'd be so amazed, you'd believe how I needed you . . . *and I would believe it too!* And maybe we'd really fall in love again.

LEAH (*covering her face, weeping*): Oh God, Lyman . . . !

LYMAN: I got back in the car to stop the dying. So I know the kind of suffering you're feeling now. (*Looks at all of them.*) It's far too late, but I swear I've never felt the love for you that's in me now. (*On the verge of collapse.*) And thank God for that.

(*But they are silent.*)

Help me, Bessie, what should I understand!

BESSIE: There are other people.

(*A long pause.*)

LYMAN: Yes. And I'd give anything for your forgiveness. But you deserve the whole damned truth.—In some miserable dark corner of my soul I'm still not sure why I'm condemned! (*He weeps helplessly.*)

(*Pause.*)

BESSIE: Come, Mother.

THEO: . . . Say goodbye to him, dear.

BESSIE (*dry-eyed now; her feeling clearer, she has a close to impersonal sound*): I hope you're better soon, Daddy. Goodbye.

(*She takes her mother's arm—*THEO *no longer resists as they move out into darkness. He turns to* LEAH.)

LYMAN: Oh Leah, say something tough and honest . . . the way you can.

LEAH: I don't know if I'll ever believe anything . . . or anybody, again.

LYMAN: Oh no. No!—I haven't done that!

(*A great weeping sweeps her and she rushes out.*)

Leah! *Leah!*

(*But she is gone.*)

TOM: Talk to you soon.

(*He sees that* LYMAN *is lost in space, and he goes out. The* NURSE *comes from her corner to* LYMAN.)

NURSE: You got pain?

(*He doesn't reply.*)

I'll get you something to smooth you out.

LYMAN: Don't leave me alone, okay?—for a little while? Please. Sit with me. (*Pats the mattress.*) Come, don't be afraid.

(*She approaches the bed reluctantly; he draws her down to sit beside him. He takes her hand.*)

It's just two worlds, see?—women want it safe, but it's dangerous. Just is. Can't help it. And it's terrible. And it's okay.

NURSE (*not giving agreement*): Let me get you something. (*Starts to withdraw her hand.*)

LYMAN (*holding on to her hand*): Ten more seconds—I love your warmth, Logan. A woman's warmth is the last sacredness; you're a piece of the sun. The last magic.—Which reminds me . . . (*He kisses the back of her hand, then releases her.*) When you're out there fishing on the ice with your husband and your boy . . . what do you talk about?

NURSE: . . . Well, let's see . . . this last time we all bought us some shoes at that big Knapp Shoe Outlet up there?— they're seconds, but you can't tell them from new.

LYMAN: So you talked about your new shoes?

NURSE: Well, they're great buys.

LYMAN: Right. That . . . that's just wonderful to do that. I don't know why, but it just is.

NURSE: I'll be right back. (*She starts away.*)

LYMAN: Hate me?

NURSE (*with an embarrassed shrug*): I don't know. I got to think about it.

LYMAN: Come right back, huh? I'm still a little . . . shaky.

(*She leans down and kisses his forehead.*)

Why'd you do that?

NURSE: No reason. (*She exits.*)

LYMAN (*painful wonder and longing in his face, his eyes wide, alive . . .*): What a miracle everything is! Absolutely everything! . . . Imagine . . . three of them sitting out there together on that lake, talking about their shoes! (*He begins to weep, but quickly catches himself and with a contained suffering stares ahead.*)

BLACKOUT

THE LAST YANKEE

To Inge Morath

CHARACTERS

LEROY HAMILTON
JOHN FRICK
PATRICIA HAMILTON
KAREN FRICK
UNNAMED PATIENT

SCENE I

The visiting room of a state mental hospital. LEROY HAMILTON *is seated on one of the half-dozen chairs, idly leafing through an old magazine. He is forty-eight, trim, dressed in subdued Ivy League jacket and slacks and shined brogans. A banjo case rests against his chair.*

MR. FRICK *enters. He is sixty, solid, in a business suit. He carries a small valise. He looks about, glances at* LEROY, *just barely nods, and sits ten feet away. He looks at his watch, then impatiently at the room.* LEROY *goes on leafing through the magazine.*

FRICK (*pointing right*): Supposed to notify somebody in there?

LEROY (*indicating left*): Did you give your name to the attendant?

FRICK: Yes. 'Seem to be paying much attention, though.

LEROY: They know you're here, then. He calls through to the ward. (*Returns to his magazine.*)

FRICK (*slight pause*): Tremendous parking space down there. 'They need that for?

LEROY: Well a lot of people visit on weekends. Fills up pretty much.

FRICK: Really? That whole area?

LEROY: Pretty much.

FRICK: 'Doubt that. (*He goes to the window and looks out. Pause.*) Beautifully landscaped, got to say that for it.

LEROY: Yes, it's a very nice place.

FRICK: 'See them walking around out there it's hard to tell. 'Stopped one to ask directions and only realized when he stuck out his finger and pointed at my nose.

LEROY: Heh-heh.

FRICK: Quite a shock. Sitting there reading some thick book and crazy as a coot. You'd never know. (*He sits in another chair.* LEROY *returns to the magazine. He studies* LEROY.) Is it your wife?

LEROY: Yes.

FRICK: I've got mine in there too.

283

LEROY: Uh, huh. (*He stares ahead, politely refraining from the magazine.*)

FRICK: My name's Frick.

LEROY: Hi. I'm Hamilton.

FRICK: Gladameetu. (*Slight pause.*) How do you find it here?

LEROY: I guess they do a good job.

FRICK: Surprisingly well kept for a state institution.

LEROY: Oh, ya.

FRICK: Awful lot of colored, though, ain't there?

LEROY: Quite a few, ya.

FRICK: Yours been in long?

LEROY: Going on seven weeks now.

FRICK: They give you any idea when she can get out?

LEROY: Oh, I could take her out now, but I won't for a couple weeks.

FRICK: Why's that?

LEROY: Well this is her third time.

FRICK: 'Don't say.

LEROY: I'd like them to be a little more sure before I take her out again. . . . Although you can never *be* sure.

FRICK: That fairly common?—that they have to come back?

LEROY: About a third they say. This your first time, I guess.

FRICK: I just brought her in last Tuesday. I certainly hope she doesn't have to stay long. They ever say what's wrong with her?

LEROY: She's a depressive.

FRICK: Really. That's what they say about mine. Just gets . . . sort of sad?

LEROY: It's more like . . . frightened.

FRICK: Sounds just like mine. Got so she wouldn't even leave the house.

LEROY: That's right.

FRICK: Oh, yours too?

LEROY: Ya, she wouldn't go out. Not if she could help it, anyway.

FRICK: She ever hear sounds?

LEROY: She used to. Like a loud humming.

FRICK: Same thing! Ts. What do you know!—How old is she?

LEROY: She's forty-four.

FRICK: Is that all! I had an idea it had something to do with getting old . . .

LEROY: I don't think so. My wife is still—I wouldn't say a raving beauty, but she's still . . . a pretty winsome woman. They're usually sick a long time before you realize it, you know. I just never realized it.

FRICK: Mine never showed any signs at all. Just a nice, quiet kind of a woman. Always slept well . . .

LEROY: Well mine sleeps well too.

FRICK: Really?

LEROY: Lot of them love to sleep. I found that out. She'd take naps every afternoon. Longer and longer.

FRICK: Mine too. But then about six, eight months ago she got nervous about keeping the doors locked. And then the windows. I had to air-condition the whole house. I finally had to do the shopping, she just wouldn't go out.

LEROY: Oh I've done the shopping for twenty years.

FRICK: You don't say!

LEROY: Well you just never think of it as a sickness. I like to ski, for instance, or ice skating . . . she'd never come along. Or swimming in the summer. I always took the kids alone . . .

FRICK: Oh you have children.

LEROY: Yes. Seven.

FRICK: Seven!—I've been wondering if it was because she never had any.

LEROY: No, that's not it.—You don't have *any*?

FRICK: No. We kept putting it off, and then it got too late, and first thing you know . . . it's just too late.

LEROY: For a while there I thought maybe she had too *many* children . . .

FRICK: Well I don't have any, so . . .

LEROY: Yeah, I guess that's not it either.

(*Slight pause.*)

FRICK: I just can't figure it out. There's no bills; we're very well fixed; she's got a beautiful home. . . . There's really not a trouble in the world. Although, God knows, maybe that's the trouble . . .

LEROY: Oh no, I got plenty of bills and it didn't help mine. I don't think it's how many bills you have.

FRICK: What do you think it is, then?

LEROY: Don't ask me, I don't know.

FRICK: When she started locking up everything I thought

maybe it's these Negroes, you know? There's an awful lot of fear around; all this crime.

LEROY: I don't think so. My wife was afraid before there were any Negroes. I mean, around.

FRICK: Well one thing came out of it—I finally learned how to make coffee. And mine's better than hers was. It's an awful sensation, though—coming home and there's nobody there.

LEROY: How'd you like to come home and there's seven of them there?

FRICK: I guess I'm lucky at that.

LEROY: Well, I am too. They're wonderful kids.

FRICK: They still very young?

LEROY: Five to nineteen. But they all pitch in. Everything's clean, house runs like a ship.

FRICK: You're lucky to have good children these days.—I guess we're both lucky.

LEROY: That's the only way to look at it. Start feeling sorry for yourself, that's when you're in trouble.

FRICK: Awfully hard to avoid sometimes.

LEROY: You can't give in to it though. Like tonight—I was so disgusted I just laid down and . . . I was ready to throw in the chips. But then I got up and washed my face, put on the clothes, and here I am. After all, she can't help it either, who you going to blame?

FRICK: It's a mystery—a woman with everything she could possibly want. I don't care what happens to the country, there's nothing could ever hurt her anymore. Suddenly, out of nowhere, she's terrified! . . . She lost all her optimism. Yours do that? Lose her optimism?

LEROY: Mine was never very optimistic. She's Swedish.

FRICK: Oh. Mine certainly was. Whatever deal I was in, couldn't wait till I got home to talk about it. Real estate, stock market, always interested. All of a sudden, no interest whatsoever. Might as well be talking to that wall over there. —Your wife have brothers and sisters?

LEROY: Quite a few, ya.

FRICK: Really. I even thought maybe it's that she was an only child, and if she had brothers and sisters to talk to . . .

LEROY: Oh no—at least I don't think so. It could be even worse.

FRICK: They don't help, huh?

LEROY: They *think* they're helping. Come around saying it's a disgrace for their sister to be in a public institution. That's the kind of help. So I said, "Well, I'm the public!"

FRICK: Sure!—It's a perfectly nice place.

LEROY: They want her in the Rogers Pavilion.

FRICK: Rogers!—that's a couple of hundred dollars a day minimum . . .

LEROY: Well if I had that kind of money I wouldn't mind, but . . .

FRICK: No-no, don't you do it. I could afford it, but what are we paying taxes for?

LEROY: So they can go around saying their sister's in the Rogers Pavilion, that's all.

FRICK: Out of the question. That's fifty thousand dollars a year. Plus tips. I'm sure you have to tip them there.

LEROY: Besides, it's eighty miles there and back, I could never get to see her . . .

FRICK: If they're so sensitive you ought to tell *them* to pay for it. That'd shut them up, I bet.

LEROY: Well no—they've offered to pay part. Most of it, in fact.

FRICK: Whyn't you do it, then?

LEROY (*holding a secret*): I didn't think it's a good place for her.

FRICK: Why?—if they'd pay for it? It's one of the top places in the country. Some very rich people go there.

LEROY: I know.

FRICK: And the top doctors, you know. And they order whatever they want to eat. I went up there to look it over; no question about it, it's absolutely first-class, much better than this place. You should take them up on it.

LEROY: I'd rather have her here.

FRICK: Well I admire your attitude. You don't see that kind of pride anymore.

LEROY: It's not pride, exactly.

FRICK: Never mind, it's a great thing, keep it up. Everybody's got the gimmes, it's destroying the country. Had a man in a few weeks ago to put in a new showerhead. Nothing to it. Screw off the old one and screw on the new one. Seventeen dollars an hour!

LEROY: Yeah, well. (*Gets up, unable to remain seated.*) Everybody's got to live, I guess.

FRICK: I take my hat off to you—that kind of independence. Don't happen to be with Colonial Trust, do you?

LEROY: No.

FRICK: There was something familiar about you. What line are you in?

LEROY (*he is at the window now, staring out. Slight pause*): Carpenter.

FRICK (*taken aback*): Don't say. . . . Contractor?

LEROY: No. Just carpenter.—I take on one or two fellas when I have to, but I work alone most of the time.

FRICK: I'd never have guessed it.

LEROY: Well that's what I do. (*Looks at his watch, wanting escape.*)

FRICK: I mean your whole . . . your way of dressing and everything.

LEROY: Why? Just ordinary clothes.

FRICK: No, you look like a college man.

LEROY: Most of them have long hair, don't they?

FRICK: The way college men used to look. I've spent thirty years around carpenters, that's why it surprised me. You know Frick Supply, don't you?

LEROY: Oh ya. I've bought quite a lot of wood from Frick.

FRICK: I sold out about five years ago . . .

LEROY: I know. I used to see you around there.

FRICK: You did? Why didn't you mention it?

LEROY (*shrugs*): Just didn't.

FRICK: You say Anthony?

LEROY: No, Hamilton. Leroy.

FRICK (*points at him*): Hey now! Of course! There was a big article about you in the *Herald* a couple of years ago. Descended from Alexander Hamilton.

LEROY: That's right.

FRICK: Sure! No wonder! (*Holding out his palm as to a photo.*) Now that I visualize you in overalls, I think I recognize you. In fact, you were out in the yard loading plywood the morning that article came out. My bookkeeper pointed you out through the window. It's those clothes—if I'd seen you in overalls I'd've recognized you right off. Well, what do you know? (*The air of condescension plus wonder.*) Amazing thing what clothes'll do, isn't it.—Keeping busy?

LEROY: I get work.

FRICK: What are you fellas charging now?

LEROY: I get seventeen an hour.

FRICK: Good for you.

LEROY: I hate asking that much, but even so I just about make it.

FRICK: Shouldn't feel that way; if they'll pay it, grab it.

LEROY: Well ya, but it's still a lot of money.—My head's still back there thirty years ago.

FRICK: What are you working on now?

LEROY: I'm renovating a colonial near Waverly. I just finished over in Belleville. The Presbyterian church.

FRICK: Did you do *that*?

LEROY: Yeah, just finished Wednesday.

FRICK: That's a beautiful job. You're a good man. Where'd they get that altar?

LEROY: I built that.

FRICK: That altar?

LEROY: Uh huh.

FRICK: Hell, that's first-class! Huh! You must be doing all right.

LEROY: Just keeping ahead of it.

FRICK (*slight pause*): How'd it happen?

LEROY: What's that?

FRICK: Well coming out of an old family like that—how do you come to being a carpenter?

LEROY: Just . . . liked it.

FRICK: Father a carpenter?

LEROY: No.

FRICK: What was your father?

LEROY: Lawyer.

FRICK: Why didn't you?

LEROY: Just too dumb, I guess.

FRICK: Couldn't buckle down to the books, huh?

LEROY: I guess not.

FRICK: Your father should've taken you in hand.

LEROY (*sits with magazine, opening it*): He didn't like the law either.

FRICK: Even so.—Many of the family still around?

LEROY: Well my mother, and two brothers.

FRICK: No, I mean of the Hamiltons.

LEROY: Well they're Hamiltons.

FRICK: I know, but I mean—some of them must be pretty important people.

LEROY: I wouldn't know. I never kept track of them.

FRICK: You should. Probably some of them must be pretty big. —Never even looked them up?

LEROY: Nope.

FRICK: You realize the importance of Alexander Hamilton, don't you?

LEROY: I know about him, more or less.

FRICK: More or less! He was one of the most important Founding Fathers.

LEROY: I guess so, ya.

FRICK: You read about him, didn't you?

LEROY: Well sure . . . I read about him.

FRICK: Well didn't your father talk about him?

LEROY: Some. But he didn't care for him much.

FRICK: Didn't care for *Alexander Hamilton*?

LEROY: It was something to do with his philosophy. But I never kept up with the whole thing.

FRICK (*laughing, shaking his head*): Boy, you're quite a character, aren't you.

> (LEROY *is silent, reddening.* FRICK *continues chuckling at him for a moment.*)

LEROY: I hope to God your wife is cured, Mr. Frick, I hope she never has to come back here again.

FRICK (*sensing the hostility*): What have I said?

LEROY: This is the third time in two years for mine, and I don't mean to be argumentative, but it's got me right at the end of my rope. For all I know I'm in line for this funny farm myself by now, but I have to tell you that this could be what's driving so many people crazy.

FRICK: What is!

LEROY: This.

FRICK: This what?

LEROY: This whole kind of conversation.

FRICK: Why? What's wrong with it?

LEROY: Well never mind.

FRICK: I don't know what you're talking about.

LEROY: Well what's it going to be, equality or what kind of country—I mean, am I supposed to be ashamed I'm a carpenter?

FRICK: Who said you . . . ?

LEROY: Then why do you talk like this to a man? One minute my altar is terrific and the next minute I'm some kind of shit bucket.

FRICK: Hey now, wait a minute . . . !

LEROY: I don't mean anything against you personally, I know you're a successful man and more power to you, but this whole type of conversation about my clothes—should I be ashamed I'm a carpenter? I mean everybody's talking "labor, labor," how much labor's getting; well if it's so great to be labor how come nobody wants to be it? I mean you ever hear a parent going around saying—(*mimes thumb pridefully tucked into suspenders*)—"My son is a carpenter"? Do you? Do you ever hear people brag about a bricklayer? I don't know what you are but I'm only a dumb swamp Yankee, but . . . (*Suddenly breaks off with a shameful laugh.*) Excuse me. I'm really sorry. But you come back here two-three more times and you're liable to start talking the way you were never brought up to. (*Opens magazine.*)

FRICK: I don't understand what you're so hot about.

LEROY (*looks up from the magazine. Seems to start to explain, then sighs*): Nothing.

> (*He returns to his magazine.* FRICK *shakes his head with a certain condescension, then goes back to the window and looks out.*)

FRICK: It's one hell of a parking lot, you have to say that for it. (*They sit for a long moment in silence, each in his own thoughts.*)

BLACKOUT

SCENE 2

Most of the stage is occupied by PATRICIA*'s bedroom. In one of the beds a fully clothed woman lies motionless with one arm over her eyes. She will not move throughout the scene.*

Outside this bedroom is a corner of the Recreation Room, bare but for a few scattered chairs.

Presently . . . from just offstage the sound of a Ping-Pong game. The ball comes bouncing into the Recreation Room area and PATRICIA HAMILTON *enters chasing it. She captures it and with a sigh of boredom goes offstage with it.*

We hear two or three pings and the ball comes onstage again with PATRICIA HAMILTON *after it. She starts to return to the game offstage but halts, looks at the ball in her hand, and to someone offstage . . .*

PATRICIA: Why are we doing this? Come let's talk, I hate these games.

> (MRS. KAREN FRICK *enters. She is in her sixties, very thin, eyeglasses, wispy hair.*)

I said I'm quitting.

> (KAREN *stares at the paddle.*)

Well never mind. (*Studies her watch.*) You're very good.

KAREN: My sister-in-law taught me. She used to be a stewardess on the *Queen Mary*. She could even play when the ship was rocking. But she never married.

PATRICIA: Here, put it down, dear.

> (KAREN *passively gives up the paddle, then stands there looking uncomfortable.*)

I'm going to lie down; sit with me, if you like.

KAREN (*indicates Ping-Pong area*): Hardly anyone ever seems to come out there.

PATRICIA: They don't like exercise, they're too depressed.

> (PATRICIA *lies down. The woman in the other bed does not stir and no attention is paid to her.*)

Don't feel obliged to say anything if you . . .

KAREN: I get sick to my stomach just looking at a boat. Does your husband hunt?

PATRICIA: Sit down. Relax yourself. You don't have to talk, although I think you're doing a little better than yesterday.

KAREN: Oh, I like talking with you. (*Explaining herself timorously; indicating offstage—and very privately . . .*) I should go out—he doesn't like being kept waiting, don't y'know.

PATRICIA: Why are you so afraid? He might start treasuring you more if you make him wait a little. Come, sit.

> (KAREN *adventurously sits at the foot of the bed, glancing about nervously.*)

Men are only big children, you know—give them a chocolate soda every day and pretty soon it doesn't mean a thing to them. (*Looks at her watch again.*) Only reason I'm nervous is that I can't decide whether to go home today.—But you mustn't mention it, will you?

KAREN: Mention . . . ?

PATRICIA: About my pills. I haven't told anybody yet.

> (KAREN *looks a bit blank.*)

Well never mind.

KAREN: Oh! You mean not taking them.

PATRICIA: But you mustn't mention it, will you. The doctor would be very upset.

KAREN: And how long has it been?

PATRICIA: Twenty-one days today. It's the longest I've been clean in maybe fifteen years. I can hardly believe it.

KAREN: Are you Baptist?

PATRICIA: Baptist? No, we're more Methodist. But the church I'd really love hasn't been invented yet.

KAREN (*charmed, slavishly interested*): How would it be?

PATRICIA (*begins to describe it, breaks off*): I can't describe it. (*A sign of lostness.*) I was raised Lutheran, of course.—But I often go to the Marble Baptist Church on Route 91? I've gotten to like that minister.—You hear what I'm saying, don't you?

> (KAREN *looks at her nervously trying to remember.*)

I must say it's kind of relaxing talking to you, Karen, knowing that you probably won't remember too much. But you'll come out of it all right, you're just a little scared, aren't you.

—But who isn't? (*Slight pause.*) Doctor Rockwell is not going to believe I'm doing better without medication but I really think something's clicked inside me. (*A deep breath.*) I even seem to be breathing easier. And I'm not feeling that sort of fuzziness in my head.—It's like some big bird has been hovering over me for fifteen years, and suddenly it's flown away.

KAREN: I can't stand dead animals, can you?

PATRICIA: Well just insist that he has to stop hunting! You don't have to stand for that, you're a *person*.

KAREN: Well you know, men like to . . .

PATRICIA: Not all—I've known some lovely men. Not many, but a few. This minister I mentioned?—he came one day this summer and sat with me on our porch . . . and we had ice cream and talked for over an hour. You know, when he left his previous church they gave him a Pontiac Grand Am. He made me realize something; he said that I seem to be in like a constant state of prayer. And it's true; every once in a while it stops me short, realizing it. It's like inside me I'm almost continually talking to the Lord. Not in words exactly . . . just—you know—communicating with Him. Or trying to. (*Deeply excited, but suppressing it.*) I tell you truthfully, if I can really come out of this I'm going to . . . I don't know what . . . fall in love with God. I think I have already.

KAREN: You're really beautiful.

PATRICIA: Oh no, dear, I'm a torn-off rag of my old self. The pills put ten years on my face. If he was a Jew or Italian or even Irish he'd be suing these doctors, but Yankees never sue, you know. Although I have to say the only thing he's been right about is medication.

KAREN: Your husband against pills?

PATRICIA: Fanatical. But of course he can stick his head out the window and go high as a kite on a breath of fresh air. (*Looks at her watch.*)

KAREN: I really think you're extremely attractive.

PATRICIA: No-no, dear, although I did win the county beauty pageant when I was nineteen. But if you're talking beauty you should have seen my mother. She only died two years ago, age eighty-nine, but I still haven't gotten over it. On the beach, right into her seventies, people would still be staring at her—she had an unbelievable bust right up to the end.

KAREN: I cut this finger once in a broken Coke machine. But we never sued.

PATRICIA: Did your conversation always jump around? Because it could be your pills, believe me; the soul belongs to God, we're not supposed to be stuffing Valium into His mouth.

KAREN: I have a cousin who went right through the windshield and she didn't get a cent. (*Slight pause.*) And it was five below zero out. (*Slight pause.*) Her husband's Norwegian.

PATRICIA: Look, dear, I know you're trying but don't feel you have to speak.

KAREN: No, I like speaking to you. Is he Baptist too, your husband?

PATRICIA: I said Methodist. But he's more Episcopal. But he'll go to any church if it's raining. (*Slight pause.*) I just don't know whether to tell him yet.

KAREN: What.

PATRICIA: That I'm off everything.

KAREN: But he'll like that, won't he?

PATRICIA: Oh yes. But he's going to be doubtful.—Which I am, too, let's face it—who can know for sure that you're going to stay clean? I don't want to fool myself, I've been on one medication or another for almost twenty years. But I do feel a thousand percent better. And I really have no idea how it happened. (*Shakes her head.*) Dear God, when I think of him hanging in there all these years . . . I'm so ashamed. But at the same time he's absolutely refused to make any money, every one of our children has had to work since they could practically write their names. I can't be expected to applaud, exactly. (*Presses her eyes.*) I guess sooner or later you just have to stand up and say, "I'm normal, I made it." But it's like standing on top of a stairs and there's no stairs. (*Staring ahead.*)

KAREN: I think I'd better go out to him. Should I tell your husband you're coming out?

PATRICIA: I think I'll wait a minute.

KAREN (*stands*): He seems very nice.

PATRICIA: —I'll tell you the truth, dear—I've put him through hell and I know it. . . . (*Tears threaten her.*) I know I have to stop blaming him; it came to me like a visitation two weeks ago, I-must-not-blame-Leroy-anymore. And it's amazing. I lost all desire for medication, I could feel it leaving me like a . . . like a ghost. (*Slight pause.*) It's just that he's got really well-to-do relatives and he simply will not accept anyone's help. I mean you take the Jews, the Italians, Irish—they've got their Italian-Americans, Irish-Americans, Hispanic-Americans—they stick together and help each other. But you ever hear of Yankee-Americans? Not on your life. Raise his taxes, rob him blind, the Yankee'll just sit there all alone getting sadder and sadder.—But I'm not going to think about it anymore.

KAREN: You have a very beautiful chin.

PATRICIA: Men with half his ability riding around in big expensive cars and now for the second Easter Sunday in a row his rear end collapsed.

KAREN: I think my license must have expired.

PATRICIA (*a surge of deep anger*): I refuse to ride around in a nine-year-old Chevrolet which was bought secondhand in the first place!

KAREN: They say there are only three keys for all General Motors cars. You suppose that's possible?

PATRICIA (*peremptorily now*): Believe me, dear, whatever they tell you, you have got to cut down the medication. It could be what's making your mind jump around . . .

KAREN: No, it's that you mentioned Chevrolet, which is General Motors, you see.

PATRICIA: Oh. . . . Well, let's just forget about it. (*Slight pause.*) Although you're probably right—here you're carefully locking your car and some crook is walking around with the same keys in his pocket. But everything's a fake, we all know that.

KAREN (*facing* PATRICIA *again*): I guess that would be depressing.

PATRICIA: No, that's not what depressed me . . .

KAREN: No, I meant him refusing to amount to anything and then spending money on banjo lessons.

PATRICIA: Did I tell you that?—I keep forgetting what I told you because I never know when you're listening. (*Holds out her hand.*) Here we go again. (*Grasps her hand to stop the shaking.*)

KAREN: —You sound like you had a wonderful courtship.

PATRICIA: Oh, Karen, everyone envied us, we were the handsomest pair in town; and I'm not boasting, believe me. (*Breaks off; watches her hand shake and covers it again.*) I just don't want to have to come back here again, you see. I don't think I could bear that. (*Grips her hand, moving about.*) I simply have to think positively. But it's unbelievable—he's seriously talking about donating his saw-and-chisel collection to the museum!—some of those tools are as old as the United States, they might be worth a fortune!—But I'm going to look ahead, that's all, just as straight ahead as a highway.

(*Slight pause.*)

KAREN: I feel so ashamed.

PATRICIA: For Heaven's sake, why? You've got a right to be depressed. There's more people in hospitals because of depression than any other disease.

KAREN: Is that true?

PATRICIA: Of course! Anybody with any sense has got to be depressed in this country. Unless you're really rich, I suppose. Don't let him shame you, dear.

KAREN: No . . . it's that you have so many thoughts.

PATRICIA: Oh. Well you can have thoughts, too—just remember your soul belongs to God and you mustn't be shoving pills into His mouth.

(*Slight pause.*)

KAREN: We're rich, I think.

PATRICIA (*quickly interested*): . . . Really rich?

KAREN: He's got the oil delivery now, and of course he always had the fertilizer and the Chevy dealership, and of course the lumber yard and all. And Isuzus now.

PATRICIA: What's Isuzus?

KAREN: It's a Japanese car.

PATRICIA: . . . I'll just never catch up.

KAREN: We go to Arkansas in the spring.

PATRICIA: Arkansas?

KAREN: For the catfish. It's where I broke down. But I can't help it, the sight of catfish makes me want to vomit. Not that I was trying to . . . you know . . . do anything. I just read the instructions on the bottle wrong. Do you mind if I ask you something?

PATRICIA: I hope it's nothing personal, is it?

KAREN: Well I don't know.

PATRICIA: . . . Well go ahead, what is it?

KAREN: Do you shop in the A&P or Stop & Shop?

PATRICIA: . . . I'm wondering if you've got the wrong medication. But I guess you'll never overdose—you vomit at the drop of a hat. It may be your secret blessing.

KAREN: —He wants to get me out of the house more, but it's hard to make up my mind where.

PATRICIA: Well . . . A&P is good. Or Stop & Shop. More or less. Kroger's is good for fish sometimes.

KAREN: Which do you like best? I'll go where you go.

PATRICIA: You're very flattering. (*Stands, inner excitement.*) It's amazing—I'm really beginning to feel wonderful; maybe I ought to go home with him today. I mean what does it come down to, really?—it's simply a question of confidence . . .

KAREN: I wish we could raise some vegetables like we did on the farm. Do you?

PATRICIA: Oh, he raises things in our yard. Healthy things like salsify and collards—and kale. You ever eat kale?

KAREN: I can't remember kale.

PATRICIA: You might as well salt your shower curtain and chop it up with a tomato.

KAREN: —So . . . meats are . . . which?—A&P?

PATRICIA: No. Meats are Stop & Shop. I'm really thinking I might go home today. It's just not his fault, I have to remember that . . .

KAREN: But staples?

PATRICIA: What?—Oh. Stop & Shop.

KAREN: Then what's for A&P?

PATRICIA: Vegetables.

KAREN: Oh right. And Kroger's?

PATRICIA: Why don't you just forget Kroger's.

KAREN (*holds up five fingers, bends one at a time . . .*): Then Stop & Shop . . .

PATRICIA: Maybe it's that you're trying to remember three things. Whyn't you just do A&P and Stop & Shop.
(*Slight pause.*)

KAREN: I kind of liked Kroger's.

PATRICIA: Then go to Kroger's, for Heaven's sake!

KAREN: Well I guess I'll go out to him. (*Moves to go. Halts.*) I hope you aren't really leaving today, are you?

PATRICIA (*higher tension*): I'm deciding.

KAREN: Well . . . here I go, I guess. (*Halts again.*) I meant to tell you, I kind of like the banjo. It's very good with tap dancing.

PATRICIA: Tap dancing.

KAREN: There's a tap teacher lives on our road.

PATRICIA: You tap-dance?

KAREN: Well John rented a video of Ginger Rogers and Fred Astaire, and I kind of liked it. I can sing "Cheek to Cheek"? Would you like to hear it?

PATRICIA: Sure, go ahead—this is certainly a surprise.

KAREN (*sings in a frail voice*): "Heaven, I'm in heaven, and the cares that clung around me through the week . . ."

PATRICIA: That's beautiful, Karen! Listen, what exactly does Doctor Rockwell say about you?

KAREN: Well, he says it's quite common when a woman is home alone all day.

PATRICIA: What's common?

KAREN: Something moving around in the next room?

PATRICIA: Oh, I see.—You have any idea who it is?

KAREN: My mother.—My husband might bring my tap shoes and tails . . . but he probably forgot. I have a high hat and shorts too. And a walking stick? But would they allow dancing in here?

PATRICIA: They might. But of course the minute they see you enjoying yourself they'll probably try to knock you out with a pill.

(KAREN *makes to go, halts again.*)

KAREN: Did your mother like you?

PATRICIA: Oh yes. We were all very close. Didn't yours?

KAREN: No. She left the whole farm to her cousin. Tell about your family, can you? Were they really all blond?

PATRICIA: Oh as blond as the tassels on Golden Bantam corn . . . everybody'd turn and look when we went by. My mother was perfection. We all were, I guess. (*With a chuckle.*) You know, we had a flat roof extending from the house over the garage, and mother and my sisters and me—on the first warm spring days we used to sunbathe out there.

KAREN (*covering her mouth*): No! You mean nude?

PATRICIA: Nudity doesn't matter that much in Sweden, and we were all brought up to love the sun. And we'd near die laughing because the minute we dropped our robes—you know how quiet a town Grenville is—you could hear the footsteps going up the clock tower over the Presbyterian church, and we pretended not to notice but that little narrow tower was just packed with Presbyterians.

KAREN: Good lord!

PATRICIA: We'd stretch out and pretend not to see a thing. And then my mother'd sit up suddenly and point up at the steeple and yell, "Boo!" And they'd all go running down the stairs like mice!

(*They both enjoy the laugh.*)

KAREN: I think your husband's very good-looking, isn't he.

PATRICIA: He is, but my brothers . . . I mean the way they stood, and walked . . . and their teeth! Charles won the All–New England golf tournament, and Buzz came within a tenth of an inch of the gold medal in the pole vault—that was in the Portugal Olympics.

KAREN: My! Do you still get together much?

PATRICIA: Oh, they're all gone now.

KAREN: Moved away?

PATRICIA: No . . . dead.

KAREN: Oh my. They overstrain?

PATRICIA: Buzz hung himself on his wife's closet door.

KAREN: Oh my!

PATRICIA: Eight days later Charles shot himself on the tractor.

KAREN (*softly*): Oh my. Did they leave a note or anything?

PATRICIA: No. But we all knew what it was.

KAREN: Can you say?

PATRICIA: Disappointment. We were all brought up expecting to be wonderful, and . . . (*breaks off with a shrug*) . . . just wasn't.

KAREN: Well . . . here I go.

(KAREN *exits.* PATRICIA *stares ahead for a moment in a blankly reminiscent mood. Now she looks at her face in a mirror, smoothing wrinkles away . . .*)

(LEROY *enters.*)

PATRICIA: I was just coming out.

LEROY: 'Cause Mrs. Frick . . .

PATRICIA (*cuts him off by drawing his head down and stroking his cheek. And in a soft but faintly patronizing tone . . .*): I was just coming out, Leroy. You don't have to repeat everything. Come, sit with me and let's not argue.

LEROY: . . . How's your day been?

> (*She is still moved by her brothers' memory; also, she hasn't received something she hoped for from him. She shrugs and turns her head away.*)

PATRICIA: I've had worse.

LEROY: Did you wash your hair?

PATRICIA (*pleased he noticed*): How can you tell?

LEROY: Looks livelier. Is that nail polish?

PATRICIA: M-hm.

LEROY: Good. You're looking good, Patty.

PATRICIA: I'm feeling better. Not completely but a lot.

LEROY (*nods approvingly*): Great! Did he change your medication or something?

PATRICIA: No.

LEROY: Something different about you.

PATRICIA (*mysteriously excited*): You think so?

LEROY: Your eyes are clearer. You seem more like you're . . . connecting.

PATRICIA: I am, I think. But I warn you, I'm nervous.

LEROY: That's okay. Your color is more . . . I don't know . . . vigorous.

PATRICIA: Is it? (*She touches her face.*)

LEROY: You look almost like years ago . . .

PATRICIA: Something's happened but I don't want to talk about it yet.

LEROY: Really? Like what?

PATRICIA (*instant resistance*): I just said I . . .

LEROY: . . . Okay. (*Goes to a window.*) —It looks like rain outside, but we can walk around if you like. They've got a beautiful tulip bed down there; the colors really shine in this gray light. Reds and purple and whites, and a gray. Never saw a tulip be that kind of gray.

PATRICIA: How's Amelia's leg? Are you getting her to change her bandage?

LEROY: Yes. But she'd better stop thinking she can drive a car.

PATRICIA: Well, why don't you tell her?

LEROY (*a little laugh*): That'll be the day, won't it, when she starts listening to her father.

PATRICIA (*a softness despite her language*): She might if you laid down the law without just complaining. And if she could hear something besides disappointment in your voice.

LEROY: She's learned to look down at me, Patty, you know that.

PATRICIA (*strongly, but nearly a threat of weeping*): Well, I hope you're not blaming me for that.

LEROY (*he holds back, stands silent. Then puffs out his cheeks and blows, shaking his head with a defensive grin*): Not my day, I see.

PATRICIA: Maybe it could have been.

LEROY: I was looking forward to telling you something.

PATRICIA: What.

LEROY: I got Harrelson to agree to twelve-thousand-five for the altar.

PATRICIA: There, you see!—and you were so glad to accept eight. I told you . . . !

LEROY: I give you all the credit. I finally got it through my thick skull, I said to myself, okay, you are slower than most, but quality's got a right to be slow. And he didn't make a peep—twelve thousand, five hundred dollars.

(*She looks at him, immensely sad.*)

—Well why do you look so sad?

PATRICIA: Come here. (*Draws him down, kisses him.*) I'm glad. . . . I just couldn't help thinking of all these years wasted trying to get you to charge enough; but I've decided to keep looking straight ahead, not back—I'm very glad you got the twelve. You've done a wonderful thing.

LEROY (*excited*): Listen, what has he got you on?

PATRICIA: Well, I'm still a long way from perfect, but I . . .

LEROY: Patty, nothing's perfect except a hot bath.

PATRICIA: It's nothing to joke about. I told you I'm nervous, I'm not used to . . . to . . .

LEROY: He changed your medication, didn't he.

PATRICIA: I just don't want you to think I have no problems anymore.

LEROY: Oh, I'd never think that, Patty. Has he put you on something new?

PATRICIA: *He* hasn't done anything.

(*Pause.*)

LEROY: Okay, I'll shut up.

(*She sweeps her hair back; he silently observes her. Then . . .*)
. . . This Mr. Frick handles oil burners; I don't know if I can trust him but he says he'd give me a good buy. We could use a new burner.

PATRICIA: What would you say if I said I'm thinking of coming home.

LEROY (*a pause filled with doubt*): You are? When?

PATRICIA: Maybe next Thursday. For good.

LEROY: Uh huh.

PATRICIA: You don't sound very positive.

LEROY: You know you're the only one can make that decision, Pat. You want to come home I'm always happy to take you home.

(*Slight pause.*)

PATRICIA: I feel if I could look ahead just the right amount I'd be all right.

LEROY: What do you mean?

PATRICIA: I realized something lately; when I'm home I have a tendency—especially in the afternoons when everybody's out and I'm alone—I look very far ahead. What I should do is only look ahead a little bit, like to the evening or the next day. And then it's all right. It's when I start looking years ahead . . . (*Slight pause . . .*) You once told me why you think I got sick. I've forgotten . . . what did you say?

LEROY: What do I really know about it, Pat?

PATRICIA: Why do you keep putting yourself down?—you've got to stop imitating your father. There are things you know very well.—Remind me what you said . . . Why am I sick?

LEROY: I always thought it was your family.

PATRICIA (*fingers pressing on her eyes*): I want to concentrate. Go on.

LEROY: They were so close, they were all over each other, and you all had this—you know—very high opinion of yourselves; each and every one of you was automatically going to

go to the head of the line just because your name was Sor-
genson. And life isn't that way, so you got sick.

(*Long pause; she stares, nodding.*)

PATRICIA: You've had no life at all, have you.

LEROY: I wouldn't say that.

PATRICIA: I can't understand how I never saw it.

LEROY: Why?—it's been great watching the kids growing up;
and I've had some jobs I've enjoyed . . .

PATRICIA: But not your wife.

LEROY: It's a long time since I blamed you, Pat. It's your
upbringing.

PATRICIA: Well I could blame yours too, couldn't I.

LEROY: You sure could.

PATRICIA: I mean this constant optimism is very irritating
when you're fifty times more depressed than I am.

LEROY: Now Patty, you know that's not . . .

PATRICIA: You are depressed, Leroy! Because you're scared of
people, you really don't trust anyone, and that's incidentally
why you never made any money. You could have set the
world on fire but you can't bear to work along with other
human beings.

LEROY: The last human being I took on to help me tried to
steal my half-inch Stanley chisel.

PATRICIA: You mean you *think* he tried . . .

LEROY: I didn't think anything, I found it in his tool box. And
that's an original Stanley, not the junk they sell today.

PATRICIA: So what!

LEROY: So what?—that man has three grandchildren! And he's
a Chapman—that's one of the oldest upstanding families in
the county.

PATRICIA (*emphatically, her point proved*): Which is why you're
depressed.

LEROY (*laughs*): I'm not, but why shouldn't I be?—a Chapman
stealing a chisel? I mean God Almighty, they've had generals
in that family, secretaries of state or some goddam thing.
Anyway, if I'm depressed it's from something that happened,
not something I imagine.

PATRICIA: I feel like a log that keeps bumping against another
log in the middle of the river.

LEROY: Boy, you're a real roller coaster. We were doing great there for a minute, what got us off on this?

PATRICIA: I can't be at peace when I know you are full of denial, and that's saying it straight.

LEROY: What denial? (*Laughs.*) You want me to say I'm a failure?

PATRICIA: That is not what I . . .

LEROY: Hey, I know what—I'll get a bumper sticker printed up—"The driver of this car is a failure!"—I betcha I could sell a hundred million of them . . . (*A sudden fury.*) . . . Or maybe I should just drive out on a tractor and shoot myself!

PATRICIA: That's a terrible thing to say to me, Leroy!

LEROY: Well I'm sorry, Patty, but I'm not as dumb as I look— I'm never going to win if I have to compete against your brothers!

PATRICIA (*chastened for the moment*): I did not say you're a failure.

LEROY: I didn't mean to yell; I'm sorry. I know you don't mean to sound like you do, sometimes.

PATRICIA (*unable to retrieve*): I said nothing about a failure. (*On the verge of weeping.*)

LEROY: It's okay, maybe I am a failure; but in my opinion no more than the rest of this country.

PATRICIA: What happened?—I thought this visit started off so nicely.

LEROY: Maybe you're not used to being so alert; you've been so lethargic for a long time, you know.

(*She moves; he watches her.*)

I'm sure of it, Pat, if you could only find two ounces of trust I know we could still have a life.

PATRICIA: I know. (*Slight pause; she fights down tears.*) What did you have in mind, exactly, when you said it was my upbringing?

LEROY: I don't know . . . I had a flash of your father, that time long ago when we were sitting on your porch . . . we were getting things ready for our wedding . . . and right in front of you he turns to me cool as a cucumber and says— (*through laughter, mimicking Swedish accent*)—"No Yankee will ever be good enough for a Swedish girl." I nearly fell off into the rosebushes.

PATRICIA (*laughs with a certain delight*): Well, he was old-fashioned . . .

LEROY (*laughing*): Yeah, a real old-fashioned welcome into the family!

PATRICIA: Well, the Yankees *were* terrible to us.

LEROY: That's a hundred years ago, Pat.

PATRICIA (*starting to anger*): You shouldn't keep denying this! —They paid them fifty cents a week and called us dumb Swedes with strong backs and weak minds and did nothing but make us ridiculous.

LEROY: But, Patty, if you walk around town today there isn't a good piece of property that isn't owned by Swedes.

PATRICIA: But that's now.

LEROY: Well when are we living?

PATRICIA: We were treated like animals, some Yankee doctors wouldn't come out to a Swedish home to deliver a baby . . .

LEROY (*laughs*): Well all I hope is that I'm the last Yankee so people can start living today instead of a hundred years ago.

PATRICIA: There was something else you said. About standing on line.

LEROY: On line?

PATRICIA: That you'll always be at the head of the line because . . . (*Breaks off.*)

LEROY: I'm the only one on it.

PATRICIA: . . . Is that really true? You do compete, don't you? You must, at least in your mind?

LEROY: Only with myself. We're really all on a one-person line, Pat. I learned that in these years.

(*Pause. She stares ahead.*)

PATRICIA: That's very beautiful. Where'd you get that idea?

LEROY: I guess I made it up, I don't know. It's up to you, Pat—if you feel you're ready, let's go home. Now or Thursday or whenever. What about medication?

PATRICIA (*makes herself ready*): I wasn't going to tell you for another week or two, till I'm absolutely rock sure;—I've stopped taking anything for . . . this is twenty-one days.

LEROY: *Anything?*

(*She nods with a certain suspense.*)

My God, Patty. And you feel all right?

PATRICIA: . . . I haven't felt this way in—fifteen years. I've no idea why, but I forgot to take anything, and I slept right through till morning, and I woke up and it was like . . . I'd been blessed during the night. And I haven't had anything since.

LEROY: Did I tell you or didn't I!

PATRICIA: But it's different for you. You're not addictive . . .

LEROY: But didn't I tell you all that stuff is poison? I'm just flying, Patty.

PATRICIA (*clasps her hands to steady herself*): But I'm afraid about coming home. I don't know if I'm jumping the gun. I *feel* I could, but . . .

LEROY: Well, let's talk about it. Is it a question of trusting yourself? Because I think if you've come this far . . .

PATRICIA: Be quiet a minute! (*She holds his hand.*) Why have you stayed with me?

LEROY (*laughs*): God knows!

PATRICIA: I've been very bad to you sometimes, Leroy, I really see that now. (*Starting to weep.*) Tell me the truth; in all these years, have you gone to other women? I wouldn't blame you, I just want to know.

LEROY: Well I've thought of it but I never did anything.

PATRICIA (*looking deeply into his eyes*): You really haven't, have you.

LEROY: No.

PATRICIA: Why?

LEROY: I just kept hoping you'd come out of this.

PATRICIA: But it's been so long.

LEROY: I know.

PATRICIA: Even when I'd . . . throw things at you?

LEROY: Uh uh.

PATRICIA: Like that time with the roast?

LEROY: Well, that's one time I came pretty close. But I knew it was those damned pills, not you.

PATRICIA: But why would you be gone night after night? That was a woman, wasn't it.

LEROY: No. Some nights I went over to the library basement to practice banjo with Phil Palumbo. Or to Manny's Diner for some donuts and talk to the fellas.

PATRICIA (*slightest tinge of suspicion*): There are fellas there at *night*?

LEROY: Sure; working guys, mostly young single fellas. But some with wives. You know—have a beer, watch TV.

PATRICIA: And women?

LEROY (*a short beat*): —You know, Pat—and I'm not criticizing —but wouldn't it be better for you to try believing a person instead of trying not to believe?

PATRICIA: I'm just wondering if you know . . . there's lots of women would love having you. But you probably don't know that, do you.

LEROY: Sure I do.

PATRICIA: You know lots of women would love to have you?

LEROY: . . . Well, yes, I know that.

PATRICIA: Really. How do you know that?

LEROY (*his quick, open laugh*): I can tell.

PATRICIA: Then what's keeping you? Why don't you move out?

LEROY: Pat, you're torturing me.

PATRICIA: I'm trying to find myself!

> (*She moves in stress, warding off an explosion. There is angry resentment in his voice.*)

LEROY: I'd remember you happy and loving—that's what kept me; as long ago as that is now, I'd remember how you'd pull on your stockings and get a little makeup on and pin up your hair. . . . When you're positive about life there's just nobody like you. Nobody. Not in life, not in the movies, not on TV. (*Slight pause.*) But I'm not going to deny it—if it wasn't for the kids I probably *would* have gone.

> (*She is silent, but loaded with something unspoken.*)

You're wanting to tell me something, aren't you.

PATRICIA: . . . I know what a lucky woman I've been.

LEROY (*he observes her*): —What is it, you want me to stop coming to see you for a while? Please tell me, Pat; there's something on your mind.

> (*Pause. She forces it out.*)

PATRICIA: I know I shouldn't feel this way, but I'm not too sure I could stand it, knowing that it's never going to . . . I mean, will it ever change anymore?

LEROY: You mean—is it ever going to be "wonderful."

> (*She looks at him, estimating.*)

Well—no, I guess this is pretty much it; although to me it's already wonderful—I mean the kids, and there are some clear New England mornings when you want to drink the air and the sunshine.

PATRICIA: You can make more out of a change in temperature than any human being I ever heard of—I can't live on weather!

LEROY: Pat, we're getting old! This is just about as rich and handsome as I'm ever going to be and as good as you're ever going to look, so you want to be with me or not?

PATRICIA: I don't want to fool either of us . . . I can't bear it when you can't pay the bills . . .

LEROY: But I'm a carpenter—this is probably the way it's been for carpenters since they built Noah's ark. What do you want to do?

PATRICIA: I'm honestly not sure I could hold up. Not when I hear your sadness all the time and your eyes are full of disappointment. You seem . . . (*Breaks off.*)

LEROY: . . . How do I seem?

PATRICIA: I shouldn't say it.

LEROY: . . . Beaten. Like it's all gone by. (*Hurt, but holding on.*) All right, Patty, then I might as well say it—I don't think you *ever* had a medical problem; you have an attitude problem . . .

PATRICIA: My problem is spiritual.

LEROY: Okay, I don't mind calling it spiritual.

PATRICIA: Well that's a new note; I thought these ministers were all quacks.

LEROY: Not all; but the ones who make house calls with women, eating up all the ice cream, are not my idea of spiritual.

PATRICIA: *You* know what spiritual is?

LEROY: For me? Sure. Ice skating.

PATRICIA: Ice skating is spiritual.

LEROY: Yes, and skiing! To me spiritual is whatever makes me forget myself and feel happy to be alive. Like even a well-sharpened saw, or a perfect compound joint.

PATRICIA: Maybe this is why we can't get along—spiritual is nothing you can see, Leroy.

LEROY: Really! Then why didn't God make everything invisible!

We are in this world and you're going to have to find some
way to love it!

(*Her eyes are filling with tears.*)

Pounding on me is not going to change anything to wonderful, Patty.

(*She seems to be receiving him.*)

I'll say it again, because it's the only thing that's kept me
from going crazy—you just have to love this world. (*He
comes to her, takes her hand.*) Come home. Maybe it'll take a
while, but I really believe you can make it.

(*Uncertainty filling her face . . .*)

All right, don't decide now, I'll come back Thursday and
we'll see then.

PATRICIA: Where you going now?

LEROY: For my banjo lesson. I'm learning a new number. —I'll
play it for you if you want to hear it.

PATRICIA (*hesitates, then kisses him*): Couldn't you do it on
guitar?

LEROY: It's not the same on guitar. (*He goes to his banjo case
and opens it.*)

PATRICIA: But banjo sounds so picky.

LEROY: But that's what's good about it, it's clean, like a tooth-
pick . . .

(*Enter the* FRICKS.)

Oh hi, Mrs. Frick.

KAREN: He brought my costume. Would you care to see it? (*To*
FRICK.) This is her—Mrs. Hamilton.

FRICK: Oh! How do you do?

KAREN: This is my husband.

PATRICIA: How do you do?

FRICK: She's been telling me all about you. (*Shaking* PATRICIA'*s
hand.*) I want to say that I'm thankful to you.

PATRICIA: Really? What for?

FRICK: Well what she says you've been telling her. About her
attitude and all.

KAREN (*to* PATRICIA): Would you like to see my costume? I also
have a blue one, but . . .

FRICK (*overriding her*): . . . By the way, I'm Frick Lumber, I
recognized your husband right away . . .

KAREN: Should I put it on?

PATRICIA: Sure, put it on!

(LEROY *starts tuning his banjo.*)

FRICK (*to* PATRICIA): All it is is a high hat and shorts, y'know . . . nothing much to it.

KAREN (*to* FRICK): Shouldn't I?

PATRICIA: Why not, for Heaven's sake?

FRICK: Go ahead, if they want to see it. (*Laughs to* PATRICIA.) She found it in a catalogue. I think it's kinda silly at her age, but I admit I'm a conservative kind of person . . .

KAREN (*cutting him off, deeply embarrassed*): I'll only be a minute. (*She starts out, and stops, and to* PATRICIA.) You really think I should?

PATRICIA: Of course!

FRICK (*suppressing an angry embarrassment*): Karen, honey, if you're going to do it, do it.

(KAREN *exits with valise.* LEROY *tunes his instrument.*)

The slightest decision, she's got to worry it into the ground.—But I have to tell you, it's years since I've seen this much life in her, she's like day and night. What exactly'd you say to her? (*To* LEROY, *thumbing toward* PATRICIA.) She says she just opened up her eyes . . .

LEROY (*surprised*): Patricia?

FRICK: I have to admit, it took me a while to realize it's a sickness . . .

PATRICIA: You're not the only one.

FRICK: Looked to me like she was just favoring herself; I mean the woman has everything, what right has she got to start shooting blanks like that? I happen to be a great believer in self-discipline, started from way down below sea level myself, sixty acres of rocks and swampland is all we had. That's why I'm so glad that somebody's talked to her with your attitude.

PATRICIA (*vamping for time*): What . . . what attitude do you mean?

FRICK: Just that you're so . . . so positive.

(LEROY *looks up at* PATRICIA, *thunderstruck.*)

She says you made her realize all the things she could be doing instead of mooning around all day . . .

PATRICIA: Well I think being positive is the only way.

FRICK: That's just what I tell her . . .

PATRICIA: But you have to be careful not to sound so disappointed in her.

FRICK: I sound disappointed?

PATRICIA: In a way, I think.—She's got to feel treasured, you see.

FRICK: I appreciate that, but the woman can stand in one place for half an hour at a time practically without moving.

PATRICIA: Well that's the sickness, you see.

FRICK: I realize that. But she won't even go shopping . . .

PATRICIA: You see? You're sounding disappointed in her.

FRICK (*angering*): I am not disappointed in her! I'm just telling you the situation!

PATRICIA: Mr. Frick, she's standing under a mountain a mile high—you've got to help her over it. That woman has very big possibilities!

FRICK: Think so.

PATRICIA: Absolutely.

FRICK: I hope you're right. (*To* LEROY, *indicating* PATRICIA.) You don't mind my saying it, you could do with a little of her optimism.

LEROY (*turns from* PATRICIA, *astonished*): Huh?

FRICK (*to* PATRICIA, *warmly*): Y'know, she made me have a little platform built down the cellar, with a big full-length mirror so she could see herself dance . . .

PATRICIA: But do you spend time watching her . . .

FRICK: Well she says not to till she's good at it.

PATRICIA: That's because she's terrified of your criticism.

FRICK: But I haven't made any criticism.

PATRICIA: But do you like tap dancing?

FRICK: Well I don't know, I never thought about it one way or another.

PATRICIA: Well that's the thing, you see. It happens to mean a great deal to her . . .

FRICK: I'm for it, I don't mean I'm not for it. But don't tell me you think it's normal for a woman her age to be getting out of bed two, three in the morning and start practicing.

PATRICIA: Well maybe she's trying to get you interested in it. Are you?

FRICK: In tap dancing? Truthfully, no.

PATRICIA: Well there you go . . .

FRICK: Well we've got a lot of new competition in our fuel-oil business . . .

PATRICIA: Fuel oil!

FRICK: I've got seven trucks on the road that I've got to keep busy . . .

PATRICIA: Well there you go, maybe that's why your wife is in here.

FRICK (*visibly angering*): Well I can't be waked up at two o'clock in the morning and be any good next day, now can I. She's not normal.

PATRICIA: Normal! They've got whole universities debating what's normal. Who knows what's normal, Mr. Frick?

FRICK: You mean getting out of bed at two o'clock in the morning and putting on a pair of tap shoes is a common occurrence in this country? I don't think so.—But I didn't mean to argue when you're . . . not feeling well.

PATRICIA: I've never felt better.

(*She turns away, and* FRICK *looks with bewildered surprise to* LEROY, *who returns him a look of suppressed laughter.*)

FRICK: Well you sure know how to turn somebody inside out.

(KAREN *enters; she is dressed in satin shorts, a tailcoat, a high hat, tap shoes, and as they turn to look at her, she pulls out a collapsible walking stick, and strikes a theatrical pose.*)

PATRICIA: Well now, don't you look great!

KAREN (*desperate for reassurance*): You really like it?

LEROY: That looks terrific!

PATRICIA: Do a step!

KAREN: I don't have my tape. (*Turns to* FRICK, *timorously.*) But if you'd sing "Swanee River . . ."

FRICK: Oh Karen, for God's sake!

PATRICIA: I can sing it . . .

KAREN: He knows my speed. Please, John . . . just for a minute.

FRICK: All right, go ahead. (*Unhappily, he sings.*) "Way down upon the Swanee River . . ."

KAREN: Wait, you're too fast . . .

FRICK (*slower and angering*): "Way—down—upon—the— Swanee River,

Far, far away.
That's where my heart is turning ever . . ."
[*etc.*]

> (KAREN *taps out her number, laboriously but for a short stretch with a promise of grace.* FRICK *continues singing . . .*)

PATRICIA: Isn't she wonderful?

LEROY: Hey, she's great!

> (KAREN *dances a bit more boldly, a joyous freedom starting into her.*)

PATRICIA: She's marvelous! Look at her, Mr. Frick!

> (*A hint of the sensuous in* KAREN *now;* FRICK, *embarrassed, uneasily avoids more than a glance at his wife.*)

FRICK: ". . . everywhere I roam . . ."

PATRICIA: Will you look at her!

FRICK (*hard-pressed, explodes*): I am looking at her, goddammit!

> (*This astonishing furious shout, his reddened face, stops everything. A look of fear is on* KAREN'*s face.*)

KAREN (*apologetically to* PATRICIA): He *was* looking at me . . . (*To* FRICK.) She didn't mean you *weren't* looking, she meant . . .

FRICK (*rigidly repressing his anger and embarrassment*): I've got to run along now.

KAREN: I'm so sorry, John, but she . . .

FRICK (*rigidly*): Nothing to be sorry about, dear. Very nice to have met you folks.

> (*He starts to exit.* KAREN *moves to intercept him.*)

KAREN: Oh John, I hope you're not . . . [going to be angry.]

FRICK: I'm just fine. (*He sees her despair coming on.*) What are you looking so sad about?—you danced great . . .

> (*She is immobile.*)

I'm sorry to've raised my voice but it don't mean I'm disappointed, dear. You understand? (*A nervous glance toward* PATRICIA. *Stiffly, with enormous effort.*) . . . You . . . you danced better than I ever saw you.

> (*She doesn't change.*)

Now look here, Karen, I hope you don't feel I'm . . . disappointed or something, you hear . . . ? 'Cause I'm not. And that's definite.

> (*She keeps staring at him.*)

I'll try to make it again on Friday.—Keep it up. (*He abruptly turns and exits.*)

> (KAREN *stands perfectly still, staring at nothing.*)

PATRICIA: Karen?

> (KAREN *seems not to hear, standing there facing the empty door in her high hat and costume.*)

How about Leroy playing it for you? (*To* LEROY.) Play it.

LEROY: I could on the guitar, but I never did on this . . .

PATRICIA: Well couldn't you try it?—I don't know what good that thing is.

LEROY: Well here . . . let me see.

> (*He picks out "Swanee River" on his banjo, but* KAREN *doesn't move.*)

PATRICIA: There you go, Karen! Try it, I love your dancing! Come on . . . (*Sings.*) "Way down upon the Swanee river . . ."

> (KAREN *now breaks her motionlessly depressed mode and looks at* PATRICIA. LEROY *continues playing, humming along with it. His picking is getting more accurate . . .*)

Is it the right tempo? Tell him!

KAREN (*very very softly*): Could you play a little faster?

> (LEROY *speeds it up. With an unrelieved sadness,* KAREN *goes into her number, does a few steps, but stops.* LEROY *gradually stops playing.* KAREN *walks out.* PATRICIA *starts to follow her but gives it up and comes to a halt.*
>
> LEROY *turns to* PATRICIA, *who is staring ahead. Now she turns to* LEROY.
>
> *He meets her gaze, his face filled with inquiry. He comes to her and stands there.*
>
> *For a long moment neither of them moves. Then she reaches out and touches his face—there is a muted gratitude in her gesture.*
>
> *She goes to a closet and takes a small overnight bag to the bed and puts her things into it.*
>
> LEROY *watches her for a moment, then stows his banjo in its case, and stands waiting for her. She starts to put on a light coat. He comes and helps her into it.*
>
> *Her face is charged with her struggle against her self-doubt.*)

LEROY (*laughs, but about to weep*): Ready?

PATRICIA (*filling up*): Leroy . . .

LEROY: One day at a time, Pat—you're already twenty-one ahead. Kids are going to be so happy to have you home.

PATRICIA: I can't believe it. . . . I've had nothing.

LEROY: It's a miracle.

PATRICIA: Thank you. (*Breaking through her own resistance, she draws him to her and kisses him. Grinning tauntingly.*) . . . That car going to get us home?

LEROY (*laughs*): Stop picking on that car, it's all checked out!

(*They start toward the door, he carrying her bag and his banjo.*)

PATRICIA: Once you believe in something you just never know when to stop, do you.

LEROY: Well there's very little rust, and the new ones aren't half as well built . . .

PATRICIA: Waste not, want not.

LEROY: Well I really don't *go* for those new Chevies . . .

(*She walks out, he behind her. Their voices are heard . . .*)

PATRICIA: Between the banjo and that car I've certainly got a whole lot to look forward to.

(*His laughter sounds down the corridor.*)

(*The woman on the bed stirs, then falls back and remains motionless. A stillness envelops the whole stage.*)

END

BROKEN GLASS

A Play in Two Acts

To Inge Morath

CHARACTERS

PHILLIP GELLBURG
SYLVIA GELLBURG
DR. HARRY HYMAN
MARGARET HYMAN
HARRIET
STANTON CASE

The play takes place in Brooklyn in the last days of November 1938, in the office of Dr. Harry Hyman, the bedroom of the Gellburg house, and the office of Stanton Case.

ACT ONE

A lone cellist is discovered, playing a simple tune. The tune finishes. Light goes out on the cellist and rises on. . . .

Office of DR. HARRY HYMAN *in his home. Alone on stage* PHILLIP GELLBURG, *an intense man in his late forties, waits in perfect stillness, legs crossed. He is in a black suit, black tie and shoes, and white shirt.*

MARGARET HYMAN, *the doctor's wife, enters. She is lusty, energetic, carrying pruning shears.*

MARGARET: He'll be right with you, he's just changing. Can I get you something? Tea?

GELLBURG (*faint reprimand*): He said seven o'clock sharp.

MARGARET: He was held up in the hospital, that new union's pulled a strike, imagine? A strike in a hospital? It's incredible. And his horse went lame.

GELLBURG: His horse?

MARGARET: He rides on Ocean Parkway every afternoon.

GELLBURG (*attempting easy familiarity*): Oh yes, I heard about that . . . it's very nice. You're Mrs. Hyman?

MARGARET: I've nodded to you on the street for years now, but you're too preoccupied to notice.

GELLBURG (*a barely hidden boast*): Lot on my mind, usually. (*A certain amused loftiness.*) —So you're his nurse, too.

MARGARET: We met in Mount Sinai when he was interning. He's lived to regret it. (*She laughs in a burst.*)

GELLBURG: That's some laugh you've got there. I sometimes hear you all the way down the block to my house.

MARGARET: Can't help it, my whole family does it. I'm originally from Minnesota. It's nice to meet you finally, Mr. Goldberg.

GELLBURG: —It's Gellburg, not Goldberg.

MARGARET: Oh, I'm sorry.

GELLBURG: G-e-l-l-b-u-r-g. It's the only one in the phone book.

MARGARET: It does sound like Goldberg.

GELLBURG: But it's not, its Gellburg. (*A distinction.*) We're from Finland originally.

MARGARET: Oh! We came from Lithuania . . . Kazauskis?

GELLBURG (*put down momentarily*): Don't say.

MARGARET (*trying to charm him to his ease*): Ever been to Minnesota?

GELLBURG: New York State's the size of France, what would I go to Minnesota for?

MARGARET: Nothing. Just there's a lot of Finns there.

GELLBURG: Well there's Finns all over.

MARGARET (*defeated, shows the clipper*): . . . I'll get back to my roses. Whatever it is, I hope you'll be feeling better.

GELLBURG: It's not me.

MARGARET: Oh. 'Cause you seem a little pale.

GELLBURG: Me?—I'm always this color. It's my wife.

MARGARET: I'm sorry to hear that, she's a lovely woman. It's nothing serious, is it?

GELLBURG: He's just had a specialist put her through some tests, I'm waiting to hear. I think it's got him mystified.

MARGARET: Well, I mustn't butt in. (*Makes to leave but can't resist.*) Can you say what it is?

GELLBURG: She can't walk.

MARGARET: What do you mean?

GELLBURG (*an overtone of protest of some personal victimization*): Can't stand up. No feeling in her legs.—I'm sure it'll pass, but it's terrible.

MARGARET: But I only saw her in the grocery . . . can't be more than ten days ago . . .

GELLBURG: It's nine days today.

MARGARET: But she's such a wonderful-looking woman. Does she have fever?

GELLBURG: No.

MARGARET: Thank God, then it's not polio.

GELLBURG: No, she's in perfect health otherwise.

MARGARET: Well Harry'll get to the bottom of it if anybody can. They call him from everywhere for opinions, you know . . . Boston, Chicago . . . By rights he ought to be on

Park Avenue if he only had the ambition, but he always wanted a neighborhood practice. Why, I don't know—we never invite anybody, we never go out, all our friends are in Manhattan. But it's his nature, you can't fight a person's nature. Like me for instance, I like to talk and I like to laugh. You're not much of a talker, are you.

GELLBURG (*a purse-mouthed smile*): When I can get a word in edgewise.

MARGARET (*burst of laughter*): Ha!—so you've got a sense of humor after all. Well give my best to Mrs. Goldberg.

GELLBURG: Gellbu . . .

MARGARET (*hits her own head*): Gellburg, excuse me!—It practically sounds like Goldberg . . .

GELLBURG: No-no, look in the phone book, it's the only one, G-e-l-l . . .

(*Enter* DR. HYMAN.)

MARGARET (*with a little wave to* GELLBURG): Be seeing you!

GELLBURG: Be in good health.

(MARGARET *exits.*)

HYMAN (*in his early fifties, a healthy, rather handsome man, a determined scientific idealist. Settling behind his desk—chuckling*): She chew your ear off?

GELLBURG (*his worldly mode*): Not too bad, I've had worse.

HYMAN: Well there's no way around it, women are talkers . . . (*Grinning familiarly.*) But try living without them, right?

GELLBURG: Without women?

HYMAN (*he sees* GELLBURG *has flushed; there is a short hiatus, then*): . . . Well, never mind.—I'm glad you could make it tonight, I wanted to talk to you before I see your wife again tomorrow. (*Opens cigar humidor.*) Smoke?

GELLBURG: No thanks, never have. Isn't it bad for you?

HYMAN: Certainly is. (*Lights a cigar.*) But more people die of rat bite, you know.

GELLBURG: Rat bite!

HYMAN: Oh yes, but they're mostly the poor so it's not an interesting statistic. Have you seen her tonight or did you come here from the office?

GELLBURG: I thought I'd see you before I went home. But I phoned her this afternoon—same thing, no change.

HYMAN: How's she doing with the wheelchair?

GELLBURG: Better, she can get herself in and out of the bed now.

HYMAN: Good. And she manages the bathroom?

GELLBURG: Oh yes. I got the maid to come in the mornings to help her take a bath, clean up . . .

HYMAN: Good. Your wife has a lot of courage, I admire that kind of woman. My wife is similar; I like the type.

GELLBURG: What type you mean?

HYMAN: You know—vigorous. I mean mentally and . . . you know, just generally. Moxie.

GELLBURG: Oh.

HYMAN: Forget it, it was only a remark.

GELLBURG: No, you're right, I never thought of it, but she is unusually that way.

HYMAN (*pause, some prickliness here which he can't understand*): Doctor Sherman's report . . .

GELLBURG: What's he say?

HYMAN: I'm getting to it.

GELLBURG: Oh. Beg your pardon.

HYMAN: You'll have to bear with me . . . may I call you Phillip?

GELLBURG: Certainly.

HYMAN: I don't express my thoughts very quickly, Phillip.

GELLBURG: Likewise. Go ahead, take your time.

HYMAN: People tend to overestimate the wisdom of physicians so I try to think things through before I speak to a patient.

GELLBURG: I'm glad to hear that.

HYMAN: Aesculapius stuttered, you know—ancient Greek god of medicine. But probably based on a real physician who hesitated about giving advice. Somerset Maugham stammered, studied medicine. Anton Chekhov, great writer, also a doctor, had tuberculosis. Doctors are very often physically defective in some way, that's why they're interested in healing.

GELLBURG (*impressed*): I see.

HYMAN (*pause, thinks*): I find this Adolf Hitler very disturbing. You been following him in the papers?

GELLBURG: Well yes, but not much. My average day in the office is ten, eleven hours.

HYMAN: They've been smashing the Jewish stores in Berlin all week, you know.

GELLBURG: Oh yes, I saw that again yesterday.

HYMAN: Very disturbing. Forcing old men to scrub the sidewalks with toothbrushes. On the Kurfürstendamm, that's equivalent to Fifth Avenue. Nothing but hoodlums in uniform.

GELLBURG: My wife is very upset about that.

HYMAN: I know, that's why I mention it. (*Hesitates.*) And how about you?

GELLBURG: Of course. It's a terrible thing. Why do you ask?

HYMAN (*a smile*): —I don't know, I got the feeling she may be afraid she's annoying you when she talks about such things.

GELLBURG: Why? I don't mind.—She said she's annoying me?

HYMAN: Not in so many words, but . . .

GELLBURG: I can't believe she'd say a thing like . . .

HYMAN: Wait a minute, I didn't say she said it . . .

GELLBURG: She doesn't annoy me, but what can be done about such things? The thing is, she doesn't like to hear about the other side of it.

HYMAN: What other side?

GELLBURG: It's no excuse for what's happening over there, but German Jews can be pretty . . . you know . . . (*Pushes up his nose with his forefinger.*) Not that they're pushy like the ones from Poland or Russia but a friend of mine's in the garment industry; these German Jews won't take an ordinary good job, you know; it's got to be pretty high up in the firm or they're insulted. And they can't even speak English.

HYMAN: Well I guess a lot of them were pretty important over there.

GELLBURG: I know, but they're supposed to be *refugees*, aren't they? With all our unemployment you'd think they'd appreciate a little more. Latest official figure is twelve million unemployed you know, and it's probably bigger but Roosevelt can't admit it, after the fortune he's pouring into WPA and the rest of that welfare *mishugas.*—But she's not *annoying* me, for God's sake.

HYMAN: . . . I just thought I'd mention it; but it was only a feeling I had . . .

GELLBURG: I'll tell you right now, I don't run with the crowd, I see with these eyes, nobody else's.

HYMAN: I see that.—You're very unusual—(*grinning*)—you almost sound like a Republican.

GELLBURG: Why?—the Torah says a Jew has to be a Democrat? I didn't get where I am by agreeing with everybody.

HYMAN: Well that's a good thing; you're independent. (*Nods, puffs.*) You know, what mystifies me is that the Germans I knew in Heidelberg . . . I took my M.D. there . . .

GELLBURG: You got along with them.

HYMAN: Some of the finest people I ever met.

GELLBURG: Well there you go.

HYMAN: We had a marvelous student choral group, fantastic voices; Saturday nights, we'd have a few beers and go singing through the streets. . . . People'd applaud from the windows.

GELLBURG: Don't say.

HYMAN: I simply can't imagine those people marching into Austria, and now they say Czechoslovakia's next, and Poland. . . . But fanatics have taken Germany, I guess, and they can be brutal, you know . . .

GELLBURG: Listen, I sympathize with these refugees, but . . .

HYMAN (*cutting him off*): I had quite a long talk with Sylvia yesterday, I suppose she told you?

GELLBURG (*a tensing*): Well . . . no, she didn't mention. What about?

HYMAN (*surprised by* SYLVIA's *omission*): . . . Well about her condition, and . . . just in passing . . . your relationship.

GELLBURG (*flushing*): *My* relationship?

HYMAN: . . . It was just in passing.

GELLBURG: Why, what'd she say?

HYMAN: Well that you . . . get along very well.

GELLBURG: Oh.

HYMAN (*encouragingly, as he sees* GELLBURG's *small tension*): I found her a remarkably well-informed woman. Especially for this neighborhood.

GELLBURG (*a pridefully approving nod; relieved that he can speak of her positively*): That's practically why we got together in the first place. I don't exaggerate, if Sylvia was a man she could have run the Federal Reserve. You could talk to Sylvia like you talk to a man.

HYMAN: I'll bet.

GELLBURG (*a purse-mouthed grin*): . . . Not that talking was all we did—but you turn your back on Sylvia and she's got her nose in a book or a magazine. I mean there's not one woman in ten around here could even tell you who their Congressman is. And you can throw in the men, too. (*Pause.*) So where are we?

HYMAN: Doctor Sherman confirms my diagnosis. I ask you to listen carefully, will you?

GELLBURG (*brought up*): Of course, that's why I came.

HYMAN: We can find no physical reason for her inability to walk.

GELLBURG: No physical reason . . .

HYMAN: We are almost certain that this is a psychological condition.

GELLBURG: But she's numb, she has no feeling in her legs.

HYMAN: Yes. This is what we call an hysterical paralysis. Hysterical doesn't mean she screams and yells . . .

GELLBURG: Oh, I know. It means like . . . ah . . . (*Bumbles off.*)

HYMAN (*a flash of umbrage, dislike*): Let me explain what it means, okay?—Hysteria comes from the Greek word for the womb because it was thought to be a symptom of female anxiety. Of course it isn't, but that's where it comes from. People who are anxious enough or really frightened can imagine they've gone blind or deaf, for instance . . . and they really can't see or hear. It was sometimes called shell-shock during the War.

GELLBURG: You mean . . . you don't mean she's . . . crazy.

HYMAN: We'll have to talk turkey, Phillip. If I'm going to do you any good I'm going to have to ask you some personal questions. Some of them may sound raw, but I've only been superficially acquainted with Sylvia's family and I need to know more . . .

GELLBURG: She says you treated her father . . .

HYMAN: Briefly; a few visits shortly before he passed away. They're fine people. I hate like hell to see this happen to her, you see what I mean?

GELLBURG: You can tell it to me; is she crazy?

HYMAN: Phillip, are you? Am I? In one way or another, who isn't crazy? The main difference is that our kind of crazy still allows us to walk around and tend to our business. But who knows?—people like us may be the craziest of all.

GELLBURG (*scoffing grin*): Why!

HYMAN: Because we don't know we're nuts, and the other kind does.

GELLBURG: I don't know about that . . .

HYMAN: Well, it's neither here nor there.

GELLBURG: I certainly don't think *I'm* nuts.

HYMAN: I wasn't saying that . . .

GELLBURG: What do you mean, then?

HYMAN (*grinning*): You're not an easy man to talk to, are you.

GELLBURG: Why? If I don't understand I have to ask, don't I?

HYMAN: Yes, you're right.

GELLBURG: That's the way I am—they don't pay me for being easy to talk to.

HYMAN: You're in . . . real estate?

GELLBURG: I'm head of the Mortgage Department of Brooklyn Guarantee and Trust.

HYMAN: Oh, that's right, she told me.

GELLBURG: We are the largest lender east of the Mississippi.

HYMAN: Really. (*Fighting deflation.*) Well, let me tell you my approach; if possible I'd like to keep her out of that whole psychiatry rigmarole. Not that I'm against it, but I think you get further faster, sometimes, with a little common sense and some plain human sympathy. Can we talk turkey? *Tuchas offen tisch*, you know any Yiddish?

GELLBURG: Yes, it means get your ass on the table.

HYMAN: Correct. So let's forget crazy and try to face the facts. We have a strong, healthy woman who has no physical ailment, and suddenly can't stand on her legs. Why?

(*He goes silent.* GELLBURG *shifts uneasily.*)

I don't mean to embarrass you . . .

GELLBURG (*an angry smile*): You're not embarrassing me.— What do you want to know?

HYMAN (*sets himself, then launches*): In these cases there is often a sexual disability. You have relations, I imagine?

GELLBURG: Relations? Yes, we have relations.

HYMAN (*a softening smile*): Often?

GELLBURG: What's that got to do with it?

HYMAN: Sex could be connected. You don't have to answer . . .

GELLBURG: No-no it's all right. . . . I would say it depends— maybe twice, three times a week.

HYMAN (*seems surprised*): Well that's good. She seems satisfied?

GELLBURG (*shrugs; hostilely*): I guess she is, sure.

HYMAN: That was a foolish question, forget it.

GELLBURG (*flushed*): Why, did she mention something about this?

HYMAN: Oh no, it's just something I thought of later.

GELLBURG: Well, I'm no Rudolph Valentino but I . . .

HYMAN: Rudolph Valentino probably wasn't either.—What about before she collapsed; was that completely out of the blue or . . .

GELLBURG (*relieved to be off the other subject*): I tell you, looking back I wonder if something happened when they started putting all the pictures in the paper. About these Nazi carryings-on. I noticed she started . . . staring at them . . . in a very peculiar way. And . . . I don't know. I think it made her angry or something.

HYMAN: At you.

GELLBURG: Well . . . (*Nods, agreeing.*) In general.—Personally I don't think they should be publishing those kind of pictures.

HYMAN: Why not?

GELLBURG: She scares herself to death with them—three thousand miles away, and what does it accomplish! Except maybe put some fancy new ideas into these anti-Semites walking around New York here.

(*Slight pause.*)

HYMAN: Tell me how she collapsed. You were going to the movies . . . ?

GELLBURG (*breathing more deeply*): Yes. We were just starting down the porch steps and all of a sudden her . . . (*Difficulty; he breaks off.*)

HYMAN: I'm sorry but I . . .

GELLBURG: . . . Her legs turned to butter. I couldn't stand her up. Kept falling around like a rag doll. I had to carry her into the house. And she kept apologizing . . . ! (*He weeps; recovers.*) I can't talk about it.

HYMAN: It's all right.

GELLBURG: She's always been such a level-headed woman. (*Weeping threatens again.*) I don't know what to do. She's my life.

HYMAN: I'll do my best for her, Phillip, she's a wonderful

woman.—Let's talk about something else. What do you do exactly?

GELLBURG: I mainly evaluate properties.

HYMAN: Whether to grant a mortgage . . .

GELLBURG: And how big a one and the terms.

HYMAN: How's the Depression hit you?

GELLBURG: Well, it's no comparison with '32 to '36, let's say— we were foreclosing left and right in those days. But we're on our feet and running.

HYMAN: And you head the department . . .

GELLBURG: Above me is only Mr. Case. Stanton Wylie Case; he's chairman and president. You're not interested in boat racing.

HYMAN: Why?

GELLBURG: His yacht won the America's Cup two years ago. For the second time. The *Aurora*?

HYMAN: Oh yes! I think I read about . . .

GELLBURG: He's had me aboard twice.

HYMAN: Really.

GELLBURG (*the grin*): The only Jew ever set foot on that deck.

HYMAN: Don't say.

GELLBURG: In fact, I'm the only Jew ever worked for Brooklyn Guarantee in their whole history.

HYMAN: That so.

GELLBURG: Oh yes. And they go back to the 1890s. Started right out of accountancy school and moved straight up. They've been wonderful to me; it's a great firm.

(*A long moment as* HYMAN *stares at* GELLBURG, *who is proudly positioned now, absorbing his poise from the evoked memories of his success. Gradually* GELLBURG *turns to him.*)

How could this be a mental condition?

HYMAN: It's unconscious; like . . . well take yourself; I notice you're all in black. Can I ask you why?

GELLBURG: I've worn black since high school.

HYMAN: No particular reason.

GELLBURG (*shrugs*): Always liked it, that's all.

HYMAN: Well it's a similar thing with her; she doesn't know why she's doing this, but some very deep, hidden part of her mind is directing her to do it. You don't agree.

GELLBURG: I don't know.

HYMAN: You think she knows what she's doing?

GELLBURG: Well I always liked black for business reasons.

HYMAN: It gives you authority?

GELLBURG: Not exactly authority, but I wanted to look a little older. See, I graduated high school at fifteen and I was only twenty-two when I entered the firm. But I knew what I was doing.

HYMAN: Then you think she's doing this on purpose?

GELLBURG: —Except she's numb; nobody can purposely do that, can they?

HYMAN: I don't think so.—I tell you, Phillip, not really knowing your wife, if you have any idea why she could be doing this to herself . . .

GELLBURG: I told you, I don't know.

HYMAN: Nothing occurs to you.

GELLBURG (*an edge of irritation*): I can't think of anything.

HYMAN: I tell you a funny thing, talking to her, she doesn't seem all that unhappy.

GELLBURG: Say!—yes, that's what I mean. That's exactly what I mean. It's like she's almost . . . I don't know . . . enjoying herself. I mean in a way.

HYMAN: How could that be possible?

GELLBURG: Of course she apologizes for it, and for making it hard for me—you know, like I have to do a lot of the cooking now, and tending to my laundry and so on . . . I even shop for groceries and the butcher . . . and change the sheets . . .

(*He breaks off with some realization.* HYMAN *doesn't speak. A long pause.*)

You mean . . . she's doing it against me?

HYMAN: I don't know, what do *you* think? (*Stares for a long moment, then makes to rise, obviously deeply disturbed.*)

GELLBURG: I'd better be getting home. (*Lost in his own thought.*) I don't know whether to ask you this or not.

HYMAN: What's to lose, go ahead.

GELLBURG: My parents were from the old country, you know,—I don't know if it was in Poland someplace or Russia—but there was this woman who they say was . . . you know . . . gotten into by a . . . like the ghost of a dead person . . .

HYMAN: A dybbuk.

GELLBURG: That's it. And it made her lose her mind and so forth.—You believe in that? They had to get a rabbi to pray it out of her body. But you think that's possible?

HYMAN: Do I think so? No. Do you?

GELLBURG: Oh no. It just crossed my mind.

HYMAN: Well I wouldn't know how to pray it out of her, so . . .

GELLBURG: Be straight with me—is she going to come out of this?

HYMAN: Well, let's talk again after I see her tomorrow. Maybe I should tell you . . . I have this unconventional approach to illness, Phillip. Especially where the mental element is involved. I believe we get sick in twos and threes and fours, not alone as individuals. You follow me? I want you to do me a favor, will you?

GELLBURG: What's that.

HYMAN: You won't be offended, okay?

GELLBURG (*tensely*): Why should I be offended?

HYMAN: I'd like you to give her a lot of loving. (*Fixing* GELLBURG *in his gaze*.) Can you? It's important now.

GELLBURG: Say, you're not blaming this on me, are you?

HYMAN: What's the good of blame?—from here on out, *tuchas offen tisch*, okay? And Phillip?

GELLBURG: Yes?

HYMAN (*a light chuckle*): Try not to let yourself get mad.

(GELLBURG *turns and goes out.* HYMAN *returns to his desk, makes some notes.* MARGARET *enters.*)

MARGARET: That's one miserable little pisser.

(*He writes, doesn't look up.*)

He's a dictator, you know. I was just remembering when I went to the grandmother's funeral? He stands outside the funeral parlor and decides who's going to sit with who in the limousines for the cemetery. "You sit with him, you sit with her . . ." And they obey him like he owned the funeral!

HYMAN: Did you find out what's playing?

MARGARET: At the Beverly they've got Ginger Rogers and Fred Astaire. Jimmy Cagney's at the Rialto but it's another gangster story.

HYMAN: I have a sour feeling about this thing. I barely know my way around psychiatry. I'm not completely sure I ought to get into it.

MARGARET: Why not?—She's a very beautiful woman.

HYMAN (*matching her wryness*): Well, is that a reason to turn her away? (*He laughs, grasps her hand.*) Something about it fascinates me—no disease and she's paralyzed. I'd really love to give it a try. I mean I don't want to turn myself into a post office, shipping all the hard cases to specialists, the woman's sick and I'd like to help.

MARGARET: But if you're not getting anywhere in a little while you'll promise to send her to somebody.

HYMAN: Absolutely. (*Committed now: full enthusiasm.*) I just feel there's something about it that I understand.—Let's see Cagney.

MARGARET: Oh, no Fred Astaire.

HYMAN: That's what I meant. Come here.

MARGARET (*as he embraces her*): We should leave now . . .

HYMAN: You're the best, Margaret.

MARGARET: A lot of good it does me.

HYMAN: If it really bothers you I'll get someone else to take the case.

MARGARET: You won't, you know you won't.

> (*He is lifting her skirt.*)

Don't, Harry. Come on.

> (*She frees her skirt, he kisses her breasts.*)

HYMAN: Should I tell you what I'd like to do with you?

MARGARET: Tell me, yes, tell me. And make it wonderful.

HYMAN: We find an island and we strip and go riding on this white horse . . .

MARGARET: Together.

HYMAN: You in front.

MARGARET: Naturally.

HYMAN: And then we go swimming . . .

MARGARET: Harry, that's lovely.

HYMAN: And I hire this shark to swim very close and we just manage to get out of the water, and we're so grateful to be alive we fall down on the beach together and . . .

MARGARET (*pressing his lips shut*): Sometimes you're so good. (*She kisses him.*)

BLACKOUT

SCENE 2

The Lone Cellist plays. Then lights go down . . .

Next evening. The Gellburg bedroom. SYLVIA GELLBURG *is seated in a wheelchair reading a newspaper. She is in her mid-forties, a buxom, capable, and warm woman. Right now her hair is brushed down to her shoulders, and she is in a nightgown and robe.*

She reads the paper with an intense, almost haunted interest, looking up now and then to visualize.

Her sister HARRIET, *a couple of years younger, is straightening up the bedcover.*

HARRIET: So what do you want, steak or chicken? Or maybe he'd like chops for a change.

SYLVIA: Please, don't put yourself out, Phillip doesn't mind a little shopping.

HARRIET: What's the matter with you, I'm going anyway, he's got enough on his mind.

SYLVIA: Well all right, get a couple of chops.

HARRIET: And what about you. You have to start eating!

SYLVIA: I'm eating.

HARRIET: What, a piece of cucumber? Look how pale you are. And what is this with newspapers night and day?

SYLVIA: I like to see what's happening.

HARRIET: I don't know about this doctor. Maybe you need a specialist.

SYLVIA: He brought one two days ago, Doctor Sherman. From Mount Sinai.

HARRIET: Really? And?

SYLVIA: We're waiting to hear. I like Doctor Hyman.

HARRIET: Nobody in the family ever had anything like this. You feel *something*, though, don't you?

SYLVIA (*pause, she lifts her face*): Yes . . . but inside, not on the skin. (*Looks at her legs.*) I can harden the muscles but I can't lift them. (*Strokes her thighs.*) I seem to have an ache. Not only here but . . . (*She runs her hands down her trunk.*)

My whole body seems . . . I can't describe it. It's like I was just born and I . . . didn't want to come out yet. Like a deep, terrible aching . . .

HARRIET: Didn't want to come out yet! What are you talking about?

SYLVIA (*sighs gently, knowing* HARRIET *can never understand*): Maybe if he has a nice duck. If not, get the chops. And thanks, Harriet, it's sweet of you.—By the way, what did David decide?

HARRIET: He's not going to college.

SYLVIA (*shocked*): I don't believe it! With a scholarship and he's not going?

HARRIET: What can we do? (*Resignedly.*) He says college wouldn't help him get a job anyway.

SYLVIA: Harriet, that's terrible!—Listen, tell him I have to talk to him.

HARRIET: Would you! I was going to ask you but with this happening. (*Indicates her legs.*) I didn't think you'd . . .

SYLVIA: Never mind, tell him to come over. And you must tell Murray he's got to put his foot down—you've got a brilliant boy! My God . . . (*Picks up the newspaper.*) If I'd had a chance to go to college I'd have had a whole different life, you can't let this happen.

HARRIET: I'll tell David . . . I wish I knew what is suddenly so interesting in a newspaper. This is not normal, Sylvia, is it?

SYLVIA (*pause, she stares ahead*): They are making old men crawl around and clean the sidewalks with toothbrushes.

HARRIET: Who is?

SYLVIA: In Germany. Old men with beards!

HARRIET: So why are you so interested in that? What business of yours is that?

SYLVIA (*slight pause; searches within*): I don't really know. (*A slight pause.*) Remember Grandpa? His eyeglasses with the bent sidepiece? One of the old men in the paper was his spitting image, he had the same exact glasses with the wire frames. I can't get it out of my mind. On their knees on the sidewalk, two old men. And there's fifteen or twenty people standing in a circle laughing at them scrubbing with tooth-brushes. There's three women in the picture; they're holding their coat collars closed, so it must have been cold . . .

HARRIET: Why would they make them scrub with tooth-brushes?

SYLVIA (*angered*): To humiliate them, to make fools of them!

HARRIET: Oh!

SYLVIA: How can you be so . . . so . . . ? (*Breaks off before she goes too far.*) Harriet, please . . . leave me alone, will you?

HARRIET: This is not normal. Murray says the same thing. I swear to God, he came home last night and says, "She's got to stop thinking about those Germans." And you know how he loves current events. (SYLVIA *is staring ahead.*) I'll see if the duck looks good, if not I'll get chops. Can I get you something now?

SYLVIA: No, I'm fine, thanks.

HARRIET (*moves upstage of* SYLVIA, *turns*): I'm going.

SYLVIA: Yes.

> (*She returns to her paper.* HARRIET *watches anxiously for a moment, out of* SYLVIA*'s sight line, then exits.* SYLVIA *turns a page, absorbed in the paper. Suddenly she turns in shock—* PHILLIP *is standing behind her. He holds a small paper bag.*) Oh! I didn't hear you come in.

GELLBURG: I tiptoed, in case you were dozing off . . . (*His dour smile.*) I bought you some sour pickles.

SYLVIA: Oh, that's nice! Later, maybe. You have one.

GELLBURG: I'll wait. (*Awkwardly but determined.*) I was passing Greenberg's on Flatbush Avenue and I suddenly remembered how you used to love them. Remember?

SYLVIA: Thanks, that's nice of you. What were you doing on Flatbush Avenue?

GELLBURG: There's a property across from A&S. I'm probably going to foreclose.

SYLVIA: Oh that's sad. Are they nice people?

GELLBURG (*shrugs*): People are people—I gave them two extensions but they'll never manage . . . nothing up here. (*Taps his temple.*)

SYLVIA: Aren't you early?

GELLBURG: I got worried about you. Doctor come?

SYLVIA: He called; he has the results of the tests but he wants to come tomorrow when he has more time to talk to me. He's really very nice.

GELLBURG: How was it today?

SYLVIA: I'm so sorry about this.

GELLBURG: You'll get better, don't worry about it. Oh!—there's a letter from the captain. (*Takes it out of his jacket.*)

SYLVIA: Jerome?

GELLBURG (*terrific personal pride*): Read it.

(*She reads; his purse-mouthed grin is intense.*)

That's your son. General MacArthur talked to him twice.

SYLVIA: Fort Sill?

GELLBURG: Oklahoma. *He's going to lecture them on artillery!* In *Fort Sill*! That's the field-artillery center.

(*She looks up dumbly.*)

That's like being invited to the Vatican to lecture the Pope.

SYLVIA: Imagine. (*She folds the letter and hands it back to him.*)

GELLBURG (*restraining greater resentment*): I don't understand this attitude.

SYLVIA: Why? I'm happy for him.

GELLBURG: You don't seem happy to me.

SYLVIA: I'll never get used to it. Who goes in the army? Men who can't do anything else.

GELLBURG: I wanted people to see that a Jew doesn't have to be a lawyer or a doctor or a businessman.

SYLVIA: That's fine, but why must it be Jerome?

GELLBURG: For a Jewish boy, West Point is an honor! Without Mr. Case's connections, he never would have gotten in. He could be the first Jewish general in the United States Army. Doesn't it mean something to be his mother?

SYLVIA (*with an edge of resentment*): Well, I said I'm glad.

GELLBURG: Don't be upset. (*Looks about impatiently.*) You know, when you get on your feet I'll help you hang the new drapes.

SYLVIA: I started to . . .

GELLBURG: But they've been here over a month.

SYLVIA: Well this happened, I'm sorry.

GELLBURG: You have to occupy yourself is all I'm saying, Sylvia, you can't give in to this.

SYLVIA (*near an outburst*): Well I'm sorry—I'm sorry about everything!

GELLBURG: Please, don't get upset, I take it back!

(*A moment; stalemate.*)

SYLVIA: I wonder what my tests show.

>   (GELLBURG *is silent.*)

>   That the specialist did.

GELLBURG: I went to see Doctor Hyman last night.

SYLVIA: You did? Why didn't you mention it?

GELLBURG: I wanted to think over what he said.

SYLVIA: What did he say?

>   (*With a certain deliberateness,* GELLBURG *goes over to her and gives her a kiss on the cheek.*)

>   (*She is embarrassed and vaguely alarmed.*) Phillip! (*A little uncomprehending laugh.*)

GELLBURG: I want to change some things. About the way I've been doing.

>   (*He stands there for a moment perfectly still, then rolls her chair closer to the bed on which he now sits and takes her hand. She doesn't quite know what to make of this, but doesn't remove her hand.*)

SYLVIA: Well what did he say?

GELLBURG (*he pats her hand*): I'll tell you in a minute. I'm thinking about a Dodge.

SYLVIA: A Dodge?

GELLBURG: I want to teach you to drive. So you can go where you like, visit your mother in the afternoon.—I want you to be happy, Sylvia.

SYLVIA (*surprised*): Oh.

GELLBURG: We have the money, we could do a lot of things. Maybe see Washington, D.C. . . . It's supposed to be a very strong car, you know.

SYLVIA: But aren't they all black?—Dodges?

GELLBURG: Not all. I've seen a couple of green ones.

SYLVIA: You like green?

GELLBURG: It's only a color. You'll get used to it.—Or Chicago. It's really a big city, you know.

SYLVIA: Tell me what Doctor Hyman said.

GELLBURG (*gets himself set*): He thinks it could all be coming from your mind. Like a . . . a fear of some kind got into you. Psychological.

>   (*She is still, listening.*)

>   Are you afraid of something?

SYLVIA (*a slow shrug, a shake of her head*): . . . I don't know, I don't think so. What kind of fear, what does he mean?

GELLBURG: Well, he explains it better, but . . . like in a war, people get so afraid they go blind temporarily. What they call shell-shock. But once they feel safer it goes away.

SYLVIA: What about the tests the Mount Sinai man did?

GELLBURG: They can't find anything wrong with your body.

SYLVIA: But I'm numb!

GELLBURG: He claims being very frightened could be doing it. —Are you?

SYLVIA: I don't know.

GELLBURG: Personally. . . . Can I tell you what I think?

SYLVIA: What.

GELLBURG: I think it's this whole Nazi business.

SYLVIA: But it's in the paper—they're smashing up the Jewish stores . . . Should I not read the paper? The streets are covered with broken glass!

GELLBURG: Yes, but you don't have to be constantly . . .

SYLVIA: It's ridiculous. I can't move my legs from reading a newspaper?

GELLBURG: He didn't say that; but I'm wondering if you're too involved with . . .

SYLVIA: It's ridiculous.

GELLBURG: Well you talk to him tomorrow. (*Pause. He comes back to her and takes her hand, his need open.*) You've got to get better, Sylvia.

SYLVIA (*she sees his tortured face and tries to laugh*): What is this, am I dying or something?

GELLBURG: How can you say that?

SYLVIA: I've never seen such a look in your face.

GELLBURG: Oh no-no-no . . . I'm just worried.

SYLVIA: I don't understand what's happening . . . (*She turns away on the verge of tears.*)

GELLBURG: . . . I never realized . . . (*sudden sharpness*) . . . look at me, will you?

(*She turns to him; he glances down at the floor.*)

I wouldn't know what to do without you, Sylvia, honest to God. I . . . (*Immense difficulty.*) I love you.

SYLVIA (*a dead, bewildered laugh*): What is this?

GELLBURG: You have to get better. If I'm ever doing something wrong I'll change it. Let's try to be different. All right? And you too, you've got to do what the doctors tell you.

SYLVIA: What can I do? Here I sit and they say there's nothing wrong with me.

GELLBURG: Listen . . . I think Hyman is a very smart man . . . (*He lifts her hand and kisses her knuckle; embarrassed and smiling.*) When we were talking, something came to mind; that maybe if we could sit down with him, the three of us, and maybe talk about . . . you know . . . everything.
   (*Pause.*)

SYLVIA: That doesn't matter anymore, Phillip.

GELLBURG (*an embarrassed grin*): How do you know? Maybe . . .

SYLVIA: It's too late for that.

GELLBURG (*once launched he is terrified*): Why? Why is it too late?

SYLVIA: I'm surprised you're still worried about it.

GELLBURG: I'm not worried, I just think about it now and then.

SYLVIA: Well it's too late, dear, it doesn't matter anymore. (*She draws back her hand.*)
   (*Pause.*)

GELLBURG: . . . Well all right. But if you wanted to I'd . . .

SYLVIA: We did talk about it, I took you to Rabbi Steiner about it twice, what good did it do?

GELLBURG: In those days I still thought it would change by itself. I was so young, I didn't understand such things. It came out of nowhere and I thought it would go the same way.

SYLVIA: I'm sorry, Phillip, it didn't come out of nowhere.
   (*Silent, he evades her eyes.*)
   You regretted you got married.

GELLBURG: I didn't "regret" it . . .

SYLVIA: You did, dear. You don't have to be ashamed of it.
   (*A long silence.*)

GELLBURG: I'm going to tell you the truth—in those days I thought that if we separated I wouldn't die of it. I admit that.

SYLVIA: I always knew that.

GELLBURG: But I haven't felt that way in years now.

SYLVIA: Well I'm here. (*Spreads her arms out, a wildly ironical look in her eyes.*) Here I am, Phillip!

GELLBURG (*offended*): The way you say that is not very . . .

SYLVIA: Not very what? I'm here; I've been here a long time.

GELLBURG (*a helpless surge of anger*): I'm trying to tell you something!

SYLVIA (*openly taunting him now*): But I said I'm here!

> (GELLBURG *moves about as she speaks, as though trying to find an escape or a way in.*)

I'm here for my mother's sake, and Jerome's sake, and everybody's sake except mine, but I'm here and here I am. And now finally you want to talk about it, now when I'm turning into an old woman? How do you want me to say it? Tell me, dear, I'll say it the way you want me to. What should I say?

GELLBURG (*insulted and guilty*): I want you to stand up.

SYLVIA: I can't stand up.

> (*He takes both her hands.*)

GELLBURG: You can. Now come on. Stand up.

SYLVIA: I can't!

GELLBURG: You can stand up, Sylvia. Now lean to me and get on your feet.

> (*He pulls her up; then steps aside, releasing her; she collapses on the floor. He stands over her.*)

What are you trying to do? (*He goes to his knees to yell into her face: What are you trying to do, Sylvia!*)

> (*She looks at him in terror at the mystery before her.*)

BLACKOUT

SCENE 3

The Lone Cellist plays. Then lights go down . . .

DR. HYMAN'*s office. He is in riding boots and a sweater.* HARRIET *is seated beside his desk.*

HARRIET: My poor sister. And they have everything! But how can it be in the mind if she's so paralyzed?

HYMAN: Her numbness is random, it doesn't follow the nerve paths; only part of the thighs are affected, part of the calves, it makes no physiological sense. I have a few things I'd like to ask you, all right?

HARRIET: You know, I'm glad it's you taking care of her, my husband says the same thing.

HYMAN: Thank you . . .

HARRIET: You probably don't remember, but you once took out our cousin Roslyn Fein? She said you were great.

HYMAN: Roslyn Fein. When?

HARRIET: She's very tall and reddish-blond hair? She had a real crush . . .

HYMAN (*pleased*): When was this?

HARRIET: Oh—NYU, maybe twenty-five years ago. She adored you; seriously, she said you were really *great*. (*Laughs knowingly.*) Used to take her to Coney Island swimming, and so on.

HYMAN (*laughs with her*): Oh. Well give her my regards.

HARRIET: I hardly see her, she lives in Florida.

HYMAN (*pressing on*): I'd like you to tell me about Sylvia;—before she collapsed, was there any sign of some shock, or anything? Something threatening her?

HARRIET (*thinks for a moment, shrugs, shaking her head*): Listen, I'll tell you something funny—to me sometimes she seems . . . I was going to say happy, but it's more like . . . I don't know . . . like this is how she wants to be. I mean since the collapse. Don't you think so?

HYMAN: Well I never really knew her before. What about this fascination with the Nazis—she ever talk to you about that?

HARRIET: Only this last couple of weeks. I don't understand it, they're in *Germany*, how can she be so frightened, it's across the ocean, isn't it?

HYMAN: Yes. But in a way it isn't. (*He stares, shaking his head, lost.*) . . . She's very sensitive; she really sees the people in those photographs. They're alive to her.

HARRIET (*suddenly near tears*): My poor sister!

HYMAN: Tell me about Phillip.

HARRIET: Phillip? (*Shrugs.*) Phillip is Phillip.

HYMAN: You like him?

HARRIET: Well he's my brother-in-law . . . You mean personally.

HYMAN: Yes.

HARRIET (*takes a breath to lie*): . . . He can be very sweet, you know. But suddenly he'll turn around and talk to you like you've got four legs and long ears. The men—not that they don't respect him—but they'd just as soon not play cards with him if they can help it.

HYMAN: Really. Why?

HARRIET: Well, God forbid you have an opinion—you open your mouth and he gives you that Republican look down his nose and your brains dry up. Not that I don't *like* him . . .

HYMAN: How did he and Sylvia meet?

HARRIET: She was head bookkeeper at Empire Steel over there in Long Island City . . .

HYMAN: She must have been very young.

HARRIET: . . . Twenty; just out of high school practically and she's head bookkeeper. According to my husband, God gave Sylvia all the brains and the rest of us the big feet! The reason they met was the company took out a mortgage and she had to explain all the accounts to Phillip—he used to say, "I fell in love with her figures!"

(HYMAN *laughs.*)

Why should I lie?—personally to me, he's a little bit a prune. Like he never stops with the whole Jewish part of it.

HYMAN: He doesn't like being Jewish.

HARRIET: Well yes and no—like Jerome being the only Jewish captain, he's proud of that. And him being the only one ever worked for Brooklyn Guarantee—he's proud of that too, but at the same time . . .

HYMAN: . . . He'd rather not be one.

HARRIET: . . . Look, he's a mystery to me. I don't understand him and I never will.

HYMAN: What about the marriage? I promise you this is strictly between us.

HARRIET: What can I tell you, the marriage is a marriage.

HYMAN: And?

HARRIET: I shouldn't talk about it.

HYMAN: It stays in this office. Tell me. They ever break up?

HARRIET: Oh God no! Why should they? He's a wonderful provider. There's no Depression for Phillip, you know. And it would kill our mother, she worships Phillip, she'd never

outlive it. No-no, it's out of the question, Sylvia's not that
kind of woman, although . . . (*Breaks off.*)

HYMAN: Come, Harriet, I need to know these things!

HARRIET: . . . Well I guess everybody knows it, so . . .
(*Takes a breath.*) I think they came very close to it one time
. . . when he hit her with the steak.

HYMAN: Hit her with a *steak*?

HARRIET: It was overdone.

HYMAN: What do you mean, hit her?

HARRIET: He picked it up off the plate and slapped her in the
face with it.

HYMAN: And then what?

HARRIET: Well if my mother hadn't patched it up I don't know
what would have happened and then he went out and
bought her that gorgeous beaver coat, and repainted the
whole house, and he's tight as a drum, you know, so it was
hard for him. I don't know what to tell you.—Why?—you
think *he* could have frightened her like this?

HYMAN (*hesitates*): I don't know yet. The whole thing is very
strange.

> (*Something darkens* HARRIET*'s expression and she begins to
> shake her head from side to side and she bursts into tears. He
> comes and puts an arm around her.*)

What is it?

HARRIET: All her life she did nothing but love everybody!

HYMAN (*reaches out to take her hand*): Harriet.

> (*She looks at him.*)

What do you want to tell me?

HARRIET: I don't know if it's right to talk about. But of course,
it's years and years ago . . .

HYMAN: None of this will ever be repeated; believe me.

HARRIET: Well . . . every first of the year when Uncle Myron
was still alive we'd all go down to his basement for a New
Year's party. I'm talking like fifteen, sixteen years ago. He's
dead now, Myron, but . . . he was . . . you know . . .
(*small laugh*) . . . a little comical; he always kept this shoe-
box full of . . . you know, these postcards.

HYMAN: You mean . . .

HARRIET: Yes. French. You know, naked women, and men with
these great big . . . you know . . . they hung down like

salamis. And everybody'd pass them around and die laughing. It was exactly the same thing every New Year's. But this time, all of a sudden, Phillip . . . we thought he'd lost his mind . . .

HYMAN: What happened?

HARRIET: Well Sylvia's in the middle of laughing and he grabs the postcard out of her hand and he turns around screaming—I mean, really screaming—that we're all a bunch of morons and idiots and God knows what, and throws her up the stairs. Bang! It cracked the bannister, I can still hear it. (*Catches her breath.*) I tell you it was months before anybody'd talk to him again. Because everybody on the block loves Sylvia.

HYMAN: What do you suppose made him do that?

HARRIET (*shrugs*): . . . Well if you listen to some of the men—but of course some of the dirty minds on this block . . . if you spread it over the backyard you'd get tomatoes six feet high.

HYMAN: Why?—what'd they say?

HARRIET: Well that the reason he got so mad was because he couldn't . . . you know . . .

HYMAN: Oh really.

HARRIET: . . . anymore.

HYMAN: But they made up.

HARRIET: Listen, to be truthful you have to say it—although it'll sound crazy . . .

HYMAN: What.

HARRIET: You watch him sometimes when they've got people over and she's talking—he'll sit quietly in the corner, and the expression on that man's face when he's watching her—it could almost break your heart.

HYMAN: Why?

HARRIET: He adores her!

BLACKOUT

SCENE 4

The cellist plays, and is gone.

STANTON CASE *is getting ready to leave his office. Putting on his blazer and a captain's cap and a foulard. He has a great natural authority, an almost childishly naive self-assurance.* GELLBURG *enters.*

CASE: Good!—you're back. I was just leaving.

GELLBURG: I'm sorry. I got caught in traffic over in Crown Heights.

CASE: I wanted to talk to you again about 611. Sit down for a moment.

   (*Both sit.*)

We're sailing out through the Narrows in about an hour.

GELLBURG: Beautiful day for it.

CASE: Are you all right? You don't look well.

GELLBURG: Oh no, I'm fine.

CASE: Good. Have you come to anything final on 611? I like the price, I can tell you that right off.

GELLBURG: Yes, the price is not bad, but I'm still . . .

CASE: I've walked past it again; I think with some renovation it would make a fine annex for the Harvard Club.

GELLBURG: It's a very nice structure, yes. I'm not final on it yet but I have a few comments . . . unless you've got to get on the water right away.

CASE: I have a few minutes. Go ahead.

GELLBURG: . . . Before I forget—we got a very nice letter from Jerome.

   (*No reaction from* CASE.)

My boy.

CASE: Oh yes!—how is he doing?

GELLBURG: They're bringing him out to Fort Sill . . . some kind of lecture on artillery.

CASE: Really, now! Well, isn't that nice! . . . Then he's really intending to make a career in the army.

GELLBURG (*surprised* CASE *isn't aware*): Oh absolutely.

CASE: Well that's good, isn't it. It's quite surprising for one of you people—for some reason I'd assumed he just wanted the education.

GELLBURG: Oh no. It's his life. I'll never know how to thank you.

CASE: No trouble at all. The Point can probably use a few of you people to keep the rest of them awake. Now what's this about 611?

GELLBURG (*sets himself in all dignity*): You might recall, we used the ABC Plumbing Contractors on a couple of buildings?

CASE: ABC?—I don't recall. What have they got to do with it?

GELLBURG: They're located in the neighborhood, just off Broadway, and on a long shot I went over to see Mr. Liebfreund—he runs ABC. I was wondering if they may have done any work for Wanamaker's.

CASE: Wanamaker's! What's Wanamaker's got to do with it?

GELLBURG: I buy my shirts in Wanamaker's, and last time I was in there I caught my shoe on a splinter sticking up out of the floor.

CASE: Well that store is probably fifty years old.

GELLBURG: Closer to seventy-five. I tripped and almost fell down; this was very remarkable to me, that they would leave a floor in such condition. So I began wondering about it . . .

CASE: About what?

GELLBURG: Number 611 is two blocks from Wanamaker's. (*A little extra-wise grin.*) They're the biggest business in the area, a whole square block, after all. Anyway, sure enough, turns out ABC does all Wanamaker's plumbing work. And Liebfreund tells me he's had to keep patching up their boilers *because they canceled installation of new boilers last winter.* A permanent cancellation.

(*Pause.*)

CASE: And what do you make of that?

GELLBURG: I think it could mean they're either moving the store, or maybe going out of business.

CASE: *Wanamaker's?*

GELLBURG: It's possible, I understand the family is practically died out. Either way, if Wanamaker's disappears, Mr. Case, that neighborhood in my opinion is no longer prime. Also, I called Kevin Sullivan over at Title Guarantee and he says they turned down 611 last year and he can't remember why.

CASE: Then what are you telling me?

GELLBURG: I would not touch Number 611 with a ten-foot pole—unless you can get it at a good defensive price. If that neighborhood starts to slide, 611 is a great big slice of lemon.

CASE: Well. That's very disappointing. It would have made a wonderful club annex.

GELLBURG: With a thing like the Harvard Club you have got to think of the far distant future, Mr. Case, I don't have to tell you that, and the future of that part of Broadway is a definite possible negative. (*Raising a monitory finger.*) I emphasize "possible," mind you; only God can predict.

CASE: Well I must say, I would never have thought of Wanamaker's disappearing. You've been more than thorough, Gellburg, we appreciate it. I've got to run now, but we'll talk about this further . . . (*Glances at his watch.*) Mustn't miss the tide . . . (*Moves, indicates.*) Take a brandy if you like. Wife all right?

GELLBURG: Oh yes, she's fine!

CASE (*the faint shadow of a warning*): Sure everything's all right with you—we don't want you getting sick now.

GELLBURG: Oh no, I'm very well, very well.

CASE: I'll be back on Monday, we'll go into this further. (*Indicates.*) Take a brandy if you like. (CASE *exits rather jauntily.*)

GELLBURG: Yes, sir, I might! (GELLBURG *stands alone; with a look of self-satisfaction starts to raise the glass.*)

BLACKOUT

SCENE 5

The cello plays, and the music falls away.

SYLVIA *in bed, reading a book. She looks up as* HYMAN *enters. He is in his riding clothes.* SYLVIA *has a certain excitement at seeing him.*

SYLVIA: Oh, doctor!

HYMAN: I let myself in, hope I didn't scare you . . .

SYLVIA: Oh no, I'm glad. Sit down. You been riding?

HYMAN: Yes. All the way down to Brighton Beach, nice long ride—I expected to see you jumping rope by now.

(SYLVIA *laughs, embarrassed.*)

I think you're just trying to get out of doing the dishes.

SYLVIA (*strained laugh*): Oh stop. You really love riding, don't you?

HYMAN: Well there's no telephone on a horse.

(*She laughs.*)

Ocean Parkway is like a German forest this time of the morning—riding under that archway of maple trees is like poetry.

SYLVIA: Wonderful. I never did anything like that.

HYMAN: Well, let's go—I'll take you out and teach you sometime. Have you been trying the exercise?

SYLVIA: I can't do it.

HYMAN (*shaking a finger at her*): You've *got* to do it, Sylvia. You could end up permanently crippled. Let's have a look.

(*He sits on the bed and draws the cover off her legs, then raises her nightgown. She inhales with a certain anticipation as he does so. He feels her toes.*)

You feel this at all?

SYLVIA: Well . . . not really.

HYMAN: I'm going to pinch your toe. Ready?

SYLVIA: All right.

(*He pinches her big toe sharply; she doesn't react. He rests a palm on her leg.*)

HYMAN: Your skin feels a little too cool. You're going to lose your muscle tone if you don't move. Your legs will begin to lose volume and shrink . . .

SYLVIA (*tears threaten*): I know . . . !

HYMAN: And look what beautiful legs you have, Sylvia. I'm afraid you're getting comfortable in this condition . . .

SYLVIA: I'm not. I keep trying to move them . . .

HYMAN: But look now—here it's eleven in the morning and you're happily tucked into bed like it's midnight.

SYLVIA: But I've tried . . . ! Are you really sure it's not a virus of some kind?

HYMAN: There's nothing. Sylvia, you have a strong beautiful body . . .

SYLVIA: But what can I do, I can't feel anything!

(*She sits up with her face raised to him; he stands and moves abruptly away. Then turning back to her . . .*)

HYMAN: I really should find someone else for you.

SYLVIA: Why!—I don't want anyone else!

HYMAN: You're a very attractive woman, don't you know that?

(*Deeply excited,* SYLVIA *glances away shyly.*)

Sylvia, listen to me . . . I haven't been this moved by a
woman in a very long time.

SYLVIA: . . . Well, you mustn't get anyone else.

(*Pause.*)

HYMAN: Tell me the truth, Sylvia. Sylvia? How did this happen
to you?

SYLVIA (*she avoids his gaze*): I don't know. (SYLVIA'*s anxiety rises
as he speaks now.*)

HYMAN: . . . I'm going to be straight with you; I thought
this was going to be simpler than it's turning out to be, and
I care about you too much to play a game with your health.
I can't deny my vanity. I have a lot of it, but I have to face
it—I know you want to tell me something and I don't know
how to get it out of you.

(SYLVIA *covers her face, ashamed.*)

You're a responsible woman, Sylvia, you have to start helping me, you can't just lie there and expect a miracle to lift
you to your feet. You tell me now—what should I know?

SYLVIA: I would tell you if I knew!

(HYMAN *turns away defeated and impatient.*)

Couldn't we just talk and maybe I could . . . (*Breaks off.*) I
like you. A lot. I love when you talk to me . . . couldn't we
just . . . like for a few minutes. . . .

HYMAN: Okay. What do you want to talk about?

SYLVIA: Please. Be patient. I'm . . . I'm trying. (*Relieved; a
fresher mood.*) —Harriet says you used to take out our cousin
Roslyn Fein.

HYMAN (*smiles, shrugs*): It's possible, I don't remember.

SYLVIA: Well you had so many, didn't you.

HYMAN: When I was younger.

SYLVIA: Roslyn said you used to do acrobatics on the beach?
And all the girls would stand around going crazy for you.

HYMAN: That's a long time ago. . . .

SYLVIA: And you'd take them under the boardwalk. (*Laughs.*)

HYMAN: Nobody had money for anything else. Didn't you
used to go to the beach?

SYLVIA: Sure. But I never did anything like that.

HYMAN: You must have been very shy.

SYLVIA: I guess. But I had to look out for my sisters, being the
eldest . . .

HYMAN: Can we talk about Phillip?
   (*Caught unaware, her eyes show fear.*)
   I'd really like to, unless you . . .
SYLVIA (*challenged*): No!—It's all right.
HYMAN: . . . Are you afraid right now?
SYLVIA: No, not . . . Yes. (*Picks up the book beside her.*) Have
   you read *Anthony Adverse*?
HYMAN: No, but I hear it's sold a million copies.
SYLVIA: It's wonderful. I rent it from Womraths.
HYMAN: Was Phillip your first boyfriend?
SYLVIA: The first serious.
HYMAN: He's a fine man.
SYLVIA: Yes, he is.
HYMAN: Is he interesting to be with?
SYLVIA: Interesting?
HYMAN: Do you have things to talk about?
SYLVIA: Well . . . business, mostly. I was head bookkeeper for
   Empire Steel in Long Island City . . . years ago, when we
   met, I mean.
HYMAN: He didn't want you to work?
SYLVIA: No.
HYMAN: I imagine you were a good businesswoman.
SYLVIA: Oh, I loved it! I've always enjoyed . . . you know,
   people depending on me.
HYMAN: Yes.—Do I frighten you, talking like this?
SYLVIA: A little.—But I want you to.
HYMAN: Why?
SYLVIA: I don't know. You make me feel . . . hopeful.
HYMAN: You mean of getting better?
SYLVIA: —Of myself. Of getting . . . (*Breaks off.*)
HYMAN: Getting what?
   (*She shakes her head, refusing to go on.*)
   . . . Free?
   (*She suddenly kisses the palm of his hand. He wipes her hair
   away from her eyes. He stands up and walks a few steps
   away.*)
   I want you to raise your knees.
   (*She doesn't move.*)
   Come, bring up your knees.
SYLVIA (*she tries*): I can't!

HYMAN: You can. I want you to send your thoughts into your hips. Tense your hips. Think of the bones in your hips. Come on now. The strongest muscles in your body are right there, you still have tremendous power there. Tense your hips.

(*She is tensing.*)

Now tense your thighs. Those are long dense muscles with tremendous power. Do it, draw up your knees. Come on, raise your knees. Keep it up. Concentrate. Raise it. Do it for me.

(*With an exhaled gasp she gives up. Remaining yards away . . .*)

Your body strength must be marvelous. The depth of your flesh must be wonderful. Why are you cut off from yourself? You should be dancing, you should be stretching out in the sun. . . . Sylvia, I know you know more than you're saying, why can't you open up to me? Speak to me. Sylvia? Say anything.

(*She looks at him in silence.*)

I promise I won't tell a soul. What is in your mind right now?

(*A pause.*)

SYLVIA: Tell me about Germany.

HYMAN (*surprised*): Germany. Why Germany?

SYLVIA: Why did you go there to study?

HYMAN: The American medical schools have quotas on Jews, I would have had to wait for years and maybe never get in.

SYLVIA: But they hate Jews there, don't they?

HYMAN: These Nazis can't possibly last—Why are you so preoccupied with them?

SYLVIA: I don't know. But when I saw that picture in the *Times*—with those two old men on their knees in the street . . . (*Presses her ears.*) I swear, I almost heard that crowd laughing, and ridiculing them. But nobody really wants to talk about it. I mean Phillip never even wants to talk about being Jewish, except—you know—to joke about it the way people do . . .

HYMAN: What would you like to say to Phillip about it?

SYLVIA (*with an empty laugh, a head shake*): I don't even know! Just to talk about it . . . it's almost like there's something in me that . . . it's silly . . .

HYMAN: No, it's interesting. What do you mean, something in you?

SYLVIA: I have no word for it, I don't know what I'm saying, it's like . . . (*she presses her chest*)—something alive, like a child almost, except it's a very dark thing . . . and it frightens me!

(HYMAN *moves his hand to calm her and she grabs it.*)

HYMAN: That was hard to say, wasn't it.

(SYLVIA *nods.*)

You have a lot of courage.—We'll talk more, but I want you to try something now. I'll stand here, and I want you to imagine something.

(SYLVIA *turns to him, curious.*)

I want you to imagine that we've made love.

(*Startled, she laughs tensely. He joins this laugh as though it is a game.*)

I've made love to you. And now it's over and we are lying together. And you begin to tell me some secret things. Things that are way down deep in your heart. (*Slight pause.*) Sylvia—(HYMAN *comes around the bed, bends, and kisses her on the cheek.*) Tell me about Phillip.

(SYLVIA *is silent, does not grasp his head to hold him. He straightens up.*)

Think about it. We'll talk tomorrow again. Okay?

(HYMAN *exits.* SYLVIA *lies there inert for a moment. Then she tenses with effort, trying to raise her knee. It doesn't work. She reaches down and lifts the knee, and then the other and lies there that way. Then she lets her knees spread apart . . .*)

BLACKOUT

SCENE 6

The cellist plays, then is gone.

HYMAN'*s office.* GELLBURG *is seated. Immediately* MARGARET *enters with a cup of cocoa and a file folder. She hands the cup to* GELLBURG.

GELLBURG: Cocoa?

MARGARET: I drink a lot of it, it calms the nerves. Have you lost weight?

GELLBURG (*impatience with her prying*): A little, I think.

MARGARET: Did you always sigh so much?

GELLBURG: Sigh?

MARGARET: You probably don't realize you're doing it. You should have him listen to your heart.

GELLBURG: No-no, I think I'm all right. (*Sighs.*) I guess I've always sighed. Is that a sign of something?

MARGARET: Not necessarily; but ask Harry. He's just finishing with a patient.—There's no change, I understand.

GELLBURG: No, she's the same. (*Impatiently hands her the cup.*) I can't drink this.

MARGARET: Are you eating at all?

GELLBURG (*suddenly shifting his mode*): I came to talk to *him*.

MARGARET (*sharply*): I was only trying to be helpful!

GELLBURG: I'm kind of upset, I didn't mean any . . .

(HYMAN *enters, surprising her. She exits, insulted.*)

HYMAN: I'm sorry. But she means well.

(GELLBURG *silently nods, irritation intact.*)

It won't happen again. (*He takes his seat.*) I have to admit, though, she has a very good diagnostic sense. Women are more instinctive sometimes . . .

GELLBURG: Excuse me, I don't come here to be talking to her.

HYMAN (*a kidding laugh*): Oh, come on, Phillip, take it easy. What's Sylvia doing?

GELLBURG (*it takes him a moment to compose himself*): . . . I don't know what she's doing.

(HYMAN *waits.* GELLBURG *has a tortured look; now he seems to brace himself, and faces the doctor with what seems a haughty air.*)

I decided to try to do what you advised.—About the loving.

HYMAN: . . . Yes?

GELLBURG: So I decided to try to do it with her.

HYMAN: . . . Sex?

GELLBURG: What then, handball? Of course sex.

(*The openness of this hostility mystifies* HYMAN, *who becomes conciliatory.*)

HYMAN: . . . Well, do you mean you've done it or you're going to?

GELLBURG (*long pause; he seems not to be sure he wants to continue. Now he sounds reasonable again*): You see, we haven't been really . . . together. For . . . quite a long time. (*Correcting.*) I mean specially since this started to happen.

HYMAN: You mean the last two weeks.

GELLBURG: Well yes. (*Great discomfort.*) And some time before that.

HYMAN: I see. (*But he desists from asking how long a time before that. A pause.*)

GELLBURG: So I thought maybe it would help her if . . . you know.

HYMAN: Yes, I think the warmth would help. In fact, to be candid, Phillip—I'm beginning to wonder if this whole fear of the Nazis isn't because she feels . . . extremely vulnerable; I'm in no sense trying to blame you but . . . a woman who doesn't feel loved can get very disoriented you know?—lost. (*He has noticed a strangeness.*) —Something wrong?

GELLBURG: She says she's not being loved?

HYMAN: No-no. I'm talking about how she may feel.

GELLBURG: Listen . . . (*Struggles for a moment; now firmly.*) I'm wondering if you could put me in touch with somebody.

HYMAN: You mean for yourself?

GELLBURG: I don't know; I'm not sure what they do, though.

HYMAN: I know a very good man at the hospital, if you want me to set it up.

GELLBURG: Well maybe not yet, let me let you know.

HYMAN: Sure.

GELLBURG: Your wife says I sigh a lot. Does that mean something?

HYMAN: Could just be tension. Come in when you have a little time, I'll look you over. . . . Am I wrong?—you sound like something's happened . . .

GELLBURG: This whole thing is against me . . . (*Attempting a knowing grin.*) But you know that.

HYMAN: Now wait a minute . . .

GELLBURG: She knows what she's doing, you're not blind.

HYMAN: What happened, why are you saying this?

GELLBURG: I was late last night—I had to be in Jersey all afternoon, a problem we have there—she was sound asleep. So I made myself some spaghetti. Usually she puts something out for me.

HYMAN: She has no problem cooking.

GELLBURG: I told you—she gets around the kitchen fine in the wheelchair. Flora shops in the morning—that's the maid. Although I'm beginning to wonder if Sylvia gets out and walks around when I leave the house.

HYMAN: It's impossible.—She is paralyzed, Phillip, it's not a trick—she's suffering.

GELLBURG (*a sideways glance at* HYMAN): What do you discuss with her?—You know, she talks like you see right through her.

HYMAN (*a laugh*): I wish I could! We talk about getting her to walk, that's all. This thing is not against you, Phillip, believe me. (*Slight laugh.*) —I wish you could trust me, kid!

GELLBURG (*seems momentarily on the edge of being reassured and studies* HYMAN'*s face for a moment, nodding very slightly*): I would never believe I could talk this way to another person. I do trust you.

(*Pause.*)

HYMAN: Good!—I'm listening, go ahead.

GELLBURG: The first time we talked you asked me if we . . . how many times a week.

HYMAN: Yes.

GELLBURG (*nods*): . . . I have a problem sometimes.

HYMAN: Oh.—Well that's fairly common, you know.

GELLBURG (*relieved*): You see it often?

HYMAN: Oh very often, yes.

GELLBURG (*a tense challenging smile*): Ever happen to you?

HYMAN (*surprised*): . . . Me? Well sure, a few times. Is this something recent?

GELLBURG: Well . . . yes. Recent and also . . . (*Breaks off, indicating the past with a gesture of his hand.*)

HYMAN: I see. It doesn't help if you're under tension, you know.

GELLBURG: Yes, I was wondering that.

HYMAN: Just don't start thinking it's the end of the world be- cause it's not—you're still a young man. Think of it like the ocean—it goes out but it always comes in again. But the thing to keep in mind is that she loves you and wants you.

(GELLBURG *looks wide-eyed.*)

You know that, don't you?

GELLBURG (*silently nods for an instant*): My sister-in-law Harriet says you were a real hotshot on the beach years ago.

HYMAN: Years ago, yes.

GELLBURG: I used to wonder if it's because Sylvia's the only one I was ever with.

HYMAN: Why would that matter?

GELLBURG: I don't know exactly—it used to prey on my mind that . . . maybe she expected more.

HYMAN: Yes. Well that's a common idea, you know. In fact, some men take on a lot of women not out of confidence but because they're afraid to lose it.

GELLBURG (*fascinated*): Huh! I'd never of thought of that. —A doctor must get a lot of peculiar cases, I bet.

HYMAN (*with utter intimacy*): Everybody's peculiar in one way or another but I'm not here to judge people. Why don't you try to tell me what happened? (*His grin; making light of it.*) Come on, give it a shot.

GELLBURG: All right . . . (*Sighs.*) I get into bed. She's sound asleep . . . (*Breaks off. Resumes; something transcendent seems to enter him.*) Nothing like it ever happened to me, I got a . . . a big yen for her. She's even more beautiful when she sleeps. I gave her a kiss. On the mouth. She didn't wake up. I never had such a yen in my life.

(*Long pause.*)

HYMAN: And?

(GELLBURG *silent.*)

Did you make love?

GELLBURG (*an incongruous look of terror, he becomes rigid as though about to decide whether to dive into icy water or flee*): . . . Yes.

HYMAN (*a quickening, something tentative in* GELLBURG *mystifies*): How did she react?—It's been some time since you did it, you say.

GELLBURG: Well yes.

HYMAN: Then what was the reaction?

GELLBURG: She was . . . (*Searches for the word.*) Gasping. It was really something. I thought of what you told me—about loving her now; I felt I'd brought her out of it. I was almost sure of it. She was like a different woman than I ever knew.

HYMAN: That's wonderful. Did she move her legs?

GELLBURG (*unprepared for that question*): . . . I think so.

HYMAN: Well did she or didn't she?

GELLBURG: Well I was so excited I didn't really notice, but I guess she must have.

HYMAN: That's wonderful, why are you so upset?

GELLBURG: Well let me finish, there's more to it.

HYMAN: Sorry, go ahead.

GELLBURG: —I brought her some breakfast this morning and —you know—started to—you know—talk a little about it. She looked at me like I was crazy. She claims she doesn't remember doing it. It never happened.

> (HYMAN *is silent, plays with a pen. Something evasive in this.*)

How could she not remember it?

HYMAN: You're sure she was awake?

GELLBURG: How could she not be?

HYMAN: Did she say anything during the . . . ?

GELLBURG: Well no, but she's never said much.

HYMAN: Did she open her eyes?

GELLBURG: I'm not sure. We were in the dark, but she usually keeps them closed. (*Impatiently.*) But she was . . . she was groaning, panting . . . she had to be awake! And now to say she doesn't remember?

> (*Shaken,* HYMAN *gets up and moves; a pause.*)

HYMAN: So what do you think is behind it?

GELLBURG: Well what would any man think? She's trying to turn me into nothing!

HYMAN: Now wait, you're jumping to conclusions.

GELLBURG: Is such a thing possible? I want your medical opinion —could a woman not remember?

HYMAN (*a moment, then*): How did she look when she said that; did she seem sincere about not remembering?

GELLBURG: She looked like I was talking about something on the moon. Finally, she said a terrible thing. I still can't get over it.

HYMAN: What'd she say?

GELLBURG: That I'd imagined doing it.

> (*Long pause.* HYMAN *doesn't move.*)

What's your opinion? Well . . . could a man imagine such a thing? Is that possible?

HYMAN (*after a moment*): Tell you what; supposing I have another talk with her and see what I can figure out?

GELLBURG (*angrily demanding*): You have an opinion, don't you?—How could a man imagine such a thing!

HYMAN: I don't know what to say . . .

GELLBURG: What do you mean you don't know what to say! It's impossible, isn't it? To invent such a thing?

HYMAN (*fear of being out of his depth*): Phillip, don't cross-examine me, I'm doing everything I know to help you!—Frankly, I can't follow what you're telling me—you're sure in your own mind you had relations with her?

GELLBURG: How can you even ask me such a thing? Would I say it unless I was sure? (*Stands shaking with fear and anger.*) I don't understand your attitude! (*He starts out.*)

HYMAN: Phillip, please! (*In fear he intercepts* GELLBURG.) What attitude, what are you talking about?

GELLBURG: I'm going to vomit, I swear—I don't feel well . . .

HYMAN: What happened . . . has she said something about me?

GELLBURG: About you? What do you mean? What could she say?

HYMAN: I don't understand why you're so upset with me!

GELLBURG: What are you doing!

HYMAN (*guiltily*): What am *I* doing! What are you talking about!

GELLBURG: She is trying to destroy me! And you stand there! And what do you do! Are you a doctor or what! (*He goes right up to* HYMAN's *face.*) Why don't you give me a straight answer about anything! Everything is in-and-out and around-the-block!—Listen, I've made up my mind; I don't want you seeing her anymore.

HYMAN: I think she's the one has to decide that.

GELLBURG: I am deciding it! It's decided!

> (*He storms out.* HYMAN *stands there, guilty, alarmed.* MARGARET *enters.*)

MARGARET: Now what? (*Seeing his anxiety.*) Why are you looking like that?

> (*He evasively returns to his desk chair.*)

Are *you* in trouble?

HYMAN: Me! Cut it out, will you?

MARGARET: Cut what out? I asked a question—are you?

HYMAN: I said to cut it out, Margaret!

MARGARET: You don't realize how transparent you are. You're a pane of glass, Harry.

HYMAN (*laughs*): Nothing's happened. *Nothing has happened!* Why are you going on about it!

MARGARET: I will never understand it. Except I do, I guess; you believe women. Woman tells you the earth is flat and for that five minutes you're swept away, helpless.

HYMAN: You know what baffles me?

MARGARET: . . . And it's irritating. —What is it—just new ass all the time?

HYMAN: There's been nobody for at least ten or twelve years . . . more! I can't remember anymore! You know that!

MARGARET: What baffles you?

HYMAN: Why I take your suspicions seriously.

MARGARET: Oh that's easy.—You love the truth, Harry.

HYMAN (*a deep sigh, facing upward*): I'm exhausted.

MARGARET: What about asking Charley Whitman to see her?

HYMAN: She's frightened to death of psychiatry, she thinks it means she's crazy.

MARGARET: Well, she is, in a way, isn't she?

HYMAN: I don't see it that way at all.

MARGARET: Getting this hysterical about something on the other side of the world is sane?

HYMAN: When she talks about it, it's not the other side of the world, it's on the next block.

MARGARET: And that's sane?

HYMAN: I don't know what it is! I just get the feeling sometimes that she *knows* something, something that . . . It's like she's connected to some . . . some wire that goes half around the world, some truth that other people are blind to.

MARGARET: I think you've got to get somebody on this who won't be carried away, Harry.

HYMAN: I am not carried away!

MARGARET: You really believe that Sylvia Gellburg is being threatened by these Nazis? Is that real or is it hysterical?

HYMAN: So call it hysterical, does that bring you one inch closer to what is driving that woman? It's not a word that's

driving her, Margaret—she *knows* something! I don't know what it is, and she may not either—but I tell you it's real.
(*A moment.*)
MARGARET: What an interesting life you have, Harry.

BLACKOUT

INTERMISSION

ACT TWO

The cellist plays, music fades away.

STANTON CASE *is standing with hands clasped behind his back as though staring out a window. A dark mood.* GELLBURG *enters behind him but he doesn't turn at once.*

GELLBURG: Excuse me . . .

CASE (*turns*): Oh, good morning. You wanted to see me.

GELLBURG: If you have a minute I'd appreciate . . .

CASE (*as he sits*): —You don't look well, are you all right?

GELLBURG: Oh I'm fine, maybe a cold coming on . . . (*Since he hasn't been invited to sit he glances at a chair then back at* CASE, *who still leaves him hanging—and he sits on the chair's edge.*) I wanted you to know how bad I feel about 611 Broadway. I'm very sorry.

CASE: Yes. Well. So it goes, I guess.

GELLBURG: I know how you had your heart set on it and I . . . I tell you the news knocked me over; they gave no sign they were talking to Allan Kershowitz or anybody else . . .

CASE: It's very disappointing—in fact, I'd already begun talking to an architect friend about renovations.

GELLBURG: Really. Well, I can't tell you how . . .

CASE: I'd gotten a real affection for that building. It certainly would have made a perfect annex. And probably a great investment too.

GELLBURG: Well, not necessarily, if Wanamaker's ever pulls out.

CASE: . . . Yes, about Wanamaker's—I should tell you—when I found out that Kershowitz had outbid us I was flabbergasted after what you'd said about the neighborhood going downhill once the store was gone— Kershowitz is no fool, I need hardly say. So I mentioned it to one of our club members who I know is related to a member of the Wanamaker board.—He tells me there has never been any discussion whatever about the company moving out; he was simply amazed at the idea.

GELLBURG: But the man at ABC . . .

CASE (*impatience showing*): ABC was left with the repair work because Wanamaker's changed to another contractor for their new boilers. It had nothing to do with the store moving out. Nothing.

GELLBURG: . . . I don't know what to say, I . . . I just . . . I'm awfully sorry . . .

CASE: Well, it's a beautiful building, let's hope Kershowitz puts it to some worthwhile use.—You have any idea what he plans to do with it?

GELLBURG: Me? Oh no, I don't really know Kershowitz.

CASE: Oh! I thought you said you knew him for years?

GELLBURG: . . . Well, I "know" him, but not . . . we're not personal friends or anything, we just met at closings a few times, and things like that. And maybe once or twice in restaurants, I think, but . . .

CASE: I see. I guess I misunderstood, I thought you were fairly close.

(CASE *says no more; the full stop shoots* GELLBURG*'s anxiety way up.*)

GELLBURG: I hope you're not . . . I mean I never mentioned to Kershowitz that you were interested in 611.

CASE: Mentioned? What do you mean?

GELLBURG: Nothing; just that . . . it almost sounds like I had something to do with him grabbing the building away from under you. Because I would never do a thing like that to you!

CASE: I didn't say that, did I. If I seem upset it's being screwed out of that building, and by a man whose methods I never particularly admired.

GELLBURG: Yes, that's what I mean. But I had nothing to do with Kershowitz . . . (*Breaks off into silence.*)

CASE: But did I say you did? I'm not clear about what you wanted to say to me, or have I missed some . . . ?

GELLBURG: No-no, just that. What you just said.

CASE (*his mystification peaking*): What's the matter with you?

GELLBURG: I'm sorry. I'd like to forget the whole thing.

CASE: What's happening?

GELLBURG: Nothing. Really. I'm sorry I troubled you!

> (*Pause. With an explosion of frustration,* CASE *marches out.* GELLBURG *is left open mouthed, one hand raised as though to bring back his life.*)

BLACKOUT

SCENE 2

The cellist plays and is gone.

SYLVIA *in a wheelchair is listening to Eddie Cantor on the radio, singing "If You Knew Susie Like I Know Susie." She has an amused look, taps a finger to the rhythm. Her bed is nearby, on it a folded newspaper.*

HYMAN *appears. She instantly smiles, turns off the radio, and holds a hand out to him. He comes and shakes hands.*

SYLVIA (*indicating the radio*): I simply can't stand Eddie Cantor, can you?

HYMAN: Cut it out now, I heard you laughing halfway up the stairs.

SYLVIA: I know, but I can't stand him. This Crosby's the one I like. You ever hear him?

HYMAN: I can't stand these crooners—they're making ten, twenty thousand dollars a week and never spent a day in medical school.

> (*She laughs.*)

Anyway, I'm an opera man.

SYLVIA: I never saw an opera. They must be hard to understand, I bet.

HYMAN: Nothing to understand—either she wants to and he doesn't or he wants to and she doesn't.

> (*She laughs.*)

Either way one of them gets killed and the other one jumps off a building.

SYLVIA: I'm so glad you could come.

HYMAN (*settling into chair near the bed*): —You ready? We have to discuss something.

SYLVIA: Phillip had to go to Jersey for a zoning meeting . . .

HYMAN: Just as well—it's you I want to talk to.

SYLVIA: —There's some factory the firm owns there . . .

HYMAN: Come on, don't be nervous.

SYLVIA: . . . My back aches, will you help me onto the bed?

HYMAN: Sure. (*He lifts her off the chair and carries her to the bed where he gently lowers her.*) There we go.

　　(*She lies back. He brings up the blanket and covers her legs.*) What's that perfume?

SYLVIA: Harriet found it in my drawer. I think Jerome bought it for one of my birthdays years ago.

HYMAN: Lovely. Your hair is different.

SYLVIA (*puffs up her hair*): Harriet did it; she's loved playing with my hair since we were kids. Did you hear all those birds this morning?

HYMAN: Amazing, yes; a whole cloud of them shot up like a spray in front of my horse.

SYLVIA (*partially to keep him*): You know, as a child, when we first moved from upstate there were so many birds and rabbits and even foxes here—Of course that was *real* country up there; my dad had a wonderful general store, everything from ladies' hats to horseshoes. But the winters were just finally too cold for my mother.

HYMAN: In Coney Island we used to kill rabbits with slingshots.

SYLVIA (*wrinkling her nose in disgust*): Why!

HYMAN (*shrugs*): —To see if we could. It was heaven for kids.

SYLVIA: I know! Brooklyn was really beautiful, wasn't it? I think people were happier then. My mother used to stand on our porch and watch us all the way to school, right across the open fields for—must have been a mile. And I would tie a clothesline around my three sisters so I wouldn't have to keep chasing after them!—I'm so glad—honestly . . . (*A cozy little laugh.*) I feel good every time you come.

HYMAN: Now listen to me; I've learned that these kinds of symptoms come from very deep in the mind. I would have to deal with your dreams to get any results, your deepest secret feelings, you understand? That's not my training.

SYLVIA: But when you talk to me I really feel my strength starting to come back . . .

HYMAN: You should already be having therapy to keep up your circulation.

(*A change in her expression, a sudden withdrawal which he notices.*)

You have a long life ahead of you, you don't want to live it in a wheelchair, do you? It's imperative that we get you to someone who can . . .

SYLVIA: I could tell you a dream.

HYMAN: I'm not trained to . . .

SYLVIA: I'd like to, can I?—I have the same one every night just as I'm falling asleep.

HYMAN (*forced to give way*): Well . . . all right, what is it?

SYLVIA: I'm in a street. Everything is sort of gray. And there's a crowd of people. They're packed in all around, but they're looking for me.

HYMAN: Who are they?

SYLVIA: They're Germans.

HYMAN: Sounds like those photographs in the papers.

SYLVIA (*discovering it now*): I think so, yes!

HYMAN: Does something happen?

SYLVIA: Well, I begin to run away. And the whole crowd is chasing after me. They have heavy shoes that pound on the pavement. Then just as I'm escaping around a corner a man catches me and pushes me down . . . (*Breaks off.*)

HYMAN: Is that the end of it?

SYLVIA: No. He gets on top of me, and begins kissing me . . . (*Breaks off.*)

HYMAN: Yes?

SYLVIA: . . . And then he starts to cut off my breasts. And he raises himself up, and for a second I see the side of his face.

HYMAN: Who is it?

SYLVIA: . . . I don't know.

HYMAN: But you saw his face.

SYLVIA: I think it's Phillip. (*Pause.*) But how could Phillip be like . . . he was almost like one of the others?

HYMAN: I don't know. Why do you think?

SYLVIA: Would it be possible . . . because Phillip . . . I mean . . . (*a little laugh*) . . . he sounds sometimes like he doesn't like Jews? (*Correcting.*) Of course he doesn't *mean* it, but maybe in my mind it's like he's . . . (*Breaks off.*)

HYMAN: Like he's what. What's frightening you?

> (SYLVIA *is silent, turns away.*)

Sylvia?

> (HYMAN *tries to turn her face towards him, but she resists.*)

Not Phillip, is it?

> (SYLVIA *turns to him, the answer is in her eyes.*)

I see.

> (*He moves from the bed and halts, trying to weigh this added complication. Returning to the bedside, sits, takes her hand.*)

I want to ask you a question.

> (*She draws him to her and kisses him on the mouth.*)

SYLVIA: I can't help it. (*She bursts into tears.*)

HYMAN: Oh God, Sylvia, I'm so sorry . . .

SYLVIA: Help me. Please!

HYMAN: I'm trying to.

SYLVIA: I know! (*She weeps even more deeply. With a cry filled with her pain she embraces him desperately.*)

HYMAN: Oh Sylvia, Sylvia. . . .

SYLVIA: I feel so foolish.

HYMAN: No-no. You're unhappy, not foolish.

SYLVIA: I feel like I'm losing everything, I'm being torn to pieces. What do you want to know, I'll tell you!

> (*She cries into her hands. He moves, trying to make a decision . . .*)

I trust you. What do you want to ask me?

HYMAN: —Since this happened to you, have you and Phillip had relations?

SYLVIA (*open surprise*): Relations?

HYMAN: He said you did the other night.

SYLVIA: We had *relations* the other night?

HYMAN: But that . . . well he said that by morning you'd forgotten. Is that true?

> (*She is motionless, looking past him with immense uncertainty.*)

SYLVIA (*alarmed sense of rejection*): Why are you asking me that?

HYMAN: I didn't know what to make of it. . . . I guess I still don't.

SYLVIA (*deeply embarrassed*): You mean you believe him?

HYMAN: Well . . . I didn't know what to believe.

SYLVIA: You must think I'm crazy,—to forget such a thing.

HYMAN: Oh God no!—I didn't mean anything like that . . .

SYLVIA: We haven't had relations for almost twenty years.

> (*The shock pitches him into silence. Now he doesn't know what or whom to believe.*)

HYMAN: Twenty . . . ? (*Breaks off.*)

SYLVIA: Just after Jerome was born.

HYMAN: I just . . . I don't know what to say, Sylvia.

SYLVIA: You never heard of it before with people?

HYMAN: Yes, but not when they're as young as you.

SYLVIA: You might be surprised.

HYMAN: What was it, another woman, or what?

SYLVIA: Oh no.

HYMAN: Then what happened?

SYLVIA: I don't know, I never understood it. He just couldn't anymore.

> (*She tries to read his reaction; he doesn't face her directly.*)
You believe me, don't you?

HYMAN: Of course I do. But why would he invent a story like that?

SYLVIA (*incredulously*): I can't imagine . . . Could he be trying to . . . (*Breaks off.*)

HYMAN: What.

SYLVIA: . . . Make you think I've gone crazy?

HYMAN: No, you mustn't believe that. I think maybe . . . you see, he mentioned my so-called reputation with women, and maybe he was just trying to look . . . I don't know—competitive. How did this start? Was there some reason?

SYLVIA: I think I made one mistake. He hadn't come near me for like—I don't remember anymore—a month maybe; and . . . I was so young . . . a man to me was so much stronger that I couldn't imagine I could . . . you know, hurt him like that.

HYMAN: Like what?

SYLVIA: Well . . . (*Small laugh.*) I was so stupid, I'm still ashamed of it . . . I mentioned it to my father—who loved Phillip—and he took him aside and tried to suggest a doctor.

I should never have mentioned it, it was a terrible mistake, for a while I thought we'd have to have a divorce . . . it was months before he could say good morning, he was so furious. I finally got him to go with me to Rabbi Steiner, but he just sat there like a . . . (*she sighs, shakes her head*)—I don't know, I guess you just gradually give up and it closes over you like a grave. But I can't help it, I still pity him; because I know how it tortures him, it's like a snake eating into his heart. . . . I mean it's not as though he doesn't like me, he does, I know it.—Or do you think so?

HYMAN: He says you're his whole life.

(*She is staring, shaking her head, stunned.*)

SYLVIA (*with bitter irony*): His whole life! Poor Phillip.

HYMAN: I've been talking to a friend of mine at the hospital, a psychiatrist. I want your permission to bring him in; I'll call you in the morning.

SYLVIA (*instantly*): Why must you leave? I'm nervous now. Can't you talk to me a few minutes? I have some yeast cake. I'll make fresh coffee . . .

HYMAN: I'd love to stay but Margaret'll be upset with me.

SYLVIA: Oh. Well call her! Ask her to come over too.

HYMAN: No-no . . .

SYLVIA (*a sudden anxiety burst, colored by her feminine disappointment*): For God's sake, why not!

HYMAN: She thinks something's going on with us.

SYLVIA (*pleased surprise—and worriedly*): Oh!

HYMAN: I'll be in touch tomorrow . . .

SYLVIA: Couldn't you just be here when he comes. I'm nervous —please—just be here when he comes. (*Her anxiety forces him back down on the bed. She takes his hand.*)

HYMAN: You don't think he'd do something, do you?

SYLVIA: I've never known him so angry.—And I think there's also some trouble with Mr. Case. Phillip can hit, you know. (*Shakes her head.*) God, everything's so mixed up! (*Pause. She sits there shaking her head, then lifts the newspaper.*) But I don't understand—they write that the Germans are starting to pick up Jews right off the street and putting them into . . .

HYMAN (*impatience*): Now Sylvia, I told you . . .

SYLVIA: But you say they were such nice people—how could they change like this!

HYMAN: This will all pass, Sylvia! German music and literature is some of the greatest in the world; it's impossible for those people to suddenly change into thugs like this. So you ought to have more confidence, you see?—I mean in general, in life, in people.

(*She stares at him, becoming transformed.*)

What are you telling me? Just say what you're thinking right now.

SYLVIA (*struggling*): I . . . I . . .

HYMAN: Don't be frightened, just say it.

SYLVIA (*she has become terrified*): You.

HYMAN: Me! What about me?

SYLVIA: How could you believe I forgot we had relations!

HYMAN (*her persistent intensity unnerving him*): Now stop that! I was only trying to understand what is happening.

SYLVIA: Yes. And what? What is happening?

HYMAN (*forcefully, contained*): . . . What are you trying to tell me?

SYLVIA: Well . . . what . . . (*Everything is flying apart for her; she lifts the edge of the newspaper; the focus is clearly far wider than the room. An unbearable anxiety . . .*) What is going to become of us?

HYMAN (*indicating the paper*): —But what has Germany got to do with . . . ?

SYLVIA (*shouting; his incomprehension dangerous*): But how can those nice people go out and pick Jews off the street in the middle of a big city like that, and nobody stops them . . . ?

HYMAN: You mean *I've* changed? Is that it?

SYLVIA: I don't know . . . one minute you say you like me and then you turn around and I'm . . .

HYMAN: Listen, I simply must call in somebody . . .

SYLVIA: No! You could help me if you believed me!

HYMAN (*his spine tingling with her fear; a shout*): I do believe you!

SYLVIA: No!—you're not going to put me away somewhere!

HYMAN (*a horrified shout*): Now you stop being ridiculous!

SYLVIA: But . . . but what . . . what . . . (*Gripping her head; his uncertainty terrifying her.*) What will become of us!

HYMAN (*unnerved*): Now stop it—you are confusing two things . . . !

SYLVIA: But . . . from now on . . . you mean if a Jew walks out of his house, do they arrest him . . . ?

HYMAN: I'm telling you this won't last.

SYLVIA (*with a weird, blind, violent persistence*): But what do they do with them?

HYMAN: I don't know! I'm out of my depth! I can't help you!

SYLVIA: But why don't they run out of the country! What is the matter with those people! Don't you understand . . . ? (*Screaming.*) . . . This is an *emergency!* What if they kill those children! Where is Roosevelt! Where is England! Somebody should do something before they murder us all!

(SYLVIA *takes a step off the edge of the bed in an hysterical attempt to reach* HYMAN *and the power he represents. She collapses on the floor before he can catch her. Trying to rouse her from her faint . . .*)

HYMAN: Sylvia? Sylvia!

(GELLBURG *enters.*)

GELLBURG: What happened!

HYMAN: Run cold water on a towel!

GELLBURG: What happened!

HYMAN: Do it, goddam you!

(GELLBURG *rushes out.*)

Sylvia!—oh good, that's it, keep looking at me, that's it dear, keep your eyes open . . .

(*He lifts her up onto the bed as* GELLBURG *hurries in with a towel.* GELLBURG *gives it to* HYMAN, *who presses it onto her forehead and back of her neck.*)

There we are, that's better, how do you feel? Can you speak? You want to sit up? Come.

(*He helps her to sit up. She looks around and then at* GELLBURG.)

GELLBURG (*to* HYMAN): Did *she* call *you?*

HYMAN (*hesitates; and in an angry tone*): . . . Well no, to tell the truth.

GELLBURG: Then what are you doing here?

HYMAN: I stopped by, I was worried about her.

GELLBURG: You were worried about her. Why were you worried about her?

HYMAN (*anger is suddenly sweeping him*): Because she is desperate to be loved.

GELLBURG (*off guard, astonished*): You don't say!

HYMAN: Yes, I do say. (*To her.*) I want you to try to move your legs. Try it.

(*She tries; nothing happens.*)

I'll be at home if you need me; don't be afraid to call anytime. We'll talk about this more tomorrow. Good night.

SYLVIA (*faintly, afraid*): Good night.

(HYMAN *gives* GELLBURG a quick, outraged glance, HYMAN *leaves.*)

GELLBURG (*reaching for his authority*): That's some attitude he's got, ordering me around like that. I'm going to see about getting somebody else tomorrow. Jersey seems to get further and further away, I'm exhausted.

SYLVIA: I almost started walking.

GELLBURG: What are you talking about?

SYLVIA: For a minute. I don't know what happened, my strength, it started to come back.

GELLBURG: I knew it! I told you you could! Try it again, come.

SYLVIA (*she tries to raise her legs*): I can't now.

GELLBURG: Why not! Come, this is wonderful . . . ! (*Reaches for her.*)

SYLVIA: Phillip, listen . . . I don't want to change, I want Hyman.

GELLBURG (*his purse-mouthed grin*): What's so good about him?—you're still laying there, practically dead to the world.

SYLVIA: He helped me get up, I don't know why. I feel he can get me walking again.

GELLBURG: Why does it have to be him?

SYLVIA: Because I can talk to him! I want *him*. (*An outburst.*) And I don't want to discuss it again!

GELLBURG: Well we'll see.

SYLVIA: We will not see!

GELLBURG: What's this tone of voice?

SYLVIA (*trembling out of control*): It's a Jewish woman's tone of voice!

GELLBURG: A Jewish woman . . . ! What are you talking about, are you crazy?

SYLVIA: Don't you call me crazy, Phillip! I'm talking about it! They are smashing windows and beating children! I am talking about it! (*Screams at him.*) I am talking about it, Phillip!

(*She grips her head in her confusion. He is stock still; horrified, fearful.*)

GELLBURG: What . . . "beating children"?

SYLVIA: Never mind. Don't sleep with me again.

GELLBURG: How can you say that to me?

SYLVIA: I can't bear it. You give me terrible dreams. I'm sorry, Phillip. Maybe in a while but not now.

GELLBURG: Sylvia, you will kill me if we can't be together . . .

SYLVIA: You told him we had relations?

GELLBURG (*beginning to weep*): Don't, Sylvia . . . !

SYLVIA: You little liar!—you want him to think I'm crazy? Is that it? (*Now she breaks into weeping.*)

GELLBURG: No! It just . . . it came out, I didn't know what I was saying!

SYLVIA: *That I forgot we had relations?! Phillip?*

GELLBURG: Stop that! Don't say any more.

SYLVIA: I'm going to say anything I want to.

GELLBURG (*weeping*): You will kill me . . . !

(*They are silent for a moment.*)

SYLVIA: What I did with my life! Out of ignorance. Out of not wanting to shame you in front of other people. A whole life. Gave it away like a couple of pennies—I took better care of my shoes. (*Turns to him.*) —You want to talk to me about it now? Take me seriously, Phillip. What happened? I know it's all you ever thought about, isn't that true? (*What happened?*) Just so I'll know.

(*A long pause.*)

GELLBURG: I'm ashamed to mention it. It's ridiculous.

SYLVIA: What are you talking about?

GELLBURG: But I was ignorant, I couldn't help myself. —When you said you wanted to go back to the firm.

SYLVIA: What are you talking about?—When?

GELLBURG: When you had Jerome . . . and suddenly you didn't want to keep the house anymore.

SYLVIA: And?—You didn't want me to go back to business, so I didn't.

(*He doesn't speak; her rage an inch below.*)

Well what? I didn't, did I?

GELLBURG: You held it against me, having to stay home, you know you did. You've probably forgotten, but not a day passed, not a person could come into this house that you didn't keep saying how wonderful and interesting it used to be for you in business. You never forgave me, Sylvia.

(*She evades his gaze.*)

So whenever I . . . when I started to touch you, I felt that.

SYLVIA: You felt what?

GELLBURG: That you didn't want me to be the man here. And then, on top of that when you didn't want any more children . . . everything inside me just dried up. And maybe it was also that to me it was a miracle you ever married me in the first place.

SYLVIA: You mean your face?

(*He turns slightly.*)

What have you got against your face? A Jew can have a Jewish face.

(*Pause.*)

GELLBURG: I can't help my thoughts, nobody can. . . . I admit it was a mistake, I tried a hundred times to talk to you, but I couldn't. I kept waiting for myself to change. Or you. And then we got to where it didn't seem to matter anymore. So I left it that way. And I couldn't change anything anymore.

(*Pause.*)

SYLVIA: This is a whole life we're talking about.

GELLBURG: But couldn't we . . . if I taught you to drive and you could go anywhere you liked. . . . Or maybe you could find a position you liked . . . ?

(*She is staring ahead.*)

We have to sleep together.

SYLVIA: No.

(GELLBURG *drops to his knees beside the bed, his arms spread awkwardly over her covered body.*)

GELLBURG: How can this be?

(*She is motionless.*)

Sylvia? (*Pause.*) Do you want to kill me?

(*She is staring ahead, he is weeping and shouting.*)

Is that it! Speak to me!

(SYLVIA's *face is blank, unreadable. He buries his face in the covers, weeping helplessly. She at last reaches out in pity toward the top of his head, and as her hand almost touches . . .*)

BLACKOUT

SCENE 3

CASE's *office.* GELLBURG *is seated alone.* CASE *enters, shuffling through a handful of mail.* GELLBURG *has gotten to his feet.* CASE's *manner is cold; barely glances up from his mail.*

CASE: Good morning, Gellburg.

GELLBURG: Good morning, Mr. Case.

CASE: I understand you wish to see me.

GELLBURG: There was just something I felt I should say.

CASE: Certainly. (*He goes to a chair and sits.*) Yes?

GELLBURG: It's just that I would never in this world do anything against you or Brooklyn Guarantee. I don't have to tell you, it's the only place I've ever worked in my life. My whole life is here. I'm more proud of this company than almost anything except my own son. What I'm trying to say is that this whole business with Wanamaker's was only because I didn't want to leave a stone unturned. Two or three years from now I didn't want you waking up one morning and Wanamaker's is gone and there you are paying New York taxes on a building in the middle of a dying neighborhood.

(CASE *lets him hang there. He begins getting flustered.*)

Frankly, I don't even remember what this whole thing was about. I feel I've lost some of your confidence, and it's . . . well, it's unfair, I feel.

CASE: I understand.

GELLBURG (*he waits, but that's it*): But . . . but don't you believe me?

CASE: I think I do.

GELLBURG: But . . . you seem to be . . . you don't seem . . .

CASE: The fact remains that I've lost the building.

GELLBURG: But are you . . . I mean you're not still thinking

that I had something going on with Allan Kershowitz, are
you?

CASE: Put it this way—I hope as time goes on that my old
confidence will return. That's about as far as I can go, and I
don't think you can blame me, can you. (*He stands.*)

GELLBURG (*despite himself his voice rises*): But how can I work if
you're this way? You have to trust a man, don't you?

CASE (*begins to indicate he must leave*): I'll have to ask you to . . .

GELLBURG (*shouting*): I don't deserve this! You can't do this to
me! It's not fair, Mr. Case, I had nothing to do with Allan
Kershowitz! I hardly know the man! And the little I do
know I don't even like him, I'd certainly never get into a
deal with him, for God's sake! This is . . . this whole thing
is . . . (*Exploding.*) I don't understand it, what is happening, what the hell is happening, what have I got to do with
Allan Kershowitz, just because he's also a Jew?

CASE (*incredulously and angering*): What? What on earth are
you talking about!

GELLBURG: Excuse me. I didn't mean that.

CASE: I don't understand . . . how could you say a thing like
that!

GELLBURG: Please. I don't feel well, excuse me . . .

CASE (*his resentment mounting*): But how could you say such a
thing! It's an outrage, Gellburg!

(GELLBURG *takes a step to leave and goes to his knees, clutching his chest, trying to breathe, his face reddening.*)

What is it? Gellburg? (*He springs up and goes to the periphery.*) Call an ambulance! Hurry, for God's sake! (*He rushes
out, shouting.*) Quick, get a doctor! It's Gellburg! Gellburg
has collapsed!

(GELLBURG *remains on his hands and knees trying to keep
from falling over, gasping.*)

BLACKOUT

SCENE 4

SYLVIA *in wheelchair,* MARGARET *and* HARRIET *seated on either
side of her.* SYLVIA *is sipping a cup of cocoa.*

HARRIET: He's really amazing, after such an attack.

MARGARET: The heart is a muscle; muscles can recover sometimes.

HARRIET: I still can't understand how they let him out of the
hospital so soon.

MARGARET: He has a will of iron. But it may be just as well for
him here.

SYLVIA: He wants to die here.

MARGARET: No one can know, he can live a long time.

SYLVIA (*handing her the cup*): Thanks. I haven't drunk cocoa in
years.

MARGARET: I find it soothes the nerves.

SYLVIA (*with a slight ironical edge*): He wants to be here so we
can have a talk, that's what it is. (*Shakes her head.*) How
stupid it all is; you keep putting everything off like you're
going to live a thousand years. But we're like those little
flies—born in the morning, fly around for a day till it gets
dark—and bye-bye.

HARRIET: Well, it takes time to learn things.

SYLVIA: There's nothing I know now that I didn't know twenty
years ago. I just didn't say it. (*Grasping the chair wheels.*)
Help me! I want to go to him.

MARGARET: Wait till Harry says it's all right.

HARRIET: Sylvia, please—let the doctor decide.

MARGARET: I hope you're not blaming yourself.

HARRIET: It could happen to anybody—(*To* MARGARET.) Our
father, for instance—laid down for his nap one afternoon
and never woke up. (*To* SYLVIA.) Remember?

SYLVIA (*a wan smile, nods*): He was the same way all his life—
never wanted to trouble anybody.

HARRIET: And just the day before he went and bought a new
bathing suit. And an amber holder for his cigar. (*to* SYLVIA.)
—She's right, you mustn't start blaming yourself.

SYLVIA (*a shrug*): What's the difference? (*Sighs tiredly—stares.
Basically to* MARGARET.) The trouble, you see—was that
Phillip always thought he was supposed to be the Rock of
Gibraltar. Like nothing could ever bother him. Supposedly.
But I knew a couple of months after we got married that he
. . . he was making it all up. In fact, I thought I was stron-
ger than him. But what can you do? You swallow it and

make believe you're weaker. And after a while you can't find a true word to put in your mouth. And now I end up useless to him . . . (*starting to weep*), just when he needs me!

HARRIET (*distressed, stands*): I'm making a gorgeous pot roast, can I bring some over?

SYLVIA: Thanks, Flora's going to cook something.

HARRIET: I'll call you later, try to rest. (*Moves to leave, halts, unable to hold back.*) I refuse to believe that you're blaming yourself for this. How can people start saying what they know?—there wouldn't be two marriages left in Brooklyn! (*Nearly overcome.*) It's ridiculous!—you're the best wife he could have had!—better! (*She hurries out. Pause.*)

MARGARET: I worked in the pediatric ward for a couple of years. And sometimes we'd have thirty or forty babies in there at the same time. A day or two old and they've already got a personality; this one lays there, stiff as a mummy . . . (*mimes a mummy, hands closed in fists*), a regular banker. The next one is throwing himself all over the place . . . (*wildly flinging her arms*), happy as a young horse. The next one is Miss Dreary, already worried about her hemline drooping. And how could it be otherwise—each one has twenty thousand years of the human race backed up behind him . . . and you expect to change him?

SYLVIA: So what does that mean? How do you live?

MARGARET: You draw your cards face down; you turn them over and do your best with the hand you got. What else is there, my dear? What else can there be?

SYLVIA (*staring ahead*): . . . Wishing, I guess . . . that it had been otherwise. Help me! (*Starts the chair rolling.*) I want to go to him.

MARGARET: Wait. I'll ask Harry if it's all right. (*Backing away.*) Wait, okay? I'll be right back.

> (*She turns and exits. Alone,* SYLVIA *brings both hands pressed together up to her lips in a sort of prayer, and closes her eyes.*)

BLACKOUT

SCENE 5

The cellist plays, the music falls away.

GELLBURG*'s bedroom. He is in bed.* HYMAN *is putting his stethoscope back into his bag, and sits on a chair beside the bed.*

HYMAN: I can only tell you again, Phillip,—you belong in the hospital.

GELLBURG: Please don't argue about it anymore! I couldn't stand it there, it smells like a zoo; and to lay in a bed where some stranger died . . . I hate it. If I'm going out I'll go from here. And I don't want to leave Sylvia.

HYMAN: I'm trying to help you. (*Chuckles.*) And I'm going to go on trying even if it kills both of us.

GELLBURG: I appreciate that. I mean it. You're a good man.

HYMAN: You're lucky I know that. The nurse should be here around six.

GELLBURG: I'm wondering if I need her—I think the pain is practically gone.

HYMAN: I want her here overnight.

GELLBURG: I . . . I want to tell you something; when I collapsed . . . it was like an explosion went off in my head, like a tremendous white light. It sounds funny but I felt a . . . happiness . . . that funny? Like I suddenly had something to tell her that would change everything, and we would go back to how it was when we started out together. I couldn't wait to tell it to her . . . and now I can't remember what it was. (*Anguished, a rushed quality; suddenly near tears.*) God, I always thought there'd be time to get to the bottom of myself!

HYMAN: You might have years, nobody can predict.

GELLBURG: It's unbelievable—the first time since I was twenty I don't have a job. I just can't believe it.

HYMAN: You sure? Maybe you can clear it up with your boss when you go back.

GELLBURG: How can I go back? He made a fool of me. It's infuriating. I tell you—I never wanted to see it this way but he goes sailing around on the ocean and meanwhile I'm foreclosing Brooklyn for them. That's what it boils down to.

You got some lousy rotten job to do, get Gellburg, send in the Yid. Close down a business, throw somebody out of his home. . . . And now to accuse me . . .

HYMAN: But is all this news to you? That's the system, isn't it?

GELLBURG: But to accuse me of double-crossing the *company*! That is absolutely unfair . . . it was like a hammer between the eyes. I mean to me Brooklyn Guarantee—for God's sake, Brooklyn Guarantee was like . . . like . . .

HYMAN: You're getting too excited, Phillip . . . come on now. (*Changing the subject.*) —I understand your son is coming back from the Philippines.

GELLBURG (*he catches his breath for a moment*): . . . She show you his telegram? He's trying to make it here by Monday. (*Scared eyes and a grin.*) Or will I last till Monday?

HYMAN: You've got to start thinking about more positive things—seriously, your system needs a rest.

GELLBURG: Who's that talking?

HYMAN (*indicating upstage*): I asked Margaret to sit with your wife for a while, they're in your son's bedroom.

GELLBURG: Do you always take so much trouble?

HYMAN: I like Sylvia.

GELLBURG (*his little grin*): I know . . . I didn't think it was for my sake.

HYMAN: You're not so bad. I have to get back to my office now.

GELLBURG: Please if you have a few minutes, I'd appreciate it. (*Almost holding his breath.*) Tell me—the thing she's so afraid of . . . is me isn't it?

HYMAN: Well . . . among other things.

GELLBURG (*shock*): It's me?

HYMAN: I think so . . . partly.

(GELLBURG *presses his fingers against his eyes to regain control.*)

GELLBURG: How could she be frightened of me! I worship her! (*Quickly controlling.*) How could everything turn out to be the opposite—I made my son in this bed and now I'm dying in it . . . (*Breaks off, downing a cry.*) My thoughts keep flying around—everything from years ago keeps coming back like it was last week. Like the day we bought this bed. Abraham & Straus. It was so sunny and beautiful. I took the whole day off. (God, it's almost twenty-five years ago!) . . . Then we had a soda at Schrafft's—of course they don't hire Jews but the chocolate ice cream is the best. Then we went over to Orchard Street for bargains. Bought our first pots and sheets, blankets, pillowcases. The street was full of pushcarts and men with long beards like a hundred years ago. It's funny, I felt so at home and happy there that day, a street full of Jews, one Moses after another. But they all turned to watch her go by, those fakers. She was a knockout; sometimes walking down a street I couldn't believe I was married to her. Listen . . . (*Breaks off, with some diffidence.*) You're an educated man, I only went to high school—I wish we could talk about the Jews.

HYMAN: I never studied the history, if that's what you . . .

GELLBURG: . . . I don't know where I am . . .

HYMAN: You mean as a Jew?

GELLBURG: Do you think about it much? I never . . . for instance, a Jew in love with horses is something I never heard of.

HYMAN: My grandfather in Odessa was a horse dealer.

GELLBURG: You don't say! I wouldn't know you were Jewish except for your name.

HYMAN: I have cousins up near Syracuse who're still in the business—they break horses. You know there are Chinese Jews.

GELLBURG: I heard of that! And they look Chinese?

HYMAN: They are Chinese. They'd probably say you don't look Jewish.

GELLBURG: Ha! That's funny. (*His laugh disappears; he stares.*) Why is it so hard to be a Jew?

HYMAN: It's hard to be anything.

GELLBURG: No, it's different for them. Being a Jew is a full-time job. Except you don't think about it much, do you.—Like when you're on your horse, or . . .

HYMAN: It's not an obsession for me . . .

GELLBURG: But how'd you come to marry a shiksa?

HYMAN: We were thrown together when I was interning, and we got very close, and . . . well she was a good partner, she helped me, and still does. And I loved her.

GELLBURG: —a Jewish woman couldn't help you?

HYMAN: Sure. But it just didn't happen.

GELLBURG: It wasn't so you wouldn't seem Jewish.

HYMAN (*coldly*): I never pretended I wasn't Jewish.

GELLBURG (*almost shaking with some fear*): Look, don't be mad, I'm only trying to figure out . . .

HYMAN (*sensing the underlying hostility*): What are you driving at, I don't understand this whole conversation.

GELLBURG: Hyman . . . Help me! I've never been so afraid in my life.

HYMAN: If you're alive you're afraid; we're born afraid—a newborn baby is not a picture of confidence; but how you deal with fear, that's what counts. I don't think you dealt with it very well.

GELLBURG: Why? How did I deal with it?

HYMAN: I think you tried to disappear into the goyim.

GELLBURG: . . . You believe in God?

HYMAN: I'm a socialist. I think we're at the end of religion.

GELLBURG: You mean everybody working for the government.

HYMAN: It's the only future that makes any rational sense.

GELLBURG: God forbid. But how can there be Jews if there's no God?

HYMAN: Oh, they'll find something to worship. The Christians will too—maybe different brands of ketchup.

GELLBURG (*laughs*): Boy, the things you come out with sometimes . . . !

HYMAN: —Some day we're all going to look like a lot of monkeys running around trying to figure out a coconut.

GELLBURG: She believes in you, Hyman . . . I want you to tell her—tell her I'm going to change. She has no right to be so frightened. Of me or anything else. They will never destroy us. When the last Jew dies, the light of the world will go out. She has to understand that—those Germans are shooting at the sun!

HYMAN: Be quiet.

GELLBURG: I want my wife back. I want her back before something happens. I feel like there's nothing inside me, I feel empty. I want her back.

HYMAN: Phillip, what can I do about that?

GELLBURG: Never mind . . . since you started coming around . . . in those boots . . . like some kind of horseback rider . . . ?

HYMAN: What the hell are you talking about!

GELLBURG: Since you came around she looks down at me like a miserable piece of shit!

HYMAN: Phillip . . .

GELLBURG: Don't "Phillip" me, just stop it!

HYMAN: Don't scream at me Phillip, you know how to get your wife back! . . . don't tell me there's a mystery to that!

GELLBURG: She actually told you that I . . .

HYMAN: It came out while we were talking. It was bound to sooner or later, wasn't it?

GELLBURG (*gritting his teeth*): I never told this to anyone . . . but years ago when I used to make love to her, I would almost feel like a small baby on top of her, like she was giving me birth. That's some idea? In bed next to me she was like a . . . a marble god. I worshipped her, Hyman, from the day I laid eyes on her.

HYMAN: I'm sorry for you Phillip.

GELLBURG: How can she be so afraid of me? Tell me the truth.

HYMAN: I don't know; maybe, for one thing . . . these remarks you're always making about Jews.

GELLBURG: What remarks?

HYMAN: Like not wanting to be mistaken for Goldberg.

GELLBURG: So I'm a Nazi? Is Gellburg Goldberg? It's not, is it?

HYMAN: No, but continually making the point is kind of . . .

GELLBURG: Kind of what? What is kind of? Why don't you say the truth?

HYMAN: All right, you want the truth? Do you? Look in the mirror sometime!

GELLBURG: . . . In the mirror!

HYMAN: You hate yourself, that's what's scaring her to death. That's my opinion. How it's possible I don't know, but I think you helped paralyze her with this "Jew, Jew, Jew" coming out of your mouth and the same time she reads it in the paper and it's coming out of the radio day and night? You wanted to know what I think . . . that's what I think.

GELLBURG: But there are some days I feel like going and sitting in the *schul* with the old men and pulling the *talles* over my head and be a full-time Jew the rest of my life. With the sidelocks and the black hat, and settle it once and for all. And other times . . . yes, I could almost kill them. They infuriate me. I am ashamed of them and that I look like them. (*Gasping again.*) —Why must we be different? Why is it? What is it for?

HYMAN: And supposing it turns out that we're *not* different, who are you going to blame then?

GELLBURG: What are you talking about?

HYMAN: I'm talking about all this grinding and screaming that's going on inside you—you're wearing yourself out for nothing, Phillip, absolutely nothing!—I'll tell you a secret —I have all kinds coming into my office, and there's not one of them who one way or another is not persecuted. Yes. *Everybody's* persecuted. The poor by the rich, the rich by the poor, the black by the white, the white by the black, the men by the women, the women by the men, the Catholics by the Protestants, the Protestants by the Catholics—and of course all of them by the Jews. Everybody's persecuted— sometimes I wonder, maybe that's what holds this country together! And what's really amazing is that you can't find anybody who's persecuting anybody else.

GELLBURG: So you mean there's no Hitler?

HYMAN: Hitler? Hitler is the perfect example of the persecuted man! I've heard him—he kvetches like an elephant was standing on his pecker! They've turned that whole beautiful country into one gigantic kvetch! (*Takes his bag.*) The nurse'll be here soon.

GELLBURG: So what's the solution?

HYMAN: I don't see any. Except the mirror. But nobody's going to look at himself and ask what am *I* doing—you might as well tell him to take a seat in the hottest part of hell. Forgive her, Phillip, is all I really know to tell you. (*Grins.*) But that's the easy part—I speak from experience.

GELLBURG: What's the hard part?

HYMAN: To forgive yourself, I guess. And the Jews. And while you're at it, you can throw in the goyim. Best thing for the heart you know.

> (HYMAN *exits.* GELLBURG *is left alone, staring into space.* SYLVIA *enters,* MARGARET *pushing the chair.*)

MARGARET: I'll leave you now, Sylvia.

SYLVIA: Thanks for sitting with me.

GELLBURG (*a little wave of the hand*): Thank you Mrs. Hyman!

MARGARET: I think your color's coming back a little.

GELLBURG: Well, I've been running around the block.

MARGARET (*a burst of laughter and shaking her finger at him*): I always knew there was a sense of humor somewhere inside that black suit!

GELLBURG: Yes, well . . . I finally got the joke.

MARGARET (*laughs, and to* SYLVIA): I'll try to look in tomorrow. (*To both.*) Good-bye! (MARGARET *exits.*)

(*A silence between them grows self-conscious.*)

GELLBURG: You all right in that room?

SYLVIA: It's better this way, we'll both get more rest. You all right?

GELLBURG: I want to apologize.

SYLVIA: I'm not blaming you, Phillip. The years I wasted I know I threw away myself. I think I always knew I was doing it but I couldn't stop it.

GELLBURG: If only you could believe I never meant you harm, it would . . .

SYLVIA: I believe you. But I have to tell you something. When I said not to sleep with me . . .

GELLBURG: I know . . .

SYLVIA (*nervously sharp*): You don't know!—I'm trying to tell you something! (*Containing herself.*) For some reason I keep thinking of how I used to be; remember my parents' house, how full of love it always was? Nobody was ever afraid of anything. But with us, Phillip, wherever I looked there was something to be suspicious about, somebody who was going to take advantage or God knows what. I've been tip-toeing around my life for thirty years and I'm not going to pretend—I hate it all now. Everything I did is stupid and ridiculous. I can't find myself in my life. (*She hits her legs.*) Or in this now, this thing that can't even walk. I'm not this thing. And it has me. It has me and will never let me go. (*She weeps.*)

GELLBURG: Sshh! I understand. I wasn't telling you the truth. I always tried to seem otherwise, but I've been more afraid than I looked.

SYLVIA: Afraid of what?

GELLBURG: Everything. Of Germany. Mr. Case. Of what could happen to us here. I think I was more afraid than you are, a hundred times more! And meantime there are Chinese Jews, for God's sake.

SYLVIA: What do you mean?

GELLBURG: They're *Chinese!*—and here I spend a lifetime looking in the mirror at my face!—Why we're different I will never understand but to live so afraid, I don't want that anymore. I tell you, if I live I have to try to change myself.— Sylvia, my darling Sylvia, I'm asking you not to blame me anymore. I feel I did this to you! That's the knife in my heart. (GELLBURG*'s breathing begins to labor.*)

SYLVIA (*alarmed*): Phillip!

GELLBURG: God almighty, Sylvia forgive me! (*A paroxysm forces* GELLBURG *up to a nearly sitting position, agony on his face.*)

SYLVIA: Wait! Phillip! (*Struggling to break free of the chair's support, she starts pressing down on the chair arms.*) There's nothing to blame! There's nothing to blame!

    (GELLBURG *falls back, unconscious. She struggles to balance herself on her legs and takes a faltering step toward her husband.*)

Wait, wait . . . Phillip, Phillip! (*Astounded, charged with hope yet with a certain inward seeing, she looks down at her legs, only now aware that she has risen to her feet.*)

LIGHTS FADE

THE END

THE RYAN INTERVIEW, OR
HOW IT WAS AROUND HERE

AUTHOR'S NOTE

Here and there in the American countryside are still a few people with memories of a different time entirely, when—in a word—porches still had people on them talking across railings from house to house rather than crouching in the dark peering at the screen. There is another country in these old guys' heads, one they can't return to or quite leave behind.

SETTING

The porch of a small house in the country.

CHARACTERS

REPORTER
RYAN

The REPORTER, *a woman, is seated in an old chair on* RYAN*'s front porch.* RYAN *enters from inside the house and hands her a cup of water.*

RYAN: Here you are.

REPORTER: Thank you.

RYAN: Yes ma'am. (*Sits in his chair.*)

REPORTER: I'd like to thank you for agreeing to talk to me, Mr. Ryan.

RYAN: I never mind talking, what'd you want to ask me? I didn't know they had women doing this.

REPORTER: Oh, there are lots of us, yes. Do you mind?

RYAN: No, I don't mind.—I worked down a lot of basements but never inside the house. That's women's work. But I guess that's all changed by now.—Go ahead, I'm not due anywhere. This is my hundredth birthday, you know.

REPORTER: Gonna have a party?

RYAN: Oh, no. They're all dead and gone.

REPORTER: A hundredth birthday is a very special occasion, that's why we wrote you a letter about an interview.

RYAN: I guess I have it on my bureau. Is this going to be in the paper?

REPORTER: Oh, yes. Would you mind if I tape-recorded this?

RYAN: Well . . . I guess it won't do any harm. I lost my glasses but I'll read the letter some other time.

REPORTER: I'll just put it right here as a backup. (*She sets the tape recorder on a crate in front of him.*)

RYAN: You're probably surprised that I'm a hundred.

REPORTER: You certainly don't look it.

RYAN: I got stuck at sixty and never looked a day older. When I was seventy they thought I was sixty. When I was eighty and ninety they still took me for sixty. But I sure feel like I'm a hundred. You got any idea what it feels like to be a hundred?

REPORTER: That's one of the things I wanted to ask you.

RYAN: Well, there's nothing like it. Not even ninety-nine.

REPORTER: Well could you describe it?

RYAN: Well, let's see. (*Pause.*) No, I don't guess I could.—You can ask me more if you like, I'm not due anywhere.

REPORTER: You were never married I understand.

RYAN: Never met anybody who'd have me.

REPORTER: Why not? Even now you're a good-looking man.

RYAN: I was always good-looking, but to tell you the truth, women mostly made me nervous.

REPORTER: Really. Have you any idea why?

RYAN: Well, let's see. (*Pause.*) Nope.

REPORTER: But there must be some reason.

RYAN: I always thought they was peculiar.

REPORTER: In what way?

RYAN: Oh, I don't know—the usual way. How about you?

REPORTER: What do you mean?

RYAN: You married?

REPORTER: Well, not really. I mean no, I'm not. I mean, I was until a few months ago. So I'm still not used to saying that I'm not married I mean.

RYAN: I didn't mean to—

REPORTER: No, no that's okay.—So then you lived alone your whole life?

RYAN: Well . . . I guess so, but they was always a lot of people around that . . . I mean it wasn't like I was alone, don't you know.

REPORTER: Yes, I see. Could I ask you about the area? This was mostly farmland, wasn't it.

RYAN: That's right, they mostly made milk. And apples too, and pears. Sheridan had the maple syrup. But it was mostly pasture and milk.

REPORTER: And did you ever farm?

RYAN: I worked for farmers, but never run a place of my own, no.

REPORTER: How come? I'm told your family once owned thousands of acres.

RYAN: That's right, six thousand more or less. I had five sisters, you see.

REPORTER: I don't understand.

RYAN: Well everytime they wanted a new hat they'd sell a

couple hundred acres. We ended up with a whole heap of hats but all I've got left is this three acres I'm sittin' on. Who'd you rather work for, Jew or Italian?

REPORTER: . . . I have no idea, who would you?

RYAN: Jew. Jew'll pay you.

REPORTER: I'm Jewish.

RYAN: Oh? Well, no offense, you couldn't help it.

REPORTER: I guess you're of Irish descent.

RYAN: I guess so—my name's Ryan.

REPORTER: I believe your people first came here around the Irish potato famine of 1848?

RYAN: No, before that—the regular famine.

REPORTER: I understand you worked right into your nineties. What were you doing?

RYAN: That would depend on who was watchin'. (*Laughs.*) After the farms give out I mowed lawns for the city people, rakin' leaves come Fall. Last few years I mostly worked for Doctor Campbell—first house bottom of the hill.

REPORTER: You suppose I could talk to him?

RYAN: You could try but he died three years ago. (*Leans toward her, lowered voice, with a glance right and left.*) Won't be missed.

REPORTER: Oh. He treat you badly?

RYAN: Campbell never treated anybody, he was tighter than a witch's . . . well, no use goin' into that.

REPORTER: I'm interested in how it was, living here fifty years ago. Could you talk about that?

RYAN: Fifty wasn't too different; seventy was, though, eighty, ninety . . .

REPORTER: You can remember ninety years ago?

RYAN: Sure I do, what do you want to know?

REPORTER: Well, for instance—I suppose these roads were all dirt.

RYAN: Oh yes—they only paved the State Highway in 1932, 33 . . . that was the WPA. My brother worked on that.

REPORTER: And how did you get to town when it snowed—there were no plows then, were there?

RYAN: Never bothered with the road once it snowed; you went right across country with the horses. It was quicker. Had to bring the milk to town every three days, y'see.

REPORTER: But in really deep snow?

RYAN: You'd start up here and shovel out in front of the horses till you got to the woods. Snow never gets real deep in the woods.

REPORTER: How far'd you have to shovel?

RYAN: Depends—half a mile, mile.

REPORTER: God! Takes about ten minutes to town now, how long'd it take you then?

RYAN: In Winter?—about three, three-and-a-half hours. But comin' back up was faster, bein' you had your path all cut.

REPORTER: I bet you were hungry when you got down there.

RYAN: Well, you might carry a chunk of smoked bacon in your pocket.—Might not, though.

REPORTER: That's very interesting.—I notice you have quite a bit of junk out front there.

RYAN: Oh no, that's not junk, that's just nothing. I *used* to have *real* junk, but I got to where I couldn't lift. Anyways, the State Police give me so much trouble I had to give it up.

REPORTER: Why'd they give you trouble?

RYAN: Well, you supposed to have a license to sell junk, specially auto parts.

REPORTER: Couldn't you get one?

RYAN: Never tried; don't believe in it. Never wanted the Government to have my name. They wanted me to mow lawns for the school one time, but I'd have had to put my name down for social security. Next thing they'll be comin' around for income tax or something.

REPORTER: You're really not on any government form?

RYAN: Nope. U.S. Government don't know I exist. Not the FBI, not the CIA; here I've been around a hundred years and none of them even knows I was born.

REPORTER: Well, that's kind of wonderful.

RYAN: Dr. Campbell used to say he'd have done the same thing if he'd thought of it in time. Well . . . I thought of it in time.

REPORTER: Don't you believe in *any* tax?

RYAN: Well, let's see. (*Pause.*) Can't think of any.

REPORTER: Tell me, were you in any of the wars?

RYAN: Nope, missed every one of them. I was always too young or too old. But you might have heard what old man Cartwright said—he had that big farm on the North side of

Route . . . (*Realizes.*) . . . Well, it's gone now, but it was way back in the woods, y'see . . .

REPORTER: What did he say?

RYAN: Well, the first War had just started—back in . . . was that 1914?

REPORTER: Yes, the First World War.

RYAN: Yes. Well, Cartwright only come down into town every couple months or so, and this time he stepped off his wagon in front of the store and met a fella and they got talking and the fella said, "Ain't it a terrible thing the way they're killing each other by the thousands over there in Europe?" And old man Cartwright says, "What are they doin' that for?" And the fella says, "Haven't you heard?—they've got a world war goin' on over there." Well, old Cartwright looks up in the sky—it was a beautiful summer's morning, and not a cloud up there, and not too hot either, and he says, "Well, they've got a nice day for it!"

(*They laugh together.*)

You can ask me more, I'm not due anywhere.

REPORTER: It must have been pretty isolated up here in those days . . . did it seem that way to you?

RYAN: Personally? I don't know—I tell you, my best friend for a long time when I was a young fella was Fred Thompson, used to live over there by Haven's Bridge? And he was a couple of years older and they took him for the first War. And when he came back I asked him, and he'd been to New York and France and all over, and he said I hadn't missed much.

REPORTER: But you must have felt some attraction for the city as a young man.

RYAN: I went to Hartford once. But there was no place to sit down.

REPORTER: But didn't you want to see shows in the city? And what about women there? Weren't you curious?

RYAN: Well I don't think I can say a thing like this front of a woman.

REPORTER: Don't be shy, go ahead.

RYAN: Well, they used to say they was all dancers, the women in New York City.

REPORTER: Dancers?

RYAN: Dance on one foot, then dance on the other and make a living between them.—Sorry, I didn't mean any offense . . .

REPORTER (*rigidly*): Well I asked you to tell me and you did. What about newspapers . . . did you get to read any?

RYAN: Oh, every few days. Of course I got up to Canterbury more often in later years when I was selling my junk there, and I did see one or two of those old fashioned shows they had there.

REPORTER: What do you mean?

RYAN: Well, you know—where these actors come on the stage and talk.

REPORTER: You mean plays.

RYAN: The old-time shows. I see one or two when I bring my junk up to Canterbury.—Had a awful time avoiding the cops, though. But one day . . . I was in my eighties then, or just about . . . and I had this great big Oldsmobile rear end sticking out the back of my truck 'cause it was too long to get into the car. And I stopped at the store for a loaf of bread, and when I come out this State Cop, John Burnside, is standing behind the car looking down at this rear end . . . naturally he knew I didn't have no license for auto parts. And I come to get into the car, and he says, "Hya Bob," and I said, "Hya John," and he says, "Nice day," and I said—"It was." (*Laughs.*) And that was the end of my junk business.

REPORTER: I'm trying to visualize the area without so many houses up here—what'd you used to see from this porch?

RYAN: Well, Isaacson's farm was down there about a mile and nothing between here and his barns; and Jonas Bean's place was out that way but you couldn't see it through the trees . . . fire a rifle pretty near anywhere and no danger to anybody. I made my living hunting fox through World War II. Four dollars a skin.

REPORTER: How many could you get in a day?

RYAN: Many as three a night, maybe—hunt at night for fox; in fact, I was walkin' down that road out there one night looking for fox; and I had this bright moon, and I remember thinking how they were bombing London at the time especially when the moon was bright—and I hears this sawing.

REPORTER: Sawing?

RYAN: That's right—zim, zim, zim—and I come around the pond up there, and it's gettin' closer. Who could be sawin' wood in the middle of the night? And then I see this Polack in the moonlight, sawing off this horse's head right there in the middle of the road.

REPORTER: Good God—why!

RYAN: Well, it'd dropped dead and he had no horse or tractor to move it with, so he cut it up for his pigs.

REPORTER: And where was this?

RYAN: Opposite the pond, where that piano player lives . . .

REPORTER: Sokolow's house!

RYAN: Well yes, but it was no mansion like it is now . . . the Polack kept pigs under the porch.

REPORTER: No pigs under that porch now.

RYAN: Oh, no pigs allowed at all in the township now. No roosters either, y'know—liable to wake people up before noon. (*Chuckles in reminiscence.*) I don't know why it reminds me, but just up the road from there Bruce Tynan had his farm. And he decided to get married when he turned sixty. His father was Charley, about in his eighties then and ate nothin' but raw clams . . . had no teeth, y'see. Old Charley stank a lot, specially in summer carryin' those clams around in his pocket, but that's here nor there. But old Bruce got married and one weekend he had this shivaree . . .

REPORTER: What's a shivaree?

RYAN: Don't know a shivaree?

REPORTER: I never heard the word.

RYAN: Wedding celebration. It goes on . . . well, till everybody drops out. They kept going a night and a day and on the second night . . . Bruce was kind of proper, you know, went to church and all . . . makin' up for all the men he killed in the first War. And I turned around, and my arm knocked over this bottle of whiskey, and old Bruce stood there lookin' at this puddle on the floor, and he says, (*gruffly*) "I'd rather see a church burn than waste good whiskey." (*Laughs, shaking his head.*) Old Bruce . . .

REPORTER: And what about church, were you religious?

RYAN: Well, my father was in the Winter.

REPORTER: Only in the Winter?

RYAN: Well, there was too much to do in the good weather. One winter was so cold—before I was born, this was—my father didn't show up in church four or five Sundays so they sent up a committee to see if there was something wrong. And when they got there they found my grandfather laid out in the front parlor. He'd been dead for three weeks but the ground was frozen three feet down and my father couldn't dig a grave.

REPORTER: It must have been pretty cold in your house.

RYAN: Oh, you could say that.

REPORTER: Still, it sounds like a pretty good life around here.

RYAN: Well, we certainly had a lot of characters. There was somebody peculiar in darn near every house. Maybe there still is but I don't know them anymore. Like old Stanley Beach who ran the general store. This woman . . . Russel Pound's widow . . . they were well-to-do, and she always had to have her stuff delivered. This was way back before the first War, and I was a young fella and I'd work for Beach now and then when he was shorthanded. And one morning she comes in—Russel Pound's widow . . . and orders a spool of sewing thread. And Stanley Beach says, "Will that be all?" And she says, "Yes. Will you deliver it?" And Beach says, "Why certainly, Mrs. Pound, I'd be happy to." Well, she leaves, and he goes out to his team, those horses must've been fifteen hands high, and hitches them to his big lumber wagon that was at least twenty feet long—they used to carry logs to the sawmill on it—and then he sets the spool on the wagon bed and drives up to her house and doesn't he back that enormous wagon right up to her front door; and he knocks and she comes and opens it and he sort of raises his arm out toward the spool and says, "Where do you want it?"

(*They both laugh together.*)

I don't know why, but you just don't hear things like that anymore.

REPORTER: Will it ever happen again, people living like that?

RYAN: Well, if you notice when you go down to town—most of the old houses on Main Street has those big porches?

REPORTER: They're lovely, yes. They're sort of inviting.

RYAN: Well you know—once upon a time people used to sit on them. Right on Main Street. And talk back and forth from one house to another. You don't see that anymore.

REPORTER: Why is that? They want privacy more now?

RYAN: I couldn't say.

REPORTER: Tell me, Mr. Ryan, when you look out at all these houses in every direction, and the cars going up and down the road out there, and all the people around—what goes through your mind?

RYAN: Tell you the truth, I do wonder sometimes—being there's so many of them and they're moving so fast—I wonder how do they get to meet anybody.

REPORTER: Would you mind if I took a picture of us together?

RYAN: No, not at all. Where do you want me?

REPORTER: Just stay right there. (*She draws closer and aims the lens at the two of them together. Clicks.*) Just one more. Smile. (*Clicks.*) Happy birthday Mr. Ryan.

RYAN: Thank you.

BLACKOUT

MR. PETERS' CONNECTIONS

CHARACTERS

CALVIN, *Mr. Peters' dead brother*
HARRY PETERS, *retired airline and military pilot and lecturer*
ADELE, *a black bag lady*
CATHY-MAY, *Mr. Peters' dead lover*
LARRY, *her husband as Peters imagines him*
LEONARD, *a guitarist and lover of:*
ROSE, *Mr. Peters' daughter*
CHARLOTTE, *Mr. Peters' wife*

A broken structure indicating an old abandoned nightclub in New York City.

A small, dusty upright piano, some chairs, a couple of tables, a few upended.

Three chairs set close to the piano with instruments propped up on them—a bass, trumpet, saxophone.

Seated on a banquette, ADELE, *a black bag lady, is ensconced amid her bags; she is reading* Vogue *magazine, and sipping from a bottle of wine. She occasionally examines her face in a hand mirror.*

CALVIN *enters.* PETERS *enters, looking around. Halts.*

CALVIN: Well, here it is.
> (*Silence.* PETERS *very slowly looks at everything. Then goes still.*)

PETERS (*undirected to anyone*): To be moved. Yes. Even once more to feel that thunder, yes. Just once! (*Slight pause.*) Lust aside, what could hit me? Novels? Model airplanes, movies, cooking, the garden? (*Shakes his head, dry grief.*) And yet, deep down . . . deep down I always seem on the verge of weeping. God knows why, when I have everything. (*Slight pause; he peers ahead.*) What is the subject?
> (PETERS *goes to the piano, plays the first five notes of "September Song," then walks a few steps. The piano continues playing; both men stare into space; piano subsides into silence. Now* CALVIN *gestures toward the structure.*)

CALVIN: Needs some work, of course.

PETERS: My wife should be here in a few minutes, I believe.

CALVIN: She'll like it, most women do.

PETERS: I'm very tired. I've been walking. Why women?

CALVIN: Hard to say. The powder room, maybe.

ADELE (*not looking away from her mirror*): Gorgeous.
(*Neither man seems to hear her.*)

PETERS: I take it you're not from here?

CALVIN: You have a good ear. Russia, I guess.

PETERS: You guess!

CALVIN: Who can be sure? In my mother's bed, I suppose, same as everybody else.

PETERS: Mother's bed.

CALVIN: Where I'm from. Actually, Sheepshead Bay, Brooklyn.

PETERS: Actually. But people from Sheepshead Bay, Brooklyn, do not say "actually," it's too . . . I don't know, high-class. But it doesn't matter; if you'd told me in the first place I'd have forgotten it by now. My personal situation these days is trying to paddle a canoe with a tennis racket . . . I am thinking, who does he remind me of?

CALVIN: I tend to do that. Some people, all they do in life is remind people of somebody.—Generally I remind people of somebody nice and reliable.

PETERS: Why don't we leave it right there.

CALVIN: I'm not trying to be facetious . . .

PETERS: Listen. Let's settle this—conflict is not my game anymore; or suspense; I really don't like trying to figure out what's going on. Peace and quiet, avoid the bumps, I'm perfectly content just to raise the shade and greet my morning. Not that I'm depressed; in fact, I feel I am an inch away from the most thrilling glass of water I ever had. On that order.

(CATHY-MAY *is lit.*)

Oh my. (*Going toward her; sad amazement.*) My-my-my. The flat broad belly, the spring of thighs, how the fire flares up just before it dies . . . ! (*He recognizes her, gasps.*) Good God, Cathy-May! (*Mystified.*) —Then you're not . . . you're not . . . dead? (*Turns from her.*) How can we go on seeing them if they . . . ? Or . . . say now, can she not have d . . . ? (*Breaks off, thinks.*) But of course she did! (*Freshly affected.*) Of course she did! (*Nearly weeping.*) Of course she did! It snowed on her funeral . . . (*Peers for a clue, then glances at her.*) But where is she, then? (*Barely smiling, shakes his head, mystified, excited.*) —Why am I so happy?

(*A tinkling of Mozart is heard.* CATHY-MAY *comes to him; she is naked, in high heels; a big smile breaks onto his face as she approaches. She is giggling.*)

Ah yes, how proud of your body—like a new party gown.

(*Giggling, with finely honed mock solemnity, she does a formal curtsy with thumbs and forefingers pressed together as though lifting a wide skirt. Laughing softly he bows formally, with one foot thrust forward. They are like two mating birds. Laughing.*)

You can't do this kind of dancing dressed like that, darling!

(*Still curtsying, she retreats into darkness. Music dies. His laughter sours.*)

Or am I depressed?

CALVIN: You've been around.

PETERS: And around again, yes—Pan Am captain twenty-six years. I'm really much older than I look. If you planted an apple tree when I was born you'd be cutting it down for firewood by now.

CALVIN: I was going to say, you don't look all that old.

PETERS (*a chuckle*): I am older than everyone I ever knew. All my dogs are dead. Half a dozen cats, parakeets . . . all gone. Every pilot I ever flew with. Probably every woman I ever slept with, too, except my wife. I doubt there's a government in the world that hasn't been overthrown at least once since I was born, except for us and England. I still pick up the phone to call some old friend, until I realize . . . (*Chuckles.*) —Maybe some broken nerve in my brain won't register the vacant pillows and the empty chairs. I wonder sometimes, have I without knowing it been embalmed? Or maybe death is polite, and we must open the door to let him in or he'll just hang around out there on the porch. (*Frowns, mystified.*) —Why am I so fluent? I'm not, usually. I'm known for not saying anything for eight hours at a time.—What about this powder room, why are women so crazy about it? . . . I'm enjoying this, but what is the subject?

CALVIN: Women love to redecorate.

PETERS: Oh, of course, yes. A man will never notice the paint floating off the ceiling onto his head, but a woman can count dust.—You always have an answer, don't you.

CALVIN: Not always.

PETERS: Often, though.

CALVIN: Pretty often.

PETERS: Do you enjoy being so right?

CALVIN (*shrugs*): I can live with it.

PETERS: I'm very different; I enjoy being right but you have to let the woman think they're right so you can take your nap in peace. The older you get, you know, the more you tend to chuckle. I do a lot of it. I mean, who can hit a man when he's chuckling, right? I had a dream, many years ago: this enormous fireplace; and I got up from my chair and said goodbye to my wife, and walked into it. The back of it swung open and I stepped out into the most perfect room I'd ever seen. Everything in that room—the furniture, the color of the walls, the carpet—it was all absolutely right. Not a single thing out of place or painful to me. And I looked out the window and the street was perfect. And I felt perfect too. It was all so satisfying, as though that is where I really belong. In fact, I begin to yearn for that house every now and then until I realize—and with some surprise—that it never existed. And the subject, you said, was . . . ? Well, never mind. (*Looks about.*) . . . I can't imagine anyone thinking he belonged in this place, can you? You absolutely remind me of someone, don't you.

CALVIN: Show your wife the powder room, she'll love you for it.

PETERS: Let's not go into it any further, okay? I have no interest whatsoever in this place. It's not my kind of place at all.

CALVIN: Maybe give it a little time, you might get used to it.

PETERS (*chuckles angrily*): I don't want to get used to it, will you stop irritating me? The only reason I'm even in this neighborhood is . . . I can't recall . . . oh yes.

(CALVIN *is motionless, unaffected.*)

I decided to buy shoes. I have very narrow feet.

CALVIN: Not as narrow as mine, betcha—triple-A.

PETERS: Quadruple-A. (*Extending a foot.*) Narrow as herrings. —So I said I'd meet her here.

CALVIN: I used to take a quintuple-A but I don't have time to go running all over the city looking for them anymore . . . I am busy!

PETERS: Well I'm busy too . . .

CALVIN: Not as busy as I am.

PETERS: I assure you, I am just as busy as you are. I got these in that shoe store right on the corner.

CALVIN: You went in *there*?

PETERS (*shamed*): . . . Well only for a couple of minutes.

CALVIN: Phew! Well, it's your funeral.

PETERS (*embarrassed*): Why?—what's wrong with going in there?

CALVIN: There isn't time now; I really need to know what you think of this place? Yes?

PETERS: Well let's see. . . . Oh, the hell with this, I'm leaving. (*Starts to go.*)

CALVIN: You can't!

PETERS: Don't you tell me I can't, I have very low cholesterol! (*He turns and starts out.*)

CALVIN: What about your wife?

PETERS: God, I almost forgot. (*Sits meekly.*) Thanks for reminding me. . . . You always need a reason to stay. I have to stay because of my wife. Why because of my wife?

CALVIN: You're meeting her here.

PETERS: Right, yes! (*Short pause.*) Why am I meeting her here?

CALVIN: Probably because that was the arrangement.

PETERS: But why here?

CALVIN: What's the difference? One has to meet somewhere.

(CATHY-MAY *appears in a filmy dress;* PETERS *goes to her, hesitantly.*)

PETERS: Could we walk together, darling? Just side by side? I'm sure you can get out of this if you exercise. Please—concentrate, darling! (*Desperately.*) You must try to move more! Here, let me help!

(*He gets in front of her, grasps a thigh and gets her to take a stiff, doll-like step.* —*Alarm in his voice.*)

Relax! You must stop being so stiff. (*Angered.*) Why are you doing this, are you spiting me?! Here, do this and stop being an idiot! One-two, one-two . . .

(*He jumps up and down flapping his arms. She remains inert. He turns to* CALVIN.)

Could you applaud?—she loves me, but she's forgotten.

(CALVIN *claps his hands; she doesn't change.*)

He's applauding, dear . . . listen!

(*To* CALVIN, *indicating her.*) Are you sure we're both in the same place?

CALVIN: How can two occupy . . . ?

PETERS: . . . the same space, yes, that's right. (*Moves away from her.*) That's one thing you have to say for the war, you always knew where you had to be . . . you had to be where you could get killed, you see. Taking off after a couple of dozen missions you'd naturally wonder, "Is this my last moon?" And so on. But funny, you know?—remarkably little fear—I don't recall actual fear; I suppose because we knew we were good and the Japs were evil, so the whole thing was necessary, and that can soak up fear like a blotter. On that order. (*Desperation, loudly.*) —Whereas now, I just cannot find the subject! Like I'll be strolling down the street, and suddenly I'm weeping, everything welling up. —What is the subject? Know what I mean? Simply cannot grasp the subject.—I can't understand why I'm so fluent here!

ADELE: Something you forgot hasn't forgotten you. You should take up drinking, it might all come pouring out.

PETERS: But I had a wonderful childhood.

ADELE: Famous last words.

PETERS: No-no, in fact, as a kid of sixteen . . . good God, I'd bicycle out to Floyd Bennett Field and wash airplanes for the Army pilots. Dollar a plane, plus they taught me to fly those little Stinsons all over the clear Brooklyn sky. Imagine that nowadays, a kid handed the stick of a fighter plane?—things are never going to get that good again, I tell you we had the best of it, the sweetness. Take Pan Am; Pan Am was not an airline, it was a calling, a knighthood. A Pan Am Captain . . . hell, we were the best of the best and when you took off, the sweaty little corporate statistician, for Christ's sake, did not climb into your lap, they stayed back there on the ground where they belonged. And God—when you got suited up in your whites and your gold epaulettes, the girls inhaled and puffed their feathers and achieved womanhood right in front of your eyes. (*Chuckle.*) I cannot understand why I'm so fluent in this building.

CALVIN: And what about this place?

PETERS: I don't flaunt my opinions, but I'd say the best way to redecorate this place would be a small bomb . . .

CALVIN: Some people think this could be a gold mine.

PETERS: Oh I'm sure! 'Specially the powder room, probably.

CALVIN: Then why do you have this browbeaten attitude?

PETERS (*angering*): Absolutely not! If I were younger I'd be champing at the bit to get in there . . .

CALVIN: But you're skeptical.

PETERS (*suddenly in distress*): I'm asking you to stop talking about this . . . you're disturbing me!

CALVIN: Listen, you've got to start facing reality.

PETERS: No-no, I'm too old—facing reality is for the young who still have time to avoid it. An old man talking about a . . . a *woman's powder room*—?—it's obscene! Look at the veins in the back of my hands?—shall these warped fingers stroke a breast, cup an ass . . . ? And you call life fair? No . . . no-no . . . (*Fumbling.*) Why don't I just sit here acting my age, quietly reading my paper till my wife comes? Tell you the truth, I've just had lunch and it makes me drowsy . . . (*Head raised, eyes shut.*) But I'll be okay in a minute . . . (*Begins panting in anxiety.*)

CALVIN: I really don't mind, I like explaining, and I have a right to explain.

PETERS (*panting anxiously, nearly shouting*): I respect your rights but whose nap is this? (*Breaks off.*)

CALVIN: It's why I've always felt just slightly . . . you know . . . under par.

PETERS (*anxiously*): Oh no, Calvin, you musn't say that; you don't look at all under par. In fact, I wish I looked as successful and vigorous and trustworthy as you.

CALVIN: But you are successful. Although I am, in my way.

PETERS: Of course you are. We're both equally successful and promising.

CALVIN: Yes. Although in a way, I am more.

PETERS: It's a relief to hear you say that.

CALVIN: You're relieved because it's not true.

PETERS: If you feel it's true, it's true.

CALVIN: I'd feel it more if it *was.* True, that is.

PETERS: We're depressing one another, don't you think? Why don't we both be quiet and, if necessary, just think about each other, okay? Shhh. Shhh. And maybe the time has come to forget this powder room. (*Sleeps, breathes deeply.*)

ADELE: Those toilet seats are solid African mahogany. Ask any detective—the imprint of woman's flesh on solid mahogany can never be entirely washed away.

PETERS: I can't bear not understanding this.

ADELE: Think of it—if science could come up with a way of reading those mahogany seats, we could identify women who went to their reward over a hundred years ago. We could inquire about their lives, their shoes, and their deaths. When I enter that powder room it's like the silence of a cathedral, a place of remembrance where dead women linger. It's always three o'clock in the morning in that room, and thoughts come up from the depths. And the dusty oval mirrors still reflect the forgotten beauty of long-departed women in their sweeping satin gowns.

PETERS: This fluency is alarming—can they all be dying?

(LARRY TEDESCO *enters.*)

CALVIN: Yes? Can I help you?

LARRY: I'm from Posito's. (*Indicates.*) The shoe store?

PETERS (*sits up*): Yes!—I was just in there, you sold me these shoes! (*Raises a foot.*) Quadruple-A! (*Alarmed.*) My God, I paid you, didn't I?

LARRY (*to* CALVIN): My wife come in here?

PETERS (*to himself*): But he can't be dead, he just sold me these . . . (*Breaks off, looking at his shoes, then looks about.*) Listen, please—these are real shoes! I paid with money! (*to* LARRY.) . . . Or rather a credit card, didn't I?

LARRY: You got some kind a problem?

PETERS (*intimidated*): . . . No. No problem.

CALVIN: Do I know your wife?

LARRY (*suspiciously*): I wouldn't be surprised; I'll look around, okay?

CALVIN: . . . Go ahead, but I don't know what she'd be legitimately doing in here; you can see for yourself, it's all torn apart.

LARRY (*indicates off*): Okay?

CALVIN: But what would she be doing here?

LARRY (*shrugs—not saying*): You mind?

PETERS: Please let this man look for his wife, if he loves her he might hear her call and jump into the water and save us all!

CALVIN (*to* LARRY): Well, okay, go ahead. But no fooling around back there, wife or no wife, got it?

(LARRY *saunters off.—Suggestive sneer.*)

You know that broad?

PETERS: Me? (*Embarrassed.*) I've never been in this neighborhood before. Not that I'm trying to deny her—she's very lovely, I say that openly.

CALVIN: She's juicy. A prime sirloin. A ripe pomegranate. A Spanish blood orange. An accordion pleated fuck.

PETERS (*recalling*): Yes, I know, but please; I hate talking like this about a woman behind her back . . .

CALVIN: What's the difference?—she'll never know.

PETERS: Why won't she? Oh! You mean . . . (*Breaks off.*) Oh . . .

CALVIN: All her underwear has been sold, stolen, or given away. And the phones don't ring that deep.

PETERS: Yes. I see.—And where she is . . . ?

CALVIN: She's nowhere.

PETERS: Yes, but is she older now? Has she grown into herself at last?

(CATHY-MAY *appears, in a middle-aged woman's coat.*)

Glasses?

(*She takes out a pair and puts them on.*)

Would it be a little less angry between us now that she's complete and her fires are banked?

(*She turns slowly to him. A calm, slow smile spreads across her face. He smiles back familiarly. They both rise.*)

Oh yes, darling, smile . . . do that!

(*Music: a Big Band—"Just One of Those Things." They dance close, the music speeds, they separate with hands clasped, and when he moves to draw her back she disappears into darkness.*)

CALVIN: Anyway, once upon a time this building was a bank.

PETERS (*desperation*): Oh don't, I beg you do not start explaining this building, will you? I'm too old for sad stories!

CALVIN: Why sad? I'm telling about a bank!

PETERS: Yes, but recalling a dead bank is painful. In those days . . . in those days . . . banks were built like fortresses, not salad bars. They had those gigantic, beautifully filigreed brass gates, and they did not go around shystering people, begging them to borrow money. No, they sat behind their little brass grills and *suspected* you. So you had to be upright, honest, and good or you were practically under arrest the minute you walked in from the street! And the clerks—what about their cute white blouses with those little rounded collars—you don't call it sad that all that is no more?

CALVIN: But think of the high-class ladies who used to come in to talk over their inheritance, and also, incidentally, to have a pee. And the dense perfumes those women wore! And the way they crossed and separated their legs!

PETERS (*clapping his ears shut*): Stop it, I beg you!

CALVIN: Well then don't go on saying you have no interest in this place! Sooner or later, as I said, these rich ladies, after spending the afternoon shopping or having coffee or tea . . .

PETERS: Or probably a sip of champagne . . .

CALVIN: Right. They had to pee, so they stopped at the bank . . .
    (PETERS *sighs openly, rests head tiredly on hand.*)
    This is very important. —As early as the turn of the century—
        (PETERS *stretches out in the chair, arm over his eyes*)
    —the women already held most of the money in this country. Probably all countries. Because they live longer. Because of the salads, in my opinion. Without women you could forget lettuce.
        (PETERS *sleeps.*)
    Sir?

PETERS (*awakened*): What?—Oh no, I enjoy salads, my father was Italian. Especially arugula and even some nice fresh spinach. My mother was Spanish as a matter of fact. God knows what I am anymore.

CALVIN: I personally crossed the River Don with two hundred pounds of the family silver under my shirt, I was twelve and very brave, and the weight built up my legs.

PETERS: None of that is true, is it.

CALVIN: Well in a way . . .

PETERS: It's all right; it's just that you remind me of somebody who used to make up stories like that. But I can't remember who he was.

CALVIN: Then let's say it was me.

PETERS: Okay.

CALVIN: Look, you're not flying anywhere, are you?

PETERS (*sitting up*): Flying! They haven't let me into a cockpit for eighteen years! I had at least five years of flying left in me when they dumped me like a bag of shit! And the Democrats are no better!

CALVIN: Then let me finish; this could soothe you, it's very educational.

PETERS: Is this the subject?

CALVIN: Let me finish.

PETERS: No! I have a right to know the subject! Precious days are passing! Hours! I will need this time!

CALVIN: After the bank it was a library. The Morris family, the largest privately owned public library in America, I was told —the idea was to educate the working class.

PETERS: Whose idea? (*Quickly amending.*) —Unless you're not supposed to tell.

CALVIN: Rich people; they had ideas like that in those ancient times. You know—the Frick Museum, the Astor Forty-second Street Library, Morgan, Rockefeller—

ADELE: Carnegie?

CALVIN (*reluctantly*): Carnegie is correct.

ADELE: The Frick has very nice toilets too . . . lots of marble.

CALVIN: Right. Those bastards stole but they gave back; now they steal and they fly the coop. And what's the answer?— religion; those old-time crooks were afraid of God. Anyway . . .

PETERS: Not that I love the rich; in fact, between their greed and stupidity they wrecked the greatest airline in the world.

CALVIN: Are you serious?

PETERS: Am I serious!—For generations my family were the only chiropractors in Naples! One of them is buried in the marble floor of the cathedral; yes, and a yard away from the king . . . who incidentally had terrible arthritis, so you'd think they'd have buried him in a warmer place.

CALVIN: I'm glad you're feeling better. Anyway, the Morris family died off and then you had the Depression and where you're sitting now was a cafeteria through the thirties. The famous Eagle Cafeteria, open twenty-four hours.

PETERS (*almost, not quite remembering*): Ah yes!—where I'm

sitting now. Philosophical Marxist discussions going through the night. Leon Trotsky was supposed to have been a waiter, which I'd like to believe, but who ever heard of a waiter in a cafeteria? Anyway, the dates don't work out; by the thirties Trotsky was already the head of the Red Army.

CALVIN: So, that's more or less the history. Was that so bad?

PETERS: No-no, I'm beginning to enjoy it. Why don't you rest now, you must be pretty old, too, aren't you?

CALVIN: Me? I stopped getting old a long time ago.

> (*Pause.*)

PETERS: . . . *Stopped getting old*, did you say?

> (CALVIN *is silent, motionless, stares front.*)
>
> (*Something horrifying dawns on* PETERS.) Ohhh . . . (*Covers his face.*) Oh my God, yes!—Then where is this? Say, you're not all dead here, are you?

CALVIN: Don't let it bother you; life is one to a customer and no returns if you're not satisfied.

PETERS: Listen, I really have to leave; I don't belong here! Just because a man decides to buy a pair of quadruple-A shoes . . . is that fair? (*Struggling to rise.*) I am leaving!

CALVIN: What will I do with your wife!

PETERS: My wife? Oh God, I don't know, just . . . just . . . kiss her and tell her . . . to . . . to . . . sadly die. (PETERS *lies back, falling asleep again.*)

CALVIN: —It's important to know that up until the Vietnam War the place was a real money-maker, but those little fellas in their black pajamas killed all the nightclubs.

PETERS: Vietnamese killed the nightclubs?

CALVIN: Destroyed all the optimism. And the pessimism. No optimism, no clubs; no pessimism, no clubs.

PETERS: Then what's left?

CALVIN: Vacillation, indecision, self-satisfaction, and religion— all enemies of nightclubs. In London, on the other hand . . .

PETERS: Wait! Before you get to London . . . could you give me an idea of the subject.

CALVIN (*angrily*): I'm explaining—I said I don't mind.

PETERS (*desperately*): I know you don't mind but I am not happy when I don't know even what the subject is! (*Shouting.*) Can't I have a hint! I ask you . . . a hint! A hint!

CALVIN (*frustrated*): For God's sake, man, they have clubs in London that go on for a hundred, two hundred years! Can you imagine anything like that here? Anyway, that's the history.
(PETERS *stands up, peers out in silence.*)
What is this misery of yours?

PETERS (*sings softly*): "I've got a crush on you, sweetie-pie . . ." (*Sings another line, then it dies.*) You're not from Moscow, by any chance?

CALVIN: Odessa. Name a great violinist and you can bet he came from Odessa. I'm talking Mischa Elman, I'm talking Sasha Schneider, and Mischa Auer . . .

PETERS: Mischa Auer did not come from Odessa, but that's all right.

CALVIN: Well, the greatest olives in the world come from Odessa.

PETERS: It's all right, just go on lying, why shouldn't you? Can I believe that during the war I delivered our P-40 fighter planes to Odessa? I had some great hopes for Russia then, but terribly puritanical—I inadvertently learned you must never get into bed with two Russian women. And incidentally, every adventurous woman I met there carried a bath-tub stopper in her purse.

CALVIN: I was never conservative enough to be a Communist. Seriously—soon as a girl joined the party she'd cross her unshaven legs and you might as well go to the library.

PETERS (*sits*): I think the subject is—humiliation. Give up the gin, then the vermouth, and end up having to explain to a Princeton class which war you were in. Talk about futility. Christ's sake, behind our propellers we were saving the world! And now, "Which war . . ." So you end up staring into space, with maybe some woman's wonderful ass floating by, or a banana split. Remember banana splits; four balls of ice cream on a sliced banana, covered with hand-whipped cream, chocolate sauce, and a maraschino cherry on top . . . for twenty-five cents? That, my friend, was a country, huh? I mean *that was a country!*—And who ever had a key to their front door?

CALVIN: Unheard of. You said you had a question?

PETERS: A question? Oh yes, yes . . . (*Takes out a tabloid paper.*) Why are you so untruthful? Are you trying to destroy the world?

CALVIN: Destroy the world!—I'm just talking!

PETERS (*springing up*): That's it!! That's what I think I've been trying to say since I walked in here!—"Just talking" is . . . is . . . There is no subject anymore! Turn on the radio, turn on the television, what is it—just talking! It can sink the ship! (*Breaks off, bewildered. Gripping his forehead.*) Something's happening to me.

CALVIN: Something like what?

PETERS (*holds up his paper as though just discovering it in his hand*): . . . I found this on the train. Amazing ads; pages and pages . . . look: breast augmentation, $4,400. And guess how much breast reduction is.

CALVIN: How much?

PETERS: Same price. That seem strange to you?

CALVIN: . . . No, seems about right.

PETERS: My father paid five thousand for the eight-room house our whole family lived in for thirty years! And a pair of tits is five thousand?

CALVIN: Yes. But houses are not as important; put a house on one magazine cover and a pair of tits on another, which one'll sell?

PETERS: And here we have penile augmentation for four thousand dollars and hymen reconstruction for two thousand. I can't imagine why hymens are cheaper.

CALVIN: There's not as much to a hymen. And they're nothing but trouble.

PETERS: Ah! But isn't it odd that penile augmentation costs four hundred dollars *less* than breast augmentation.

CALVIN: Well, I wouldn't take it personally.

PETERS (*turning pages*): But you have to, don't you?! I read these ads and I wonder—"Why don't I understand this?" You see? WHY DON'T I UNDERSTAND THIS! (*A sudden quizzical expression.*) Please don't be offended, but are you asleep?

CALVIN: Me?

(LARRY *reenters.*)

LARRY: Thanks. If you see her let me know, would you? I'm Larry, in Posito's near the corner.

CALVIN: What's she look like?

LARRY: What she looks like? . . . She looks perfect. With a white angora sweater. And pink plastic spike-heel shoes. A little on the pudgy side but not too fat . . . just . . . you know, perfect.

PETERS: What made you think she would be in here?

LARRY (*he shrugs*): She could be. (*Nods.*) She could be anywhere. The neighborhood's got a lot of Jews, you know. And Koreans now and Chinks.

PETERS (*in Italian*): *E italiani.*

LARRY: I'm Italian.

PETERS (*in Italian*): *Certo; non sono sordo?* (*In English*): You know, Larry, Italians have always been a tolerant people.

LARRY: Fuck that, sir.

PETERS: Excuse me but fuck that sir is not a way to talk intelligently. Italian tolerance comes from the Roman era when so many different races flooded into the empire . . . Arabs, Gauls, Spanish, Nordics, Russians . . .

CALVIN: Lithuanians.

PETERS (*sharply*): Not Lithuanians.

LARRY: In March the niggers busted our window, robbed forty-one pairs of shoes.

CALVIN: I heard about that.

LARRY: You heard about it? We're fed up. Fed up!

ADELE: Us too.

LARRY: I didn't hear that. (*Leaning angrily toward* PETERS.) Fuck the tolerance, sir, that's all over. Finished! Now we protect ourselves! (*To* CALVIN.) Thanks. (*To* PETERS.) Good luck with the shoes. By the way, her name is Cathy; Cathy-May.

PETERS: Yes, I know . . . But is she the same Cathy-May who used to be alive?—I don't mean "alive" in that sense, I mean . . .

(LARRY *exits.*)

(PETERS *leans his elbows on his thighs and holds his head in despair.*)

It didn't used to get to me—but lately . . . almost every time I take my nap . . . it's like a long icicle slowly stabbing down into my balls.

CALVIN: When I lived in Florence . . .

PETERS (*open fury*): For God's sake, don't say one additional thing, will you?! (*Eyes shut, hand on forehead.*) I wonder if I'm eating too much for lunch. (*Suddenly turning on* ADELE.) Excuse me, but may I ask what you are doing here?

ADELE (*puts on a nurse's cap*): Thank you for your interest. With God's permission I live here. I hope none of you has the idea of tearing this building down.

PETERS: Why are you putting on a nurse's cap?

ADELE: Could it be I'm a nurse? And before you mock me, be sure you don't get sick and need my services.

PETERS: I'm not at all mocking you, but a nurse sitting around drinking like that . . .

ADELE: You mock everyone! Look at how you mocked that handsome shoe salesman!

PETERS: But it's a mistake, she can't have married a lout like him! She's not really a common slut, you know—and she's . . . well I won't say she's . . . (*A choked cry.*) She's dead? (*A realization.*) Or not? . . . Not? (*High hope suddenly.*) Please! Is she? What is her situation!

ADELE: I'm not a nurse; sorry.

PETERS: Then what are you doing with that cap!

ADELE: I just found it on the sidewalk outside the Lenox Hill Hospital, probably some nurse lost it jumping into a cab to meet her date, probably a well-to-do elderly man who was going to fix her up for life. But if I was a nurse would I have the right to sit around drinking booze?

PETERS: Of course, just as he . . . (*To* CALVIN.) I've forgotten, what was your right . . . ?

(LEONARD *and* ROSE *enter. He carries a guitar case. He is holding her by the elbow.*)

LEONARD: Excuse me, can she sit down?

CALVIN: We're closed. We only open the second floor around six-thirty.

LEONARD: She's pregnant.

CALVIN: Oh! Well, have a chair. They've all been re-glued.

(LEONARD *and* CALVIN *quickly seat her.*)

ROSE (*sitting*): Don't worry, I'm not having it, I just walked too much.

CALVIN: Relax, we're all on the side of the pregnant woman. (*Asking.*) You're not the father.

LEONARD: How'd you know!

CALVIN: What's to know?—nobody's the father anymore. (*To* PETERS.) So that's the history. (*To* ROSE.) If you need the powder room, it's straight that way.

ROSE: Thank you, I will in a minute.

LEONARD: I've passed this place a hundred times and never knew it was a nightclub . . . it is, isn't it?

CALVIN: That's our style, or it was—no sign outside, no advertising; people either want to be here or they don't. Most didn't, obviously. (*To* PETERS.) I'll be in my office if your wife is interested. (*Slows beside* ROSE.) I hope you know the father.

ROSE: Of course I know the father!

PETERS: Of course!

CALVIN: Just kidding—it's only that they used to say—I'm talking forty, fifty years ago—"A man who betrays his wife will betray his country."

PETERS (*simultaneously*): ". . . Will betray his country."

CALVIN: I figured you knew that saying.

PETERS: Haven't heard it in fifty years, and it's still idiotic. What has screwing a woman got to do with betraying your country?

CALVIN: Nothing, but nobody even *says* things like that anymore. (*To* ROSE.) Morals count, you know, even if you just say them. (*Making to leave.*) Excuse me, Professor.

PETERS: How did you know I was a professor?

CALVIN: What else could you be?—I can smell the chalk. (*Touching his temple.*) Nobody forgets chalk.

> (*He exits.* PETERS *stares after him, perplexed, deeply curious. Silence.* ROSE *takes out a bottle of Evian and drinks. Finally . . .*)

PETERS: How old are you people now, if you don't mind my asking?

LEONARD: I'm twenty-seven.

ROSE: Twenty-eight now.

ADELE (*unasked*): Thirty-four.

PETERS: And you're all . . . (*Embarrassed chuckle.*) I feel a little funny asking, but . . . you're all awake, aren't you.

ROSE: Awake?

PETERS: Forget it. Maybe it's that I don't see many young

people anymore, so it's hard to guess their ages. . . . To me, everybody looks about twenty-two. Do you find it hard to follow what people are saying?

LEONARD: Well . . . not really. (*To* ROSE.) Do we? (*Before she can answer.*) Except she never listens anyway.

ROSE: I do listen, but I have my own thoughts and it's hard to listen while I'm thinking.

PETERS: Let me put it another way—do you find you get sleepy after lunch, or when do you start?

ADELE: Getting sleepy? The minute I wake up.

PETERS: It struck me the other day that everyone I know is sleepy—I wonder if it's something about the times.

ROSE: Maybe you're low on potassium. You should eat bananas.

PETERS: I do eat two or three a week for breakfast. Actually I rather like bananas.

ROSE: You should try to love them. Motivation is important in the diet; bananas are there to be loved. Try eating five a week. Seven or eight would be even better. Or ten.

PETERS: Isn't that quite a lot of bananas?

ROSE (*raises one leg in a stretch*): You only have enough bananas when one more would make you want to throw up. I know about such things, I'm a dancer, dancers need trace elements for the knees.

PETERS: *Trace elements for the knees?*

ROSE: They're tiny but important.

PETERS (*nods with a certain alarm*): *Trace elements for the knees?* You see, this is what I mean; when I was young no human being from one end of the United States to the other would have uttered that sentence. For example, my father and grandfather—I don't recall them ever in the presence of a banana. And they lived into their nineties.

ADELE: Same thing with my mother; she can gross down two, three at a time, a woman over ninety and no bigger than a thimble and still driving an eight-cylinder Buick loaded with extras—air bags, defrosting side mirrors, tinted glass . . . (*Continues mouthing.*)

PETERS: In fact, nobody ate bananas when I was young. You make me wonder how we managed.

ADELE: . . . Fifteen-inch wheels, leather trim, non-skid brakes, moon roof, lighted trunk . . . (*Continues mouthing.*)

ROSE: People had different thoughts then, and there was nothing around to get them so exhausted.

ADELE: Upholstered armrest, front and rear utility lights, metallic paint . . . V6, three-and-a-half-liter engine, automatic transmission . . . (*Goes on mouthing.*)

PETERS (*nods in silence for a moment*): Please forgive my curiosity, but does this conversation revolve around some . . . subject that I am unaware of?

LEONARD: A subject? I don't think so . . . (*To* ROSE.) Does it?

ROSE: What? Excuse me, I was thinking of something.

LEONARD: You know, darling, it's not very polite to drop out of a conversation without telling anybody.

PETERS: . . . Unless we don't need a subject anymore . . .
(*They look at him blankly.*)
I mean do you people ever wonder . . . as you're getting into bed, what you were talking about all day?

LEONARD: I don't think so. (*To* ROSE.) Do we?

ROSE: When we're getting into *bed*?

PETERS: Or for example, I do enjoy the movies, but every so often I wonder, "What was the *subject* of the picture?"

ROSE: The subject of a *picture*?

PETERS: I remember my mother—washing machines were rather rare in those times—and she'd have the maid boil the sheets and the laundry on the stove and lug it all up to the roof of the apartment house to dry. Have you ever heard of that?

ROSE: Boiling sheets?

LEONARD: On a gas stove? That's a fire hazard!

ROSE: Water is fireproof, Leonard.

PETERS (*forcing concentration; peering*): No-no, I think what I'm trying to . . . to . . . find my connection with is a . . . what's the word . . . *continuity* . . . yes, with the past, perhaps . . . in the hope of finding a . . . yes, a subject. That's the idea, I think, but I'm exhausted . . .

ROSE: Boiling sheets?

LEONARD: But that's not really a *subject*.

ROSE: Well then, going up to the roof?

PETERS: That's it! Yes! Maybe!

ROSE: But wouldn't wet sheets weigh a ton?

PETERS: Right! And nobody would do that anymore! So maybe

that's a real subject, because one thing reveals another. What else about that?

ROSE: Maybe that's why you need more bananas now.

PETERS (*to* LEONARD): Say now! She makes a lot of sense! You've relieved me a lot.

ROSE: Really? Why?

PETERS: Because you have added to what I said! Rather than exhausting me by starting a whole new unrelated conversation. That's really glorious! Thank you so much. (*Tears flow, he wipes them.*)

ROSE: Don't be upset.

PETERS: It's just that when you've flown into hundreds of gorgeous sunsets, you want them to go on forever and ever . . . and hold off the darkness . . .

   (*The trumpet plays a loud blast of "My Blue Heaven." His anxiety soars.*)

How like sex the trumpet is—it always leaves you kind of sad when it's finished. You know, every spring . . . every spring the Polish maids would carry our carpets up to the roof and hang them out on wires, and they'd beat them for hours until their blouses were dark with sweat. When April came and early May, hundreds of rooftops all over the city had those big fair-haired Polish girls walloping clouds of carpet dust to drift out over the avenues.

ROSE: Was this before vacuum cleaners?

PETERS (*frowning, disturbed, he pants*): Oh, God, imagine dying in the midst of a conversation about vacuum cleaners!

LEONARD (*passionately*): But would it be any better talking about differential calculus? The thing is not to be afraid . . .

ROSE (*covers his hand*): That's right, dear.

PETERS: But you're so young—how can you know!

LEONARD: We're afraid.

PETERS: Oh, good, then we can talk without my risking your disdain—yes, we did have a vacuum cleaner; but it screamed like a coal truck and it frightened the Polish girls. Actually, though, I think it was virtue that made people go lugging those carpets up to the roof. Discomfort was righteous in America; when Teddy Roosevelt went sweating through the jungle hunting tigers he wore a tie; Woodrow Wilson, Warren

Harding, Calvin Coolidge, Herbert Hoover—those men went fishing in the same itchy dark suits they wore at their inaugurations; they waded into wild rivers wearing cuff links, stiff collars, and black high-topped shoes. The President of the United States was above all morally righteous, you see, rather than just entertaining. Even after President Harding was exposed as the father of an illegitimate daughter he continued to take precisely the same virtuous photographs. And Grover Cleveland likewise. And for that matter, George Washington was in and out of so many beds they finally called him the father of his country. But no one ever questioned his dignity, you see. Or his virtue. And he was never exhausted. I can't remember my point.

ROSE: I definitely think something very tiring is in the air now.

LEONARD: It's lead.

(*All turn to him.*)

It's a proven fact, there's more lead than ever in the air.

PETERS: But we seem to be living longer than ever.

LEONARD: But in a poisoned condition.

ROSE: Like you being so sleepy. You might live to a hundred, but half asleep.

LEONARD: You know?—I just realized—I've been getting up later and later in the mornings.

ROSE: Maybe you're just a teeny bit depressed, Leonard.

(*She kisses his cheek lightly.*)

ADELE: Depression'll do it every time.

LEONARD: Like do you find you're a little more slow-witted than you used to be?

ADELE: You can count me in there.

PETERS: Definitely, yes. But couldn't it be this constant changing of the subject that's wearing out our brains?

LEONARD (*to* ROSE, *indicating* PETERS): Sounds like lead. You know the Romans used lead pipes in their water systems and also wine storage, and one emperor after another was nutty as a fruitcake.

ROSE: And lots of subnormal children.

LEONARD: The Teutonic tribes, on the other hand . . .

PETERS (*gripping his forehead*): Would you mind not talking about the Teutonic tribes?

LEONARD: It's just that they drank out of lakes and clear streams . . .

PETERS: Yes, I know, but I am much older than I look and there is just so much irrelevant information that I am able to . . .

LEONARD: But everything is relevant! If you don't mind my saying it, that's what you don't seem to understand and what is making you rather pessimistic. You are trying to pick and choose what is important, sir, like a batter waiting for a ball he can hit. But what if you have to happily swing at everything they throw at you? The fact is—those Germanic tribes were drinking fresh water and came down and just wiped out the Roman Empire! Which was drinking wine loaded with lead! I think that's kind of relevant, isn't it? Incidentally, we never picked up the laundry. Or maybe wait till tomorrow?

ROSE: There's still time. Where'd he say that powder room was?

PETERS: That way, I believe, in the back.

(ROSE *exits*.)

LEONARD (*calling after her*): Maybe I should try to pick it up now? (*To* PETERS.) I just hate leaving laundry overnight. On the other hand, I've never lost any. Although I did get a wrong shirt once. (*Getting up to leave.*) Maybe tell her I left, would you?—Well, never mind, I'll wait. (*Sits again.*) Except one of those shirts belongs to my brother, it's very expensive. I'd better go. (*Stands.*) . . . Well, I'll wait, to hell with it, he's got fifty shirts. (*Sits. Pause.*)

PETERS: You may have read the Babylonian myth explaining why there are so many different languages in the world?

LEONARD: No.

PETERS: God was extremely annoyed by the racket in the streets, so he invented all the different languages to keep people from talking to each other so much.

LEONARD: That's pretty funny.

PETERS: Are you in business?

LEONARD: No, I'm a composer. And investor.

ADELE: You may as well ask why I started drinking.

PETERS (*a bare glance at* ADELE): Then what are you doing here?

LEONARD: My friend had to urinate.

PETERS: Of course!—My God, I think I'm just swinging at random from limb to limb.

LEONARD: Are you in business?

PETERS: No, I flew for Pan Am for many years, then some lecturing at Princeton till I retired.

LEONARD: May I ask your subject?

PETERS: Oh, mysterious things—like the suicidal impulse in large corporations. Are you a college man?

LEONARD: Harvard, yes.

PETERS: Well, that's not a bad school. Incidentally, are you asleep? I only ask because it just occurs to me that I may be awake. (*Chuckles.*) . . . Horrible as that would be. But that's impossible, isn't it—a person awake can't talk to one who's asleep. You are, aren't you—asleep? . . . But that's not right either, is it; two sleeping people can't converse can they. (*Chuckles.*) You can't share sleep, can you. Any more than death, right? So . . . I'm asleep. But you—what's your . . . you know . . . situation? What bothers me is that—look at these shoes; they're obviously brand-new, right?

(LEONARD *looks at them.*)

So all this must be happening, right? I didn't produce these shoes out of thin air, correct? Look at the soles . . . not even soiled.

(LEONARD *looks at soles, but almost de-animatedly, totally uninterested.*)

And I couldn't have bought them in my sleep, could I. You walk into a store with your eyes closed they're not going to let you walk out with a new pair of shoes. . . . What's begun to haunt me is that next to nothing I have believed has turned out to be true. (*Breaks off in a surge of fear.*) IF SHE DOESN'T COME, DOES IT MEAN I CAN'T LEAVE?! WHERE IS MY POOR GODDAMNED WIFE! (*He is on the verge of weeping. The piano plays loud and fast, for a moment, "If You Knew Suzie" and stops.*)

LEONARD: Is she ill?

PETERS: We are both ill; we are sick of each other. (*Shouts.*) Her imagination is destroying me! (*Moment.*) We're happy. (*Takes*

a few deep breaths.) —I'm much obliged to you for listening.
Are you Jewish?

LEONARD: Yes.

PETERS: I thought so; Jews and Italians are happy to allow a
person to mourn.

ADELE: Yes, we cry them into the grave.

PETERS: Tell me . . . this Calvin guy here . . . the owner or
manager or whatever he is . . . Did you notice anything
odd about his eyes?

LEONARD: His eyes? (*A moment; thinks.*) Say now . . . yes.
It's almost like . . . I can't describe it, almost like there's
nothing in his eye sockets. No!—it's that his eyes . . . can
it be they have no color?

(PETERS *stares, silent.*)

Is that what you mean?

(PETERS *says nothing.*)

What is it, some disease?

PETERS (*motionless*): He's my brother.

LEONARD: Your brother! Did you know he was here?

PETERS: Oh no, no, it just came to me. (*Pause.*) He's dead.

(LEONARD *astonished.*)

Drowned almost twenty years ago.

LEONARD: You mean he's *like* your brother.

PETERS (*shakes his head*): No.

(LEONARD *is silent, terrified.*)

His eyes . . . they're almost translucent, like jellyfish; the
sea in winter; the insides of oyster shells . . .

LEONARD: Well, I . . . I don't know what to say . . . Does
he know you're his brother?

PETERS: I'm not sure. It's hard to know how much the dead
remember, isn't it . . . But that's not quite right . . . (*Stares
in silence, smiles now.*)

LEONARD: I understand.

PETERS: . . . You see, he was always a great kidder and practical joker. Once he was driving us down the Rocky Mountains and pretended the brakes had failed. Darn near a
hundred miles an hour and heading straight for the rail
when he pretended the brakes came back. A cruel streak,
but full of life.

LEONARD: You mean he pretended to drown, as a joke?

PETERS: I'm wondering that. He was capable of anything. But that can't be right, we were all at his funeral.—I'm wondering if my wife got lost. Could you be a good fellow and take a look outside? She's very short . . . although you might not agree . . .

LEONARD (*gets up*): What's her name?

PETERS: Her name? (*Touches his head.*) I'm so embarrassed.

LEONARD: Well it doesn't matter . . .

PETERS: Oh it does, it does!—What I do in these circumstances is start with *A* and go down the alphabet. Anna, Annabella, Augusta, Bernice, Beatrice . . .

LEONARD: Well what's your name . . . just so I can approach her.

(PETERS *stares in deepening anxiety.*)

It's all right, I'll just look for a short woman . . .

PETERS: It's not all right! (*Suddenly.*) Charlotte! Charlotte Peters!—My God this is terrible.

LEONARD: No-no, maybe I shouldn't have asked . . .

PETERS: This is the worst I've had. It's not Alzheimer's, I've been examined . . . I wonder if it's just a case of not wanting to be around anymore.

LEONARD: I'd look into lead.

PETERS: Oh, my boy, I wish it were lead, but in the end I'm afraid one arrives at a sort of terminal indifference, and there is more suspense in the bowel movement than a presidential election.

LEONARD: But I often forget things . . . In fact, as a child I used to wonder why we needed to remember at all. Wouldn't it be wonderful if we got up in the morning and everyone was a complete stranger?

PETERS: Are your parents divorced?

LEONARD: Yes, that's where I got the idea. Do you think things are worse than years ago?—Although I'm glad there's penicillin.

PETERS: Penicillin is definitely better, yes, but things have been getting worse since Eden; it's not lead, however.

LEONARD: What then?

PETERS: Washington, Jefferson . . . most of the founding fathers were all Deists, you know; they believed that God had wound up the world like a clock and then disappeared. We are unwinding now, the ticks are further and further apart. So instead of tick-tick-tick-tick-tick we've got tick—*pause*—tick—*pause*—tick. And we get bored between ticks, and boredom is a form of dying, and dying, needless to say, takes an awful lot out of a person.

LEONARD: But so many things are happening.

PETERS: But not the main thing. The main thing is emphatically not happening at all and probably never will again.

LEONARD: And what is that?

PETERS: Redemption.

LEONARD: I've never really understood that word.

PETERS: That's all right, no one understands love either, but look how we long for it.

LEONARD: Then you believe in God?

PETERS: I'm quite sure I do, yes.

LEONARD: What would you say God is? Or is that too definite?

PETERS: Not at all—God is precisely what is not there when you need him. And what work of beauty have you created this week?

LEONARD: I haven't done much this week.

PETERS: Well, I suppose that can happen in the creative life.

LEONARD: I'm not having much of a creative life these days.

PETERS: Lover trouble?

LEONARD: As a matter of fact, I recently split up with somebody.

PETERS: Too bad. Boy or girl?

LEONARD: Girl.

PETERS: Well, cheer up and pray that you run into a girl who makes you imagine you've forgotten the other fifty million single American women walking around loose.—Charlotte! Here I am!

(*He has spotted his wife. She enters, looking all around.*)

CHARLOTTE: For Christ's sake.

PETERS: Yes, it's pretty awful.

CHARLOTTE: Awful!—it's marvelous! Look at those moldings, look at that ceiling, look at these floors. Gimme a break, this is heaven!

(ROSE *enters.*)

And who is this lovely young pregnant woman?

(ROSE *looks at* CHARLOTTE *and laughs.*)

LEONARD: She's not so short.

CHARLOTTE (*to* PETERS): What is this again?

PETERS (*covering his eyes*): I'm terribly sorry, I had a vision of you as being quite . . .

CHARLOTTE: He said I was *short*?

LEONARD (*to* PETERS): I'm awfully sorry! (*To* CHARLOTTE.) He asked me to go out and look for you and he couldn't think of your name, so he . . .

CHARLOTTE (*laughing angrily, to* PETERS): Couldn't think of my *name!*

LEONARD (*tortured*): Only for a minute!

CHARLOTTE: In my opinion it's his flying for three solid years in World War II; the Essex Class Carrier had a very short flight deck and it blew his nerves. (*To* PETERS.) I'll bet something here reminded you of the war, didn't it.

PETERS: . . . as a matter of fact . . . (*Looking around.*) . . . I think I said this place could use a small bomb.

CHARLOTTE: There you go.—Where's this Mister Calvin?

PETERS: He said he'd be in his office if you were interested. He said you should see the powder room.

CHARLOTTE: Gimme a break—the *powder* room?

ROSE: It's glorious. I was just in there—I've never been like . . . kissed by a room, or felt such good-hearted *safety*, or like a room was hugging me. It's like you suddenly didn't have to . . . like defend yourself. It's a sort of *courteous* room, you know? I mean the energy I use up just keeping people from . . . *bothering* me, you know what I mean?

CHARLOTTE: I know exactly what you mean, I'm a decorator.

LEONARD: Really!—we were just thinking of calling a decorator for her apartment.

ROSE: But it's so tiny . . . practically a closet.

PETERS: It doesn't matter, if it's vertical she'll happily decorate it.

CHARLOTTE: You're not the father?

PETERS: They're only friends. He just brought her in here to pee.

CHARLOTTE: He did? Well, that is one of the most encouraging things I've heard in I don't know how long.—I must have a look at this powder room.

ROSE: It's straight that way. Watch out for the lumber on the floor.

CHARLOTTE: I know how you feel, we have four daughters. All four are flight attendants on major airlines.

PETERS (*to* LEONARD): I truly wonder whether the country could be saved if people could stay on the same subject for more than twenty seconds.

CHARLOTTE: So if you're planning on flying anywhere let us know and one of the girls might be able to look after you. Now let's see this famous powder room. (*She exits.*)

ROSE: Actually, I was thinking of flying to Oregon to see a friend; maybe I could have one of your daughters' phone numbers.

PETERS (*chuckling*): I'm afraid the girls are not connected to the airlines.

LEONARD: But didn't she say . . . ?

PETERS: Sometimes she is simply overwhelmed by a burst of comprehensive enthusiasm. A little like heels and skirts— one year high, next year low. Women have visions. Now, she has a vision of our four young women in those snug uniforms and cute little hats, feeding the multitudes. She's a very emotional woman, as you know by now, and she means no harm, but she has powerful longings.

LEONARD (*to* ROSE): That's really weird.

ROSE: I don't know. I mean here I'm carrying around this, I assume, baby which could end up not even liking me . . .

LEONARD: Rose, how can you say a thing like that?

ROSE: But how many of our friends really like their parents?

LEONARD: Parents!

ROSE: Yes! I'm going to be a *parent*, Leonard.

LEONARD: Oh, right. (*Stares, shaking his head in amazement.*) This is turning out to be a really strange day.

(CHARLOTTE *enters, inspired, amazed.*)

CHARLOTTE: Wow. Did you see it?

PETERS: I don't normally go into powder rooms.

CHARLOTTE (*pointing off imperiously*): Go. GO!

PETERS: I absolutely refuse! I have no conceivable interest in . . .

CHARLOTTE: Gimme a break, Harry, I insist you see that powder room! Now will you or won't you!

PETERS (*rising*): But I have no viewpoint toward powder rooms!

CHARLOTTE: Well how about participating for once *without* a viewpoint! I mean gimme a break, Harry, be human, this place is fantastic!

PETERS (*peering into air*): I simply don't understand anything anymore. When I woke up this morning, I did not plan to shop for shoes, and I certainly did not expect to end the day inspecting a ladies' bathroom. (*To* LEONARD.) Would you mind?—I'd like another man with me.

CHARLOTTE: Oh, Harry darling, aren't you feeling well?

PETERS: Let me put it this way . . . (*He begins to weep.*) Are you feeling well, Charlotte?

CHARLOTTE: I'm feeling wonderful.

PETERS: I'm so glad for you. (*To* ROSE.) She's everybody's mother . . . as I'm sure you realize, and her happiness—(*sighs*)—is inexhaustible. (PETERS *turns and goes, taking out a handkerchief as he exits.*)

LEONARD (*as he goes*): I'm worried about my brother's shirt.

ROSE: Leonard please, try to have some faith, it's only away in the laundry for the afternoon. Maybe think of it like a vacation it's on.

   (LEONARD *exits following* PETERS.)

CHARLOTTE: How far along?

ROSE: Six weeks, I think.

CHARLOTTE: Did you want it or . . . ?

ROSE (*shrugs*): It wants me, I know that much.

CHARLOTTE: You sound alone.

ROSE: I am, I guess. He can't quite make up his mind.

CHARLOTTE: Men! If they were in charge of the sun it would go up and down every ten minutes. What happened!—a good man is so hard to find anymore.

ROSE: My friend Leonard thinks it's something in the water.

CHARLOTTE: He's not the father?

ROSE: Sometimes he seems to think he is. But sometimes he doesn't.

CHARLOTTE: What stories the world is full of! So are you telling him he is or he isn't?

ROSE: I want to see what it looks like first.

CHARLOTTE: Why! Tell him it's his and you can change your mind later.

ROSE: But we always end up fighting like brother and sister. And that can't be right, can it.

CHARLOTTE: You young people—why are you always digging away at each other for the truth? We never dreamed of telling the truth to a husband and the result was practically no divorces.—Well, thank God for the airlines! You know, if something drops on the uniform the company pays the cleaning.

ROSE (*near tears*): How can you be so happy!—you're wonderful!

CHARLOTTE: I can't help myself—I've been happy since I was a baby and I never changed. It irritates my husband but what can I do?—First thing in the morning I open my eyes and I'm so overjoyed I could eat the whole world for breakfast. Listen, I like your Leonard; I would let him be the father.

ROSE: It's strange, I think I feel older than you.

CHARLOTTE: Italians love to cook, that's my salvation. And I'm in pretty fair shape—I used to dance, you know.

ROSE: Professionally?

CHARLOTTE: Radio City Rockettes nine years. We met in the alley of the theater. He was a Navy pilot, stage-door Johnnie, he'd come back from bombing Asia and go banging through that chorus line . . . eighteen girls on a thirty-day leave! But a delight, a dee-light! Funny? Gimme a break, the man was sheer humongous wit. I weighed one-eighteen those days, till the bread did me in. I lost twelve pounds last year but who's kidding who, I'm still everybody's mother.

(LEONARD *and* PETERS *enter; rather expressionless, even solemn looks.*)

Well?

(*The men glance uneasily at each other.*)

So?

(*They still hesitate.*)

LEONARD: Well it's a washroom, right?

CHARLOTTE: A *washroom!*

PETERS: Where you wash up.

CHARLOTTE: Mama mia . . . (*To* ROSE.) They don't see anything! He walks around the house like a blind man— "Where's my glasses? Where's my suspenders? Where's my bathrobe?"

ROSE: By the way, how did you know I was pregnant?

CHARLOTTE: I'm part Gypsy.

LEONARD (*to* PETERS): Is that true?

(PETERS *sighs and looks away.*)

CHARLOTTE: What does he know? To him nothing is true unless you can hammer it, fuck it, or fly it around.—Gypsy women, darling, can tell you're pregnant just by looking into your eyes. Not only that, but I can tell you it's a girl.

PETERS: Now how could you know *that*, for God's sake?

CHARLOTTE: Because the air is full of *things!* (*Gesturing between* ROSE *and herself.*) And we are looking at each other through the air, aren't we?

PETERS: I feel I have lived my life and I eagerly look forward to a warm oblivion.

LEONARD: May I ask whether you intend to start a new night-club or is this a . . . ?

CHARLOTTE: Depends; if this man's deal is good I would certainly consider a new club . . . why?

LEONARD: I'm not trying to pressure you but if it's going to be a club I'd like to talk to you about the music.

ROSE: He has a great little band. She danced in Radio City.

LEONARD: Really, a Rockette? (*To* PETERS.) Is that true?

CHARLOTTE: Why do you keep asking him if it's true! You think I'm off my nut, or something?

LEONARD: Oh no-no, please don't think I . . .

ROSE: No-no! He didn't mean anything like that . . .

CHARLOTTE (*to* PETERS): Well aren't you going to answer him?

PETERS (*shuts his eyes, sighs, then* . . .): Yes, it's true.

CHARLOTTE: Well I'll go find this Calvin and see what kind of deal he has in mind. Tell them your philosophy. (CHARLOTTE *exits.*)

LEONARD: We should really pick up the laundry . . .

ROSE: Your philosophy?

PETERS: No-no, it was only a dream I had many years ago. After my wing was destroyed.

ROSE: I love dreams, could you tell it?

PETERS: I'm afraid I have to rest now. Why don't we all?

ROSE: I'd love to, frankly. What was your dream?

LEONARD: Shouldn't I pick up the laundry?

ROSE: Try to rest, Leonard.

LEONARD: Should you be on the floor?

ROSE: It's okay.

LEONARD: Should I look for a pillow?

ROSE: You've got to try to have a little confidence, Leonard.

LEONARD (*self-blame*): I know.

ROSE: I mean try to assume that whatever is going on out there will go on without us for a while. So you might as well rest.

ADELE: This is my kinda thing, I tell ya. It's been going on without me for a long, long time.

ROSE: All right then . . .

> (*She stretches her legs. All lean back and close their eyes. Pause.*)

I don't think you're resting, are you?

LEONARD: I want to be the father, Rose.

ROSE: We'll see. I don't like deciding right now.

LEONARD: But when you do, will you think of me?

ROSE: Of course. (*Slight pause.*) If not, you could be its brother.

LEONARD: A brother twenty-eight years older?

ROSE: Well, an older brother. It happens.

ADELE: Appearance is everything; my older sister's got those hips, those eyes, and those ambitious legs—the girl could raise a man from the dead just by stepping over his grave. And now she's down Wall Street with her own office at Bear Stearns.

PETERS: I dreamed of another planet; it was very beautiful— the air was rose, the ground was beige, the water was green, the sky was the fairest blue. And the people were full of affection and respect, and then suddenly they grabbed a few defectives and flung them into space.

LEONARD: Why were they defective?

PETERS: They were full of avarice and greed. And they broke into thousands of pieces and fell to earth, and it is from their seed that we all descend.

LEONARD: Well that's very strange . . . I mean we usually assume that man is born good . . .

PETERS: Not if you look sharply at the average baby.

ROSE (*hand on her belly*): How can you say that?

PETERS: If a baby had the strength, wouldn't he knock you down to get to a tit? Has a baby a conscience? If he could tear buildings apart to get to a suck, what would stop him?

We tolerate babies only because they are helpless, but the alpha and omega of their real nature is a five-letter word, g-r-e-e-d. The rest is gossip.

(CALVIN *enters with* CHARLOTTE, *both studying papers of figures. She sits down absorbed in papers, and working a pocket calculator.*)

CALVIN (*absorbed in his figures*): Harry.

PETERS: Yes?

(CALVIN *still doesn't look up.*)

. . . Did you call me Harry?

CALVIN (*surprised at himself*): What?

PETERS: Charley . . . come on . . .

(CALVIN *stares at him as he approaches.*)

It's me!

(CALVIN *stares front.*)

Mother and Dad . . . remember Mother and Dad? Fishing in Sheepshead Bay? The fluke? . . . I know!—the bluefish, when you gutted that big bluefish and brought it over to . . . what was her name!—Marcia . . . yes, Marcia Levine!

CALVIN: Marcia Levine?

PETERS: In that shingle house on the corner! You said she had . . . (*To the others.*) Excuse me, please—(*To* CALVIN.) . . . the best ass on the East Coast.

CALVIN (*very doubtfully, striving to recall*): Marcia *Levine*?

PETERS: For God's sake, Calvin, you'd be in there whole *days* with her! (*Frantically—to all.*) Am I the only one who remembers anything? I'm going to fall off the earth! (*Furiously to* CALVIN.) For God's sake, man, you'd lie on your bed looking up at the ceiling endlessly repeating, like a prayer, "Marcia Levine's ass, Marcia Levine's ass . . . Marcia Levine has the most beautiful ass in America!"

CALVIN: I don't remember her . . .

PETERS (*laughing happily*): You have to step out of this . . . this forgetfulness, Calvin! It's a terrible, terrible thing to forget Marcia Levine! . . . Listen, you do know I'm Harry, don't you?

CALVIN (*a remoteness coming over him*): You're mistaking me for somebody else.

PETERS: No! Charley, I will not accept that! Charley? Please . . . if you forget me . . . don't you see? If you forget

me—who . . . (*with a desperate cry*) who the hell am I!
Charley, save me!

(CALVIN *is staring front, eyes dead.* PETERS *roars in terror into his face.*)

Man . . . wake up your dead eyes!

(CALVIN *doesn't move. A moment.*)

. . . Sorry for troubling you. (*Closes his eyes in pain; slumps down on a seat. Pause.*) God, if no one remembers what I remember . . . if no one remembers what I . . .

(CATHY-MAY *enters. She is in a tight white miniskirt, transparent blouse, carries a white purse and a brown shopping bag . . . and wears a dog collar.*)

Why are you wearing a dog collar?

CATHY-MAY: Case I get lost, he said.

PETERS: Dear . . . listen . . . could I ask you . . . ?

CATHY-MAY: Don't ask me too much, I might not be here by the end.

PETERS: Could I just listen to you?

CATHY-MAY: But don't take too long. And please don't hurt me.

(*He presses his ear to her breast. She breathes in deeply, and exhales.*)

You were loved, Harry. But I'm very tired.

PETERS: Please; more . . .

(*She inhales again.*)

Yes! More!

(*She does it again.*)

Oh, glorious . . . to hear a woman's deep breathing again!
(*She breathes in and out again and again, her breaths coming faster and faster . . . and now he is breathing with her.*)

Oh Cathy-May, Cathy-May, Cathy-May . . . !

(LARRY *enters, walks over to her and rips the shopping bag out of her hand, turns it over—it is empty.*)

LARRY: This is shopping? Where's the stuff, left it on the counter again? (*Feels her for panties.*) And where's your underwear? (*To* PETERS.) And this woman votes! Walks around bareass on New York streets? Bends over in the fruit market to test tomatoes in front of *Koreans?*—a married woman? What am I a fuckin' ox, I don't have feelings? Take her to a counselor and

I'm behind her on the stairs and she's wearing no panties!—
for a conference with a *counselor*? Meantime I'm overdue for
a heart operation, so I'm not supposed to be stressed! Can
you believe a fucking doctor telling me not to be stressed in
the City of New York? And that idiot is going to operate on
me!—Look at this! (*Shaking the bag.*) Look at this! . . .
Where's your underwear? You belong to me or not? I said you
belong to me or not! Where is your underwear, stupid!!

> (*With a sweeping gesture he sends her onto her back, legs in
> the air, and looks under her skirt; she is struggling ineffectu-
> ally to free herself.*)

You see underwear, Mister? Look, everybody!

> (*He is trying to spread her legs apart.*)

Forget your shoes and take a look at this! How can this belong to anybody!—Look at it!

CATHY-MAY: You were loved, Harry!

LARRY (*struggling with her legs*): Show them, show them! Look
at this, Professor!

> (PETERS, *crying out, tries to intervene but the horror of it sends
> him away, rushing about, covering his eyes and yelling.*)

PETERS: Nonononono!

LARRY (*to* PETERS): What are you scared of, come here and
open your eyes!

> (*The struggle stops;* LARRY *is kneeling beside* CATHY-MAY
> *now, kissing her gently. She has become inert.* PETERS *comes,
> bends, and presses his ear to her breast.*)

LEONARD: What do you hear?

PETERS: Footsteps. And darkness. Oh, how terrible to go into
that darkness alone, alone!

> (CATHY-MAY *emits one last exhale.* PETERS *kisses his finger
> and touches it to her mouth.*)

CATHY-MAY: C-aaaaaaahh! (*And then she is still.*)

ADELE: I was a substitute teacher for six years in Weehauken
New Jersey. But little by little I came to realize that I am a
brokenhearted person. That's all there was to it—I'm brokenhearted. Always was and would always be. At the same
time I am often full of hope . . . that for no particular
reason I will wake up one morning and find that my sorrow
has left me, just walked away, quiet as a pussy cat in the

middle of the night. I know it can happen . . . (*She picks up her mirror and examines her face.*) I know it. I know it.

PETERS (*slight pause*): —Rest now. All rest. Quietly, please. Quietly rest. While we think of the subject. While breath still comes blessedly clear. While we learn to be brave.

> (ROSE *and* LEONARD *sit on either side of* PETERS. *Farther upstage, frozen in time,* LARRY *is looking into the empty shopping bag,* CHARLOTTE *is working her calculator,* CAL-VIN *is staring into space,* ADELE *is examining her face in her mirror, turning from side to side.*
>
> *Light begins to die on these.* ROSE *opens her eyes. Light dies on* LEONARD *now, and only* ROSE *and* PETERS *are illuminated.*)

ROSE: Papa?

PETERS (*opens his eyes, listens*): Yes?

ROSE: Please stay.

PETERS (*straight ahead*): I'm trying!

ROSE: I love you, Papa.

PETERS: I'm trying as hard as I can. I love you, darling. I wonder . . . could that be the subject!

> (*For a moment he is alone in light. It snaps out.*)

RESURRECTION BLUES

A Prologue and Two Acts

CHARACTERS

GENERAL FELIX BARRIAUX, *chief of state*
HENRI SCHULTZ, *his cousin*
EMILY SHAPIRO, *a film director*
SKIP L. CHEESEBORO, *an account executive*
PHIL, *a cameraman*
SARAH, *a soundwoman*
POLICE CAPTAIN
JEANINE, *Schultz's daughter*
STANLEY, *a disciple*
SOLDIERS, WAITERS, PASSERSBY, PEASANTS

PLACE

Various locations in a far away country

Dark stage. Light finds JEANINE *in wheelchair; she is wrapped in bandages, one leg straight out. She addresses the audience.*

JEANINE: Nothing to be alarmed about. I finally decided, one morning, to jump out my window. In this country even a successful suicide is difficult. I seem to be faintly happy that I failed, although god knows why. But of course you can be happy about the strangest things . . . I did not expect failure in my life. I failed as a revolutionary . . . and come to think of it, even as a dope addict—one day the pleasure simply disappeared, along with my husband. We so badly need a revolution here. But that's another story. I refuse to lament. Oddly, in fact, I feel rather cheerful about it all, in a remote way, now that I died, or almost, and have my life again. The pain is something else, but you can't have everything.

Going out the window was a very interesting experience. I can remember passing the third floor on my way down and the glorious sensation of release. Like when I was a student at Barnard and went to Coney Island one Sunday and took that ride on the loop-the-loop and the big drop when you think it won't ever come up again. This time it didn't and I had joined the air, I felt transparent, and I saw so sharply, like a condor, a tiger. I passed our immense jacaranda tree and there was a young buzzard sitting on a branch, picking his lice. Passing the second floor I saw a cloud over my head the shape of a grand piano. I could almost taste that cloud. Then I saw the cracks in the sidewalk coming up at me and the stick of an Eskimo ice cream bar that had a faint smear of chocolate. And everything I saw seemed superbly precious and for a split second I think I believed in god. Or at least his eye, or *an* eye seeing everything so exactly.

(*Light finds* HENRI SCHULTZ.)

My father has returned to be of help. I am trying to appreciate his concern after all these years. Like many fools he at times has a certain crazy wisdom. He says now—despite being a philosopher—that I must give up on ideas which only lead to other ideas. Instead I am to think of specific, concrete things. He says the Russians have always had more ideas than any other people in history and ended in the pit. The Americans have no ideas and they have one success after another. I am trying to have no ideas.

Papa is so like our country, a drifting ship heading for where nobody knows—Norway, maybe, or is it Java or Los Angeles? The one thing we know for sure, our treasure that we secretly kiss and adore—is death—

(*Light finds* EMILY SHAPIRO *and* SKIP L. CHEESEBORO.)

—death and dreams, death and dancing, death and laughter. It is our salt and chile pepper, the flavoring of our lives.

We have eight feet of topsoil here, plenty of rain, we can grow anything, but especially greed. A lot of our people are nearly starving. And a bullet waits for anyone who seriously complains.

(*Light finds* STANLEY.)

In short—a normal country in this part of the world. A kind of miraculous incompetence, when you look at it.

I had sixteen in my little brigade, including two girls. We were captured. They shot them all in thirty seconds.

(*Light finds* FELIX BARRIAUX.)

My uncle Felix, the head of the country, spared me. I still find it hard to forgive him. I think it is one of the contradictions that sent me out my window. Survival can be hard to live with. . . . None of my people was over nineteen.

(*Light finds nothing.*)

I have a friend now. When I woke on the sidewalk he was lying beside me in my blood, embracing me and howling like a child in pain. He saved me. His love. He comes some nights and brings me honor for having fought.

(*The last light brightens.*)

Up in the mountains the people think he is the son of god. Neither of us is entirely sure of that. I suppose we'll have to wait and see.

(*Brightens further still. Slight pause.*)

What will happen now, will happen: I am content.

(*She rolls into darkness. The last light brightens even further, widening its reach until it fully covers the stage.*)

SCENE I

Office of the Chief of State, FELIX BARRIAUX. *He is seated at a window near his desk, studying a letter while filing his nails. Intercom barks.*

FELIX (*to intercom*): My cousin? Yes, but didn't he say this afternoon? Well, ask him in. . . . Wait. (*Tension as he studies the letter again.*) All right, but interrupt me in fifteen minutes; he can go on and on. You know these intellectuals.— Anything in the afternoon papers? The radio? And the Miami station? Good. . . . Listen, Isabelle . . . are you alone?—I want you to forget last night, agreed? Exactly, and we will, we'll try again soon. I appreciate your understanding, my dear, you're a fantastic girl . . .

You can send in Mr. Schultz. (*In conflict he restudies the letter, then . . .*) Oh, fuck all intellectuals! (*He passionately, defiantly kisses the letter and stashes it in his inside pocket.*)

(HENRI *enters. Wears a cotton jacket and a tweed cap.*)
Henri! Welcome home! Wonderful to see you; and you look so well!

HENRI (*solemn smile*): Felix.

FELIX (*both hands smothering* HENRI'*s*): —I understood you to say this afternoon.

HENRI (*confused*): Did I? (*Touching his forehead.*) . . . Well I suppose I could come back if you're . . .

FELIX: Out of the question! Sit! Please! (*Shaking his head, amazed—before* HENRI *can sit.*) I can't help it.

HENRI: What?

FELIX: I look at you, cousin, and I see the best years of our lives.

HENRI (*embarrassed*): Yes, I suppose.

(*Now they sit.*)

FELIX: You don't agree.

HENRI: I have too much on my mind to think about it.

FELIX (*grinning feigns shooting with pistol at* HENRI): . . . You sound like you're bringing me trouble . . . I hope not.

HENRI: The contrary, Felix, I'd like to keep you out of trouble . . .

FELIX: What does that mean?

HENRI: I didn't want to take up your office time, but there was no answer at your house . . . have you moved?

FELIX: No, but . . . I sleep in different places every night.— No guarantee, but I try to make it a little harder for them.

HENRI: Then the war is still on? I see hardly anything in the European press . . .

FELIX: Well, it's hardly a war anymore; comes and goes now, like a mild diarrhea. What is it, two years?

HENRI: More like three, I think.

FELIX: No. There was still major fighting three years ago. You came afterward.

HENRI: That's right, isn't it.—God, my mind is gone.

FELIX: Listen, I lied to you—you're not looking good at all. Wait!—I have some new vitamins! (*Presses intercom.*) Isabelle! Give my cousin a bottle of my new vitamins when he leaves. (*To* HENRI.) French.

HENRI: What?

FELIX: My vitamins are French.

HENRI: Your vitamins are French?

FELIX: —What's the matter?

HENRI: I'm . . . very troubled, Felix.

FELIX: Jeanine.

HENRI: Partly. . . . It's that . . . at times nothing seems to follow from anything else.

FELIX: Oh, well, I wouldn't worry about a thing like that.

HENRI: I've always envied how you accept life, Felix.

FELIX: Maybe you read too many books—life is complicated, but underneath the principle has never changed since the Romans—fuck them before they can fuck you. How's Jeanine now?

HENRI: What can I say?—I'm with her every day and there are signs that she wants to live . . . but who knows? The whole thing is a catastrophe.

FELIX: I know her opinion of me, but I still think that girl has a noble heart; she's a Greek tragedy. . . . You remember my son-in-law, the accountant? He calculates that falling from the third floor—(*raises his arm straight up*)—she must have hit the sidewalk at sixty-two miles an hour. (*Slaps his hand loudly on desktop.*)

HENRI (*pained*): Please.

FELIX: But at least it brought you together. Sorry. Incidentally, where's your dentist?

HENRI: My dentist?

FELIX: I am practically commuting to Miami but my teeth keep falling apart. Where do you go?

HENRI: It depends. New York, London, Paris . . . wherever I happen to be. Listen, Felix . . . (*Breaks off.*) I don't know where to begin . . .

FELIX: . . . I hope it's not some kind of problem for me because I'll be frank with you, Henri—I'm not . . . completely myself these days.—I'm all right, you understand, but I'm just . . . not myself.

HENRI: . . . I didn't come to antagonize you.

FELIX (*in a flare of anger-alarm*): How the hell could you antagonize me! I love you, you bastard. . . . Tell me, you still living in New York?

HENRI: Mostly Munich. Lecturing on Tragedy.

FELIX: Tragedy is my life, Henri—when I was training in Georgia those Army dentists were the best, but I didn't have a cavity then. Now, when I'm paying the bills I'm full of holes. —How do you lecture on Tragedy?

HENRI (*inhales, exhales*): Let me tell you what's on my . . .

FELIX (*now a certain anxiety begins to seep out more openly*): Yes! Go ahead, what is it? . . . Isn't that cap too hot?

HENRI: It helps my arthritis.

FELIX: Oh, right! And how does that work again?—Oh yes!—it's that most of the body heat escapes through the skull . . .

HENRI: Exactly . . .

FELIX (*suddenly recalling*): . . . So it keeps your joints warm! —this is why I always loved talking to you, Henri!—you make my mind wander. . . . Wait! My god, I haven't congratulated you; your new wife.

HENRI: Thank you.

FELIX: I read that she's a concert pianist?

HENRI (*a strained smile*): . . . You're going to have to hear this, Felix.

FELIX: I'm listening!—But seeing you again always . . . moves me. (*Reaches over to touch* HENRI*'s knee.*) I am moved. (*Collects himself.*) How long will you be staying this time?

HENRI: A month or two; depends on how Jeanine progresses . . .

FELIX: Doctor Herman tells me she'll need another operation.

HENRI: Two more, possibly three. The whole thing is devastating.

FELIX: . . . I have to say, I never thought you were this close . . .

HENRI: No one can be close to a drug addict; but she's absolutely finished with that now. I was never much of a father but I'm going to see her back to health if it's the last thing I ever do.

FELIX: Bravo, I'm glad to hear that.—How a woman of her caliber could go for drugs is beyond me. What happened, do you know?

HENRI (*sudden surge*): What happened!—she lost a revolution, Felix.

FELIX: All right, but she has to know all that is finished, revolution is out . . . I'm talking everywhere.

HENRI: . . . Listen, don't make me drag it out—I haven't the strength.

FELIX: Yes. Please.—But I must tell you, it always amazes me how you gave up everything to just read books and *think*. Frankly, I have never understood it. But go ahead . . .

HENRI: Day before yesterday I drove with my wife up toward Santa Felice to show her the country.

FELIX: According to this *Vanity Fair* magazine that is one of the finest views in the world, you know.

HENRI: As we were passing through the villages . . .

FELIX: . . . Also the *National Geographic*.

HENRI: When we got up there, Felix . . . it all came back to me . . . remember when we were students and hiked up there together? Remember our shock and disgust that so many of the children had orange hair . . .

FELIX (*a happy memory; laughs indulgently*): Ah yes! The blood fluke . . . it's in the water. But it's practically harmless, you know.

HENRI: Not for children. It can destroy a child's liver . . .

FELIX: Well now, that's a bit . . .

HENRI (*sudden sharpness*): It is true, Felix! And the symptom of course is orange hair.

FELIX: What's your point?

HENRI: What's my point! Felix, blood fluke in the water supply in the twenty-first century is. . . . My god, you are the head of this country, don't you feel a . . . ?

FELIX: They won't boil the water, what can I do about it!— What is all this about the fluke suddenly? The British are definitely going to build a gigantic warehouse on the harbor, for god's sake!

HENRI (*distressed*): A warehouse! What's that got to do with . . .

FELIX: Because this country's starting to move and you're still talking blood fluke! I assure you, Henri, nobody in this country has the slightest interest in blood fluke!—Is this what you wanted to talk to me about?

HENRI: You probably won't remember, but on my last visit I brought home an eighteenth-century painting from Paris, cost me twenty-six thousand dollars. The pollution in our air has since peeled off about a third of the paint.

FELIX: That couldn't happen in Paris?

HENRI: It's been sitting in Paris for two hundred and fifty years! . . . I had a grand piano shipped from New York for my wife . . .

FELIX: The varnish cracked?

HENRI: The varnish did not crack but my architect is afraid the floor may collapse because of the underground leakage of water from the aqueduct, which has undermined the foundations of that whole lovely neighborhood. And brought in termites!

FELIX: I'm to chase termites?

HENRI: —My wife has to practice in the garage, Felix! When she plays for me I have to sit listening in the Mercedes!

FELIX: But cousin, a grand piano—you're talking three-quarters of a ton!

HENRI: I was getting out of a taxi yesterday on Avenue Fontana, our number-one shopping street . . .

FELIX: Did you see the new Dunhill store . . . ?

HENRI: . . . I nearly stepped on a dead baby lying at the curb. (FELIX *throws up his hands and walks away, steaming.*) Shoppers were passing by, saw it, and walked on. As I did.

FELIX: What is all this suddenly? None of this has ever been any different!

HENRI: I don't know! I suppose I never really *looked* at anything. It may be Jeanine; she was so utterly beautiful, Felix.

FELIX: Oh god, yes.

HENRI: I think I never really *saw* what I meant to her. Sitting with her day after day now . . . for the first time I understood my part in her suffering. I betrayed her, Felix. It's terrible.

FELIX: Why? You always gave her everything . . .

HENRI: A faith in the revolution is what I gave her . . . and then walked away from it myself.

FELIX: I hope I'm not hearing your old Marxism again . . .

HENRI: Oh shit, Felix!—I haven't been a Marxist for twenty-five years!

FELIX: Because that is finished, they're almost all in narcotics now, thanks be to god; but the Americans are here now and they'll clean out the whole lot of them by New Years! Your guerillas are done!

HENRI: These are not my guerillas, my guerillas were foolish, idealistic people, but the hope of the world! These people now are cynical and stupid enough to deal narcotics!

FELIX: Listen, after thirty-eight years of civil war what did you expect to find here, Sweden? Weren't you in analysis once?

HENRI: Yes. I was. Twenty years ago at least. Why?

FELIX: I'm seeing a man in Miami.

HENRI: Well, that's surprising. I always think of you in control of everything.

FELIX: Not the most important thing.

HENRI: . . . You don't say. Maybe you have the wrong woman.

FELIX: They can't all be wrong. My dog just won't hunt.

HENRI: Imagine. And analysis helps?

FELIX (*hesitates*): Semi. I'm trying to keep from letting it obsess me. But I have this vision, you know?

HENRI: Oh? Someone you've met?

FELIX: No, just imaginary—like those women you see in New York. Tall, you know? Fine teeth. Kind of . . . I don't know . . . nasty. Or spirited . . . spirited is the word. Is your wife tall?

HENRI: No. She's Viennese. Rather on the short, round side.

FELIX: I've tried short and round, but . . . (*Shakes his head.*)

It's torturing me, Henri. Listen, how would you like to be ambassador to Moscow again?

HENRI (*gripping his head*): Do you see why I am depressed?— nothing follows!

FELIX: —The reason you're depressed is . . .

HENRI (*grips his head*): I beg you, Felix, don't tell me why I'm depressed!

FELIX: . . . It's because you're a rich man in a poor country, that's all . . . but we're moving, by god!

(*Intercom.* FELIX *bends to it.*)

Thank you, my dear. (*To* HENRI.) —I have a meeting. . . . What'd you want to tell me?

HENRI (*a pause to organize*): On our little trip to Santa Felice —Hilda and I—we were struck by a . . . what to call it? . . . a kind of spiritual phenomenon up there. Really incredible. Wherever we went the peasants had pictures of this young man whom they . . .

FELIX: He's finished. We've captured him, Henri, he is history, all done.

HENRI: They keep candles lit before his photograph, you know . . . like a saint.

FELIX: This saint's gunmen have shot up three police stations and killed two officers and wounded five more in the past two months.

HENRI: They say he personally had nothing to do with the violence.

FELIX: The man is a revolutionary and he is responsible! —Listen, Henri, two of my brothers died fighting shits like these and he will have no mercy from me. Is this what you wanted to talk to me about?

HENRI: There is a rumor—which I find hard to believe—that you intend to crucify this fellow?

FELIX: I can't comment on that.

HENRI: Beg your pardon?

FELIX: No comment, Henri, that's the end of it.

HENRI: And if this brings on a bloodbath?

FELIX: Don't think it will.

HENRI: Felix, you are totally out of touch. They really think he is the Messiah, the son of god!

FELIX: The son of god is a man named Ralph?

HENRI: But a crucifixion! Don't you see?—it will prove they were right! These are simple people, it could bring them roaring down out of the mountains!

FELIX: Shooting doesn't work! People are shot on television every ten minutes; bang-bang, and they go down like dolls, it's meaningless. But nail up a couple of these bastards, and believe me this will be the quietest country on the continent and ready for development! A crucifixion always quiets things down. Really, I am amazed—a cretin goes about preaching bloody revolution, and you . . .

HENRI: Talk to the people! They'll tell you he's preaching justice.

FELIX: Oh come off it, Henri! Two percent of our people—including you—own ninety-six percent of the land. The justice they're demanding is your land; are you ready to give it to them?

HENRI: . . . To tell the truth, yes, I just might be. I returned to try to help Jeanine but also . . . I've decided to put the business and both farms up for sale.

FELIX: Why!—those farms are terrific!

HENRI: They've been raising coca and it's impossible to police my managers when I'm away so much; in short, I've decided to stop pretending to be a business man . . . (*Breaks off.*)

FELIX: Really. And what's stopping you?

HENRI: Courage, probably. I lack enough conviction . . .

FELIX: No, Henri, it's your common sense telling you that in ten years the land you gave away will end up back in the hands of two percent of the smartest people! You can't teach a baboon to play Chopin.—Or are you telling me this idiot is the son of god?

HENRI: I don't believe in god, let alone his son. I beg you, Felix, listen to what I'm saying . . . you crucify this fellow and our country is finished, ruined!

FELIX: Henri, dear friend . . . (*draws the letter out of his jacket pocket*) . . . not only are we not ruined—I can tell you that with this crucifixion our country will finally begin to live!

This fax arrived this morning.

(*A gigantic fax unspurls.*)

You've heard of Thomson, Weber, Macdean and Abramowitz of Madison Avenue?

HENRI: Of course . . . Thomson, Weber, Macdean and Abramowitz. They're the largest advertising agency for pharmaceutical companies.

FELIX: So I'm told. How they got wind of it I don't know, unless General Gonzalez contacted them for a finder's fee— he's our consul in New York now; anyway, they want to photograph the crucifixion for television.

HENRI: What in god's name are you talking about?

FELIX (*hands the letter to* HENRI): This is an offer of seventy-five million dollars for the exclusive worldwide rights to televise the crucifixion.

HENRI (*stunned, he reads the letter*): Have you read these conditions?

FELIX: What do you mean?

HENRI (*indicating letter*): They will attach commercial announcements!

FELIX: But they say "dignified" announcements. . . . Probably like the phone company or, I don't know, the Red Cross.

HENRI: They are talking underarm deodorants, Felix!

FELIX: You don't know that!

HENRI (*slapping the letter*): Read it! They hardly expect a worldwide audience for the phone company! They're talking athlete's foot, Felix!

FELIX: Oh no, I don't think they . . .

HENRI: They're talking athlete's foot, sour stomach, constipation, anal itch . . . !

FELIX: No-no!

HENRI: Where else does seventy-five million come from? I'm sure they figure it would take him four or five hours to die, so they could load it up—runny stool, falling hair, gum disease, crotch itch, dry skin, oily skin, nasal blockage, diapers for grownups . . . impotence . . .

FELIX: God no, they'd never do that!

HENRI: Why not? Is there a hole in the human anatomy we don't make a dollar on? With a crucifixion the sky's the limit! I forgot ear wax, red eyes, bad breath . . .

FELIX: Please, Henri, sit down for a moment.

HENRI (*sitting*): It's a catastrophe! And for me personally it's . . . it's the end!

FELIX: Why?—nobody will blame you . . .

HENRI: My company distributes most of those products, for god's sake!

FELIX: I think maybe you're exaggerating the reaction . . .

HENRI: Am I! As your men drive nails into his hands and split the bones of his feet the camera will cut away to . . . god knows what . . . somebody squirming with a burning asshole! You must let the fellow go . . . !

FELIX: He's not going anywhere, he's a revolutionary and an idiot!

HENRI: You're not visualizing, Felix! People are desperate for someone this side of the stars who feels their suffering himself and gives a damn! The man is hope!

FELIX: He is hope because he gets us seventy-five million! My god, we once had an estimate to irrigate the entire eastern half of the country and that was only thirteen million! This is fantastic!

HENRI: Felix—if you sell this man, you will join the two other most contemptible monsters in history.

FELIX: What two others?

HENRI: Pontius Pilate and Judas, for god's sake! That kind of infamy is very hard to shed.

FELIX: Except that Jesus Christ was not an impostor and this one is.

HENRI: We don't know that.

FELIX: What the hell are you talking about, the son of a bitch is not even Jewish!—Good god, Henri, with that kind of money I could put the police into decent shoes and issue every one of them a poncho. And real sewers . . . with *pipes!*—so the better class of people wouldn't have to go up to the tops of the hills to build a house . . . we could maybe have our own airline and send all our prostitutes to the dentist . . .

HENRI: Stop. Please. (*Slight pause.*) Do you really want our country blamed for a worldwide suicide?

FELIX: *What?*

HENRI: A crucifixion lasting possibly hours on the screen—use your imagination! To a lot of people it will mean the imminent end of the world . . .

FELIX (*dismissing*): Oh that's nonsense . . . !

HENRI: I can see thousands jumping off bridges in Paris, London, New York . . . ! And California . . . my god, California will turn into a madhouse.—*And the whole thing blamed on us?—We'll be a contemptible country!* I know you'll call it off now, won't you.

(FELIX *stares.*)

Felix, think of your children—their father will be despised through the end of time, do you want that stain on their lives?

(*Pause.* FELIX *in thought.*)

FELIX: I disagree. I really do. Look at it calmly—fifteen or twenty years after they kicked Nixon out of the White House he had one of the biggest funerals since Abraham Lincoln. Is that true or isn't it?

HENRI: Well, yes, I suppose it is.

FELIX: Believe me, Henri, in politics there is only one sacred rule—nobody clearly remembers anything.

HENRI: I've seen him.

FELIX: Really! How'd that happen?

HENRI: The police happened to have caught him in the street outside my window. Terrible scene; four or five of his . . . I suppose you could call them disciples stood there, weeping. One of the cops clubbed him down and kicked him squarely in the mouth. I was paralyzed. But then, as they were pushing him into the van—quite accidentally, his gaze rose up to my window and for an instant our eyes met.—His composure, Felix—his poise—there was a kind of tranquility in his eyes that was . . . chilling; he almost seemed to transcend everything, as though he knew all this had to happen . . .

FELIX: I thank you for this conversation, it's cleared me up . . .

HENRI: Let me talk to him. I take it you have him here?

FELIX: He won't open his mouth.

HENRI: Let me try to convince him to leave the country.

FELIX: Wonderful, but try to feel out if we can expect some dignity if he's nailed up? I don't want it to look like some kind of torture or something . . .

HENRI: And what about our dignity!

FELIX: Our dignity is modernization! Tell him he's going to die for all of us!

HENRI: . . . Because we need that money!

FELIX: All right, yes, but that's a hell of a lot better than dying for nothing! (FELIX *opens the door; a blinding white light pours through the doorway through which they are peering.*)

HENRI: What is that light on him?

FELIX: Nothing. He just suddenly lights up sometimes. It happens, that's all.

HENRI: It "happens"!

FELIX (*defensive outburst*): All right, I don't understand it! Do you understand a computer chip? Can you tell me what electricity is? And how about a gene? I mean what is a fucking gene? So he lights up; it's one more *thing*, that's all. But look at him, you ever seen such total vacancy in a man's face? (*Pointing.*) That idiot is mental and he's making us all crazy! Go and godspeed!

HENRI (*takes a step toward doorway and halts*): You know, when I saw him outside my window a very odd thought . . . exploded in my head—that I hadn't actually been *seeing* anything . . . for most of my life. That I have lived half blind . . . to Jeanine, even to my former wife . . . I can't begin to explain it, Felix, but it's all left me with one idea that I can't shake off—it haunts me.

FELIX: What idea?

HENRI: That I could have loved. (*Slight pause.*) In my life.

(HENRI, *conflicted, exits through the doorway.* FELIX *shuts the door behind him.*)

FELIX: Odd—one minute I'd really love to blow that moron away. But the next minute . . . (*He stares in puzzlement. He goes to his phone. Picks up the letter.*) Isabelle. Get me New York. 212-779-8865. Want to speak to a Mr. . . . (*Reads letter.*) Skip L. Cheeseboro, he's a vice president of the firm.—Well, yes—if they ask you, say it's in reference to a crucifixion. He'll know what it means.

BLACKOUT

SCENE 2

Mountain top. EMILY SHAPIRO *enters with* SKIP L. CHEESEBORO. *She is in jeans and zipper jacket and baseball cap, he in bush jacket, carrying a portfolio and a shooting stick. They bend over to catch their breaths. Now she straightens up and looks out front, awed.*

EMILY: My god! Look at this!

SKIP: Yeah!

EMILY: That snow. That sun. That light!

SKIP: Yeah!

EMILY: What a blue! What an orange! What mountains!

SKIP: What's the date today?

EMILY: Seventeenth.

SKIP: Huh! . . . I think she's getting the divorce today and I completely forgot to call her.

EMILY: Well maybe she'll forgive you. (*Looking into distance.*)— This is absolutely awesome. How pure.

SKIP: A lot like Nepal—the Ivory Soap shoot.

EMILY: Like Kenya too, maybe . . . Chevy Malibu.

SKIP: The Caucasus, too.

EMILY: Caucasus?

SKIP: Head and Shoulders.

EMILY: Wasn't that Venezuela?

SKIP: Venezuela was Jeep.

EMILY: Right!—No!—Jeep was the Himalayas.

SKIP: Himalayas was Alka Seltzer, dear.

EMILY: Oh right, that gorgeous bubbling fountain.

SKIP: I think the bubbling fountain was Efferdent in Chile.

EMILY (*closing her eyes in anguish*): God, what a mush it all is! (*Looking out again.*) Human beings don't deserve this world. (*Spreading out her arms.*) I mean look at this! Look at this glory! . . . And look at us.

(*The* CAPTAIN *enters.*)

CAPTAIN: Everything is fine?

SKIP: Beautiful, thank you very much, Captain. Our crew will be arriving shortly . . .

CAPTAIN: We will help them up . . . (*Important news.*) Mr. Schultz is already arriving.

EMILY: Mr. Schultz?

CAPTAIN: Very famous; his company is making the medicine for the feet.

EMILY and SKIP (*uncomprehending*): Ah!

EMILY: Oh!—athlete's foot!

CAPTAIN: And for the ears . . . to remove the wax.

SKIP: Really. And what connection does he have with . . . ?

CAPTAIN: He is cousin to General Barriaux . . . very important. (*A wide gesture front.*) This is the perfect scenery, no?—for the crucifixion?

EMILY (*laughs*): For the what?

SKIP: Thank you, Captain . . .

CAPTAIN: Yes! I must go down; I am speaking English?

SKIP: Oh yes, you speak very well.

CAPTAIN: How you say "lunch"?

SKIP: Lunch? Well . . . lunch.

CAPTAIN: We also. You say lunch and we say lunch.

EMILY: That's really remarkable.

CAPTAIN (*pleased with himself*): Thank you, Madame. (*He leaves.*)

EMILY: That wonderful?—a great spot for a crucifixion!

SKIP (*empty laugh*): Yes . . . Darling, what exactly did Atcheson tell you?

(CAPTAIN *reenters with* HENRI.)

CAPTAIN: Ah, here is Mr. Schultz!! (*To* HENRI.) Here is our director!

HENRI (*to* EMILY *and* SKIP): How do you do?

CAPTAIN: I am honored, sir. My wife and daughter are taking "Schultz's" every month!

HENRI (*trying to get back to* EMILY): . . . Thank you, but I have very little to do with the company anymore.

CAPTAIN: You also have very good pills for the malaria.

HENRI (*turning to* SKIP): I am Henri Schultz . . .

EMILY: Emily Shapiro. Director. This is my producer, Mr. Cheeseboro. We're making a commercial up here.

HENRI: So I understand. I believe the General will be coming up; I have something I'd like to say to you both if you have a moment . . .

EMILY: We're just laying out possible backgrounds . . . (*Turning to* SKIP.) . . . Although I still haven't been told what exactly we're shooting . . .

SKIP: . . . May I ask your involvement, sir? Or should I know?

HENRI: Well let me see—my involvement, I suppose, is my concern for the public peace or something in that line.

SKIP: I don't understand.—If you mean good taste, Miss Shapiro has given the world some of its most uplifting commercial images. And luckily, the beauty of this location practically cries out for a . . . ah . . .

HENRI: A crucifixion, yes. But if you can give me five minutes, I'd like to speak to you about . . .

EMILY: What is he talking about?

SKIP (*to* HENRI, *walking her away*): Excuse us, please. (*To* EMILY.) What exactly did Atcheson tell you?

EMILY: Practically nothing.—Phoned from his limo and said to get my crew right over to Kennedy and the company jet and you'd fill me in when I got here . . .

SKIP: That's all?

EMILY: Wait a minute—yes; he sort of mentioned some kind of execution, but I didn't get the product . . . —What is it, somebody making an execution movie, is that it? And I grab some footage?

HENRI: Candidly, I wouldn't rule out a certain danger . . .

SKIP: There is no danger whatsoever; they have troops all over the mountain.

CAPTAIN: . . . Everything is absolutely covered.

EMILY: Why?

SKIP: Well, let's see. There is this sort of revolutionary terrorist.

EMILY: *Terrorist?* A real one?

HENRI: Actually, he himself is apparently not a . . .

SKIP: The man is totally vicious! His gang have killed some cops and blown up government buildings. And he goes around claiming to be the . . . like, you know, the son of god. (*Turning on* HENRI *nervously.*) —Is there something I can help you with, sir . . . I mean, what is it you want?

EMILY: I'm confused—what's the product? (*To* HENRI.) What are all those soldiers doing down below?

SKIP: They always have soldiers . . . even around weddings . . . rock concerts . . . anything.

HENRI: This is a bit different, they are there in case of a protest.

EMILY: Protest about what?

SKIP: Sir? We are here under an agreement with General Barriaux, and you are interfering with our work; I'm afraid I really must ask you to leave . . .

(*Soldiers enter, dark local men; two carry spades, and a long beam which they set down. One carries a submachine gun and a chainsaw—he stands guard.*)

EMILY: What's this now?

SKIP: They're putting up a little set. (*To the soldiers.*) Very good, gentlemen, but don't do anything yet, okay? Just sit down and wait a few minutes, okay? We'll be with you in a few seconds, okay?

(*The soldiers nod agreeably but begin unpacking tools—an electric drill, bolts. One of them lays a beam across another.*)

HENRI: You know it's to be a crucifixion?—

EMILY: A crucifixion. Really. But what's the product? (*Calling to the soldiers.*) Wait gentlemen! Don't do anything till I tell you, okay?

(*The soldiers nod agreeably and one of them begins digging a hole.* SKIP *grasps the shovel handle.*)

No, wait, fellas; for one thing, I've got to decide on the camera angle before you build anything, okay?

(*The guard shifts his gun nervously.*)

Oh well, go ahead.

(*They proceed with the digging as she turns to* SKIP *with beginning alarm.*)

Will you kindly explain what the hell is going on here? And what am I shooting, please?

SKIP: . . . It's a common thing with murderers here . . . they attach the prisoner . . .

EMILY: Attach? What do you mean? To what?

(*A very short burst from an electrical drill interrupts.*)

Please stop that!

(*Drill cuts out and in the momentary silence the* CAPTAIN, *to* HENRI . . .)

CAPTAIN (*patting his own stomach*): Also you have the best for the gas . . . "Schultz's"!

HENRI: Captain, please—I inherited the company but I have very little to do with running it. I am a philosopher, a teacher . . .

SKIP: Darling, you must understand—this fellow has blown up a number of *actual* buildings, so they're quite angry with him . . .

EMILY: Wait, Skip—I don't know where I got the idea but I thought somebody was shooting a movie and we were just hitchhiking onto it . . .

SKIP: There's no movie.

EMILY: So . . . is that a cross?

SKIP: Well . . . (*Takes a fortifying breath.*) In effect.

EMILY: It's really a *crucifixion*?

SKIP: Well . . . in effect, yes, it's very common here . . .

EMILY: "In effect"—you mean like with nails?

HENRI: That's correct.

SKIP: It is not! I was told they'll most likely just tie him onto it! (*To* EMILY.) They do that quite a lot in this country. I mean with death sentences.

EMILY: But he's not actually going to like . . . die . . .

SKIP (*frustration exploding*): I cannot believe that Atcheson . . . !

EMILY: Atcheson told me to get here, period! He didn't say "die"! Nobody dies in a commercial! Have you all gone crazy?

SKIP: We're only photographing it, we're not *doing* it, for god's sake!

EMILY (*clapping hands over ears*): Please stop talking!
(*A soldier starts up a chainsaw. She rushes to him, waving her arms.*)
Prego, Signor . . . No, that's Italian. Bitte . . . not bitte . . . stop, okay? What's Spanish for "stop"?

HENRI: Stop.

EMILY: Yes. (*To the men.*) Stop!
(*They stop.*)
Gracias. Muchos. (*To* SKIP.) I'm sorry, Skip—I think maybe I'm just out.

SKIP: Now you stop being silly!

CAPTAIN: This is going to be a very good thing, Madame. It will frighten the people, you see.

EMILY: And that's good?

CAPTAIN: Oh yes . . . it's when they are not frightened of the government is when they get in trouble. Of course, it would be even better if they were allowed to say whatever they want. Like in the States.

HENRI: Well that's a surprise, coming from the police.

CAPTAIN: Oh, but is a very simple thing—if the troublemakers are allowed to speak they are much easier to catch. (*His handheld intercom erupts. He holds it to his ear.*) The General has arrived! (CAPTAIN *rushes out.*)

HENRI: You may start a bloodbath in this country, sir, I hope you realize that.

SKIP: You are endangering this woman's career! (*To* EMILY.) This could move you into a whole new area. I mean just for starters, if you shot him against the view of those incredible mountains . . .

EMILY: You mean on the cross?

SKIP: Emily dear, you know I adore you. Have I ever steered you wrong? This is a door to possibly Hollywood. There's never been anything remotely like this in the history of television.

EMILY: —And when are we talking about? For it to happen? Just out of curiosity.

SKIP: Toward sundown would be best, but it has to be today.

EMILY: Why?

SKIP: . . . Well, basically . . .

EMILY: Don't tell me "basically," just tell me why.

SKIP: Well, basically because the story is bound to jump the border and we'll have CNN here and ABC and every goddam camera in Europe. So it has to be done today because we have an exclusive.

HENRI: I beg you both, let us discuss this rationally.

EMILY: My head is spinning.

SKIP: I share your feelings, believe me, but . . .

EMILY: . . . I mean there's something deeply, deeply offensive, Skip.

HENRI: That's the point precisely.

EMILY: Really. I think it like . . . disgusts me. Doesn't it you?

SKIP: In a way, I suppose, but realistically, who am I to be disgusted? I mean . . .

(*Suddenly, the gigantic cross is raised, dominating the stage.* EMILY, *struck, raises her hand to silence* SKIP, *who turns to look as it rises to position while soldiers observe to figure if it is the right height.*)

All right, dear, let's parse this out head-on, okay?

(*She is staring into space now, into herself. Sudden new idea.*)

Showing it on the world screen could help put an end to it forever!

(*Warming.*)

Yes! That's it! If I were moralistic I'd even say you have a *duty* to shoot this! Really. I mean that.

(*Soldiers take down the pole and start up a chainsaw again, which stops their talk. The pole is sawed shorter.*)

In fact, it could end up a worldwide blow against capital punishment, which I know you are against as I passionately am. Please, dear, come here . . .

(*She doesn't move.*)

Darling, please!

(*He goes upstage of the soldiers and the beams. Half in a dream she reluctantly joins him and he holds arms out.*)

Look at this!—if you shot from here, with that sky and the mountains . . .

EMILY: But, Skip, I've never in my life shot anything like . . . real—I do commercials!

SKIP: But your genius is that everything you shoot *becomes* real, darling—

EMILY: My genius is to make everything comfortably fake, Skip. No agency wants real. You want a fake-looking crucifixion? —call me.

SKIP: Dear, what you do is make real things look fake, and that makes them emotionally real, whereas . . .

EMILY: Stop. Just stop it, Skip. Please. I'm totally lost. All I know is that somebody actually dying in my lens would melt my eyeball.—I have to call New York . . . (*She takes out cell phone.*)

SKIP: No, dear, please . . .

EMILY: I can't call my mother?

SKIP: Your mother!—Of course. (*Handing her his cell phone.*) Use mine, charge it to us. And darling, please don't feel . . .

EMILY (*punching the numbers, yells, outraged, scared*): Skip, I beg you do not use ordinary beseeching language to me, okay?! This is death we're talking about! (*She dials.*)

SKIP (*suddenly turning on* HENRI): Sir, I appreciate who you are, but if you refuse to leave I will be forced to call the police!

HENRI: Sir, my family has been in this country since the Conquistadors.

SKIP: Really. Conquistadors named Schultz?

HENRI: Cortez had a German doctor.

SKIP (*one-upped, growing desperate*): You don't say!

EMILY (*in phone*): Mother! Yes! Hello? (*To* SKIP.) Now listen, I haven't agreed to anything, okay?—Hello?
 (CAPTAIN *enters, glancing about;* EMILY *mouths a conversation into the phone.*)

CAPTAIN: My excuses, please! General Barriaux is approaching below. I am to ask if there are any firearms . . . pistols, long knives, please to hand them to me. I am speaking English.

HENRI: Don't bother, Captain . . . I'm sure they're not armed.

CAPTAIN (*salutes*): Very good, sir! From Mister Schultz I accept this reassurance! You know, since I was a little child . . . when I was coughing . . . my mother always gave me . . .

HENRI: Will you stop that? Just stop it. This is a serious event, Captain!
 (SKIP *settles onto his shooting stick, takes out a magazine and affects to blithely work a crossword puzzle.*)

EMILY (*in phone*): . . . Mother, please! Listen a minute, will you? . . . It is, yes, it's beautiful. And the birds, yes, they're sensational. I saw a condor, twelve-foot wingspread, unbelievable, it can carry off a goat!—Listen, I left in such a hurry I forgot my cleaning woman doesn't come today so could you go over and feed my cats? Thanks, dear, but just the one can for both, I mean don't have pity, okay? What?

SKIP (*to* HENRI): Sir, we are trying to work here . . . I'd be happy to meet somewhere later . . . tomorrow, perhaps . . .

EMILY (*in phone*): —Do I? Well I am nervous, they've just thrown a whole pail of garbage at me and I don't know what to do with it. Well it turns out it's a . . . well, a crucifixion.

Some kind of Communist, I suppose. Not as far as I know—
(*Louder.*) I said he's not Jewish as far as I know!

SKIP (*glancing up from his puzzle*): But she mustn't mention . . .

EMILY: But you mustn't mention this to anybody, you understand? —Of course it's a problem for me! I'd be on the next plane but I just signed for my new apartment and I was depending totally on this check.

SKIP: You'll have walked twice in one year, darling—case closed.

EMILY: This'd be my second time I walked off a shoot . . . well the slaughter of the baby seals last year. So I'm a little scared.—And it's also that I'm a little late.—Well, who wouldn't be edgy! I mean I don't know, do I want it or don't I?—Well . . . to tell you the truth I'm not sure, it could have been Max Fleisher.—What marry?—I should marry Max Fleisher? I'm not sure it was him anyway.—Mother, please will you listen, dear; I have no interest in marrying anybody.—I profoundly don't know why! Except I can't imagine being with the same person the entire rest of my life.—But I do believe in people—it's just myself I have doubts about.

(*The crew enters:* PHIL, *cameraman;* SARAH, *soundwoman.*)
Got to run, don't forget the cats and give Daddy a kiss for me. I'll call tomorrow. 'Bye!

PHIL (*sets camera on the ground*): Skip. Good morning, director, what are we shooting?

SARAH: Emily, please could I use your cell phone, I've got to call New York.

EMILY: Is it all right, Skip?

SKIP: Why can't you call from the hotel?

SARAH: Because it's just after nine and they said I could get my pregnancy report after nine and I can't wait.

EMILY: Sarah, really! Isn't that fantastic!

SARAH (*jumping up and down*): Please!

EMILY (*hands her the phone*): Here! Can you say who the father is?

SARAH: Well, ah . . . actually, yes. My husband . . .

EMILY: You have a *husband*?

SARAH: Last Tuesday.

EMILY: How fantastic! Make your call!

(*Watches with unwilling envy as* SARAH *goes to a space and calls.*)

PHIL: Listen, I'm trustworthy, can you tell me the secret?— what am I shooting?

EMILY (*indicates the cross*): That.

PHIL: What am I supposed to do with that?

EMILY: Well, nothing, until they nail a man to it.

(*Soldiers lower the cross to the ground and start attaching a footrest . . . as . . .*)

PHIL: I always knew you were gutsy, but doesn't this crowd insanity? You're not serious, are you?

EMILY: I may not be your director in about ten minutes, Phil. (*To* SKIP.) . . . Which reminds me, do you have a doctor?

SKIP: Oh god, you're not feeling well?

EMILY: Not for me, for him!—You've really gone crazy, haven't you . . .

SKIP: I am not at all crazy! . . . In all the thousands of paintings and the written accounts of the crucifixion scene I defy anyone to produce a single one that shows a doctor present! I'm sorry but we can't be twisting the historical record! (*Great new idea.*) . . . And furthermore, I will not superimpose American mores on a dignified foreign people. The custom here is to crucify criminals, period! I am not about to condescend to these people with a foreign colonialist mentality!

EMILY: What about a hat?

SKIP: A hat?

EMILY: If I know mountains it'll probably be a hundred degrees up here by noon.

SKIP: Yes, but a hat—is that the look we want?—on a cross with a hat? I mean we're not here to make some kind of a *comment*. I defy anyone to find a painting where he's wearing a . . .

EMILY: And what do you plan on giving him?

SKIP: Giving him . . . ?

EMILY: For the pain!

SKIP: If you're talking light drugs, okay, but we can't have him staggering up to the cross or something. Especially in like dry states . . . Kansas or whatever.

SARAH (*holding the phone*): They gave him wine, you know—the Romans . . .

SKIP: Well a little wine, but he can't look stoned. I mean we've got several million born-agains watching. Actually, I was thinking aspirin . . . or Tylenol if he's allergic . . .

EMILY: Aspirin with nails through his hands and feet? Skip dear, are you out of your fucking head?—I mean I personally am on the verge of disappearing here, but. . . . Look, I don't know why I'm even talking to you!

SKIP (*terror raised a notch*): Emily, dear, in all solemnity—if you walk on this one you'd better forget about any more work from us! And probably most if not all the other agencies. Now that's candid. It's simply too late to get somebody else, and your career, I can assure you is a wipeout.

EMILY: You are threatening me, Skip.

SKIP: I'm in no way threatening, dear, but if I know Thomson, Weber, Macdean and Abramowitz a lawsuit is not out of the question, and you'll be total roadkill in the industry!

(*Enter* FELIX *in uniform, with the* CAPTAIN.)

FELIX: Henri! Good!—you've decided to come, what a nice surprise. Good morning all!—Have you met Mr. Cheeseboro? Mister Cheeseboro, Mr. Schultz, my cousin.

SKIP: We've met.

HENRI (*taking* FELIX's *elbow—intimately*): Felix, I beg you . . . we must talk before you commit to this.

FELIX: Later. I have a problem.

HENRI: What do you mean?

FELIX: Everything is under control . . .

HENRI: What are you talking about?

(*But* FELIX *has spotted* EMILY *and is instantly vibrating.*)

FELIX (*both open hands toward her*): And who is . . . ?

SKIP: . . . Our director, sir—Emily Shapiro.

EMILY: How do you do.

FELIX (*sweeps his hat off his head, lowering it for an instant, hiding his "enthusiasm"*): Wonderful! I hadn't expected a *woman* . . .

SARAH (*at one side with her phone*): Why not! I assure you women can film crucifixions as well as anybody else!

FELIX: I'm sure, but . . . (*to* EMILY, *while putting his hat back on*) . . . watching them, you know, can make even strong men uncomfortable.

EMILY: Oh? . . . Is this something you do fairly often?

FELIX (*points skyward*): That depends on the weather . . .

SKIP (*warm academic objectivity*): Now isn't that *interesting*.

FELIX: Most of our people are peasants, you see. (*A shake of the fist.*) When the crops are good, people are content. (*Points skyward.*) But it's hardly rained for twenty-six months, so there is a certain amount of unrest; we have an old saying, "when the rain stops the crosses sprout." It is not something we enjoy, I assure you, but there is either order or chaos. Are you taken for dinner?

EMILY: I hadn't thought about it. . . . I hope you won't mind too much, but I've half decided to try to stop this travesty from happening.

SKIP: That is not for you to . . . !

EMILY (*over-shouting him*): . . . Just so my crew and I—and especially Mr. Cheeseboro—know what to expect—when they're being nailed up do they like . . . *scream*?

HENRI: Certainly.

EMILY: And for how long?

FELIX: Not very; usually they're given a couple of bottles of tequila beforehand. Incidentally, I particularly admire your haircut.

SKIP: But you don't mean they're like . . . staggering.

HENRI: Of course.

FELIX: That is nonsense, Henri. Occasionally they have to be carried to the cross, but . . .

SKIP: Well that's out of the question . . .

FELIX: Oh? Why?

SKIP: Carrying him up to the cross would be like . . . I don't know . . . blasphemous in the United States!

EMILY: Sounds terrific to me . . . piggyback!

SKIP: Now wait, dear . . . !

EMILY: . . . Stop calling me "dear," my name is mud. Miss Mud. Emily Mud. (*To* FELIX.) I'm sorry, General Whatever, but I've lost my brain.

FELIX: Haha—it's certainly not noticeable!

SKIP: Moving on to screaming, Mr. President—just to reassure our director—I assume it's important to this man what kind of public impression he makes, right?

FELIX: I have no idea; he has refused to say a word since he was caught.

SKIP: —But I should think if he is confident that he is about to . . . like meet his father in heaven, you could put it to him as a test of his faith that he not scream on camera. The camera, you see, tends to magnify everything and screaming on camera could easily seem in questionable taste.

FELIX: I understand. I will certainly try to discuss it with him.

SKIP: He cannot scream on camera, sir; it would destroy the whole effect. And I'm afraid I'll have to go further—I mean, sir, you have deposited our check, right? I mean as a man of honor . . .

FELIX: I will certainly do all I can to convince him not to scream.

HENRI (*turning* FELIX *by the elbow—sotto*): What problem were you talking about?

EMILY: Well let's not nail him, so screaming is not a problem, right? (*To both.*) I said is that right?

SKIP (*to* EMILY): All I'm trying to say, dear . . .

EMILY: Mud. When Emily is sued her name is Mud, so make it Mud, please!

SKIP (*momentarily put down*): I am simply saying that even though he was nailed—the Original, I mean—he is always shown hanging up there in perfect peace.

FELIX: The paintings are not like it is.

SARAH (*still with the phone*): What about the little sign over his head?

SKIP: What sign?

EMILY: Say that's right, they mocked him and stuck this hand-painted sign on the cross over his head—I believe it said "King of the Jews."

SKIP: No!! Absolutely out of the question . . . this has nothing to do with the Jews! Or Jesus either!

HENRI: Excuse me, but it will inevitably have that connotation.

SKIP: Nonsense! This is simply the execution of a violent criminal!

HENRI: Yes, but isn't that what they said the first time?

SARAH (*phone to her ear*): Speaking of Jews, they called him "rabbi," I think.

SKIP: Stop it!—Excuse me, Emily, no reflection on your personal heritage, but I mean, this will run in like Mississippi and even the Middle East, like Egypt . . . we do a lot of business in Egypt and Pakistan, and there's no point irritating the world's largest religion—I mean, from their viewpoint it's bad enough implying the son of god was Christian without making him Jewish, for Heaven's sake.

EMILY: All right, but I'm just saying—he . . . *was* . . .

SKIP: You know it and I know it, dear, but what's the point of rubbing it in worldwide, darling? (*Turning to* FELIX.) Now sir, have you decided what time of the day you are going to . . . ah . . . there's a question of the light, you see.

FELIX: I'm not sure we will be able to proceed today. It is possible, but perhaps not.

SKIP: I don't understand, sir.

FELIX: He's escaped.

EMILY: Our guy?

HENRI (*a clap of his hands*): Felix!

FELIX: He will certainly be captured, there's no question, but it may be a day or two . . .

EMILY (*to the crew*): He's escaped!

CREW: Attaway, baby! Hurray! etc. . . .

SKIP: Shame on you! The man's a criminal! (*To* FELIX.) This is terrible, terrible news, General! CNN, NBC . . .

(*Soldier starts up a screaming chainsaw.*)

FELIX: Para! Esta puta cosa. Para! [English: Stop that goddam thing! I said stop it!]

(*Soldier, dumbfounded, cuts saw.*)

CAPTAIN: No ves que están hablando? [English: Can't you see they're talking?]

(*Soldier salutes in terror.*)

Eres un imbécil? [English: Are you an idiot?]

(*Soldier salutes again.*)

HENRI (*touching* FELIX's *arm*): Listen, Felix . . .

FELIX (*freeing his arm*): I want to offer to pay for the extra time you will be here, Mr. Skip, but he will absolutely be found by tomorrow, maybe tonight.

SKIP: I am only concerned about our exclusivity, any delay is dangerous. (*To the crew.*) I want everyone at the hotel . . .

we meet let's say noon, or make it eleven, and we'll see where
we are. And don't wander off in case he's caught sooner.

FELIX: . . . I believe we will catch him even this afternoon,
maybe.

(*As crew packs, preparing—with uncertainty—to leave, he
turns back to* SKIP.)

Not to worry about the exclusivity, I have the Army blocking the only road up this mountain; no other crew can get
up here.

SKIP: There are helicopters.

FELIX: I have forbidden any takeoffs.

SKIP: What about from over the border?

FELIX: They cross the border they will be shot happily down.

SKIP: Well that's a relief. (*To* EMILY.) How about lunch and let's
talk?

EMILY: I think I'll have a look around the country for a bit . . .

SKIP: Don't go far . . . please. (*To* FELIX.) I'm expecting your
call the moment you have any news, sir.

FELIX: Rest assured.

(SKIP *exits.*)

(*To* EMILY.) Then may I expect you for dinner, Miss Shapiro?
I was serious about your haircut, I find it very moving in a
way that is particularly important to me.

EMILY: A moving haircut!—in that case, yes, I'd love dinner . . .

FELIX: Until tonight then, Miss Shapiro!

(*He gets to the periphery where* HENRI *intercepts him—
intimately.*)

HENRI: What happened?

FELIX: I can't talk about it.

HENRI: Well, how did he get out?

FELIX: He paid off the guards.

HENRI: Where'd he get the money?

FELIX: How the hell would I know!—They're trying to hand
me this bullshit that he walked through the walls. They're
calling him a magician, but he paid them off and I've locked
them all up and I'm going to find that little bastard if I do
nothing else in my life!

(*He starts out;* HENRI *grabs his arm.*)

HENRI: Felix! Do nothing! Thank your lucky stars, it's a blessing.

FELIX (*loudly, angered*): A blessing? It's chaos!—And I'm going to miss my analysis day in Miami!

(FELIX *throws off* HENRI's *hand, goes to* EMILY, *kisses her hand.*)

Again!—Until tonight, Miss Shapiro!

(*With a gallant wave he exits.* HENRI *starts to follow, but halts and turns to* EMILY.)

HENRI: You could stop this, you know.

EMILY: Me!

HENRI: Couldn't you try to dissuade him? Seriously—he can be very affected by good-looking women. He's undergoing psychoanalysis now. I've never known him to be quite this ambivalent about things—last year he'd have shot this man by now. And to be candid, I thought his reaction to meeting you was amazingly genuine . . . I mean his feeling.

EMILY: And he did like my haircut.

HENRI: He's a big baby, you know; his mother nursed him till he was seven.

EMILY: I hope you don't expect me to pick up where she left off.

SARAH (*closing her phone*): I'm pregnant!

EMILY: Oh, Sarah! (*She bursts into tears.*)

SARAH: What's the matter?

(*Taking her hand as she weeps loudly, uncontrolled.*)

Oh Emily, what is it!

EMILY: I'm so glad for you! I mean you look so happy and I'm all fucked up! Kisses Sarah. Drink milk or something . . .

HENRI: I do admire your irony!

EMILY: Yes, I'm famous for it. Miss Irony Mud.—Okay, I'll margarine the General.

HENRI: Thank you, my dear.

EMILY: Tell me, Henri, as a truth-loving philosopher—wouldn't you gladly resign from the human race if only there was another one to belong to?

HENRI: Oh, of course. But are we sure it would be any better?

BLACKOUT

SCENE 3

STANLEY, *an apostle, softly plays a harmonica in* FELIX*'s office. Sneakers, unkempt ponytail, blue denim shirt, backpack.*

FELIX *enters.*

FELIX: Thank you for coming.

STANLEY: Well, I was arrested.

FELIX: What's your name again?

STANLEY: Stanley.

FELIX: You know who I am.

STANLEY: Of course. You're the head.

FELIX: Tha-a-a-t's right, I am the head. I'm told you're very close to him.

STANLEY (*cautiously*): You could say that.

FELIX: Asshole buddies.

STANLEY: . . . I never put it quite that way.

FELIX: I'm told you did some . . . service for us a while back.

STANLEY: I've made some mistakes in my life, that was one of the big ones.

FELIX: We need to know where he is. There's good money in the information.

STANLEY: Thanks, but I really don't need money right now.

FELIX: Then tell me gratis—where is he?

STANLEY: I've no idea. Honest.

FELIX: A neighbor claims he saw him going into your house in the middle of last night.

STANLEY: How did he know it was him?

FELIX: He'd seen him earlier, standing on the corner staring into space for over an hour like a crazy man.

STANLEY: He only stayed with me a little and left.

FELIX: . . . Tell me, does *he* think he's the son of god?

STANLEY: That depends.

FELIX: Really! On what?

STANLEY: Hard to say.

FELIX: Let's put it this way, Stanley, if you're going to fuck around with me we'll be happy to knock your teeth out,

469

starting with the front. This would not be my preference, but we are a military government and I am only one of five officers running things. Now please answer my questions before some really bad personalities get into this. The question is whether he believes he is the son of god.

STANLEY: Some days he's sure of it and then he . . . suddenly can't believe it. I mean it's understandable.

FELIX: Why is it understandable?

STANLEY: Well, a man facing crucifixion'd better be pretty sure what he believes.

FELIX: Why? If he's the son of god crucifixion shouldn't bother him too much.

STANLEY: Yeah, but if it turns out he's not the son of god it'll bother him a lot.

FELIX: What's your opinion? Is he?

STANLEY: . . . I better fill you in before I answer that. I've ruined my life believing in things; I spent two and a half years in India in an ashram; I've been into everything from dope to alcohol to alfalfa therapy to Rolfing to Buddhism to total vegetarianism, which I'm into now. So you ask me do I believe he's the son of god, I have to be honest—yes, I believe he is . . . kind of.

FELIX: Kind of.

STANLEY: Well, with a background like mine how do I know what I'm going to believe next week?

FELIX (*thinks for a moment*): What did you talk about with him last night?

STANLEY: Last night? Well, let's see—women, mainly. They're a mystery to him. Men also, but not as much.

FELIX: He's bisexual?

STANLEY: I would say he's more like . . . tri.

FELIX: Trisexual.

STANLEY: Yes.

FELIX: Well let's see now—there's men, and women, and what?

STANLEY: Well . . . vegetation.

FELIX: He fucks cabbages?

STANLEY: No-no, he loves them.

FELIX: Loves cabbages.

STANLEY: Well they're alive.

FELIX: I see. What about a girlfriend?

STANLEY: Well, yeah, one. But she jumped out of a window recently.

FELIX: . . . You don't mean Henri Schultz's daughter.

STANLEY: Oh, you know him?

FELIX: We're cousins.—So this son of god is banging Schultz's daughter?

STANLEY: I don't think so, frankly. My impression is that it stays kind of—you know—remote. Although I picked him up one morning at her apartment and she looked like a woman who . . . you know . . .

FELIX: Had had it.

STANLEY: But I think it was different. I think he may have just . . . laid down next to her and . . . you know . . . lit up.—Because you know he can just light up and . . .

FELIX: I know, I saw him do it. So you mean if he lights up it makes her . . . ?

STANLEY: Definitely.

FELIX (*truly fascinated*): Huh! That's very interesting. That's one of the most interesting things I've heard lately.—And how long can he stay lit up?

STANLEY: Seems like . . . I don't know . . . a few seconds.

FELIX: Is that all.

STANLEY: Well of course I never actually saw . . .

FELIX: So it could have been longer.

STANLEY: Who knows? I mean . . .

FELIX: Yes. (*Exhales, blows out air.*) This is really amazing. (*Worried but curious.*) I was wondering why Schultz was so fascinated by him.

STANLEY: Oh but I doubt she'd have mentioned Jack to her father.

FELIX: That's his name—Jack?

STANLEY: Well one of them. Jack Brown. But he's got others . . . depending.

FELIX: We believe his name is Juan Manuel Francisco Frederico Ortuga de Oviedo. Although up in the villages some of them call him Ralph.

STANLEY: Possible. He changes names so he won't turn into like . . . you know . . . some kind of celebrity guru.

FELIX: Well, that's unusual, isn't it. Now tell me how he escaped from jail.

STANLEY: I really can't talk about that.

FELIX: How did he get out, Stanley?

STANLEY: He doesn't like people talking about it.

FELIX: About what?

STANLEY (*conflicted, shifts in his chair*): I'm really not comfortable talking about that part of it.

FELIX: I don't want to have to persuade you, Stan. How did he escape?

STANLEY: Well . . . is this something you're insisting on?

FELIX: This is something I'm insisting on.

STANLEY: . . . He went through the walls.
     (*Pause.*)

FELIX: And how did he do that?

STANLEY: You're asking me so I'm telling you, right? He has terrific mind control, he can see space.

FELIX: Anybody can see space.

STANLEY: No. What you see is the borders, like the walls of a room, or mountains. Pure space is only an idea, so he can think it out of existence. But he doesn't want it spread around too much.

FELIX: Why's that?

STANLEY: If he gets known as a magician he thinks it could take away from his main message.

FELIX: Which is what, in a few words?

STANLEY: Well, you know . . . just don't do bad things. Especially when you know they're bad. Which you mostly do.
     (*Pause.*)

FELIX: You like women?

STANLEY: Well I'm . . . yeah, I guess I'm kind of on the horny side.

FELIX: You ever light up with them?

STANLEY: Me? Well there've been times when I almost feel I have, but . . . I guess I've never *blinded* any of them.

FELIX (*some embarrassment*): I want to talk to him, Stanley. For personal reasons.

STANLEY: Well, if he shows up, I'll tell him.

FELIX (*attempting cool*): . . . I want you to emphasize the personal. Let him pick a place and I'll meet him alone.

STANLEY (*realizing*): . . . Oh!

FELIX: I'm interested in discussing the *whole* situation. You understand?

STANLEY: —Okay, I'll tell him.—You want to be any more specific?

FELIX (*hesitates*): . . . No, that's . . . that's about it. (*Suddenly suspicious, hardens.*) He didn't send you to me, did he?
 (STANLEY *looks away.*)
Stanley?
 (*No response.*)
Did he send you?
 (*No response.*)
Why did he send you?
 (*No response.*)
Answer me! Did you get yourself arrested?

STANLEY: It's complicated.—I can't stand the idea of him being . . . you know . . . hurt. So I thought maybe I could talk to you about it.—See, I think in some part of his mind he thinks it would help the people.

FELIX: If he's executed.

STANLEY: Crucified.

FELIX: He wants it.

STANLEY: . . . In a way, maybe.

FELIX: How would it help them?

STANLEY: Well, now that the revolution's practically gone, people are pretty . . . you know . . . cynical about everything.

FELIX: What about it?

STANLEY: To see a man tortured for their sake . . . you know . . . that a man could actually like care that much about anything . . .

FELIX: You're telling me something . . . what are you telling me?—Does he want it or not?

STANLEY: Oh no! No. It's just that . . . you see—(*rapidly overwhelmed by the vision's horror*)—he gets to where he just can't like bear it—

FELIX: Bear what!

STANLEY: Well . . . the horror!

FELIX: What horror, what the hell are you talking about!

STANLEY: Well like—excuse the expression—living in this

country! Like when he takes a walk and sees some—some
guy sending out eight-year-old daughters to work the streets,
or those little kids a couple of weeks ago killing that old man
for his shoes . . . Or, excuse the expression, the Army
opening up on that farmers' demonstration last spring . . .

FELIX: Those people had no permission to . . . !

STANLEY (*more and more stridently*): Well you asked me so I'm
telling you, right? A massacre like that can start him shivering and he can't stop crying! I've seen him go for . . . like
two hours at a time, crying his heart out. Then he stops and
he's cool for a while. We even have fun. Then he sees something and it like hits him again and he begins talking like in
. . . Swedish, sounds like, or Russian or German—he once
told me in a joke that he's trying to find out what language
god understands. Then he falls asleep, and wakes up sounding like anybody else—and that's when he doesn't know.

FELIX: Doesn't know what?

STANLEY: Well . . . whether maybe he really is supposed to
die, and . . . like cause everything to change.—I mean, for
your own sake, sir, I would definitely think about just letting
him go, you know? I mean this can be dangerous!

FELIX: I think you know where he is, Stanley. I asked you in a
nice way, now we'll try something else. (*Goes to the door,
grasps the knob.*)

STANLEY: You going to hurt me?

FELIX: I'm stashing you away until you make up your mind to
lead us to him. And incidentally, there's some hungry live-
stock in there that I don't think you're going to enjoy. Get
in! (FELIX *opens the door and the blinding white light flies out;
he raises his hands to shield his eyes.*) My god, he's back!

(STANLEY *falls to his knees facing the open door.* FELIX *steps
to his desk, presses a button, loud alarm bells go off as he
shouts into his intercom* . . .)

Captain! Come quick, he's back, he's back!

(CAPTAIN *and two soldiers come in on the run.*)

(CAPTAIN *and soldiers rush out through the door.* FELIX
yanks STANLEY *to his feet.*)

Why did he come back? What's this all about, Stanley?

STANLEY (*scared, elevated*): God knows!

FELIX (*grabs* STANLEY, *shakes him*): Answer me! Answer me!

STANLEY (*almost lifted off the floor by the throat*): —I think he just can't make up his mind, that's all—whether he really wants to—like die. I mean it's understandable, right?—
(FELIX *releases him.*)
. . . with this great kind of weather we're having?
(CAPTAIN *and two soldiers back out of the cell doorway; they are trembling, trailing their rifles, staring in at the cell.*)
FELIX: What's this now! (*He rushes to the cell, looks in. Then turns to the soldiers.*) How'd he get out!
(*They are speechless. Whirls about to* STANLEY.)
Talk to me! Why'd he come back! Why'd he escape?
STANLEY: I don't know! . . . Maybe to get your mind off me? I mean . . . it's possible, right?—for a friend?

BLACKOUT

Café table. HENRI *seated with a bottle of water and glass.* SKIP *enters, looking about.*

HENRI: Mr. Cheeseboro!

SKIP: Hi. (*Sitting.*) I don't have much time. What can you tell me?

HENRI: Can I order something?

SKIP: I'll have to leave in a few minutes.

HENRI: No news, I take it.

SKIP: Nothing. And you?

HENRI (*a shake of the head*): I thought an exchange of ideas could be useful—the two of us, quietly . . .

SKIP (*slaps his own cheeks then lets his head hang*): I'm beginning to smell the dead-dog stink of disaster. (*Straightens up.*) Tell me—why'd the General let this man escape?

HENRI: It was a complete surprise to him. I spoke to him shortly after it happened; he was absolutely shocked . . .

SKIP: But he had him locked in a cell.—We've made a large down-payment, you know. . . . Or may one appeal to logic in this country?

HENRI: This is why I thought you and I ought to talk.

SKIP: About what?

HENRI: Have you any interest in history? Or philosophy? Where did you go to school?

SKIP: Princeton. But my interest was business, frankly. No philosophy, no culture, mainly the market.

HENRI: Oh, but poetry and the stock market have a lot in common, you know.

SKIP: *Poetry and the market!*

HENRI: Oh yes. They are both based on rules that the success-ful never obey.—A few years ago I spent some time in Egypt . . . you've probably been there?

SKIP: Egypt?—I've shot commercials all over Egypt . . . Chrysler, Bayer Aspirin, Viagra . . .

HENRI: . . . Then you know some of the wall paintings and sculpture.

SKIP: Of course.—What's this about?

HENRI: I want to tell you about a surprising discovery I made there. I am far from expert on the subject, but . . .

SKIP: What are you, a businessman or an academic?

HENRI: I retired from the pharmaceuticals business some years ago. I still breed fighting bulls but I'm getting out of that too; I'm basically a scholar now. In Egypt . . .

SKIP (*takes out a cell phone and punches numbers from notebook*): Excuse me.

HENRI: If you're making a local call . . .

SKIP: The General's office. To tell him I'm here.

HENRI: Doubt that'll work . . . (*glances at watch*) . . . this close to lunch.

SKIP: Good god, why don't they fix it?

HENRI: They? There is no "they" here; hasn't been in most of the world since the fall of Rome.

SKIP (*snaps his phone shut*): What can you tell me about this guy's escape?

HENRI: —I know how absurd this is going to sound, but I ask you to hear me out. (*Slight pause.*) I had a very distinct feeling at the time they found him gone, that he had never been in that cell.

SKIP: But they had him, they'd captured him.

HENRI: They believed that, yes.

SKIP: What are you talking about?

HENRI (*considers*): . . . It struck me one day in Egypt . . .

SKIP (*starting to rise*): Look, I have no interest in Egypt . . .

HENRI (*voice hardly raised*): This may save your neck, Mr. Cheeseboro! Do sit; please.—

    (SKIP *goes still.*)

It struck me one day; that there were lots of images of the peoples the Egyptians had conquered, but none showing Jewish captives. I am far from expert in the subject but I couldn't find more than one or two menorah—candelabra —a vague star of David . . . almost nothing, really. Which is terribly strange when the Jews are supposed to have drowned the whole Egyptian army, don't you think? And Joseph was the Pharaoh's chief adviser and so on? It would be, let's say, like writing the history of Japan with no mention of the atomic bomb.—

SKIP: But what is the connection with . . . ?

HENRI: One day the thought hit me—could the whole story of
    the Jews in Egypt have simply been a poem? More or less
    like Homer describing magical cattle, and ravenous women
    and so on? Ancient peoples saw no difference between a
    vivid description of marvels and what we call reality—for
    them the description itself *was* the reality. In short, the Jews
    may never have been literally enslaved in Egypt; or perhaps
    some had been, but the story as we know it may have been
    largely fictional, an overwhelmingly powerful act of the
    imagination.

SKIP: If you're telling me this guy doesn't exist, I'm . . .

HENRI: That depends on what you mean by "exist"; he cer-
    tainly exists in the mind of the desperately poor peasant—he
    is the liberator; for the General his crucifixion will power-
    fully reinforce good order, so he must exist . . . and I
    know a suicidal young woman of high intelligence who in-
    sists that he has restored her will to live, so for her he cer-
    tainly exists. And needless to say, for you, of course . . . his
    execution will sell some very expensive advertising, so you
    are committed to his existing.

SKIP: But he can't be imaginary, the General spoke with him.

HENRI: Not quite. According to the General the fellow never
    said a single word. Not one. The General spoke *at* him.

SKIP: But didn't I hear of this . . . apostle of his they've just
    jailed? *He's* certainly spoken with him.

HENRI: A fellow named Stanley, yes. I understand he is a drug
    addict. I needn't say more; he could be put away for the rest
    of his life unless he cooperates. Drug-taking is a felony in
    this country.

SKIP: Really. But they export tons of it.

HENRI: They do indeed. The logic is as implacable as it is be-
    yond anyone's comprehension.

SKIP: Then what are you telling me?—Because you've gotta
    believe it, the money we paid the General is not a poem.

HENRI: But it may turn into one as so many other important
    things have done. The Vietnam War, for example, began . . .

SKIP: The Vietnam War!

HENRI: . . . Which was set off, mind you, by a night attack upon a United States warship by a Vietnamese gunboat in the Gulf of Tonkin. It's now quite certain the attack never happened. This was a fiction, a poem; but fifty-six thousand Americans and two million Vietnamese had to die before the two sides got fed up reciting it.

SKIP: But what is this light . . . not that I'm sure I believe it . . . but he emits a light, I'm told.

HENRI: Yes. I saw it.

SKIP: You saw it!

HENRI: At the time I thought I did, yes. But I was primed beforehand by my two days in the upper villages where everyone is absolutely convinced he is god—so as I approached that cell door my brain *demanded* an astonishment and I believe I proceeded to create one.

SKIP: Meaning what?

HENRI: Mr. Cheeseboro, I have spent a lifetime trying to free myself from the boredom of reality.—Needless to say, I have badly hurt some people dear to me—as those who flee reality usually do. So what I am about to tell you has cost me. —I am convinced now apart from getting fed, most human activity—sports, opera, TV, movies, dressing up, dressing down—or just going for a walk—has no other purpose than to deliver us into the realm of the imagination. The imagination is a great hall where death, for example, turns into a painting, and a scream of pain becomes a song. The hall of the imagination is really where we usually live; and this is all right except for one thing—to enter that hall one must leave one's real sorrow at the door and in its stead surround oneself with images and words and music that mimic anguish but are really drained of it—no one has ever lost a leg from reading about a battle, or died of hearing the saddest song. (*Close to tears.*) And this is why . . .

SKIP: I don't see why . . .

HENRI (*overriding*): . . . This is why this man must be hunted down and crucified; because—*he still really feels everything*. Imagine, Mr. Cheeseboro, if that kind of reverence for life should spread! Governments would collapse, armies disband, marriages disintegrate! Wherever we turned, our dead unfeeling shallowness would stare us in the face until we shriveled up with shame! No!—better to hunt him down and kill him and leave us in peace.

SKIP: . . . You're addressing me, aren't you.

HENRI: Oh, and myself, I assure you a thousand, thousand times myself.

SKIP: On the other hand, shallow as I am I have twins registered at Andover; maybe some need to be shallow so that some can be deep. (*He starts to rise.*)

HENRI: Please! Go home!

SKIP: I can't go home until this job is done!

HENRI: You could tell your company there was nothing here to photograph! It was all imaginary, a poem!

SKIP: It's impossible, I can't pull out of this. (*Starts off.*)

HENRI: I hope you won't take offense!

(SKIP *halts, turns, curious.*)

Our generals are outraged, a cageful of tigers roaring for meat! *Somebody* may get himself crucified—and not necessarily a man who has done anything. Do you want the responsibility for helping create that injustice!

SKIP: I've been trying hard not to resent you, Mr. Schultz, but this I resent.—I am not "creating" anything! I am no more responsible for this situation than Matthew, Mark, Luke and John were for Jesus' torture!

HENRI: But Jesus was already long dead when they wrote about him, he was beyond harm!

SKIP: Well, I can't see the difference.

HENRI: But Mr. Cheeseboro, this man is still alive!

SKIP: We are recording a preexisting fact, Mr. Schultz, not creating it—I create nothing!

HENRI: But the fortune you've paid the General has locked him into this monstrous thing! Your money is critical in his decision!

SKIP (*exploding*): You have utterly wasted my time! (*He exits.*)

HENRI: And so the poem continues, written in someone's blood, and my country sinks one more inch into the grass, into the jungle, into the everlasting sea.

BLACKOUT

SCENE 5

Darkness. A moon. A palm tree. Light rises, gradually revealing a candelabra on a café table, with FELIX *and* EMILY *eating lobsters and drinking wine.*

At all the dim edges of the stage, riflemen sit crouched, weapons at the ready, backs to the couple.

Music; very distant strains of a guitar and singers serenading.

EMILY: I've never in my life eaten three lobsters.

FELIX: But they're very small, no?

EMILY: Even so.

FELIX: Of course, small things can be better than big sometimes.

EMILY: Oh? (*Catches on.*) Oh, of course, yes!

FELIX: I beg you to forgive my forwardness.

EMILY: Not at all—I like it.

FELIX: I can't help myself, I am desperate for you not to slip away.

    (*They eat in silence, sucking the lobster legs.*)

EMILY: You're a contradictory person, aren't you?

FELIX: I have never thought so; why am I contradictory?

EMILY: Well, you seem so tough, but you're also very sentimental.

FELIX: Perhaps, yes. But with very few people. This is a hard country to govern.

EMILY: —I must say, your face seems softer than when we met.

FELIX: Possibly because something grips my imagination as we converse.

EMILY: Grips your imagination?

FELIX: Your body.—I beg you to forgive my frankness, it's because I am sure, Emily, that I could . . . how shall I say . . . function with you.

EMILY (*equivocally*): Well now . . .

FELIX: How fantastic—you are blushing!

    (*She laughs nervously.*)

    My god, how your spirit speaks to me! There is something

sacred in you, Emily—for for me it's as though you descended from the air. —I must sound like I have lost my mind, but could you stay on some weeks? Or months? I have everything here for you . . .

EMILY: I'm afraid I have too many obligations at home. And I'm going to have to get busy saving my career. (*Pointedly.*) . . . Unless you'd decide to do what I asked.

FELIX: I beg you, my dear, you can't ask me to call off the search. The General Staff would never stand for it . . .

EMILY: But if you insisted . . .

FELIX: It's impossible; the honor of the Armed Forces is at stake. This man is trying to make fools of us.

EMILY (*reaches out and touches his cheek. Surprised, he instantly grasps her hand and kisses her palm*): Why do I think you don't want to catch him, Felix . . . you personally?

FELIX (*cradles his face in her palm*): . . . To tell you the truth I'm not sure anymore what I want.

EMILY: . . . Just out of curiosity, you really think my haircut started it?

FELIX: Oh yes, absolutely, it went straight to my heart.

EMILY: Imagine. And here I was thinking it was too short.

FELIX: No—no, it's perfect! I had one look and it was as though I . . . I was rising from the dead.

EMILY: . . . Could we talk about that?

FELIX: About what, my dear?

EMILY: The . . . ah . . . difficulty you have that you've been . . . alluding to.

FELIX (*fear and eager curiosity*): What about it?

EMILY: . . . Unless you don't feel . . .

FELIX (*steeling himself; deeply curious*): . . . No—no, of course not, I have no fear!

EMILY: Well, what I think, is that you have to seem invulnerable to the world, and so you suppress your feelings.

FELIX: I am running a country, Emily, I cannot expose my feelings to . . .

EMILY: I know, but that suppression has spread down and down and down . . . (*running her finger up his arm and down his chest*) until it's finally clobbered . . . your willy. (*Quickly.*) You're simply going to have to let your feelings out, Felix, is all I'm saying.

FELIX (*aroused and confused*): I am . . . I am . . . I . . . I
. . . (*disarming himself*) . . . must talk to you . . . I can
come to New York, I have money there and an apartment . . .

EMILY: Why wait? Like if you feel you really don't wish to pur-
sue this fellow, just don't do it and see what happens.

FELIX: Darling, the General Staff would tear me apart, they are
hungry lions . . .

EMILY (*reaches for his hand*): Felix dear . . . I don't know
where this is going between us, but I must tell you now—if
you go through with this outrage you'll have to find yourself
another girl.—Not that I'm promising anything in any case.

FELIX: But what are your feelings toward me? You never speak
of them.

EMILY: I like a man to be a man, Felix—which you are. And I
have enormous curiosity.

FELIX: About men.

EMILY: Yes. Powerful men, especially . . . to tell the truth.

FELIX: About what in particular?

EMILY: Well, frankly, for one thing—how they are making love.

FELIX: I have never known a woman with such courage to
speak her mind.

EMILY: One needs it when one is not marvelous to look at.

FELIX (*kisses her hand*): You are more marvelous to look at
than . . . than six mountains and a waterfall!

EMILY: That's very sweet of you, Felix.—I'd love to walk along
the beach. Could we, without all these guards?

FELIX: I'm afraid not. But come, we can take a few steps
through the garden.

(*They walk together.*)

EMILY: Who exactly would want to kill you, Communists?

FELIX: The Party is split on this question. One side thinks
somebody worse would replace me if I am eliminated.

EMILY: And I suppose the Right Wing people love you . . .

FELIX: Not all—some of them think I am not hard enough on
the Communists . . . those might take a shot at me too.
Then there are the narco-guerillas; with some we have an
arrangement, it's no secret, but there are others who are not
happy for various reasons.

EMILY: It all seems so utterly, utterly futile. Or do you mind?

(*He halts, holds her hand.*)

FELIX: I mind very much, in these hours since I know you. Very much. You have made me wish that I could live differently.

EMILY: Really!

FELIX: Emily, I will confess to you—when I imagine myself making love to you, entering into you, I . . . I almost hear a choir.

EMILY: A choir! Really, Felix, that is beautiful!

(FELIX *suddenly turns away, covering his eyes.*)

What is it? You all right? Felix?

(FELIX *straightens up, grasps her hand, kisses it, holds it to his cheek.*)

What is it?

FELIX: I will divorce.

EMILY (*blurting*): Oh no, you mustn't do that! . . . I mean you're a Catholic, aren't you?

FELIX: I am ready to go to hell! I cannot lose you!

EMILY: But my dear, I'm not prepared for . . . I assume you're talking commitment?

FELIX (*striking his chest*): You have exploded in my mind like a grenade! I have never had such a feeling . . . it is like all my windows have blown out and a fresh breeze is passing through me . . . I must not let you go, Emily—what can I give you! Anything! Tell me!

EMILY: Ralph!

FELIX: Ralph?

EMILY: Let him go!

FELIX (*at the height of tension—dives*): That is what you truly wish?

EMILY: Oh yes, Felix—yes! It would solve everything for me! And he sounds like such a dear person!

FELIX: And you will surely see me in New York.

EMILY: Of course, I'll be happy to!—I mean not necessarily on a permanent basis . . . I mean I travel a lot, but . . . yes, of course!

FELIX: All right, then—it is done!

EMILY: Done! Oh, Felix, I'm overwhelmed!

FELIX: I have fallen in love with you, Emily! Come—let me take you to my best house.

EMILY: Your best?

FELIX (*solemnly*): It was my mother's. I have never brought anyone there before. It is sacred to me. I haven't been there since I was seven.

EMILY: That's very touching. But first could we go into the mountains? I would like to see one of those high villages where they love this Ralph fellow so. It's just an experience I've never had, have you?—to walk in a place full of love? (*Up close to him, face raised.*) Take me there, Felix?

FELIX (*sensing her distant surrender*): My god, woman—yes, anything! Come . . . come to the mountains!

(*He grips her hand and they hurry off with all the guards following, their heads revolving in all directions in the search for killers.*)

BLACKOUT

SCENE 6

JEANINE *rises from her wheelchair with help of a cane, and walks with a limp to a point.* HENRI *enters, stands, astonished.*

HENRI: Jeanine!
    (*She turns to him.*)
JEANINE: I don't understand it. I woke up, and I was standing.
HENRI: And the pain?
JEANINE: It seems much less. For the moment anyway.
HENRI: This is absolutely astonishing, Jeanine. This is marvelous! How did this happen?
JEANINE: The lightning this morning shot a lot of electricity into the air—
HENRI: —Could that have affected you?
JEANINE (*cryptically*): I . . . don't know, really.
    (*Pause.* HENRI *settles in.*)
HENRI: I'm sorry, dear, but we have to talk about Felix.
JEANINE: Oh god, why?
HENRI: He called me this morning—woke me at dawn. He's convinced you can lead him to this god-fellow.
    (JEANINE *is silent.*)
  He'll be here to see you this morning. He insisted. (*Coming to his point.*) . . . Do you know a fellow named Stanley?
JEANINE (*hedging*): Stanley.
HENRI: They have him.
    (*She stiffens.*)
  He has apparently told Felix you and this . . . god-fellow are lovers.
    (*She is silent.*)
  Felix is convinced you would know where to find him.
JEANINE: Papa, I have no way of contacting this man, so let's just forget it, will you?
HENRI (*a moment; swallows resentment*): According to Felix this Stanley fellow has hinted that your friend may actually welcome crucifixion. In order to accomplish his . . . whatever it is . . . his mission.
    (JEANINE *is silent.*)

In any case, I'm not sure I can keep you from being arrested for harboring him and failing to turn him in.

JEANINE: But how can I turn him in! I don't know how to contact him!

HENRI: . . . For one thing, darling—how shall I put it?—he clearly had to have been here last night . . .

JEANINE: Why!

HENRI (*patience gone*): Well look at you! Felix is not stupid, Jeanine—he knows your spine was crushed, it could only have been this man's hand on you that has brought you to life like this!

JEANINE: . . . You believe then!?

HENRI: . . . I don't know what I believe! I only know that Felix intends to kill this man and that can't be allowed to happen!

JEANINE: Oh Papa, why do you go on caring so much when you know you will never act! You'll never stand up to these murderers!

HENRI: Act how! Who do I join! How can you go on repeating that political nonsense? There is no politics anymore, Jeanine—if you weren't so tough-minded you'd admit it! There is nothing, my dear, nothing but one's family, if one can call that a faith.

JEANINE: Late one night you came into my room and sat down on my bed. There was a storm. Tremendous! The wind broke limbs off the oak behind the house. It groaned, like pieces of the sky breaking off! And you said you had decided to go into the mountains and join the guerillas to fight against Felix! Lightning seemed to flash around your head, Papa. You were like a mountain, sitting there. At last you would do something, at last you would answer the idiots and fight against Felix! And I knew I would follow you . . . and high up in the mountains I found you in your tent with a rifle on your lap, reading Spinoza.

HENRI: The world will never again be changed by heroes; if I misled you I apologize to the depths of my heart. One must learn to live in the garden of one's self.

JEANINE: Even if one has seen god?

HENRI: . . . Then you really do believe?

JEANINE: I think so, yes.

HENRI: Very well. I'm glad.

JEANINE: You are!

HENRI: I'm happy for the love I see in you, my dear, your hair flowing so gently around your face, and the softness that I haven't seen in so many years in the corners of your eyes. I love you, Jeanine, and if it's he who brought you back to life . . . —Why not? I think now it is no more impossible than the rest of this dream we live in. (*Glances at watch.*)—Felix will be here soon. I'll wait with you, is that all right?

(*She suddenly weeps; he goes to his knees beside her.*)

(*Embracing her*): Oh my darling, my darling . . . !

(*Enter* FELIX, *with* EMILY—*her hand tucked under his arm.* HENRI *springs up.*)

Felix! Miss Shapiro! Good morning! Miss Shapiro, this is my daughter, Jeanine.

FELIX (*going to* JEANINE *in surprise*): Why Jeanine, how wonderfully well you look! My god, this is amazing—what's happened?

HENRI: Nothing. She often has more energy in the mornings.

FELIX: We must talk, Jeanine . . .

HENRI: She's really not up to it, Felix.

FELIX: There's a couple of things I'd like this man to understand. It's important.

HENRI: But she has no contact with him.

FELIX: Well, if you happen to see him—

HENRI (*glancing from one to the other*): —Something's happened, hasn't it . . . with you.

EMILY: Oh yes! We hardly slept all night.

HENRI: How nice!

EMILY: Yes . . . it was.

HENRI: Well! May one congratulate the old dog?

FELIX: Definitely!—he's back hunting over hill and dale. This is the strangest twenty-four hours I've ever been through. (*Drapes an arm around* EMILY.) . . . She wanted to drive up and look around in the villages . . .

EMILY: It's like walking on the sky up there—the purity of the sunbeams . . . that strangely warm, icy air . . .

FELIX: It's been years since I was up there in our last campaigns. I was absolutely amazed—his picture really is everywhere in the villages. They paint halos around his head. I

had no idea of the devotion of the people—it's a real phenomenon, he's like a saint. (*To* HENRI): You remember,
Henri—that whole back country was always so . . . what's
the word . . . ?

HENRI: Depressing.

EMILY: They've taken out the ancient instruments that nobody
has played for years, and they dance the old dances again.
. . . It was so absolutely delightful, we didn't want to leave.

JEANINE: Then you've decided what?—not to kill him?

FELIX: I must have a meeting with him. I was hoping you
could arrange it.

HENRI (*instantly*): She really has no idea where he . . .

FELIX (*charmingly to* JEANINE): One thing I'm never wrong
about is the face of a satisfied woman.—When he comes to
you again I would like him to understand the following: I
have talked to a number of his people now and they say he
has always told them to live in peace. Some of my own people say otherwise but I'm willing to leave it at that. What I
want him to consider—I mean eventually, of course—is a
place in the government.

JEANINE: In *your* government? *Him?*

FELIX: I'm serious. The military is not as stupid as maybe we've
sometimes looked, Jeanine. We must get ready for some
kind of democracy, now that the revolution is finished. He
could help us in that direction.

JEANINE: I'd doubt that.

EMILY: He's released Stanley.

JEANINE: Really.

FELIX: Stanley's agreed to deliver my message to your friend,
but I don't know how much weight he carries with him. I
would feel better if you spoke to him yourself.

JEANINE: But I know his answer. He will tell you to resign.

FELIX: Resign.

JEANINE: —Let's be honest, Felix; this man is full of love—I
think you realize that now, don't you; all he is is love. But we
aren't. I'm not and neither are you. You've killed too many
of us to forget so quickly.

FELIX: I have changed, Jeanine. This woman has opened my
eyes.

JEANINE (*to* EMILY): Imagine!—in one night!

FELIX: No, not one night; I've been thinking about it for some time now . . . that we've been fighting each other almost since I was born. It has wasted us all. I want a normal country. Where people can walk safely in the streets at night; sleep in peace, build a house . . . I can't tell you how exactly it happened, but this woman has made me wonder—maybe if your friend could help us begin to come together I am ready to give it a try. (*He sees she is not convinced.*) What can I do to prove I have changed, Jeanine?

EMILY (*to* JEANINE): I have an idea . . . suppose he announced on television that your friend was no longer a wanted man?

FELIX: Excuse me, dear—I can't do that unless he agrees in advance to disarm *his* people . . .

JEANINE: He personally has not armed anybody . . .

FELIX (*composure rattling*): Now look, dear . . .

JEANINE: Don't call me dear!—Why can't you make that announcement?

FELIX: They have tons of hidden arms, goddamit!

EMILY (*to* FELIX): Don't, darling, please . . .

FELIX (*to* EMILY, *indignantly*): No! I can't pretend I am dealing with Jesus Christ here! I'm trying my best but the man is not just a hippie, he's also a guerilla . . . !

EMILY (*patting his head*): And he has also managed to walk through your prison wall.

FELIX: So what?—am I supposed to have an explanation for everything?

HENRI: Felix, listen; if you announce that he is no longer a wanted man you take the moral high ground, and if . . .

FELIX: Do we have laws or not? There's a homicide sentence on the man! In return for what am I lifting his sentence? (*His anger returning.*) I am not turning this government into a farce! I'm asking you, will he promise to keep the peace?—

JEANINE: But shouldn't you promise first? You have the tanks.

FELIX: Yes, I have the tanks and he doesn't, so he's the one who has to make the promises!

JEANINE: Well now!—So much for all this high spiritual change you've gone through . . .

HENRI: I have an idea; for just this moment, right now, try to think of this problem as though you did not have a gun.

FELIX: Right. Okay, I'm ready! You want me to talk?—here I am. (*To* JEANINE.) So where is he? (*Slaps his hips.*) No guns! I'm all ears! Where's god?

(STANLEY *enters.*)

JEANINE: Stanley!

(STANLEY *comes and embraces her.*)

STANLEY: How you doin', Jeanie, you're lookin' good.

JEANINE: Is . . . everything all right?

FELIX: Have you spoken with him?

STANLEY: . . . Here's the thing. (*Pause.*) What it all comes down to is—he's having big trouble making up his mind.

HENRI: About . . . ?

STANLEY: Getting crucified.

FELIX: What's his problem?

STANLEY: Well . . . if he doesn't, will people feel he's let them down?

JEANINE: I'm surprised at you, Stanley; his deciding to be crucified is not going to depend on whether he's disappointing people's expectations!

STANLEY: He is serious about changing the world, Jeanie, everything he does he's got to think of the effect on people. What's wrong with that?

JEANINE: What's wrong is that it changes him into one more shitty politician! Whatever he does he'll do because it's right, not to get people's approval!

FELIX: So where does that leave matters? (*Violently.*) . . . And try not to use so many words, will you?

STANLEY: My candid, rock bottom opinion?

FELIX: What.

STANLEY: Ignore him.

HENRI: Brilliant.

FELIX: I can't ignore him, he's broken the law, he's . . .

STANLEY: General, I don't have to tell you, even now up in the villages the crime rate's been dropping since he showed up, people are getting ready for heaven, right? A lot of them like starting to boil the water, right? And much less garbage in the street and whitewashing their houses and brushing their teeth—and the number screwing their daughters is like way down, you know.—In other words, this is a very good thing he got going for you, so how about just turning your attention . . . elsewhere?

HENRI: Brilliant. Absolutely brilliant.

FELIX: And will he "turn his attention elsewhere"? His people will go right on agitating against me, won't they. As though I had nothing to do but go around murdering people; as though I'd done nothing to improve the country, as though the British are not building two hotels, and the Dutch and Japanese weren't starting to talk to us. . . . What the hell more does he want of me!

STANLEY: Well for one thing . . . I don't know like maybe let's say, if you like stopped—you know, like knocking off union organizers . . .

FELIX: I have no outstanding orders against organizers!

JEANINE: Of course not, they're all dead.

FELIX: I'm sorry, decent people don't join unions!

EMILY: I'm in a union.

FELIX: *You!*

EMILY (*smoothing his cheek*): Don't take it to heart, dear, it's only the Directors Guild of America.

FELIX: I can't believe this, Emily . . . *you* are in a *union*?

EMILY: Felix dear, you really do have to start thinking differently . . .

FELIX (*furious*): How can I think differently if nobody else is thinking differently?—So where are we, Stanley—the war goes on? Yes or no?

STANLEY: . . . Could I please ask a favor, General? Would you leave us alone for a couple minutes?

FELIX: No! We've got to settle this!

STANLEY: I can't talk to her otherwise, okay?

EMILY: There's nothing to lose, dear. (*Holding out her hand to him.*) Come. Let's both have a glass of water.

FELIX (*hesitates*): . . . But I hope we understand each other.

STANLEY: We do, sir, just give me five.

EMILY: Come, Felix dear.

FELIX (*sotto, as she leads him off*): I don't know why everybody's being so fucking stupid!

(FELIX *and* EMILY *leave.* HENRI *starts to move.*)

STANLEY: You can stay if you want—it's just I didn't want to say it in front of him but in my personal opinion this thing is getting pretty nasty out there—

JEANINE: Nasty how?

STANLEY: A lot of the folks—they don't say it out loud, but they're hoping their village will be picked.

JEANINE: Picked?

STANLEY: For the crucifixion.

HENRI (*grips his head*): Oh my god!—why!

STANLEY: Well—like you know the honor of it and . . . well, the ah . . . property values.

JEANINE: *Property* values!

STANLEY: Well, face it, once it's televised they'll be jamming in from the whole entire world to see where it happened. Tour buses bumper to bumper across the Andes to get to see his bloody drawers? Buy a souvenir fingernail, T-shirts, or one of his balls? It's a whole tax base thing, Jeanie, y'know? Like maybe a new school, roads, swimming pool, maybe even a casino and theme park—all that shit. I don't have to tell you, baby, these people have *nothing*.

HENRI: We are living in hell.

STANLEY: Well yes and no; I think he figures it could also like give people some kind of hope for themselves.

JEANINE (*incredulously*): *Hope*? From seeing a man crucified?!

STANLEY: From seeing somebody who means it when he says he loves them, honey. So that's why—at least when I left him—he's like thinking death.

JEANINE (*bursts into tears*): Oh god . . .

STANLEY: —So what I'm hoping . . . can I tell you?—Cause you're the only one he'd possibly listen to . . . I guess because you tried to die yourself.

(JEANINE *lifts her eyes to him.*)

. . . I really wish you'd tell him he's got to live . . . and just maybe forget about . . . you know, being god. I mean even if he is.

(JEANINE *moans in pain.*)

We've got to face it, Jeanie, in a couple weeks people forget, you know? Nothing much lasts anymore, and if they nail him up it'll eventually blow away like everything else. I mean he's just got to . . .

JEANINE: . . . Give up his glory.

STANLEY: Maybe not quite—he's already waked up a lot of people that things don't have to be this way. He could settle for that.—You're the only one who could save him, Jeanie. Please, for all of us. Make him live.

HENRI: And of course, to return to basics, we still don't know for sure . . . who and what he really is, do we.
    (*Pause.*)

JEANINE: Do we know, Stanley? Tell me the truth.

STANLEY: Oh, Jeanie, I wish I knew! Some days it's like he walked straight out of the ocean or a cloud or a bush full of roses. Other days . . . (*Shrugs.*) . . . he smells a lot like anybody else.

JEANINE: Then what do you want me to say to him, exactly?

STANLEY: . . . I think he has to . . . well . . . agree to a deal that if Felix will stop persecuting people he'll . . . you know . . . disappear.

JEANINE: Forever?

STANLEY: Well . . . I guess so . . . yeah.

JEANINE: I'm to ask him not to be god.

STANLEY: No—no, he could be god like . . . in a more general inspirational way. I mean the actual improvements would just have to be up to us, that's all.

HENRI: Wonderful! He's still god but he goes away and there's no bloodbath! Peace!

JEANINE: And each for himself.

HENRI: Peace! Or the country is done, finished, a heap of bones!
    (*Long pause.*)

JEANINE (*to* STANLEY): All right, I want him alive. We haven't the greatness to deserve his death.—I just hope I never hear that he's mowing the lawn.

STANLEY: Nobody's pure, baby—if that's what's bothering you . . .

JEANINE: So if he comes again. . . . Tell me what to say.

STANLEY: . . . Just say . . . like—"Charley darling . . ."

JEANINE: Charley?

STANLEY: He changed it last night. Said it was really Charley from now on, not Jack. Although he's changed it on me a dozen times. Vladimir once, Francisco . . . Herby for a week or two . . . Just say, like . . .

(*The light comes on, but dimly. He looks about. A music very distant, subliminal.*)

Charley? Is that you?

(*The light brightens sharply. All straighten, look slightly upward.*)

(FELIX *enters with* EMILY.)

FELIX (*feeling the air*): Something is happening . . . !

STANLEY: Ssh—please!

FELIX: Who are you telling to sshh!

EMILY (*end of her patience*): For god's sake, will you control yourself! (*To* STANLEY, *pointing up to the light.*) Is that . . . ?

STANLEY: I think so.

JEANINE (*facing upward*): How I love you, darling. Now please, please listen to me!

FELIX (*looking about combatively*): Well where is he, goddamit!

EMILY (*pointing up*): The light, dear, the light!

FELIX (*realizing now, looking up with dawning fear*): Holy shi . . .

STANLEY (*upward*): I've got an idea, baby, if you'd like to consider it.

JEANINE: Whatever you decide you are my life and my hope, darling.

STANLEY: You've like turned the country inside out, you know? There's lots of changes since you showed up . . . compared, you know? So maybe, just as—you know, a suggestion —we're thinking maybe the best thing right now, would be for you to . . . just let it hang the way it is. Stand pat. Don't make your move, you know? Bleiben sie ruhig, baby; vaya con calme; ne t'en fais pas; spokoine-e gospodin; nin bu yao jaoji—dig?

(*As* SKIP, *the two soldiers, and the crew all appear, looking up and about.*)

SKIP: We've got thirty-five minutes of sun . . . where is he?

FELIX (*finger raised*): Ssh—that's him!

SKIP (*looking up*): What's him?

JEANINE (*to the air*): Adore you, darling.

FELIX (*to* STANLEY): Are you talking to him or not?

STANLEY: I'm not sure, I think so.

FELIX: Tell him I'll call off the search and we can forget the whole thing if he goes away and never comes back!

SKIP: Goes away!—we have a contract, sir!

JEANINE (*furious*): And empty the jails, of course. And the torturers are to be prosecuted!

FELIX: What torturers?

JEANINE (*to Heaven*): Come down, Charley!

FELIX (*to Heaven*): Wait!! Hold it!—Okay, you stay up there indefinitely, and I'll . . . fire the torturers.

SKIP: This is a contractual breach!—he's got to come down!

FELIX (*to* SKIP, *retrieving authority*): . . . Will you shut up? I've still got him under arrest, don't I?!

STANLEY: . . . That's about it, Charley, okay? I mean we're going to miss you, baby, especially those fantastic conversations on the beach, but . . . you know, maybe it's all for the best, right? I mean, could you give us a sign?

Maybe you tell him, Jeanie, could you?

JEANINE: Oh my dear, my darling, it cuts my heart to say this but I think maybe you better not come back! I'm going to miss you terribly, nothing will be the same . . . but I guess you really have to go!

STANLEY: I'm not trying to rush you, baby, but can we have some kind of an answer?

SKIP: Just a minute, I'd like a word with him. (*Comes down, center—sotto.*) What's his latest name again?

STANLEY: Charley.

SKIP (*looking up*): Charles? You simply have to return, there's no question about it. I will only remind you that my agency has a signed contract with this government to televise your crucifixion and we have paid a substantial sum of money for the rights. I will forebear mentioning our stockholders, many of them widows and aged persons, who have in good faith bought shares in our company. I plead with you as a responsible, feeling person—show yourself and serve your legal sentence. I want to assure you that everyone from the top of my company to the bottom will be everlastingly grateful and will mourn your passing all the days of our lives. —A practical note: the sun is rapidly going down so may I have the favor of a quick reply? Thank you very much.

(*All look about expectantly, but nothing happens.*)

FELIX (*stepping up to the center*): Now listen, Charley, I'm

having some second thoughts about this deal I mentioned—
you just have to come down and get crucified.

JEANINE: You just promised not to . . . !

FELIX: The country's desperate! If he stays up there I will have
to return some of the money!

SKIP: All of it, General.

FELIX: Well, we'll discuss that.

JEANINE: So much for your word!

FELIX (*to* JEANINE): That money will mean hundreds of
jobs . . . ! (*Upward.*) I'm planning on school upgrading,
health clinics, lots of improvements for the folks. Whereas if
I have to return some of the money . . .

SKIP: All of it!

FELIX: I am not returning that goddam money!

(EMILY *steps up.*)

EMILY: May I, Skip?

(SKIP *steps aside, gesturing to her to move in. She looks up.*)
I'm afraid I have to differ with my friend Skip, and my dear
friend General Barriaux.—Wherever you are, Charley, I beg
you stay there.

FELIX: This is terrible stuff you're telling the man! You are
condemning this country to ruin!

EMILY (*persisting to the light*): Don't make me photograph you
hanging from two sticks, I beg you, Charley! Stay where you
are and you will live in all our imaginations where the great
images never die. Wish you all the best, my dear . . . be
well!

FELIX (*to the light*): All right now, just listen to me . . .

HENRI (*to the light*): Whoever you are!—I thank you for my
daughter's return to life. And before your loving heart I
apologize for ignoring her for so many years, and for having
led her in my blind pride to the brink of destruction.

PHIL: Speaking for the crew—(*sees* SKIP *react*) . . . this is not
a strike! (*To the light.*) But we'd appreciate it a lot if you, you
know, just didn't show. . . . (*Sees* SKIP *react.*) We're ready
to go as the contract calls for! But . . . (*upward*) well,
that's the message.

SKIP (*upward*): Now look here, Charles—we have fifteen minutes of sun . . . !

(*He is stopped by the low, rumbling bass of a great organ heard as from a distance.*)

STANLEY: Sshh!

(*He looks around for the source of the sound—the others too. Then upward again.*)

Am I hearing the ocean in the background, Charley? I visualize you on the beach, right? Staring out at the sea, making up your mind?—Let me say one more final thing, okay?—the country's like nice and quiet at least for the moment, right?—give or take a minor ambush here and there? After thirty-eight years of killing, so they tell me, it's almost normal now, right?—So the thing is, Charley—do you want to light the match that'll explode the whole place again?

FELIX: Don't worry about the country, Charley, I'll take care of it. You come down, you hear me? I'm talking syndication, this is one big pot of money! I'm talking new hotels, I'm talking new construction, I'm talking investment. You care about people? Come down and get crucified!

JEANINE (*starting to weep*): For all our sakes, my darling, don't come down . . . !

SKIP and FELIX (*upward*): You can't do this to us! (*They look about, wait . . . then . . .*)

SKIP (*to FELIX*): You will return that check, or I'm calling the Embassy!

FELIX: Fuck the Embassy, I'm keeping the money . . . !

(*They continue shouting at each other, vanishing into the crowd . . .*)

SKIP: This is larceny! I'll call Washington! You are destroying my career!

FELIX: I did my good-faith best!

STANLEY: Go away, Charley, before they all kill each other! You gotta give us a sign, baby, what's it gonna be!

(*The light slowly fades to black, as they all look upward and about in wonder and apprehension.*)

(*In the silence, tentatively.*) Charley?

(*All wait, all glancing about. Nothing happens.*)

We're not seeing the light, okay?

(*Silence; all listening.*)

Don't hear the ocean, okay?

(*Silence . . . then . . .*)

(*They are weeping, immensely relieved and sorry.*)

HENRI: Good-bye, Charley.

EMILY: Good-bye, Charley.

FELIX: Good-bye, Charley.

SARAH: Good-bye, Charley.

PHIL: Good-bye, Charley.

(SKIP *turns and angrily walks out.*)

JEANINE: Good-bye, my darling! . . . But could you think about . . . maybe trying it . . . another time?

(*Silence.* HENRI *takes* JEANINE*'s arm and they move; each of the others now leaves the stage silently, in various directions, each alone.*)

STANLEY (*lifts a hand in farewell, looking forward and up*): Always love you, baby. And look, if you ever feel like, you know . . . a cup of tea, or a glass of dry white, don't hesitate, okay? . . . I'm always home. (*Salutes.*) Thanks. (*He walks off alone.*)

END

FINISHING THE PICTURE

CHARACTERS

EDNA
OCHSNER
KITTY
DEREK
FLORA
CASE
PAUL
JEROME

ACT ONE

The spacious veranda of a penthouse hotel apartment. Outdoor furniture. A western dawn. Sky turning colors. PHILLIP OCHSNER *enters; trousers, bedroom slippers, and buttoning a sport shirt. Goes directly to phone.*

OCHSNER: This is Mr. Ochsner in the Penthouse. Tell me, the horizon is all red, what is that? No kidding! Since when? Huh!—okay, thanks dear. And you keep ringing Miss Meyers, heh? Thank you. (*Hangs up, walks to railing, looks off at the distant horizon. Now he takes newspaper off the breakfast tray, peels impatiently through pages and gives up on it and stands there pulling on his cheek, brains racing. Shakes his head at a misfortune.*) Shit.

   (*Turns at a sound from upstage toward apartment.* EDNA MEYERS *enters: a petite, shy but determined woman in her forties.*)

EDNA: Good morning. (*Indicates upstage.*) Your door's open, shall I shut it?

OCHSNER: Leave it, I'm expecting Clemson. (*He goes to her, lifts up her chin, kisses her gently, but no embrace; then grins at her.*) Care for coffee?—I was just ringing you. Please sit, I'd like to try a memo to Clemson.

EDNA: I was down buying a few things for Kitty in the drug store.

OCHSNER (*indicating chair*): Please.—You're sure Kitty doesn't mind my borrowing you like this?

EDNA: Not at all; she's glad I'm being kept busy. She likes you, you know. (*Sits.*)

OCHSNER: Am I wrong? You seem as amazed as I am.

EDNA (*laughs, tense*): I don't know what to say. I don't know what happened to me.

OCHSNER: I think it was our mutual surprise that we were not only from Brooklyn but two blocks apart.

EDNA: Yes, well, that did surprise me, but why it should have led to . . . (*Breaks off with a charmingly shy laugh.*)

OCHSNER: As long as there are no regrets.

EDNA: Certainly not from me.

OCHSNER: Me neither, certainly.

EDNA (*pause*): Did you wish to dictate?

OCHSNER: I want to try something to Clemson.

(*Thinks; then a personal tone.* EDNA*'s pencil is poised.*)
Wait, this is not the memo. You know, when my wife died I
kind of cemented myself in a wall; you naturally assume
you're supposed to be lonely to the end. But candidly I
think I got more sensitive to everything. Maybe because
death is constantly at your elbow once someone you care
about disappears. There's music now that can almost make
me cry. And frankly I feel like eating up all the women.
Which I don't do, but . . . Well, thank you, Edna.

EDNA: I was totally unprepared. Something burst through me.

OCHSNER (*broad smile*): You know, you still haven't called me
Phillip.

EDNA: There's so much gossip on location like this, and I simply detest it. (*A shy chuckle.*) Maybe give me more time.

OCHSNER: How is your tooth now?

EDNA: The pain disappeared as quickly as it came.—I'm so
sorry; it was very embarrassing . . .

OCHSNER: No-no. In fact . . . (*Chuckles.*) I hope you don't
think it's cruel but I enjoyed your intensity—till I realized
what it was.

EDNA (*a gentle laugh*): I assure you it wasn't only my tooth.

OCHSNER (*reassuringly*): I know that, Edna. (*Stands, hikes
pants.*) By the way, you see all that red.

EDNA: It's a forest fire in California, yes.

OCHSNER: Amazing—must cover a couple hundred miles.

EDNA: More. Distance is deceptive here. They say it was an
arsonist.

OCHSNER: Huh! I guess there's not a single rotten thing
human beings aren't capable of doing.

EDNA: Think of the animals in there.

OCHSNER (*points*): Look at that smoke out there—the whole
sky is turning black.

EDNA: Terrible.

OCHSNER: I'd like to try a memo, just to clarify my mind before Clemson gets here.

(*She takes a pad out.*)

How's Kitty seem this morning? Chance she'll work today?

EDNA: She didn't sleep again but . . . it's hard to say. I might try waking her in a while.

OCHSNER: How long'd you say you been with her?

EDNA: Over five years now.

OCHSNER: It speaks well for her that she picked you for a secretary—she's lucky.

EDNA: I never had any problems with Kitty.

OCHSNER: Well, you're a loving woman. All right, let me try it. "Dear Mr. Clemson." (*Pause.*) Suppose I could call him Derek?

EDNA: Oh, I'm sure—you had a talk with him yesterday, didn't you?

OCHSNER: Only briefly when I arrived. Well. "Dear Derek."— Listen, Edna, I want you to let me know whenever you think I'm being too rough on these people.

EDNA: I think you're doing just fine.

OCHSNER: I'm a little out of my depth here, I never dealt with artistic types. You're always at a disadvantage when the other guy knows what you know but you don't know what he knows.

EDNA: Actually, they feel inferior to you in a sense; really— they're all terribly insecure. Life isn't real to movie people— not like it is to you.

OCHSNER: All I want is to just get this picture finished, preferably without stepping on too many toes.

EDNA: You're a sensitive man, you won't go wrong.

OCHSNER: For the life of me I can't understand why you're not married.

EDNA (*with a shy laugh*): Do I have to be?

OCHSNER: That's a point too, isn't it. Okay . . .

(*She readies her pad.*)

"Dear Derek. I saw the roughcut of the first seventy minutes last night, and while I have no claim to being a critic I do have a retentive and logical mind; frankly, I think I'm probably a representative audience, if there is such a thing.

(*Reaches out and kisses her hand, then smiles at her.*)

"The picture is always interesting, but I wonder if it will move people. It's kind of beautiful but cool as a rose. (*Pause.*) In fairness, I should say that I'm not moved much by most pictures I've seen in recent years. But I'm not asking for sentiment, sentiment turns me off even worse. I have read the screenplay, which I find somewhat confusing. The movie is clearer, but remote, with less feeling. Is this Kitty's fault? She's got a kind of spooky underwater look sometimes." Too rough?

EDNA: Well of course the coldness isn't all her fault. Derek is very macho and doesn't really relate to women and it freezes her up. She's a girl of tremendous sensitivity, Mr. Ochsner.

OCHSNER: Why can't you call me Phillip?

(EDNA *looks down, too upset to speak.*)

How emotional you are.

EDNA: I feel so for her.

OCHSNER: Tell me the truth, Edna, you think I'm wasting my time trying to save the picture?

EDNA: No! You could do it. But you must not let them blame everything on Kitty.

OCHSNER: But she's the one who's caused the delays.

EDNA: But maybe that's the price you have to pay if you want her.

OCHSNER: Well that's certainly a different way to look at it. But this picture is now almost five weeks over schedule, that's coming up on about four and a half million dollars in the hole.

EDNA (*with difficulty admitting*): I know.

OCHSNER: Did I hear somebody . . . ?

(*Starts through glass doors toward the apartment, then stops cold. She leaps up at what she sees through doorway.*)

EDNA: Oh God! (*Turning back to* OCHSNER.) You have a robe to put on her?

OCHSNER: In my bathroom.

(*He starts in toward the apartment, but she stops him.*)

EDNA: Don't. Please. Let me put her in your bed.

OCHSNER: Sure, go ahead.

(EDNA *exits into apartment, he goes to railing.*)

KITTY'S VOICE (*off*): Where is this?

EDNA'S VOICE (*off*): Come, dear, we can use this bedroom till you . . . (*Her voice dies away.*)

KITTY'S VOICE (*fading*): But where is this place? Where is Flora? What happened to my strawberries . . . ?

(*Silence.* OCHSNER *turns to look toward the apartment. Worried.*)

OCHSNER: Horrible.

(*Moves at random, shaking his head. Picks up a shaver for something to do, turns it on and thoughtfully runs it over his face, looking at the horizon.* DEREK CLEMSON *appears in doorway.*)

DEREK: Good morning.

OCHSNER: Oh. Sorry. I didn't hear you. Come in, Derek. I can call you Derek, can't I?

DEREK: The poor thing has apparently been cruising through the halls with nothing on this morning.

OCHSNER: She's in my bedroom.

DEREK: Really!

OCHSNER: Just walked in a minute ago. Edna's with her.—She had kind of a . . . I don't know, a big funny stare.

DEREK: That funny stare has cost you a few million so far.

OCHSNER: Is that from the drug?

DEREK: Pills, yes, and a bad life.

OCHSNER: I noticed it in a couple of shots last night.

DEREK: Yes. And it probably means we can't shoot her today. I hope not but I may have to cancel again. But I'll have Terry Case look at her.

OCHSNER: Can't shoot around her, huh?

DEREK: There's nothing left to shoot except her final scenes. (*Glance at watch.*) I'd better have a look at her. Is Flora in there too?

OCHSNER: Only Edna.

DEREK: Well that's a mercy.

(*Starts upstage.* FLORA *appears. He walks past her.* FLORA *is a round woman in a black sack-dress. In her early sixties.*)

FLORA: Wait! I can't find Kitty.

DEREK: Can't find her? Really? (*Pointing toward the apartment.*) Try his bedroom.

FLORA (*wide-eyed, to* OCHSNER): Here?

OCHSNER: Just walked in from the hall. Edna's with her.

FLORA (*falls into a chair*): Oh thank God. I'll let Edna handle it for a minute. I'm washed out. What a night I had with her. This was Waterloo. The Battle of the Bulge, the Brothers Karamazov. (*Focuses on one of the five small watches hanging on chains from her neck, and with alarm.*) Five o'clock?

OCHSNER: No-no, six-thirty.

FLORA (*focuses closer*): Oh!—I'm reading London.

OCHSNER: It wouldn't be five o'clock in London.

FLORA: Then Tokyo. (*Peers at another watch.*) Here, here's London, I think. I can't see anything anymore . . . So, Mr. Ochsner, what good news have you brought to rescue us if I may ask?—You know who I am, don't you?

OCHSNER: Of course, we shook hands last night in the lobby.— Why all the watches?

FLORA: I collect. I can't help myself. Some people smoke, I collect. If I have one I have to have a pair; have two, I must have three. Like Vladimir Horowitz has bow ties, hundreds. He's a friend for thirty years, y'know. But it's practical, sometimes I have to know what's the time in London or Madrid or Sydney because the curtain goes up all over the world on our people practically every night.

OCHSNER: Your pupils, you mean.

FLORA: Would you believe we have people shooting on three, at least that I know of, three continents at this very instant? Including the Arctic Circle, if that's a continent—they're remaking *Nanook of the North* with Louella Hirsh.

OCHSNER: Wasn't that with all Eskimos?

FLORA: But they've put in a Canadian Mounted Policeman, Louella Hirsh will be the first woman Mounty. We have got to talk, Mr. Ochsner—I just called my Jerome and he said we should all be thankful that you came. I thought you'd want to know. Terrible and unprofessional things are happening here. I mean if you're serious about finishing this picture. Tell me, are you, or shouldn't I ask? I'm naive, forgive me, are you now President of Bedlam International instead of Cooperman?

OCHSNER: Yes.

FLORA: But you were not in pictures.

OCHSNER: No.

FLORA: I heard you were in the trucking business?

OCHSNER: That's right. We merged with Bedlam.

FLORA: Well listen, stranger things have happened. I ran the Orange Julius stand on Broadway and 47th Street for six years before I crashed through. I suppose you know the chaos we're in here; this motion picture is out of control, and I don't say that lightly. May I ask how long are you staying?

OCHSNER: As long as I can be useful—what are you referring to specifically?

FLORA: I don't know where to start. I mean how do they come to give me a double room?

OCHSNER: Beg your pardon?

FLORA: This is the first picture in my entire life where I didn't have a suite.

OCHSNER: I don't get the connection.

FLORA: But what else am I talking about? Mr. Ochsner, you are not of the theatre, you are from some logical kind of industrial world. For which incidentally thank God in a sense, mainly that you might bring some business intelligence to bear here. But if you were of our world you would understand that as the star's coach it reflects on her that I am stuffed into some room.

OCHSNER: I'll see what I can do.

FLORA: It's not for myself, believe me, I didn't even mention it to her—she'd be so furious—but if we want to work on a scene and God forbid her suite is not made up yet we end up in my room with one of us sitting on the bed like an immigrant and the other on the floor. I mean can you imagine Garbo learning lines on a floor? It's an unprofessional insult to her.

OCHSNER: I'll see what I . . .

FLORA: Fine—a corner suite so I have light. But for instance, the car, I mean you ask me for examples. Not in ten years have I coached a star (what am I talking about, "star"?—an actor, any actor) where I wasn't provided with a car and a chauffeur.

OCHSNER: But I believe I saw some bills for a . . .

FLORA: Finally, sure! I had to threaten to quit the picture till Billy McGuire got me one.

OCHSNER: But why couldn't you share Kitty's limousine?

FLORA: But is that the way on a first-class film?

OCHSNER: But don't you ride together to the location every morning?

FLORA: To go over the lines together.

OCHSNER: So why do you need another limousine?

FLORA: So I'm independent. It's not that I use it that much, but there's a principle here.

OCHSNER: I can see that. (*Unabashed mocking laugh.*) You're a real woman of principle, Flora!

    (DEREK *enters.*)

DEREK: My cameraman is coming up to look at her eyes. Then we can decide whether to cancel the day . . .

OCHSNER: Everybody's already been called?

DEREK: I'm trying to reach McGuire—he's head of production, but he's not picking up his phone.

FLORA: McGuire is in the shower a lot.

DEREK: He's just below here; I want to check some shots with him anyway. I'll be right back.—We'll have to talk, Phillip. (*He goes out.*)

FLORA: You notice? Not so much as a good morning to me. There goes one of the greatest directors of our age, but . . . and I beg you on bended knee to believe that I'm not talking for myself . . . but if Derek Clemson had treated me with professional respect, Kitty would not have arrived at this condition now.

OCHSNER: Why? How does he treat you?

FLORA: It's difficult when you don't know the business.

OCHSNER: Well, think of part of your salary as going for my education.

FLORA (*big smile*): You're witty. (*No smile.*) What can I say?— He treats me like an enemy instead of using me as a transmission belt from him to Kitty. Don't ask me why—maybe I'm a threat to his masculinity, I don't know. I mean it's a famous non-secret, for his third wife's fortieth birthday present the man brings her home an unhousebroken chimpanzee. A live ape! This is my twenty-sixth picture, and believe me with no director did I start out with such indescribable respect for his genius, including Visconti, may he rest, and De Sica—I can show you a bundle of his letters that thick, in English. With Derek we're literally afraid to talk in front of him, Kitty and I, we have to hide someplace so I can tell her what to do. He's crazy about horses.

OCHSNER: But why must you tell her what to do, isn't he clear?

FLORA: Is the Internal Revenue clear? Sure, if you understand it; if not, you need a lawyer. I'm the actor's lawyer. I turn the director's caviar philosophy into a slice of bread and butter.

OCHSNER: I think I understand.

FLORA: Forgive me, you don't understand because I don't. The actor's performance is a process of such complication, not on a par with the atom bomb but close. And my Jerome is the only one who I would say—yes, he understands. The rest of us, no; we do our best, here and there now and then we hit on the key, the button, the procedure whereby something comes out right. But I am only Jerome's deputy, I do my best, but I have no illusions that I understand. Any more than any artist understands how he does what he does.

OCHSNER: I see now why you could easily get into conflict with a director.

FLORA: Wrong again, forgive me—I could supply a Mafia funeral with the tons of flowers that grateful directors have sent me in gratitude. All a director needs to do is come to me and say, look Flora, what I want her to do is so and so; and I will go to her and justify his idea, you see?

OCHSNER: But why can't he justify his own directions? He has directed dozens of pictures and some great actors.

FLORA: Because Kitty's tradition and Derek Clemson's tradition are

(DEREK *enters*)

practically not on speaking terms.

DEREK (*with a laugh*): Indeed—and as a consequence the girl lies gasping for life like a landed salmon.

FLORA (*to* OCHSNER): I don't want to keep it a secret—he terrifies me.

DEREK: She was wandering around naked in the corridors. Or did I misunderstand that you were watching her?

FLORA: I left the room for two minutes, Derek! I had to go out and send flowers to Larry Olivier. (*To* OCHSNER.) He just opened, you know. If I don't send something I don't hear the end of it for . . .

DEREK: We have something to discuss, Flora.

FLORA (*stands*): The lobby is full of rumors that you're canceling today, is that on? I should know.

DEREK: Try to get her on her feet. I think I might be able to shoot over her shoulder, quarter-profile, I don't know yet. Go in, see what you can do.

FLORA (*going*): She is in terrible need of a rest, you know, Derek.

DEREK (*sprawling on a chair*): Aren't we all. See if you can get her going.

FLORA (*to* OCHSNER): I have a good feeling for some reason about you, Mr. Ochsner.—But you mustn't be discouraged —the truth is we all love each other. (*Points at his face.*) You would love my Jerome. (*She exits.*)

OCHSNER: Is she crazy?

DEREK: Like a fox. A fox who chases horses.

OCHSNER: How do you find Kitty?

DEREK: Nearly *non compos mentis.*

OCHSNER: I don't know Latin.

DEREK: Blotto. But she has incredible powers of recuperation. You've seen the rushes, I understand.

OCHSNER: I started a memo but I can tell you—you mustn't give up on this picture. I feel it could use some warmth, but I think if you could get some of that into the final scenes it would lift the whole story. I think it could make a highly unusual film. Although I doubt it'll make a dollar.

DEREK: What do you have in mind to do?

OCHSNER: It depends entirely on her condition. I suppose we'll really have to look at a shutdown.

DEREK (*pained*): I'll be completely straight with you, Mr. Ochsner . . .

OCHSNER: Phil, please.

DEREK: I have never in my life been beaten by an actor but this girl has me on the ropes.

OCHSNER: Does anyone have any idea what is exactly wrong with her?—I mean to look at her she's the picture of health.

DEREK: She is a case of terminal disappointment. With herself, her husband, the movies, the United States, the world.

OCHSNER: Well that sounds like most of us. But why? It seems to me she's got everything. She must be the envy of ninety percent of humanity.

DEREK: So is the United States—why are so many of us unhappy? —But there's really no time for this, Phil. What do you want to do?

OCHSNER: You are now forty-seven or forty-eight days over schedule. Actual loss if we decide to scuttle the picture would be in the neighborhood of nine, probably ten. The board leans heavily toward a shutdown.

DEREK: Really.

OCHSNER: Oh, they're totally pissed off, ya. But I decided to come and spend a day or two and see if anything can save it.

DEREK: I guess I don't have to say how sorry I am about this.

OCHSNER: I tell you frankly, this woman bewilders me. Kitty to me is the most beautiful woman I ever laid eyes on . . . there's a miracle in her face. I look at her and for some reason I feel glad inside. How can she be so depressed?

DEREK: She's had a frightful life . . . she's been stepping on broken glass since she could walk. She is pure survival.— Which could be why she moves you.

OCHSNER (*sighs, shakes his head at a loss*): You can finish in eight days, or is that real?

DEREK: Provided she gives me a full day's work every day— some days she doesn't show up at all or can't get herself out of her trailer for hours.

OCHSNER: Now tell me about this idea of a week's rest . . . you really think it would make the difference? And by the way, I talked to her analyst in New York for a few minutes. He's in favor of a hospital.

DEREK: I know. Look . . . if she rests for a week and I get her back here alert and clear-eyed for seven or eight days, you've got a picture.

OCHSNER (*smiles*): Do I hear some uncertainty?

DEREK: What can I say?

OCHSNER (*nods*): I should tell you . . . the board, against my vote, I might add—has notified the insurance company that we may apply for payment on her policy—we've got her insured for a million.

(*Pause.*)

DEREK: That would end her career, of course.

OCHSNER: I know. And I would hate for that to happen.

DEREK: She'd be uninsurable anymore, she'd never work again.

OCHSNER (*pause*): I know.

DEREK: In fact, that might turn out to be the least of it; you understand me.

OCHSNER: Really.

DEREK: Oh yes.

> (*Silence.* OCHSNER *stares ahead.*)

She's chinning on a bar with hundred-pound weights tied to her ankles.

OCHSNER (*looks off, thinks*): I'm asking you to tell me if it's hopeless.

DEREK: Phillip, I've never failed to complete a film, and this is my forty-third. Just the idea of walking away is an abomination to me.

OCHSNER: It comes down to betting maybe a million additional dollars that she's going to come back ready to work, and I'm looking for evidence.

DEREK: Incidentally, my cameraman, Terry Case, will be coming by shortly—he's known Kitty since she started out. I think you should talk to him, too.

OCHSNER: Okay. But what do you think? Rock bottom, Derek. It won't help either of us to kid this.

> (*Pause.*)

DEREK: I believe she'd come back ready to work if she had a week's rest. I believe it because—as naive as it sounds and romantic—deep inside Kitty is a woman of honor. Where there is honor anything is possible.

OCHSNER: But then how could she have let a whole company stand around like this day after day, week after week?

DEREK: She has ghosts sitting on her chest; ghosts of things she's done, or been done to her; she can't breathe, can't sleep, can't wake, fleeing the hounds of hell. But if I can reach her sense of honor I believe she'll come back and finish the picture.

OCHSNER (*moves in deep tension; halts*): I'm trying to believe that.

DEREK: It could come to nothing, but I do think I . . .

OCHSNER: Someone at the door? Yes! Come in!

> (*Enter* TERRY CASE.)

DEREK: This is Terry Case, our cinematographer. Phillip Ochsner, Terry.

CASE: Glad to meet you, sir.

OCHSNER: Sit down, Terry.

CASE (*finding a seat*): I hope you won't mind if I get a phone call, it's an emergency.

DEREK: It's come through?

CASE: I was cut off, but it sounded good.

DEREK: He's got a big piece of an oil well in Texas.

OCHSNER (*eager fascination*): Drilling it now, you mean?

CASE: Right. (*To* DEREK.) Possible gusher, he said, but the connection was bad. He's calling back.

DEREK: Christ, what are you going to do?

CASE: Get on my boat and bye-bye till the next life. Caribbean and Gulf of Mexico. Maybe a seaplane perched on the deck. Fly up to Vegas now and then, and screw.

OCHSNER: We've been trying to decide to shut down for a week or so till she can work.

CASE: Uh-huh.

OCHSNER: What's your opinion? I understand you photographed her in years past.

CASE: Oh, Kitty and I go back to the beginning. She's a good kid. But if you're asking my opinion, it's like the wranglers say about horses—nobody knows what a horse is going to do next because the horse don't know.

OCHSNER: Derek feels he could reach her if she got off the pills. But I'm told he's a man who climbed Mount Blanc and went six rounds with Billy the Bomb Martinez.

CASE: Yeah well, friend Derek is not your average judge of real life—wrestled a crocodile in Guatemala, you know. (*Glance at* DEREK.) Nearly lost that one, baby . . .

 (DEREK *chuckles.* CASE *considers, then* . . .)

See, I got a different way, Mr. O. Actors respond best to threatening gestures. Any director they really admire, if you look at him close, turns out to be a rough, tough dude . . . in other words, a thug in sheep's clothing. (*Of* DEREK.) Like this one. Kitty was great until she read in the papers that she was this fragile, pitiable little girl.

DEREK: That's true, but it's more complicated.

CASE: Kitty is tough, like every real star I ever knew. A star is an animal; you control an animal with love and threats. That's why people are so fascinated by them, because most people are afraid to be animals or forgot how. Not that I'm a great authority on the psychology.

DEREK: He is, though.

CASE: All I know is what I see through the lens. And I've been looking through the lens over thirty years. A star has a certain skin, it's living skin, it acts. You can have a beautiful girl but her skin don't act, the lens won't stick to her. The lens sticks to a star. This has nothing to do with brains, goodwill, or anything but animalism. Nothing photographs like ass. You can add tits but ass is what's essential. Kitty has the skin and the ass. It may have something to do with matching the curvature of the lens, I don't know, but ass stops the traffic every time, and she's got it.

OCHSNER (*hearing from within, calls*): Yes! Come out here!
 (PAUL *enters.*)

DEREK: Hiya, baby, work on that scene?

PAUL: Yes, I guess it's better now, I don't know anymore.

OCHSNER: We're just discussing a shutdown for a week till she can work again.

PAUL: Ah. (*Falls onto a chaise.*)

OCHSNER: The question, of course . . .

PAUL: . . . Whether she'll come back.

OCHSNER: . . . Any better than she is now.

PAUL: Well, I wouldn't know—I've been trying not to upset her so I've been staying clear of her lately. I heard you were canceling today?

DEREK: Haven't decided. I may try shooting over her shoulder to avoid her eyes . . . provided she comes to now.

OCHSNER: Would you like to talk to her? She's in my bedroom.

PAUL (*surprised*): How's that?

DEREK: She just wandered in, been walking the halls with nothing on.

PAUL: Where the hell was Flora?

DEREK: Out sending flowers to Larry Olivier.

PAUL: Christ, that woman!

DEREK: But she and Edna are in there with her now.

PAUL: . . . So what's the program?

DEREK: We're talking. Abandoning the picture is on the agenda, Paul.

PAUL: Not altogether. (*Beat.*) Altogether?

OCHSNER: It depends on her condition. We can't continue missing whole days.

PAUL (*blows out, shakes his head. To* DEREK): That would devastate her. It could kill her.

DEREK: He put two years into that screenplay plus this year on production.

PAUL: That doesn't matter anymore.

OCHSNER: Derek feels that once she's back to herself after a week off he could appeal to her sense of honor. What do you think?

PAUL: Oh, she has that. In fact, if she had less of a sense of honor she would be less ill—the world is an affront.

DEREK: Exactly what I was saying.

PAUL: But these are all words, of course; she lives with emanations. Mysterious streams of insight, subterranean shifts of feeling . . .

OCHSNER: . . . But she ends up more real to more people than any of us types.

PAUL: I don't think she's real to people, she's poetry. Speaking of poetry, did any of you see the Nixon–Kennedy debate last night?

DEREK: Only a minute at the end. What'd you think? All I could get from the commentators is that Nixon needed to shave closer.

PAUL: Of course! That was the issue. His five o'clock shadow.

OCHSNER: Nixon could win, you know. He owns anti-Communism. But don't you think Kennedy was better on the issues?

PAUL: I had a bottle of Scotch so I can't remember any issues. All I remember is that Kennedy's suit really fitted him, and Nixon, as somebody said, looked like they forgot to take the hanger out of his jacket. (*Laughter.*) It's serious; the fate of the world could hang on this vaudeville. The whole thing has turned into show business.

CASE: Which it's always been.

PAUL: I don't know, I think Roosevelt had real feelings about helping people . . .

CASE: Roosevelt's real feeling was that he should be elected four times.

OCHSNER: Maybe it was always a beauty contest and the television is just proving it.

DEREK: But it did seem to have a certain . . . dignity in the old days.

PAUL: I wonder if it's the television doing it to them, but they all come over with the sincerity of car salesmen. The presidency is the prize we give to the actor who does the best imitation of a president.

CASE: Never been different.

PAUL: Jesus, Terry, Jefferson was not a performer; Lincoln certainly wasn't . . .

OCHSNER: Maybe we ought to . . .

CASE: Good thought, sir—let's get back to the art of photography. (*To* DEREK *and* OCHSNER.) I think you've got to threaten her. I would go in there right now and tell her she's fired, and you're remaking the picture with another actress.

DEREK: She knows we can't do that.

CASE (*suddenly bare outrage*): Well goddam you, Derek, if it was my picture I wouldn't be sitting out here wondering what to do, with a forty-man crew in the lobby waiting to go to work! She's making you a laughing stock, for Christ's sake!

(FLORA *enters.*)

FLORA: You can be heard in there, Terry.

CASE: We used to have a saying in the Salvation Army—"Fuck 'em all but six and save them for pall bearers."

FLORA: Well, that's one way to look at it. But if you want a picture, you should keep your voice down.

DEREK: Is she awake?

FLORA: She's eating some ice cream.

DEREK: Is that grounds for hope or despair?

FLORA: We are all motivated by different motivations; if ice cream does it, be happy. (*To* OCHSNER, *spreading out her arms.*) What can I tell you? Babe Ruth didn't always get a hit, right?

CASE: But he always came to the plate.

FLORA: Listen, don't ask me about baseball. (*She goes out.*)

PAUL: When must you decide?

OCHSNER: Last night.

CASE: They ought to send Flora to Japan to fertilize the lettuce.

(*They all laugh.*)

Dear God, ring that phone.

PAUL (*looking off*): You know, it's still burning out there.

OCHSNER: They say it may go on for a week. One crazy man with a match.

CASE: That doesn't necessarily hurt, y'know. Fire invigorates the seed buried in the soil. Some seed won't sprout without fire.

PAUL: That's an interesting metaphor.

CASE (*to* PAUL): You can't talk to her?

DEREK: She goes into a frenzy when she sees him.—That's a wonderful line—Flora in Japan fertilizing the lettuce; I can just see her.

CASE: Oh sure—and telling the Japs what time it is in Philadelphia.

PAUL: She's right out of Molière.

OCHSNER: Molière?

PAUL: A French seventeenth-century playwright.

OCHSNER: Oh.

PAUL: She's such a perfect fraud it finally comes out as something genuine.

DEREK: A genuine fraud.

PAUL: Yes. Her consistency is so flawless you almost have to admire it; if there is the slightest choice between the truth and a lie she will always choose to tell a lie.

OCHSNER: I'm thinking. Or rather wondering . . .

(EDNA *enters.*)

Yes?

EDNA: Nothing. She's kind of dozing. . . . Derek, I suppose you know there's a man been standing at your door with a package from Mexico, he says.

DEREK (*great surprise and joy, leaping up*): Right! (*To* OCHSNER.) Back in a minute.

(DEREK *exits. A short silence, a sense that something has entered the air.*)

EDNA (*to* CASE, *anxiously*): He's being careful, isn't he?

CASE: It can't be smoked, honey—no problemo.

OCHSNER: Something happening?

CASE: Derek collects pre-Columbian pottery, nuts about it.

OCHSNER: Sculpture?

CASE (*minimizing*): Some.—Not to worry, Derek always knows what he's doing.

OCHSNER: But he does it anyway, I hear.

CASE: It's not illegal.

OCHSNER (*a wry twist to his face*): Exporting antiquities? You sure?

CASE: I stand mute. But really, it's nothing for you to worry about.—Edna!—do I see makeup on you this morning?

EDNA (*shyly*): Not really. Just trying to cover up my lack of sleep. Your call come in?

CASE: I'm waiting. (*To all.*) If it's a gusher, I'm going to set up Edna as a madam in Acapulco.

(*Laughter, including* EDNA.)

OCHSNER: What do you think?—could she be appealed to through Flora?

EDNA: To do what?

CASE: To go to work, honey; that's why we all signed up to leave our homes and loved ones and come here to a hundred and five degrees in the shade.

EDNA: Don't be rotten, Terry. (*To* OCHSNER.) You're mistaken to think Flora has any great weight with her.

CASE: In case you missed it, I said Flora should be shipped to Japan to fertilize the lettuce.

(*She and all laugh.*)

EDNA: Look, the poor thing only tolerates Flora because Jerome isn't here.

(DEREK *enters.*)

OCHSNER: Jerome is Flora's husband.

EDNA: Yes, her teacher. He's her real . . .

PAUL: God.

EDNA: Not God but . . .

PAUL, DEREK *and* CASE: God.

OCHSNER: Well, that's interesting—how about getting him here to talk to her?

EDNA: That would certainly help, if he'd agree. But I don't know how Derek would feel about it.

DEREK: I don't care. Let him come if she wants him. I don't think he will, of course.

OCHSNER: Why not?

DEREK: I only shook Jerome's hand once—but my distinct impression was of a man who does not board sinking ships. He will never risk his magic by failing to get her back to work.

PAUL: Kitty's tried to get him to come out several times, you know.

DEREK (*quickly interested*): Has she!

PAUL: That I know of. (*To* EDNA.) Right?

EDNA: I don't feel I ought to be . . .

DEREK: There's no disloyalty to her, Edna—we have to find a solution, for her sake as well as ours. They're on the edge of scrapping the picture.

EDNA: Oh dear God!

> (*She suddenly bursts into tears.* DEREK *goes and embraces her. They mourn in silence.*)

DEREK: Oh, honey . . .

OCHSNER (*helplessly*): I'm doing my best, dear.

EDNA: Oh I know!—Well, she has asked Jerome to come.

PAUL: Edna, dear—she begged him to come half-a-dozen times.

EDNA: —Look, I'm no partisan of Jerome's, but you really ought to talk to Kitty about him, not me.

OCHSNER: But do you feel his presence could get her back to work?

EDNA (*tense about telling secrets*): To tell you the truth, I never understood what she got from Jerome; he's like Flora, as far as I can see—they talk in circles, round and around. But you have to be fair—he excites her imagination somehow.

DEREK: Flora has certainly not excited her on this picture; she has confused and depressed her.

EDNA (*blurting out*): I'm sorry, Derek, but without Flora here she wouldn't be able to work at all! It may be unbelievable but what isn't?

OCHSNER (*coming to a decision*): All right, then we . . .

CASE: . . . Excuse me, sir; I love the girl, so I'm going to say this—she's simply got to be told to get off her mattress or she's back modeling underwear.

OCHSNER: You mean that seriously.

CASE: I mean it because I love her. (*To* DEREK, *of* OCHSNER.) And he's the boss, he ought to deliver the ultimatum—believe me, she'll be saddled up and away pronto.

OCHSNER (*pause*): Edna?

EDNA: I can't imagine how she could possibly be expected to act when she's being threatened.

OCHSNER: Paul—I'd like to know what you think—personally, as her husband.

PAUL: What I think? Her life has her by the throat. There is no way to reach into her that I know of. We're all a little bit angry at her, that's inevitable—but the key to this lock is probably love. Which she can't accept.

OCHSNER: Derek?

DEREK: I'm thinking. I'm wondering if she's capable of making a decision; it's like asking a drunk to whistle.

CASE: Except she's far from a drunk.

DEREK: What do you mean?

CASE (*silent for a moment; then decides*): . . . I had her face in closeup yesterday when she started blowing lines. Her eyes were alert at that moment and clear, and I could swear she decided to blow.

EDNA: Oh go on!

CASE: Edna, she's the Virgin Mary to you, but I saw those eyes with a calculated look if ever I saw a calculated look in my life.

PAUL: Why would she purposely blow lines!

CASE: Because Derek made her do six takes of the same scene to get the lines straight, and she was going to remind him who sells the tickets!

EDNA: That's ridiculous, Terry! (*To* PAUL.) How can he say that!

PAUL: If she looked alert, Terry, she was probably trying to hold on to one of Flora's instructions . . . (*To* OCHSNER.) . . . You see, they teach that only emotions count, the lines are incidental.

OCHSNER: What should they teach?

PAUL: That the emotion is in the language, not despite it. She's so busy looking for the emotions she sometimes loses the lines.

CASE: Okay. I'll say it again and you can hammer it into Mount Rushmore—the girl is confused because the one thing God gave her like nobody else was that darling face and a spectacular ass, which was her glory and her power, and which everybody's been snickering at and trying to teach her to think *thoughts*!

PAUL: That's only half true, Terry, she's a great actress.

OCHSNER (*to* CASE): How about you talking to her?

EDNA: She can't stand him. (*Making a face to* TERRY.) Especially his vulgarity.

CASE: Since when is ass vulgar? I mean what is going on, Edna—who do these classy European directors pick to act out their profound spiritual dramas? Does Bergman cast some flat-chested, buck-toothed sack of bones? And Rossellini, and Renoir, and Kurosawa and you name them? How come they all pick the best ass in their countries to carry the spiritual message? I'm just a cameraman, but this right now is why I think she's stupefied in her bed at seven in the morning instead of shooting her picture—because she's got some idea from her intellectual and artistic friends that the best piece of capital she has is some kind of puritanical disgrace.

EDNA: Nobody's said that. But she does have a mind, you know.

CASE: I'll try anything, Edna, but I can't photograph minds. (*To all.*) I mean, what are we making here, some fucking French movie? This is America!—The girl's got to glory in her flesh again! (*To* DEREK.) Christ, remember years ago—she could knock around all night, bounce onto the set straight from some party and her face shining like a brand new apple . . . Remember, Derek?

DEREK: Yes, yes. She had one dress and the constitution of a horse.—Which she still has if she could only . . .

EDNA (*crying out*): Why can't you understand? She just doesn't think she's wonderful anymore!

(*Silence. All turn to her clear emotion.*)

Why is that so difficult? Whatever she wore, whatever she said, people'd look at her and say, "My God, this girl is simply glorious!" She tries, you can't imagine how she tries, and sometimes she almost has it again, but . . .

DEREK: The first time I saw her . . . we were casting a small part . . . she'd never acted before . . . walked in and I remember thinking—this is real, this is the Rocky Mountains, the Mississippi . . .

EDNA: Oh yes! And now she thinks everything is fake . . . herself most of all. And it's terrible. (*She blows her nose.*)

(*Pause.*)

PAUL: Maybe we go in together . . . she's got to work today.

EDNA: Please, Paul—let Derek.

(DEREK *stands, steps toward the bedroom, halts.*)

DEREK (*frustrated—directed toward* CASE): How simple it all was! Remember, Terry? When nobody in pictures talked about art? Certainly not in America. We just did it.

CASE: The European bullshit took over. We made the pictures the whole world wanted, and they couldn't make them, so they talked about art. The Germans send me treatises that long about my camera work, my philosophy. I can't understand word-one. They invited me to lecture in Sweden someplace; I said I'd be finished in five minutes. What's there to say?—Get close so you can see the faces, get low so you get the ass.

EDNA: But why do your pictures always look so marvelous?

CASE: Who the hell knows?

(*Pause.*)

You had a bird here who naturally sang. Then they started to teach her how to sing, and so naturally she can't sing anymore.

OCHSNER: All right.

(*Pause. All turn to him.*)

What it seems to come down to then, is how to make her feel glorious. 'Cause frankly, to me that's what she is. I'm speaking personally, not as the money—I look at her on the screen and life is a miracle.

PAUL: Well . . . her analyst has been trying for a long time.

CASE: Psychoanalysis is the world's most expensive fertilizer.

EDNA: Why is everything to you some form of shit?

CASE: Because I'm in the movie business, darlin'.

OCHSNER: I can't believe there is no way to encourage her. How about we give it a try?

PAUL: Maybe it's not encouragement she wants.

OCHSNER: What then?

PAUL: I don't know, maybe the right to express her grief.

OCHSNER: Grief! About what?

PAUL: About having to pretend she's the happy, radiant, carefree girl she was before she had a thought in her head.

OCHSNER: I admire your coolness under the circumstances.

PAUL: Not cool, exhausted; waste is exhausting.

OCHSNER (*a glance at his watch*): All right then . . . I'll go in and propose the week off if she'll guarantee to come back and finish the picture.

DEREK: She may give you a little fight—it means admitting she's incapable of going on.

OCHSNER: But she is incapable, isn't she?

DEREK: Admitting it is something else. Life on this film is not simple, Phil.

PAUL: It's really my responsibility to . . .

EDNA: No, Paul . . . you'd better not, you know? (*To* OCHSNER.) I wouldn't mind, if you want me to, Mr. Ochsner.

OCHSNER: Won't you ever call me Phil?

(*Slight pause.*)

DEREK: No, I'll tell her.

EDNA: Shall I go in with you?

DEREK: No, she'll simply have to trust me.

OCHSNER: I don't understand it—why is there such fear of her? I feel it myself. We're only trying to help her.

PAUL: Well, that's not quite the message that comes through, though.

OCHSNER: Why? What is the message?

PAUL: That we need her.

OCHSNER: Instead of?

PAUL: That we love her.

OCHSNER: But I do! I honestly think she is marvelous in every way!

PAUL: She won't believe that, quite.

OCHSNER: Why!

PAUL: Because you need her.

OCHSNER: So what's the solution?

PAUL: Love! What else? (*Sudden thought.*) —Derek, listen— Maybe he's the one ought to talk to her. He comes to her with clean hands, she might trust him.

DEREK: It's my picture, kid.

OCHSNER: You don't think a new face might encourage her?

DEREK (*hesitates*): . . . Okay. But keep it to five minutes. I'll come and interrupt you.

EDNA (*to* PAUL): This could solve everything!

PAUL: Yes. (*A frustrated sigh.*) Provided the thing we can't see doesn't barge in and take over.

OCHSNER: The thing we can't see.

PAUL: I hardly slept last night trying to see all this as she does. There's a kind of monster walking step for step behind her whispering in her ear never to trust anyone; and the trouble is he has a point. Everyone wants something from her; we're no exceptions; we want a beautiful film, so we insist she wake up bright and fluffy even when she feels like dying— our careers, the months and years we put into this project are redeemed by her fluffiness. Or that crowd of our technicians wandering around the lobby waiting to go to work— they also want fluffy. To say nothing of your stockholders and their families—more fluffy. Plus the magazines and newspapers that sell her fluffiness, and the salaries of *their* staffs, and distributors and truck drivers; plus of course her agents and their lawyers, plus movie-house stockholders and their staffs, in addition to the Internal Revenue Service that tax her fluffiness, not to mention the churches, synagogues and mosques and their staffs who live by condemning her fluffiness . . .

OCHSNER (*deeply disturbed*): . . . I still can't understand this! —She's the envy of half the world!

PAUL: But what they are envying doesn't exist! . . . She doesn't feel loved, Phil, so the fluffy Kitty the world adores is a mockery, a phantom, a curl of smoke. And she certainly is surrounded with resentment now.—I think she's not sure she really exists. So she stays in bed—this is all unconscious, I think, not a strategy; but knowing that forty workers are praying in the lobby for you to appear has to mean you exist, right? And if powerful executives and their bankers from New York to LA are stomping up and down, chewing their resentful cigars and cursing her—she must certainly exist even if only as a figure to hate.—She keeps phoning her analyst, but I know he's baffled. But it's too late for reason anyway. I tell you, I'm down to wishing for some kind of magic now. Some arrival out of the blue. Like a lightning strike of love. Like God walking in.

OCHSNER: What about you?

PAUL: We're far too angry at each other, the bridge is burned. We each promised to cure the other of his life, but we turned out to be exactly who we were. That's a very large disappointment, ordinary as it is.—I wish you'd give it a try, Phil—go in.

OCHSNER (*stands up*): I'm still not sure what to say but I'll try it.

PAUL: Just be your adoring, sympathetic self; swing with her mood, go light on logic and agree and agree and agree.

OCHSNER: Well, here goes . . . (*Starts upstage.*)

DEREK (*stands*): Stay here, Phil, I'll talk to her. (*Starts away.*)

PAUL: Derek, *listen* . . .

DEREK (*anger peeping out*): She's an actor; she owes us a performance!

CASE: That's the ticket!

(FLORA *enters.*)

FLORA: I just talked to my Jerome!—He'll come! (*To* EDNA.) You better tell McGuire to authorize a first-class ticket, and he'll have to negotiate a substantial per diem with our agent because he's canceling two days of classes.

(*Phone rings.*)

CASE (*instantly moves toward phone—and to* OCHSNER): You mind?—I'm expecting.

OCHSNER: Go right ahead, hope it's a gusher.

CASE: Hello, Case here. What!—No kidding! (*Looks off toward sky.*) Thank you, I'll tell him. (*Hangs up.*) They may have to cut off the electricity because of the fire, so if you want to use the elevator it might be out in twenty minutes for at least the day.

OCHSNER: Huh!

(*They all move toward the railing, looking out and upward.*) Look at that—one lousy little match! (*To* CASE.) Must mean the whole town is stopped, then.

CASE: This whole section of the state. That fire's at least two hundred miles away, but it's moving.

OCHSNER: God, I can smell it now!

EDNA: Yes! Is it getting closer?

(*They are all standing, sniffing the air.*)

Well, is it? (*To* OCHSNER.) Maybe we should get her out?

DEREK: You know, Phillip—you might check your insurance. This is an Act of God, right? You might be covered for the week's shutdown.

CASE: Right! And if it gets any blacker I can't shoot—the sky won't match. That's an Act of God for sure.

OCHSNER: I'll check. (*Shake of his head.*) You begin to wonder if somebody up there doesn't want this picture finished.

DEREK (*a quiet, absolute quality*): It'll be finished.

(*All turn to look at him, feeling his certainty.*)

BLACKOUT

ACT TWO

JEROME's suite. He is pulling on new cowboy boots, which he takes from a new box. Difficulty. Finally gets feet in. Sets cowboy hat on head, admires in mirror. Tries buttoning shirt collar, unbuttoning. Walks, testing a John Wayne stride. Fails. FLORA enters, clasps her hands in admiration.

FLORA: Fantastic. But a little uncomfortable? The boots?

JEROME: Most comfortable boots I ever had. (*Takes painful step.*) All cowboy boots have to be broken in, they make them that way. How do I look?

FLORA: Gorgeous. John Wayne with a brain. (*Waving air over her face with both hands.*) Thank God for air conditioning, it's a hundred and four outside. I've ordered ice water. I have a pain in my side from lifting her.

JEROME: I saw some ice water in the fridge.

FLORA: Let them bring fresh, the production can afford it. She seems to be restful but she's desperate to see you.

JEROME (*one finger raised*): The most important thing is rest. (*Glance at watch.*) Ochsner said eight, no?

FLORA: They'll be here. (*Looks around.*) Beautiful suite, I could move in for life. See?—soon as you come people straighten up. They had me practically in a dungeon.

JEROME: But be careful—I don't want them to assume I'm taking responsibility.

FLORA: God forbid. You're here to help out of . . . a sense of responsibility.

JEROME: Absolutely not.

FLORA: What then?

JEROME: Friendship. Professional friendship. I am not taking responsibility—she sounds very sick to me.

FLORA: I meant friendship.

JEROME: So tell me—the breakup is definite?

FLORA: Who knows? I think so.

JEROME: And she's relieved, or what?

FLORA: She's experiencing professional and spiritual outrage.

Paul was very hard, he kept telling her she had to stop blaming people and look at herself.

JEROME: That can be destructive. He never looks me in the eye. Paul dislikes me, doesn't he.

FLORA: Well who wouldn't—I don't mean who wouldn't, but he'd dislike anybody who got between him and his wife. She's his wife, after all. But let me clarify—the issue, I mean, is that Derek practically ordered me off the set.

JEROME: We were talking about Paul, not Derek.

FLORA: I changed the subject.

JEROME: Tell me the truth. You talked to her on the set in front of Derek, didn't you?

FLORA: Well, what can I do? Soon as they set up a shot she comes over to me for help . . .

JEROME: He is the director! The director resents third parties between himself and his actors! You have to stop being such a schmuck, Flora! I do not want to antagonize Derek! This is one of the world's greatest directors!

FLORA: I'm trying!

JEROME: Stupidity is never an excuse!

(*Doorbell.*)

Please. Keep your mouth shut.

FLORA: It could be the ice water.

(*She goes to exit. He wriggles his feet, grimaces with pain.*)

(*Enter* OCHSNER *and* EDNA *with her notebook.*)

Ah, Mr. Ochsner! We were just thanking our stars that you were here! This is Jerome.

OCHSNER: Yes.

(*He approaches* JEROME *who offers one hand, palm down.*)

Phil Ochsner . . .

(*He holds out a hand;* JEROME's *hand slowly proceeds to touch his.*)

JEROME: Very glad.

OCHSNER: Bad back?

JEROME: Bad back?

OCHSNER: Excuse me . . . (*Touches his own back.*) Takes me for ever sometimes to get up . . . you know, to meet somebody, so I thought you . . .

JEROME: No, my back is fine.

FLORA: Sit! Please! I've ordered ice water.

OCHSNER: Don't bother, I'm okay.—You know Edna.

EDNA: Oh of course. Good morning, Jerome!

> (FLORA *and* JEROME *nod to her and mutter suspicious hellos.*)

OCHSNER: . . . To take notes if necessary. So. First of all, Mr. Fassinger, I'm very glad you could come out . . .

JEROME: My opinion of Kitty is well known; she is one of five, perhaps six actors whose names will live for ever. I'm talking of the world now.

OCHSNER: Have you spoken to her this morning?

FLORA: He only got off the plane at midnight; he was so tired I made him go shopping. You can pick up some great buys here . . . provided you like Western . . .

JEROME: Flora.

FLORA: Yes. (*To* OCHSNER.) Don't let me interrupt.

JEROME: . . . I needed some time to myself before I saw her.

OCHSNER: Let me get to my point and you can take it from there. My board is ready to shut the picture down . . .

JEROME: Temporarily or completely?

OCHSNER: Completely. The costs are out of sight.

JEROME: That would be a death blow to her career.

OCHSNER: End it, possibly, yes.

FLORA: She . . .

JEROME: Flora.

OCHSNER: I am new to pictures, but . . .

JEROME: You merged . . .

OCHSNER: Yes. I know something about trucks, but I'm still feeling my way in this business. Time is of the essence is what I am trying to tell you. She is insured for a million; we will eat the remaining losses but a shutdown will at least stop the hemorrhage. The question is, what assurance is there that she can finish in eight days. Because the board's budgetary limit will cover the next seven or at most eight days, no more. In other words . . .

JEROME: Well, certainly *I'm* in no position to give you assurances. I can't be responsible for Kitty.

OCHSNER: I see.

JEROME: I don't know where you got the impression . . .

OCHSNER (*turns to* FLORA): Well, your wife . . .

JEROME: . . . She couldn't have said I was responsible . . .

FLORA: I never . . . !

OCHSNER: Not responsible exactly, but she said you were the only one who could talk to her and . . .

JEROME: Talk yes, but . . .

FLORA: What I said . . . excuse me . . . was that *if* . . . if, mind you, there was a person in the entire world who could . . .

OCHSNER: That's not . . . pardon me . . .

JEROME: She could not have said that I . . .

FLORA: Never!

OCHSNER: . . . WILL YOU KINDLY LET ME FINISH?

JEROME: Who are you addressing!

OCHSNER: Sorry, but I have paid your first-class fare here, Mr. Fassinger, plus an outrageous per diem, if I may say so, and I have to ask you straight—can you get Kitty to work this afternoon or latest tomorrow morning or can you not? If you say no, I take your word and we will take it into consideration as to whether or not to shut down this morning.

JEROME: I . . .

OCHSNER: I'm not finished, excuse me. I am not an acting expert, but I have run two of her movies and seen some of the rushes on this one—nobody has ever moved me like her. She is adorable, goddamit, and there has to be a way to keep her from destroying herself! Can you do it or can't you?

JEROME: Now listen to me.

OCHSNER: Yes.

JEROME: Kitty is not a truck. And I am not a mechanic who can fly in with a replacement part and put her back on the road.

OCHSNER: There are some trucks you can't do that with either; some trucks need special understanding . . .

JEROME: What are we talking about trucks for?

OCHSNER: I'll repeat my question . . .

JEROME: I cannot guarantee anything!

OCHSNER: Will you talk to her this morning?

JEROME: . . . I will try. If she is amenable.

OCHSNER (*pause*): I understand she trusts you more than anybody else in the world.

JEROME: That is true.

OCHSNER: Okay. So you will be seeing her this morning.—
Because I have a call in to my board at one o'clock to give
my estimate of the situation. If I have no reason for optimism they will pull the plug today.

JEROME: This is intolerable. Suddenly, everything depends on
me? I have never said I was responsible for her!

OCHSNER: Well, my assumption . . .

JEROME: You have no right to assume anything!

OCHSNER: I see. I guess I assumed that as her teacher and
longtime friend you were very close . . .

JEROME: We are very close but that doesn't mean I am responsible for her.

OCHSNER: I see. To put it bluntly, it was also that your wife's
coaching fee on this picture is almost as big as Kitty's
salary . . .

JEROME: My wife's fee is not my business.

OCHSNER: Right. I think I understand.—I will tell you candidly in view of all this, that my hopes for this picture have
practically evaporated.

JEROME: That will have to be up to you.

OCHSNER (*studies his watch*): It's seven-forty. If let's say by ten
you have had your talk with her . . . is that feasible?

JEROME: If she feels up to it I will certainly try.

OCHSNER: All right; I'll expect your call at ten, one way or the
other; if you tell me she can't go, it's all over; if you think she
can, I will do everything possible to convince my board, and
we shoot for seven or eight days to the end. Do we understand each other?

JEROME: Mr. Ochsner, there is no similarity between an actor
and a truck.

OCHSNER: There is one—they both have to work. But I'll tell
you a funny thing about trucks. There are trucks that come
fresh off the assembly line and they're never right. Engineers
try, mechanics . . . nothing doing. The truck is junk. Some
simple-minded guy comes along and *falls in love with that
truck*. He buys it for five dollars, fools around with it, and it
starts up and sings Dixie. Frankly, I love this woman; given
the trust she has in you I think between us we can get her on
the road. Okay?—Talk to you at ten.

(*He turns and exits,* EDNA *after him.*)

FLORA: What a nerve!

JEROME (*profoundly worried*): Will you please stop?!

FLORA: But to talk to *you* that way!—I could have slapped his face!

JEROME: You made me responsible for her, don't you understand that?

FLORA: All I said . . .

JEROME: . . . Was that if I came I could get her to work! Like I was Jesus Christ or something!

FLORA (*tears*): But you are, Jerome . . . to me.

JEROME (*big frustrated exhale*): Go to her room. Get her cleaned up. Tell her I'm coming in a few minutes. Tell her . . . that I will straighten her out so she can go back to work.

FLORA: Oh God, Jerome . . .

JEROME: Shut up. Tell her to get washed, and put on some makeup, and get her dressed. I am leaving for New York tonight . . .

FLORA: You just got here! Stay a few days . . .

JEROME: Do as I say, Flora!—If she cannot believe in herself in an hour she won't do it in a week. Tell her I will only see her for an hour, hour and a half; it will peak her concentration, so what I tell her will be more precious; this is a fifteen-round fight, she can't add more rounds.

FLORA: But supposing . . .

JEROME: No further comments. Go.

FLORA: God bless you, Jerome.

(FLORA *exits. He sits and tries bending his new boots. Stands, puts on his western hat, looks at himself in the mirror with a noble, stern expression . . . ending in a look of alarm.*)

BLACKOUT

ACT THREE

OCHSNER's *bedroom. A stray beam of light from the edges of heavy drapes leaves the bed area nearly pitch dark, revealing only* KIT-TY's *motionless form covered by a light blanket. A ladder-backed chair blocks the view of her upper body so that only an occasional movement of her legs under the blanket is clearly visible.*

The door opens, letting in a quick blast of daylight from the adjoining living room, and EDNA *slips in and shuts the door, leaving near-darkness again. She approaches the bed.*

EDNA: Kitty dear?—Hi, it's Edna.—About quarter past eight. —Well yes, they are, they're still hoping to shoot this morning. —Derek's in the other room . . . Yes, with Paul and Mr. Ochsner, and Terry—and guess what—Jerome is here! Of course to see you, that's why he came!—He's resting up but he'll be down in a few minutes to talk to you.—Oh, please, Kitty, don't take anything just now, could you? Because Terry's going to have to look at your eyes to see if he can shoot today. Well yes, dear—they were a bit—you know— unfocused in the last rushes, so Derek hopes you won't take anything for a while.—Paul? What can I say, to me it's tragic that this could happen between you two.—Contempt? Paul? Really?—Darling, please don't ask me to take sides, I've known Paul for so many years now . . . Well, he's a writer, dear, and I suppose writers can be a bit oblivious.—I don't know, maybe because they're constantly thinking.—Oh, please don't feel that way, people do respect you, Mr. Ochsner certainly does.—Mr. Ochsner? (*Embarrassed giggle.*) How in the world did you guess that? You see through everything!—Well, yes, we did. Last night.—It was—well, interesting. (*Giggles.*) Well, no, his wife died. Imagine?—she got some paralysis, and he went home every day for more than a year to have lunch with her and personally bathed her, took her to the toilet . . . He moved me so, I . . . (*laughs*) couldn't say no!—Oh, my dear, how wonderful to hear you laughing! What do you say we get you showered and . . .

(*Door opens and* DEREK *enters, approaches the bed.* EDNA *leaps up and shutting the door behind him* . . .)

I'm sorry, the light disturbs her . . .

DEREK: Kitty? It's Derek.

EDNA: I'll be outside, dear. (*She opens the door; the light flashes through the room; she exits. Door shuts, darkness again.*)

DEREK: Heard you laugh, kid, feeling better?—Well, that's too bad.—Me angry? No, kid, I haven't time—we're on the ropes, they may close us down today.—Oh they're serious, honey.—The Sistine Chapel? What are you talking about?— I know, honey, but Michelangelo could go six *months* over schedule, but his boss was the Pope—all we've got is Bedlam Pictures and Phillip Ochsner. Now here's my plan . . . Kitty, dear, I beg you don't ask me to discuss your private life. Paul, as far as I am concerned, is a hard-working writer and that's all I care to know. (*Listens for a moment.*) —Yes, okay, okay . . . Slow down, darling, I want you to listen to me. I take it you want to finish this picture, is that correct?— Jerome? Oh. Well, sure, if that's what you want, he can come onto the set—but of course he's not to be getting between you and me. But I doubt he'd have very much to say to *me*, dear.—Well, because our problem is the condition of your soul, not my direction or your acting.—Of course I understand that, why the surprise?—But I need you to answer my question first—are you absolutely committed to finishing?— Good then, I'll bring Terry in to have a look at your eyes . . . And cheer up, kid, you've done some really fine work on this one.

(*Goes and opens the door: the daylight pours in. He beckons to someone outside.* TERRY CASE *enters, passes* DEREK *and goes to the bed as* DEREK *shuts the door and the room goes dark again.*)

CASE: Hey baby, what's the good news this morning? Hold still for a sec so I can have a peek.—No, I'm still waiting on a call from my partners.—That's right, a gusher is possible. If it comes in I'll buy you a solid gold alarm clock. Open the eyes, okay? (*He switches on a pencil flashlight and shines it down at her face, holds it there for a moment.*) Great, thanks.

(*Switches flashlight off, turns to* DEREK, *and they leave the bedside together.*)

Marginal. But if she'll saddle up and stays clean for a couple hours it's possible—that body's still strong as a horse, as you know . . . (*Turns back to the bed.*) —Now hold it, honey, I did not say horse's ass, I said you have the *strength* of a horse. Anyway, I bend my knee.

(CASE *exits.* DEREK *goes back to the bed, stands looking down at* KITTY *in thought.*)

DEREK: Honey . . . ? I want you to tell me straight—how bad is it with you?

(*Light knock on the door. He goes and opens it to* OCHSNER, *who gestures whether he can come in.* DEREK *gestures for him to enter and they go to a corner away from the bed.*)

OCHSNER: Terry says he can photograph her, what do you think?

DEREK: I don't have the key to this lock, Phillip; I'm not sure she isn't too exhausted to do a day's work. It'd be very bad if I had to break off in the middle of the day. (*Looks back toward the bed.*) It's hard to judge her condition, she always looks like dawn over the Garden of Eden.

OCHSNER: What about a doctor?

DEREK: She's gone through two of the best analysts in the country and left both of them talking to themselves. She's floating out there somewhere beyond science. She is frightened and resentful and angry—(*glances at his watch*) and we've got about half an hour to cure all three. So I would say we need a miracle, Phillip, or an accident or the intervention of a higher power.

OCHSNER (*deliberates, then*): I'd like to talk to her.

DEREK (*gestures toward bed*): All yours. I'll make a few calls. (*Starts for the door.*)

OCHSNER: . . . Derek?

(DEREK *halts.*)

I'd rather not be saying this, but since we're hanging by a very thin thread I feel obliged to ask you . . . not to have any more deliveries from Mexico until you've finished the picture?

DEREK (*between embarrassment and anger*): There's absolutely no danger . . .

OCHSNER: Forgive me; I've had dealings down there with my trucks, so I'm probably being too pessimistic, but be careful not to put yourself at the mercy of some blackmailing official —export of antiquities is heavy jail time. I've dealt with some real beauts down there, they'll stop at nothing.

DEREK: I apologize, Phil.

OCHSNER: I'm only trying to protect the picture. For that, I'll do anything.

DEREK: As you should. I'm sorry, Phil.

OCHSNER: There's one more thing.—And please understand, there's nothing personal . . . But the management contacted me when I arrived . . . (*Hesitates, then plunges in.*) He asked whether the production was intending to make good on a pretty sizeable crap table debt you'd rung up. I got a strong hint that they were not letting you leave town until it was paid. I didn't get a figure . . .

DEREK: Thirty.

OCHSNER: You owe thirty thousand?—My only concern is that you have to be back in LA for the editing . . .

DEREK (*suppressing irritation now*): Took care of that this morning.

OCHSNER: Did you! Great . . .

DEREK: Cost me a night's sleep, though. I didn't finish up till quarter to five this morning.

OCHSNER: You mean . . .

DEREK: Won it back plus three thousand six-fifty-five.

OCHSNER (*short laugh*): God, you are something else, aren't you.

(OCHSNER *extends hand,* DEREK *takes it.*)

DEREK: Let's never have this conversation again, Phillip—I will always be where I need to be.

OCHSNER: Yes!—I'm sorry, Derek, but I . . .

DEREK (*returns to the bed*): Be right back, honey. This is Phil Ochsner, our producer. Good man.

(DEREK *exits.* OCHSNER *looks toward the door, shaking his head. Now goes to the bed.*)

OCHSNER: Could you open your eyes, Miss? Hello?—Hi, we met yesterday . . . I'm Phillip Ochsner, Bedlam Pictures? —Edna? Oh yes, she's a fine person.—That's right, we had a wonderful evening, I have great regard for Edna.—I've been thinking about you a lot . . . can I call you Kitty?—Good. (*Draws up a chair, sits.*) Kitty, I don't pretend to understand your frame of mind but I want to. I come out of a whole different kind of world and I'm not too sure on my feet yet, but I thought you might be interested in some of my experiences.

(*Slight pause.*)

My eldest son—I have two—or I had—the older one committed suicide last year.—With pills, yes.—Why? That's the question, of course. I can only guess; to be honest, he was not a lucky boy. Small, you know? And not really great looking. And I have to face it, I lost patience with him last couple of years.—Well, because the boy wins the Mathematics Prize at Harvard, has a tremendous future, and suddenly . . . turns inward, lays around listening to rock music, living like some kind of monk. "I have a misunderstanding with my life," he said. So I said to him, "Who doesn't?" I mean . . . do I understand how I start out dirt poor in Brooklyn, become a militant Marxist, a union organizer for twenty-three years and now I'm rich and employ over six hundred people? No, I can't understand it. How can this be me? Am I so brilliant? Do I have such a good smell? Or is it luck or just incomprehensible? I think I know what you're doing, Kitty, may I tell you? And please, don't be offended.—When you look in the mirror, it's like somebody else got inside you. But where are *you*, right? Who and where is Kitty!—How I know?—Because I'm exactly the same, or I was.—Well, I finally decided to stop wrestling with my fate. It's like wrestling a cat, you'll never pin him down and you can lose an eye in the bargain. A person, Kitty, is dealt a hand, he's got to play that hand, not somebody else's. This now is your hand, whoever you are is whoever you are, you can't drop your cards and step out of the game. Which I have a feeling is what you're trying to do.—How I know? I don't know how I know; I just ask myself, how does a woman who looks like that get so depressed? It has to be a very big answer.—The alternative? Acceptance, my dear. Any human life is a damaged apple—you just have to nibble around the spoiled spots and be thankful for the rest. That is my experience. . . . Just one more thing and I'll stop bothering

you.—Think about this, it's important: I was reading where
the whole universe may have originated because certain molecules happened to accidentally crash into other molecules,
and the explosion created everything. But it may not have
been inevitable, you follow me?—All the stars could have
floated around up there, like dead rocks for ever. In other
words, chance was built in from the beginning, so how about
taking a chance that you're going to be wonderful today and
get up, and let's go to work and explode the screen!

(*Slight pause. He listens with sadness.*)

Oh, I understand, but I beg you to believe me—if I was a
religious person I would say that when I look at you I know
why God made the world; just to look at you is to feel hope,
my dear. But if you don't work today my board will pull the
plug.—Have I made any impression at all?

(*Door opens,* DEREK *enters.*)

DEREK: How are we doing?

OCHSNER: I don't know. (*Turns to the bed.*) How are we doing,
Kitty?

DEREK: You might give Fassinger a call to come down.

OCHSNER: I'll call him. (*Sotto voce.*) . . . Talk to her. (OCHS-
NER *exits.*)

DEREK: What do you say, kid? (*Listens at length; an angry frown
growing.*) Yes, of course he respects you, we all respect you.—
(*His voice barreling out.*) Kitty! What on earth are you . . . ?
Have you forgotten who you're talking to? Who gave you
your first speaking role and picked you out of that roomful of
girls?—Exactly. And who supervised your costumes as though
you were already a star when nobody but your agent even
knew your name? And did I try to fuck you?—Then what is
all this about disrespect?—Oh, Flora!—But really my dear,
you can't ask me to talk to Flora.—No-no, my dear, I direct
actors not their coaches!—Interpreted! But darling, I don't
need to be interpreted, and you don't either! This game has to
stop, Kitty, it's outrageous and it's destroying you . . . and
this picture!

(*Light knocking, door opens and* EDNA *sticks her face in.*)

EDNA: Flora's here, and Jerome.

DEREK (*silently gestures for her to come in, and she closes the door
behind her*): I want you to stay in here with them.

EDNA: Where will you be?

DEREK: Right outside.

EDNA (*indicating the bed*): She may not want me listening here.

(*Knocking on the door, which opens and* TERRY CASE *sticks his head in.*)

TERRY: His Holiness is here, and Mrs. Holiness.

EDNA: We know, Terry.

TERRY: . . . Just telling you that the crew is ready to go.

DEREK: Thanks. I'll be out in a minute.

TERRY (*with a quick glance behind him*): I'd like to invite them both for high tea on a leaky Lithuanian submarine.

(TERRY *exits.* DEREK *returns to the bed.*)

DEREK: Kitty? We have approximately fifteen minutes to notify the crew to start moving out. I'll be in the other room.

(*He opens the door, gestures to* FLORA *and* JEROME *in the other room and they enter, he in his cowboy suit.*)

FLORA: Good morning, Derek dear. (*Gesturing weightily toward* JEROME.) This is my husband, Jerome Fassinger.

DEREK (*handshake*): Yes! How do you do? We did say hello once, I believe.

JEROME (*holding the hand importantly*): Only for a moment, yes. This is an honor. A great honor.

DEREK: Well! (*Laughs.*) Thank you very much!

JEROME: I will remember this moment.

DEREK (*an impatient glance toward the bed*): Yes, well . . .

FLORA (*pointing* at JEROME): There is a fan to end all fans, you know.

DEREK: We're pressed for time, Mr. Fassinger, so . . .

(*Gestures toward the bed as* FLORA *goes to it.*)

JEROME: Yes. Will you be available?

DEREK: In the other room. (*Glances at watch.*)

JEROME: Surely you can postpone any decision to shut down . . .

DEREK: Afraid it's now or never. Good luck.

(DEREK *exits.* JEROME *hesitates, glancing anxiously toward the bed.*)

FLORA: She wants you, Jerome. She . . .

JEROME (*his quick angered look silences her. He walks to the bed*): Yes, dear, I've come. (*Bends downward for a kiss.*) You look so tired. You must be completely exhausted.—Yes, of course, it's what we discussed, it's not the body that tires, it's the spirit, so what must we do?—Correct, we must address the spirit. (*Removes his Western hat and fondles it, smiles.*) —Do I? Well, maybe it's the hat; makes me *feel* handsome, so I look it.

FLORA (*pouring from a pitcher*): Have some water, darling. (*Hands over a glass.*)

JEROME: You giving her ice? You out of your mind?

FLORA: Leave the ice, darling! (*To* JEROME.) It cools her throat.

JEROME (*to* KITTY): You want ice?—So have ice. I just wanted to avoid a shock to the body. But your feeling is always the arbiter. What you feel is right is right for you, period. We don't have much time, dear, so . . . —No, no, dear, I am not here to get you back to work, I want that understood. I am here as your teacher and your friend. Whatever comes of my visit, so be it, I can't control. I never control; I speak; if a person listens he listens, if he doesn't he doesn't. (*Clears his throat.*)

FLORA: The air conditioning clogs his throat.

JEROME: My sinuses.

FLORA: I meant sinuses, but it drips down into the throat.

(JEROME *implores the ceiling with an impatient sigh.*)

I didn't mean to interrupt; forgive me; please. I'm just so nervous, I . . .

JEROME (*to* EDNA): I wish to be alone with her.

EDNA: Derek asked me to stay in case she . . .

JEROME: Flora can help if she needs it.

EDNA: . . . Well, all right. (*To the bed.*) I'll be right outside, Kitty!

(EDNA *exits.*)

JEROME: Kitty, I want to talk to you about Eleanora Duse, the great nineteenth-century Italian actress.—Thank you, dear, I had my breakfast.—No-no, I'd rather stand. Remember the book I gave you about her life.—Well, when you have time you must read it.—It's not important when she died, I think in the twenties. Or maybe earlier, I forgot. The thing is, people say "Eleanora Duse" like some kind of deity. A statue. Some kind of *object*. But she was a woman. A woman who knew hunger, disappointment, sex, thirst . . .

FLORA: Menstruation.

JEROME (*furiously*): Flora, I forbid you to . . . !

FLORA: I'm so happy you're here I can't contain myself! (*To the bed.*) God has blessed this man! If there were Jewish saints there he is.

JEROME (*starting to ride her praise despite himself*): What is important about Eleanora Duse? Not the greatest beauty, you realize. Beautiful, yes, but not extraordinary. A voice? Yes. But again not outstanding. What was it, Kitty! What made this ordinary . . . not ordinary in the ordinary sense, but she could walk down the street without people turning to look. This was no . . . no model, no movie star. Not that a movie star can't be extraordinary in the sense of sensitivity, but Duse, Duse . . . listen, the woman could sit alone on a stage, alone mind you, in an ordinary dress and shawl with no lines, not a word coming out of her mouth, Kitty, and just sit there motionless, motionless, Kitty, simply staring into space, and have her audience in tears. People moaning with sadness, people, people swaying from side to side as they joined with her, Kitty, joined with this human being in her spiritual isolation, you understand? Her existential loneliness was stripped naked to the world . . . (*To* FLORA.) Get her a handkerchief . . .

(*To* KITTY, *as* FLORA *produces kerchief and hands it to* KITTY.)

Don't blow too hard, it's bad for the brain.—So what is the point? Why do we revere this Italian woman? This woman of Italy with an ordinary voice, and face, and . . . and so on. What accounts for the incredible hold she has had on people of the theatre for something like a hundred years? People go around saying, "Duse this, Duse that," but it's all nonsense! We revere this woman, Kitty, BECAUSE SHE WAS AN ARTIST!

(*Door opens and* PAUL *enters.*)

Paul! Good morning!

PAUL: Hello, Jerome.

JEROME (*to the bed*): Ssh, darling, there's no need to scream! No-no, now wait a minute, please! Kitty, I am asking you to stop this!—I know, dear—I know, dear;—I know—yes, dear—I know . . .

FLORA (*indicating* JEROME): I told him everything, dear . . .

JEROME (*to* PAUL): Was there something you . . . ? (*To* KITTY.) —Let me *talk* to him, dear! (*To* PAUL.) Yes?

PAUL (*indicating* KITTY): I have your permission?

JEROME: Now, Paul, there's no reason to . . .

PAUL: I just wanted to be sure . . .

JEROME: I think you *ought* to talk, you two, I've always thought that. You *must* talk. Come, Flora . . . (*Starts toward the door, but then turns back to the bed.*) All right, dear.—Yes, okay, I'll stay. (*He turns to* PAUL *with a helpless "What can I do?" shrug.*)

PAUL: Derek and I are thinking that the best thing might be to shut down for say a week, and get her into a hospital where she could really rest . . .

JEROME: Will they go for that—the company?

PAUL: Ochsner is calling New York now.

FLORA: Now *that* sounds to me like . . .

JEROME (*throws* FLORA *his look and she shuts up, then, stalling for* KITTY's *reaction*): Well it's certainly something worth a discussion . . .

PAUL (*to the bed*): Would you agree to that?

JEROME (*to the bed*): . . . There's no need to scream, dear!—I know, I know, but . . .

PAUL (*to the bed*): Because Derek is busy on the phone trying to keep this production from collapsing so he asked me to propose it to you! I wouldn't have disturbed you otherwise!

JEROME: Ssh! There's no need to . . .

PAUL: Are you instructing me, Jerome? Please don't do that.

JEROME: I was simply trying to keep her from getting too excited.

PAUL: Yes, well, you're a bit late with that.

JEROME: And what is that supposed to imply?

PAUL: She's been almost two months trying to get you to . . . to bestir yourself and come and help her out here.

FLORA: How dare you!

JEROME: I've spoken with her practically every day on the phone!

PAUL (*indicating the bed*): Yes, and here she lies. (*Responds to* KITTY.) —I didn't say it was his fault.—That's right . . . or Flora's either. Or yours, certainly.—Right, so that leaves me. And maybe some day God will punish me for going along with all this idiocy!

(*He turns away in anguish, and* JEROME *steps in.*)

JEROME: . . . Darling, you'll destroy your voice screaming like this!—I know, dear.—Yes, I know.—Yes.—I will. (*To* PAUL.) I guess you'd better leave.

PAUL (*thinks for a moment*): Jerome . . .

JEROME: Yes, we should have a talk.

PAUL: Why not now? There's really only one question, seems to me.

JEROME: But she wants you to leave . . .

PAUL: In a minute. The question is, who is responsible for her? That needs to be settled.

JEROME (*to the bed*): —Kitty, you can't go on like this, you will have no voice! Now please! (*To* PAUL.) Clearly, I can't take responsibility in that sense.

PAUL: Right. And Flora certainly can't. And Derek has a production to look out for, and she doesn't want me around . . . (*Responding to the bed.*) —You're damned right—I don't *want* to be around. So you have nobody, is all I wanted you to understand! And nobody means nobody. Especially not him and not her, so you'd better stop thinking they're looking after you! (*Shouting over* KITTY*'s screams.*) You are alone in this world, Kitty! Everything else is bullshit!

JEROME: Now just a minute! I was not implying that I . . .

PAUL: It's all perfectly clear now, Jerome, why muddy it up? You are her teacher, it's perfectly right that she look to you for instruction—except that you can't be here, so you won't be! And that means she has to stop depending on you, doesn't it.

JEROME: She knows she can call me at any time day or night! And Flora is here!

PAUL (*indicates the bed*): But clearly this absentee supervision hasn't worked, has it. (*Shouting directly to the bed.*) I would scream too if I were in your spot, I would shake heaven! . . . I just wanted to clear it up, Kitty, so now you know exactly where you are and who you can look to for help! (PAUL *goes to the door, yanks it open, exits.*)

FLORA (*pouring*): Here, darling, take water. (*Indicating the door and departed* PAUL.) Now you see why she's suffering; he's hard as nails.

JEROME: Shocking. Absolutely shocking. And seeing her condition. (*To the bed.*) —I wish I could, dear, I'd gladly stay; it pains me to say I can't, darling, but I have important meetings in New York in the morning. Now listen, about this idea of a week's rest. And I want to be clear, I am not advising, but if it's an idea you have in your mind I would say, yes, take the week.—Good. (*To* FLORA.) Go out and tell Derek she agrees.

FLORA: Wonderful! (*Points at bed; commandingly.*) You are going to rest!

(FLORA *exits.* JEROME *sits at bedside.*)

JEROME: I have to talk to you more about Duse, I think it helps you formulate something, doesn't it.—Good.—She was, yes, she was married couple of times, divorced and many lovers.—Oh, I don't know, a dozen maybe . . . at least. More, I think.—Yes, two, a boy that died after a few months and a girl who she treasured. But the biggest problem was exhaustion.—Oh yes, she'd often work herself into a collapse. (*Gesture toward* KITTY.) Exactly the same thing.— How she'd come out of it? Work. "Work is my life," she said. But of course she had a culture that supported her, people around her who understood that this was a great artist not some kind of chopped liver. You see, they couldn't take her seriously for a long time.—Well, because she was not posing. The great Sarah Bernhardt had worked out about twenty-five different poses which she could take out of her pocketbook, exactly the same for each performance. You want anger? Here's anger. (*Strikes a pose for each feeling.*) Pity? Danger? Love? Admiration? Contempt! Terror! What I call early technological, cookie-cutter acting. But very expert; she is definitely not to be put down. Bernhardt was the IBM of acting. For a while she even fooled George Bernard Shaw. And along comes this Italian non-beauty . . . maybe five feet tall . . . five-two, maybe . . . and practically no makeup . . . and refuses the big entrance. I mean Bernhardt, when she entered the stage it was—you know, Moby Dick, the National City Bank—with the white full-length satin gowns and ten pounds of makeup and the whole ta-da! . . . Duse practically entered by accident. Like she wandered in from the street. And she understood silence. Bernhardt dominated the stage, Duse loved it. I don't have to tell you, darling—to act, Duse had to be in love. With something

. . . her child, her room, a man, her part, the city, the country, a quilt—life! You, darling, are not surrounded by culture or by love but exploitation, by people digging out pieces of your flesh! So you are left, trying to sing intimately in a roaring wind, a gale, a typhoon of greed and insensitivity!—But darling, how could I not know! I know you down to the back of your spine and I'm the only one who does!

(*Slight pause.*)

Now about this week-off idea. Consider it carefully. I can't advise, it's up to you. But I think it's okay to try, but I have to be honest, darling, there is one element to watch out for.—I sense they are trying to get me to say that I guarantee you'll come back, ready to start work, or something of this kind. My sense of what's going on here, in other words, is that they would like to tell the board of directors in New York that Fassinger is taking responsibility for you. Which in a sense I am . . . between the two of us, but not publicly.—Because darling I have to think of my school and my students, are you following me? Their faith in me is all-important to these young people, Kitty, and if, God forbid, let's say the worst happens and you can't get yourself to go back to work it'll be all over the papers and who are they going to blame? Me! I know it seems impossible to you but there are people who hate me.—Of course it's envy, but nevertheless . . . And besides, out of sheer respect for your art—this is important, darling—I refuse to make it look like you're some kind of automated personality that I push a button and you come out dancing. (*Leans in closer.*) —What? I can't hear you.—*Today!* My God, you really think you can?—Yes, of course, it would be fantastic for me too. I mean that I came out here and you were suddenly able to . . . ! But you sure now? You don't want to try walking around first? Shall I notify Derek?—You are a phenomenon! Duse would go down on her knees to you! (*Starts for the door, stops.*) —No! The credit is yours, not mine. All I did was come and remind you of who you are and what you are and forge the link between your work and the whole cultural history of your art! Kitty, your greatness to me is like a country!

(*Hurries to the door and exits. The silhouette stirs on the bed. Now it struggles to rise, but falls back as* EDNA *enters.*)

Kitty! Is it true? How wonderful! But . . . forgive me,
dear, but do you really feel up to it? I mean . . . I don't
know how to say this . . . but I hope you're not doing it
for Jerome's sake. I mean you *are* strong enough, right?—
Well, that is just great! Wait, the air conditioning is very
high in here, let me get your robe and get you a shower.—
Oh! I didn't know you'd taken one. (*Goes to a point, picks up
a white robe.*) —Paul? Could we wait till later to talk about
that?—Well, I'm not comfortable talking about Paul, I've
known him so many years.—I won't deny that, I've always
admired Paul.—But what can I say?—He's devastated.—
Well, that it turned out like this between you. Oh darling,
you mustn't believe that!—You've been tremendously important to him, dear, I think you underestimate yourself. I
mean he adores you, darling—well he did anyway, and I
really think he still does.—But Kitty, how could I be blaming you when I know what you go through every day with
your problems.—But we all have problems, dear, I'm not
criticizing.—Me? Of course I do—I don't have anybody for
one thing, and here I am forty-five and counting, (*chuckles*)
that's a problem, isn't it?—I don't know why, I suppose I'm
maybe too shy, or just not attractive enough in that way. But
it's no great tragedy, I have a lot in life.—Well, for one thing
I have you to look after. (*Chuckles.*) That's a lot.—Of course
I enjoy it, it gives me great pleasure when you're happy with
yourself, and to feel I may have helped—it thrills me,
frankly.—Honesty? Well, darling, (*laughs*) when you're not a
knockout you can at least be honest. (*Laughs.*) It's something to hang on to!—Could what "work again"—you
mean with you and Paul? . . . Please, dear, I'd really rather
not have to say . . . Well, I guess I do wonder if it could
work, dear. Maybe you both owe each other more forgiveness than it's possible to give.—But I'm *not* blaming you,
Kitty. Oh, please don't be angry with me, I'm doing all I
can, darling . . . ! (*She is weeping, holds up the robe.*) Come,
dear, let's get you started, they're all waiting . . . (*Outcry.*)
Please don't ask me to blame him, Kitty, I can't blame anyone! For anything! It's this damned business! It's terrible!

    (*A knock. She goes to door,* OCHSNER *enters.*)

She'll be right there, Phillip.

OCHSNER (*throwing up his arms*): At last she calls me Phillip! (*Cups her face.*) You are beautiful today, Edna.—You mentioned you like lobsters; I'm flying in lobsters from Maine for dinner, if she doesn't need you . . . (*Turns quickly to the bed.*) Huh? (*Back to* EDNA, *pointing at bed.*) You hear? She says you're free for dinner! (*Goes to bed.*) I got my board to agree to a week off, but Fassinger says he got you to agree to work today?—Yes, he must have great insight. I just wanted to tell you how happy I am. So I'll let you get dressed . . . By the way, I've ordered Mrs. Fassinger her own limo . . .

(DEREK *enters with* TERRY CASE, *goes to bed.*)

DEREK: Great news, kid. I'd like Terry to have one more look.

TERRY (*opens his flashlight*): Want to have you lookin' great, babe. (*Shines it down on her.*) Good. Better than before. Here's a couple drops for the eyeballs. (*Squeezes a bottle over her eyes.*) Great. (*To* DEREK.) Let's go. (*To the bed as he opens door.*) Proud of you, Kit! See you at the set!

(CASE *exits.*)

DEREK (*to the bed*): Anything I can do?—Forget it, kid, no need to thank me . . . whatever helps finish the picture, that's all.—Darling, if Jerome helped, he's got my gratitude, I don't hold grudges . . . Kitty? (*Bends closer.*) Is she falling asleep?

EDNA (*comes to bed*): Kitty?

DEREK: Oh. Christ! Kitty!

EDNA: Ssh!—please don't yell . . . !

DEREK: Is she out? What's happening!

EDNA: Darling? Are you sleeping?

DEREK: Goddamit, we've called the whole crew and the extras!

EDNA: Derek, please! She can't help it!

DEREK: What is this, some kind of power trip? She's trying to humiliate everyone!

EDNA: That's not true, Derek, you mustn't think that! (*To the bed.*) Darling! Can we try to get ready? Kitty dear?

(KITTY *suddenly sits up, her back to us. She gets out of bed and stands straight for a moment, then dashes for the bathroom, pushes the door open and disappears within.* EDNA *calls at the door.*)

Can I help you, dear? (*Listens.*) Are you all right?

DEREK: Now what!

EDNA: I beg you, Derek, hold on. She'll come through for you, I know she will. Please, don't let yourself get angry . . .

DEREK: This is outrageous, it's humiliating and outrageous! In thirty years of directing I have never . . .

EDNA: I know, I know. But maybe one can't expect people who've been kicked around to suddenly behave like people who've had love and affection.

DEREK: Edna, this is all vengeance! And on me! And all I ever did was . . .

EDNA: . . . It's fear, Derek, it's terror! The bottom drops out; she's afraid she's going to be ridiculous; she has no . . . no . . . what the hell is the word?—*resources*! She is like a sensitive poet! Yes, an abused, wounded poet! But she is strong too, Derek, I promise you she is going to finish this picture! But you must hold on, try to be as kind . . . As kind as you've been!

(*Door opens,* FLORA *enters, goes to the bed.*)

FLORA: Where is she?

EDNA: In the bathroom.

FLORA (*to* DEREK): Jerome is making an earlier plane so he had to go.

DEREK (*preoccupied*): Of course.

FLORA: He told me to tell you how honored he was to meet you.

DEREK: What? (*Focusing.*) Oh . . . he told me.

FLORA: He is constantly using you in his classes as an example of . . .

DEREK: Flora, I am preoccupied with a problem that I don't think this is contributing to, okay? You have a limo of your own now, right? Why don't you go out to the set and wait for her there?

FLORA: We always go over lines together on the way out.

DEREK: This time I will take her in my car, I have things to discuss with her, okay?

FLORA: Absolutely, Derek, but she needs me with her . . . Jerome ordered me to go out together with her every morning so that she feels supported by a . . .

DEREK: Flora, go out of this room!

FLORA (*alarmed*): What is this attitude! Jerome got her back on her feet, didn't he?

DEREK (*profoundly menacing*): Go out of this room, Flora!
     (*Door opens and* OCHSNER *enters.*)

FLORA: Well, I wish someone would tell me what this is all about!

     (FLORA *exits, passing* OCHSNER, *who looks a bit bewildered by the emotion in the room.*)

OCHSNER: What's happening?

DEREK: She's in the bathroom.

OCHSNER (*to* EDNA): You look pale.

EDNA: It's so early, that's all.

     (*A pause.* OCHSNER *looks from* EDNA *to* DEREK, *who both look blankly into space.*)

OCHSNER: So . . . it's going to happen, isn't it? Because everyone's been called.

EDNA: Give her a few minutes.

DEREK: I think it will, yes. Happen.

OCHSNER: I had no idea . . . (*A smiling head-shake, shielding his fears.*) It's fascinating, but it's some far cry from the trucking business.

DEREK: It's not a business, Phillip. It's an art pretending to be a business. But it's never been any different; the artist dies in his work, the businessman carries his work into the world. Like ants carrying off the rotting twigs of a fallen branch to feed the other ants.

OCHSNER: It's hard to put all this together with what she's like on the screen. The woman is so glorious.

DEREK: Yes, she is, that's why we're here.

OCHSNER: And she's so witty. So packed with . . . with . . .

EDNA: Life.

OCHSNER: Yes, life. (*Looks at his watch. Then to* DEREK *with a fallen look.*) Is it over? Tell me.

DEREK: Not yet.

     (*Door opens,* CASE *enters, goes to* DEREK.)

CASE: I came back, Derek, because . . .

DEREK: I know.

CASE: If you want to continue the last shot . . .

DEREK: . . . You need the morning light.

CASE: Right. So she's got an hour for makeup, and I'd say we'd have another forty-five minutes and that's it. So she starts off right now or we lose the day.

DEREK: Yes. (*Looks at him stoically; sounding like farewell.*) Thanks, kid.

> (*A moment; they stand staring at one another;* CASE *is gradually realizing that* DEREK *is punch drunk and his alarm darkens his face.*)

CASE: We're still in the ring, aren't we?

> (DEREK *is silent, staring.*)

Derek baby, we still in there?

> (DEREK *is silent.*)

It'll kill the kid, Derek. She's all done if we close this thing. (*He comes close to* DEREK's *face.*) She's got ten more years in that body if we get her through this, you gotta hold on, baby!

> (DEREK *is silent.*)

I want you to tell me. We still in there?

DEREK (*inhales, closing his eyes*): Yes.

> (CASE *and* DEREK *embrace in silence.*)

CASE: Edna?

> (*A quick salute to her and he exits. No one moves for a long moment.*)

DEREK (*stiffening*): Has she locked that door, Edna?

EDNA (*goes to the door, tries the knob*): Yes.

DEREK: She wouldn't be doing anything to herself, would she?

OCHSNER: God!

EDNA (*calls at the bathroom door*): Kitty? (*Silence.*) Kitty dear? (*Silence.*) Kitty!

KITTY (*from within*): Yes!

EDNA: Can I help?

> (*Door to the other room opens and* PAUL *enters.* KITTY's *muffled voice is heard but what she is saying is only understood by* EDNA *who has her ear pressed to the door.*)

I'll get it, dear! (*She rushes to a point, opens a drawer, pulls out a bandana and rushes back to the door, knocks, we hear it being unlatched and she hands in the bandana and a pair of sunglasses and the door shuts.*)

> (PAUL *sits.*)

PAUL: Well, Jerome's left anyway. Maybe we're gaining on it.

> (*Another pause.* EDNA *comes to* PAUL.)

EDNA: Paul, dear, can we talk for a minute?

PAUL: Go ahead . . . (*Indicating* OCHSNER *and* DEREK.) I'm too tired to hide anything, what is it?

EDNA: I'm just wondering if it won't upset her again . . .

PAUL: Seeing me?

DEREK: Stay where you are, kid. (*To* EDNA.) Let us all resolve to end humiliation, hers and ours. And yours, too.

EDNA: I don't feel humiliated, I feel . . .

DEREK: Edna, my dear, we can only help her by being ourselves and not the dream creatures her desperation sometimes turned us into. I wish you'd stay right here, Paul—reality has to intervene sooner or later.

> (*A moment. No one stirs. Then he gets up and goes to the bathroom door.*)

Kitty? I want you to come out now and let's go to work. (*Silence.*) Kitty, do you hear me?

> (*The bathroom door slowly opens.* KITTY *comes out. She is in a bathrobe, her entire head wrapped in the bandana and she is wearing black sunglasses.*)

Hi, kid.

> (*She steps over to him looking up into his face.*)

Ready?

> (*He offers his elbow, she slips her hand under his arm, they walk a few steps toward the door when she slides down beside him and* EDNA *catches her.*)

EDNA: Here!

> (DEREK *picks her up with* PAUL*'s help and she is set down on the bed.* EDNA *leans down to her.*)

—What?—Yes, of course.

> (*She comes to* DEREK *who has walked from the bed.* PAUL *and* OCHSNER *remain staring down at her.*)

She wants to start this afternoon.

OCHSNER: No. (*All turn to him. To* DEREK.) She'll rest in the hospital for six days as we discussed. I'll call everything off till then. (*He starts for the door.*)

EDNA: Thanks, Phillip.

OCHSNER (*surprised*): Thank *you*, Edna.

> (OCHSNER *exits.* DEREK *goes to the bed, looks down for a moment.*)

DEREK: Poor thing.

EDNA: Oh, she'll be marvelous when she comes back! . . . You see?—She's already asleep without a single pill; her mind is beginning to rest.—Maybe all she needed was a little . . . you know . . . consideration.

(DEREK *and* PAUL *look at her with mouth-dropping incredulity. She breaks the moment with an almost hysterical burst of laughter, registering the absurdity of her remark; the two men join in this laughing release, and* DEREK *reaches out and takes her in his arms and she nearly goes limp there, trying to stop this crazy laughter.*)

Oh Derek, dear, I'm so sorry.

DEREK (*cupping her cheek*): Darling, we're all going to look back at this like a walk in the garden. (*Releasing* EDNA *he turns to* PAUL.) And so our revels are ended, kid.

PAUL: Want to thank you for your patience, Derek.

DEREK: And I for yours. (*To* EDNA.) Call me when she wakes; I'll take her there tonight, if possible.

(DEREK *exits. Pause.*)

EDNA: She didn't blow up when she saw you.

(PAUL *nods vaguely. She comes and sits beside him.*)

May I tell you my feeling?

(PAUL *turns to her.*)

I feel that once this tension is over . . .

PAUL: It can't work anymore, dear.

EDNA: But deep down I think she . . .

PAUL: It's all gone, Edna. What we had that was alive and crazy has been pounded into some hateful, ordinary dust.

EDNA: I have to go by my feelings, Paul—Kitty loves you.

PAUL: But she doesn't *like* me, Edna. And how could she—I didn't save her, I didn't do the miracle I kind of promised. And she didn't save me, as she promised. So nothing *moved*, you know? It was like we kept endlessly introducing ourselves to one another. I'm afraid of her now—I have no idea what she's going to do next. (*Slight pause.*) I wonder if maybe there was just too much hope; we drank it, swam in it. And for fear of losing it didn't dare look inside. A sad story. (*He goes to the bed, looks down at* KITTY.) Isn't she something? In a week she'll come back all fresh and new—like spring. And wondering what all the excitement was about. Derek said it—he calls her the Mississippi. He's right. (*Goes to* EDNA, *hugs her.*) Thanks, dear.

(*She grasps his face and buries a kiss in his cheek.*)

EDNA: Try, can't you?

PAUL: No more. Just . . . no more. For both our sakes.

(*He goes to the door and exits. She sits rocking her body forward and back.*)

(OCHSNER *enters, comes and sits beside her.*)

OCHSNER: Just spoke to the manager—we don't have to move her out; the fire's going down.

EDNA: Oh thank God.

OCHSNER: Derek'll be up shortly; he'll take her to the hospital.

EDNA (*starts to rise*): I'll get her ready.

OCHSNER (*detains her with his hand; she silently sits*): Sit for a moment.

(*They sit in silence for a beat.*)

The sky's turning all nice and blue again.

EDNA: You must be exhausted.

OCHSNER: Not too bad. (*Glance toward the bed.*) —Is she asleep?

EDNA: Up and down.

OCHSNER: It's like childbirth . . . a movie. The baby is cleaned up, the sheets are changed, the mother is bathed . . . and everybody forgets the screaming.

EDNA: They have to, I guess, or they wouldn't make another one.

OCHSNER: I'll call you in New York, may I?

EDNA: Do. Please.

(*They rise together, hands joined.*)

OCHSNER: How about a lobster tonight?

EDNA: Yes! Lovely.

(*He touches her face, kisses her.*)

OCHSNER: You know, I just realize—I've been relying on you through this whole thing.

EDNA: That's funny—I was just thinking the same about you.

OCHSNER: . . . Thank you, Edna. See you tonight.

EDNA: Yes . . . Phillip!

(*They share a laugh; he exits. She goes to the bed.*)

Derek will be here in a few minutes, darling, so we have to get you dressed, okay?—Well, for the hospital.

(*She nearly breaks down, then reaches to* KITTY *and helps her to her feet.*)

There we are.

(*Opening the bathroom door and ushering* KITTY *in.*)

Who? Oh that was Mr. Ochsner . . . just to say the emergency is over, the fire's going down. The sky's clear and bright. (*Alone, she goes to the window and looks up and out into the distance.*) Isn't it wonderful? We forgot all about it and the whole state could have burned. (*She finds her pocketbook and takes out a mirror and a brush, sits and with a sigh at the sight of her tired self, gives her hair a few brushes, then leaves off, and plucks at her cheeks to bring color into them. Then she stares ahead.*) . . . But Terry says it makes the seeds germinate. (*She turns upstage.*) —The fire, darling . . . the heat opens up the seeds.

EARLY PLAYS

THE GRASS STILL GROWS

A Comedy

CHARACTERS

ABE SIMON, *a coat manufacturer*
ESTHER, *his wife*
BEN SIMON, *their eldest son*
ARNOLD SIMON, *their younger son*
GRAMP, *Esther's father*
SAM ROTH, *a wealthy manufacturer*
HELEN ROTH, *his daughter*
LOUISE, *Abe's bookkeeper*
MR. MARTIN, *a coat buyer*
DAVE SIMON, *Abe's brother*
MAX SCHNEEWEISS, *Abe's shop foreman*
And a furrier's clerk

ACT ONE

The living room of the Simon home in New York City. In the left wall, upstage, is the door to the street. Next to it, further downstage, is a large window with eggshell-colored curtains, and beside it is a cabinet radio. Nearest the front on the left is a large maroon chair, very comfortable. A line of small windows runs along the back wall. Under these, flush against the wall, is a long couch which might be called green. On the right of it, in the corner, is another armchair, and in this same upstage right corner is the landing of the stairway to the second floor. The doorway to the dining room and kitchen is in the right wall, and beside this on the downstage side stands a carved, high-backed chair. There are small rugs and a few lamps.

This is a seven-room house, vintage 1929. The furnishings are old but in good taste and they were probably expensive. At the moment, however, they are distinguished mainly by the fact that they are too many.

On the rise, ESTHER SIMON *is sitting on the couch knitting, as usual, and listening to the voice of a sentimental crooner coming through the radio. Behind her through the small open windows, the new twilight can be seen. She is dressed fit for a bridge game in good company. She knits in time, taps her feet in time, and her head sways in time with the rapturous song. As she is beginning to conduct the music with her needle,* ABE SIMON *comes into the house from the left door. He walks heavily not only because he is heavy and tall, but because it is a very warm June evening, and it has been a hot June day. His jacket is on his arm and he tosses it next to his wife, drops his newspaper on it, and kisses the lady with one deft movement. He straightens up, stretches, shows a pained face, and goes to the radio lumberingly.*

ABE: You want this on? (*Turns radio off.*)
ESTHER: No, you can turn it off.
ABE (*sitting in chair next to radio*): Hear from Arnold?
ESTHER: Not yet. I'm worried, Abe.

ABE: He'll be in soon. It takes time from Baltimore. (*Stretches out in chair.*) Ahhh. (*Bends his feet.*)

ESTHER: Hot in the city today?

ABE: Awful. (*Deep breath.*) I seen a man drop dead on Thirty-Ninth Street this afternoon.

ESTHER: No! Who is he?

ABE: I don't know. I couldn't look at him.

ESTHER: I don't want you to walk in the sun. Go up and take a shower. You'll cool off.

ABE: I'll wait a little.

ESTHER: Where's Ben?

ABE: On the corner talking to Louise. He'll be right home.

ESTHER: I wish he wouldn't walk so slow with that girl.

ABE: Ah, don't worry, Esther, nothing'll come of it.

ESTHER: She's after him. I can see it, Abe.

ABE: So what'll I do, fire her? She's the best bookkeeper I ever had. (*Closes his eyes.*) For the twelve dollars a week I pay her I'll have to expect a little romance.

ESTHER (*smiles*): Then I'd rather you paid more money and got a married woman.

ABE: You're right, you're right. But let's not start anything now.

ESTHER: Did you have anything for supper? (*Certain he didn't.*)

ABE: Just a bite, but cool. It's good to eat out Monday nights for a change. Ben enjoys it.

ESTHER: You ate potatoes, though, didn't you.

ABE: Not a one. Not even a smell of it. When I tell you I'm on a diet, I'm on a diet. I had sour cream and coffee with one sugar.

ESTHER (*ready to laugh*): And no potatoes with the sour cream?

ABE (*pause*): So I ate a piece of potato. I'm starving to death, Esther. (*Smiles.*)

ESTHER: You wouldn't starve. You're eating too much.

ABE: Really, I don't see why it can hurt me.

ESTHER: No? Look at your heart.

ABE (*concerned*): Potatoes is bad for my heart?

ESTHER: Sure, it presses . . . and it clogs the vessels. You think if you close your eyes and eat a potato it don't count.

ABE: All right. I'll only drink water. I'll become a nun.

ESTHER: Don't become a nun. Just don't eat what you're not supposed to. (*She watches him closely, then looks off.*) How was it today, busy?

ABE (*nods*): Had a very good day. We got a nice order for three hundred coats, and . . . (*softly*) . . . why don't you listen to me?

ESTHER (*apologetically, with some sarcasm*): I'm listening, Abe.

ABE (*looks at her searchingly*): What's the matter, Esther?

ESTHER: Nothing. Nothing's the matter.

ABE: Why are you all dressed up? What happened?

ESTHER: Must something happen for me to put on a clean dress?

ABE: Why don't you believe me?

ESTHER: I do believe you. What makes you think I don't believe you?

ABE (*rises*): Because you didn't ask me who I sold the coats to. Esther, I said we were busy. I said we sold three hundred coats today.

ESTHER: Then that's all there is to say.

ABE: But you don't believe me! Why?

ESTHER: Because you're not telling the truth! (*Turns away. Pause.*)

ABE (*softly*): Then I'm a liar?

ESTHER: Sam Roth called up before.

ABE (*stands still*): And?

ESTHER (*looks straight at him*): He'll be over tonight. Abe, you didn't tell me you needed money.

ABE: Oh, so that's why you think the world is ending tonight.

ESTHER: Abe, you've got to tell me . . . how bad is it?

ABE: Is Roth bringing his daughter?

ESTHER: Abe, you're not answering me! How bad is it?

ABE: . . . I seen it worse. Esther, take my word for it, the world will be here tomorrow, and the day after, and the day after that, so why get yourself excited? Is Roth bringing his daughter?

ESTHER (*brightens*): Yes, Helen is coming along too.

ABE: Ben is not gonna like that, Esther.

ESTHER: Well I assure you I didn't invite the girl. . . .

ABE (*nods*): Assure me, assure me.

ESTHER (*laughs, waves her hand*): Oh, go on.

ABE: Go on, but you oughta know that when a rich man goes visiting with his daughter it ain't to give her exercise.

ESTHER: Well if a man tells me he's bringing his daughter can I refuse?

ABE (*quieting her*): I'm just sayin' that if Ben smells a rat he's gonna shoot off fireworks.

ESTHER: I still say that Sam Roth, rich as he is, doesn't forget his friends, and you don't appreciate it.

ABE: Esther . . . Lady . . . Sam Roth has no friends. . . . (*Enter* LOUISE *and* BEN *from left.* BEN *carries jacket and paper like his father.*)

LOUISE: Good evening, Mrs. Simon, did Arnold arrive yet?

ESTHER: No, Louise, and we didn't hear a word either.

LOUISE (*sympathetically clucks her tongue*): Well . . . he'll get in all right, don't worry.

BEN (*to* LOUISE): Oh, you're just as bad as she is. He's not flying the Arctic . . . it's only Baltimore. You get out of here, Lou, before you get her excited.

LOUISE: And I suppose you're not excited.

BEN: I never am, am I?

LOUISE: Not much. You haven't done a stitch of work all day.

ABE (*laughs*): That's right, Louise, you tell him.

LOUISE (*admiring* BEN *and smiling. To* ABE): He thinks he's such a stoic.

ABE (*laughs*): Yeh.

LOUISE (*moves to go. To* ESTHER): I may be in later.

BEN: If he's not too tired, I'll bring him over.

LOUISE (*as she goes*): Don't forget.

BEN: So long, Lou.

(*Exit* LOUISE *left.*)

ABE (*as* BEN *is tossing his jacket and paper down*): What's that . . . stoic?

BEN (ESTHER *and* BEN *laugh*): Ah, you wouldn't remember if I told you.

ESTHER: No, tell him, Ben. He's always saying wrong words. (*To* ABE.) A stoic is somebody that never gets excited.

ABE: Oh . . . that's a good word, stoic. But who never gets excited?

BEN: You can't teach him words because he doesn't believe them.

ESTHER: Then you should take more time with him. Where can Arnold be?

BEN (*sitting*): Are you starting that again? He's been hitch-hiking home from school for seven years: he won't get killed the last time.

ESTHER: Thank God it's the last time.

ABE: Who would believe that seven years would fly by so fast? I still can't get it in my head that he's a doctor.

ESTHER: I remember like today the first day he went down to school.

ABE (*laughs*): To look at you it was the end of the world.

ESTHER (*smiling*): And to look at you? I remember we met you downtown to buy him a suit the day before Arny left and you were crying like a baby.

ABE (*smiles embarrassedly*): I would've liked to send him off better.

BEN: Ta, ah . . . I forgot to return that library book. I take out one book a year and I can't even return it on time.

ESTHER: You should've seen him, Ben, he cried right on Thirty-Sixth Street. I'll never forget it. As big as he is.

ABE: Well . . . I never really believed he would go away. (*A little ashamed.*) It was . . . sudden to me.

ESTHER: It wasn't sudden to me but if I'd have known that he'd have to hitch-hike home every year I wouldn't have let him go so quick.

BEN: A million kids come home from college by thumb every year and your son is going to get killed.

ESTHER: Kids from college, yes, but not a boy who just got his medical degree. (*Warily.*) Believe me, it's a marvellous thing that Abe Simon can't send his son carfare to come home like a human being . . . and it's even better that we couldn't go to see him graduate. That's all I got to say.

BEN: Why Abe Simon? There're richer men than he ever was who can't even get a salesman's job today, let alone a business. The war is over, Mom.

ESTHER: Yeh? How about Joe Baum? His wife don't still wear mink?

BEN (*smiles*): Sure, Mom, but what is Joe Baum wearing? Stripes.

ABE (*laughing. To* ESTHER): *That* was a mistake. You should never've mentioned Joe Baum.

ESTHER: All right, laugh, but I still say Arny should be home by now and he ain't, and God knows what happened to him.

ABE: Well what can I do? If I could get blood from a stone I'd get blood. But the stones is all dry so I can't get no blood. I feel worse than you do about it.

ESTHER: You could at least have tried to put something aside for him so he wouldn't have to. . . .

BEN: Put aside! From what?

ABE: Don't bark at her, she can hear.

BEN: Oh I'm tired of coming home and having her think that the business is the same as it was in 1928. It's time she knew.

ESTHER: What should I know?

BEN (*looks at her. Pause*): Forget I said anything.

ESTHER: What is it that I ought to know?

ABE: He didn't mean anything.

ESTHER: What do you expect me to do if you never tell me anything? Ben, tell me what's the matter!

BEN: All right, I'll tell you. . . .

ABE (*warningly*): That's all, Ben!

BEN (*to* ESTHER, *ignoring* ABE): We need three thousand dollars in a hurry, Mother. We've got our backs to the wall. If we don't get help we'll be out. Now you know.

ABE: We wouldn't be out!

BEN: Stop making it easy for her! If it comes it'll send her to the hospital! The trouble with you is that you see the handwriting on the wall and you suddenly forget how to read. I can't stand seeing her walking around on a bubble, and it's going to stop right now.

(*Pause.*)

ESTHER (*shaking her head*): That's fine. (*To* ABE.) What's the matter, haven't I got the brains to understand, that you don't tell me anything? Am I a three-year-old child that you put me to sleep?

ABE (*looks away*): I don't like to tell you because we always got out of it before and we'll get out of it again.

ESTHER: Yeh, but in the meantime. . . .

ABE (*rises quickly*): Because every time I tell you something you go crazy, that's why. Because I got enough to worry about without thinking how miserable you are too. (*Angrily to* BEN.) And I don't like you to talk when I tell you not to talk!

Over thirty years I ran that business myself and she was happy here at home! She doesn't have to know and it's my affairs what goes on downtown . . . and . . . and it's my affairs!

BEN: All right, it's your affairs.

ABE: Don't mimic me!

ESTHER (*glancing at the windows above her*): Quiet, quiet . . . the neighbors.

(*Pause.* ABE *sits slowly.*)

Abe, I think you oughta change your shirt and put on your white pants.

ABE: I can talk to him the way I am. Roth knows I'm not a millionaire anymore.

BEN (*a bit startled*): Sam Roth coming over tonight?

ESTHER (*fearful*): Yeh, isn't that nice?

BEN: I don't know yet. What does he want?

(ABE *laughs.*)

ESTHER: Does he have to want something? He called up and he says he wants to help you out.

BEN (*to* ABE): What is she talking about?

ABE: Yeh, he's coming over.

BEN: But you asked him for money twice. Why the sudden philanthropy?

ESTHER: I don't know why you both look like somebody died in the house. If it's unhealthy to talk to a rich man anymore then throw him out when he comes in. The world is in a wonderful condition if a man can't visit with his daughter once in. . . .

BEN: Oh, his daughter! So that's the story!

ESTHER (*smiling, about to cry*): Is it a crime to invite such a fine. . . .

BEN: You invited her!

ESTHER (*failing*): No! She wanted to come along!

BEN: Helen is not the kind of a girl to *want* to come along and you know it!

ESTHER: Sure, she's a fine girl!

BEN: Are you agreeing with me or arguing?

ESTHER: I don't know, leave me alone! (*Holds her ears.*)

BEN (*to* ABE): Did you ever hear of a thing like that? He knows that down the place we're too busy to talk about nonsense like that so he's got a new tactic now. Corner me where I live. (*To* ESTHER.) Well he's sadly mistaken, that fat ass . . . I'm going to sleep.

ESTHER: Don't go to sleep yet.

ABE (*to* BEN): Why do you act like that? The girl ain't gonna eat you up.

BEN: You too, eh?

ABE: What me too? I got married long ago, I ain't even interested.

ESTHER (*outraged*): What are you talking . . . married? The girl is simply coming with her father . . . for the ride. Is that so terrible?

ABE (*chuckles*): Sure it's just for the ride. Girls always liked to ride. I remember even when I was a girl. . . .

BEN: Now listen, both of you. And get it through your heads because I'm not repeating. I have no intention of getting married, you are not going to arrange my wedding when I am ready, and I will not stand for any horse-trading tonight!

ABE (*laughs*): Horse-trading is good.

ESTHER: Ben, you're so silly. Would I think of such a thing?

BEN: Yes. You had no business telling a man who wants to marry off his daughter that I'd be home tonight.

ESTHER: What do you want me to do, lie? To listen to you the girl has bowlegs and eczema. Does it hurt to say hello to her? If you ask me you never gave yourself a chance to find out what she's like. She's a college graduate, Ben.

BEN: I have nothing against the girl. I met her, I've taken her out and I think she's . . . a . . . a . . . fine person. I just don't like the idea of you arranging me. I . . . I feel like a cue-ball that everybody's aiming at.

ABE: Listen, why do you act like a kid? Nobody is going to force you into anything. . . .

BEN: But you're in on this too, aren't you. . . .

ABE: I'm not in on nothin'. I'm just . . . a . . . a worker here. All I know is that before you can get married you gotta sign a marriage license and nobody can do it for you. That's the law . . . even your mother can't change that. But if she says she ain't trying to hook you, then believe her. What does it cost you? Say hello to the girl . . . be nice to her . . . and maybe he'll loan us a few thousand. You went to college . . . you oughta be able to figure these things out.

BEN: Is this why Roth hedged whenever we asked him?

ABE: I suppose so.

BEN: And you knew all the time that I was supposed to go for his daughter?

ABE: Sure I knew. And you shoulda knew too . . . that is, if you wasn't such a professor. (*Laughs.*) Look at him, he's sweating like a horse. (*To* BEN.) There's no rope around your neck, for God's sake . . . take it easy.

BEN: Sure I'm sweating. Because you're not. You're on the rocks and you're laughing. And I know why you're laughing.

ABE: What'll I do, wear a black tie?

BEN: No, but you should be worried.

ABE: I am worried. I'm worried that you're not gonna be sensible about this. . . .

BEN: Oh, sensible!

ABE: What're you barking for?

(*Slight pause.*)

There ain't a reason in the world why Roth shouldn't help us out. I been through this kinda thing before. If you act like not a college man for once, and you keep your head on your shoulders, we can . . . well we can get some help without . . . without.

ESTHER: Sure.

BEN (*to* ESTHER): I know what you want so you just be a spectator, please.

ABE: My advice is to treat the girl like she's a lady, don't jump up and down like a Senator every time somebody says something, and make him think what he wants to think, y'understand? When a man wants to believe something as bad as he does, he just needs a little touch to convince them. Your job is to provide the touch. Not a shove, mindya, but a touch, and maybe he'll go the rest of the way himself. He likes you, Ben. He thinks you know the coat business better than any other bachelor . . . so keep your head on you. . . .

(*Sound of the left door-latch. They become electric. Enter* GRAMP *and they relax. He carries a small box.*)

(*On sight of* GRAMP.) Uh! . . . the General is here.

ESTHER (*loudly, in order to penetrate his hearing device*): Hello, Poppa!

GRAMP: Good evening, good evening.

> (*He carefully removes his jacket and panama hat and goes right.* ABE *only looks at the old man when the latter's face is turned away.*)

ESTHER (*calling through right doorway*): Did you get the cards, Poppa?

GRAMP (*enters from right without coat and hat, and meticulously smooths himself as he talks*): I got the calling cards for Arnold. Look, Abe.

ABE (*as* GRAMP *is opening box and showing him a card. To* ESTHER): That's nicer than the last batch.

ESTHER (*rises*): Let me see. (*Goes left to take card.*) Beautiful.

GRAMP (*proudly*): I think they're nicer than even the other ones. See . . . I ain't got my glasses . . . but the letters is more fancy.

BEN (*reaches over and takes a card*): "Arnold Simon, M.D." That's swell, you know?

ESTHER: I can't wait to see him. (*Ecstatically.*) Abe, your son is a doctor! How much did they cost, Poppa?

GRAMP: Heh?

ESTHER (*points to card*): How much?

GRAMP: Oh, I got a bargain . . . four dollars.

ABE: The others was three and a half. Where's the bargain?

ESTHER (*for the peace*): These are better, these are better.

ABE: Sure . . . they saw him comin'.

ESTHER: You wouldn't give him credit if he got them free.

GRAMP (*seats himself majestically,* ESTHER *following*): I said to the man, "I want the best card you got because it's for my grandson." And (*to* ESTHER) I said like you told me, "I want M.D.," like you said. M.D. is on there?

ESTHER (*nodding*): Yes, Poppa.

GRAMP: See? I didn't make one mistake. (*Settles back.*) So, Abe, you're selling?

ABE (*looking off*): Yap.

GRAMP: Heh?

ABE (*swings his head toward* GRAMP): YAP!

GRAMP: Good. (*To* BEN.) I was here when Sam Roth called. . . .

> (ESTHER *takes his arm but he throws it off, annoyed.*)

BEN: Well! Now we'll get to the truth. What did he say?

GRAMP (*as* ABE *laughs*): It's a good idea. He's got a nice girl for you. . . .

ESTHER: Poppa, no . . .

BEN: The army is growing.

GRAMP: Heh? . . . What?

ESTHER (*to* BEN): He didn't mean anything by it . . . Poppa, go inside and take some tea!

GRAMP (*annoyed*): I had tea.

    (*To* BEN. ABE *chuckling.*)

He's got a wonderful business there, Ben . . . I knew him when he was a boy . . . he came to work for me when I had my business on Forsyth Street yet. . . .

ABE: And I wouldn't be a bit surprised if Sam Roth is so big today only because the old man told him how to run his business. Yes sir. . . .

GRAMP: What?

ABE: I was just sayin'.

GRAMP: Oh. (*To* BEN.) You know, Sam is old already. He's lookin' for somebody to take over for him . . .

    (BEN *rises as* ABE *laughs and* ESTHER *is trying to shut* GRAMP.)

. . . and let me say, Ben, you're the boy for the job.

BEN: Well, well, well. Lovely, lovely. I'm just so happy you've all settled it so nicely. . . .

ESTHER: He don't know what he's talking about. . . .

BEN: Oh yes he does, yes he does. You talk it all over between you and it's settled like the Versailles Treaty. We're all going to be rich and I'll be married and we'll roll around in mink coats and stinking perfume and Florida six times a year! . . . I'm losing my mind but somebody is going to be awfully disappointed! (*To* GRAMP.) What else did she say!

GRAMP: Heh?

BEN: Yeh, "heh." He knows when to hear all right.

    (*Looks to* ABE *who is enjoying it all.*)

Oh my God. . . .

GRAMP: Listen, Ben. My advice, if you ask me. . . .

ABE: Listen to him, Ben. When the Chairman of the Chamber of Commerce is talking you dasn't not listen. (*To* GRAMP.) Go ahead, Chairman.

GRAMP: My advice . . .

ABE: You're not listening, Ben. This is advice.

GRAMP: When Roth comes you should not argue with him. Let him to understand that it's substantial here. And give him room he should talk. Even when he was a boy in my place on Forsyth Street he used to talk like a . . . like a steam engine.

ABE: Yeh, steam engine. That's good.

ESTHER: Poppa . . .

(*He throws her arm off.*)

GRAMP: And Abe, if you'll take my advice, you'll ask him how he does his merchandizing . . . he knows his business.

ABE: I'll make a note of that. What else should I ask him?

ESTHER: Abe, he. . . .

ABE (*to the others*): I don't see nobody listening. After all, it ain't every day the President of the United States gives advice. . . .

GRAMP: Who?

ABE: I was just sayin'! Go ahead!

ESTHER: Poppa, take some tea for God's sake!

GRAMP: I don't want no tea! I can't drink tea all day!

(*Left door opens, a labelled valise enters followed by* ARNOLD. *Everybody at him.* ESTHER *hugging him,* BEN *pumping his hand,* ABE *trying to get through to him. Only* GRAMP *stands off awaiting a more dignified moment. After the shouting and kissing die down. . . .*)

ESTHER: You got thinner, Arny.

ARNOLD: No I didn't. I gained three pounds.

ABE: Leave it to her to think of your stomach first. . . .

ARNOLD: Dad looks fine. (*To* ABE.) How've you been?

ABE: I feel good. But I wouldn't mind being a little sick with a professor in the house.

ARNOLD (*pats his shoulder*): I'd rather you didn't get sick until I get a little more practice. Why . . . Gramp! I didn't see you. How are you?

(GRAMP *just smiles under the spotlight.*)

Oh, you got a new phone. How does it work?

GRAMP: What?

ARNOLD: How does it work?

GRAMP: Don't yell! You'll blow my head off!

ARNOLD: Oh, I'm sorry. (*To the others.*) How must you talk to him?

ABE: Just salute, he'll understand . . . the General.

ARNOLD (*laughs*): Ah, stop kidding him.

BEN: He's the biggest pest on the Eastern Seaboard.

ARNOLD (*looks about, smiling*): Gosh, it's good to be home. Everything looks just the same as last year. But the furniture's placed differently, isn't it?

ESTHER: Yeh, we moved the couch so that. . . .

ABE: Wait a minute, wait a minute. Why do you tell him ghost stories. (*To* ARNOLD.) We didn't move nothin'. The adjutant chief of staff over there, decided, y'see, that the furniture is all. . . .

GRAMP: Hah?

ABE (*to* GRAMP *with finger raised*): Just a minute. (*To* ARNOLD.) He made up his mind that the furniture is in the same place too long. So he moved it around. That's six times in the past month. He's afraid, y'understand, that the chairs is gonna drill holes through the floor, so. . . .

ESTHER (*laughing with them*): He's like a Japanese Beetle . . . he never knows when to stop. You'd think Gramps was chopping the legs off the furniture or something. . . .

ABE: Oh he'll get around to that . . . give him time, that's all, give him time. After all, he's an old man, it takes time. . . .

BEN (*to* ARNOLD): Better open your valise and take your stuff out.

ARNOLD: Doesn't matter . . . oh, wait a minute, I've got something to show you all. (*Opens valise.*)

ABE: Y'hear? "You all." A regular colonel from Kentucky.

ARNOLD (*rummaging in valise*): Dirty laundry, dirty laundry, and . . . (*Lifts out framed diploma, holds it up.*)

ESTHER (*all standing admiring it*): It's gorgeous! Look, Abe, (*points with her finger*) "Arnold Simon . . . and all the rights and privileges . . . to practice . . ." (*Hugs* ARNOLD.) It's gorgeous!

ABE (*takes the diploma. In awe*): This makes it . . . legal, heh?

ARNOLD: Well it still smells from sox, but it's legal enough.

ABE (*religiously*): Takes a long time to get that. You oughta hang it up where people can see it. How does it feel, Arny? The truth.

ARNOLD (*sits,* ESTHER *cuddling up next to him.* ABE *sits*): Well, really. . . .

ABE (*to* ESTHER, of her cuddling): Hey, none a that with a medical man.

ARNOLD (*laughs*): Well I really don't know how it feels yet. My first reaction when somebody asks me what's wrong with them, is to tell them to see a doctor.

ABE: That's a good way. You'll get rich quick doin' that.

BEN: Say, how were your marks this year?

ARNOLD: I meant to write. I graduated with honors. . . .

ESTHER: No! Abe, give me that diploma.

ABE: No, let me hold it now.

BEN (*to* ARNOLD): That's pretty damn good.

ARNOLD: It doesn't mean much. Ten do it every year.

BEN: How do you stand in the class?

ARNOLD: Well, two fellows tied for first. I'm second out of a hundred and twenty. That's what I like. The honors business doesn't count much.

ESTHER: Don't belittle yourself so much. I'll make you supper.

ARNOLD: I just ate an hour ago.

ESTHER: Some milk . . . and I made a cake.

ARNOLD: All right . . . but not a gallon.

ESTHER: I ain't got a gallon. (*Exit* ESTHER *right.*)

ABE: Y'know you look different . . . something like a doctor.

GRAMP: No, to look like a doctor he's got to have a moustache. I remember, Arny, when they couldn't be a doctor unless they had a Van Dyke beard. (*Rises, smiles.*) I remember: but they don't require it anymore. (*Exit* GRAMP *right.*)

ARNOLD (*laughs*): He's some guy. Healthy as a bull.

ABE: Why shouldn't he be? What is he got to worry about?

ARNOLD: I think you like him.

ABE: But he's a pest sometimes.

BEN: And I suppose you're never a pest. (*To* ABE.)

ARNOLD: Say, Ben, when are you finishing your novel? I want to read it.

BEN (*smiles, hurt.* ABE *begins to swing his leg*): There ain't no novel, Arny.

ARNOLD (*quietly, alarmed*): What happened? It was almost done. . . .

BEN: I tore it up, Arnold.

ARNOLD: Good God, why did you do a thing like that? It was good stuff, Ben.

BEN: I tore it up . . . and then I threw it into the furnace. It made a good fire . . . didn't it, Dad . . . it warmed the whole house.

ARNOLD: Dad, you didn't make him. . . .

BEN (*rises quickly, hands toward* ABE): I'm sorry, Dad. I didn't mean it. (*To* ARNOLD.) I don't mean anything.
(*Pause.*)
I can't write anymore.

ARNOLD: Why?

BEN: I can't see the point in it anymore. You've been to school Arnold, but I've been with a lot of tough people. I was walking on Eighth Avenue some time ago and it suddenly occurred to me that to write is for a fool. That is, the world doesn't need writing to fix it. It needs men like you.

ARNOLD: You're not right, Ben. . . .

BEN: No . . . I'm no good for writing. And I think I'm not very good for the world either. I'm too sentimental. I look for a loveable trait in everybody and when I find it, I hang on to it for dear life. That is, I have no perspective because at the time of my life when I should have been learning to hate small things within reason, I was pulled out of boyishness and dumped into a business where the things to hate are much, much too big for a boy with nerves, so I fell back on a weltanschauung that has blinded me to hate and to perspective, and the result? I cannot appreciate real evil. I don't know what to do when it confronts me and I either fall apart and burn my book . . . yes, Arn, I burned that book!—or I continue loving in a childishly blind way. Arnold, I'm afraid you're looking at a fool and a boy who is growing into an old man . . . but without wisdom.

(*Enter* ESTHER *right with tray and milk as* ABE *rises suddenly startling her.*)

ABE: I don't understand these things. I . . . you fellows got away from me. I . . . I never read a book in my life. I don't understand. (*Exit* ABE *right, hurriedly.*)

ESTHER (*puts tray down*): Why did he say that? What doesn't he understand?
(*Silence.*)

What were they talking about, Arnold?

(*Pause.*)

The business is worse than they said, heh.

(*They stand watching her.* BEN *breaks into a smile and hugs her. . . .*)

ARNOLD: Don't, Ben!

BEN (*breaks from* ESTHER. *Trifle angry*): What?

ARNOLD: No . . . I meant. . . .

BEN: What did you mean?

ARNOLD: That . . . you shouldn't drop from one thing to another so suddenly. Here, take some milk. (*He drinks slowly.*)

ESTHER: You too, Ben, here. (*Gives him glass.*)

BEN (*ignoring glass*): You know what would happen to him if I left him? Flat on his face like Max Schmeling.

ESTHER: You're going someplace, Ben?

BEN (*takes milk to assuage her*): No, Mother.

ESTHER: What is happening in this house? I live here but nobody talks to me. Am I really so stupid? I've got some brains too. Why don't you tell me something? (*Begins to cry.*)

BEN (*distressed*): Mother, what are you crying for. . . .

ESTHER: Everything is upside down. Where did Poppa go? You probably got him all worried now. Oh. . . .

(*She waves her hand despairingly, begins to go right, when enter* ABE *carrying old armchair with* GRAMP.)

ABE: He's got me doing it already. Esther, when does this end?

ESTHER: Well what are you helping him for? (*Laughing.*)

ABE: He'll get a hernia. You want him to get a hernia?

GRAMP (*they put chair down*): Imagine? I forgot all bout this chair.

ABE (*falling into another chair*): What a shame.

GRAMP (*wondrously*): Seventeen years I didn't see it. (*To* ESTHER.) I remember how Momma used to sit in this chair at night, and I was wondering, where could that chair be? How did you remember to take it when I moved from the old house?

ESTHER (*speaks into his device*): I got all the stuff. Momma's sewing baskets are downstairs too. Abe, I want to talk to you.

GRAMP (*shakes his head*): Yeh, she used to sew in this chair. It'll

look good up here. (*Moves it.*) See, we can put it right here
so it'll look nice. No . . . here. See? Seventeen years old.
That's some piece of furniture. They don't make them like
that anymore.

ABE: We got that to be thankful for.

GRAMP (*tilts back the chair*): Look at the way the joints is put
together.

ABE (*to* ARNOLD): He's a forestry expert. He knows all about
wood.

ESTHER: You make too much of a fuss. Who does he harm?

ABE: Sure look at the fuss. But who's gotta clean up the dirt
again? You. Who's gotta cart it all downstairs again? You. He
only does the engineering, Herbert Hoover there.

    (*Exit* GRAMP *in a huff.*)

Ah! He's going for something else. He never gets tired. The
United States Trucking Company in person. Day and night
service. He works while we sleep.

ESTHER: I can't understand you, Abe. Something terrible is
going on here and everybody's laughing. It's a madhouse!
And look at this room! We're expecting company and my
house looks like a pigsty!

ARNOLD: Why, is somebody coming?

BEN: Oh, that's right, you don't know. I'm getting married
tonight.

    (ABE *laughs.*)

ESTHER: Why do you prejudice him? (*To* BEN, *then to* ARNOLD.)
All that happened is that Sam Roth, you know, Poppa's
old friend, called up that he's coming over to lend them
some money because God only knows what's left of the
business. . . .

BEN: She forgot to say, though, that the man is bringing his
daughter.

ESTHER (*to* ARNOLD): All he can say is daughter, daughter. I
had no idea in my head that anybody was thinking of a
match, I should live so, Arnold.

ARNOLD (*smiles*): Don't they believe you?

ESTHER: No, can you imagine?

ARNOLD: Very easily.

ESTHER (*to the air*): Him too! (*To* ARNOLD.) Don't you understand that. . . .

ARNOLD: Now listen, Mother. . . .

ESTHER: But Arny. . . .

ARNOLD: Wait, wait, wait!

(*Slight pause.*)

I guess I should have arrived tomorrow night because I see that somebody is going to try to enlist me. . . .

ESTHER: Don't be silly, Arnold, I just. . . .

ARNOLD: Please, Mother.

(*She stops. He pats her on the head.*)

(*To All.*) From now till the time that Roth goes home you will regard me as a neutral observer. I don't want anyone to look to me for support. If you, Mom, want Ben to marry somebody, fight with Ben; and Ben, if you don't want to marry somebody, fight with Mom; and Dad, if you don't give a damn, don't give a damn, but please don't anybody try to pull me in on this because I'm out. It sounds pretty theoretical I know, but that's the way I am. I assume that everybody in this room has a conscience and that they'll act accordingly. That's my first and last dictum and the only rule I can advance. Beyond that, to all intents and purposes, I am contemplating my navel.

ABE (*laughs*): Good for you, Arny! You hear that, Esther? He's gonna look at his navel all night, how do you like that?

ESTHER: I can see now where nobody is going to believe me as long as I live. To look at them you'd think that God knows who's coming to the house. You'd think a bandit was coming to burn us in our beds. Why can't you be civil? The man isn't a thief. . . .

BEN: Exactly. That's exactly what he is.

ESTHER: Oh, don't talk like that.

BEN: He is a thief! (*To* ABE.) Why don't you tell her something?

ABE: I'm like Arny. The umpire.

BEN: All right, but I'm not. (*Stands.*) First of all. . . .

ABE (*his index finger goes up. To* BEN): Just a minute, just a minute. Before you deliver your message to Congress, let me say a few words.

(BEN *sits. To* ESTHER.)

What the Senator was going to tell you . . . you know the Senator here is very hard to understand. He talks only for college men, but that's all right because he's a Senator. What he's trying to say . . . the Senator . . . is that Roth is a crook. . . .

ESTHER: Abe, you're talking like a. . . .

ABE: Just a minute, Mrs. Perkins, I got the floor.

(*Pause.*)

I been in the coat business now, close to thirty-three years, and after all that time I'm on my back. Sam Roth is been in business only since 1922 and he's standing up . . . he's even running. All right. You listening, Mrs. Perkins, or am I talking to myself?

ESTHER: I'm listening!

ABE: But not so loud.

ESTHER (*clenches her fists next to her ears*): He's such a pest!

ABE: All right. Why is he standing and I'm sitting. Why is it that after all these years of my labor, I'm worth the price of a wet pretzel? I'll tell you why, Mrs. Perkins. I gotta pay union wages on my stuff, but Sam Roth . . . he don't pay union wages.

ESTHER (*excited*): How can that be? I don't see why you. . . .

ABE: Why? Because when I was big I wouldn't stand for no gangsters to protect an open shop, but Roth . . . it never bothered him.

ESTHER: Yeh, but the union must know. . . .

ABE: Little girl, he's big enough to produce most of his stuff in scab shops outa town where there ain't no union. The net result is, that me and the rest of the little guys is all made up of a big eight-ball, and Roth and a few other big boys is shootin' at us. Like the Senator says, he don't like to be a cue ball, so I'm an eight-ball. The whole business is one big billiard game.

ESTHER: So . . . you can't compete.

ABE: Now you get the idea.

ESTHER (*slight pause*): So the moral is you gotta be big.

ABE: No, the moral is not that you gotta be big. The moral is . . . you wouldn't understand what the moral is.

ESTHER (*angry*): Why wouldn't I understand?

ABE: Why? Because you're a little girl. And because . . . I don't understand it myself.

(*Enter* GRAMP *right with footstool.*)

Uh huh! The moving man is here again!

GRAMP (*joyously*): Look! I found the footstool what belonged with that chair!

ABE: Now you got something!

(*To* ARNOLD *as* GRAMP *sets stool.*)

Arnold, you're a doctor, did you ever hear of such a thing?

ARNOLD (*laughs*): Well what the hell, he only does it once in a while. . . .

ABE: Is that so . . . ?

ESTHER: Poppa, I think there's too much furniture in here. . . .

ABE: Ask the Senator. Today is Monday. Last Tuesday he brought up a vase, musta been seven feet high. For my bedroom, he says.

(*They laugh.*)

Wait a minute. Thursday he found a table musta weighed half a ton. But mind you, Arnold, this is all because he's got memories. God help us if he remembers the coal bin; he'll bring that up too. . . .

GRAMP (*drags chair to middle of stage*): I think it looks much more presentable here. Heh, Abe?

ABE: Esther, if I can have a word edgewise, it looks like a furniture store. . . .

ESTHER (*grasps chair*): Poppa, there's too much furniture!

GRAMP (*holds chair*): No, you gotta have room to sit down!

(DOORBELL.)

BEN: There's Roth, I'm going to sleep! (*Rises.*)

ESTHER: Please, Ben! Poppa, I'm taking it out! (*Pulls chair.*)

GRAMP (*holding on*): I will not permit it!

BEN: Goodnight! (*Goes toward landing.*)

ESTHER: Ben, you'll kill me! (*Laughs and cries.*)

GRAMP: Leave the chair alone!

(DOORBELL.)

ESTHER: Arnold, will you take in the tray?

(*Exit* ARNOLD *with tray.*)

Abe! Help me!

ABE: I'm like Arny . . . a neutral navel.

(BEN *laughs with her.*)

(DOORBELL.)

ESTHER: Poppa, leave the chair alone!

(*Enter* ROTH *stepping over footstool, noticed only by* BEN *and* ABE.)

ROTH (*smiling*): I thought there was an explosion!

ESTHER (*turns, shocked*): Oh . . . hello, Sam.

ROTH (*calls out left*): Come in, Helen, they're home! (*To All.*)
I thought something was wrong so I walked in. Excuse me.

ESTHER: That's all right, Sam, we were just moving some
furniture.

ABE (*extends hand*): How are you, Sam.

ROTH: So so. How's tricks with you? (*He turns to* BEN.) What
are you hiding for, Ben? Don't you say hello?

BEN (*smiles*): I was just waiting. Hello.
(*Enter* HELEN.)

HELEN: I've told you over and over again, Daddy, this key is
not the right one for that car. It won't lock the door. . . .

ROTH (*to* HELEN): You remember everybody, don't you?

HELEN: Of course. Hello, Mrs. Simon.

ESTHER: You look wonderful, Helen. Don't you think so, Abe?

ABE: She's got a lot of color.

HELEN: We were riding with the windows open.

BEN (*comes center*): You do look well, Helen.

HELEN: Oh, Ben, I didn't notice you.

ABE: Here, sit down, Sam. I'll move this away.
(*Takes* GRAMP's *chair.*)

GRAMP: I'll move it, please!

ABE (GRAMP *moves it right*): Sit down, everybody. . . .

ROTH (*as they are seating themselves*): What's the matter, Ben,
you look tired. Working too hard?

BEN: That's part of it, I guess.

ROTH (*half to* ESTHER): I didn't see your father. Hello, Mr.
Steiner!

GRAMP (*just sitting in his chair. Matter-of-factly*): Hello. You
know, Sam . . . (*arranging himself*) . . . you look like an
old man already.

ROTH (*laughs angrily*): Me? I don't look old.

GRAMP: I ain't seen you since twelve years . . . at your wife's
funeral.

ROTH (*loudly*): That's right! (*Winks.*) I saw him six months ago
and he don't remember. He's gettin' old, poor fellow . . .
(*Shakes his head with sympathy.*) Helen, let me sit in that
chair. You sit here. (*Beside* BEN.)
(*He rises with effort as enter* ARNOLD *right.*)

ABE (*to* ROTH): You remember my son, Arnold. He just got in
from school.

ROTH: No, I ain't seen you since you were that high. (*Very low.*)

ARNOLD (*smiles*): It must have been quite a time ago. How do you do.

ROTH (*sitting where he arose from*): He's got a sense of humor.

GRAMP: Believe me,

    (ARNOLD *sits on landing*)

this chair is more comfortable than all a them you got in the house. Look at the way I sit with my feet . . . (*Places feet on stool.*)

ROTH (*smiles quickly to* GRAMP): So, Abe . . . what's the bad news?

ABE (*uncomfortably*): It ain't so bad . . .

ROTH: Ben, why don't you and Helen take a spin in my car? (*To* ABE.) Did you notice my car outside?

BEN: I'm very tired . . .

ABE: What car've you got?

ROTH: What car would I put in my garage? Packard.

ESTHER: Sure, Packard is good.

ROTH: Good? It's the best. I just traded in the Cadillac convertible sedan. I wouldn't have it another day. You know you sit in the back seat and you think you're gonna be locked in a chicken coop. You like a convertible?

ABE (*as though deciding*): Ah . . . what is that?

ROTH: You know, with the top comes down?

ABE (*but definitely*): Oh no . . . I wouldn't stand for it. You never know. . . .

ROTH: That's what I figured. And besides . . . I gotta have space.

ESTHER: Naturally.

ROTH: Sure. Ben, why don't you take a ride?

HELEN (*riled*): Well, after all, Daddy, maybe Ben doesn't feel like riding!

ROTH (*as though she were a child*): Do *you* feel like riding, darling?

HELEN (*turns from him*): I don't know.

ROTH (*laughs*): You see? As soon as you send them to college they can't make up their mind. (*To* BEN.) You know, Helen went to . . . where'd you go, darling?

HELEN (*crosses her legs, bored*): Wisconsin.

ARNOLD: Is that a fact? You know Doc Peterson in physiology?

ROTH (*to* ABE): Wisconsin. That's the best school in the country.

HELEN (*to* ARNOLD): No, I've heard of him though. I was in child psychology. I never took Peterson's class.

ARNOLD: Oh. Any luck with a job in psychology?

HELEN (*smiles*): No, my father doesn't approve of careers for women.

ROTH (*to All*): I ask you. Is it right for a girl like Helen to slave away her life taking care of other people's children?

ARNOLD: Why not? It's a good way to earn a living.

ROTH: Listen to him! (*Deprecating.*) And where did you go?

ARNOLD: Johns Hopkins.

ROTH (*laughs*): Sounds like a cough medicine. Where is that, some place . . . (*Up the creek.*)

ARNOLD: Baltimore.

ROTH: Oh, Baltimore. I got a customer there. Ain't so far. (*To All.*) Wisconsin, you know, is hundreds of miles.

ESTHER: Baltimore was far enough for me.

ROTH: Yeh, I guess you miss him. (*To* ARNOLD.) So now that you're finished what do you think you're gonna do?

ARNOLD: Intern, I suppose.

ROTH (*laughs*): Intern? You gotta be a doctor first, don't you?

ARNOLD: I am a doctor.

ROTH (*half laugh*): *You're* a doctor? (*To* ABE.) He's a doctor?

ABE: Sure, Doctor Arnold Simon.

ROTH (*weakly*): You don't say. (*Looks* ARNOLD *over.*) Why don't you put on some weight? . . . you're so thin?

(*To* ABE *as* ARNOLD *smiles.*)

Y'know, I can't understand why all the kids are skinny as a rail.

HELEN (*angrily*): He's not skinny.

ROTH: Sure he is, darling . . . can't you see . . . he looks like a ghost.

ESTHER (*apology*): Now that he's home I'll fatten him up.

GRAMP (*rises suddenly*): Oh, I forgot! A dog followed me home before. I bet he's still waiting out there for something to eat. (*Goes to left window.*)

ABE: The old man feeds dogs.

GRAMP (*looking out window*): No, he went away. You know, if you feed one dog in the street, every dog knows it. All the dogs know me. (*Continues looking out window.*)

ESTHER: I can't get over how lovely Helen looks.

ROTH: Well, she's got a life. She lives like a queen.

HELEN: Don't listen to him, Mrs. Simon. I looked the same when I was living in Wisconsin where they don't permit queens.

ROTH (*confidentially*): She plays tennis. . . .

GRAMP: Say, that's a wonderful looking car. That's yours, Sam?

ROTH: Ben, what's the matter, why don't you take a spin. You'll have twelve cylinders in front of you.

BEN: I'm really very tired. I had a hard day.

ARNOLD: I'm not tired.

ROTH (*quickly*): Let me hear your opinion, Mrs. Simon, is that dress or is it not made for a schoolteacher. (*Of* HELEN's *dress.*)

ESTHER: Well, it is a little tailored. . . .

ROTH: What do you think, Ben? Shouldn't she wear something with more style?

BEN: I . . . I really wouldn't know . . . I. . . .

ROTH: Stand up, Helen, I want to show them how you. . . .

HELEN (*stands quickly*): Wouldn't *some*one like to ride in our new Packard? It has six horns.

ROTH: What's the matter, darling, did I. . . .

BEN: How would Arnold do?

ARNOLD (*stands*): He'd do fine. Come on, Helen . . . (*Walks toward door.*)

ROTH: Go along, Ben, the air'll do you good. . . .

GRAMP: In a car like that I would like to ride before I die.

ESTHER: No, Poppa, your kidneys.

HELEN (*as* ARNOLD *opens door*): We'll be back soon.

ROTH (*smiling with anger*): Arnold, you won't. . . .

ARNOLD: I won't drive. . . .

(*Exit* HELEN.)

ROTH (*to* HELEN *through door*): Don't be long . . . Darling! I gotta take the car for inspection!

ARNOLD (*bows*): Very shortly, very shortly. (*Exit* ARNOLD.)
(*Pause.*)

ROTH (*to* ABE): How long is he gonna be in town, the younger one?

ABE: Ah . . . he don't go back no more.

ROTH: No more, heh?

ESTHER: It's nice that he's home, though. We missed him.

ROTH (*not impressed*): M, hm.

ESTHER: He'll be very busy, though, in the hospital.

GRAMP: That car wouldn't do no harm to my kidneys. (*Still looking out window.*)

    (*Pause.*)

    (ESTHER *scans the room for a word.* BEN *sits looking straight ahead. Finally.* . . .)

ABE: So . . . Sam, how is business?

ROTH: Not so good, but I get my share. Y'know, Abe . . . (*Takes out a cigar.*) I . . . Esther, will you get me a match, please?

ESTHER: Sure. (*Rises and going right.*) How about some nice cake and. . . .

ROTH: No thanks, I'm full. Just a match if you got it.

ESTHER: We got plenty of matches. (*Exit* ESTHER.)

ROTH (GRAMP *sits and listens and during the conversation, when he is not using his voice, he speaks adamantly in pantomime*): I wanna say, Abe, I'm terribly sorry I couldn't help you out when you asked me. The first time, I had all the taxes on my buildings to pay and I was up to my neck. The second time, it was something else. Do you understand me, Abe?

ABE (BEN *looks at him*): I understand, Sam. Listen, you can't always do what you wanna do. That's an old story.

ROTH: I'm glad you see it my way.

    (*Enter* ESTHER.)

ESTHER: Here, Sam. (*Gives him matches and sits.*)

ABE: Well, there's no other way to see it.

ROTH: Thanks, Esther. (*To* ABE.) If you woulda come to me at the end of the month, I woulda had it for you, but the way it was, everything was in a . . . confusion.

    (*Lights his cigar,* BEN *watching him.*)

Ahh . . . there's nothin' like a good cigar. Three for a half. I came tonight, Abe . . . have a cigar?

ABE: I don't smoke, thanks.

ROTH: Still don't smoke . . . how about you, Ben?

BEN: No thanks.

ROTH (*to* ESTHER): Like father like son.

ESTHER: The neither of them got a taste for it.

ROTH: And I can't do without it. . . .

GRAMP: That cigar smells good. What kind is that?

ROTH (*looks at him like a buzzing fly*): Here, light up.
(GRAMP *looks it over and lights it carefully. Sits in his chair.*)
So . . . how much did you need, Abe?

ABE: Well . . . I'll tell you, Sam. A lotta money I wouldn't ask you for. Today is Monday, right?

ROTH: Monday is right.

ABE: On Wednesday, day after tomorrow, we got two notes coming due. Not due, but, man to man, overdue. We already got an extension, but Wednesday is the deadline.

ROTH: So soon? How big are the notes?

ABE: Ah . . . what are they, Ben?

BEN: Twenty-nine hundred dollars . . . That's both together.

ROTH (*to* ABE): Well . . . that ain't so big . . . What are you worried about?

ABE: Sure it ain't so big . . . if ya got it. But if you ain't, it's the world.

ROTH (*pause*): So. Twenty-nine hundred.

ABE: Yeah . . . Twenty-nine hundred. I tell ya, Sam, I wouldn't ask you if I didn't need it but you know the way the season was and. . . .

ROTH (*liberally*): That's all right, Abe. I don't want you to hesitate to come to me. (*Looks up in the air as though computing the population. Pause.*)

GRAMP (*out of the silence*): Ahh . . . this is some smoke. Such a cigar I bet you can't buy for under ten cents.

ESTHER: Poppa . . . sshh.

GRAMP: What?

ESTHER (*finger to mouth*): Sshh.

GRAMP (*nods*): Oh. (*Sotto voce.*) Wonderful smoke. . . .

ROTH: You don't mean, Abe, that if you can't raise the money by Wednesday that you're out of business.

ESTHER: No, he just. . . .

ABE: Just a minute please. (*To* ROTH.) It means that . . . Well . . . yeh, I suppose, if we can't get another extension.

ROTH: Ts. That's too bad, Abe. (*Leans back and looks off like one embarking on a narrative.*) You know, Abe, I ain't a young man anymore. Y'understand me, Ben?

BEN: Oh yes.

ROTH: With me, business was always first, and I never took a
day off for vacation. You know that, Abe.

ABE: Absolutely.

ROTH: Next year, with God's help, I'll be sixty. That's not old,
of course, but it ain't young either. You know that, Abe.

(ABE *nods.*)

For the last five years, I been thinkin': "Sam," I been thinkin',
"maybe it's time you should get out and *live* the rest of your
life." Y'understand me, Abe . . . I don't mean go crazy, I
mean just enjoy myself. I already built myself up a good
solid business, my daughter is old enough to take care of
herself, a wife I haven't got, . . . so what am I waiting for?
Y'understand? Well . . . I got a lot of responsibility. It
would kill me if anything happened to Roth Coat. So the
time passes, and I'm still in the rut. What I'm trying to say, I
mean, is that I still ain't enjoying myself.

ABE: Well what would you do with yourself all the time?

ROTH: I'll tell you, Abe. I . . . sure you don't want to smoke,
Ben?

BEN: I'd tell you if I did.

ROTH (*tolerantly*): All right.

(*Slight pause.*)

Abe, I'd like to go to Hollywood.

ABE: Y'mean the movies? You wanna go in. . . .

ROTH: No, no movies. I ain't no Clara Bow. I just wanna buy
myself a house and live out the rest of my life with . . .
nice people . . . in the sunshine. Hollywood, I understand,
is a regular paradise.

ABE: That's some idea. I wouldn't mind that myself.

ROTH: But not to go crazy, y'understand. Just to enjoy
myself.

ABE: No, you don't have to go crazy . . . just . . . quiet.

ROTH: That's what I figured. But I only know one man I
would have in my place.

(*Pause.*)

GRAMP: Look, blue smoke. . . .

ROTH: What do you think, Ben?

BEN (*rises and leans against the wall*): Why . . . yes. In fact I
think that would be just the place for you . . . Hollywood.

ROTH: No, I meant. . . .

BEN: Mr. Roth, we have no collateral for you.

ROTH (*outrageous*): Ah! Collateral! What am I, a bank?

BEN: Well no . . . I didn't say that.

ROTH: I don't want you to worry anything about collateral . . . or even interest. As a matter of fact, whenever Pop is got the money, he can give it to me back. What do you think of that?

BEN: But there's absolutely no guarantee that you'll ever get your money back.

ROTH: Please. Let me worry about that.

BEN: Good enough. You worry about it. But . . . well . . . let's not decide on your trip to Hollywood yet, eh?

ROTH (*puts up his opened hand as though it's all right*): Anytime you say the word, Ben, and I buy my ticket for the coast.

BEN: Because I've never borrowed money on these terms before.

ROTH (*complete sympathy*): Listen, Ben, who do you think you're dealing with? I wouldn't hurry you for the world. I want you to think it over. That's why I like you. You think careful. What you can do, is when you make up your mind, give me a ring, and we'll talk further. Fair enough?

BEN: But look. Our notes are due day after tomorrow. Supposing I can't decide by then. Will you cover us?

ROTH (*draws minutely on cigar*): That, Ben, I'm afraid is entirely up to you.

BEN: But I can't let Dad go out of business.

ROTH: You shouldn't, Ben. You could see to it that he doesn't. (BEN *walks across the room and looks out the window.*)

ABE: Sam, what's the use of talking now? He . . . he . . . what's the use? I tell you what you can do. You don't have to lay out a nickel and you can do me a big favor. You know Dawson at the bank?

ROTH (*carefully*): Yes?

ABE: Would you go down tomorrow and ask him, as a personal favor to you, to hold off calling in my notes for another two weeks? Would you do that for me, Sam?

ROTH (BEN *turns and looks at him, pause. Slaps his thigh*): Fair enough. I'll see Dawson tomorrow four sharp.

ABE: I appreciate that, Sam. Just tell him what's what.

ROTH: Don't worry. Dawson'll do it for me.

ABE: You're a friend, Sam.

ESTHER (*reverently*): I should say so.

ROTH: Listen, whenever Sam Roth can help out a friend like you, Abe, he's only too glad to do it. So think it over, heh, Ben?

ESTHER (*rises*): Don't worry about him, Sam. He's sensible. *Now* how would you like a beautiful piece of home-made cake?

ROTH: Now I could appreciate it. With nothing on my mind I can eat. Home-made cake is the biggest reason I miss my wife so much. (*Laughs.*)

ESTHER: There's nothing like it. (*Exit* ESTHER.)

ROTH: You got a good housekeeper there, Abe.

ABE: As soon as a person opens his mouth with her around she's got something to shove down.

ROTH: I like Esther. I wonder where those two could be?

ABE: Who, Arnold?

ROTH: Yeh, Helen. We shouldn't have let them go.

ABE (*smiles*): Ah, I suppose they're speeding it up.

ROTH (*alarmed*): No, they shouldn't speed! I'm still breakin' that car in.

ABE: So, it'll break in faster.

ROTH (*as* ESTHER *enters with a piece of cake*): No, you don't understand how it works, Abe. You ain't allowed to run it fast or . . . or if y'do, y'understand, the gasoline don't . . . develop, y'see?

ABE: Oh, I see, I see.

   (BEN *is smiling.*)

ROTH (*takes cake and shoves it in his mouth*): Thanks. Y'see, Abe, it's just like a person. If you jump quick into something . . . you're liable to give yourself a good strain y'understand? You gotta go slow in the beginning.

ABE (*to* ESTHER): Imagine that? It's like a person.

ROTH (*to* ESTHER): Sure.

ABE: How did you ever pick up that stuff?

ROTH (*with some hauteur*): Well, y'know, I take out books from the library. I got a regular card. And then I watch the man when he fixes my car . . . y'know I keep wide awake. I'm a regular mechanic.

ABE: I could see . . . by the way you know these things. To me a car is a closed ledger.

ROTH (*with sudden impatience*): Where can those two be?
(*Begins to go to the window left.*)

ESTHER: They'll be here. How is Abe's brother, Dave, doing
with you?

ROTH (*slight pause. He looks at her seriously*): Dave? Why?

ESTHER: I just like to know.

ROTH: He's doing all right.

ABE: What kind of job did you give him?

ROTH (*goes to window*): If I remember, he's a salesman now. I
figured I'll take him off the street. After all, he's a friend and
your brother . . . I couldn't see him in such shape.

ABE: I'm glad he found a place finally.

ROTH (*looking out window*): Why? The car is still there! . . .

ABE: They must've gone for a walk.

ROTH: But they. . . .

ESTHER: Sit down, Sam . . . some milk. . . .

ROTH: But I didn't *tell* them to go for a walk!

ESTHER: Ben, go out and see if they're coming.

ROTH: Never mind, never mind. I'll take the car, and when she
comes have her take a taxi home.

ABE: O.K. They'll be right in and I'll tell her. Don't worry,
Sam.

ROTH: I just like people to be on time, that's all. Good night,
be sure and tell her. Good night, Ben.

GRAMP: Have a nice time, Sam.

ROTH: Heh?

ABE: You won't forget about the bank, Sam, eh?

ROTH (*absently*): The bank?—oh, no, don't worry. Goodby,
Abe.

ABE: Good night.

ROTH (*sotto voce, as he goes*): Some walk . . . I never . . .
(*Exit ROTH left.*)

ESTHER (ABE *and* BEN *begin to laugh*): What are you laughing
at? He knows the man wants to go home and he keeps her
out all night! He needs a good talking to when he comes in!
(*Enter* ROTH *flushed.* HELEN *and* ARNOLD *follow him in,
blinking at the light.*)

ROTH (*glares at* ARNOLD. *To* All): On the front porch all the
time!
(*He grabs* HELEN *and snatches her off left.* ARNOLD *stands*

as though he had been dropped there. They look at him, ES-
THER *scandalized, at a loss for words,* ABE *and* BEN *ready to
burst out laughing.*)

ARNOLD (*looks around at them*): What the hell is the matter
with that guy?

(ABE *and* BEN *roar laughing.*)

ESTHER: Don't you know that the man is waiting for his
daughter! . . . that you should come in when the time is
. . . is up?

ABE (*laughing*): Well to him the time wasn't up yet, that's all!

BEN: Do you look like a fish! (*Laughs.*)

ARNOLD: What the hell, must I declare my intentions before I
can talk to a girl in the dark? Would it have been any better
if I went for a ride?

ABE: No, just as good, just as good!

GRAMP: Heh, Abe?!

ABE: Just as good I said!!

GRAMP (*edging his way in*): Arny, you made a damn fool outa
that man and you should apologize.

ARNOLD: I came too late to make a fool out of him!

GRAMP: You did not!

ESTHER (*to* ARNOLD): He's right! You should've known enough
to. . . .

ARNOLD: Wait a minute! Let me make myself clear. I'm neutral
in every possible way. . . .

ABE: I should so say! (*Laughs.*)

ARNOLD (*exasperated*): I am! Including the matter of Helen
Roth. For God's sake all she did was talk about Ben all the
time.

ESTHER (*slight pause*): You see, Ben? You oughta give her more
of a tumble. A girl likes to be rushed around.

BEN: All right, I'll go over with my little hand-truck and rush
her around!

ESTHER: Helen is a lovely girl!

BEN: Stop that, will you!

ABE (*raises both arms*): He! No!

(ESTHER *exits right, angry.*)

You're screaming as though somebody was gonna leave us.
Nobody is gonna leave us. I been in worse scrapes than this
and I get out . . . and nobody had to marry me out either.

You know your mother. She likes to dream. Then let her dream. But don't forget while she's dreaming, that Sam Roth was my shipping clerk and he'll never be my boss. . . .

ARNOLD: I don't know anything about it, but I hope you're right.

ABE: You need a guarantee, Doctor? Well it's right in here. (*Taps his chest.*) I'm a bigger man than Sam Roth, that's the guarantee. So you can come inside, Neutral, and finish up the cake. Come on, Neut, the war's over.

(*Exit* ARNOLD *right.*)

You too, Senator, and don't stand there like you lost your last vote.

BEN: Oh, Dad, you're not doing this right . . . you're not doing it right.

ABE: Let me worry about it, will you? I'm older than you. Come on.

(*He goes to door with* BEN *who goes through. Turns to* GRAMP.)

(*To* GRAMP.) Come on in, Pop, have some cake.

GRAMP (*gravely*): Be careful, Abe.

ABE (*looks at him closely*): What do you mean?

GRAMP: I mean that Sam Roth is a smart man.

ABE (*nods. Softly, almost to himself*): Yeh. (*Beckons.*) Come.

(GRAMP *walks toward the door and* ABE *follows him very thoughtfully, his hand almost touching* GRAMP'*s back as* . . .)

SLOW CURTAIN

ACT TWO

The following afternoon at about four o'clock, in the office and show-room of the Simon Coat and Suit Company. A large window in the left wall looks out on a cavern twelve stories to the street. Along this same side are ranged two small glass-topped tables, stained brown, sturdy chairs, small and the same color, an old coat hanger which flourishes brazen arms, also somewhat brown. At the back, center, two large and almost red swinging doors are set, giving access to the hallway and elevators. At the right of these, a partition extends downstage from the back wall a distance of about seven feet where it is joined by another partition from the right wall. The space within this enclosure, known as the office, is visible through a good-sized clerk's window in its downstage side. It is entered by a door in its left side. In it may be seen a telephone, commercial books, etc., and the upper section of LOUISE, *who, at the moment is bent over the desk therein, working, we suppose. Next to this office, in the right wall, is the doorway to the shop, and perhaps another chair is stranded hereabouts. Somewhere, there may be a chrome sign explaining that we use so-and-so's woolens, but not necessarily. However, there is certainly a short rolling rack supporting ten or twelve sample coats, with and without fur, all tagged. This is an old loft. It has been renovated many times. The general color is tobacco.* ABE SIMON *does not buy new fixtures.*

On the rise, ABE *is standing, hands in pockets, glaring out the window. Near him, facing right* MAX, *his ancient shop-chairman, sits hunched over his crossed legs, squinting through his thick lenses at the smoke he is permitting to leak through his nose. His cigarette is held 'twixt second knuckle of the forefinger and the flat of the thumb, ashes up,—like a flag. He opens his hand to draw. A moment, and* ABE *turns on* MAX, *and looking down at him. . . .*

ABE: Two dollars and ten cents.

MAX (*apologetically*): It can't be done, Mister Simon. Two dollars and thirty is the union scale and I cannot cut it . . . if I beg your pardon.

ABE: Max, I ask you for the last time. Will you be reasonable, or must I stop manufacturing coats?

MAX: Mister Simon. . . .

ABE: Don't Mister Simon me. Give me an answer.

MAX (*pleading*): I'm giving you an answer. . . .

ABE: That's no answer. An answer like that I can get from my enemies not my shop-chairman . . . Max, look at those threads stuck on your lip. You dassn't put a cigarette near there, you'll start a fire.

MAX: I wouldn't burn. I been smoking with thread on my lips for forty-five years. (*But he makes a stab at picking off the longest one.*)

ABE (*turns toward office*): Louise?

LOUISE: Yes?

ABE: What time you got?

LOUISE: Just about four.

ABE: Call up the bank, will you, and see if Sam Roth was in to see Dawson.

LOUISE: I thought you were going to wait for him to call you.

ABE: No. Call him, will you?

LOUISE: Do you want to speak to Dawson?

ABE: No . . . just ask his secretary if Sam Roth was in to see about my notes . . . Abe Simon's notes.

LOUISE: O.K. (*She picks up phone.*)

MAX: Mister Simon. Ain't I been your foreman going on fifteen years, ain't I? Would it be good for me if I told you something . . . that ain't right? We depend on you for work . . . we understand this, don't we?

ABE: How am I gonna know you understand? From the way you're acting it don't look like you understand my language even. I can not operate on such a labor cost, Max, and I'm telling it to you with a . . . a open heart.

MAX (*leans over troublously*): Mister Simon. If we worked on that coat for a cent less than two thirty, we'd be breaking union scale on that coat. . . .

ABE: Yeh, but how about. . . .

MAX: Mister Simon!

(*Slight pause.*)

Look, I call you still Mister Simon. After all these years I never even took the liberty I should call you Abe, like you call me Max. And only because I never wanted you should feel that Max Schneeweiss is lookin' for something what don't belong to him.

ABE: But Max, them bastards is cutting into the scale and I can't sell my goods on the market. You know what I get now? The leavings. The crap orders that the big guys happen to miss . . . and maybe a friend of mine who'll do me a favor and buy my merchandise. Max . . . you got to do it for me!

MAX (*very emotionally, as though he can't stand shouting*): I can't break a scale, I'm chairman of the shop!

ABE: You know you made more than I did last year? . . . Max!

MAX (*covers his ears*): Don't yell . . . please.

   (*Pause. He relaxes.*)

I know we made more than you did. I know it's hard for you to sell. I know these things, Mister Simon. But I also know that when I was nine years old they grabbed me off the boat and put me to work in a sweatshop for six dollars a week, seven in the morning to midnight. And I slept in the shop on a table where we cut the coats. And you remember that too . . . because you did the same thing. I am not arguing over two dollars and thirty cents, if you'll pardon me. I am arguing because my eyes are going blind and my back is crooked, and because I will not see that my son, and my son's son, should be pitied for old men when they're only fifty-four. That's why I argue, not for the two dollars and thirty cents. Nobody will protect us, Mister Simon, we've got to protect ourselves . . . and our children too.

   (*Pause.* ABE *is still. He begins to turn to* MAX . . .)

LOUISE (*in phone*): You're sure? Thank you. (*To* ABE.) Mr. Roth hasn't been in to see Dawson yet.

ABE: What time is it?

LOUISE: A little after four.

ABE (*pause. He shakes his head slightly*): All right, Louise.

   (*Pause. He breaks his thought . . .*)

Then that's the last word, eh, Max?

MAX: That's all I can say. (*Rises and goes toward right.*)

   (ABE *begins to go up toward office.*)

   . . . only . . .

ABE (*turns*): Yah?

MAX: Mister Simon, we are not your enemies. Is thirty dollars . . . or even thirty-five too much for a man to make when he works his life out on a machine? Will that make us rich? But there are people who are getting rich, Mister Simon . . . by cutting wages and threats! Them big guys (*kiss*) with the Pierce-Arrow cars! Whatever we get, we worked for . . . hard.
> (*Enter* BEN *with samples on his arm.*)

I'm sorry I talk so much . . . I'm sorry. (*Exit* MAX *right.*)
> (BEN *sits tiredly, discouraged as* ABE *looks at him and begins to walk about. . . .*)

ABE: What do you do with a guy like that? Can I yell at him? Can I throw him out? Sure he went half-blind already on the goddam machines . . . I watched it happen. But did I tell him to lose his eyes? Did I want it? For God's sake you'd think I wanted his eyes!

BEN: Why are you talking like this?

ABE: Heh? I'm through talking. Did you sell anything?

BEN (*slight pause*): No.

ABE: Did you see my friend at Nelson Shops?

BEN (*rises*): Dad . . . I don't blame them for not buying from us . . . or anybody like us.

ABE (*angering*): That's fine. . . .

BEN: Because we can't deliver a big order like Roth can! And, what's more, we can't meet his prices.

ABE: Don't give me that kinda stories! If you worked my friend right at Nelson Shops you woulda sold him!

BEN: Listen, your friend at Nelson Shops told me just now that we've got to put a dime in his pocket on every coat we sell him. A dime on every coat . . . for him! How are you going to sell coats? We can't give graft when we only make a lousy quarter on the garment! And if we could I wouldn't do it!

ABE (*pause*): He asked you for a dime?

BEN: On each coat he buys.

ABE (*flushed*): Ten cents. The honorable member of the community. Plays golf. Drives a big car. Demands a dime before he'll buy a coat from me! Me! Who did I steal the dime from that I could give it to him? Where's the man in this city who'll say I stole from him! Where is he Goddammit! A dime, I'll give him! A punch in the nose better!
> (*Pause.*)

BEN: Did Roth see Dawson at the bank for you?

ABE (*slight pause*): No. Not yet.

BEN: Dad, listen to me this time. Sam Roth didn't see Dawson for you, and he never had the slightest intention to see him.

ABE: Don't talk like that.

BEN: He wanted us to trust everything to him so that we wouldn't try elsewhere for an extension. He'd like to come here tomorrow when they're closing us down, and have us right up against the wall, where he wants us.

ABE: I know him too long for that! Did you see Martin of Freeport Stores?

BEN: Yes. He said he'll be up to see the line later.

ABE: Well why didn't you tell me? What's it, a secret?

BEN: It slipped my mind, I meant to tell. . . .

ABE: It slipped your mind. It looks like everything is slipping your mind. You're laying down too, but that don't slip my mind!

BEN: Oh, I'm quitting! I give you seven years in this hole and I'm quitting! What the hell do you want me to do, arrest them if they don't buy?

ABE: At your age I woulda pushed down doors to sell them if I had to! Doors! You got no guts, that's the matter with you! You got no fire, no push! (*Fist against palm.*) You're not working against college men here. These are beasts . . . animals, you understand? We gotta sell coats, Ben, and we won't if we can't push our way in!

(*Enter* FURRIER'S CLERK.)

Yah?

CLERK: Mister Simon?

ABE: What is it?

CLERK (*gives him a paper*): From Simpkin Fur.

(ABE *reads.*)

Mister Simpkin says I should tell you that he needs the money and could you pay it now. . . .

ABE: Ben.

(BEN *comes to him.*)

This is due next week, ain't it?

BEN (*looks at bill*): Next Wednesday.

ABE (*to* CLERK): You know anything about this?

CLERK: Well . . . yeh . . . but not much.

ABE: Not much, heh? Well you go back and find somebody who knows "much" about this, see and tell him that when Abe Simon's bills is due, Abe Simon pays them, and when they ain't due, Abe Simon don't pay them, you follow me?

CLERK: I . . . I only know that I'm supposed to tell you that. . . .

ABE: It's all right. It's all right. Just go back and tell Mister Simpkins. . . .

CLERK: Simpkin.

ABE: Simpkin, Simpkins, it's the same guy. Go back and tell him that the Simon Coat and Suit Company don't live in a tent that they're not gonna fold up and run away. Let him know that the Simon Coat and Suit Company is been in business since 1906 and it's gonna stay in business 'til 1966. Let him know, y'understand?

CLERK (*ashamed*): All right . . . I'll . . . I'll . . . (*Goes to door. Frightened.*) But how about the bill?

ABE: The bill? Tell Simpkins, that if he needs the twelve dollars so bad that he's gotta come to me before it's due . . . tell him I'll lend him the money . . . no interest, you got that?

CLERK: All right . . . (*Turns to go.*)

ABE: Goodby!

CLERK (*just before he quickly goes. Shakes his head*): I'll tell him. (*Exit* CLERK *center.*)

ABE: It's getting around. Every dime we owe is coming up. The vultures, Ben . . . they won't give us a chance . . . we gotta do something, Ben . . . quick!

BEN (*slight pause*): I want to say something to you. Sit down?

ABE (*impatiently*): I can hear better standing up. What've you got to say?

BEN: There's no use fooling ourselves, Dad. I think . . . maybe we ought to . . . liquidate.

ABE (*he is shocked. He stands stock-still, then shakes his head sarcastically*): Liquidate. You think maybe we oughta liquidate. (*Pause.*)

Well maybe I think we ought not! Maybe that's what I think!

BEN: Don't blow up like that! And don't look at me as though I did it! We can go out now, and maybe in time we'll get enough money to come back and make a go of it. I know the books better than you, Dad. We're through.

ABE (*his head goes back and forth. Very softly at first*): Well. That's easy to say. It's always easy to say that. But it's harder to say that you're not through! And that's what I say! I'm not a professor but that's what I say!

(BEN *turns away from him.*)

Ben. Ben, listen to me. Max tells me he came over on a boat and that he slaved in a sweatshop. Max tells me he slept on wood. Well I slept on wood too! And when I opened them doors in 1906 I still slept on wood! Why?

(*Pause.*)

You. Only you, Ben. For me a board was good enough but not for you. Nothin' was gonna be good enough for you. I was gonna see to that . . . My God, you don't understand me. . . .

BEN: I do, I do! Why would I have stayed all this time if I didn't understand?

ABE: All right. That's something. If you understand, that's a little anyway.

(*Pause.*)

Ben, I know you don't want the business. . . .

BEN: Dad, it's not that I. . . .

ABE: It's all right, Ben. I *understand* that you don't want it. You never built. How could you want it? But whatever you are, if you ain't a cloak man, you're still my son, Ben, . . . and as my son I'd like you to take this from me that I made. It ain't very much, I'll admit, but I'm in it like I'm in you, and I don't want to see it die, like I don't want to see you die. If it's worth twenty-five cents, Ben, I gotta give it to you, because that's the only reason why it's here. Just let me sign it over to you when the time comes . . . just let me give you that piece of paper. And then, if it's gotta be taken apart, then you do it . . . because I can't. It's . . . these walls, Ben . . . and that chair . . . and that coathanger, too. Whatever they are, that's what I am; whatever they'll become, that's what I'll become too.

BEN: I know that, Dad. I won't leave you.

ABE: It sounds like . . . like a kid, Ben. I know that. It's a language that they don't speak anymore in this country. It's a language that went out thirty years ago. But it's the only kind I can speak, Ben . . . because it's the only one I ever learned. I know you don't belong in it, Ben . . . but try, try to belong. Or at least . . . help me hold on to it. Make believe . . . it's only for me.

BEN (*pause*): What do we do now?

ABE (*stands erectly and tightly*): *We* don't do nothin', Ben. You just stay here, and when Martin comes, sell him what we made . . . like I taught you to sell.

BEN: Where are you going now?

ABE (*slight pause*): To the bank. I'm going to see Dawson. And he's gonna let me go on.

(*He turns and goes toward center exit when* LOUISE *comes out of office and stands before him.*)

What . . . you been crying, Louise.

LOUISE: No. I have some money, Mr. Simon,—nearly five hundred dollars that my father left me when he died. I'm not using it. Why not take it, and you can return it whenever you're able.

ABE (*smiles*): You know . . . you might never get it back?

LOUISE: I know that.

ABE (*shakes his head*): No, Louise. Five hundred is not even a quarter of what I need. And anyway, there's banks to lend money to honest people. There's a bank downstairs . . . and I'm honest people.

LOUISE: Don't go to the bank. . . .

ABE: Why, you're afraid they'll turn me down?

(*She nods.*)

Don't be afraid. I been turned down before, by better people. No, Louise, you hold on to your money.—That's your dowry, ain't it.

LOUISE: No. . . .

ABE: But it is, isn't it.

LOUISE: . . . Yes.

ABE: Then use it as a dowry. How do you know, you're liable to marry to a guy who'll need it . . . say a poet? You can't tell, you're liable to marry a poet. People do it. And a poet can always use five hundred dollars. It's old-fashioned, and the poets I know don't believe in dowries, but take it from me, Louise, it's still a good idea.

(*He touches her shoulder in appreciation and walks to the doors. Center, turns . . . Points to* LOUISE.)

See, Ben? That's what I'm talking bout. People used to speak like that . . . in that language. But not anymore. (*Exit* ABE.)

LOUISE (*comes down to* BEN *quickly*): He can't get anything from the bank.

BEN: I know. (*He doesn't look at her.*)

LOUISE: Then why do you let him go down?

BEN: He's a dynamo. He must prosecute every lead to its finish, and if I tried to stop him he'd say I was laying down. He knows his chances, Lou, but he hopes secretly that somehow the odds'll change by the time he gets downstairs.

LOUISE: People shouldn't fool themselves that way.

BEN: People must fool themselves. If they didn't, life would hardly be liveable.

LOUISE: Then . . . I've been fooling myself too?

BEN: No. With us it's real. It's real, Louise! I don't think we fooled ourselves . . . so let's not start now.

(*Pause.*)

LOUISE: Ben . . . you're not thinking of that girl. . . .

BEN: How do I know what I'm thinking! How do I know!

LOUISE: . . . When did you decide?

BEN: I never decided! I was brought here, and I looked around, and I saw. And now I'm telling you what I saw.

LOUISE: But this is so small that you're holding. It's something that can be made again. Again and again!

BEN: I know that! I knew it the first time I walked into this place more than six years ago. But look at me. I'm in deeper now than ever before. It's just . . . Lou, I never had the guts to go up to him and tell him that I hate it here, that I loathe this damned thing, and I haven't the courage, the fact of sheer courage, to march you out and meet him on that elevator right now.

(*Pause.*)

No. That's not true. I've told him . . . many times. And I *could* take you away now . . . but I won't, Louise. I guess it's simply . . . that I love him . . . that's all.

LOUISE (*pause*): I suppose I might even be able . . . to love you for that too . . . I'm that big a fool. (*Turns away.*) If it happens . . . with that girl . . . I'll only stay a while . . . till you get another girl here and then I'll . . . I can't believe it, Ben!

(*He takes her and they kiss severely, frantically. . . .*)

BEN: It won't happen . . . I'll get out of it . . . some way . . . there must be a way!

LOUISE: But if there isn't?

BEN: There must be!

LOUISE: You're fooling yourself, Ben!

BEN: I'm not! I'll divorce her afterwards . . . I'll . . . !

(*Enter* ARNOLD *frightening them. He saunters in, his pipe in his mouth and throughout, burns matches. But he is very serious.*)

ARNOLD (*on entering*): No you won't.

BEN (*as they break*): What are you doing here?

ARNOLD: Me? I was waiting for a train outside the door . . . and people kept looking at me, so I thought I'd wait in here. You don't mind, do you?

BEN: Listen, go home, will you? . . .

ARNOLD: I heard . . . the whole thing. It was beautiful . . . really. I was touched. But you're not going to marry Helen, because if you do, you'll stay married. She won't divorce you. She loves you.

BEN: Oh . . . (*Deprecating.*)

LOUISE: Ben! . . .

ARNOLD: No . . . it's not his fault. Everybody loves Ben, because Ben loves everybody . . . or most everybody. He's soft, that's his trouble. He never learned that sometimes, in order to benefit some people, you've got to hurt them first.

BEN: Now, listen, if you think. . . .

ARNOLD: I do. Shut up.

BEN: Arnold, if . . .

ARNOLD: You're older than I am but I'm talking now!

(*Pause. He walks about, thinking. Then stops. Extends hand expressively.*)

Now . . . I should be in Baltimore. That's where I belong. But since I'm here, and the trains always run on time in God's country, I'll put in my chunk and scram, because this is a very unhealthy climate for me. (*To both.*) You've got something . . . rare. Do you grasp my meaning? It's something that doesn't happen every day, or every year. It's something . . . special. Like . . . like . . . dinosaur eggs.

(*They laugh.*)

All right, it doesn't matter . . . it's rare. Now . . . if you break this up, neither of you will ever get an equal value in return, ever.

BEN: I know that. What the hell, are you coming here to. . . .

ARNOLD: But what you don't know is that our father won't get a commensurate value either! Because when this thing gets cool, our father, who is a lot of things but not stupid, will realize that he was stuck on this deal. And he'll regret it. And so will our mother. And as for me, I'm already regretting . . . many things. But to the point. This is at the stage where cell-division hasn't taken place yet, so to speak, so a man can still analyze. I'm very tired now but if you don't stop it here, it'll become so complicated, that only God . . . will be making trees . . . if you get what I mean.

BEN: I get what you mean, and if you don't leave I'll throw you right out that window. This is my affair!

ARNOLD: You're telling me!

BEN: Then what the hell are you doing here?

ARNOLD: If I knew I wouldn't be here!

BEN: They did something to him down there. He's crazy.

ARNOLD: Not yet. When I'm crazy I'll go into the coat business. But before I do lose my senses, let me state, Louise, that if you permit him to do what he thinks he's got to do, you should have your brain examined in the morning. But you know that. You're a woman. (*Half to* BEN.) I'm tired now so I won't quote authorities, but it appears that a woman is born with certain fundamental concepts, while a man is born when he's twenty years old and consequently holds on to many ideas that he should have lost when he was one . . . and things become very difficult. However . . . what the hell, you both know what I'm talking about. Why don't you just go out and get married? It only takes a minute. Do it simply . . . do everything simply . . . like grass, and trees. You'll live longer.

BEN: Arnold.

ARNOLD: Yes?

BEN: You're talking through your hat. This place means. . . .

ARNOLD: I know what this place means. After all, I've only been in Baltimore a few years. But as a matter of fact, not of sentiment, mind you, but of fact, this place is by no means the culmination of all civilized effort. It's not the bud, so to speak, of the stem of . . . you know what I mean. The conclusion to the lecture is, then, that you hie ye hence in a helluva hurry, get yourselves a license to practice the much-touted profession come hell and father-in-law . . . and I'll stay here and hold the fort . . . but come back. Because I don't want to be left here alone too long. I have a bad astigmatism and I see bars in no time at all. So . . . (*switches his hand*) . . . go.

BEN: You sit there as though this were a problem in mathematics. It's not that simple. I'm here because . . . !

ARNOLD: You're here because you made a mistake! You have an idea that fate points the finger. Fate is dead, you understand! An unhappy man can never make anyone else happy, and you're going to learn that before you try it yourself. You made one mistake, my brother, but I'll be damned if you're going to make the same one again!! Now get the hell out of here before I throw you out!

LOUISE: What do you say, Ben? Is he right?

BEN: Sure he's right. He's always right. But my father doesn't understand these things . . . and I don't know that I want him to understand. . . .

ARNOLD: Louise, what's the matter with you? Why do you let him think that way?

LOUISE: I know it's wrong. But I understand him too well, Arnold, and your father too. I mean . . . when you know why people act the way they do it's hard to condemn them. We're different from you. At least I am.

ARNOLD: Well that's fine, Louise, because I'm no good at all.

LOUISE: No, I meant that our ambitions are completely divorced from what we expect to happen in our lives. We try to live with as little noise as possible, and yet we hope always that without making a sound we'll be heard and somehow lifted up.

ARNOLD: But that will never happen, Louise. Why don't you make noise? Why not live louder? Live at the top of your lungs! For God's sake get the hell out of here and sing your way to the marriage bureau!

LOUISE: But your father. . . .

ARNOLD: You leave Pop to me. Now go, and take my blessing from my own private church. . . .

(*Enter* ABE *downcast. Sits slowly.*)

(*Pause*): Hello . . . Dad.

ABE (*looks up at him*): Hello, Doc.

BEN: What did they say?

ABE: Very little, very little. In fact, just a word. No.

BEN: Roth hasn't been down there?

ABE: Roth didn't lift a finger for me.

   (*Looks at* BEN.)

What a dope I am, heh, Ben.

ARNOLD: Dad.

ABE: Yes, Doctor,

   (LOUISE *goes to office*)

you came home just in time for a big celebration.

ARNOLD: About Ben, I want to say that. . . .

ABE: Oh. I know what you want to say, Arny. You want to tell me that it ain't worth it for him to think of somebody he don't like. That's it, ain't it?

ARNOLD: . . . Yes.

ABE (*slight pause*): I agree with you. So what should I do?

ARNOLD: Tell him to go ahead and do as he likes.

ABE (*slight pause*): All right, Arny. Ben? Go ahead. Do what you like.

BEN: But, Dad . . .

ABE (*to* ARNOLD): See? He argues with me. I tell him to do what he likes and he argues with me. He thinks it's a fake and he don't believe it. He knows this is a hard world where nobody does what they like to do . . . except you. The rest of us don't know how.

ARNOLD: That's nonsense.

ABE: What?

ARNOLD: I said it's nonsense. He knows you don't mean what you're saying.

ABE: I do mean it, Arnold. I want you to understand that, Ben.

BEN: I understand it.

ABE (*to* ARNOLD): And I believe him. But just like you can't use a house for an automobile, so you can't use a responsible man like was not responsible. People are built a certain way. . . .

ARNOLD: Responsible, eh? (*To* BEN.) Well, what are you standing there for? I know why. You believe deep in your secret heart, that some great event will solve everything for you before the notes are due tomorrow. You've seen too many movies, all of you! You've watched, too many times, how a girl rides along on a Fifth Avenue bus and a sixty thousand-dollar sable coat falls on her head from a building, and she meets a banker. Well that's only the movies! You've got to collide with life, you've got to go out yourself and crash into it! Go on out and bang into a marriage license right now, because it won't walk up here itself. The great event that you're all waiting for is only potential, and that's all it will ever be.

BEN: And you don't believe . . . in that great event?

ARNOLD: Sure I do. But I always keep reminding myself that statistically, it can't happen, so if it does I'll be very happy, but if it doesn't, I won't be caught without my pants. Dad? Let me hear you say this. "Ben, go out right now and marry Louise before you tempt me."

(LOUISE *comes out of office.*)

ABE (*ridiculing*): Ah. . . .

ARNOLD: Go on!

ABE (*pause*): Wait. (*He tries to hide his head.*)

ARNOLD: No, say it!

ABE: I said wait!

ARNOLD: Say it!

LOUISE (*to* ABE): Don't you dare!

(*Pause. They turn to her.*)

When I want to marry Ben, and when Ben wants to marry me, we'll get married. Until then, we'll take care of all the details ourselves. (*Walks upstage into office.*)

ARNOLD: Well, I guess that settles something . . . I'm not sure what.

ABE (*rises quickly*): Come on, for Chrissakes, let's go to work! I'm sick and tired of listening to all this crap being thrown around! (*To* BEN.) Look at these samples laying there on the table. What are they made outa, burlap? Get some life in you! Here, unfold them and hand them to me . . . I'll hang them up.

(BEN *begins to do so* . . .)

A little life! A little life!

(*Snaps his fingers and* BEN *takes a sample and briskly hands it to him. He shakes it out and hangs it carefully.* . . .)

ARNOLD: A little life, but what's going to be done?

ABE (*looks up a moment*): This is a place of business. We got work to do here, if you don't mind. (*Goes back to work.*)

ARNOLD (*they are moving about under his nose and they continue vigorously as he talks. Loudly*): Here the most important problem in all your years is staring you in the face and what do you do? You hang up samples! For God's sake, the great event is not going to happen! I'll guarantee it! I'll put money on it!

(*They continue oblivious.*)

People, People, when the hell are you going to learn that it's entirely up to you! When will you stop this waiting? What are you waiting for? This is not the movies, People!

ABE (*stops and turns to him quickly. Loudly*): Arnold?

(*Enter* MAX *from right.*)

MAX: Mister Simon. (*He stands awaiting command.*)

ABE: What, Max?

(BEN *stops working.*)

MAX: Could I speak to you a minute?

ABE (*goes closer to him*): What is it?

MAX: Sit down, heh?

ABE: I hear better standing up. What's on your mind?

MAX (*pause. Cigarette smoke envelops his head*): We got a little proposition for you.

ABE: Who's we?

MAX: The shop and me . . . if I beg your pardon.

ABE (*impatiently*): Don't beg my pardon. Talk.

MAX: So . . . we know, Mister Simon, what's doing here. The men is none a them been here less than eight years. I'm right?

ABE: Well what's on your mind?

MAX: We don't want to see you go under like this.

ABE: Well . . . I'm glad to hear that, Max. It's good to see the men come to their senses.

MAX: No . . . we don't mean to cut the price on labor, Mister Simon.

ABE: Only?

MAX: Only . . . we got a proposition.

ABE: Well for God's sake what is it?

MAX: I'm just afraid you're going to bite my head off!

ABE: I don't bite heads off! Go ahead.

MAX: So . . . between us all . . . the shop, I mean, we got saved something like forty-three hundred dollars.

ABE: Yeh, Max?

MAX: And we figured to ourselfs, could we put it in the business and. . . .

ABE: You mean that, Max?

MAX: Yeh, but. . . .

ABE: Sure you can put it in, Max. I'll pay you regular interest. . . .

MAX: No, wait. Interest we don't want.

ABE (*carefully*): Only?

MAX: Only . . . well, Mister Simon . . . if I beg your pardon, we feel . . . the shop, I mean . . . that any more money put in this business, the way things is, would be thrown in the river . . . if I beg your pardon.

ABE: Is that so?

MAX: Now please don't get mad on me. I just tell you. . . .

ABE: Who's getting mad? I just said, is that so?

MAX: All right. We don't want no interest, and we ain't lending money. We'll put it in the business on the condition that you'll what they call, reincorporate with us as equal partners . . . you're getting mad and I didn't finish.

ABE: I'm listening, Goddamnit!

MAX: All right . . .

ABE: You talk as if the words tasted so good you didn't want to get rid of 'em.

MAX (*slight pause*): So . . . if there's profits, we all share even-Steven. Everybody gets a salary.

ABE: Yeh, so you think that just because you share the profits, there's gonna be any? Don't kid yourself, Max, I don't milk this business.

MAX: That ain't it. What we mean, is that if we're all cooperative, what they call, we'll be willing to work for a scale low enough to run out the scab shops from the industry and when that's done, we'll bring up the level . . . and it wouldn't be possible, you understand, for anybody to undersell us. The result will be, that either the scab shops will go out, become like us cooperative with the workers sharing, or they'll unionize, and in either case, the whole industry will be paying about the same scale, and then you'll compete. And mark my words, Mister Simon, it wouldn't pay to cut throats no more, and there won't be a racketeer left in the industry.

ABE (*long pause.* MAX *wants to fly*): In other words, Max, I'll be a manager.

MAX: Right. And we'll make the coats.

ABE: But a manager I'll be.

MAX: But you'll do the same work you do now.

ABE: But a manager.

MAX: Yeh . . . a manager.

ABE (*shakes his head with the information*): I'll think it over, Max.

MAX: Fine. I hope you'll consider, Mister Simon, because . . . well, we don't want to see you go under . . . and also we don't want to work somewhere with people we don't know. (*Exit* MAX *rather quickly.*)

(ABE *turns to* BEN *and waits for his opinion.*)

ARNOLD: That's a brilliant idea. . . .

ABE (*palm out*): When I'm sick I call a doctor, but now I'm not sick!

(*Turns again to* BEN.)

What do you think, Ben?

BEN: Take it. It's a way out.

ABE: You thought it over so quick? You didn't need no time?

BEN: I thought of that many times. I didn't tell you because I know you like to think of yourself as a boss. . . .

ABE: Well, ain't I?

BEN: You're not, Dad. You're simply . . . a working man; you aren't very much more independent, and you certainly haven't made much more than working men. What they're saying, Dad, is that you really belong with them, but that until now you've been fighting them instead. Overall, I think they're right.

ABE: But, Ben . . . it means my place ain't mine anymore.

BEN: No. It means that you're recognizing a fact which says that the place has been theirs too. Why, if we can believe Max, it means that they even hate to leave it as you do.

ABE (*long pause. He stands still with small eyes*): It's upside down. I never heard of nothin' like it. I . . . I don't know where to start to tell you. . . .

(*Phone. They turn to it.*)

LOUISE: Hello. Just a moment please.

(*Pause. She covers the receiver. To* ABE.)

It's Mr. Roth. He'd like to know . . . whether he can have some time with you . . . now.

ARNOLD (*pause.* ABE *silent. They all watch him*): Say no, Dad. Tell him to go to hell.

(*Pause. To* LOUISE.)

Give me that phone! (*Begins to go to her.*)

ABE (*pause. He looks at* BEN *as though for forgiveness. He raises his head to* LOUISE): Tell Mr. Roth . . . that I'm waiting for him.

LOUISE (*stares at him, then*): Mr. Simon will be waiting for you. (*Hangs up, comes out of the office.*) He'll be over soon to see you. I don't feel well. I'd like to go home.

(*They stand looking at her,* ARNOLD *begins to talk but doesn't; she turns and goes through the doors.* BEN *makes a step and stops;* ARNOLD *glares at him and rushes out after her.*)

ABE (*to* BEN): Why don't you do what you want? Why do you look at me? Do what you like and leave me alone!

(*Enter* ARNOLD *holding* LOUISE*'s arm.*)

LOUISE: Let go of my arm! . . .

ARNOLD: Shut up and wait a minute! Pardon me. (*He turns to* ABE *and* BEN *and brings his fingers to his temples.*) Now, everybody stand still and see if I can find some logic here. Roth is coming up here to make a final deal, isn't he?

ABE: I guess so.

ARNOLD (*to* BEN): Do you want to marry this person some day, or do you not?

BEN: . . . I do.

ARNOLD (*to* LOUISE): Do you still want to marry that guy?

LOUISE (*pause*): I suppose I do.

ARNOLD (*takes down his hands*): Well we've got that. Don't move yet.

(*Pause.*)

Maintaining all the rights of neutral . . . (*Angrily.*) . . . You see I'm speaking legally so that you won't get this Goddamned thing balled up as you usually do for no reason at all! Maintaining all the rights of a neutral, with no obligations of a belligerent, I am willing, with your cooperation, to inveigle Mr. Roth into believing that I am a suitable husband for his daughter.

LOUISE: Arnold!

(*She kisses him as* BEN *comes quickly and pumps his hand* . . .)

BEN: Arn, you're a guy!

(ABE *stands not joyfully.*)

ARNOLD: Wait a minute! (*He wipes them off.*) The sable coat hasn't fallen from the window yet! But if he does accept me, I will neglect to marry his daughter sometime after he comes across with whatever he is supposed to come across with aft. . . .

LOUISE: Arnold, you're adorable.

ARNOLD: After which! After which I am going straight back to Baltimore because this is entirely against my principles! (*To* ABE.) And why are you so unhappy?

ABE: Because it won't work. Sam Roth don't just want a son-in-law, he wants Ben.

ARNOLD: That's a good statement. Now, why does he want Ben?

ABE: Because Ben knows the coat business. And you don't!

ARNOLD (*pause*): Don't I?

(BEN *turns to* ABE, ABE *to* BEN.)

ABE (*palpitating softly*): Does he?

BEN: Sure he does. What the hell is there to learn in the coat business?

ABE (*walks about, fingers through his hair*): There's plenty to learn, there's plenty to learn, don't worry . . . (*To* ARNOLD.) What the hell did you come down here for? You'll disgrace me!

ARNOLD: But you're liable to eat.

ABE: I can eat without this, I can eat. (*Keeps walking.*)

BEN (*to* ABE): He can stay away from technicalities and speak generally. We can dope him up. At least Roth might hold us over tomorrow and then we can figure out something permanent later on. . . .

ABE (*stops walking, snaps his fingers*): Martin is coming up right away to look at merchandise, is he?

BEN: He promised.

ABE (*as though* BEN *is stupid*): Well? Arny can sell Martin a bill a goods and we can sell Roth a bill a goods. What do you say, Arny?

ARNOLD: You mean actually I've got to sell something . . . to somebody?

ABE: Well Roth ain't gonna think you're a business man just because you put your hands together.

LOUISE: Oh, leave him alone, he'll never be able to do it. I'm going.

ABE: You're going into the office and finish your work, young lady. You ain't so sick no more. This is gotta look like a place a business even if it ain't.

(*She looks at him and goes in office.*)

(*To* ARNOLD.) Well? You wanna work or you fainting?

ARNOLD: I'm not fainting . . . but I never sold a thing in my life. . . .

ABE: Sure. Just let a college man talk and he's in heaven. But give him something to *do*? Bango, he faints.

ARNOLD: I'm not fainting!

ABE (*prodding him*): Well! Well! Make up your mind, make up your mind . . . (*snaps his fingers*) . . . come on, come on, come on. . . .

ARNOLD: O.K.!

ABE: Fine! (*Quickly.*) Bring over the rack, Ben. . . .

ARNOLD (*as* BEN *sets the rack*): But remember, I'm not signing anything and this is just to help you out.

ABE: It's all right, you're neutral, you're neutral, don't worry so much about it. (*Hand on rack.*) Now, listen. You're listening, Baltimore, or am I talking to myself?

ARNOLD: Yes, I'm listening.

ABE: All right. (*A breath.*) We got a couple a minutes before Roth gets here and Martin ain't due yet for awhile in this neighborhood. Listen, and what you don't know, ask. You got it?

ARNOLD: I got it.

ABE: Fine. This is our line. You know what a line is?

ARNOLD: Yes . . . samples.

ABE (*correcting him*): A line. Samples . . . it's samples, but a line.

ARNOLD: A line. A man can buy any one of these coats.

ABE: You got it. Now look. There's eight coats here. One, two, three . . . so forth. Y'understand me?

ARNOLD: Yes, sure.

ABE: But we don't wanna sell these eight coats. We only want to sell two. This one, and this one.

ARNOLD: Why?

ABE: Why? Because it's the only ones we can make something on. The rest is crap. Now here . . . I'll put these two right in front so you don't make no mistakes. This is 649 . . . that's the number of the coat; and this is 722. You got it?

ARNOLD: This is 649, and this is 722.

ABE: Fine. The numbers is on the sleeve-tags. This is a sleeve-tag. Now go ahead . . . take 649 off the rack.

(ARNOLD *begins to take it off with fear.*)

Nononono. Arnold, put it back. You ain't taking the wheel off a car. This is a coat, it's gotta be *handled*, y'understand? Take it easy, lift it up, tender, y'know? . . . like you were delivering a baby . . . slow. Now go ahead, left hand on the hanger, right hand behind the coat. Hold it out, don't hide it. Ahh, that's nice, that's nice. See, Ben? He's all right. (*To* ARNOLD.) O.K. give it to me. (*Hangs it up.*)

ARNOLD: But. . . .

ABE: Just a minute. Now . . . You wanna ask something?

ARNOLD: Yes. How about suits?

ABE: What suits? We don't sell no suits this time a year. (*To* BEN.) He's liable to sell suits. . . .

BEN (*to* ARNOLD): No. . . .

ARNOLD: I'm not trying to sell suits. . . .

ABE: I know, but y'see. . . .

ARNOLD: I'm not trying to sell anything! I'll just. . . .

ABE: Oh yes you are. You're selling coats.

ARNOLD: I mean.

ABE: You mean, you mean. Don't sell no suits because we don't have 'em. (*To* BEN.) He'll sell suits yet he'll put us on the street.

ARNOLD: I'll only sell what he wants!

ABE: That's the ticket. All right.

(*They stand before a coat.*)

Now here's a coat . . . not a suit. You see it?

ARNOLD: Yes, I see it!

ABE: O.K. There's the top, there's the bottom. . . .

ARNOLD: For God's sake I know that!

ABE: Just a minute, I'm comin' to it! I'm in business thirty-five years and I'm tryin' to teach you everything I know in five minutes. Gimme a chance, will ya?

ARNOLD: I'm sorry. Go ahead.

ABE: Now look. (*Picks up bottom of coat.*) This coat is got a . . . what they call, a hand-felled bottom.

ARNOLD: No.

ABE: You don't understand. (*Scratches his head.*) All right, I'm glad you told me. Hand-felled, is open, y'see? The lining on the bottom here ain't attached to the coat with stitching. If it's stitched, it's a machine bottom. This is open.

ARNOLD: I see. What's the difference?

ABE: This is better.

ARNOLD: Why?

ABE (*enraged*): Because it's better!

ARNOLD: All right, I'm sorry.

ABE: It's better, why the hell do you care why? (*Begins to go on to another topic but . . .*) It's better because if the lining shrinks in the cleaners it can pull up free without rolling up the bottom of the coat . . . that is, if it's a hand-felled bottom. But if it's stitched across and it shrinks, it'll pull the bottom right up with it, and it'll look like hell. Y'see?

ARNOLD: Gosh, that's pretty clever.

ABE: What then, only medicine? Now look . . . this lining is rayon. Not silk, but rayon.

ARNOLD: Is silk better?

ABE: Don't better! For God's sake, you ain't buyin' it you're sellin' it!

ARNOLD: But I want to know!

ABE: I'll tell ya later!

(*Pause.*)

Yeh, silk is better. So . . . this coat comes in these shades on the swatches here . . . see, on these pieces of cloth.

ARNOLD: Oh, that's simple.

ABE: You know what I'm talking about?

ARNOLD: I'm right with you.

ABE: Be sure. Now. What I'm gonna tell you is important, see, so if you already forgot the rest of it, remember this, because this is what counts. Price, understand? Price.

ARNOLD: I understand.

ABE: This coat . . . mind ya this one not the rest, costs Mister Martin eight seventy-five, less eight percent. What did I say?

ARNOLD: This coat . . . mind you this one and not the rest . . . costs Martin eight seventy-five, less eight.

ABE (*smiles*): Where did you learn to say "less eight"?

ARNOLD: Well I used to live with a family named Simon.

ABE (*to* BEN): He was born with a needle in his mouth. (*To* ARNOLD.) All right, now look. This coat is eight seventy-five, but the other one . . . see, 722, is ten seventy-five less eight and it comes in the same colors. It costs more because it's got a better cloth and a silk lining, y'understand?

ARNOLD: Why is that cloth better?

ABE: Arnold, do us a favor and forget about better. Better don't count in this business. Whatever one he likes is better and what he don't like ain't better, y'get me?

ARNOLD: I get you.

ABE: O.K. Now you're gonna sell him only the 649 and the 722 because the rest is lemons, y'understand? What's the rest?

ARNOLD: Lemons.

ABE: You got it. Now, he's gonna try to. . . .

ARNOLD: But. . . .

ABE: But what?

ARNOLD: But supposing he likes one of these.

ABE: You gotta see to it that he don't like one a these.

ARNOLD: But if he insists.

ABE: He won't insist.

ARNOLD: But if he does.

ABE (*to* BEN): A regular leech! Use your head! Have a feeling for it!

ARNOLD: All right, I'll have a feeling for it. What else?

ABE: He's gonna try to get ten percent off instead of eight off. That, you don't stand for.

ARNOLD: I see. But if he insists?

ABE: Don't be such a professor! He's out for your skin. You're selling merchandise here. Don't *let* him insist. (*Snaps his fingers.*) The head, the head, use it, y'know? O.K. now, let me see you work. Take it off the rack and go ahead.

(ARNOLD *lifts a coat from the rack with infinite care.*)

A little respect for the merchandise . . . it ain't burlap, it ain't burlap . . . lift it up, you're wiping the floor with it . . . we got brooms for that.

ARNOLD: Mr. Martin, this is number 649. . . .

ABE: Good, good, go on, but don't move around so much, he ain't gonna run after ya. . . .

ARNOLD: This has a rayon lining. . . .

ABE: No! You don't *tell* him it's rayon. Silk you say loud, but rayon you whisper.

ARNOLD (*nods*): Ah . . . we're selling this in great quantities now. It's a very good number here.

(ABE *nods O.K.*)

Now Mr. Martin, I think that. . . .

ABE: No, you don't think either. No thinks, no maybes, no seems to me's . . . no college stuff here. Only be definite. Whatever you say, stick to it, because if you can't believe yourself he ain't gonna believe you neither. It's yes or no, top or bottom, me or you . . . no in-betweens.

ARNOLD: But if I'm not sure.

ABE: Right or wrong, be sure. He'll have respect, because he don't know a helluva lot either.

ARNOLD: And are there sizes in these things?

ABE: What, is every woman the same size, Doctor? These coats is made in 12, 14's, 16's and 20's. But no 18's.

ARNOLD: 12, 14, 16, 20. Is that all I have to know?

ABE: No, but that's all you do know, so make use of it.

ARNOLD (*walks, memorizing quickly*): 12, 14, 16, 20 . . . Now about . . . when can you deliver?

ABE: One week.

ARNOLD: O.K.

(*Looks in air, his expressive hand extended.* LOUISE *looks on from the office, smiling;* BEN *and* ABE *observing him as he walks . . .*)

Mr. Martin, on these numbers we can give you immediate delivery, because. . . .

ABE: Since when is a week immediate delivery? Immediate is tomorrow morning!

ARNOLD: Well I . . . was . . . I was just trying to put something over.

(*Others laugh.*)

Now you see, Martin, this color blends well with almost any complexion and . . . and . . . 12, 14, 16 . . . (*To* ABE.) What's after sixteen?

ABE: You losing your mind? Is that the trouble?

ARNOLD (*looks blank*): I . . . I can't remember anything. What's after sixteen? My God, what's after sixteen? I can't do it! I don't know anything about it!

ABE: That only could happen to a full-blooded professor!

BEN (*takes* ARNOLD'*s shoulders*): Arn! Don't listen to him. You don't need to know anything but the price. The rest is garbage. He's just trying to complicate it so he can justify his thirty years in the business. . . .

ABE: Is that a fact?

BEN: Yes! (*To* ARNOLD.) It's not an art, it's not a science, it's all bull and it can be mastered by an imbecile . . . so go ahead and knock him dead.

ARNOLD: Thanks, Ben. Eight seventy-five less eight . . . but what comes after sixteen?

ABE: There's the elevator door!

ARNOLD (*stiffens*): All right. Bring him in.

ABE: What, bring him in. Loosen up, loosen up . . . you're fainting again.

ARNOLD: One question, Dad.

ABE: Quick, what is it?

ARNOLD: Ah . . . I suppose there are linings in the sleeves.

ABE: You suppose . . . ! (*Hits his head (his own) with his palm.*) What's the matter, ya thick!(?)

(*Enter* DAVE SIMON, *a little man with the intonation of a taxi-driver and the walk of a sailor. They are silent for a moment, then* . . .)

ARNOLD: Uncle Dave!

DAVE (*beams at* ARNOLD. *Half to* ABE): The kid! Arny! (*Hugs him.*)

(*They laugh; he pulls away and looks.*)

Gee, you got to be such a big guy. You're a doc?

ARNOLD: I'm a doc.

DAVE: Gee, he's a doc!

ABE: Yep, we're gettin' old, Dave.

DAVE (*glowing*): Look at him, Ben. Arny, when I look at you I see myself when I was in law school. One year in law school and then I walked out into a mud pile. I'm still in it. Listen to me, Arnold . . . no, don't listen to me. Don't take anybody's advice. You get advice from two kinds a people. The big success and the failure. The big success don't tell you the truth because he's proud, and the failure don't tell you the truth because he's ashamed. Who started me off?

ABE (*looks at him closely*): Why ain't you been around, Dave? What's on your mind!

DAVE: You got a minute for me?

ABE: Well, some people are coming in, but tell me. . . .

DAVE (*begins to go*): Then I won't bother you.

ABE (*grabs him*): Don't be so sensitive, for God's sake! What're you got on your mind!

DAVE (*pause*): I want to ask you advice.

ABE: Then go ahead. Dave, I'm still a brother.

DAVE: All right, Abe. (*A breath.*) I wanted to ask you if I should go away. I got a chance for something big in Florida.

ABE: I thought you're making good money here. You are, aren't you?

DAVE: Yeh . . . yeh, I'm makin' good money, but I figure I could maybe do better in Florida.

ABE: You're still selling for Roth, aren't you?

DAVE: Selling? . . . yeh, I'm selling for Roth.

ABE (*pause. He goes closer*): Dave, what's the story? Why don't you look at me?

(DAVE *turns.*)

What'd you do now, Dave?

DAVE: What do you mean, what I did! Am I a thief! I'm a thief!

ABE: What the hell are you talking about!

DAVE (*turns to go*): O.K. g'by, g'by, I'm sorry I bothered you. . . .

(*Enter* ROTH.)

ROTH (*looks at* DAVE): Hello. What are *you* doing here?

DAVE (*looks up at him and down at his shoes*): Hello.

(*Exit* DAVE. ABE *runs to doors and calls out.*)

ABE: Come to the house on Sunday! Dave!

    (ARNOLD *exits quickly thru doors.*)

ROTH: How are you, Ben.

ABE: What happened to him? Is he still selling for you?

ROTH: I guess so, Abe.

ABE: Well don't you know?

ROTH (*sits*): Yeh, he's selling, but between you and me, he ain't exactly what he might be. He's a . . . ah, but what's the use of talking about it? I meant to see Dawson for you at the bank, but I didn't have a minute.

ABE: Oh. I didn't know what to think, Sam. You should've called and told me. If it's not paid before tomorrow I'm closed down.

ROTH: Don't worry, Abe, nobody's gonna close you down. Here, take a cigar. I got my name on the cellophane.

ABE (*takes cigar*): Thanks. But will you be sure to take care of that, Sam? You know I got no pull in that bank anymore. . . .

    (*Enter* ARNOLD.)

ROTH: Forget it, Abe. (*Of* ARNOLD.) What's he doing here?

ABE: Oh . . . he helps me out every once in a while.

ROTH: Don't say. That's nice. But I thought he's a doctor.

ABE: A business head never hurts, even on a doctor.

ROTH: Specially a doctor. So, Ben . . . what did you decide?

ARNOLD: Ah, Dad . . . I think I'd better tell the cutter not to cut until he rearranges that pattern.

ABE: Ah . . . yeh, yeh, you better tell him . . . why?

ARNOLD: Well he'll waste three inches on every coat.

ABE: Oh . . . yeh, don't let him do that.

    (*Exit* ARNOLD *right.*)

ROTH: He talks like he knows something.

ABE (*offhand*): Him? If I knew at his age what he knows about the coat business, I'd be better off today.

ROTH: You mean he knows silks . . . and furs?

ABE: Of course he's still got plenty to learn, but he's on his way.

ROTH: But furs . . . ?

ABE: I said he's on his way, Sam.

ROTH: You mean . . . he don't know.

ABE: Oh, he knows . . . but he's on his way. You know he worked plenty of summers here. He ain't no amateur. . . .

ROTH: You must feel like an old man with such sons walking

around. Y'know, Abe, you look much older than I do. Tell me, Ben, how is it you don't come over more often to see Helen?

ABE: I could answer that, Sam. If times was good, he'd feel like celebrating at night, but times is bad so he's got no time for it. (*Enter* ARNOLD.)

ROTH: I know, Abe, but to come to my house he don't have to celebrate. . . .

ABE (*index finger up*): Granted. But still . . . times is bad.

ROTH: Times *is* bad, yes.

ABE: Well? What more is there to say? I tell ya, Sam, if it was Arnold, for instance, you'd have a different story. . . .

BEN: There's the elevator! Your customer, Arn!

ARNOLD: Heh? Oh . . . (*Goes toward doors.*)

ABE (*discreetly*): No, Arny, just wait in here . . . (*To* ROTH, *confidentially.*) He's still breakin' in on the sales end.

ROTH (*amazed*): You're gonna let him wait on a buyer?

ABE: Him? I would trust that guy with R. H. Macy.

ROTH: And a doctor in the bargain! Hm!
(*Enter* MARTIN, *a dumpy man.*)

ABE (*goes to* MARTIN *vigorously, shakes his hand*): Good to see ya, Martin, how are you, you're lookin' fine.

MARTIN (*looks up at* ABE *sourly. Monotone. Hard*): I can't listen to no crap today, Mister Simon, I'm a sick man.

ABE: What happened?

MARTIN: You know you don't give a damn what happened. Just show me your merchandise. If I like it I'll buy it, if I don't I won't buy it.

ABE: Martin, since when do I crap you?

MARTIN: All right, Simon, I'm sorry. But Jeziz, I bought eleven thousand coats today and I'm sick and tired of all the bull I gotta wade through before I can buy a goddam garment. Just show me your stuff, will ya, I wanna go home and go to sleep. I got a headache.

ABE (*pause. He turns to* ARNOLD, *wetly*): This is my son, Arnold, Mr. Martin . . . (*As he goes to his seat.*) He'll wait on you.

MARTIN: All right, Arnold, come on will ya, what're you got? (*Puts down his portfolio.*)

ARNOLD (*goes to rack, takes off coat.* ROTH *looks on waiting for the kill, ready to laugh*): This is number. . . .

MARTIN (*holds his head*): I don't wanna know your numbers. I got a headache. Numbers don't mean a thing to me, boy, just put it out. Hang it up, will ya? No, not on the rack, over here on the hook so I can see it.

(ARNOLD *hangs it on hook;* MARTIN *looks it over.*)

O.K. now, what else you got? I'm in a hurry.

ARNOLD: Sure. Here's our best number. (*Hangs second coat.*) They don't come any nicer than this. . . .

MARTIN: Listen, boy, I know when they come nicer and when they don't. If it's nice I'll say it's nice and when it ain't nice I'll say it ain't nice so don't go telling me when it's nice!

(*Looks it over, turns to* ARNOLD.)

All right, next.

(ARNOLD *just stands and looks at him.*)

What's the matter, boy, move, will ya?

ARNOLD: You shouldn't be buying coats today.

MARTIN (*struck*): What? You tryin' to tell me my business?

ARNOLD (ABE *is almost on his feet*): Yes. You should be in bed.

MARTIN: Listen, I pay good money for my medical advice. Bring out your stuff or. . . .

ARNOLD: Well if you pay you're getting stuck.

MARTIN (*to* ABE, *his hand pointing to* ARNOLD): What'd you do to me here?

ABE: Ah . . . he's a doctor, Martin.

MARTIN: What is this, a circus?

ARNOLD: I am a doctor. I just graduated recently. What's wrong with your eye?

MARTIN (*pause. Looks at him sideways*): You kidding me?

ARNOLD: I could be arrested if I am. Let me see your eye.

MARTIN (*pulls down his face*): Yeh, look at that eye, will ya?

(ARNOLD *is looking into it.*)

You're really a doctor, aren't you?

ARNOLD: Of course. Look up at the ceiling.

MARTIN: I was comin' out of a cafeteria on Thirty-Sixth Street one o'clock in the afternoon and I'll be damned if I didn't catch something in my eye. It feels like a truck.

ARNOLD: It's not a truck. Just hold still.

MARTIN: You can't walk around in this goddamned garment center five minutes without getting something in your eye. Look at the way it swelled up, huh.

ARNOLD: Not very much. Now look down at the floor. There we are. How does it feel now?

MARTIN (*blinking*): Well I'll be God damned, I can see! Thanks, a helluva lot, Doc. (*Shakes his hand.*) Y'know I was afraid to go into one a these drug stores . . . they'll take your eye out, heh.

ARNOLD: No, they perform a simple operation like that.

MARTIN (*laughs*): Imagine? I bought eleven thousand coats today . . . with one eye.

ABE (*laughing*): I hope you didn't get stuck.

MARTIN: Go on. I can buy better with one eye than any of 'em with four.

ARNOLD: How's your headache?

MARTIN (*softly*): I still got it, I guess. On this side. Y'know, I got a bad stomach.

ARNOLD: What did you eat today?

MARTIN: Nothin' much. Lemme see . . . I had a little crab-meat for lunch.

ARNOLD: Well that's enough. Open your mouth and let me see your tongue.

MARTIN (*mouth open*): Maybe I oughta come to your office.

ARNOLD: I'm not settled yet. Stick out your tongue.

(MARTIN *does.*)

Ah, hah . . . all right, close your mouth. Give me your wrist, please.

MARTIN (*as he pulls up his sleeve*): Y'know, I can't seem to find a good doctor. . . .

ARNOLD (*takes his wrist*): Sshh!

(*Silence.* MARTIN *very anxious.*)

MARTIN (ARNOLD *drops his hand. With fear*): How is it?

ARNOLD (*looks at him seriously*): What's your blood pressure, do you know?

MARTIN: Pretty high, Doc.

ARNOLD: What's the rating?

MARTIN (*sheepishly*): 210.

ARNOLD: How old are you?

MARTIN: Thirty-nine.

ARNOLD (*feels his forehead*): Feel chilly at all?

MARTIN (*realizing the seriousness*): Yeh . . . I was hot and cold before.

ARNOLD: You may have a fever.

MARTIN (*frightened*): No!

ARNOLD: Yes. You go right home, Mr. Martin, take some magnesia, go to bed, cover up, and if you feel any worse call a physician immediately. And don't eat crabmeat if it makes you ill.

MARTIN: Am I sick?

ARNOLD: Quite. And you'll be sicker if you don't go to bed.

MARTIN (*hurriedly picks up his portfolio*): Jeeze, thanks, Doc, I kinda thought it was something, but (*apologizing*) . . . I'm awfully busy.

ARNOLD: That's not an excuse.

MARTIN: Yeh, I know. Well . . . (*Goes for the door, stops at the coat hanging next to it.*) Oh. You still selling coats?

ARNOLD: Are you sure you feel up to it?

MARTIN: Well I gotta fill my quota today. This one'll do. What do you get?

ARNOLD: Eight seventy-five, less eight.

MARTIN (*with a guilty smile*): I can get less ten, Doc.

ARNOLD (*politely, but warningly*): You'll get pneumonia if you try to buy any more coats today.

MARTIN (*hurriedly*): O.K. . . . let's see, I'm short 240 . . . can you send me up 240 a these?

ARNOLD: As many as you like.

MARTIN: When can I get them?

ARNOLD: Monday at the earliest, Mr. Martin.

MARTIN (*slight pause*): O.K. Monday. Thanks for everything, Doc, let me wish you all the luck in the world. I feel like a new man already.

ARNOLD: You'd better take a taxi home.

MARTIN: I'll do that, Doc. So long, I hope to see you again.

ARNOLD: The feeling is mutual, Mr. Martin.

MARTIN: Thanks. (*Goes to door, stops, turns slowly.*) S a y. Why are you selling coats if you're a doctor?

ARNOLD: Oh, I come down occasionally. I enjoy the work. (*Smiles.*) Just for the hell of it.

MARTIN (*smiles wistfully*): Oh. Yeh, I guess it would be nice if you didn't have to do it for a living. (*Stands in a haze for a moment.*) Say, Simon, you got a good kid here.

ABE: You're telling me?

MARTIN (*to* ARNOLD): But stay outa the business, son, look what it did to your old man.

> (*They laugh, including* ABE.)

> (*Quickly.*) Jeez, I'm sweatin' like a pig. Goodby.

>> (*Exit* MARTIN. ARNOLD *turns to them, the conqueror. Reenter* MARTIN.)

> (*His head appearing through the doors*): Did you say magnesia?

ARNOLD: Magnesia is right, Mr. Martin.

MARTIN: Any drug store?

ARNOLD: Any drug store.

MARTIN (*salutes broadly*): Thanks.

>> (*Exit* MARTIN. ABE *and* BEN *rush to him and wring his hands.*)

ABE: I never seen nothin' like it in my life!

BEN: Beautiful job, kid!

>> (*Laughs, hitting him on the back.* LOUISE *is ready to climb through the window.*)

ABE (*to* ROTH): Man to man, how did you like that?

ROTH (*rises with dignity, but he is beaming*): I would never believe it if I didn't seen it with my own eyes. You notice Martin didn't talk to me? He's such a tough guy we're on the outs. I can't get near him he's such a holdup. Arnold, (*his hand on* ARNOLD's *shoulder*) I felt for you when that bastard walked in, like as if you was my own son with lions . . . if I had a son. (*To* ABE. *Growing enthusiasm.*) Really, I felt almost like it was my merchandise he sold.

ARNOLD: Well . . . it wouldn't be hard to sell if we could always spot a character like that. The man obviously wanted sympathy, and I simply gave it to him.

ABE: You hear, Sam? Notice the way he figures this out? That's college for you.

ROTH (*ecstasy*): Listen, Abe, I always said . . . college, is . . . college. There simply ain't nothin' like it. Tell me, Arnold . . . is he really sick? (*Smiles wryly.*)

ARNOLD: Why, yes . . . but a little magnesia'll never hurt him anyway. (*Smiles.*)

ROTH (*turns to* ABE, *his hand on* ARNOLD): Abe? (*Taps his own skull.*) . . . A head. Come, sit down everybody.

> (*As they do.*)

And believe me, there's plenty buyers walkin' around needin' a physician.

ABE: Plenty? All a them. That's the biggest trouble with the coat business.

ROTH: Well not all, Abe. I know a few who's all right.

ABE: A few, yes . . . but they don't buy for the big houses.
（*Laughs.*）
You can't tell, it might pay the manufacturers to put Arnold on a full-time basis. A regular buyers-clinic. We'd last longer, and I'd have my hair today.
（*They laugh,* ROTH *included. He leans back comfortably, everyone smiling for various reasons.* LOUISE *smiles in from the office window.*）

ROTH: In the excitement I almost forgot what I came for. (*Laughs at himself.*) Without beatin' the bush . . . Ben, did you come to a decision yet. (*Looks at* BEN *pleasantly, comfortably.*)

ARNOLD (*rises*): Mr. Roth.

ROTH: What is it, Arnold . . . I should say, Doctor Cloak-man.

ARNOLD (*laughs with* ROTH. *Slight pause*): What would you say . . . if I should ask you . . . if I could take . . . Ben's place.

ROTH (*looks up genially*): You mean. . . .

ARNOLD: For Helen.
（ROTH *smiles less.*）

ABE: He just . . . wants to know . . . Sam.

ROTH: Yeh, I see. (*Pause. Looks at his cigar's side.*) Well, Arnold . . . I'll tell you. A thing like this . . . I feel we got no right to mix in.

ARNOLD: Oh, I agree with that.

ROTH: In many ways we're two of a kind, Arnold. So a thing like this . . . why should we . . . turn over the whole apple truck? Let bygones be bygones is my way of lookin' at it. I'm a conservative man. Y'understand me?

ARNOLD: Yes, but I simply thought that . . .

ROTH: There's no hard feelings, Arnold. In fact, if you're a good boy, maybe when you open up in practice I'll buy you one a those machines . . . that they burn you with. What do you call them?

ARNOLD: Heat therapy.

ROTH: Therapy. What do you think of that?

ARNOLD (*solemnly*): I hope I'll be a good boy. (*Smiles but weakly.*)

ROTH (*lightly hits* BEN*'s thigh, smiling*): Well, Ben?

BEN (*pause. He stands and turns from the office. Looks down*): All right.

ROTH (*stands suddenly*): You mean that, Ben?

BEN: Yes . . . I mean it.

ROTH (*takes his hand*): Congratulations.

(*Takes* ABE*'s hand.*)

Congratulations, Abe.

(*Takes* ARNOLD*'s hand.*)

Same to you, Arn. (*Takes a breath, smiling, but exhausts it.*) What's the matter you're all so sad?

ABE: Well . . . you know, as much as you prepare for it, it's still a shock.

ROTH: I know. I feel the same way all of a sudden. (*Brightly.*) Let's all get a drink! You got a bottle Abe?

ABE: I ain't got a thing.

ROTH (*turns suddenly to the office*): Girl! Girl! Call Algonquin 6-9910, my friend's store. Tell him to send up a bottle a port wine . . . for Sam Roth, tell him.

(*She stares at him.*)

Well?

LOUISE (*picks up the phone.* BEN *steps toward her, stops. To* ROTH): That's . . . Algonquin-6 . . . 9 . . . ?

(*Breaks into tears and rushes out.* ROTH *turns to them.*)

ROTH (*sincerely*): What's the matter with her?

(BEN *rushes out past him. He follows* BEN *with his eyes and when* BEN *is gone, keeps looking at the doors for a moment. He turns to* ABE *who is sitting and looking off blankly. Softly.*)

That's . . . his girl, Abe?

(ABE *nods slowly.*)

(*Softly and a little sadly*): Ah. (*Pause. He does not blink. Softly.*) Well, that's the way it goes. Love . . . is a terrible thing. (*A breath.*) I'll go home now, Abe. You want to drink?

ABE: I don't feel like it, Sam.

ROTH: Me neither. (*Moves.*) I'll be over Sunday. Esther can set the date. All right?

ABE (*nods without looking at him*): All right, Sam.

ROTH (*looks at* ABE *a moment*): I'll hold off Dawson for a week.

ABE: Thanks, Sam.

ROTH (*almost testing*): Well, goodby, Abe.

ABE (*only half relieving his doubts*): Goodby, Sam.

> (ROTH *waits a second then quickly goes.* ARNOLD *stands center,* ABE *sits leaning on his knees, looking off.* ARNOLD *looks down at him. Pause.*)

ARNOLD (*hands on hips*): Well? (*Slowly and softly.*) I guess that sable coat isn't going to fall on our heads today. I guess that great event never bothered to occur. This is not the movies, Dad. This is us.

> (*He turns and walks leisurely but heavily toward the doors,* ABE *immovable, as* . . .)

SLOW CURTAIN

ACT THREE

SCENE I

*Sunday morning at seven o'clock in the Simon home. The curtain
rises and there is a pause long enough to tell of people sleeping in
this house, and of the intense quiet just before a family awakens.
The sun is streaming in through the windows. A bird may be
heard talking somewhere outside. The old chair and stool that*
GRAMP *brought up in the first act are no longer here.*

*After a time, there is heard a very, very light tapping on the door
to the street,—as though the visitor feared his or her own presence
at this unearthly hour. A pause in complete silence. The tapping
again. A pause. Then a light tinkle of the doorbell. Pause again.
A light, restrained effort is felt at the left window. Slowly, it goes
up, and as it rises, shuffling is heard at the head of the stairs. As
the leg of* HELEN ROTH *is uncomfortably preceding her through
the opened window,* ARNOLD SIMON *is, with equal temper, making his bleary way down the stairs, irregularly, rubbing his eyes
and shading them in an effort to see whatever needs seeing. He
seems almost drunk as he makes his way, like a blind man, toward
the door, and as he opens it and looks out,* HELEN *stands behind
him inside the room, arranging herself. He peers out, east and
west, and satisfied, closes the door and begins to go back to bed.*

HELEN: Pardon me.
ARNOLD (*frightened, he jumps and turns*): Ha!
HELEN: Sshh!
ARNOLD (*with secrecy*): Yeh. Good morning.
HELEN: Good morning.
ARNOLD: Ah . . . (*Waving his hand aimlessly.*) Did I . . . let
    you in?
HELEN: I came in myself.
ARNOLD (*smiling weakly in supposed recognition*): Oh . . .
    you have a key.
HELEN: No, I came through the window.
ARNOLD: I see . . . (*Looks at window.*) The window. (*Turns
    back to her.*) Yourself?

628

HELEN: Yes, alone.

ARNOLD: Oh. (*Hits his head to shake it awake.*) Good morning.

HELEN (*smiling*): We said that once.

ARNOLD: Oh, did we? What time is it?

HELEN: Not seven yet.

ARNOLD: Not seven? Pretty early isn't it. (*Smiles weakly.*)

HELEN: I always get up early.

ARNOLD: Yeh? It's nice, I guess. (*Holding his head.*) I've never been up before ten in my life.

HELEN: It's the best part of the day.

ARNOLD: That's what I heard. I've got to try it sometime. But my eyes don't open before ten. I . . . astigmatism. Ah . . . is there . . . something I can do for you?

HELEN: Are you awake?

ARNOLD: Oh no. I . . . I don't expect to be for a few hours. You just tell me whatever is on your mind . . . and I'll go to sleep and try to remember it when I get up. I'll attend to everything.

HELEN: I have something very important to ask you, Arnold. I hoped you'd be the one to answer the door. I knew your bedroom was nearest the hall.

ARNOLD: Oh yes, my bedroom. Nice room.

HELEN: When nobody answered the door I decided to break in and wake you.

ARNOLD: Yeh, that would be the best thing . . . I appreciate. . . .

HELEN (*he seems about to fall over. She supports him and talks in his ear*): Arnold. Wake up! I want to tell you something!

ARNOLD: Yes . . . yes. Just give me a minute . . . I can't breathe right yet . . . (*He holds his eyes open and takes breath.*) There we are. Now . . . what were you saying?

HELEN: Can you hear me?

ARNOLD: Oh yes. Almost every word now.

HELEN: Well try to listen, won't you? This is hard for me too.

ARNOLD: But not as hard as it is for me. I'm a . . . a late sleeper, Helen . . . my whole system. . . .

HELEN: But you've got to listen!

ARNOLD: I'm listening.

HELEN: I went shopping yesterday.

ARNOLD: Stores must've been crowded, heh.

HELEN: I mean I met Louise in Macy's.

ARNOLD: You did.

HELEN: She's a very unhappy girl, Arnold.

ARNOLD: Yeh, I know. She's. . . .

HELEN: I had a long talk with her, Arny.

ARNOLD (*nods*): M. Hm.

HELEN (*looks around, swallows*): Arnold, would you marry me?

ARNOLD (*pause. He stands there nodding with his eyes shut*): Sure, sure. . . .

HELEN: I . . . I . . . asked if you'd *marry* me, Arnold!

ARNOLD: Sur—Oh *Marry* you! Oh no, I couldn't do a thing like that. (*Awakens.*) Marry you! Are you crazy!(?) It's seven o'clock in the morning!

HELEN: Sshh! (*She presses his lips.*) You'll wake your mother and she won't like this.

ARNOLD (*whispers*): Yeh. But Helen, (*strained whisper*) are you sure you . . . you've got the right party? I'm Arnold, don't you see?

HELEN: I know you're Arnold.

ARNOLD: Then one of us is wrong, Louise . . . Helen, I'm not Arnold . . . I mean I'm Ben . . . I'm Arnold I mean!

HELEN: Here, sit down. That's better. Now, you're Arnold Simon, and I'm Helen Roth. I'm asking you to marry me. Is that clear?

ARNOLD: You're asking me to . . . But couldn't you wait till this afternoon?

HELEN: No, because then I'd find it hard to get you alone, and anyway, it might be too late by this afternoon.

ARNOLD: Yes, it might be . . . Why?

HELEN: This is Sunday, Arnold, and. . . .

ARNOLD: Seven o'clock.

HELEN: Seven o'clock. This afternoon my father's coming here and they're going to set the date for Ben and me. Ben doesn't want me. He wants Louise. He told me that himself.

ARNOLD: Oh, I see. That's right. He wants Louise. She's a nice girl.

HELEN: Well . . . doesn't anything suggest itself to you?

ARNOLD (*thinks*): There's only one thing could suggest itself to me at this hour—a bed. But you just go right ahead. Now . . . what is it I'm not doing?

HELEN: You're not listening to me. My God, are you like this every morning?

ARNOLD (*smiles at how remarkable it is*): Yeh, imagine?

HELEN: Well try, won't you? Try to understand what I'm saying before they get up.

ARNOLD: I am trying, Louise . . . Helen. Go on.

HELEN: There's only one thing that can stop my father from trying to marry me to someone who doesn't want me. And he's tried it before, Arnold . . . he's tried it before!

ARNOLD (*shakes his head from side to side*): That's horrible, Louise.

HELEN: Arnold, if you would marry me. . . .

ARNOLD: You mean now?

HELEN: Right away. If you would do that, we could come back here and break it all up. And that horrible thing couldn't happen.

ARNOLD: I guess it couldn't at that. Yeh, but . . . *we'd* be married!

HELEN: Yes . . . we would.

ARNOLD: Well . . . do you . . . this is ridiculous at seven o'clock in the morning, Helen . . . do you love me?

HELEN: Why . . . that's beside the point.

ARNOLD: Oh it is, eh??

HELEN (*quieting him*): I mean we could divorce.

ARNOLD: But maybe we couldn't. You know they don't give divorces to every Tom, Dick, and Harry just like that.

HELEN: Well . . . mental cruelty.

ARNOLD: Who, me? Oh no you don't. I'm going to practice medicine, you know. You expect people to call in a maniac? . . . especially when they're sick? No sir. . . .

HELEN: All right . . . Reno.

ARNOLD: That costs a lot of money, Helen.

HELEN: I have money.

ARNOLD (*rises seriously and walks about*): That's another thing. You know I've spent a good part of my life preaching to people on the evils of marriage for money.

HELEN: I know, but. . . .

ARNOLD: How is that going to look if I myself go off and marry a rich girl . . . at seven in the morning no less.

HELEN: Then I won't take a cent from my father. He'll probably cut me off anyway.

ARNOLD (*he stops moving. Pause*): You mean . . . completely?

HELEN: Without a cent.

ARNOLD: Gee.

   (*Pause.*)

   Well that's better. Because you know I can take care of myself in this world.

HELEN: I know that, Arnold.

ARNOLD: Without anybody's help.

HELEN: I know that too.

ARNOLD (*stops again*): You mean . . . actually . . . without a cent?

HELEN: Well, I have four hundred dollars of my own.

ARNOLD (*relieved*): Oh, well that's close enough. No use being childish about these things. You know you'd have to support yourself for quite a while.

HELEN: Until the divorce.

ARNOLD: . . . Yes, until the divorce. Because an intern doesn't get paid . . . and I didn't plan on a wife quite so soon.

HELEN: But, Arnold, it isn't as though I were asking you to support me.

ARNOLD: Yes, but I'll have no wife of mine supporting me.

HELEN (*impatiently*): Oh, that's all irrelevant. In a few minutes your mother'll be up and it'll be too late. Will you do it or not?

ARNOLD (*he grabs his hair, looks down, paces*): I want you to understand, Helen, that it's entirely too early in the morning for me to know what I'm doing, but I can tell you, that to my mind, marriage is . . . is a consummation devoutly to be wished, but it must also be devoutly consummated. I mean . . . (*His voice cracks.*) I don't feel healthy fooling with it this way!

HELEN (*rises*): Would it make any difference if I said that I. . . .

ARNOLD (*turns from her*): Yes, it would.

HELEN: Well . . . do you?

ARNOLD: I . . . how do I know? After all, love isn't a steam room that you walk into and suddenly feel warm.

HELEN (*smiles*): Then what is it?

ARNOLD: It's . . . it's an ordinary room, in an ordinary house, where you sit for a time, and become convinced that you're . . . overheated. And I haven't been inside long enough to know.

HELEN: If I didn't like you I wouldn't have asked. You know I don't come through people's windows every day in the week.

ARNOLD: Well I should hope not!

HELEN: I mean . . . it's quite uncomfortable for me here!

ARNOLD: Sshh!

HELEN: I won't sshh!

ARNOLD: I'm an ass. (*Looks at her long.*) Forgive me, eh? How long does a divorce take?

HELEN: . . . Months.

ARNOLD: . . . But maybe we could expedite it, eh?

HELEN: Maybe we could.

(*They stand looking into each other.*)

ARNOLD: Wait here. I'll get some clothes on. How will we go?

HELEN (*smiles*): Of all ways, the new Packard.

ARNOLD: Oh, and what will Papa Roth do to me?

HELEN: Reverse English on a shotgun, I think.

ARNOLD: That'll be interesting. I think I'd better tell my father now, because if we don't get back before your old man gets here. . . .

HELEN: Don't call him old man, please.

ARNOLD: Sorry. If your father gets here before we do, I'll want my old man to be here. We'll go to Connecticut, eh?

HELEN: Yes, hurry.

ARNOLD (*crosses to stairs*): I'll be right down.

HELEN: Be careful not to wake your mother.

ARNOLD: Don't worry. (*Stops at landing, turns.*) Say . . . (*Returns across to her.*) You're a pretty swell girl for doing this. I mean somebody else would have run off. By the way, why don't you just beat it.

HELEN: I may still be able to get some money for your father.

ARNOLD (*smiles*): Gee. Pretty clever. A girl as sympathetic as you are is rare. Like . . . like dinosaur eggs.

(*Looks mystical.*)

You know, I think I said that before, some time. Did you

ever feel that you were doing a new thing the second time? Oh no, I remember. I'll be right down. (*Quickly to stairs, stops, turns.*) Say. . . .

HELEN: What is it now?

ARNOLD (*returns to her*): Has there been any venereal disease in your family?

HELEN: How dare you!

ARNOLD: Please! We're going to Connecticut. I want to know your health!

HELEN: Did I ask about yours?

ARNOLD: Well you should've! People should. . . .

HELEN: What's the difference? We'll be divorced soon!

ARNOLD: Yes, but it's liable to take time!

HELEN (*pause. She relents but slowly*): Well, have you?

ARNOLD (*pause*): No.

HELEN: Good for you. Hurry and dress.

ARNOLD (*begins to go right, turns*): You aren't insulted, are you?

HELEN: I haven't decided yet. You'll know when you're dressed.

ARNOLD (*sheepishly*): O.K.

> (*Goes to the landing and takes the first step as* GRAMP *comes through the right doorway with a tremendous vase in his arms.*)

Oh, God. Keep him amused, Helen. He's on my mother's side.

GRAMP (*loudly and benignly*): Where are you going, Arny?

ARNOLD (*comes down quickly, fingers to his mouth*): Sshh!

GRAMP (*alarmed. Softly*): What's the matter?

> (*They both cringe as* ARNOLD *seeks his ear.*)

ARNOLD (*hoarse whisper*): Don't make any noise.

GRAMP (*softly*): Why not?

ARNOLD (*waves toward* HELEN): We're going for a walk.

GRAMP (*as though aware*): Oh.

> (ARNOLD *stands erect.*)

But why shouldn't I make any noise?

ARNOLD: . . . Because we can't go for a walk if you make any noise.

GRAMP: Eh, heh. Why do you walk so early? It's only about seven o'clock.

ARNOLD: Because . . . it's . . . it's nicer early. We like it.

GRAMP: Oh. (*Smiles.*) Summertime.

ARNOLD (*smiles*): That's it, summertime.

GRAMP (*nods wisely*): I can understand it. Ben is goin' too?

ARNOLD: No . . . Ben is sleeping.

GRAMP: Well I'll wake him up for you.

ARNOLD: No . . . no, he's tired.

GRAMP (*definitely. Shakes his head*): No he ain't. He went to sleep early. You shouldn't walk with Helen alone, Arny.

ARNOLD: I know, but it's our last walk together.

GRAMP (*doesn't understand, but . . .*): Oh. (*Reaches into pocket.*) Do me a favor and get my paper for me on your way back. Just tell the candy store man it's for me. Here.

> (*Offers money, but* ARNOLD *refuses it and begins to go to landing.*)

ARNOLD: I'll pay for it.

GRAMP (*loudly*): No, I can pay, I can pay!

ARNOLD (*rushes back to him*): All right, you pay, you pay. (*Takes the money.*)

GRAMP (*as* ARNOLD *is trying to get to the stairs*): How do you like the vase, Arny?

ARNOLD: Beautiful, Gramp. (*Kisses his fingertips.*) Just right.

GRAMP (*to* HELEN, *smiling*): I brought that up special for today.
> (ARNOLD *steps on stair.*)

HELEN: It's very lovely.

GRAMP (*smiles*): Today is a big day for you.

HELEN: Yes, it certainly is, Mr. Steiner.

ARNOLD (GRAMP *putters with vase . . .*): Helen.

HELEN: What?

ARNOLD: Don't you think it'd be better if I wrote a note and asked Gramp to give it to Dad?

HELEN (*points to* GRAMP): Does he read English?

ARNOLD: Oh, that's right. (*Goes to* GRAMP.) Gramp.

GRAMP: Heh?

ARNOLD: . . . If they haven't any Jewish papers this morning should I bring an English paper?

GRAMP: No, Jewish is better papers. More news.

ARNOLD (*smiles. Casually*): Why . . . can't you read English?

GRAMP: I . . . (*Looks at* ARNOLD, *then at* HELEN. *To* ARNOLD, *shrewdly.*) What do you care if I can read English?

ARNOLD: I . . . I just thought, that if they didn't have Jewish papers. . . .

GRAMP: You know they got Jewish papers seven o'clock in the morning. How old do you think I am?

ARNOLD (*trying to brush it off*): No, Gramp. . . .

GRAMP: No Gramp, no Shramp, where you going, Arny?

ARNOLD (*explaining*): Just for a walk. . . .

GRAMP: You shouldn't like that girl, she's for Ben!

ARNOLD: Sshh!

GRAMP: Don't shush me! I'm going up to tell Momma!

(*He marches toward the landing and* ARNOLD *grabs him.*)

ARNOLD: Momma wants to sleep. . . .

GRAMP: Let me go! Momma wants to get up, but she don't know it yet!

HELEN: Come, Arny, they'll stop us!

GRAMP (ARNOLD *is bewildered*): Esther! Esther!

ARNOLD (*still holding* GRAMP *who struggles*): But I haven't any pants on!

GRAMP: Esther! Esther!

HELEN: It doesn't matter, come!

ESTHER (*from above, as though awakened*): What! What! Abe!

HELEN (*as a tumult is rising above and* GRAMP *is struggling and gasping,* HELEN *grasps* ARNOLD's *pyjama collar and pulls him toward the door*): Come on!

ARNOLD (*on the way*): But I need clothes!

HELEN (*as* ESTHER *is galloping down the stairs* ABE *behind her, both yelling incoherently*): We'll get a suit from my father's closet!

ARNOLD: Yeh, but . . . !

(*But she yanks him out the door as* ESTHER *comes running on with* ABE *behind her, all yelling at once, "What's the matter," etc., and* GRAMP *is pulling them to the door.*)

GRAMP: I think they're getting married!

ESTHER: God in heaven!

(*She fights to go out, but* ABE *holds her fast.*)

ABE: You can't go out that way!

ESTHER: They're in the car! Let me go, Abe!!

(GRAMP *is running back and forth trying to see between them.*)

ABE: Not the way you are!

ESTHER: Look, there they go! (*Roar of a motor is heard.*) Let go of me!! (*Roar fades.* ESTHER *relaxes dumbly. To* ABE.) If you'd let me go out I would've stopped them!

GRAMP (*backing her up*): Yeh!

ABE (*to* GRAMP): That's enough!

(BEN *appears on the landing, dopey.*)

(*To* ESTHER.) I will not permit you to go out in the street that way!

ESTHER (*beginning to cry, and falling into a chair*): But for the garbage pail I can go out every morning, *that way*?

ABE: That is not a garbage pail!

ESTHER (*leaning forward, head in hands*): All right, Abe . . . all right. But what will you tell Roth this afternoon?

ABE: I'll tell him to go to hell, that's what I'll tell him.

BEN (*sleepily*): What happened to her?

ABE: It looks like they went off together for a little wedding.

BEN: Who?

ABE: Arny and Helen. (*Smiles.*)

BEN (*relaxes. Smiles*): Ahh. What a guy. (*He lumbers upstairs.*)

ESTHER (*full of tears, looking off, leaning forward*): For a garbage pail . . . yes. But for my son who shouldn't be married yet for five years at least . . . no. That's fine, Abe, you're a good father.

ABE: Oh, Esther, it won't be so bad. . . .

GRAMP (*adamantly, with his finger. He stands center and does not physically address anyone in particular*): College. That's what it is. In my time a thing like that would never happen. I told you not you shouldn't send him to college . . . Both! They don't believe in God, they don't believe in nothin'! The world is going crazy because there's too many college people already. They don't do what you tell them . . . they wouldn't listen! . . . (*Suddenly stops and looks at the rug.*) And I'll bet you . . . (*with utter disappointment . . .*) he wouldn't bring me back my paper either . . . five cents on Sunday. Hm! (*He turns right and flat-footedly trudges off as the . . .*)

CURTAIN FALLS

SCENE 2

That afternoon about four o'clock in the Simon home. On the rise,
ESTHER *and* ABE *are alone in the room. She sits on the couch, knitting almost viciously, and frankly, she is mad as hell.* ABE, *of course, is aware of this and he sits on the armchair at the left, near the radio, trying to occupy as little space as possible in this super-charged atmosphere. It is some time before either party utters a syllable, and in this interval* ABE *sneaks a glance at her, and when he is looking at the rug, she makes a very short observation of him, only to resume her knitting with a deft jab. Finally, he turns on the radio, and as soon as the warmup hum is heard. . . .*

ESTHER: I don't need music, now, please.

ABE: Pardon me. (*He turns it off and crosses his legs. Pause. He swings his foot slightly, then begins to whistle, "My Bonnie Came Over the Ocean."*)

ESTHER: Of any kind.

ABE (*shuts his eyes and nods, and stops whistling. Enter* GRAMP *looking for something important. He goes around the room, his head bent toward the floor like a hound's.* ABE *watches him closely, with interest and sarcasm. After* GRAMP *has circled the room, whistles loudly*): Pop!

(ESTHER *starts.*)

GRAMP: What?

ABE: Time is it?

GRAMP: Heh?

ABE (*draws swift circles on his own wrist, whistling circularly at the same time*): Time, time, time! (*Puts his wrist to his ear.*)

GRAMP (*he understands something*): Oh. (*Waves his hand.*) Not any more today. (*Continues his quest.*)

ABE: Clock! Time!

GRAMP: Oh, time. (*Taking out his onion watch.*) Well why didn't you say so? Sixteen . . . sixteen and a half minutes past four.

ABE (*salutes and nods thanks.* GRAMP *searches on*): What're you looking for??

GRAMP (*sadly*): The vase. I brought it up this morning and now I can't locate it.

ABE: Oh you can't locate it. Well then it ain't big enough! (*Gets up and goes to the massive vase and pats it.*) Here.

GRAMP: Oh yeh, I can't even see no more.

(*Goes to vase and lifts it as* ABE *returns to chair.*)

ABE (*smiles hopefully*): You're gonna take it down?

GRAMP: No, I'll move it. It needs . . . adjustments.

ABE: Oh, adjustments.

(*As* GRAMP *is tugging it.*)

Well that's fine. That means I can expect it in my lap any minute now. (*Sotto voce.*) The adjuster. Look, Esther, am I a liar? He's puttin' that . . . that horse right in front of the door. Somebody'll break their neck comin' in and I'll have a law suit!

GRAMP: Temporary, temporary. (*Surveys the room majestically.*)

ABE: Oh, temporary. Pardon me. I'm wrong again. Look at him the way he's watching for an empty square inch . . . the Secretary of the Interior there. (*To* GRAMP.) Mr. Ickes, that's enough for today!

GRAMP: I'm just doing it for the house. It don't look substantial yet.

ABE: Well we're only here twelve years; another thirty and it'll look substantial. Like a warehouse.

(GRAMP *lugs the heavy vase to his chosen spot.*)

Look at him, Esther. That bargain he found must weigh a thousand pounds. He's a specimen, believe me . . . at his age. A doctor would love to look him over . . . the brain too.

(GRAMP *goes off right.*)

He's insulted. I insulted him. But he never gets so mad that he moves out. The warehouse merchant. Always right. Only I'm wrong. The garbage man's best friend. Never throws nothin' out.

(*Pause.*)

Esther, I'm not joking. I caught him today puttin' umbrella handles in my closet. Worth money, he says. He's losin' my mind for me, Esther.

(*Pause.*)

What did I do?

ESTHER: I don't want to talk to you.

ABE: That I know. I'm just talkin' to myself, but make believe you overheard me. I wanna know, what did I do?

ESTHER: Plenty.

ABE: That's a beginning. Now what else besides plenty?

ESTHER: I . . . I can't talk to you.

ABE: Try. I gotta know.

ESTHER: You gotta know? All right you gotta know.

ABE: Esther, I'm not a child.

ESTHER: That's what you say. It's still an open subject.

ABE: Are you gonna tell me, or must I go away . . . for a walk?

ESTHER (*pause*): You ruined his life. That's why I'm not happy.

ABE: Whose life?

ESTHER: Ben's.

ABE: How about Arnold's life?

ESTHER: Arnold too.

ABE: Well now we're gettin' somewhere. Explain me.

ESTHER: I'll explain you, don't worry. Arnold shouldn't be married before he sets himself up. I want him to intern with at least a few cents in his pocket. Now, not only is he broke, but he's also got a wife on his books.

ABE: Ain't Helen the same girl you were gonna marry Ben to?

ESTHER: She is not. Don't try to tell me that Sam Roth'll give her a cent. He wanted Ben and still wants Ben. Just because Arnold can sell a few coats to a sick buyer don't change the matter.

ABE: So where is my fault?

ESTHER: You didn't utter a word to stop it all. You like it just the way it is, and what's going to stop Ben from running off with the wonderful book-keeper? That's also your fault.

ABE: Oh. Well, y'see? It's always good to talk a thing over. Now let me have my say.

ESTHER: Have your say, but let me tell you, Abe, I don't understand what's come over you. In a few weeks you turned yourself inside out.

ABE: I didn't turn myself inside out so quick. And it's not only the last few weeks . . .

ESTHER (*jumps up*): You realize Roth is coming soon!

ABE: Sit down, please.

(*She does.*)

And let me tell you something. I sat in my office, the other day, and I saw a girl bust into tears . . . for love, and for sadness. And I also saw my son run out after her when she ran out. And I'm proud of him. I'm proud of him, Esther!

ESTHER: Yeh, I know you're proud.

ABE: I'm proud, because for one of the few times in my kind of life, I saw a man obey himself.

ESTHER: With a book-keeper.

ABE: Even with a servant girl. It don't matter. Because I come to realize, Esther, that I ain't God and that there are still plenty things I don't understand. Now am I so clever, so wise, that when my son comes to me and tells me he loves a girl, that I should take his life in my two hands and tell him no. Who am I to say no? Am I God? *He* loves the girl. *He* knows her. I don't. And if you'll pardon me, neither do you.

ESTHER: Abe, I am not trying to take anybody's life in my hands. But all I know is, that in this world it's very few people who can be poor and happy. And I want them to be happy. And they're poor. You tell me love. I know what love is. . . .

ABE: But not in these circumstances. We got married because the old man arranged with my old man, he should rest in peace, and they traded us.

ESTHER: But I knew what it was later.

ABE: Sure you knew. So do I. We got used to each other.

ESTHER: So why can't Ben get used to Helen?

ABE: Why should he? He's already used to Louise.

ESTHER: Because with Helen, he'll eat. With Louise, he won't.

ABE: Oh, he'll eat. He's not crippled. And anyway, how much can he eat? For God's sake, you don't marry a jar of pickles, you marry a woman . . . that is, you should, because if you don't a jar of pickles becomes much more important than it's got a right to be.

ESTHER: In other words . . . you get stuck.

ABE: No, I hate to say it right now, but I didn't. I seen it happen, though, in my time, and I don't like the looks of it.

ESTHER: And the business? Down the river?

ABE: It ain't down the river yet.

ESTHER: It's not down the river but Roth is coming and you might be able to get help from him, and you're not even dressed.

ABE: From now on, when the King of England comes for

supper, I'll get dressed. But I don't expect the King for the next couple a days, so I'll stay comfortable. Roth don't lend money according to the shine on my pants.

ESTHER: Why is Roth such a louse all of a sudden? What's the matter, you got it against him because he held off the bank for you?

ABE: I got nothin' against Roth. His trouble is just that he ain't a man, and I got no respect for him.

ESTHER: What is he, if he ain't a man?

ABE: He's a ledger. A walking ledger. Black on one side, red on the other. His whole life is to try and get everything black.

ESTHER: And you're getting redder every day. A regular Communist.

ABE: No, Esther, I'm not a Communist. I'm a damn fool. And if you don't mind, sweetheart, so are you.

ESTHER: Thank you.

ABE: That's all right. Where is the time when we were gonna start to live? Where is it?

ESTHER: You're talking already like a movie actor.

ABE: I am not talking like a movie actor. I'm talking sense. All these years we been denying ourselves. All these years we been saving . . . not only in money, but in time. We're always afraid that we're enjoying ourselves too much. We're always saving for something . . . some wonderful day that's gonna happen. Meantime, the days go by. Meantime every day that passes is not added to the end of the total, it's gone. Esther, you talk as if we had a hundred and ninety-five years to live. You talk as if our sons had three hundred to live. They haven't, so let them live what have the way they want to live it, because once you start to put away your enjoyments in the bank, and expect to come back when you're sixty and withdraw them for use, you're signing away your life, because that's a one-way bank. It don't do business by the paying desk.

ESTHER (*slight pause*): But what will you tell Sam Roth? Here the man is coming to arrange a wedding for a daughter already married; here you need his help like you need air, and you're walking around the house like a rag-picker. What will I say to him? Abe, I'm . . . I'm going crazy! I don't understand anything!

ABE: First of all, I am not a rag-picker, second of . . .
(*Doorbell.*)
ESTHER (*jumps up*): There he is! And where did Ben go!
ABE: With Louise, I suppose.
ESTHER: Do me a favor, Abe. Put a suit on.
ABE: I'm too tired and I'm comfortable.
(*Goes to door, opens it as* ESTHER *puts on her best smile.
Enter* DAVE.)
Why, Dave! Esther, it's Dave!
ESTHER (*not happily*): I see.
DAVE (*to* ABE): Why, was I supposed to be somebody else?
ABE: No, I'm glad you came. Sit down.
DAVE: I don't sit down till Esther says hullo to me.
ESTHER: Hello.
DAVE: Not like to a bill collector. Come on, Es, say it like you
meant it.
ESTHER (*smiles*): Hello.
DAVE: That's better.
(*As they sit. To* ESTHER.)
Do I get my glass a milk?
ESTHER: You still drink milk. You don't look any fatter since
the last time I saw you.
DAVE: Milk don't fatten. It strengthens. I'm strong.
ESTHER (*as she goes right*): Samson. (*Exit* ESTHER *right.*)
DAVE: After twenty years Esther still don't like me.
ABE: She likes you. What made you run out like that last
Tuesday?
DAVE: I didn't run out. I walked out.
ABE: Dave . . . why do you come to me only to argue? What's
between you and Roth?
(*Enter* ESTHER *with milk.*)
ESTHER: It's nice and cold. Grade A for you, Dave.
DAVE: That's fine, Es, sit down. (*Drinks.*) Best drink in the
world. (*Smacks lips, looks at both.*) I came . . . to say yiz
g'by.
ESTHER: You don't come for months and then you say good-
bye. Where are you going so quick?
ABE: I thought you didn't make up your mind yet.
ESTHER (*to* ABE. *Hurt*): You knew he was going somewhere?
DAVE: I'm going to Bermuda.

ESTHER: But, Dave, how about Marian?

DAVE (*avoids* ABE's *eyes*): I figger I'll be worth more to her as a husband when I get back. I need a change.

ABE: But what happened to the job you had in Florida?

DAVE: I got a better proposition in Bermuda . . . that is . . . going to Bermuda . . . I mean . . . well, a friend a mine, I don't have to tell you who. . . .

ESTHER: Who?

DAVE: I don't have to tell you.

ESTHER: Oh.

DAVE: This guy I know sez to me, he sez, "you want a job on a boat?" So what can I answer him? Sure I want a job on a boat, I sez. (*Seems to expect ridicule. Overloud.*) So is that such a disgrace that I'm workin' on a boat!

ABE (*a little angered. Draws back*): What are you yelling for? If you'd like to work on a boat and you can get the job, take it. Why not?

DAVE (*apologetically*): Well, it's only seventeen a week.

ABE (*looks at him closely*): Is this what "Florida" meant down the place, Tuesday? Is this what you wanted to tell me?— that you're ashamed to work with your hands? Dave, I don't like that kinda stuff!

DAVE: Sure, you can talk. . . .

ABE: Since when is it honorable not to work? What the hell is comin' over the world? You wanna sit on your behind and clip coupons? That's honorable? Honorable is sweat! Honorable is blisters on the fingers! Honorable is eight hours a day! If you're crying to me because you gotta be a worker, you're talking to the wrong man, Dave!

DAVE (*rises*): Then . . . g'by.

ABE: Good luck. (*Takes* DAVE's *hand.*) And take care of yourself. (*Pulls him close.*) Davy, you made enough mistakes in your life! You're sure you thought it over.

DAVE: Yeh . . . yeh, I'm sure.

ABE: . . . Then, goodbye. (*Releases his hand.*)

DAVE (*looks longingly about the room, then at* ABE *and* ESTHER): So long. (*Goes to door. He opens the door, steps out and quickly returns, closing the door.*) Sam Roth comin' in here?

ABE: Yeh, is he out there already?

DAVE: He's payin' his cabby. I'll take the back door.

ABE (*stops him and holds his shoulder*): What happened, Dave.

DAVE: Lemme go, Abe!

ESTHER: My God!

ABE: What happened first?

DAVE: I never hit a man in my life, Abe, you know that. But if I see that man I'll knock him down! I'll knock him down!

ABE: Why?

DAVE (*eyeing the door*): I'm no salesman. I'm a scab. A lousy scab, Abe! Twenty-one bucks a week he gives me! Twenty-one a week for a man and his wife! Marian's gone, Abe. My Marian left me. My wife, Abe!

(*Doorbell.*)

Lemme go, Abe, or there'll be trouble.

(ABE *releases him, staring at him.* DAVE *goes to right doorway, turns.*)

I'm never comin' back. That's why I came here. I wanted to look at the house once more . . . and the boys. . . .

ABE: Stay! Tell him to his face!

DAVE: I made up my mind. (*To* ESTHER.) Workin' on a boat *is* a disgrace. I should have a business . . . (*At the point of tears, he turns right . . .*) I should have a business.

(*Exit* DAVE *right. Doorbell.* ABE *goes to the door and turns to* ESTHER. *He turns from her, opens the door. Enter* ROTH, *very worried.*)

ABE (*levelly*): Hello, Sam.

ROTH: Is Helen here?

ABE (*factually*): Helen? No.

ROTH: I can't make head or tail of it. I get up this morning and there's a note. She says she'll meet me here.

ESTHER: Then I suppose she'll be here soon.

ROTH: Yeh, but she ain't been home all day. And then I went to the garage. Is another note. She took the car.

ESTHER (*jovially*): Ah, I suppose she's got a little surprise for you.

ROTH (*as they sit*): That's what I'm afraid of. You know my Helen is . . . they don't come better, but she ain't . . . for me she ain't reliable. I mean, y'know what happened once. Two years ago when she was in Wisconsin, I write telling her I'm calling for her to take her home for the summer. So I drive out . . . Wisconsin, mind you . . . and when I get there, she left a note. She likes to write notes. Says she went by train. I tell you, Abe, I wore out a new automobile on that trip. You know Wisconsin is with mountains first, and deserts, and God knows what.

ABE (*a bit disgusted*): Well, don't worry yourself. She didn't go to Wisconsin.

ROTH: I was thinkin', though, maybe she took Ben for a ride?

ABE: No. Ben was here a little while ago.

ROTH: Where is he now?

ABE: With a friend.

ROTH: Maybe Arnold then?

ABE: Sam, I got something to tell you.

ROTH: What Abe?

(*Enter* GRAMP *with bunch of flowers in his arms.*)

GRAMP: Look, Esther, I found flowers in the lot next door.

ESTHER (*relieved*): They're pretty.

GRAMP: But I can't find a vase for them.

ESTHER: Put them in a bottle in the kitchen, then.

GRAMP: No, they must be in here. The house has not got enough flowers and pretty soon they'll build a house next door and then there wouldn't be any.

ABE: We're talking here, Pop.

GRAMP: Oh, pardon me. Hello, Sam, I didn't see you. Did you hear?

ROTH: What.

ESTHER (*rises*): Take the flowers inside, Poppa. Come! (*Takes his arm.*)

GRAMP (*shakes her off*): I can go by myself. I'll put them in a bottle for the meantime. I'll get enough for the whole house.

ESTHER: That's right, Poppa. . . .

GRAMP: You remember, Sam, people used to have more flowers in their houses. Nowadays people forget all about flowers. The florist business must be in a pretty bad shape.

ABE: We're talking, Pop!

GRAMP: Pardon. I'll get more flowers. (*Exit* GRAMP.)

ABE: Sam.

ESTHER (*nervously*): A little milk, Sam?

ROTH (*graciously*): No, Esther, I don't care for none. (*To* ABE.) Always milk. (*Laughs.*) I'd think I was a cow or something.

ABE: Yeh. (*Goes grimly to left window.*)

ROTH (*pause. He looks about and then at* ABE): What's the matter, Abe, you don't look right.

ESTHER: Well . . . he's got a lot on his mind. . . .

(*Enter* BEN *from left, smiling.*)

BEN: Oh, hello, Mr. Roth.

ROTH: Hello, Ben. Ain't it about time you called me Sam?

BEN (*looks at* ABE *who turns away. Nervously*): All right, Sam.

ROTH (*smiles*): Where were you just now?

BEN (*glances at* ABE): Taking advantage of my remaining freedom.

ROTH (*begins to laugh, but stops*): What's the matter here? It's . . . it's . . . (*Sentence hangs.*)

ABE (*turns to* ROTH *directly*): I want to say, Sam, that. . . .

ESTHER (*apologizing*): Sam, he. . . .

ABE: I'm talking now, please! (*To* ROTH.) I want to thank you for holding off the bank that way.

ROTH (*growing alarm*): Why do you talk so . . . so formal . . . like I was a judge or something. Why don't you sit down, Abe?

ABE: I feel like standing.

ROTH: But when you stand I feel like it's . . . temporary.

(ABE *begins to sit at leisure as . . .*)

I decided, Abe, that'll pay both your notes on Monday. On the day of the wedding, I'll. . . .

ABE (*rises suddenly. With some bitterness and contempt*): Why did you tell me Dave was a salesman?

(*Exit* ESTHER *quickly.*)

ROTH (*knits his brows*): What's that got to do with it? I'm talking about. . . .

ABE (*growing impatience*): I asked you a question, Sam.

ROTH (*touch of indignation*): What do you mean, you asked me a question . . . ?

ABE (*insulted*): Are you too big to answer me? Why did you tell me a lie?

ROTH (*rises, hurt*): You know what you just said?

ABE: I know what I said. You made him ashamed of himself. You made a man like that run away from his wife! You told me a lie, Sam! I don't like nobody to lie to me!

ROTH (*warningly*): I won't stand for that, Abe!

ABE: You made him a scab in your scab shop!

ROTH (*moves to go*): Then I guess that settles everything, Abe Simon.

ABE (*as* ROTH *nears door*): Your daughter's married, Sam.
(*Silence.* ROTH *just stands for a moment facing the door. He turns slowly, lifts his hand slightly, smiles, frowns. Softly, dazed* . . .)

ROTH: She wouldn't . . . she wouldn't do that to me . . . (*Roar.*) She wouldn't do that to me! Where's Arnold!

ABE: With Helen.

ROTH: You're lying!
(*Enter* GRAMP *hurrying.*)

GRAMP: Arnold's back?(!)

ROTH (*in* GRAMP's *ear*): Where is Arnold!

GRAMP: Don't yell so loud!

ROTH: Where's my daughter!

GRAMP (*holds his head*): Stop that yelling!

ROTH: Answer me!
(GRAMP *looks up at him angrily, rips out connecting wire of his device, and stomps out, right.*)

BEN: It's true. Arnold married her.

ROTH (*wide-eyed, breathless*): I won't permit it! I'll go to court! I'll sue the life out of you! I'll. . . .
(HELEN *bursts in, swinging door wide, rushes to* ROTH, *throwing her arms around him.*)

HELEN: Daddy!

ROTH (*unclasps her arms*): What did you do to me?

HELEN (*laughing, yet ready to weep*): I drove home . . . you weren't home.

ROTH (*laughing with high hope*): No, darling, no, I was here. . . .

HELEN: We went to Connecticut. . . .

ROTH (*horrified*): You got married?(!)

HELEN: We stood before the Justice of Peace, and . . . (*with love*) I looked at Arnold. . . .

ROTH: For God's sake tell me!

HELEN: Daddy, he's a wonderful man! (*Falls on him laughing, crying.*)

ROTH (*pushes her away*): Helen! What *did you do*?

HELEN: He looked at me, and he said, "Helen, are you sure you're sure?" And then I looked at him, Daddy, and I said,

"I don't know." And then he said,—and he smiled—, "You know, Helen, your father's a son-of-a-bitch but I think we ought to ask him first."

ROTH (*ecstatic smile*): Arnold said that?!

HELEN (*equal ecstasy*): Yes, Daddy!

ROTH (*embraces her hugely*): Oh . . . my darling, my darling. (*Smooths her hair.*)

ABE: So what happened to Arnold?

HELEN: He took the car. . . .

ROTH (*disengages her. Angrily*): You gave Arnold the car!?

HELEN: He put me in a cab and he said he had to go some place for somebody . . . I don't know, he just took it, and. . . .

ABE: Esther! Ben, find your mother!

BEN (*goes quickly right*): Hey, Mom! . . . Mom! (*Exit* BEN.)

ROTH: You should not give anybody that car . . . specially that fella!

ABE: What do you mean, that fella? He's a better driver than you ever was!

ROTH (*faces* ABE): He's good for nothing! He's. . . .

(*Enter* ARNOLD *in suit too large for him. Safety pin holding up pants, as enter* ESTHER *from right.*)

ESTHER (*rushes at him*): Arnold! Thank God!

ARNOLD (*pecks a kiss*): Wait a minute, Mother. (*Thru door.*) Come in, Max.

(*Enter* MAX *fearfully.*)

MAX (*smiles warily*): Hello, Mr. Simon. (*Nods his head testily.*)

ABE: Max, what are you. . . .

ARNOLD: Wait a minute, Dad. (*Walks about.*) You're all insane. Utterly, completely insane.

ROTH (*indignantly*): Who are you to. . . .

ARNOLD: Please!

(*Silence.*)

I've decided that . . . my mind in good condition is worth more to me than a lot of other things. So I'm going to eliminate all the hours of aggravation . . . all the weeping. All the garbage goes right out the window. Mr. Roth? You have no intention of lending my father . . . this man here . . . any money now, have you?

(ROTH *is silent.*)

Then it all equals this.

(*Points to* ABE.)

You're broke.

ROTH: A genius. Come on, Helen.

ARNOLD: Look, Mr. Roth, make believe this is all make believe. Make believe nobody but me is crazy. All right. So the score is (*to* ROTH) you're out, and (*to* ABE) you're in the hole up to your chin. Everybody: silence. Max? Now.

MAX: I should . . . ?

ARNOLD: Say it. (*Closes his eyes and bends his neck down.*)

MAX (*hat in hands*): I didn't come myself, Mr. Simon, Arnold brought me. I was going to tell you Monday, but I might as well tell you now, because he says to me everything is in a bad condition. . . .

ABE: Max, what are you trying to say?

MAX: I'm trying to say that if you'll agree that the men and you and me should work together,—equal equal—, like partners, for the wage that's gonna knock out the scabs and open-shops from the industry, I can personally guarantee that the men will put in not forty-three hundred, like I said last week, but five thousand dollars in the business. (*Looks down, hands on stomach.*)

ROTH (*steps toward him, very concerned*): What business?

MAX: Mr. Simon's, if you'll pardon me. . . .

ROTH (*angered*): Since when does a shop-foreman make propositions?

MAX: I'm . . . Max. . . .

ROTH (ABE *stands silent,* ROTH *goes to him*): You're taking this man serious? You know he's crazy, of course. . . .

ARNOLD: You're out of turn!

ROTH: Shut up, you!

(*To* ABE, *very anxiously.* ABE *doesn't move.*)

You're not thinking of such a thing, are you?

(*Silence.*)

Abe, you realize what it'll mean? They'll take your business away from you . . . they'll . . . Abe! You'll ruin the industry!

ABE (*level*): Why will I ruin the industry?

ROTH (*preposterous question*): What do you mean, why? They'll . . . they'll. . . .

ABE: They'll compete with you, Sam? Sam Roth you mean that they'll run the scabs and gangsters out of your shop? That don't bother me.

ROTH: I don't like that talk, Abe!

(ESTHER *exits right*.)

ABE: But I said it don't bother me, Sam! It don't bother me (*snaps his fingers*) that much if they run the blackjacks outa the coat industry! In fact it don't bother no honest man for that to happen!

ROTH: Abe . . . (*almost pleading*) . . . why make an enemy for yourself?

ABE: I know who my friends are, Sam!

ROTH: Yeh? . . . then why do you talk like this? Why . . . how do you know . . . maybe . . . maybe *I'd* give you five thousand dollars?

ABE: And how do you know, maybe *I* wouldn't take it!

ROTH: You crazy!(?)

ABE: You're not talking to a boy, Sam! I'm old enough not to jump up and down when you throw five thousand dollars in my face! I'm old enough for that! I'm old enough to remember that I had more than five thousand last year and look where I am today!

ROTH: Because you're ten years behind the times!

ABE: I can not stand no gangsters in my shop and I will not stand them and if blackjacking workingmen is up-to-date then I'm gonna be old-fashioned! I started that business without a gun and it's gonna go on without a gun because I don't want a Packard car bad enough to make it any other way!

ROTH: But, Abe. . . .

ABE: I don't want to listen!

ROTH: Let me. . . .

ABE: Not a word! (*Turns to* MAX.) O.K. Max. I'll see you Monday eight o'clock down the place.

MAX (*struck*): You mean?

ABE: Yeh, I *mean*. What's the matter? You're white. . . .

MAX: No . . . I'm all right. I just ain't used to riding in a car. The smell from gasoline gets in my nose . . . I'll go . . . goodby. (*Opens door.*)

ABE: Goodby, Max. Eight o'clock. I want everybody there.

MAX (*looks at him adoringly*): Everybody'll be there. (*Smiles.*)
Goodby . . . Abe.

ABE (*seriously and gravely*): Goodby.

(*Exit* MAX.)

ARNOLD (*grabs his hand*): Congratulations!

ABE: Thanks, Arnold. (*To* ROTH.) You don't wish me luck?

ROTH (*pause*): Sure . . . I'll wish you luck . . . (*shakes hands*)
. . . workingman.

ABE (*drops* ROTH*'s hand. Shortly*): Goodby, Sam.

ROTH (*smiles victoriously*): Well y'are a workingman, ain't you?

ABE: I want you to understand something. I am not disgraced.

ROTH (*smiles knowingly, turns to* HELEN): Come, darling. . . .

ABE (*loudly*): But understand it, Sam! And when you meet
people and talk, make it clear! Abe Simon is not disgraced!

ROTH (*ignores* ABE, *opens door*): I only thank God I found out
in time what kind of people live here. Come, Helen. (*Steps
over threshold.*)

HELEN: No, Daddy.

ROTH (*turns*): What?

HELEN: I'll be home to sleep, but I'm staying here now.

ROTH (*takes her arm. Consternation on his face*): What's here
for you?

HELEN: I think you'd better get used to being without me,
Daddy, because . . . I'm going to marry Arnold soon. I
wanted to tell you first.

ROTH: You wanted to . . . (*Floored.*)

ARNOLD: See, Helen, I told you he wouldn't appreciate it. . . .

ABE: Sam, take it easy!

ROTH: You came back to let me appreciate it!—you . . . So!
(*To* ABE.) So this is the story, heh! So the doctor is going to
live on my money! Well put this in your pipe, Abe Simon,
not a cent goes with that girl!

ABE (*turns away*): I heard enough screaming for today.

ROTH (*turns on* HELEN): Come home with me!

HELEN: I'm not coming home, Daddy.

ROTH (*warning command*): Helen!

HELEN: Please don't speak like that to me anymore! I am not
for sale! The car is waiting for you outside.

ROTH: Well, it's nice of you to leave the car, at least. Thank
you, thank you . . . but it will never happen! I will not

allow it! (*Shakes his fist under* ARNOLD*'s nose.*) You won't get away with it! I'll . . . !

HELEN: Don't make a fool of yourself!

ROTH (*brought up short. Turns to her. Tears in his eye*): Helen . . . darling . . . why must you do this to me? Why do I deserve it? Didn't I give you whatever you wanted? Didn't I let you go to Wisconsin even?

HELEN: Yes, Daddy, but go home now. I'll explain some other time. Go home.

ROTH (*looks long at her, then to door*): Home. What's waiting for me home? Twelve rooms . . . no people. Helen, please come with me.

(*Silence.*)

Darling. . . .

HELEN: There's nothing to say now, Daddy.

ROTH: You're sure, darling?

HELEN: I'm sure, Daddy.

ROTH: You know, darling, you made a damn fool outa me?

ABE: Sam, I don't want you to go away mad.

ROTH (*turns to* ARNOLD): Then . . . at least if you're gonna be my son-in-law, don't go around looking like a bum.

ARNOLD (*touches his lapel*): Oh, this. . . .

ROTH: That suit, y'know, looks like you picked it out of a garbage pail.

ARNOLD (*softly*): Ah . . . this is yours, Mr. Roth.

ROTH (*pause. Shakes his head slightly, turns up his palm*): Well. (*Exit* ROTH.)

ABE: Ach, poor fella. Maybe you shoulda gone with him for now, Helen.

HELEN: No. It's got to start sometime. . . .

(ESTHER *enters. Silent on her entrance. She and* HELEN *look at each other. Finally* ESTHER *smiles slightly* . . .)

ESTHER (*looking at* HELEN): All right.

HELEN (*rushes and hugs her*): Oh, Mrs. Simon, Mrs. . . .

(ARNOLD *kisses* ESTHER . . .)

ABE: Hey! That's enough, that's enough!

(*Enter* BEN *and* LOUISE.)

Ah! You got more comin', Esther!

BEN (*to* ABE): Max said you told him . . . !

ABE: I did it, Ben!

LOUISE: Good luck, Mr. Simon!

BEN: Mother. . . .

(*Silence.*)

ESTHER (*closes her eyes*): Go ahead. Tell me.

BEN: Louise and I were talking and . . . we'd like to get married.

ESTHER (*opens her eyes*): Why not? (*Smiles.*) It looks like a lot of people are doing it.

BEN (*ready to laugh*): Arny?!

ARNOLD: Yeh!

(*Both bust out laughing and shake hands furiously.*)

ESTHER: But don't either of you ask your father?

BEN (*silence*): Is it all right, Dad?

ABE (*to* ARNOLD): Doctors don't ask?

ARNOLD: Consider yourself asked.

ABE: That's respect for a father. "Consider yourself asked." Now that I come to think of it, why didn't either of you ask me?

LOUISE: Well we thought. . . .

ABE: Yes, you thought. Well I refuse. What good it'll do me I don't know, but I refuse. (*Laughs.*)

LOUISE: Mrs. Simon, you're crying. . . .

HELEN: Oh, don't cry. . . .

ESTHER: I'm not.

ARNOLD: You are, Mother. . . .

ESTHER: And if you can't cry when two sons tell you they're getting married, when can you cry? I just hoped, since the day they were born, that at least for one of the boys we could make a wedding. A pretty wedding, with nice people in lovely clothes, dancing and laughing . . . like my wedding. But I suppose that's a dream for children. Like a child plays with dolls I played with these dreams. Ah . . . but I guess you can't always play with dolls. We've got to grow up some day. Dolls are like big weddings, I suppose. When you grow up in these times you can only remember them . . . and maybe cry. Come here, young ladies. (*She takes their hands.*) I can't advise you because what I know, I can't say . . . and it came so fast. . . . I bet neither of you can cook. (*Smiles.*)

HELEN: We can learn.

ESTHER (*smiling*): And what will they eat while you're

learning? I'll make a list of meals you could cook for them. They both like the same things . . . except Arnold. He can't stand scrambled eggs.

(*She laughs with them.*)

That's all I can tell you. You know the rest. Just be good wives to them, and wherever you are, no matter where, let us know if you're in trouble . . . and whenever you want to come back, all of you, the house is yours. Just be happy, live long, and give them strong children. (*She kisses the girls.*)

ARNOLD: Come on, everybody, let's go for a walk!

ESTHER: That's right. Go, all of you.

(*Enter* GRAMP *with a great bunch of flowers.*)

GRAMP (*to* ESTHER): In the whole house there ain't one place to put flowers! Arny's here!

BEN: We're getting married, Gramp!

GRAMP (*wisely, to* ARNOLD): Did you do it?

ARNOLD (*nods*): Almost!

GRAMP (*amazed, turns to* ESTHER): Then we must have a party! Look! I'll move the couch over here, and the. . . .

ABE: Oh will he have a good time now!

GRAMP (*excited*): Louise . . . here. Take some . . . (*Gives her some flowers.*) (*He hurries to the door and then hurries back to* HELEN.) Take the rest, Helen. (*Gives them to her quickly.*) . . . Wait . . . I got the decorations from the party when Arny graduated high school . . . I saved them . . . wait, I'll show you. . . .

ESTHER (*as he hurries to right door*): Not now, Poppa. . . .

GRAMP (*stops*): Heh? (*Turns.*) Did somebody call me?

ESTHER: I said to wait with the decorations.

GRAMP: I can't hear. I tore the wire out when Roth was yelling. I gotta get it fixed by the man . . . wait . . . (*Exit* GRAMP.)

ABE (*to* ARNOLD, BEN): If you're gonna walk you'd better get outa here before he comes back with his merchandise. (*Pushes them.*) Go on, get outa here. . . .

BEN (*as they move toward door*): We'll be back soon.

LOUISE: Come, Helen.

HELEN (*waves to* ABE *and* ESTHER): Goodby.

(*Exit* HELEN, BEN, LOUISE.)

ARNOLD: You mustn't cry, Mom.

ABE: Well? You're still neutral?

ARNOLD: O.K., you win.

ABE: O.K., Baltimore, but when she needs something to eat don't be too neutral.

> (*He pushes* ARNOLD *who laughs as he goes out.* ABE *and* ESTHER *come to window and watch them as they pass in the street.*)

ESTHER (*softly*): They're so young, Abe, they're so young.

ABE: They're men and women, Esther.

ESTHER: Then we must be old.

ABE: Why old? Come, we can take a walk too! We ain't too old to walk!

ESTHER: You think they'll be all right, Abe?

ABE: Why not? They got the main thing.

ESTHER (*almost to herself*): I don't know . . . it should have been planned more. It should have taken more time.

ABE (*with vigor*): No, it shouldn't! Let them *do*, let them *do*. We can learn a little from them, Esther. We can learn to stop saving the time. Time is for spending! Come, we'll walk like them in the fresh air! The grass still grows, and the trees are still there, and there's still enough sun for us to look at! What are we waiting for, Esther, let's walk with the time instead of trying to stand on it!

ESTHER: All right, Abe, we'll walk with the time. At least nobody can stop us from that kind of spending.

ABE: We'll have more to spend than time. I still got my two hands, and the heart is still strong. That's enough, Esther.

ESTHER (*looks down at herself*): I'll put on another dress.

ABE: That dress is nice. It covers you, and it's clean. That's all I care about as long as you're in it.

ESTHER (*slight pause*): Come then.

> (ABE *opens the door.*)

ABE: Yes, Esther, there's new ways to live . . . young ways, and we gotta learn them. . . .

> (*Enter* GRAMP *from right.*)

GRAMP (*he has rolls of red and white paper bunting in his hands. He enters excitedly*): I found them . . . I . . . (*Disappointedly.*) Oh . . . they went away. (*To* ESTHER.) They went away?

ESTHER (*nods*): Yes.

GRAMP: I found them in the trunk downstairs. (*Holds up bunting.*) You see, it pays to save things.

ESTHER (*goes to him*): We'll be back soon!

GRAMP: All right, I'll . . . (*Smiles.*) I'll have a surprise for you.

ESTHER (*smiles*): All right. (*Waves to him, goes to door.*)

ABE: But whatever happens to us or to the cloak business or to the country even, I'm afraid there will never be a place for that man.

ESTHER: Let's go, he's going to surprise us.

ABE: That's what I'm afraid of. I just hope that when we come back there'll be a place to sit down. Come.

(*Exit* ABE *and* ESTHER.)

(GRAMP *goes to the window, watches them pass. He lays down the rolls, takes one to the corner of the room, moves a chair, stands on it, catches the end of the roll to the moulding, gets down and walks, unrolling the paper. The end falls from the wall, he goes to put it back in place, gets one foot on the chair, but stops suddenly as though tired, sits with faint strength, the red and white bunting in his hand trailing over his thigh and onto the floor . . . and he gazes at nothing, tired, wondering as . . .*)

SLOW CURTAIN

THE END

THE HALF-BRIDGE

A Play in Three Acts

CHARACTERS

Policeman
Mark Donegal
Captain Schulenberg
Dr. Luther
Rocko
Bosch
August Kruger
Doped-up Man
Anna Walden
Dennis
Carrol
Nelson
Jack Biggers
Dino

ACT ONE

The front of a pier in New Orleans Harbor, at nearly three o'clock in the morning.

The entrance to the pier, which occupies more than half of the back of the stage, is composed of two enormous doors,—now shut,—in one of which is set a normal-sized door. Over this small door hangs a yellow bulb.

Beside the pierface, at its right, looms the outline of a ship's prow which is almost touching the bulkhead at the edge of the street. A rope from the prow is lashed to an iron capstan which humps up from the water-edge of the street. A short stretch of open water is seen to the right of the ship, and the night sky above.

Down stage and left is a watchman's shack the interior of which is dimly lighted by a single kerosene lamp. In it are a board "bed," a few chairs, and a shelf across the back. The extreme right and left edges of the stage are in blackness.

On the rise, we find BARRET, *a policeman in uniform,—light blue shirt and trousers,—sitting tipped back in a chair against the shack, dozing. For a moment there is silence but for the creaking of the ship's hawsers and an occasional boat whistle far off.*

Presently, the tapping of a cane on pavement is heard from the right, and JACK BIGGERS, *a blind man enters along the street. A tray of razor blades is suspended from his shoulders. When he enters, the* COP *starts slightly.*

COP: I told you not to come so early tonight.

JACK: I'll go away if you've got business.

COP: 'Cause it ain't even three o'clock, Jack.

JACK: Crowds gave out. Can't sell any more tonight. People drunk or sleeping.

COP: You'll have to beat it right away. I'm meetin' somebody private.

JACK: All right. Just like to rest. (*He walks a step or two, tapping his cane, then stops, and standing before the hall, taps his cane, testingly, on the pavement.*) New ship in, Barret.

COP: Yeh, *Bangkok Star.* Pulled in at sundown.

JACK: Big ship?

COP: Can't you tell?

JACK (*taps ground*): Feels big.

COP: 8,000 tons.

JACK: Big. (*He listens to the ship.*) Hear that? She's breathing. Nice when a ship's in her berth. Nice to hear her breathe. Makes you want to sleep.

(JACK *goes into shack, removes blade-box.* COP *remains seated.*)

COP: Anything doin' in town tonight?

JACK (*taking a bottle of seltzer from shelf, and glass*): Feller said there was a big fight.

COP: Where?

JACK: Rampart Street, some house.

COP: Killed?

JACK: Don't know. Just heard. (*He presses lever, gets glass of seltzer.*)

COP: How the hell do you keep drinkin' that stuff?

(JACK *drinks.*)

JACK: Stomach. I get pains. On my feet too much. Bad for the stomach. (*He drinks again.*) Too much killin' going on in this town.

COP: Always did in New Orleans.

JACK: No. More now. Lotta people fighting, gettin' killed. (*He puts bottle and glass back on shelf.*)

COP: Don't go to sleep yet.

JACK: I'll go way. Just say it.

COP: You can set a while. Think I'll take a look around. (*Rises from chair, stretches.*)

JACK: What's the name of that ship?

COP: *Bangkok Star.* Comes from Chile. (*Pushes shirt into trousers.*)

JACK: Pretty name.

COP (*going right*): You can come back later and get your sleep.

JACK: Thanks, Barret, thanks a lot. I'll go soon as you say.

(COP *goes off right, sauntering off.* BLIND MAN *sits in chair, sighs with tiredness. The sound of the hawsers creaking. He*

*turns his head toward the sound . . . listening calmly.
From the shadows at left,* ANNA *comes, goes directly to the
little door in pierface,—hurriedly, quietly. She tries the door.
It is locked . . .)*

Can't open that.

(ANNA *turns to him startled.*)

Got to have a pass to get in there. . . .

ANNA (*comes toward him warily*): How come they don't let the crew off?

JACK: Should think they'd be off by now. Ship's in since sundown.

ANNA: Nobody's come out though.

JACK: Been waiting here all the time?

ANNA: . . . Yes.

JACK: Better come back in the morning.

ANNA: I heard they're sailing in the morning.

JACK: Well you can't get in there now.

(ANNA *turns from him. She takes a few steps toward the door
again.*)

You *can't*, Miss.

ANNA (*she looks around, then up at the ship's prow. It's almost as
though she were looking for a way to climb on board. She turns
back to the blind man, goes toward him*): I've got to get on
board. . . .

JACK: You just have to wait.

ANNA (*points to shack*): Is the key in there?

JACK (*gets up quickly*): You can't do that, Miss. . . .

ANNA (*quieting him*): It'll be all right, I've got to see one of
the officers. . . .

JACK (*points off right*): Barret's coming, ask Barret. . . .

(ANNA *looks quickly toward the right. Sound of men talking
is heard.*)

Barret's in charge, he'll. . . .

ANNA (*frightened, she touches the blind man's arm*): Listen. I'll
be back. Don't tell anyone I was here, will you?

JACK: Well, what do you want . . . ?

ANNA: Don't say anything, heh? I'll give you something. . . .

JACK: Just so you don't do any harm. . . .

ANNA: I won't. Promise, will you?

JACK: . . . All right, yes . . . all right, but don't do any harm.

ANNA: I'll give you something. Please. (*Glances right, and hurries left.*)

(Blind man *nervously follows her a few steps, halts as* COP, DENNIS, NELSON *and* CARROL *come on from right. The three sailors are drunk,*—CARROL *being merely fuzzed and getting sick,* DENNIS *loud and challenging,* NELSON *querulous.*

They come on thus: DENNIS *is holding the* COP's *shoulder and talking into his ear. The* COP *is obviously patronizing him, laughing at his every joke, quickly turning serious when* DENNIS *seems to be heading that way. Right behind them* CARROL *and* NELSON *follow,* NELSON *listening critically and* CARROL *shaking his head "no" but hardly listening.* . . .)

DENNIS: You aren't. . . .

COP: I am, I tell you. . . .

DENNIS: No, you're sayin' it 'cause you got some ridiculous idea that I'm drunk!

COP: I tell you I'm Irish! My mother was Irish, my father was Irish . . . I'm Irish!

DENNIS (*they stop walking.* DENNIS *steps back, holding the* COP *at arm's length, inspecting him*): All right then. Reply to this. Ireland is bounded on the North . . . by what?

COP: The ocean.

DENNIS: Right. And on the East!

COP: Uh . . . the ocean.

DENNIS: When the hell were you in Ireland!

NELSON: Dennis! We're supposed to be in a hurry!

DENNIS (*goes to* CARROL, *links his arm, speaks into his face*): How're you doin', Carrol?

CARROL: I don't feel so good.

DENNIS: Have you been breathin' like I told you?

CARROL: How?

DENNIS: Shortly . . . don't inhale deeply 'cause it activates your . . . your animosities, understand?

NELSON (*indicating offstage left*): Dennis, we're in a hurry to get back to the ship!

COP: You ain't sailin' tonight.

NELSON: We just gotta go on board a minute then we gotta go back to town.

COP: Oh, goin' back again, eh?

DENNIS: Yes, and don't be giving us any more addresses, please.

COP: Why, what's the matter?

DENNIS: It destroys all my faith in law and order.

COP: I just like to help the fellas out sometimes. Girls were nice, weren't they?

DENNIS: Ignorant women!

COP (*to* NELSON): Did you go in? I like to know. . . .

NELSON: Yeh, they were all right.

DENNIS: Ignorant!

COP: You told them I sent you, didn't you?

NELSON: Yeh, we told them . . . Come on Dennis.

COP: Say look, fellas, if you're goin' back to town again I got another place for you . . . real women . . . I mean they come out and you can look 'em over . . . don't have to stay if you don't like them, see?

DENNIS: Ah, what the hell are you talkin' about that for?

NELSON (*to* COP): Dennis gets embarrassed. . . .

DENNIS: I got a terrible feelin' my poor mother is dying!

COP: What do you say, Dennis . . . I got another nice place. . . .

DENNIS: *Another* nice one! In the last place I ask the girl "Who composed the poem entitled, 'The Ship of State'?" Not a twitter out of her! So I recite it . . . (*Assumes elocution pose.*)

> The Ship of State
> *Oh Captain my Captain our fearful trip is done*
> *Our ship has weathered every rack*
> *The goal we sought is won.*

. . . and still she don't know it was Walt Whitman done it!

COP: Well you can't expect. . . .

DENNIS: I do expect! A feller's got to talk when he goes ashore, don't he?

NELSON: Come on, Dennis, we're in a hurry.

DENNIS: Yes, sure . . . what the hell are we goin' back to the ship for?

NELSON: We gotta bring my moose horns to that saloon where I promised them; and then I got that dress I want to give to that girl. . . .

DENNIS: Oh yes, we'd better hurry . . . Come on, Carrol. . . .

CARROL: Did I ever show you this? (*He takes out wallet.*)

DENNIS (*sees him removing picture*): Yes, she's a very lovely looking girl . . . Come on.

CARROL: But you don't see me getting married. . . .

DENNIS: I should say not, Carrol! Come will you?

> (CARROL *walks toward the* Bangkok Star.)

That's the wrong ship, ours is two piers down. . . .

CARROL (*holds his head*): Somebody hit me.

DENNIS: You just been breathin' too deep . . . come on. . . .

> (*He links his arm.*)

BLIND MAN: Any of you boys interested in some razor blades? Got some nice Swedish steel . . . nickel a box. . . .

NELSON: We gotta go. . . .

DENNIS: I'll have a dozen boxes.

> (*Takes out a bill, goes toward the shack into which* JACK *goes for blades.*)

COP: What do you say, boys, like a nice place?

CARROL: I'd like a nice place . . . (*Walks toward the* COP.)

DENNIS: You'll do better with a nice physic, young feller. . . .

> (*Grabs him back.*)

COP: What are you telling him what to do . . . ?

> (*Enter* BOSCH *a few steps from right: stands watching* COP.)

DENNIS (*goes up to the* COP): Did you ever know that a man's home is his castle?

COP (*laughs. To* NELSON): He's a great one. . . .

DENNIS (*seriously*): And a stitch in time saves nine? And too many cooks sp'il the broth . . . ?

> (COP *laughs.*)

CARROL: If at first you don't succeed, try, try again.

> (COP *sees* BOSCH. *Stops laughing.*)

DENNIS: Oh, Officer, all those wonderful sayin's and nobody knows them any more.

COP (*glancing at* BOSCH): Why don't you go back to your ship, I'll see you later?

DENNIS: Nobody believes the old things and we've got no new things, Officer. The bars are down, and we're adrift, adrift, on the wide, wide sea . . .

> (JACK *comes to* DENNIS *with box.*)

JACK: How many packages you want . . . ?

DENNIS: I'll. . . .

COP: Don't come back for a while, Jack.

JACK (*realizing* BOSCH *has come*): Oh . . . will you fellows come this way . . . ? (*Off left.*) I got a nice Swedish blade. . . .

NELSON: They'll be waiting for us to get back, Dennis!

DENNIS: Come, Carrol. . . .

(*Leading* CARROL . . . *To* JACK *who is starting left.*)

And how did you lose the sight of your eyes, if I may ask the question?

JACK (*as they walk off left. Takes a package from the box*): It's a nice blade, everybody compliments it. Guaranteed five shaves each. . . .

DENNIS: You don't say!

JACK: Not likely to rust either when you're out on the water. Contains manganese, cellulose and fits any razor; all the men like it. . . .

DENNIS: Was it an accident you had . . . ?

JACK: Guaranteed five shaves each and if you don't get that many. . . .

(*Exit* JACK, DENNIS, NELSON, CARROL—*left.*)

COP (*watches them go, then turns to* BOSCH, *goes to him at right*): I guess it's all right now.

BOSCH: Keep them away from here.

COP: Their ship is two piers down. I'll go on board, have a drink with them.

BOSCH (*nods. Looks at* COP *a moment. Then takes a bill from a wallet in his breast pocket, gives it to* COP *who puts it away*): Go ahead. (*Motions off left where sailors went.*)

(COP *goes across, turns.*)

COP: Try not to take too long.

BOSCH: Go ahead.

(COP *goes off left.*)

(BOSCH *watches him go a moment. Then turns his head slightly to the right, behind him.* ROCKO *comes from the darkness behind him. Then* LUTHER *comes. Stands between them. All three look at the door in the pierface.* LUTHER *motions toward the door.* ROCKO *goes up to it, knocks on it. A pause. From above on the prow,* CAPTAIN SCHULENBERG's *form appears. He is looking down at them. They do not notice him. The door in the pier opens.* MARK DONEGAL, *in mate's uniform steps through, closes the door behind him. He looks at* ROCKO, *then at* LUTHER *and* BOSCH. LUTHER *walks*

up to him, BOSCH *walking with him.* LUTHER *and* BOSCH
stop a yard in front of MARK.)

MARK: Who's the boss?

LUTHER: Es wirt ein neuer tag, nicht wahr?

MARK: Warum nicht? Deutschland ist stark.

LUTHER: Wo ist der man?

MARK: Talk English, please. German words echo near water.

LUTHER: Where is the man?

MARK: Where's my money?

LUTHER: You'll get it.

MARK: Before I give you the guy.

(LUTHER *is silent.*)

Come on, chum, I'm not playing house.

LUTHER (*takes out wallet, bills*): How do I know you have him
here?

MARK: You don't.

LUTHER (*slight pause. Gives him bills*): Two hundred.

MARK: I told them in Valparaiso I don't ship them under three
hundred dollars any more.

LUTHER: You'll get nothing if I say so.

MARK: You'll get a bullet if I say so. Three hundred American.

LUTHER (*holds out a bill*): You should trust me.

MARK (*takes the bill*): Ditto for you.

(*He turns, looks into the little doorway,* AUGUST KRUGER
comes out supporting a DOPED-UP MAN *hardly able to hold
up his head,* LUTHER *tips the man's chin up, examines his
face, lifts an eyelid.*)

Get him out of here.

LUTHER: Morphine.

MARK: That's how they delivered him to me.

LUTHER (*to his aides*): Put him in the car.

(*They drag the man off.*)

MARK: What was his misdemeanor?

LUTHER: He wrote letters to the wrong people.

MARK: What do you do? Cut him open for the addresses?

LUTHER: Did he talk to you?—said something perhaps?

MARK: You'd like to know?

LUTHER: I must know what a traitor knows.

MARK: A hundred more.

LUTHER: Your American blood. . . .

MARK: When Hitler works for nothing I will.

LUTHER: We can trust Hitler.

MARK: Certainly. Everybody else pays cash. Good night. (*Turns away.*)

LUTHER: I want to talk to you.

MARK: Talk.

LUTHER: I'll be back in twenty minutes.

MARK: I'm going into town.

LUTHER: Wait for me.

MARK: If you find me here then I waited.

LUTHER: This will be worth your while.

MARK (*to* KRUGER): Want to wait, August?

LUTHER: August? August what?

MARK: August September, what's it to you?

LUTHER: I like to know the German personnel.

MARK: Wipe your nose.

LUTHER: You might try to please me!

MARK (*approaches him*): That wouldn't be a threat, would it?

LUTHER: And if it should be?

MARK: I don't like you. Not for one cent, understand? I got one glimpse of your face and I knew you were a wrongee.

LUTHER: I merely. . . .

MARK: Now go away, and if you got business come back, but don't threaten me or I'll beat your Goddam brains out.

LUTHER (*smiles*): See you in twenty minutes. My name is Dr. Luther. Be careful with me. (LUTHER *goes off right.*)

MARK (*to* KRUGER, *taking a flask from his hip*): What'd I tell ya? Three hundred bucks!

KRUGER (*looking where* LUTHER *went*): Why didn't you tell me *he* was going to meet you?

MARK: I didn't know. It used to be another guy. . . .

KRUGER (*very nervously*): You should have known, Mark!

MARK: What're you shivering for? (*Drinks.*)

KRUGER: That man is Gestapo! I am wanted in Germany, Mark.

(*Pause.*)

MARK: So what?—you're in the USA, you're all right. . . .

KRUGER: I am not all right. They take a person from any place. You shouldn't have told him my name, Mark—never!

MARK: You never told me nothin' about politics, Gussy.

KRUGER: I am finished with politics, I want only you should remember what you promised me.

MARK: I told you a million times; we're going down there together. What do you think I'm runnin' these guys in for?

KRUGER: Yes, what for? How much money have we got from eleven months of this . . . ?

MARK: Don't talk like that!

KRUGER: I will talk like that, Mark! Let me hold that three hundred dollars before you drink it away!

MARK: You don't understand me, August, I gotta have money in my pocket, even if I don't spend it I gotta walk with it. . . .

KRUGER: Walk with it! In Mobile last month you also walked with six hundred dollars, where is it now?

MARK: Don't gimme discipline, will ya? Don't!

KRUGER (*grabs his arm*): Wait, Mark, wait.

MARK (*turns from him*): We're goin' down to Brazil, August, together we're goin'. I made up my mind. I'll have the thousand in a couple of weeks. . . .

KRUGER: That's all we need is a thousand. . . .

MARK: I'll make a lotta scores, big scores. . . .

KRUGER: Remember always what I told you, Mark. There is a fortune in emeralds there. . . .

MARK: I know, I believe it. . . .

KRUGER: You could be rich again, you could live again . . . I seen these stones with my own eyes. No white man but me has ever been in there . . . if you would come we could take them out, I need you. . . .

MARK: Kruger, don't talk to me like I was a child, will ya? I wanna go down there, I gotta go, I can't stand this tiny existence any more, I told you that. . . .

KRUGER: But you run, you run like. . . .

MARK: We'll have the dough, this ain't even folding money. That's a sleeping country, I wanna break it open big, I wanna push against jungle, I wanna come back and spread myself over a lotta people, like I used to, and you can only do that with money; you don't have to sell me a bill, this country's too small for me, it's lost its *daring*, I gotta go where they need big men!

KRUGER: And I will take you to see these ruins that I only know where they are.

MARK: Sure.

KRUGER (*ecstatic*): You will see, an idol sits in the forest five hundred years old!

MARK: Jeeze, that'll be something to see.

KRUGER: You will look once on that idol's face, Mark, and you will want to live there forever, to die there . . . ja, you will forget even the emeralds when you see that face! You will feel, Mark, like there is no use to move further, that you should forget everything and only sit and look.

MARK: We're on our way, Kruger, leave it to me.

KRUGER (*takes* MARK'*s hand*): I believe you. Come on the ship, we talk more about it.

MARK: I want to go into town for a while.

KRUGER: Why, Mark. You'll only spend the money.

MARK: For Christ's sake, Kruger, I been on the ship five weeks! I gotta see people, I wanna hear noise, see what a woman looks like. There's a thousand souls in the French Quarter . . . I gotta see! Don't be . . . !

(ANNA *comes from the shadows at the left.*)

ANNA: Excuse me.

MARK (*looks her over*): But of course. Out late aren't you?

ANNA: Are you an officer on this ship?

MARK: First Mate, *Bangkok Star*. Mark Donegal is how they named me . . . (*He moves toward her.*)

ANNA (*slightly frightened by his move*): I came . . . I'm looking for someone.

MARK (*stops moving, smiles*): Then what're you afraid of?

ANNA: He's the Second Engineer. . . .

MARK: Babson?

ANNA: No, he's the Second Engineer, Lester Kimball. . . .

MARK: You're seven months too late, sister. Kimball's been off the ship since May.

ANNA: I know he's on the ship, he. . . .

MARK (*smiling*): But I know he ain't. . . .

ANNA: He must be on the ship . . . !

MARK: Take it easy, Jesus. . . .

ANNA (*ready to weep*): You made a mistake, he must be. . . .

MARK: Hey . . . hey. (*Takes her arm.*)

ANNA (*disengages her arm at his touch*): Please!

MARK (*steps back*): O.K. . . .

(*Pause.*)

You want something . . . drink? . . . (*Reaches for hip.*)

ANNA: This ship goes to South America, doesn't it?

MARK: Chile, yeh . . . can I help you? Your friend got off at Galveston.

ANNA: Oh. . . .

MARK: Lemme give you a help . . . my name is Mark Donegal, Elmira New York . . . known around the hemispheres, I'm all right . . . Donegal.

 (ANNA *looks at him silent.*)

I got you wrong for a minute, I thought you were. . . .

ANNA (*bitterly*): I'm not.

MARK: I'm sorry kid, I. . . .

ANNA: I'm not.

MARK: Forgive me . . . it's after three in the morning . . . What's your name?

ANNA: . . . Anna.

MARK: Where do you belong? This ain't your scenery is it?

ANNA: I'm from another state.

MARK: Georgia, heh?

ANNA: No, not. . . .

MARK: I can tell, it's all over your mouth. . . .

 (*She turns and starts walking away.*)

  (*Goes after her.*)

Wait, wait!

 (*Turns her around. Deeply worried.*)

You're all nerves, what's the matter with you?

CAPTAIN (*from the prow of the ship*): Mr. Donegal!

 (MARK *startled, looks up, as do* KRUGER *and* ANNA.)

Come up on board, please.

MARK (*slight pause*): I'll be back in the morning, sir.

CAPTAIN: At once, in my cabin, please!

MARK (*turns slowly from* CAPTAIN *to* ANNA): Lemme take you into town, I'll get a cab. . . .

CAPTAIN: Mr. Donegal!

MARK (*ignoring* CAPTAIN. *To* ANNA): Come on, we'll dance, sing, play musical instruments. . . .

CAPTAIN: Mr. Kruger!

KRUGER: Yes, Captain?

CAPTAIN: Board the ship.

KRUGER (MARK *and* ANNA *watching him, he turns to* MARK, *then back up to the* CAPTAIN): Yes, sir.

CAPTAIN: At once.

(*He disappears on deck behind the prow.* KRUGER *starts for the door of the pier.*)

MARK (*strides to* KRUGER): I told you not to listen to him.

KRUGER: I've got to go up.

MARK: His brains are swimming, he's gotta be walked on!

KRUGER: Mark, I've got to go up.

MARK: All right, but don't crawl to him, let him know who he's talking to! (*Looks up at prow.*) That hophead!

KRUGER: Don't go into town without me . . . please, Mark. (KRUGER *goes into pier.*)

ANNA: When do you sail?

MARK (*turns to her from door, stands watching her a moment*): You're floating loose, heh?

ANNA: What do you mean?

MARK: You got a place to stay?

ANNA: Sure, I've got a room. . . .

MARK: Your stockings are torn.

ANNA: I like my stockings torn.

MARK (*comes a step toward her*): What are you after?

ANNA: I was sure Kimball was on that ship. . . .

MARK: But he ain't.

ANNA: I've been waiting here a week. . . .

MARK: Kimball's in Texas. Start from that.

(*Pause.*)

ANNA: You . . . take passengers on that ship? I thought Kimball would make it easier to get on. . . .

MARK: But we go to Chile, South America.

ANNA: I know that. I want to go to South America.

MARK: You gotta go, eh?

ANNA: I said I'd like to go to South America.

MARK: You're pretty local, aren't you.

ANNA: What do you mean by that?

MARK: I mean you don't know who to be afraid of. I'm a right guy, Anna!

(*Men's voices heard from left.*)

(ANNA *steps back, glancing left.*)

What's got you scared?

ANNA: Who said I'm scared?

MARK: The cop, heh?

ANNA: No. . . .

MARK: He's just a punk, he don't even scare the rats.

ANNA (*glancing off left*): Look. I . . . I've got thirty dollars, could you get me on?

MARK (*looks at her closely*): Talk more.

ANNA: I've got nothing more to say. . . .

MARK: No, you know how to talk . . . you. . . .

ANNA: Why do you look at me like that?

MARK: Why do I think I've seen your face, Anna?

ANNA: You're drunk, aren't you?

MARK: Why don't you come into town with me?

ANNA: No, I don't want to do that. . . .

MARK: We're not gonna "do that," I'll buy you a beer. I've been talking to the wind five weeks and I'm bored, Anna! Come on, we'll find out who we are! . . .

> (*He reaches toward her, she draws back as* DENNIS, NELSON, CARROL *come from left.* DENNIS *and* CARROL *are carrying a moose head by the horns suspended between them, while* NELSON, *a cardboard box in his hand is overseeing carefully.*)

DENNIS: All right, Carrol, now it's my turn to get on the windward. The bloody beast is stinkin' something fearful!

NELSON: Careful, now . . . !

> (DENNIS *starts to circle around to get in front. . . .*)

MARK (*Irish brogue*): The Ship of State!

DENNIS (*drops the horns in fright*): Mark!

NELSON (*alarmed at dropping moose*): Dennis you. . . .

MARK: Nelly, for Christ's sake!

> (CARROL *sits on the moose, holding his head.*)

NELSON: Well, Mr. Donegal, you're alive!

DENNIS (*as they grab his arms shake his hands*): We thought you were dead surely . . . !

NELSON: We really did, we. . . .

MARK: Well, I ain't, forget it . . . what're you doin' here?

DENNIS: We're on the *Swordsman* over there . . . (*Indicates left.*)

NELSON: God, we never expected to see you again. . . .

DENNIS: They told us they buried you!

MARK: Yeh, but I didn't stay covered . . .

DENNIS (*hitting* NELSON): Leave it to the Irish! They told us you beat up on seven navy fellers.

MARK: Yeh, I woke up in the basement. . . .

DENNIS: But still in Shanghai?

MARK: Yeh, same town, this whore brought a Chink doctor, bandaged me up fine. . . .

NELSON: That was very decent. . . .

MARK: Stayed there nine days, fed me, everything, wouldn't take a nickel.

DENNIS: I always said it, the Chinese is an upright people!

MARK (*points to moose*): What the hell are you doing with that?

DENNIS (*turns to* CARROL *on the moose*): Well, if it's the upper part you're referrin' to, we're trying to keep him from floating away!

NELSON: I promised a moose to Bill that runs the Black Cat saloon?—so we gotta get it to him so he can hang it behind the bar. . . .

(COP *enters smiling.*)

COP: Doin' all right, boys?

MARK: Yeh, swell. . . .

(*Goes to* ANNA *as he talks, links her arm. She is frightened of the* COP, MARK, *draws her toward the group.* . . .)

Nelson is gonna be a famous collector. . . .

ANNA: Is that so?

MARK: Yeh, he's got tigers and lions, tell her, Nelly. . . .

DENNIS: And one is as odiferous as the other!

NELSON: I bought a beautiful leopard this trip. Johannesburg. . . .

MARK: So what've you seen that would make you want to live another year?

DENNIS: Well, Nelson met a woman. . . .

MARK: What? Another one?

DENNIS: This one promised to buy him a roadhouse in Mobile! How's that!

MARK: What do you know, Nelly!

NELSON: It's true.

MARK (*to* ANNA): Nelson goes for society women. Senior League stuff.

ANNA (*laughs*): And do they go for him?

MARK: That's no mahoofus. (*To* NELSON.) So what the hell are you doing in New Orleans?

NELSON: Well see, I had in mind a fine place, where fine people would like to come and have a friendly drink together, and I'd hang up my old guns and arrows and knives and things. . . .

DENNIS: With bronze labels under them. . . .

NELSON: Yes, with bronze labels under them. I was going to name it the "Museum Inn," get it?

MARK: Yeh, that's a swell title. Like that title, Officer?

COP: Sounds good to me.

MARK: Thought you'd like it. (*To* NELSON.) Then what happened . . . ?

COP: Say I don't like to seem like a butt-in guy. . . .

MARK: You're doin' all right, that's all right . . . (*Glances at* ANNA.) So what, Nelly?

NELSON (DENNIS *glances at* COP, *then at* ANNA): So I get to Mobile and she rides me out there in her car, Packard . . . and she bought a very run down place, unpainted, you know? A dive. It . . . it wasn't what I had in mind. So I left . . . and that's all.

MARK: Your luck was with you. . . .

NELSON: No, I'm out to get a place, Mark. . . .

DENNIS: He is, Mark. . . .

MARK: You make me nervous, Nelly, you make me sad.

NELSON: That's facts, Mark, I'm gettin' a place, I already got my eye on a nice stove for the winter. . . .

MARK: Man, you're a sailor! You'll bust out of a restaurant and be smellin' for water in ninety days! It's not big enough for you Nelly, it ain't important enough when you spent your life watching stars. Am I right?

NELSON: Yeh, but . . . I thought I wanted a place.

MARK (*to* DENNIS): What'd you sell him this?

DENNIS: No, but it's a helluva life, Mark, bangin' around, gettin' nowhere.

MARK: That's because you lost your timber, your imagination, Dennis.

DENNIS: I have too imagination!

MARK: You're turning into a bloody Mick hayseed plowboy.

DENNIS: I'm not no plowboy, by God!

MARK: Back to the farm for you, you lost your rhyme!

DENNIS: Don't say that, Mark! It's just that . . . by God, what's the end of it all? Workin' a month, and gettin' drunk, and workin' again, and takin' a goddam moosehead to . . . (*suddenly turns to* NELSON) . . . what the hell are we doin' with that animal!

NELSON: It's for Bill. . . .

DENNIS: And who the hell is Bill, and what the hell am I drunk for! You know where we're gonna end? (*To* MARK.) You and me and Nelly and this foolish child here?—all of us side by side in the gutter, monkey-drunk!

MARK: So what're you going to do about it?

DENNIS: Man, you get me crazy every time I see you!

MARK: Yeh? How, Dinny?

DENNIS: Ah . . . you always make me think I'm wastin' me life when I could be doin' some strange, wonderful deeds.

MARK: Maybe you could, Dinny. I've been thinking about you guys, and some of the other fellas that made that Far East trip last year with us. Nice bunch on that voyage.

NELSON: Every one of them.

MARK: Why don't you boys see me tomorrow on board? I think I got an idea for you.

DENNIS (*fascinated*): What sort of an idea, Mark?

MARK: I don't know, maybe we'll bust open a piece of geography, go someplace where nobody's been before, do something special.

DENNIS: Come on with us! We'll have a drink!

MARK: No, I'm busy now . . . tomorrow on the ship, and bring the baby if he's got any stuff. (*Of* CARROL.)

(DENNIS *springs over to* CARROL, *as* JACK *comes tapping on, and goes to shack. He catches* MARK'*s eye.* MARK *watches him absorbed from this point on.*)

DENNIS (*shaking* CARROL): Wake up there, Montana!

CARROL (*rising*): What? What?

DENNIS (*to* MARK): Two drinks and he looks like a poster of the Temperance Society!

(COP *laughs heartily.*)

(*To* CARROL.) Grab hold there! (*To the moosehorn.*)

CARROL (*dizzy*): They gypped me out of four hundred acres.

NELSON (*of moosehorn*): I'll take it, Dennis.

(*Takes one horn,* DENNIS *the other.*)

DENNIS: See you tomorrow, Mark!

MARK (*watching* JACK *in shack pouring seltzer. Absently*): Yeh, yeh. . . .

CARROL (*turns unsteadily to follow* DENNIS *and* NELSON *and moose, suddenly sees his wrist sticking out of his jacket*): Hey!

NELSON: Carrol, we gotta get to town!

CARROL (*holding his wrist*): I'm growing! (*He staggers toward the water.*)

COP: Hey, don't fall in there!

(*Rushes to* CARROL, *turns him straight.*)

DENNIS: Would you be good enough to follow him a ways, Officer? He's like to be floatin' into the Gulf before we know it.

COP (*leading* CARROL): Easy son, easy. . . .

CARROL (*as* DENNIS, NELSON, *precede him off*): I'm only twenty, there's plenty of time for me . . . I want to see all the things . . . not like the people, the people who . . . who . . . the people. . . .

(MARK *continues to study blind man who sits before the shack.*)

COP: Yeh, watch that there. . . .

CARROL: Then I'm goin' back home and. . . .

(*Exit* SAILORS *with* COP.)

(*As soon as the* COP *goes,* ANNA *starts left.* MARK *pulls his eyes from blind man.*)

MARK (*to* ANNA, *going to her*): What're you going for?

ANNA: Thanks, I want to go. . . .

MARK: Wait, come here will ya?

ANNA (*turns from watching the departed* COP. *To* MARK): Say . . .

(MARK *turns to her.*)

. . . who are you?

MARK (*smiling wondrously*): Isn't it a funny night?

ANNA (*feeling a substance, as though dreaming*): Yes.

MARK: You never heard of a guy like me.

ANNA: I don't know, who are you?

MARK: Mark Donegal, they know me all over the world. I'm a swell crazy guy.

ANNA: Are you drunk?

MARK: Sure, I'm always drunk . . . on what I see and what I hear and what I think about. What's your education? High school?

ANNA: You ask the funniest questions.

MARK: High school, heh? Georgia.

ANNA (*of* JACK): What are you looking at him for?

MARK: I've been thinking of something for three months. That's a long time for me. I got a feeling you're going to help me out.

ANNA: I don't know very much.

MARK: No, you got good eyes, you know what trouble is. I want you to stay around with me . . . I'm trying to figure something out, something enormous . . . stay . . . (*Turns to* JACK.) Hey, fella.

    (JACK *does not react.*)

What's your name, blind man?

    (JACK *turns his head slightly.*)

Jack.

JACK (*turning his head slightly*): Yeh?

MARK (*moving to him*): Your name is Jack, isn't it?

JACK: What do you want?

MARK: I saw your walk.

    (*Takes* JACK*'s head in his hands.*)

Jack Biggers, heh?

JACK (*removing* MARK*'s hands*): Yes, Jack Biggers.

MARK: This is Mark Donegal, Jack.

    (JACK *is blank.*)

Donny.

    (*Pause.*)

Donegal. You remember me.

    (*Pause.*)

My old man was Kerry Donegal, made parts for aircraft.

    (*Pause.*)

JACK: You've got the wrong party.

ANNA: He doesn't know you.

MARK: This is my past, Anna . . . (*Smiles.*) . . . yeh . . . my past is a blind man that don't remember me . . . (*Turns to* JACK.) . . . yeh . . . you know who this is? Jack Biggers, Anna, that's like sayin nothing to you. This was the greatest lightheavyweight that every lived . . . am I right, Jack?

JACK (*nervously*): Please, go away, will you?

MARK: Jack, we flew to Washington together, don't you remember? 1925.

JACK: I wish you'd go away!

MARK: I want you to remember like I remember! Madrid, remember the fight in Madrid? 1924! (*To* ANNA.) You know who used to come to his fights? Not touts and sportsmen and fast women,—the finest artists in Europe—, he had a Greek body, didn't you Jack!

JACK: I don't remember you, go will you, please?

MARK: I don't want all the old wires down, Jack . . . you taught me how to box in Paris, Soisante Deux, Rue St. Quentin!

JACK: I . . . I don't know, I don't know. . . .

MARK: Your birthday . . . 1926 . . . I brought two hundred people and bought up the Luxembourg Cafe for five days!

   (JACK's *head sways from side to side as though in pain.*)

I was selling propellers to the Dutch, Ralph Barnes was laying out the plans for the University of Miami, I was going to set you up teaching boxing there. . . .

   (JACK *continues to sway, saying no,* MARK *speaks with rising excitement as though to drill into* JACK's *mind, meantime a note of self-laughter is in his voice.*)

Then I was cracking oil land in Mexico for Connie Verne's old man, when you came to Honolulu I met you at the pier in that green Cadillac I had and we had a blowout in that house I built with the blue stone roof and you had a fight with George Kidder from Standard Oil, and I was running the Fairchild Plantation, sugar, remember? Jack, open your mouth!

JACK: There's a great many things. . . .

MARK (*kneels down, takes* JACK's *arm*): Look, fella. I want you to remember, you gotta. Marseilles. I ran outa dough, my old man wouldn't send me any more, I was running all over Europe with Senator Lawson's boy . . . played tackle at Colgate with me . . . and you got me my first sailor job, *Leviathan*, remember. The boiler room, Jack, you sat there laughing at me all the way across!—and then I went to St. Louis, football, the first professional team . . . This is Donny . . . for Christ's sake!

JACK: There's a great many things.

MARK (*rises slowly. To* ANNA): This looks like a reunion in the gutter, don't it. Jesus, Anna, you don't know what we lost in this country. Those climbing years, the enormous men, people weren't so three-for-a-penny and the country was moving like a train like the biggest thing in the world, a clean thing it seemed like, and you believed in it and you belonged, you *belonged*! . . . Yeh, I'm drunk but I'm clear . . . I've been around the world fifty times, know all the kinds of people, I'm just trying to get what it means, where we're heading, to find a way to do the great thing again, to feel you're steering your own life, to pull out of the mob and walk the earth like a giant again to make new roads into brand new places! . . . Why do I think I've seen your face!

ANNA: No, you haven't.

MARK: You think I'm a queer stick, heh? I'm all right . . . I'm just gonna figure out where I belong . . . why do I think I've seen your face?

(KRUGER *comes through door in pier and comes quickly to* MARK.)

KRUGER: Mark.

MARK (*suddenly looks up at the sky, the ship, the pier, at* ANNA): Jesus, it's a . . . funny night. I feel like it's going to stay dark till I pull the sun up with my hand! (*He laughs.*)

KRUGER: Captain Schulenberg is coming down.

ANNA: Can I talk to you . . . tomorrow maybe? It's important.

MARK: Yeh . . . don't go away . . . (*To* KRUGER.) What does he want?

KRUGER (*rapidly*): He's carrying a gun in his pocket—here. (*Touches his breast.*)

(Blind man *hurries out, frightened.*)

MARK: What're you . . . ?

(CAPTAIN *quickly steps through the pier door, stops, when he sees* MARK.)

(*Pause.*)

CAPTAIN: I asked you to come to my cabin.

MARK: This is my time off. I don't go aboard till sailing.

CAPTAIN: We never leave ship in these cities, you know that.

MARK: I'm goin' into town, the lady and I. . . .

CAPTAIN (*coming downstage a little*): But I gave these orders five months ago. . . .

MARK: Come on, Anna. . . .

CAPTAIN: I want to speak with you before you go.

MARK: Then say it now. . . .

CAPTAIN: We are not precisely alone. . . .

MARK: Then don't say it. (*He takes* ANNA'*s arm, starts left.*)

CAPTAIN: Wait!

  (MARK *stops. Pause.*)

MARK (*a deep anger controlled*): I'm sorry, Anna, will you wait over there? I'll be right along . . . don't let him frighten you . . . please, heh? I gotta settle something.

  (ANNA *glances at the* CAPTAIN *wonderingly, goes to the far upstage left corner almost in shadow, stands at the edge of the water.*)

(*Turns to* CAPTAIN.) Ran outa long cigarettes, heh?

CAPTAIN: I want to discuss some business with you.

MARK: You're jumpy, Schulenberg. Why don't you go down to Bourbon Street, basement, it's fresh stuff?

CAPTAIN (*not looking at* MARK): Before you shoot your money in the French Quarter, I would like you to pay me the two hundred dollars you owe to me.

MARK: What two hundred dollars?

CAPTAIN: Dr. Luther just gave you three hundred. Two of that is mine.

MARK (*searching him*): I thought you wouldn't touch that kind of money?

CAPTAIN: I've changed my mind.

MARK: Why? It's still beneath your dignity, isn't it?

CAPTAIN: I take the responsibility for bringing these men in, I deserve a share.

MARK: Don't con me around, what's on your mind, Schulenberg!

CAPTAIN (*glancing around*): Please! You owe me two hundred. . . .

MARK: Don't pull that on me, Captain, you're not on a U-Boat any more!—

CAPTAIN: I said you . . . !

MARK: Get that through your haircut, Schulenberg!
  (*Pause.*)

CAPTAIN (*suddenly a new tone, whining a little, deferential*): You could be a great man, Mark. This Brazil expedition, why don't you go through with it . . . ?

MARK: What's that to you?

CAPTAIN: I hate to see you wasting your talent, your wonderful energy, when you could make something of yourself down there. I want to hold your money for you, that's why.

MARK: Yeh, heh?

CAPTAIN (*a slight pleading in his voice*): Look, you could have been already on your way with that six hundred dollars they stole from you in Mobile! Where will you end?
(*Pause.*)

MARK (*stiffening* . . . KRUGER *moves closer to them*): How did you know they took six hundred from me in Mobile?

CAPTAIN (*a real nervousness beginning—tries to laugh—indicates the prow*): I confess I was eavesdropping . . . Mr. Kruger was saying. . . .

MARK: He didn't say it was stolen, Schulenberg, he said I shot it away.

CAPTAIN (*slight pause*): As a matter of fact you told me yourself when you came on board in Mobile. . . .

MARK: You weren't on ship when I came on in Mobile. . . .

KRUGER: Mark. . . .

MARK (*to* KRUGER, *flying up*): No, wait a minute!

CAPTAIN: What are you trying to say!

MARK (*advances on* CAPTAIN): How did you know they stole my money! Come on!

CAPTAIN: You weren't in a condition to remember, you told me yourself! They fixed your drink and robbed you!

MARK (*advancing on the* CAPTAIN): Where's my dough?

KRUGER: Mark, please . . . !

MARK: Where's my dough, goddamit!

CAPTAIN (*he suddenly limps a few steps back, limps slightly*): Kruger . . . !

ANNA: Please! (*She comes down a few steps, halts, frightened.*)

MARK (*glances up at her, halts—to* CAPTAIN): All right . . . all right, now I'll see you later . . . down here or on ship . . . I'll see you. (*Goes to* ANNA.) Come on, I'll take you to a cab, they're up a block here. . . .
(*He hustles her off left, she glancing back at* CAPTAIN.)
(*Pause.*)
(CAPTAIN *stands wringing his hands slightly, staring at where* MARK *went.* KRUGER *looks at him.*)

CAPTAIN (*helplessly*): He likes this girl?

KRUGER: Now he knows you took his money, he will ask why.

CAPTAIN (*still staring left*): Then I will tell him why.

KRUGER: You must never tell him; he will kill you!

CAPTAIN: No, he will understand, he must *understand*!

KRUGER: Return him his money, let him go with me away!

CAPTAIN (*looks at* KRUGER): He does not go to Brazil! You will not take him from me!

KRUGER: Captain Schulenberg!

CAPTAIN: No, he will never go . . . soon I will tell him and he will belong to me!

KRUGER: He'll murder you for an unnatural thing!
      (*Pause.*)

CAPTAIN: He will come to me, Kruger . . . I think already in his great heart, he begins to understand! (*Suddenly turning on* KRUGER.) And you will not talk so insubordinate to me. . . .

KRUGER: I only. . . .

CAPTAIN: Because I permit him to speak like that does not mean I cannot put you in your place!

KRUGER: Yes sir. . . .

CAPTAIN (*with a cry*): The whole world comes down!!
      (*Enter* LUTHER, ROCKO *and* BOSCH *from the right.*)
      (CAPTAIN *senses them, turns with shock.*)

LUTHER: Good evening, Herr Schulenberg.

CAPTAIN: Oh, Doctor Luther.

LUTHER: Where is Mr. Donegal, on board?

CAPTAIN: No, he will be right back, he went . . . (*Indicates left.*)

LUTHER: M, hm. (*Looks at ship.*) She will need a painting.

CAPTAIN: Yes, I wanted to speak to you about that. . . .

LUTHER: Well, we let her go for a while. . . .

CAPTAIN: I like to have a clean ship.

LUTHER: You had a fine voyage?

CAPTAIN: Very calm, yes.

LUTHER (*of* KRUGER): I see you have a new member of the crew?

CAPTAIN: Mr. Kruger is bos'n. We took him on a few months ago in Valparaiso. . . .

LUTHER: Kruger?

KRUGER: Yes sir.

LUTHER: August Kruger.

KRUGER: Yes sir.

LUTHER: That is a good German name, Herr Kruger.

KRUGER: I am a good German.

LUTHER: Oh yes, we are all good Germans. You have been to sea very long?

KRUGER: Sixteen years.

LUTHER: And a citizen?

KRUGER: Of Germany, sir.

LUTHER: And when were you last home?

KRUGER: Oh . . . must be three, four years.

LUTHER: You can't remember?

KRUGER: Three years I think.

LUTHER: You must not like your home. . . .

KRUGER: Oh no, this is simply my profession to sail. . . .

> (*Enter* MARK *from left.*)

LUTHER: Hello, we've been waiting for you.

> (MARK *comes toward center looking at* CAPTAIN, CAPTAIN *looking at him.*)

CAPTAIN: Well, I will say goodnight. . . .

LUTHER: No, stay please, and you too, Mr. Kruger. . . .

MARK: What's on your mind?

LUTHER: Can we go somewhere and talk?

MARK: Where I'm going I go alone.

CAPTAIN: I'm sorry I can't offer you the ship, but you can't go aboard until the customs inspection. . . .

MARK (*indicates shack*): This is private, nobody comes here this time of night.

LUTHER (*looks around*): Very well. Herr Schulenberg?

> (*Extends hand toward the shack.* CAPTAIN *goes to it, goes in.* MARK *follows him as . . .*)

> (*Going to shack with* KRUGER.)

How did you like the new buildings in Bremen, Herr Kruger?

KRUGER: Bremen? I never lived in Bremen.

LUTHER: Oh, I thought you told me. . . .

> (*The lights dim on the stage as they enter shack.*)

KRUGER: No, you're mistaken.

> (LUTHER *and* KRUGER *enter shack,* BOSCH *and* ROCKO *approach.*)

MARK: I got nothing to say to your gorillas.

LUTHER (*to* ROCKO *and* BOSCH): Go.

> (*They go off, stand and watch silently.*)
>> (*As* MARK, CAPTAIN, KRUGER *sit.*)

Shall we cast some more light on the subject? (*Strikes match, lights kerosene lamp.*)

MARK: What's the subject?

LUTHER (*finishes lighting lamp, blows out match*): You.

MARK: What do you know about me?

> (LUTHER *takes a bottle of whiskey from his coat pocket.*)

I had enough, thanks.

LUTHER: It's your brand.

MARK: I had enough, I said!

LUTHER (*laughs*): Well, there's no reason to. . . .

MARK (*stands suddenly, nervously*): What's the gag?

LUTHER: Won't you be seated?

MARK: Stop glomin' around, will ya? What's on your mind?

LUTHER (*pause—puts flask on chair*): Donegal, I have developed a great admiration for your family.

MARK: What does that mean?

LUTHER: A splendid aggregation of talented people. Your brother John, a rare architect; Michael, an accomplished industrial engineer, and Mary, I have heard her voice on the radio. . . .

MARK: And in the old sod my father cut blank verse in tombstones. So you looked me up, I get it.

LUTHER: Personally yourself, you have an amazing history.

MARK: So what?

LUTHER: So I need you, Mark Donegal, you. (*He rises, walks about.*) I need the son of the wealthy father who walked out of his university to see what it was like to be an ironworker. I need the man who went to Waukeegan Illinois with his football team and stayed to fly in the air corps,—and got cashiered for flying figure-8's between the smokestacks of the powerhouse on Lake Michigan. . . .

MARK (*smiles*): Oh, you got that, heh?

LUTHER: Are you sorry for those things?

MARK: Why? They don't fly any more, they travel by air, they put tracks in the sky, that's not flying and I wouldn't have it. Wings were made for men who couldn't live without wings.

We had to see what the back of a cloud felt like, or how close you could get to a star, or if you could fly under a bridge when the tide was up . . . like Bert LaCost. They broke me and they broke LaCost because the little people wanted lawyers in those planes, not artists who could land like a sparrow on the head of a nail. They've got no more use for the man who plants the flag;—he's got no address, he's not in the groove. Yeh, they made the world a room with a view.

LUTHER: You should have been in Germany.

MARK: Is that what you're selling tonight?

LUTHER: Oh, not at all. . . .

MARK: Because I've been to Germany. And I don't like it. I don't like your high school conquistadors with the plaster-cast brains. No, I'm going where I belong.

LUTHER: Where is that?

MARK: Where? Up the Amazon, Brazil.

LUTHER: I've been to Brazil, you don't belong there. . . .

MARK: I know!

LUTHER: You don't know! The giants are dead in every land, the little people inherit the earth. But the oceans remain, the sea where your wild blood brought you. Donegal, you have lived four life-times, you can live another.

(MARK *is silent.*)

What I have to say will of course never be repeated. I have information. I know the cargo of every ship that leaves any port in the Western Hemisphere. And I know what that cargo's worth.

MARK: I don't get it.

LUTHER: The world is falling apart, Donegal, and the wealth of the world rides on the seas. The future time belongs not to the man in the room with a view, not to the man in the counting house, but to the man who'll sail the seas and take, take what he's got the wit and daring enough to take!

MARK: What, what?

LUTHER: The *Bangkok Star* has new engines. She can overtake any freighter on the seas.

MARK: Nineteen and a half knots.

LUTHER: When the war started, three eight-inch guns were stowed away on your ship.

(MARK *rises.*)

Yes, Donegal . . . a raider. To gather up the floating fragments of the world! This is for the giant to do!

MARK: Go on, go on.

CAPTAIN: Luther, what are you saying?

LUTHER: Did I ask you to speak, Herr Schulenberg?

(CAPTAIN *is silent.*)

Then why do you speak? (*To* MARK.) I tell you the name of the ship, her course. You meet her on the high seas. You radio that you have some very sick men on your ship and ask her to take them to port, for you are headed out. You board her armed, smash her radio, and transfer her cargo to the *Bangkok Star.*

CAPTAIN: And so soon as she gets to port every destroyer in the world goes out hunting for us!

LUTHER: She never reaches port. (*To* MARK.) She leaves no trace.

(*Pause.*)

(MARK *reaches over, takes the bottle, opens it, pours a drink.*)

KRUGER: Mark! (*Softly, pleading.*)

(MARK *gulps it down.*)

LUTHER: I will dispose of the merchandise. . . .

MARK: I'm not talking about merchandise!

LUTHER: I recognize the danger is. . . .

MARK: I'm not talking about danger!

LUTHER: I guarantee you twenty five thousand on the first voyage. . . .

MARK: When you sail a ship into port at night you know the buoys are going to be in the right place, you know the reefs are marked, the lights haven't been moved. That's . . . we believe that, that's civilization. . . .

LUTHER: I am. . . .

MARK: You talk, Luther, and I feel the plaster falling around my head. I see dogs dragging children along the streets, and man pulling his daughter into bed, and a lie is the truth and the truth is a lie. Is that what I *mean*? You're a clever guy, Luther, is that what my life adds up to?

LUTHER: That's what the world adds up to! That's why I come to you, Donegal, because the very blood of these decades has pounded through your veins;—when America drove in

Packard cars, you drove them faster, when they aimed for the clouds you flew to the stars, when the gangster ruled the cities you were his fabulous friend, and you drank with police who tracked him down. You were the traveler, the writer in Paris, the salesman in Hong Kong, the American tapping Mexican oil . . . what were you looking for, for what were you searching but this, this?

MARK: I don't know what for. All I know is that I was always trying to do the hardest thing, the biggest thing, the thing with the power, the thing with the glory. Always I wanted to be my own master, to feed my own daemon and let it carry me wherever it would, to live each day like it was the last, to make myself like nobody else in the world, but only like Mark Donegal. And the guys who drank with me, and flew drunk with me are all rich now, or dead and I feel like there's only two things left in the world, me and the mob trying to pull me into their miserable lives. And I look in the mirror now, and there's a drunken sailor there on a third-rate scow, and I'm wondering what turn I missed when everything changed.

LUTHER: This is your year, Donegal.

MARK: Sometimes I wonder if there's any year left for me.

LUTHER: No, *this* is your year! The mob is bewildered, frightened behind locked doors. Take the time in your hands, sail out alone, cut across channels, break through the sealanes and write your own rules with your giant hand!

MARK: Give me time, will you?

LUTHER: Now is the time! The world waits for you like a ship without master, like a lost woman!

MARK: I've got to think!

LUTHER: A Greek ship leaves Porto Barrios Wednesday for Indo-Chinese ports. I must know tonight, now.

> (MARK *picks up whiskey bottle, begins to pour, bangs it down.*)

MARK: I'll go.

LUTHER (*goes to him quickly, hand extended*): I'll see you on board tomorrow.

> (MARK *slowly takes his hand.*)

Good night.

> (*Quickly turns to* KRUGER *and* SCHULENBERG.)

Of course none of this is repeated. None of it.—I will arrive at the ship in the afternoon, four o'clock.

(LUTHER *goes out.* ROCKO *and* BOSCH *follow him off right.*)

CAPTAIN: Mark, you can't do it.

MARK: Get out of here.

CAPTAIN: Mark!

MARK: I said get out, Schulenberg!

(SCHULENBERG *goes out, eyes down.*)

KRUGER (*rises slowly*): All we needed was a thousand . . . (*voice shaking*) . . . you could have gotten a thousand. . . .

MARK: There's a big score in this, a lot of money. . . .

KRUGER: It's too dangerous, you can make your fortune down there!

MARK: Maybe not.

KRUGER: I swear to you, Mark, on my honor you can be rich again!

MARK: I'm not after money, I never was!

KRUGER (*pause*): Then . . . then what are you doing this for?

(MARK *turns from him, wringing his fists.*)

Mark . . . you want to die!

MARK (*quickly*): No, don't say that, Kruger!

KRUGER: It's true, you know it!

MARK: Stop that, Goddam you . . . !

(*As they talk* ANNA *enters hurrying from left, hears them, goes to shack.*)

KRUGER (*almost weeping*): Mark! Mark!

MARK (*clamping his ears*): Shut up!

(ANNA *appears before* MARK.)

ANNA: I couldn't go home, I was afraid something was going to . . . (*Stops, looking at* MARK.) Are you all right?

(MARK *stares at her.*)

. . . Mark?

(*Pause.*)

MARK (*comes out of the shack*): How would you like to bust this town wide open tonight, I mean bust it open!

ANNA: Well there isn't much night left!

MARK: Then we'll make a night! Come on, I know all the dancing people in this town, all the sad ones . . . (*Grasps her.*) . . . Anna, I know all the kinds of people there are!

ANNA: Excepting me.

MARK: Yeh . . . that's right, Anna . . . how would you like to dance?

ANNA: I'd love to dance!

MARK (*as they go left*): Come on, we'll sing, and we'll dance, and we'll tell each other everything we know . . . (*Suddenly pulls back from her.*) Jeeze, Anna, you got a wonderful stride!

> (*He sweeps her off, both laughing.*)
>
> > (KRUGER *goes slowly toward the pier door, upstage, watching them disappear. The* COP *comes sauntering on from the right.*)

COP: Evening.

KRUGER: Good evening.

COP: Looks a little like rain, I guess.

KRUGER (*looks up*): No, maybe little, not much.

COP: How do you tell?

KRUGER: Oh, stars. The way you feel. Can tell many things by what you feel, after a while.

COP: Must be nice to travel all the time.

KRUGER: No, I don't think so. There is no peace in it. Makes in a person a hunger . . . to see too many things is bad. Better to stay in little place. A person must belong. (*Laughs.*) Don't worry, you don't miss nothing. (*Turns toward door, opens it.*)

COP: Well, I'll see you.

KRUGER: Yes. Good luck to you.

> (*Goes into pier.* COP *goes to his chair beside the shack, sits, leans back, lights his cigar, exhales, and while he turns his head to look again at the weather in the sky . . .*)

SLOW CURTAIN

ACT TWO

The Chart Room of the Bangkok Star *the following afternoon at about four o'clock. This is a well-worn section of a well-worn ship. The right wall is a series of windows looking toward the aft of the ship. There is oak paneling below them. In the right corner of the back wall is a paned sliding door which gives access to a landing, and from this landing one can climb upward to the bridge and down to the deck. There are three windows in the back wall, beyond which can be seen the line of the pier roof. An oak door opens out of the upstage corner of the left wall and leads into the* CAPTAIN*'s cabin. In this left wall which is solid, are a number of drawers, and from its center at chest height a shelf extends. This, the size of a small desk-top, has great charts strewn upon it. There are a few chairs scattered about, and a small table. Over the windows a fine mist is clinging, and the occasional sounding of a warning whistle from boats on the river through the act suggest a heavy day.*

On the rise, we find DINO, *the steward, cleaning the room. He is a small Chilean, with a shiny brown face. His jacket was once white and starched but that was some time ago. At the moment he is polishing a brass water bottle. He hangs it back on the rack which is screwed into the wall at the back, then goes to a shelf below the windows at the right, and dusts it. A small cigarette box is on the shelf. He picks it up and dusts under it. The door at the left opens, and* CAPTAIN SCHULENBERG *comes in.* DINO *turns around quickly, straightens his posture.*

CAPTAIN: Good afternoon, Steward.

DINO: Good afternoon to you, sir.

> (CAPTAIN *starts to go upstage, right, toward the paned door.* DINO *resumes dusting.* CAPTAIN *stops, watching him, then goes to him and turns him around.* DINO *has the cigarette box in his hand.*)

Yes, sir?

CAPTAIN (*takes box from his hand*): What are you doing with this?

DINO: I was cleaning under it.

CAPTAIN: I notice you always make it very clean under this box.

DINO: Not specially, sir, no.

CAPTAIN (*looking at* DINO, *opens box*): You never steal these?

DINO: No, sir, I never smoke that kind.

CAPTAIN: I don't ask if you smoke this kind,—whatever you might mean by "this kind,"—I ask if you steal these.

DINO: I don't steal, sir.

CAPTAIN: Then they have been walking away by themselves.

DINO: I don't know, sir.

CAPTAIN: Just so you know that I am not blind like you think.

DINO: Yes, sir.

CAPTAIN (*motions toward shelf*): Go on.

(DINO *dusts further along shelf.*)

(*Rubs an area* DINO *has just cleaned.*) Now look, Dino. (*Shows dust on his fingers.*) This is what I am talking about. You call this clean?

DINO: This ship is all cracked,—the wood, the paint,—hard to clean.

CAPTAIN (*feeling a vague insult*): I didn't ask your comment on the ship!

DINO: I don't feel so good, sir. I want to go ashore.

CAPTAIN: For what?

DINO: Want to look around, buy things.

CAPTAIN: For instance?

DINO: I can't stand on a ship so long, five months.

CAPTAIN: For instance what will you buy!

DINO: Sox, underwear, things. . . .

CAPTAIN: Oh dear yes, sox, underwear! They think below I am a madman, eh? The captain is crazy, eh? Well you can tell them they will not go ashore and bring me back the filth from these whores they lay with, I shall have to wash my hands if I touch something here!

DINO: Yes, sir. . . .

CAPTAIN: Yes, sir, and you can get yourself a clean cloth once in a while, you animal! (*He grabs the cloth from* DINO's *hand, throws it to the floor.*) Get out of here. And you can tell the rest of them that they shall not get off the ship until they get back to Valparaiso! And if I catch you again stealing, I'll . . . !

(*The door at the right opens,* MARK *comes in, ready to laugh at what* DENNIS, *who is just behind him, is saying.* NELSON *and* CARROL *follow* DENNIS *in.*)

DENNIS: . . . Get that beast out of this saloon, he says! Imagine, afraid of a dead moose as though it was goin' to bite . . . !

(*He stops, seeing* MARK, *whose laugh is gone, watching* DINO *picking the rag off the floor.* DINO *is obviously sullen, picking it up slowly. The* CAPTAIN *is uneasy under* MARK*'s eyes.*)

MARK: Finished in here, Dino?

DINO (*straightening up*): Yes, sir.

MARK: Because we can go somewhere else.

DINO: No, I'm all finished. (*He goes right, and out.*)

CAPTAIN (*affably*): A farewell party? (*Takes a coat from a hook on wall.*)

MARK: I don't know how long they're gonna stand for that.

CAPTAIN: Your Doctor hasn't come yet?

MARK: He'll come. Sit down, boys.

CAPTAIN (*nervously, overloudly*): Well, that's how it goes with important men. They let the help know who is important in the corporation. Tell the deck man he shall tighten up on the number three winch. I take a walk around the deck. (CAPTAIN *goes out, pulling door shut behind him.*)

NELSON: Say, is it all right for us to be up here?

MARK: What do you mean? You got important business. Sit down, what'll you have? Scotch or rye?

NELSON (*as they take chairs*): Make mine scotch.

DENNIS: Same here. Say, how the hell do you keep this boat so filthy?

MARK: Yeh, you'd think the Greeks were running her. (*To* CARROL.) What's yours?

DENNIS: Nothin for Carrol till he practices his breathin'.

CARROL: I'll wait with mine.

NELSON (*as* MARK *opens back cabinet, pours drinks*): What's the matter, Mark, don't nobody work on this ship?

MARK (*pouring drinks*): Sure, but it's a broken-down crew on a broken-down ship. We got what you call discipline here, see? If a guy's workin' with a broom and he's doing all right, the mate's gotta go down and tell him to get a brush for no goddam reason. Then the guy knows who's boss, get it?

CARROL: That captain's sort of a whack, ain't he.

MARK: Well, you can't do much with this banana, it's thirty two years of old age . . . (*giving out drinks*) . . . propellor's ready to fall into the coffee.

DENNIS (*lifting glass*): Let's have a toast! I love a toast!

MARK (*lifts glass with* NELSON): To the *Bangkok Star*, her voyage to glory. Non comp a mentis tempus fugit. (*Drinks.*)

DENNIS (*laughing*): Oh, Mark, you're some feller! Where in the world did you learn Latin?

MARK: My father had me all set to be a priest, you know. Thought it would be the best way to keep me out of reform school. (*Laughs.*)

NELSON: Dennis was going to be a cardinal.

DENNIS: Oh, go on now, Nelly.

NELSON (*to* MARK): That's what he said! But he couldn't make it on account of the oldest in the family wouldn't give up the linen shirt!

DENNIS: If you knew anything about Ireland, you'd know the only citizen that's got a linen shirt is the Pope, and he's in Italy! How's your mother these days, Mark?

MARK (*a bright smile*): You remember about her, eh? That's nice, Dinny.

DENNIS: I love to talk about mothers!

MARK (*feeling warm, leaning against shelf*): Yeh, Mom's still goin'. Seventy one years old. Y'know,—I got one sister and four brothers. All successful, pullin' down some important money. Me? I'm a bust. But who do you think my mother wants to see the most? Donny!

NELSON: I'll bet! (*Laughs.*)

MARK: That's true, and you know why? She has *fun* with me! Sure, I come home, and we go over to the Washington Heights Bar and Grill . . . she lives up there . . . they call her Queen Marie in that joint! Yeh, she drinks me under the table. Loves to hear me tell stories, y'know? Where I been, the people I met, yeh . . . (*staring, the smile departs*) . . . it was the old man believed in me, though. Never gave him a minute's peace, spent all his dough . . . he was all right, the old man . . . yeh. . . .

(*Pause.*)

DENNIS: Say, Mark. . . .

MARK (*suddenly bursts out, very seriously*): I like you guys! I
    could bust the world open with you guys! (*Strides about full
    of energy.*) I got a terrific idea for all of us.

DENNIS: Before we talk, Mark.

MARK: Don't interrupt me.

DENNIS: What the hell is wrong on this ship?

MARK: Why, you seeing ghosts?

DENNIS: Those gunmen on the pier ain't no ghosts. What're
    they doin' there. You said you'd explain.

MARK: I don't know what they're doing, is that enough?

DENNIS (*turning away*): I don't want no trouble on a ship.
    Ashore, all right, but not on a ship.

MARK: All right, so cut it, will you?

DENNIS: Every time I meet you you're on some kind of a mess!

MARK: I'm not in a mess!

DENNIS: I wish to hell I was sure of that!

MARK: What are you losing your juice?

DENNIS: Don't kid me, Mark! What are gangsters doin' on that
    pier!

MARK: I said I don't know, that's all!

DENNIS: But you're nervous!

MARK: Then I'm nervous!

    (*Silence.*)

    (MARK *sits slowly, turns to* CARROL.) How old are you?

CARROL: Twenty one next month.

MARK: When'd you go to sea?

CARROL: Year and a half about.

MARK (*to* DENNIS *and* NELSON): I'm doing you fellas a favor.
    I'm not asking you to pull me out of anything. Nelly, you've
    been sailing almost twenty years, right?

NELSON: Just about.

MARK: And you, Dennis.

DENNIS: It's eight years come February.

MARK (*slight pause*): What'd it get you? Come on, talk it out.

DENNIS: What's it supposed to get ya. A taste for strong liquor
    and a crick in the back. So what?

MARK: And when you hit your fifties you start learnin' how to
    sew up the seat of your pants, right?

NELSON: That's the way it goes.

DENNIS: What are you driving at, Mark?

CARROL: You guys just stayed in it too long, that's all. Take me: I'm going to save my money, and then. . . .

MARK: How much've you got now?

CARROL: Well . . . I didn't start yet, but. . . .

MARK: Yeh. How much've you got, Dennis?

DENNIS: I'm not much for savin'.

NELSON: Somehow . . . it's pretty hard.

MARK: The word is impossible, Nelly. When you get paid off and you go ashore, you want to live, you want to gobble it all up,—getting off a voyage is like lifting out of a grave, it's death on a ship. You *gotta* spend your money,—you need a woman, a drink, you gotta dive into the middle of the noise. That goes back to Ulysses. So this is what I've got to say, and it dies with the four of us.

DENNIS: You can trust us, Mark.

MARK (*sits*): I've got a man coming on board any minute now.

DENNIS: This doctor?

MARK: Yeh, he's a doctor. He's got an idea. It's going to make me a lot of money, and if you want to come in on it, you'll be counting in hundreds, maybe thousands.

NELSON (*his throat constricts*): What do we do?

MARK (*to* CARROL): You don't shoot your mouth off, do you?

CARROL (*embarrassed*): No, I'm all right.

MARK (*gets up*): The crew here is all half-breeds from Chile. They're all right, see, but they've been taking an awful beating from the bridge. I'm afraid they've got no stuff left, know what I mean?

DENNIS: Why, you expecting a fight sometime?

MARK (*slight pause*): Maybe.

DENNIS (*crosses his legs uneasily*): Well?

MARK: So I want a couple a guys with me who can understand me in a hurry, and know how to handle themselves. Guys I can trust.

(*Pause.*)

NELSON: What . . . what is it going to be?

MARK: It's something that'll buy you the swellest beer garden on the Mobile road, and you, Dennis, you'll have yourself a farm in Ireland, the kind without rocks.

DENNIS (*smiles*): Is that so?

MARK: And Carrol, you can set up a photograph joint with all the cameras and all the stuff.

DENNIS: Well come on, what the hell is it?

MARK: I want you to sail with me.

NELSON: But we're not allowed to sail a foreign ship.

MARK: Leave that to me. Nobody's going to know. Nobody.

DENNIS: Where do we sail to?

MARK: I'm meeting another ship at sea. I'm boarding her. She's got a valuable cargo.

   (*The men lean forward.*)

We transfer the stuff and beat it. The rest is taken care of. (*Rises.*) I need you. You'll make a real score. Thousands. . . .

   (DENNIS *rises, goes across the room, eyes wide.*)

(*To* DENNIS.) . . . Thousands of dollars. And when you're old you'll know you lived without a bit in your mouth.

CARROL (*jumps up*): I'll go. I want to go, let me go with you!

   (MARK *looks from* DENNIS *to* NELSON.)

Let me go, I'm not afraid. I'll go back home, there's four hundred acres belonged to me when Pop died and they gypped me out of everything . . . I'll go back, it's swell sheep land, I know how to make them grow! You can't get it slow, you've got to scoop it up in one bunch . . . like harvest, you've got to cut it quick or it rots, it rots, it. . . .

   (*Goes quickly to* MARK, *grabs his arm.*)

Take me with you, I'm ready now.

MARK (*turns to* DENNIS): Well? Talk, Irish.

   (*Long pause.*)

DENNIS (*turns slowly to* MARK): I would never've believed, Mark, that I could even consider such a thing. But I am considerin' it, yes, I am. It's a terrible hatred we carry around with us, all of us who work like this, a hatred and a shame that frightens me to feel. You work your life out like a mule never knowin' what for, but in the quiet hours, the tired hours, it comes up like a fire, the knowin' that as big as you are they're laughin' at you behind their big bronze doors, laughin' at your sweat and laughin' at the dreams you make, collectin' on you when you float and collectin' when you sink. . . .

MARK: And what are you going to do about it?

DENNIS: I don't know, Mark! I'd have to believe I was doin'

right, in a way, to keep courage on a thing like this, I'd have to keep remembering that hatred, I'd have to believe that we're only takin' back what belongs to us, what we worked for and never got, what we got drunk a thousand times for not having got!—and I don't know if this is the way to get it back . . . I don't know if I could keep feelin' that I'm right in doin' it,—I don't know, Mark!

MARK: You'll have to make up your mind. I think I'm sailing tonight.

CARROL: Well I'm ready, I'm all set.

DENNIS: You're ready and you don't know what you're talkin' about!

CARROL (*embarrassed*): And what do you know?

DENNIS: I know that you're scared and that's why you're ready!

CARROL (*turning from him*): Scared, heh?

DENNIS: Scared, yes! Scared you'll end up like we are, Nelly and I and Mark, with all your wonderful plans up the chimney and your future a-wanderin' over the face of the earth, lost like a fish in the sea, and that's not the reason to be goin' into a terrible thing like this!

CARROL: You know everything!

DENNIS (*going toward* CARROL, *losing his temper*): I know you, and you're goin' to think it over again before you. . . .

MARK (*to* DENNIS): Hey, hey . . . !

(*Enter* BOSCH. DENNIS *stops.* BOSCH *stands looking at each of the men.*)

(*To* BOSCH): Hello. Finished talking to the crew?

(BOSCH *just keeps looking at the men.*)

Friends of mine.

BOSCH (*as though memorizing their faces, still not looking at* MARK): All right, that's all right.

MARK: You're damned right it's all right. (*Laughs.*) What do you mean, it's all right?

BOSCH (*still looking at men*): I just like to know who comes on the ship . . .

(*Looks up at* MARK.)

. . . and so forth.

MARK (*to* MEN): Why don't you all go down to the galley, tell the cook I sent you, get a coffee and whatever you want. Think it over, go on.

DENNIS (*glancing at* BOSCH): They got any good pastry down there?

MARK: Well, Jesus, I've been eating it, don't I look pastry?

NELSON (*as they laugh*): See you later, Mark.

(*Enter* CAPTAIN *as though he had seen* BOSCH *going in here from a distant part of the ship and wanted to make sure he had seen right. He hurries in.*)

MARK: Go on, fellas. It's on the company.

(*As* MEN *go out,* BOSCH *and* CAPTAIN *stand looking at each other.*)

And don't go away.

(*Exit* DENNIS, NELSON, CARROL.)

BOSCH (*as* MARK *turns back to room*): Captain Schulenberg?

MARK (*to* CAPTAIN): This is Mr. Bosch, Captain.

(CAPTAIN *silent.*)

BOSCH (*graciously*): I am happy to know you, sir. Doctor Luther sent me ahead to. . . .

CAPTAIN: You are Hermann Bosch?

BOSCH: Hermann Bosch, sir, Doctor Luther asked me to. . . .

CAPTAIN: What is it you want here?

MARK: He came to talk to the crew.

CAPTAIN: And what did he tell the crew?

BOSCH: Only that they are going into dangerous water and they are to receive a bonus.

CAPTAIN: And what was their answer?

BOSCH: They are very happy to cooperate with us.

MARK: I told you you wouldn't have any trouble. . . .

CAPTAIN (*stiffly*): I gave no permission for this man to talk to my crew. He has no right to board this vessel.

MARK (*to* BOSCH): You wanted to tell him something?

BOSCH: Oh, no. (*Looks at* CAPTAIN.)

MARK: You said you had something to say before.

BOSCH: No . . .

(*Looking directly at* CAPTAIN, CAPTAIN *at him.*)

. . . I just wanted to make his acquaintance. (*Turns quickly to door.*) I'll wait on the pier for the Doctor.

(*Exit* BOSCH. CAPTAIN *does not move.*)

MARK: What the hell goes on here?

CAPTAIN (*goes quickly to door, pulls it shut, turns quickly to*

MARK. *Sarcastically*): You came to complete agreement with Doctor Luther? Everything is settled between you?

MARK (*a tone of resentment rising*): No, nothing's settled, I still gotta talk to Luther. . . .

CAPTAIN: *Everything* is settled!

MARK: Now look, Captain. . . .

CAPTAIN: Everything is settled, I tell you!

MARK: Just a minute!

(*Pause.*)

I been waiting for this all day, I want to settle it now. I got the crew, I got the guns, I got the ship,—everything. Only you don't fit in.

CAPTAIN: I will not fit in such a thing!

MARK: That's what I want to know. What're you going to do? You can fight it out with Luther or fire me. But one way or another there is not going to be any battling between us.

CAPTAIN: I cannot fire you.

MARK: You're the master of this ship, anytime you say.

CAPTAIN: No, not anymore, Mark.

(*Pause.*)

MARK: Why not?

CAPTAIN: Because talking to the crew was only one of Mr. Bosch's minor duties on the *Bangkok Star* today. More important was that I should see him, and that I should remember what he is.

MARK: What is he?

CAPTAIN: He is a murderer, he is a killer, he is a beast. Hermann Bosch is covered with blood! And you have now no more to say about what you will do with your life, than a prisoner in a concentration camp!

MARK: Now let me tell you something. If I was a bookkeeper or a clerk or a bankrupt junker . . . or an engineer, doctor, or anybody else in this world but me, that would scare me spitless, but it doesn't. Because this is what I want, this is what everything adds up to in my life,—listen to me, Schulenberg,—I've had a hundred jobs, good ones, and I never stuck more than two months on any one of them because I never found one that was big enough for me. I've worked in everything from steel to law to running beer and back again, and I never met one guy who could see two yards further than his belly. The poor are petty and the rich are pigs, they gotta be, it's the dollar bill wrapped around their eyes. I'm pullin' out of that now, all of it. I'm breaking the circle we were born into this year of our lord; I'm going to do the one thing that demands a guy my size!

CAPTAIN: And what of those who will die on the ship you're going to sink?

MARK: The same as the ones who blew up on the ships I didn't sink! They'll go under remembering that right and wrong went out of the world and that'll be their peace.

CAPTAIN: You don't believe that what you're saying.

MARK: Why don't I! What the hell do I care about them? And what's waiting for them on shore? Is this a world to live in? Is this anything to cling to? I'm doin' them a favor, for Christ's sake, and if I'm not, to hell with them, I'm not the horse I'm the rider for once!

CAPTAIN: You're the rider. And if you die on this ride?

MARK: I don't want to hear anymore about dying! You and Kruger! I'm trying to live! The biggest kind of living I can find!

CAPTAIN: *But if you die!*

MARK: Then I'll die, but I'll pull a star down with me when I do, and that's how I want to go! It's either this or the gutter for me, I'm not kidding myself anymore, and it won't be the gutter!

CAPTAIN: Mark, where will this end?

MARK: To hell with the end, I'm at the beginning. And a better beginning I never made, knowing that once I hit the sea I'm king of my life, riding my own daemon with the reins in *my* hands, bowing to none of the laws that small men make to make me small, knowing that I'm wearing out my life for my sake, *only mine*, and not to buy chops for some important punk with silver dollars in his ignorant eyes. You gotta crawl to live in this world; crawl to men who don't know what a rudder's for but own it just the same. Men whose perspiration falls on silk, who eat the bread you make and never know your name! Well I don't crawl, I like myself too much for that, and if blood spills on the water when this is done, blood never spilled for higher purpose,—that at least one guy might feel as tall and straight as he was made!

CAPTAIN: Mark, you are trying to build a fortress around yourself. You will end a very lonely man. I know. . . .

MARK: I am asking where you stand on this, Schulenberg, that's all.

CAPTAIN: I stand between you and this darkness. (*With a fear.*) You must find something to give yourself to, something that respects you, that is clean and not corrupt. . . .

MARK: What's clean? What's not corrupt? You're talking like. . . .

CAPTAIN (*with a rising, desperate resolution*): Something, that if it were hurt, you would be hurt. If it died, you would want to die with it.

MARK: And where is that? Where is that in this year!

CAPTAIN: I am that, Mark.

 (MARK *stops all movement, turns slowly to him; seems to be trying to pierce him.*)

We could be friends . . . good friends . . . we are the same . . . alone, alone in the rottenness.

MARK (*softly*): What does that mean, Schulenberg?

CAPTAIN: You are to me as a white column, an aspiring thing. You are to me as my country before it was defiled. . . .

MARK (*a horror rising in him*): I don't get it.

CAPTAIN: Mark, if you understood me you would respect me . . . (*Involuntarily moves away, nervously, with a very, very, slight limp.*)

MARK (*his voice trembling*): What will I understand?

CAPTAIN (*his hands moving; not looking at* MARK): I am not a monster! It is not an ugly thing. . . .

MARK (*his fists fly up*): Schulenberg!

CAPTAIN: It is not an. . . .

MARK: For Christ's sake!

CAPTAIN: Mark, you must try to understand!

MARK (*pause. He looks at nothing*): . . . Why I hated you and didn't know why. . . .

CAPTAIN: Mark. . . .

MARK: Why you trailed me around in every port . . . why my women made you puke. . . .

CAPTAIN: If you wouldn't lose your temper, I could. . . .

MARK: And this is what I'm supposed to live for?

CAPTAIN: Mark, please, listen to me. . . .

MARK: This is the only clean thing left? This is what I'll give myself to?

CAPTAIN (*tears come from his eyes*): If we could talk it over, we are reasonable people. . . .

MARK: What is there to talk? It is an ugly thing. It's a lousy, rotten, ugly thing. You're twisted around like a corkscrew. But not me. It's never going to twist me, it's me that does the twisting now! I'm going to take my piece of the world and bend it down till it kisses my feet, and I'll be my own temple and I'll make my own flag . . . !

CAPTAIN: No, Mark, you can't go through with this!

(*Enter* KRUGER.)

What do *you* want!

KRUGER: I'm sorry, sir. (*To* MARK.) The pier watchman says there is a young lady asking for you.

MARK: OK, thanks. (*To* CAPTAIN.) Then that's the last word?

CAPTAIN: I will not permit it, Mark. I don't know what I shall do, but this will never happen.

MARK: There can't be two masters on the bridge this trip.

CAPTAIN: There will be one master, Mark.

MARK: OK. (*He goes toward door.*) But I know who he's going to be.

CAPTAIN: He will not be you!

(MARK *goes out.*)

I will fight you, Mark!

(KRUGER *starts out after* MARK.)

Just a moment, Kruger. (*He walks left, wringing his hands.*) You don't try to change his mind?

KRUGER: I can do nothing with him, sir.

CAPTAIN: What's the matter, they beat you so much you have no heart left? You are dead now?

KRUGER: Yes . . . they beat me so much.

CAPTAIN (*trying to awaken him*): Did you ever see a ship go down, Kruger? Answer me.

KRUGER: Yes sir.

CAPTAIN: Did you ever sink a ship?

KRUGER: No sir.

CAPTAIN: No sir. Do you know what this does to a man to sink a ship?

KRUGER: I can't stop him, I can't!

CAPTAIN: You are going to stop him! You will accomplish this! Twenty four merchant ships I sent to the bottom in 1917! Do you see what he will become from this? (*Stands facing* KRUGER.) Look! Do you see!

    (KRUGER *silent.*)

    (*Rushes to cigarette box on shelf, pounds it again and again upon the shelf.*) This he will become! This, this! (*Stands breathing hard, looking as though at a vision.*) It screams . . . a ship can scream like an animal when she goes down . . . no . . . I will not see it again . . . he can't make me see it again!

KRUGER: If you would say to Luther you refuse to. . . .

CAPTAIN: I can refuse the Nazi nothing! But he can! And only you can make him do it! I took you on this ship because I had pity on you, but I have no more pity, there is nothing between us!

KRUGER: What do you mean, sir?

CAPTAIN: You will stop Donegal or I will tell Luther who you are.

KRUGER: No, you will never do it!

CAPTAIN: I swear to God I will tell him, Kruger!

KRUGER: He will take me back, they'll kill me there!

CAPTAIN: What good are you here! Make up your mind you are going to stop him . . . !

KRUGER: How, how! Is he a child that I can turn his mind around like. . . .

CAPTAIN: Yes! He is a child, a little lost boy to whom everything is a wonder, a little lost boy. There is too much good in him for this, he is too good!

KRUGER: I will try my best, Captain, but you cannot tell Luther. . . .

CAPTAIN: Hush! (*Goes quickly to right windows. Looking down outside.*) What is this woman to him?

KRUGER: They went together last night, I don't know.

CAPTAIN (*coming from window*): He likes her?

KRUGER: I suppose.

CAPTAIN (*silent a moment*): Stay with them in here. (*He goes left, toward his cabin.*)

KRUGER: And you will not mention me to Luther?

CAPTAIN (*at his door*): A man does what he has to do. Remember it, Kruger, what I said. You have little time.

(ANNA *and* MARK *are just appearing through the glass of the sliding door at right, as the* CAPTAIN *goes out right. Enter* MARK *and* ANNA. *She is talking as she comes on. She is excited, free-feeling, in a new place.* MARK *seems disquieted, although he smiles. It is as though what he has to say needs an* ANNA *prepared for disappointment and she is making it hard.*)

ANNA (*looking at everything as though it were brand new*): It's like the movies, everything is iron. What do you do in here?

MARK: This is the chart room . . . I want you to meet Kruger . . . this is Anna Walden, August.

ANNA: How do you do.

KRUGER (*a slight bow*): I am charmed to meet you, Miss Walden.

MARK (*going to cabinet at back*): Kruger's the best guy in the world. What'll you have?

ANNA: I'd feel better with my valise on the ship.

MARK: It's safe with the pier man. Have a scotch.

ANNA (*looking out right windows*): Are those what you call booms?

MARK (*going to her, looking out*): Yeh, that's what hoists up the cargo.

ANNA: And what's a jib boom?

MARK: No, that went out with Horace Greeley.

ANNA: And is there really such a thing as a poop deck, or is that a dirty joke?

MARK (*laughs with* KRUGER): Well it's the best place to tell a dirty joke, it's that raised deck at the back of the ship there. Come on, have a snort, it's a lousy day. (*He returns to cabinet, pours drinks.*)

ANNA (*to* KRUGER): Why don't you stop him from drinking so much?

MARK: He did. Gussy is a good influence.

ANNA: What's that in your hand, body-builder?

MARK (*to* KRUGER): Ain't she intelligent?! No kiddin'!

KRUGER: I think so, yes.

MARK: Anny, you got a first-class esprit de corps! Come on, a drop.

ANNA: No, it'll make me seasick. I feel funny already.

MARK (*his eyes caught by* KRUGER'*s*): No, you'll be all right, you'll . . . (*Stops. Turns back to cabinet.*)

ANNA (*seeing them looking at each other*): What's wrong?

MARK: Nothing, come on, let's tap the bottle. . . .

KRUGER (*to* ANNA): You can't sail on this ship. (*To* MARK.) What are you doing to her?

(ANNA *looks querulously at* MARK.)

MARK (*puts down his glass*): It's just this, Anna. . . .

ANNA: But you told me it was all right.

MARK: Well last night I was pretty sure I could work you in. . . .

ANNA: No, Mark, you said you were sure.

MARK: I meant it, but I've thought it over, see, and. . . .

KRUGER: He makes many promises, Miss Anna, and he means to keep them, but you must never trust this man.

MARK: Why do you talk that way, Kruger?

KRUGER: Who can speak with more experience than I? You love the human race, you don't know when to stop promising.

MARK: I don't like you to talk like that!

KRUGER: But it's true, Mark!

ANNA: It isn't true. (*To* MARK.) I'm going, isn't it so?

MARK: I'm going to help you out, see. . . .

ANNA: But there's only one way to help me. I've got to sail.

MARK: Please, you're going to sail, don't make a heel outa me. (*To* KRUGER.) And that goes for you. (*To* ANNA.) There's a ship on pier 8 sailing for Venezuela tonight.

ANNA (*with fear and impatience*): But I've only got thirty dollars, Mark, I told you that.

MARK (*taking out wallet*): Well, Jeeze, here's a hundred, and you sail in style.

ANNA (*suddenly nervous*): I don't want your money!

MARK: Come on, it's free. (*Takes her hand to put the money in.*)

ANNA (*pulling away from him*): I told you it's got to be this ship!

(*Pause.*)

MARK: But you didn't tell me why, and I want to know why.

ANNA: And I'd like to know why you suddenly won't take me.

MARK: Because I can't. This ship is rotten meat.

ANNA: "Sure, come on board tomorrow, kid, we'll fix you up. Don't worry, you're on your way."

MARK: Now look, you don't want any part of this ship, Anna!

ANNA: How do you know what I want? This ship is good enough for me.

MARK: Why, because you can't see any holes in it? Get outa here, Kruger, I got something private.

KRUGER: Why don't you tell her the truth.

MARK: There's gunguys out there . . . (*Points out back.*) . . . I don't want her in this!

KRUGER: Then why are you in this! (*Quickly, to* ANNA.) He is going out to raid a ship.

MARK: Kruger! (*Watches* ANNA.)

KRUGER: The *Bangkok Star* may never reach another port. Now. Maybe you can put some sense in his head. (*He pulls the door open and goes out.*)

ANNA (*softly, as though to herself*): Oh . . . I see.

MARK: I didn't tell you last night, so you would come back here today, because. . . .

ANNA: Because I've got something that belongs only to you.

MARK (*pause*): How did you know?

ANNA: You were drunk last night, Mark.

MARK: I had a feeling that I said something that I wanted to remember. Something I had to know. What is it, Anna?

ANNA: You said you were about to do something important.

MARK: No, something else.

ANNA: And that you were doing it, because . . . (*Stops.*)

MARK: What? Tell me, Anna?

ANNA: Because it was an important way to die.

MARK: I didn't say that!

ANNA: You did, Mark!

MARK: I didn't, I didn't, I never said such a thing!

ANNA: Then why are you so frightened?

MARK: Kruger told you to say that!

ANNA: How could he!

MARK: You saw him on the pier!

ANNA: Stop shouting at me!

MARK: No, it's not true, I never said that.

ANNA: Why isn't it true? Is there a noise you haven't heard, a flavor you haven't tasted, a woman you've wanted that you haven't had? Is there anything you believe in, and is there anything to believe anymore? Is there a soul who'd weep for you besides your silly mother and some drunken whores?

MARK: So what do you care? What're you getting mad for?

ANNA: Because you're the first decent guy I ever met! (*Goes from him, about to weep.*)

MARK (*goes to her*): Anna . . . (*puts hand in pocket*) . . . I want you to take this money. I want you to go from me.

ANNA: Why?

MARK: I got what I wanted from you: —You sized me up. Go on, I got a job to do.

ANNA: And if you didn't have? If you were coming back in a week?

MARK: I'd still send you away.

ANNA: Why, Mark?

MARK: I'm going to want you, Anna, and with a girl like you it's got to be forever.

ANNA: You kind of think I'd want you forever.

MARK: I'd make you want me, and when you did, I'd have to get out and see the colors of the world. Sooner or later I'm a guy who walks alone. Here. Take it. (*Offers her money.*)

ANNA: I told you, Mark. It's got to be this ship or none.

MARK: I don't get it, Anna, I don't get it at all.

ANNA: They'll want to see my passport . . . I won't know them. . . .

MARK: What are you running from?

ANNA (*goes from him quickly*): No, Mark. . . .

MARK: What's got you so scared!

ANNA: It's not what I'm running from that scares me now. I thought I was going *toward* something, a place, some place, where people weren't all so violent, so mean and small as the ones I knew. And when we talked last night I knew I was right, and there was such a place, and a person left who could still dream of cleaner years and a larger life,—and then you talked of dying,—*you, you*!

MARK: Go, will you? I don't want you here!

ANNA: It's these ships, this rushing from one place to another, looking for something you might have missed until there's nothing left to wonder about and you're ready for the grave!

MARK: No, you don't know what goes on in my head!

ANNA: Mark, there's a job for you somewhere, a life to live!

MARK: No, Anna, there's nothing but this. I gotta know that I can always pull out, pull away. I don't want to lock with anything, job, work, woman, because everything I ever pulled to my heart soured in a season, became a trap for me, a trap like everybody else is caught in, a trap I had to break every time, and broke the thing and the person that was holding me.

ANNA: And you're happy now? You're free now. Like the wind! You want to walk alone, you're alone now!

MARK: I'm afraid, Anna! There's no boundaries, no gauge, no rock under my feet, only me, me running wild like a river over flatland . . . Jeeze, I feel some times like I'm walking in a gas and I'm going to drop into a bottomless thing, and I want to reach out for center, for solid, for something that won't change!

ANNA: And if you touched a solid thing you'd pull your hand away.

MARK: Because I'm afraid what I catch on to will never let me go. And it'll pull me down into the life I can't stand, like the rest of the millions going round and round the mill like harnessed oxen, never knowing why they're alive, never seeing the thousand, thousand colors of the world! No, *I'm* going to weigh heavy on the scales, I'm going to leave a special print on the face of the earth, I'm going to know that I'm more than chemicals,—yeh, that I'm *Mark Donegal*, one of a kind doing a thing that even the wind will remember! Yeh, I'm going to rape that ship from bridge to keel . . . !

ANNA: Then what! What, Mark!

MARK: Then watch her blow when I give her the gun! Then I count my blood if I got any more! Then there's another day and another ship until there's no more days and I'm king of the world at the bottom of the sea, and I win! Now get off, will ya? I want to be clear and free for this, I don't want you around, you mix me up.

(*Pause.*)

ANNA: Mark, you're like a little boy. Everything in the world is there only for you to taste and try and drop when you're tired of it.

MARK: Y'know, there's one dream that keeps coming back since I was a kid. How I'm walking on an orbit way over the earth, I'm taller than towers, and the stars are like fruit that I taste in my mouth, and I walk on strings that play music under my feet, and the sky is full of thrones, and all of them are mine to sit on and look down where everything is small.

(*Pause.*)

ANNA: Goodbye, Mark.

MARK: Here . . . (*Gives her the money.*) Where will you go?

ANNA: How can you care?

MARK: I botched something up for you, didn't I.

ANNA: Sure you did. That's not new, is it?

MARK: Always that way. I drop a thing like a shell before it grows into my hand. See?

ANNA: Well, I didn't fall very far. (*Smiling.*) I guess it's good there wasn't time for you to lift me too high.

(*Enter* KRUGER, *hurrying.*)

KRUGER: Mark, Mark,—Doctor Luther is coming down the pier.

MARK: That's good, you better go, Anna.

KRUGER: That's good? You mean you're going through with this?

MARK: I'm sorry, August.

KRUGER: You're sorry! What happens to me? I don't exist? I am not a human being?

MARK: You shouldn't've trusted me! My promises are no good, you should've known that! I'm out for myself, you should've known!

KRUGER: And if they tear me to pieces because of you, you are still for yourself!?

MARK: What are you talking about?

KRUGER: Schulenberg tells Luther who I am unless you drop this thing!

MARK (*pause*): He told you that?

KRUGER: Yes, and he will do it, he's out of his head!

(*Pause.*)

MARK (*goes to back windows, looks down at pier*): I won't let him open his mouth if he comes in here.

KRUGER: How will you stop him?

MARK: I'll stop him! I won't let it happen!

KRUGER: Mark, for God's sake, you don't need this, there is still time, Mark!

MARK: Here's money, go ashore, leave the ship.

KRUGER: Where will I go! Where! I am not a citizen, I can't walk this country!

MARK: I can't take care of you, Kruger, here's money, take it!

KRUGER: No, Donegal, I will not take it. You are going to call this off, and because of me. This you made and this you will finish! For the first time in your life you will give up something you want for the sake of another person, and if you won't, then I shall know who killed me, Mark!

MARK: No, Kruger!

KRUGER: Let it lay on your head! You are building my scaffold, remember it, I will not forget! (*He rushes out.*)

MARK (*walks about looking down*): I'll get him out, see, I'll fix something up for him, I'll . . . (*Sees* ANNA.) You're crying. Why? I hurt you, heh? Did I hurt you, Anna!

ANNA: Mark, you're worth more than this.

MARK: Anna, I want to do something for you, what can I do?

ANNA: Take me somewhere, somewhere away.

MARK: Why are you running away? Tell me, Anna! Why! (*He grabs her.*)

ANNA: . . . There's a man who died, Mark. And I think I killed him.

MARK: What the hell are you talking about?

ANNA: They called it heart attack in the papers, but they know he was killed. But they don't say it because an important man is not supposed to look that way when he dies.

MARK: Who? What are you saying, Anna?

ANNA: I worked in the paper mill in Shawnee Springs, eight years. Last Christmas time they sent him down from Pittsburg with his wife . . . production . . . he was to work in the mill and learn production, before he took over for the company. Worked next to me, he was nice . . . he had blond hair . . . I let him drive me home after work . . . he talked so nice.

(*Pause.*)

One night he wouldn't stop in front of my house . . . went on to the lake . . . his face changed in the dark there . . . I jumped out and ran . . . he came after me like an animal and we fought on the rocks there and he fell on a grey stone and there was blood on me. I don't know if they're looking for me, Mark. But I want to get over the water to a place that's green . . . I want to start to live, Mark . . . I've been watching a wheel all my life . . . I'm not old, I want to live. I'm afraid they'll stop me on a strange ship and I want to go, I've got to go, Mark!

MARK: How would it be if . . . I could try to make a stop somewhere.

ANNA: Oh, Mark, you're a good man.

MARK: No there's just so many black hearts, that's all. Go on, get your valise and wait on deck . . . I'll set you down in Venezuela . . . hurry, somebody's coming up.

ANNA: And what about you?

MARK: Go on, go on!

ANNA (*takes his face in her hands*): Why must you go through with this? Maybe together, together we could. . . .

MARK (*bends slightly as though to kiss her*): No, no . . . I'll follow my star.

(*Enter* LUTHER.)

LUTHER: So sorry I'm late.

MARK: Glad to see you, Doctor. (*To* ANNA.) Go ahead, kid.
(*She looks at Doctor.*)

Go on.

LUTHER (*to* ANNA. *Sweetly, as to a child*): What is your name?
(ANNA *turns and goes out quickly.*)

(*Laughs.*) Oh, but she is a shy one!
(*Taking off his coat as* MARK *closes door.*)

Miserable day, isn't it.

MARK: Yeh, it's getting heavy.

LUTHER: I was just speaking with Mr. Bosch. You met him.

MARK: He's been on board all morning.

LUTHER: Was it fair of you to bring those sailors on board?

MARK: They're my friends.

LUTHER: I know, but I thought it was understood the extremely private nature of this thing.

MARK: So what?

LUTHER: You told them what you're doing?

MARK: I want them to sail with me.

LUTHER: Oh. They're willing to go along?

MARK: Well. . . .

LUTHER: They're willing?

MARK: Yeh, . . . yeh, they're all set.

LUTHER: Then that's different. (*Takes a leather folder from his coat, puts it on table.*) After all, a thing like this one does not want to become street gossip.

MARK (*as* LUTHER *unstraps folder*): Who am I talking to, Luther, am I talking to the boss?

LUTHER: You are talking to the boss, yes, on the gulf I am the boss. (*Indicating bedroom door.*) Anybody in there?

MARK: That's Schulenberg's cabin.

LUTHER: Pitiful old man, isn't he.

MARK: You'd better talk to him before you go.

LUTHER: Unnecessary. He does what he's told. (*Going to right windows.*) Well, on a ship like this one takes what one can get. (*Stands a moment glancing out window.*) How big a man are you, Donegal?

MARK: Big enough.

LUTHER: For instance, how much do you imagine is in this for you?

MARK: What are you doing, haggling?

LUTHER: Now wait, wait. You are very suspicious of me.

MARK (*smiles*): I never trust a fat man.

LUTHER (*laughs*): Why, there is something in avoirdupois that unnerves you?

MARK (*smiling*): No, through history the fat men have been the butchers, the guys who cut and ate what we sweated for in the woods. That goes back to the Babylonians.

LUTHER: Then I shall have to show you how big this is, Donegal, so you shall know I am not from the streets, so you shall know with whom you are dealing, with what sort of a mind. How much do you expect?

MARK: I don't sail if my share is under twenty five thousand dollars.

LUTHER: Good, that's very good. I like to hear you talk that way. Your share is forty thousand dollars.

(*Pause.*)

MARK (*his whole manner quickens*): That's all right, Luther.

LUTHER (*loudly, forcefully*): And this is only the start, this is very little!

MARK: Well let's get started, come on, talk.

LUTHER: So you realize I do not talk pennies.

MARK: No, that's a good score. Go on.

LUTHER (*looks at* MARK *a moment, then snaps his fingers, smiling with his teeth*): I think we can work together. (*Walks back to the window, leans on shelf.*) I know of a certain ship.

MARK: Yeh?

LUTHER: She is on her way from South Africa.

MARK: Yeh?

LUTHER: She is going to Buenos Aires.

MARK: Yeh?

LUTHER: She is armed. She carries uncut diamonds. (*Turns his head to* MARK.) One hundred and eighty five thousand dollars' worth of diamonds.

(MARK *walks left, his blood rushing.*)

You like that.

MARK: Go on, you got a wonderful style, you got me excited.

LUTHER: You proceed as follows. When you get to sea you mount your guns fore and aft. I will describe in detail the ship you will meet and her position. You board her. You go directly to her Master's cabin where you will find, on the righthand side of his bed, a steel safe in the wall. Force him to open it. In there is your stones. Can you do that?

MARK: Can you?

LUTHER: No.

MARK: That's why I need more than forty grand.

LUTHER: How much do you need?

MARK: Sixty.

LUTHER: On a condition.

MARK: What?

LUTHER: I have had a talk with your second and third mates. They are not right for this voyage. So I brought with me two men to replace them. Both crack gunners.

MARK: Who are they?

LUTHER: A Mr. Rocko and Mr. Bosch.

MARK: You don't trust me at all, do you.

LUTHER: That is not the question.

MARK: That is the question. We're equals in this Luther, I don't want a gun in my back.

LUTHER: Just for this voyage. They are my only guarantee, after all.

MARK: What do they know about sailing?

LUTHER: You will have to take care of that. If they could run a ship I would not need you. After all, this is business.

MARK: But to me it's not business. When I pull out of this port I want to be boss of these decks, nobody over me, but nobody.

LUTHER: They are *absolutely* under your command.

MARK: I mean I'm not working for you, Luther, I'm working with you, and I can't do that if you're going to be a picayune guy.

LUTHER: I understand positively, Mark! I would not want you otherwise. So your share is sixty thousand dollars.

MARK (*impatient suddenly*): All right. What's the name of the ship? Where do I find her? I want to get on the water right away.

LUTHER (*smiling*): I am very proud of myself.

MARK: Why?

LUTHER: I have extremely good judgement. Come here, please. (*Goes to table, takes a large chart from his folder, spreads it out.*) On the night of the sixteenth,—that is, night after tomorrow,—the ship you are to meet will pass this point. (*Draws circle on chart with a pencil.*) Nine hundred miles off the coast of Uruguay. One-thirty, Greenwich Mean Time.

MARK: What's the name of the ship?

LUTHER: Now, everything is agreed, I'm right?

MARK: Sure, what's her name?

LUTHER: And you sail at once.

MARK: I'm all set.

LUTHER: The name of the ship is the *Prince Haakon.*

MARK: That's swell.

LUTHER (*putting a calling card on table*): Meet me at this address in Valparaiso with the stones on the twenty fourth. I will be waiting with great. . . .

   (*Door to* CAPTAIN's *cabin, at left, opens.* CAPTAIN *comes out, his body tense and stiff like a man in great fear, almost terror, and yet . . . angry.*)

We did not call you, Captain.

CAPTAIN: I have a word to say.

LUTHER: You have nothing to say, now why don't you go inside? (LUTHER *moves toward him.*)

CAPTAIN: I am not afraid of you anymore.

LUTHER (*tries to laugh, and discern the meaning of the* CAPTAIN): Come now, we are not finished yet. (*He lifts his arm as though to turn the* CAPTAIN *back toward the cabin door.*)

CAPTAIN (*draws a pistol*): Don't touch me.

LUTHER (*to* MARK): What's happened to him?

MARK (*very worried, as though by one insane*): What's the trouble?

LUTHER: Come, put that away, Schulenberg.

CAPTAIN: I will put away what is to be put away, what must come out must come out.

LUTHER (*takes* MARK's *arm*): Come, we leave him. . . .

CAPTAIN: Stay where you are!

(*They stop moving. He takes a roll of bills from his pocket, holds them out to* MARK.)

Take this.

MARK: What is it?

CAPTAIN: Six hundred is yours, four hundred I give you. Take your friend and go to Brazil.

MARK: That don't interest me anymore.

CAPTAIN (*holding money out, looking at* LUTHER): Take it, I tell you!

MARK: No, that's little beans. Put it away.

CAPTAIN: I am telling you to take it from me!

(MARK *studies the* CAPTAIN *in silence.*)

LUTHER (*to* CAPTAIN, *smiling with slight relief*): Well? Now will you leave us?

CAPTAIN: Listen to what I say, Mark.

LUTHER: Don't you see he is not interested?

CAPTAIN: Doctor Luther owns sixty percent of the *Bangkok Star.*

(MARK *looks at* LUTHER.)

LUTHER (*laughs*): So this is a great secret?

CAPTAIN: Don't you move, Luther!

LUTHER (*a hidden viciousness rising in him, but restrained*): You're out of your mind, go to your cabin!

CAPTAIN: Forty percent is owned by Berlin.

LUTHER: This interests you, Donegal?

MARK: Why don't you let him talk?

LUTHER (*insulted*): I am a busy man, I can't stand here all day to hear this dope addict babbling nonsense! I am surprised at you even that you listen to him!

MARK: But I never knew you own this ship.

LUTHER (*laughs*): So what difference does it make? This is fantastic!

MARK: Well I don't know, Luther, I don't know yet.

LUTHER: Very well then. (*To* CAPTAIN.) Talk, grossvater, go grandpa-with-the-gun, talk! (*He marches away putting hands in pockets.*)

CAPTAIN: The *Prince Haakon* is a Nazi ship.

    (MARK *turns his head quickly to* LUTHER.)

LUTHER (*smiles. To* MARK): You seriously believe this idiot, this fool?—that *I* would send you against a German ship?

CAPTAIN: It is a German ship, the *Prince Haakon*!

LUTHER: I beg your pardon, she is Jugoslav. (*To* MARK.) And should you wish to prove she is Jugoslav, look into the registry for 1940 and you will find she is a Jugoslav ship.

CAPTAIN: But in 1941 she is German.

LUTHER: That is a lie!

CAPTAIN: They bought the *Prince Haakon*, you know it!

LUTHER (*frightened. To* MARK): You see, he is crazy, the man is out of . . . !

CAPTAIN: She's German, her captain is Albert Hofritz and I know this because August Kruger deserted the *Prince Haakon* in Valparaiso when the Nazis took her over! Yes, there is one or two things I can tell you, Herr Doctor!

    (LUTHER *dashes toward the right door.*)

      (*Calls out, "Bosch! Bosch!"*)

MARK (*grabs him by the coat, draws him up*): What're you trying to pull, you son of a bitch!

LUTHER: I am going to have him attended to! (*Tries to free himself.*)

MARK: You've got them waiting for us out there, haven't you!

LUTHER: Don't be a fool!

MARK: They got torpedos on the German ships, you're trying to send us under!

LUTHER: Why! Why! Have you lost your mind too!

    (*Enter* BOSCH *running.*)

CAPTAIN (*to* BOSCH): Put your hands up!

MARK (*stepping away from* LUTHER): No, no! I don't want any firing here. Put it away.

    (CAPTAIN *puts his gun in his pocket.*)

LUTHER: You must let me explain, Donegal.

MARK (*looking down*): Don't talk or I'll kick your head off!

LUTHER: But he says a lie!

MARK (*trying to collect his weeping mind*): Shut up, I said!

CAPTAIN: Get Kruger! Ask him if it's true!

MARK: Leave Kruger out of this! (*To* BOSCH.) Don't put your hand there.

> (BOSCH *moves his hand from his pocket.*)
>> (*Pause.*)

I'm leaving ship.

LUTHER: Now, please, just a minute.

MARK: You're crooked.

LUTHER: This . . . this addlebrain's word against mine is proof?

MARK: This fishhouse is worth thirty times more on the bottom than afloat. You own sixty percent. Berlin needs dollars. That's enough for me, when you took my two mates off because they wouldn't take the line of bull that I took.

LUTHER: And what about Mr. Bosch here? And Mr. Rocko on deck. They would sail out with you if they were to die at it?

MARK (*pause. He turns to* BOSCH. *Walks toward him*): I don't know. Maybe . . . maybe these guys were supposed to get off in time.

> (LUTHER *suddenly has a gun in his hand, as he dashes at the* CAPTAIN *and rips the latter's pistol from his pocket.* MARK *turns quickly to* LUTHER *who is pointing his gun at him.*)

LUTHER: Yes. That's right. Don't try anything. You can't get off the ship.

> (MARK *involuntarily, blindly, goes toward* LUTHER *raising his fists.*)

Don't move!

> (MARK *stops, his fists raised, bursting with anger at this symbol of all he hates.*)

Don't move, I said. Now . . .

> (*He starts to turn to* CAPTAIN, *as* ANNA *enters quickly.*)

ANNA (MARK *wheels about to her*): That Nelson wants to get off and they won't . . . (*She sees the gun in* LUTHER'*s hand.*)

LUTHER: Come in here, please.

> (BOSCH *steps between her and the door, closes it. She moves in, struck dumb, staring at the gun.*)

MARK (*turns quickly from her to* LUTHER): She's got to get off.

LUTHER: I did not bring her on.

MARK (*roaring, as though at a pattern which has enveloped his life from the beginning*): No, she's got to get off, I'll tear the walls down, she's got to get off!

(*He grabs her hand and starts pulling her toward the door.* BOSCH, *who is standing there, draws his gun.* MARK *and* ANNA *stop.*)

LUTHER: You have too many friends. And I will not be hanged by their tongues. (*To* CAPTAIN.) Come to the bridge. You are pulling the ship out. Come.

(CAPTAIN *walks toward door,* LUTHER *behind him with a gun in his back.*)

(*At doorway, to* MARK.) I will be with you for a while. Until you pass through the inspection at the mouth of the river. I shall draw up the papers for the young lady. (*To* SCHULEN-BERG.) Go on, make ready to sail.

(LUTHER, CAPTAIN *go out, followed by* BOSCH, *closing the door after him.* MARK *and* ANNA *stand watching the door for a moment. He turns and looks at her, pause.*)

MARK: See, it was all so I would take her out and they'd sink her under me . . . and that Rocko and Bosch'd jump before the blow . . . (*He stops, realizing he has been talking to himself. Now he* sees ANNA. *Smiles.*) You're scared, heh?

ANNA: I don't know.

MARK (*with terrible vigor, clasping her shoulders*): Never, kid! This is Mark Donegal. I always get out, look at the scars! The Houdini of the freights, I been in more trouble than the Jews! (*Laughs loudly.*) I'm gettin' you off, Anna, come on, we'll tap out the bottle and you're on your way! (*Goes, as on dancing feet to chest at back.*)

ANNA (*as he pours drinks*): You're . . . you're happy! (*A laugh escapes her.*)

MARK: Anny, for Christ's sake, this is when you're alive! Here . . . (*Puts glass in her hand.*) . . . when your blood starts pumpin'! . . . go on, pour it in! (*Gulps his drink.*)

(ANNA *lifts her glass uncertainly.*)

Go on, go on! (*Swings about the room.*) Sure, my number's been up three times,—a hundred and two miles an hour in a Packard twelve, soft shoulder, right over the bank . . . I'm quite a driver, Anna!

ANNA (*as though she must keep something from falling*): I'll bet you are! (*A short burst of laughter.*)

MARK (*his voice and manner rising to proportions of a declaration*): Owned thirty one cars! Sold them all for junk! Jeeze, Anna, you're lookin' pink in the cheeks!

ANNA (*a growing wildness in her. Laughing*): What are you thinking of! What's in your head now?

MARK: Jeeze, like sparks, Anna, like rivers!—all the ways to get you out, a million ways! Anny, girl, I feel so big I'll bust this ship out at the seams! Here, have a smoke, you're on your way. Havana cigarettes!

ANNA: I thought they only made cigars! (*Takes one, laughing.*)

MARK: That's because you don't know Cuba!

(*As he lights a match for her, the ship's whistle suddenly roars. They are both frozen. It keeps blasting without letup. The match drops from MARK's hand. The whistle continues. His head bends over as though he were being beaten. The whistle stops. They do not move.*)

(*Deeply, like a rumble.*) Everything I ever touched. . . .

ANNA (*with the fear of the thing about to fall*): Don't say that, Mark.

MARK: Everything, *everything I ever touched*!

ANNA: You didn't bring me here, I came myself!

MARK: No, no, Anna! I'm a punk, I'm a punk don't you see it!

ANNA: Stop talking! Stop it now!

MARK: Now it's all spilling down, down, down, like a sewer on top of my head! I got a trail of broken people behind me as long as this river . . . !

ANNA: Mark, stop it!

MARK: Never stuck on the downgrade, always run, Donny, run, follow your star! You're a special guy, outside the rules, stay outa harness, man, woman, child out of his way, this is Donny comin', special guy! The world is his apple, he's one in ten billion . . . !

ANNA: I don't care, Mark, I don't care!

MARK: I look good to you, heh, strong, handsome, wonderful smile, got an answer to everything, yeh . . . in the North there's a girl with a kid of mine! Got outa that too, got outa everything, run, Donny, run! Everybody suffered so I could swallow the world, my mother, father, a thousand people around the globe, but not you, Anna, not you, Anna, you're gonna get off! (*He rushes to a drawer in the left wall, pulls it open.*)

ANNA (*rushing to him*): What are you doing!

MARK (*wildly searching in the drawer*): Let me alone, I had a gun here!

ANNA: Then it's not there, that's all!

MARK (*ramming things around in the drawer*): I had a gun, a gun, dammit . . . !

ANNA: Stop it, Mark, please, stop it!

MARK (*faces her, weeping*): You wait here, I'll get you off! (*He goes toward the door.*)

ANNA (*rushing after him*): They'll kill you! (*She blocks his way at the door.*)

MARK: You think I can't swing it, heh? Big blowoff, heh! (*He starts to pull her from the door.*)

ANNA: I don't want to get off!

(*Silence.*)

Even if they let me off . . . if they told me to go.

MARK: Anna . . . I got you crazy . . . I'm a bad apple. . . .

ANNA: I know what you are, Mark, and I'm not ashamed of you.

MARK: No, there's a chance for you. . . .

ANNA: I can't go back . . . I want to go with you, Mark.

MARK: I'll be under water in two days! You want a green place, you want to live, Anna!

ANNA: I want to go with you . . . and leave it gladly behind. Two days is long enough when you've got what you want . . . and it's really forever. (*She smiles.*)

MARK (*a smile breaks on his face*): I . . . I suddenly don't feel scared of that word,—forever.

ANNA (*comes closer to him*): And you'll tell me all about the stars, like you said you would, and ships and all the things. . . .

MARK: Oh, God, Anna, the ocean sky'll make you weep when you see it! You'll cry like a baby, I tell ya!

ANNA: And we'll ride like two people from the sea—like people going home!

(*The ship's whistle roars. He pulls her to him frantically, they sway with the noise.*)

(*The whistle stops. They stand embraced.*)

MARK: Yeh, I know you, Anna, I knew you all the time . . . all my life. Under the bridge with the wings tearing; a hundred and two miles an hour when the sky turned over; when we piled up on Hatteras; when they came for me with knives in the Shanghai bar,—wherever I lay with my blood running out, your face . . . ! (*He kisses her hard.*)

ANNA: How will it be, Mark!—tell me how it'll be that night!

MARK: There'll be stars, maybe, and the black sea slick as a seal, and the engines stroking like a heart under you, and we'll stand the bridge drunk in the belly of the night, and shells come across the water like fiery stars and the cool salt rises to your lips and we sleep, kid, out of the two-penny, put-and-take world, the rich and the poor, the hangmen and the hanged . . . we'll sleep, Anna!

ANNA: Mark . . . love me, Mark!

MARK: Make it true, what it is, don't cry! Now everything is true . . . come, come. . . .

(*They go to the door of* CAPTAIN*'s bedroom.*)

ANNA: Mark. . . .

MARK (*pulls her quickly into his arms*): I'm gonna take you, Anna!

(*He presses her against the door jamb, his mouth to hers. He opens the door and they go through and the door shuts. The sound of the engines thumping. Then from the room comes a strange, soft, and yet piercing jazz tune. Another blast of the ship's whistle. It stops. The sound of engines quickens. Through the back windows the line of the pier-roof recedes, another short blast of the whistle, then only engines thumping and over them the music.*)

SLOW CURTAIN

ACT THREE

SCENE I

The same night, about twelve. This is the pilot house, situated just forward of the chart room of Act Two. The left wall is the windshield, an unbroken series of windows looking toward the bow. The back wall is not wide, contains windows, and is broken by a sliding door. The right wall is solid,—(on the other side of it is the chart room). A few feet toward the center from this wall, is the wheel, and before it is a hip-high column topped by a convex lens under which floats the compass. There are no chairs but a high stool which is tucked under a shelf in the upper right, back, corner. On this shelf is a small wooden box. As before, we can discern the roof of the pier through the windows and door in the back wall. When the door is opened, we can see the flying bridge running straight out to the port side of the ship. There are ladder-stairs running down from this bridge to the decks, one set going forward, another toward aft, but these are not seen.

On the rise, the room is dark but for the meager night-light filtering through the windows. Softly, jazz music is coming through the right wall. At the moment, CAPTAIN SCHULENBERG *is leaning against a window, smoking rapidly. He moves now, restlessly, the smoke pouring from his nostrils. He goes to the compass-column, turns a switch on it, a green light issues from beneath the lens lighting his drawn face. He takes a revolver from his jacket pocket, throws out the cartridge chamber, examines it, throws it into place, puts gun back into his pocket; takes a second gun from his shoulder holster, does the same, replaces it as he moves restlessly about the room again, smoking. He goes to the box on the shelf, takes out a flashlight and searches for something in the box, finds a key, goes to the door, pulls it tight, locks it from the inside, tests it to see if it will hold as* BOSCH *appears outside the door.* CAPTAIN *fumbles opening the lock,* BOSCH *knocks on the door, finally* CAPTAIN *gets the lock open,* BOSCH *pulls door wide, steps in, curious. . . .*

CAPTAIN (*nervously*): Hello, I merely. . . .

BOSCH: Why are you locking it on the inside?

CAPTAIN: I . . . the lock is rusty . . . what is it?

BOSCH (*watches him a moment*): You know what you're doing, don't you?

(KRUGER *appears behind* BOSCH *in the door, knocks.*)

CAPTAIN: Ja?

KRUGER (*coming in*): It's almost midnight, Captain.

CAPTAIN: Yes, make ready, go to. . . .

BOSCH: That's what I came up to tell you. You're waiting a few minutes.

CAPTAIN: Why? The schedule is midnight.

BOSCH: That's new orders. Just wait. (*Starts to go.*)

CAPTAIN: Something happened wrong?

BOSCH: Wait. You'll sail soon enough. (BOSCH *goes out.*)

KRUGER: Well, I suppose I'll . . . (*Moves to go.*)

CAPTAIN (*walking nervously from him*): Just a moment, please. (*Stands with back to* KRUGER.)

KRUGER (*stops . . . waits*): Yes, sir?

CAPTAIN: Close the door.

KRUGER (*closes door: waits*): Captain?

CAPTAIN (*a quick cry*): Just a moment, please!

KRUGER (*softly*): I'm sorry, sir.

CAPTAIN (*goes to window, not facing* KRUGER): You know something about guns?

KRUGER (*slight pause*): . . . A little, yes.

CAPTAIN (*quickly turns, goes to compass, takes revolver from side pocket, holds it over green light*): I am having trouble with this hammer spring, she sticks.

(*Pause. He looks up at* KRUGER, *from gun.*)

KRUGER (*reaching for gun*): Sometimes a little oil loosens them up, I could maybe. . . .

(CAPTAIN *has imperceptibly turned muzzle of the gun to* KRUGER.)

(*Looks up at* CAPTAIN *slowly.*) What . . . what is . . . ?

CAPTAIN: I told you something before, didn't I?

KRUGER: You're not serious. . . .

CAPTAIN: Get that girl off the ship before we sail.

KRUGER: How, how can I do . . . ?

CAPTAIN: This is a good German gun, Kruger. Get her off the ship.

KRUGER: They're watching us from the pier. Nobody can get off.

CAPTAIN (*pushes gun into him*): I will give you this!

KRUGER: Will you listen, please! If I could get her off, and you did sail with him alone. . . .

CAPTAIN: Then . . . then I will be happy.

KRUGER: No. . . .

CAPTAIN: Nobody can tell me . . . !

KRUGER: He will never turn from her to . . . to. . . .

CAPTAIN: To me, yes, he will turn to me, he will understand what I am, I will tell him in clear words and he will find a place for me . . . !

KRUGER: He'll kill when he finds out . . . !

CAPTAIN: You will not make a filthy thing of this!

KRUGER: I only tell you what I know.

CAPTAIN (*wildly*): He will take from me what I have to give, what there is no country left to take, what there is no god to take . . . I can't wait any longer!

KRUGER: Listen!—they've turned the radio off. (*Points right.*)

CAPTAIN: Go, go . . . (*points right*) . . . he'll be coming in here to sail, I'll keep him here.

KRUGER: Captain, it's impossible. . . .

CAPTAIN: You recognize this gun, it's his . . . ! (*Quickly takes out another.*) . . . there is no others on board! . . . I have these guns myself! . . . I have everything here! . . . everything here! (*Slaps his pocket as he puts gun away.*)

KRUGER: I see, I see, ja . . . all right, sir, I do my best. . . .

CAPTAIN (*suddenly kind*): Yes . . . you're a fine fellow, you can do. There is something very strong and fine in you, Kruger . . . go, please do this thing. We are all lost, we must do what we can. It's dangerous times, we must do what we can. Get her off.

> (*He looks at his hands.* KRUGER *goes out.* CAPTAIN *lights another cigarette, the flame shaking. He walks about again at a more rapid pace.* BOSCH *comes in leading* KRUGER *by the arm. Once in the room, he switches a flashlight into* KRUGER'*s face, studies it . . .*)

BOSCH (*releasing him*): Go on.

> (KRUGER *stands looking at* BOSCH.)

Go on.

> (KRUGER *goes out.*)

(*To* CAPTAIN.) What do you know about him?

CAPTAIN: . . . Kruger . . . that's August Kruger. . . .

BOSCH: You know him how long?

CAPTAIN: Long? Nine months, more. . . .

BOSCH: I don't like you this way.

CAPTAIN (*tries to laugh*): Well, we must choose our friends. . . .

BOSCH: You've got a job to do, you're going to do it, aren't you?

CAPTAIN (*flying up*): I do what I promise, I do . . . !

BOSCH: You're smoking too much. That stuff makes you crazy.

CAPTAIN (*crying out*): Don't talk to me like that!

BOSCH: Tell me your instructions.

CAPTAIN: . . . I sail for Valparaiso. . . .

BOSCH: And in the middle of the Gulf?

CAPTAIN: I . . . I know, leave Donegal to me, please.

BOSCH: Remember it. He dies with the girl. I don't want to have to do it myself. Nothing happens till we're half across the Gulf. We don't want any trouble in this port.

(*Pause.*)

You sail shortly.

(BOSCH *turns militarily, gets to door as* MARK, ANNA, *and* KRUGER *come in.*)

MARK (*wide smile*): Oh you, I forgot all about you.

BOSCH (*smiles*): Might as well, we won't be in each other's way.

MARK (*wide smile*): What're you hatchin' in here?

BOSCH: I was just telling the Captain. . . .

MARK: That's your trouble, this is the pilot house, your nose don't belong in here.

BOSCH: I beg your pardon. I told the Captain we will be delayed a few minutes.

MARK: You're running the whole aquarium, eh?

BOSCH: I wouldn't talk like that. . . .

MARK (*sharply*): I don't want you giving him (*Captain*) orders in here! I'm a very temperamental navigator, Mr. Bosch.

BOSCH: We may as well be civil.

MARK: Yeh, my birthday this week, don't forget me.

BOSCH (*loudly*): Be sure, I never forget! (*To* CAPTAIN.) I'll tell you when to sail. (BOSCH *goes out.*)

MARK (*pulling door shut*): You're takin' an awful lot of crap from that pig.

CAPTAIN: . . . These times we do what we can. . . .

MARK: You're not feeling well, Captain.

CAPTAIN: I have a little cough. . . .

MARK (*linking* ANNA*'s arm*): I want you to meet all the wisdom in the world.

>   (CAPTAIN *gives a high, short laugh.*)

ANNA: Oh, Mark, now. . . .

MARK: No, wait, Anna, you don't get me. (*To* CAPTAIN.) I want you to shake her hand, Captain . . . (*as he links their hands*) . . . go on, Schulenberg. . . .

CAPTAIN: . . . I think we met. . . .

>   (*Laughs. Drops her hand.*)

MARK (*taking* ANNA *around*): We're gonna kiss you goodbye, Captain. You're droppin' us off on the Florida Keys. I'm leaving the ship there.

>   (*Pause.*)

CAPTAIN: You're leaving the ship.

ANNA: He knows a wonderful house to live in. . . .

MARK: Kruger remembers . . . The place with the windows, Gussy. . . .

ANNA (*to* KRUGER): He tells me it's cheap, is it?

KRUGER: Oh, yes, yes. . . .

MARK: No Name Key, remember, August? You know the island, Captain, no name, we're gonna baptise the place in the name of Anna Walden and the Holy Ghost. Wish us luck, for God's sake. . . .

CAPTAIN (*swiftly to door*): Excuse me, please. . . .

MARK (*hurriedly stops him, speaks close to his face*): Nonono. . . .

CAPTAIN: I must go out. . . .

MARK: No, we're gonna do it sweetly, Captain.

CAPTAIN: Let me out!

MARK: What's that in your eyes?

>   (*Pause.*)

> We're headin' for the Keys: Don't tell Rocko and Bosch.

CAPTAIN (*avoiding* MARK*'s eyes*): I've got to go on deck.

MARK (*to* KRUGER *and* CAPTAIN): What the hell happened in here!

>   (*Silence.*)

CAPTAIN (*suddenly goes to door*): I'm going on deck. . . .

MARK (*stops him*): You're stoppin' at the Keys, I'm gettin' off with Anna. Don't let Rocko and Bosch know.

CAPTAIN: You're getting off; I understand.

MARK: That's right, Schulenberg. We're gonna live in a decent house. I say this on a rusty ship, this is not the end of my life. (*Points to* ANNA.) My woman . . . she takes me away.

CAPTAIN (*nods*): Yes.

MARK: Be nice to us, heh, Schulenberg? I couldn't live to see this botched. This is gotta work out immaculate, heh?

CAPTAIN: Yes, it will work out fine . . . fine. (*To* KRUGER.) Attend to what you have to do, Mr. Kruger. We don't have much time before sailing. (CAPTAIN *goes out.*)

ANNA: Mark!—how nicely you told him!

MARK: Wait'll you see the place, kid, ask Gussy. . . .

KRUGER: Mark. . . .

MARK: . . . the Gulf Stream runs right past your nose, there's schools of tarpon knockin' on the kitchen door . . . ask him . . . Gussy, she don't believe me. . . .

ANNA (*to* KRUGER. *Laughing*): He's out of his head!

MARK: Tell her about the sixteen-foot boat we could've bought for nineteen bucks . . . !

KRUGER: Mark, this is a fine woman, what are you doing!

MARK: Jesus, that's a swell congratulations, Gussy!

KRUGER (*to* ANNA): You don't know this man, believe me!

MARK: What don't she know!—I love this girl, Kruger, forever, all the time,—you don't know what I'm talkin' about, you don't know me anymore, I'm a different guy!

KRUGER: You will do terrible things to her, you won't stick, you'll be on a ship again in sixty days and you know it!

MARK: All right, that's all!

KRUGER (*to* ANNA): Please!

MARK: All right, Gussy, that's all!

KRUGER: For God's sake if you love this girl get her off the ship!

MARK (*takes* ANNA's *hand*): Don't listen to him, kid. We're gonna live like crown princes on the Keys, we're gonna. . . .

KRUGER: You will not live to cross the Gulf of Mexico!

MARK (*turns quickly to him*): What'd you say, August?
(*Silence.*)

KRUGER: Everything is planned. Rocko and Bosch have orders to kill both of you in the middle of the Gulf.

MARK (*with terror*): You're blowing your top. . . .

KRUGER: In twelve hours you will die with her. . . .

ANNA: What is he talking about, what did he say?

MARK (*points to* ANNA, *stunned*): Kruger . . . did you understand what I told you!

KRUGER: I don't stand between you, Mark.

MARK: Goddammit, Kruger, do you know what's come over me!

KRUGER: It is too late for that, Mark. Get her off.

(*Slight pause.*)

MARK: I knew it . . . I knew it. . . .

ANNA: What, I don't understand! Who wants to kill you? (*To* KRUGER.) What are you talking about?

KRUGER: Sssh! (*To* MARK.) I'll bring up the American seamen. I know a way to get her off with them.

ANNA: Go away, leave us alone . . . !

KRUGER: Don't let them sail yet. I'll be right up with the men.

ANNA: Don't bother, I'm not getting off . . . Mark, tell him.

MARK (*almost weeping*): Oh, Christ, kid!

(KRUGER *goes out, shutting door.*)

ANNA: Mark . . . turn your face to me. You're not sending me off. . . .

MARK: Yes.

ANNA: But why?

MARK: Because the world don't allow this to go on. Because I did a crime against you, and you against me. . . .

ANNA: What? What?

MARK: We fell in love, sister, and this is no year for lovers. We took it for granted . . . in the dark there, in your arms there . . . that we're meant to move on, to move upward. . . .

ANNA: We are. . . .

MARK: It's not so, Anna, and you made me forget with your voice in the dark you made me forget what the world looks like, but you can't change what it is . . . look out the window Anna, there's our future, the man with the gun!

ANNA: I don't care. You could come with me . . . off the ship . . . come, we'll go together!

MARK: No, wherever I am they'll find me and I don't want you there when they do!

ANNA: I'm not going without you, Mark!

MARK: I dug my own grave, what're you jumpin' in on top of me for!

ANNA: What grave? Mark, we're young, we've got a right to live!

MARK: I tell you go, there's a hand on my shoulder!

ANNA: How you talked there in the dark!—how we were going to live!—and how you lied!

MARK: Never, Anna, never to you! But the stories people make up lying in the dark don't move one pebble in the world!

ANNA: They do, they must! It can't be that we're built for the grave. . . .

MARK: What then! Are we precious to the world, are we ships that gotta be rolled and rivetted and glued before they're done? We're people, Anna, more numerous than pins, the cheapest thing in the world!

ANNA: I love you, Mark, for that we're not cheap!

MARK (*points through window at pier*): Tell them down there that we're not cheap!—you'll get a bullet in your face!
(*Pause.*)

ANNA: Then I'd rather get it like that, telling them I'm human, than to say, "Come on, world, strike me down, I'll be obedient, I'll die like a cow!" Who should pity us if the first thing we're ready to do when there's trouble, is give up our lives? All right, the world pushes you to the grave; all right, it's hard to fight death, I know. Then the world has got to be changed, Mark! It's got to be changed so we can live, and if you've gotta die, then die changing it!

MARK: Change! Anna, child, this is not from yesterday or the year before. Walk in the countries, go up the Yangtze-Kian river, whole families living on those junks, you throw your slop overboard and they scoop it out of the slimy river with nets, eat it wet, every ten minutes a dead man floats downstream! I've seen families roaming the streets in Naples all night carrying crosses, looking for a hole to sleep in! The rats feed on children in the Glasgow slums, in India the mother cracks her baby's joints so he'll make a good beggar! Men have dropped dead on the decks of this ship under the African sun, and they walked right over them all day loading the ship!—that's what people are worth, Anna, East and West, and we can't walk off the compass!—(*Turns.*)—go with Kruger, will ya, I'm gonna cry.

ANNA (*pause. She is weeping*): You're such a little guy, Donegal.

MARK (*laughs, tears in his eyes*): Yeh, kid, you got my size. I'm a nice guy though, ain't I?

ANNA (*softly, weeping*): Afraid of anything but storms.

MARK: Anna . . . you're holding my heart in your hands this minute. . . . I want to tell you something. I had a thousand women under me in my time, but every minute of my life except tonight, I've been alone. Twenty two years I've been running over the world from one noise to the next, searching, searching for what I didn't know . . . and tonight I know. We're built with half a bridge sticking out of our hearts, looking for the other half that fits so we can cross over into someone else, so we can give ourselves and say . . . all the things. But it's too late now, Anna, I had all my changes, my number's up, and all I'll ever give you is a lotta tears.

ANNA: I saw a life altogether under the open sun, giving children to the world. . . .

MARK: We can't fight this future, Anna, and I don't want to see you cry. Go on, kid, and when I'm telling the fish what a woman is, believe it, she'll be you. Go with Kruger. . . .

ANNA: Where? Where will I go?

MARK: I won't drag you down, Anna, not you.

ANNA: Somebody's coming . . . Mark. . . .

MARK: Go, please. We called for the wrong century.

(*Enter* KRUGER *with* DINNY, CARROL, NELSON. DINNY *enters last, looks fore and aft before closing door behind him.*)

KRUGER: Well? We decided something? (*Smiles.*)

MARK (*looking at* ANNA): The lady wants to get off.

KRUGER: Very sensible, Miss. The first thing. . . .

MARK: What're you gonna do, Kruger?

KRUGER (*to* ANNA): You are not afraid of water, are you? It's quite safe.

ANNA: I . . . (*Looks at* MARK.)

MARK (*to* KRUGER): What water?

KRUGER: Carrol, will you stand there, see if somebody comes.

(CARROL *goes to door, looks out. To* ANNA.)

In the very aft of the ship, you see, there is a shaft that turns the rudder. This goes through the stern and there is a steel collar around it which I will take off and this leaves you an open circle, so big, a few feet above the water. . . .

MARK: They'll see from the pier. . . .

KRUGER: No, we're loaded down, that hole is under the line of the pier. So we lower her down with a rope, the boys too, and they swim eight ten yards to the piles under the pier, and then they can creep underneath a whole block, and they're away, they can go.

(ANNA *looks at* MARK.)

MARK: Can you do that?

(ANNA *is silent.*)

(*Pause.*)

. . . All right, August.

(MARK *and* ANNA *stand looking at each other.*)

KRUGER: Fine. You better stay here so they don't turn over the engines, we'll be right above the propeller. (*To* ANNA.) Well? Shall we go?

ANNA (*slowly extends hand*): Goodbye, Donegal.

MARK: 'Bye, Walden . . . (*Smiles.*) If it's cold tomorrow I'll blow you a warm wind.

KRUGER (*pulls door open,* ANNA *goes to it*): Be quiet, please, we go down the starboard side.

(*She hesitates a moment, then goes with* KRUGER.)

CARROL (*as he leaves*): Some day, Donegal, I'm gonna figure this out.

NELSON: Sorry you're not coming, Mr. Donegal.

(CARROL *goes out.*)

MARK: Next time, Nelly; thanks for the help.

NELSON: 'Bye. (*He goes.*)

DENNIS: Well, it's the first time anyway I ever made egress from a ship through her hind quarters!

MARK: See she gets away all right, heh?

DENNIS: Gets away!—feller, I'll see she enters the city in triumph!

MARK: Get goin', this is no picnic.

DENNIS: Oh, don't let Dennis fool ya, now, I'm not as happy as I might appear. See you again, Mark.

MARK (*nods.* DENNIS *goes.* MARK *is left . . . nodding. He looks about him, and nods. He goes to the tubes, whistles down . . .*): Donegal . . . yeh, don't turn over the engines unless I give you the word . . . Remember, Dino, only me . . . there's repairs going on over the screw . . . (*Puts ear to tube.*) Any minute, just keep awake, I'll push your face in if you let anybody tell you to turn 'em over . . . (*Puts ear to tube.*) OK, Dino, be a good boy I'll read your palm. . . .

(DOCTOR LUTHER *appears in the doorway flanked by* ROCKO *and* BOSCH. MARK *rises from the tubes, turns, is startled by them . . .*)

Well what d'ya know, the native returns. Come on in.

(LUTHER *comes in with* ROCKO *and* BOSCH . . . *looks about gravely.*)

Don't look, I stole everything the first week.

LUTHER (*stops movement*): I want some information.

MARK: Sure, where do you wanna get to?

LUTHER (*with deep force*): Where is August Kruger?

(MARK *is silent.*)

Come, please, where is this man?

MARK: I got him in my other suit.

LUTHER: You will save me time. . . .

MARK: Why does he interest you?

LUTHER: Don't play with me, please, it's enough you. . . .

MARK: I'm on the line, Luther, what do you want with him?

LUTHER: You knew his name was not Kruger! . . . you knew this all the time!

(*Pause.*)

MARK: Not . . . Kruger?

LUTHER: Very well. (*Turns to go, angrily.*) (*To* BOSCH.) Come, we'll have to look. . . .

MARK: No . . . (*Goes to him.*) What's your hurry? Give me the dope, maybe I don't like him either.

LUTHER: August Kruger is Manfried Seibert.

MARK: Which is zero to me.

LUTHER: We have been searching for him nineteen months. A very clever thing for him to do, sailing on my ship.

MARK: What happens when you find him?

LUTHER: They would like to talk to him in Europe. (*He starts to go.*)

MARK: Now wait, will ya? Maybe I know where he is.

LUTHER (*turns back to him*): Yes?

MARK: Just make me sure you got the right boy.

LUTHER: He has changed his hair, his nose is straight now and he walks different without the limp, but one thing he can never change. His right eye is blind. He's coming with me, where can I find him?

(*Pause.*)

MARK (*points left*): Go forward to the prow of the ship, there's a locker in the foc'sle. He's in there painting.

LUTHER: I thank you. (*Stops at door, half-turns.*) Where is your young lady?

MARK: Playing badminton on the poop deck, why?

LUTHER: Very pretty girl.

MARK (*goes to him, smiling very wide, raising his fists, assuming a boxer's crouch . . .*): Sometime we gotta do a round together, Uncle.

LUTHER (*backs off nervously . . . laughing*): Ja . . . !

MARK (*sparring with him, wide smile*): Yeh, I'd like to bounce the bloomers off you. . . .

(*They laugh.*)

. . . Nice to hit guys like you in the belly, sounds like a watermelon.

LUTHER (*laughing*): Well, I've got to go. . . . (*Watching* MARK *closely, laughing.*)

MARK: Yeh . . . ever kill a man, Luther?

(LUTHER, *his smile lessens, but is still there.*)

I did. Terrible temper. We were walking over the Seine River, Paris, France . . . I pushed him . . . he never came up.

(*They stand opposite each other a moment.*)

LUTHER: You sail . . . in five minutes.

(LUTHER *quickly goes out, followed by* BOSCH *and* ROCKO.)

(MARK *waits a second, goes quickly to tubes . . .*)

MARK: Dino! Donegal. Wake up! Keep her hot but don't turn a valve till you hear my voice or I'll stuff you down a scupper. Hold ship till you hear from Donegal! (*Listens.*) OK, boy, I'll buy you a second-hand cigar! (*Goes to door, walks out, looks left toward bow where* LUTHER *went, then dashes away right as* the lights go down.)

SCENE 2

We see this scene by little more than flashlights. We are inside the curve of the stern . . . on the right side of the stage a steel shell bellying out and upward.

KRUGER *and* CARROL, *wrenches in hand, are on their knees rapidly unbolting a collar,—size of a manhole cover,—from around the base of a shaft which shoots up above their heads and into darkness.* DENNIS *holds a flashlight by which they work;* NELSON *stands close by holding other great wrenches.* ANNA *is farthest left, closest to the blackness of the rest of the stage. A coil of rope is on the floor.*

As the light goes up, KRUGER *is pulling on a stubborn nut while* CARROL *is tapping his wrench to turn it.* ANNA *keeps walking up and downstage a few paces, always glancing toward the darkness at left. The group is very compact in a small playing area. . . .*

KRUGER (*to* CARROL): All right, that's enough. (*Tries to pull nut, can't move it.*)

NELSON: You'll have to give her a hard whack.

KRUGER (*glancing left*): No, the noise rings down here. (*To* CARROL.) Go on, we'll leave this one, get the rest.
    (*They work on the other nuts with wrenches.*)

DENNIS (*holding light*): I hope to hell you'll be able to loosen that bugger.

KRUGER: We loosen, we loosen, move the light over here . . . good.

DENNIS: Oh dear, I've a terrible feelin' my poor mother is dyin'.
    (*Silence as they work on.* DENNIS *watches* ANNA *pacing up and down.*)

    (*To* ANNA.) That's a pretty dress to be dippin' into the Mississippi.
    (ANNA *nods, paces on.*)

    I wouldn't be worryin' myself now, Miss Walden.

ANNA: I'm not.

DENNIS: Sure.
    (*Slight pause. They work on.*)

Would y' believe it?—I'm only out of Ireland forty one months this April? Oh I tell ya, I was such a donkey when I got here, they had to back me off the boat!

KRUGER: Will you be quiet!

DENNIS: Oh yes, sir. (*Watches them a moment, turns again to* ANNA.) Have you a favorite ambition?

ANNA: Have you?

DENNIS: Indeed I have, Miss. You've been to the city of Cleveland, haven't ya?

ANNA (*glancing left*): No.

DENNIS: I've always wanted to be the mayor of Cleveland.

CARROL: Hey, will you stop movin' that light around!

DENNIS: Oh sure, Carrol. (*Readjusts light on collar.*)

KRUGER: Quiet, quiet.

(*They work on.* KRUGER *stops finally.*)

(*To* CARROL.) All right?

CARROL (*taking off last bolt*): Yep, there she is.

KRUGER (*fastening wrench on stubborn nut*): Come here, Dennis, pull this with me.

(DENNIS *bends, lays his hand to the wrench* . . .)

ANNA (*startled*): What's that!

CARROL: Cut the light!

(*Light goes out, stage is dark. Footsteps running on.*)

MARK (*in darkness*): Kruger! . . . Anna, where are you!

(*Light goes on in* DENNIS' *hand.*)

ANNA: Mark, you came!

MARK: Kruger, hurry up, Doctor Luther's on board.

KRUGER: Luther!—why?

MARK: Come on, what's holdin' it up?

KRUGER: This bolt is rusty, we can't. . . .

MARK (*of wrench*): Gimme that . . . lay a hand here, Dennis. . . .

(*He and* DENNIS *tug on wrench, nut gives.*)

All right, get that off, step on it.

(KRUGER *goes to his knees, unscrews nut.*)

(*Standing over* KRUGER.) You better go through with them, August.

KRUGER: What he said!

MARK: He knows who you are.

KRUGER: All right, she's clear . . . help me lift her out.

MARK: Everybody together, fellas . . . Dinny give that to
Anna. . . .

(*Flashlight.*)

. . . come on, drag your pants!

(*Four of them lift the collar off in two halves, a hole gapes
below them.*)

Go ahead, Carrol, you're first, we'll lower you down. (*Keeps
glancing left.*)

(CARROL *springs to rope, ties it around his chest, as . . .*)

Anna, don't stand so far . . . keep listening, they'll be
lookin' all over for him now . . . (*To* CARROL.) Here,
lemme see that. (*The knot.*)

CARROL: She's tight.

MARK: OK, get in there. (*Takes his shoulder.*) But don't flop in,
see? Just smooth, 'kay? Dennis, Nelly, take the rope-end. . . .

(DENNIS, NELSON *stand off with rope-end,* MARK *holds center as* CARROL *lowers himself into the hole up to his waist.*)

CARROL: There's an awful stink down there.

MARK: You're going back to civilization, hurry up.

CARROL: 'Bye.

MARK: Go on, go on, when you get in the water open the rope
and swim to the pier, go ahead, quiet!

(CARROL *releases his hold on the floor, they lower him down,
his head disappears,* MARK *stands over the hole watching,
raises his hand to* NELSON *and* DENNIS . . .)

Hold it.

(*They stop letting out. They listen in dead silence. Sound of a
man pushing through water is faintly heard from below.*)

He's OK, pull up.

(*They pull the rope up.*)

Come on, Nelson. . . .

NELSON: Maybe Dennis wants. . . .

MARK: Don't stand there like . . . —sh! (*Suddenly points to
ceiling.*) They're right over us!

DENNIS: Holy God!

(*Pause, silence, listening.*)

MARK: Get it on, Nelly.

(NELSON *rapidly ties rope around himself.*)

(MARK *goes to* ANNA, *takes her face in his hand.*)

Don't scare, don't scare, you're all right. . . .

ANNA: Why must . . . ?

MARK: This is the way the world moves, it's gotta be!

NELSON: I'm ready, Mr. Donegal.

MARK: Kruger, take it with Dennis.

> (KRUGER *takes rope-end with* DENNIS, NELSON *goes to hole, turns, lowers himself halfway in* . . .)

(*To* NELSON.) You wait under the pier, she'll come next, get her away. . . .

NELSON: I'm all right, I'm all right. . . .

MARK: OK, so long, Nelly . . . quiet.

NELSON (*as he passes down through*): . . . I'm all right . . . I'm all right. . . .

> (*He disappears, they keep lowering rope,* MARK *watches through the hole, the sound of water again, rope becomes slack* . . .)

MARK: Up!

> (DENNIS *and* KRUGER *pull up rope quickly,* MARK *goes to* ANNA.)

All right, kid, now it's you.

> (KRUGER *brings up end of rope, goes to them with it.*)

ANNA: I don't want that rope . . . that's not for me.

MARK: Anna. . . .

ANNA: No, you can't, no, I'm not going back, I'm not going. . . .

MARK: There's no time to talk!

ANNA: We're not this cheap, Mark!

MARK: They'll kill you, Anna, you can't sail! (*To* KRUGER, *of rope.*) Gimme that. . . .

ANNA (*pushing rope away*): No, we've got a right to live . . . !

MARK: We ain't got a chance . . . put this on. . . .

ANNA: There's something clear to fight, now, with a body and a face!

MARK (*to* KRUGER *and* DENNIS): Come here, take her!

ANNA (*backing from them*): Mark, it's not me you're dropping in the river, it's yourself!

MARK: Then it's me, and there's one noise less in the world!

> (KRUGER *suddenly leaps for the flashlight in* ANNA's *hand, puts it out. Stage is black. Silence.*)

(*After a moment*) Why'd you . . . ?

KRUGER: Ssh!

> (*Footsteps of three men coming closer. They stop. Come on stage, stop. A light flashes on in one of their hands. We discern*

LUTHER *holding it,* ROCKO *and* BOSCH *beside him. The light travels the wall, finds* KRUGER, *stops.* ROCKO *opens his light, it moves, finds* DENNIS, *stops.* BOSCH *opens his, it moves, finds* MARK *and* ANNA, *stops.* LUTHER *walks with his light up to* KRUGER, *grabs his hair, throws his head back, focuses the light into* KRUGER*'s eyes, holds it a moment.*)

LUTHER: Allll-so. (*With finality.*)

(*He releases* KRUGER *(his gun is drawn), and as he begins to move his light catches the open hole on the right and stops.*)

(*He moves to it, looks down, suddenly turns about flashing his light quickly in all directions as though searching for someone . . .*)

Bosch, quick, two sailors got through . . . find them quick, they can't be far.

(BOSCH *rushes off, left, into darkness.*)

Kruger.

KRUGER: Ja?

LUTHER (*points to collar*): Put that section on again.

KRUGER (*comes to him*): I don't think anymore of politics and these things . . . I don't fight against you anymore. . . .

LUTHER: Put that back on. . . .

KRUGER: I want only peace, let me go. . . .

(LUTHER *strikes out, hits his face.*)

MARK: You son of a bitch! (*Moves toward* LUTHER.)

LUTHER (*to* MARK): You stay where you are! (*To* KRUGER.) Put that on!

(KRUGER *goes to hole, starts with collar.*)

MARK: Put that gun down, he'd beat the hell outa you!

(*Goes at* LUTHER . . .)

(LUTHER *punches* MARK *suddenly in chest.*)

(MARK *falls back a step, his arms don't raise. . . .*)

LUTHER (*to* KRUGER): Hurry up, hurry up. . . .

KRUGER: There's a number of bolts. . . .

LUTHER: Don't bother bolting it, just cover the hole, it will keep the noise in here. . . .

MARK: What noise!

ANNA (*rushes down to* LUTHER): Put that gun away. . . .

LUTHER: Stand back!

ANNA: No, we're not dying, we're not. . . .

LUTHER: Miss, will you . . . !

ANNA: No, give me that gun . . . go away . . . (*To* ROCKO.) Who are you without a voice, without a name, who are you killing!

(*She rushes at* ROCKO *who flings her back.*)

LUTHER (*gun drawn, backs left with* ROCKO): Now, the four of you, turn your backs.

ANNA: Mark! . . . come, come!

(*Rushes to him, tries to pull him left.*)

MARK: What are you doing? . . .

(*She is crying and trying to pull him.*)

Anna, what are you doing! Anna, baby, what . . . ?

(*He looks into her face, her tears her great desire to live. She is sobbing . . . He turns to* LUTHER.)

Luther . . . let us out.

ANNA: Yes, Mark!

MARK: We'll beat it away . . . far. . . .

LUTHER: I would rather you turned your backs.

MARK (*holding* ANNA): Luther, give us a chance, for Christ's sake! I gotta live, Luther, I . . . !

LUTHER: You had your chance, Donegal. You could have been king of all the seas.

MARK: That's for frightened men, I'm not afraid now, let us go, we'll live alone!

LUTHER: Oh you fool, this was your year, you could have lived to count the treasure of the world on your fingers!

MARK: And the names of murdered men!

LUTHER: Ja, on the blood of the dead feed the enormous men!

MARK: Enormous men!—peewee guys afraid of anything but dying, that's what you are, that's what I was, tiny wreckers pullin' the world down, puffin' ourselves up like frogs with the noise of the stones falling!

LUTHER (*nervously*): Turn around . . . !

MARK: Turn around, yeh . . . ! O you forty-four-caliber rulers of the world, you slick guys in all languages, throw us to the snails, knock off a billion twenty-buck suckers, but a bridge is building, a bridge around the world where every man will walk, the Irish with the Jews, and the black with the white, stronger together than any steel, bone to the bone we'll live to hang you over the edges of the sky! Go on, ya punk, I dare you let me live, or give it to us between the eyes, we're lookin' at you till the dirt's in your mouth!

(LUTHER *lowers his gun, slowly, turns to* ROCKO *as the* CAP-TAIN *emerges from the darkness behind them.* ROCKO *raises his gun to aim, as the* CAPTAIN *pulls out a revolver and fires instantaneously.* ROCKO *falls forward, and as* LUTHER *wheels about,* MARK *rushes him from behind,* ANNA *with him. As they fall fighting to the ground* LUTHER*'s flashlight flies from his hand and goes out. There is a moment of scuffling in the dark, then a shot. Silence. A light flashes in* DENNIS*' hand;—* MARK *is half-risen over* LUTHER*'s body,* ANNA *is standing over him holding a smoking revolver . . .*)

ANNA (*wild-eyed*): I killed him. . . . I killed him, Mark!

(MARK *takes the gun from her, slowly kisses her, they stand a moment, looking into each other's eyes, thankfully . . .* MARK *turns to the* CAPTAIN *who stands staring at nothing.*)

MARK (*to* CAPTAIN. *Softly*): Thanks.

CAPTAIN (*indicating the bodies*): Give that to the river.

MARK: I'll dump them later . . . (*To* KRUGER *and* DENNIS.) We gotta cast off; his friends (*Luther's*) will be coming on to look for him. Come, Anna, we're leavin' town, we're gonna hit the sea, I'll show you what it is to live! (*To* DENNIS *and* KRUGER.) Come up to the bridge.

(MARK *and* ANNA *hurry out into the darkness at left followed by* DENNIS. KRUGER *stops beside the* CAPTAIN.)

KRUGER: Thank God it is all over, sir.

(*Pause.*)

CAPTAIN: Is it all over?

(KRUGER *looks at him, frightened, then hurries left into the dark.*)

(CAPTAIN *goes slowly to the bodies, drags* ROCKO *to the hole, removes the collar which was not bolted, lowers him down . . . sound of the body meeting the water. He goes back to* LUTHER, *drags him to the hole . . .*)

Also, Victor? . . . grosser Victor, why did you live? Your face is still surprised . . . ja, you died surprised, with all your shiny guns . . . I don't die like you, Victor . . . alone . . . (*A triumphant note comes into his voice.*) . . . to what do you belong? Come, sweets for the sweet . . .

(*Lowers him over the edge of the hole.*) . . . pah!—this river has a rotten stomach! (*Releases him . . . sound of water meeting body . . . He talks into the hole . . .*) Go down, go deep, Victor . . . is not good, eh, to die alone? To what do you belong!—alive and dead to the oysters! Not I, Victor! You could not take what is mine! I don't die alone! . . . is everything here . . . (*hits pocket containing gun*) . . . here! (*Turns to left, goes unsteadily, face upward, mumbling, weeping . . .*) . . . is everything here! . . . ja . . . ja . . . (. . . *sobbing, he disappears into the darkness at left as all lights go down.*)

SCENE 3

The pilot house again. It is lit as in Scene 1.

ANNA *and* MARK *hurry in through sliding doors.* MARK, *inside the door, looks out and down at the pier.*

ANNA: What are they doing?

MARK: Just standing around. I guess they didn't hear the shots. Stay right there, kid, and don't scare, we're pullin' out.
  (*Takes a stool and stands on it, reaches up on the back wall behind the steering wheel and takes down an axe as* DENNIS *and* KRUGER *come in.* KRUGER *is carrying another axe.*)
  (*Giving* DENNIS *an axe.*) Here's one for you, Irish. Now listen. We can't hoist the gangway off the dock or they'll know something's up. So we'll let her hang and pull her up later. You Dennis, go aft, Kruger go to the bow. When I pull my arm down like this, chop through the rope,—there's one on each end holding us to the pier. You got it? Chop through.

DENNIS: Suppose they start shooting?

MARK: Then you start duckin'. Got it?

DENNIS: I got it, but just ask me and I'll give it right back to you. Come on, Kruger.

MARK: And step on it, eh?
  (DENNIS *and* KRUGER *hurry out. Once out the door, they go in opposite directions, left and right,—fore and aft.* MARK *goes downstage to the tubes . . .*)

ANNA: You'll be careful. . . .

MARK: Careful! You're looking at an ex-package-wrapper from Abercrombie and Fitch! (*Laughs.*) Yeh, three days. (*Into tubes.*) Dino! I'm asking you for steam, but I mean steam not hot water. One minute, and I'll give you the go, then I want the works, everything, I want her to burn outa the water, we're leavin' fast. Stand by! (*To* ANNA *as he passes her going to door.*) Stay back from the windows. (*At the door, he turns his head, motions right with his thumb.*) Deep in, deep.

(ANNA *moves against the right wall.*)

(MARK *goes just over the threshold of the door, looks left, then right. He lifts his arm, looking left, and chops it down, then does the same while looking to the right. He rushes to the speed indicator, rams it down to "Full Speed," (it rings), then rushes to the wheel, stands behind it. The motors begin to throb below. The roof of the pier, seen behind the windows, begins to move slightly as the ship pulls away . . .*)

ANNA: Mark, we're moving! (*She comes left toward windshield.*) Look, we're . . . !

(*Simultaneously a shot rings out and a glass in the windshield smashes.*)

MARK: Get down, get down, I told you!

(DENNIS *comes rushing in.*)

DENNIS (*pointing down, right*): One of them is hanging onto the gangway!

(*Another shot, another window in the windshield smashes.*)

MARK: Take this!

(DENNIS *takes the wheel.*)

(MARK *goes to door drawing revolver, flattens himself against the wall beside the door, aims somewhere out, down, and right.*)

DENNIS (*looking ahead, steering*): He was climbing up, I think it was Bosch!

MARK (*fires*): Well he ain't climbin' up anymore!—gimme that wheel, Dinny. . . .

(*He takes the wheel, as . . .* KRUGER *enters, all smiles.*)

KRUGER: Oh you did good, you did so good, he was coming up!

MARK (*steering*): Yeh, hoist the gangway, will ya, before we lose it? How we doin', Anny girl?

DENNIS (*as* DENNIS *and* KRUGER *make for doorway*): Good God, I'm all perspired!

MARK (*expansively*): Come on, Anny, talk to me, we're ridin' to the sea!

> (CAPTAIN SCHULENBERG *appears in the doorway.* DENNIS *and* KRUGER *stop.*)

KRUGER: Go, I'll be right along, Dennis.

> (DENNIS *goes out.* KRUGER *goes to* MARK.)

I can take it now, sir.

> (MARK *gives* KRUGER *the wheel, slowly comes around to face the* CAPTAIN *who is standing on the threshold, his eyes wide and feverish, a revolver in his hand.* MARK *goes in his direction, pulls up the speed lever to "Slow" . . . The throb of the engines becomes slower, softer . . .*)

MARK: Everything is under control, sir.

CAPTAIN: . . . He died alone.

MARK: Get hold of yourself. . . .

CAPTAIN: Alone, sweet for the sweet, he died alone. . . .

MARK (*trying to move him out*): Come, we'll talk. . . .

CAPTAIN: I won't die alone, Mark. . . .

MARK: You're not gonna die, Schulenberg.

CAPTAIN (*suddenly goes to* KRUGER. *Into* KRUGER'S *face,* KRUGER *does not turn*): This one dies alone, heh? By Brazil he goes to lay down under the stone face of death, heh!

KRUGER (*still looking ahead*): Nein, nein!

CAPTAIN: Nein, nein, warum nein!

KRUGER: It is possible to live—to fight and to live!

CAPTAIN (*points at* MARK, *looks at* KRUGER): He will never live with the Captain, how can the Captain fight? What has the Captain Schulenberg? (. . . *turning to* MARK *as he speaks*) . . . Der Captain Schulenberg can nicht leben, der Schulenberg cannot love the filthy world, only the great good heart he can love! Only one good heart loves this world, how can I live if this heart will not come unto me! How can I learn the goodness of this world unless I touch this heart!! (. . . *raises his gun as he goes on . . .*)

MARK: Schulenberg!

CAPTAIN (*weeping, shouting*): . . . how can he teach me, he takes a woman, how can I belong to his goodness, he takes a woman . . . !

MARK: Stop that!!

CAPTAIN: I cannot live alone hating living things, die with me, Mark, let me belong, I cannot die alone!!

MARK: Give me that gun.

CAPTAIN (*pause. Quietly*): . . . Eh?

MARK (*softly; extends his hand*): Give it to me, Schulenberg.

> (CAPTAIN *looks at the gun in his hand as though he had never seen it.*)

The gun, give me. We're on the river, you don't need it now.

CAPTAIN: . . . Ja, clean it. . . .

> (*Giving the gun to* MARK.)

I killed a black hawk . . . (*Looks around him.*) Where is Luther?

MARK: He's dead.

CAPTAIN (*nods*): He was an evil man. . . .

MARK: Yeh, you're a good man. . . .

CAPTAIN (*sees* ANNA. *Goes to her peering closely*): You came finally?

ANNA: Yes, before.

CAPTAIN: I thought you wouldn't come to the ship today, it's so miserable . . . you should have told me you came, I had coffee, I would give you some. (*Goes to door, stops when he sees the sky.*) It's night time so quick?

MARK: You slept long.

CAPTAIN (*looks at sky a moment, turns. In routine manner*): I just thought I would come up, but it's clear enough now, you don't need me. A good moon you got. Wake me up when we cross the bar.

MARK: Right, sir.

> (CAPTAIN *looks at the walls, at the people, and a sob wells up in him. He keeps looking around him, his sobbing grows . . .* MARK *starts to go to him.*)

KRUGER: Let me, Mark. . . .

> (MARK *takes the wheel,* KRUGER *goes to* CAPTAIN, *takes his arm . . .*)

Come, Herr Schulenberg, you should rest a little. . . .

CAPTAIN (*in an old voice, sobbing helplessly. Looking at the sky*): When it came night? It was daytime . . . it came night so quick? . . . the night came so quick? . . . so quick the night . . . ? What happened?

(KRUGER *leads him out.* ANNA *stands watching the open doorway,* MARK *steers. An occasional tiny light passes on the distant shore.*)

ANNA (*softly*): He loves you, Mark.

(*Pause.*)

MARK: Yeh, I see now. Half the bridge sticking out of the heart, but for him there is no other half . . . and that's why so many don't care if they die . . . come here to me, will ya?

(*She comes to him, they look ahead.*)

You're never gonna die, Anna. (*Softly.*)

ANNA: You Irish with your dying!

MARK: Never . . . and we're gonna have a lotta kids!

ANNA (*nearly crying*): . . . And you'll tell them all the stories . . . and this story. . . .

MARK: How they serve you horse steaks on a stick in Belgium . . . delicious. They'll be laughing all the time, tellin' everybody,—"Me old man used to be a bum"!

(*They laugh.*)

Did I waste too many years, Anna?

ANNA: Not a one.

MARK: Believe it, heh? Y'know, I got three successful brothers, but who does my mother like the best?

ANNA: You.

MARK: Sure, and you know why?—because she has *fun* with me!

ANNA: I'll bet!

MARK: Seventy nine years old in July and she drinks me under the table! I tell her all the wonderful things,—see, that's what I wanted, Anna,—I thought all the time I was out to gobble it all up, but all I wanted . . . was to give . . . everything I got!

(*Pause.*)

ANNA: It's so quiet now. I feel so wise.

MARK: Yeh, we're beginning to smell salt.

ANNA: Do sailors always talk like this?

MARK: Naa . . . a sailor is a lonesome tree, carrying his true love tattooed on his arm. On ships they talk about whorehouses, in whorehouses they talk about ships. The roots are cut before they grow. . . .

(*Pause.*)

. . . Look ahead, kid, what do you see?

ANNA: The river, the delta, a ship . . . (*She goes to windshield.*)

MARK: Look up, woman.

ANNA: Oh, the stars!

MARK: Straight ahead, see?—Altair . . . and right up above, Vega . . . the navigable stars, Anna. Arcturus, Spica . . . the ones to go by . . . Polaris, see?—the bright one? Sirius, Achernar, Capella . . . they never change, Anna . . . some stars never change.

(*A light passes on shore. A whistle sounds in the distance. The engines beat like a heart . . .*)

SLOW CURTAIN

THE END

RADIO PLAYS

CAPTAIN PAUL

CHARACTERS

ANNOUNCER
CHIEF
JACK
SERGEANT
JONES
DOROTHEA
STACY
LOOKOUT
SECRETARY
COMMODORE
MESSENGER
MERCHANT
DOUGLAS
FRANKLIN
LOOKOUT
SAILOR
CARPENTER
COUNTESS
COUNT
KING LOUIS
CATHERINE
LANDLADY

Captain Paul

ANNOUNCER: It is a dark night in Paris, the summer of 1799. Here in this old, well-to-do section the houses snore contentedly like rows of aged ladies after a dance. Suddenly a man appears around a corner, dashes down the street, two gendarmes flying after him.

(*Breathless running.*)

He ducks into an alleyway, leaps a garden fence. He's trapped. He climbs a vine,—first story, window locked,—second, ah, open wide! He leaps into the dark room, slams the window shut.

(*Sound: window down.*)

CHIEF: Ha! What! Who's there!

JACK: Ssh! I beg y', don't talk!

CHIEF: Who is that!

JACK: Put out that light!

CHIEF: Stand away!

JACK: Don't point that gun here, lordship! . . . they're climbin' the stairs . . . don't tell 'em I'm here . . . Let me explain . . . give me a chance . . . !

(*Sound: rapid knocking.*)

CHIEF: Entrez!

(*Sound: door opening.*)

SERGEANT: Oh, here he is! A thousand pardons, Captain Ecoli. . . .

CHIEF: I'll break you for this! Don't I have enough of thieves all day in the precinct but you've got to chase them into my good night's sleep!

SERGEANT: I'm sorry, Captain, but he was the one who led us here.

CHIEF: You were the ones who chased him!

SERGEANT: Yes, Captain.

CHIEF: Bah. What's he been up to? Stealing what? What?

SERGEANT: You remember that rather poor cemetery on Rue de Parnasse. They're building a new fishmarket right on top of it. We caught him down in the foundation ripping up the beams.

JACK: They're drivin' pillars into his grave, Lordship! They're breakin' his bones with timbers . . . !

CHIEF (*sympathetically*): Ah . . . your father is buried there?

JACK: No lordship, Captain Paul. You remember John Paul Jones?

CHIEF: Indeed! I suppose George Washington is lying next to him! Captain Jones was a great American admiral, you fool, and that's a graveyard for chimney sweeps, plumbers. . . .

JACK: Oh thank heaven for your lordship. But he's there I tell ya. I helped in the buryin', I was the only one to follow his coffin. I'm Jack, Jack Stacy, one of his boys, I sailed a hundred times with him, and now they're goin' to lay a bloody fishmarket over his bones! You can't allow it, lordship, you. . . .

CHIEF: A likely excuse for stealing lumber! John Paul Jones was a Knight of the King, you blundering oaf, he'd as soon be buried there as. . . .

JACK: Aye, and there's only one way I can prove it sir. They've ripped out his headstone, but if you'd let me say a word or two you'd see how he *had* to be laid away in such a place,— aye, great hero that he was it ain't strange at all that this final mockery should be laid upon his bones. Y'see, sir, Paul Jones was a Scotsman,—(*music*) a great blonde whip of a man, born to the sea like the salt in the brine, born in Kirkudbright he was, an' sixteen years from the age of twelve he sailed about the oceans of the world, on slaver ships and merchantmen, a pirate too for a while, they say . . . and one thing and another he landed up in love with a wealthy girl in Virginia, and that's where my tale begins.

(*Music up & down.*)

JONES: Dorothea, there's a terrible thing must be said tonight, and I'd like to say it now.

DOROTHEA (*laughs lightly*): You're always filled with terrible things to say. What is it now, John?

JONES: I'm going to leave you.

DOROTHEA: Leave me? But you said. . . .

JONES: Aye, I've said my love a thousand times and meant it every one. But all our words leave us where we were;—I'm a near-pennyless seaman, and your family wants a man of wealth and name.

DOROTHEA: But we settled that, John. You're going to buy land and establish a household, and then. . . .

JONES: It's a lie, Dorothea. I'm no farmer. The land is for men with sleep in their veins, old men.

DOROTHEA: But you promised you were finished with the sea . . . !

JONES: But now there's a war to be fought, it's coming, it's here. The colonies need a navy and my head is filled with ships and guns and plans,—aye, if they'll give me a ship I'll sweep the seas for America, I know I can!—and back I'll come, rich Dorothea, and I promise you, famous enough to strike your father speechless when I ask your hand.

DOROTHEA: . . . How long before you return?

JONES: When the seas are free again for all men to sail . . . and that will take a long day. Will you wait for me, Dorothea?

DOROTHEA: Look there, John, the North star. And when you're alone on the sea look there again, for my love burns so, like that everlasting star.

(*Music.*)

(*Sound: seas on hull of sailing ship: pacing footsteps on deck: second pair of steps approaching.*)

STACY: Captain Jones?

JONES (*pacing halts*): Oh . . . good morning, Mr. Stacy.

STACY: A good morning it looks to be. You're looking bright yourself, if I might say.

JONES: Aye, it's the blessed sea, Jack. With a ship under my feet,—as small as she is,—the world falls away.

STACY: Aye, it's a good feeling.

JONES: I just thank heaven the water's got no politicians in it. A year, a whole year wasted trying to get a ship! My blood boils to think of it.

STACY: A pity you don't have an uncle or somethin' in Congress. You could've got to sea earlier.

JONES: Mention no uncles, cousins, relatives to me! The ocean teems with transports for the enemy,—shoes, uniforms, food, guns,—pouring into Boston; we could've cut their sea lanes and starved them out and the war'd be over by now! But no, I had to sit in Philadelphia while they parceled out commissions to their families!—Ah, but we're here now, and the sea is clean. There's a year's work to be done this month, Jack!—and enough treasure floating on this water to keep a dozen revolutions well supplied!

LOOKOUT (*from above*): SAIL HO TO STARB'D BOW!

JONES: At last!

STACY: What is she, can you make her out, sir?

JONES: Aye, a brigantine, and rich, I think to judge by her belly in the waves! Mr. Jackson!—close haul to the wind! Sheer to larboard! Beat to quarters, Mr. Stacy!

(*Sound: insistent drumroll: running men: shouts.*)

Stand to battle stations! She's twice our size but half as willing, boys! Stand to the guns! . . . (*Fade on drumroll.*)

(*Sound: door opening.*)

SECRETARY: Commodore Hopkins will see you now, Captain Jones.

JONES: You'd better wait out here, Jack.

JACK: My right eye to see the Commodore's face when you tell him!

JONES: And my left to have a different Commodore to face.

(*Sound: footsteps: door closing.*)

COMMODORE: Oh, Captain Jones, you're back safely! Is the ship all right? Much damage? What will it cost to repair . . . ?

JONES: In the six week cruise we destroyed eight enemy vessels, sir.

COMMODORE: Destroyed eight . . . ! Oh, come now, this is no time to. . . .

JONES: And eight more merchant ships are under way to this harbor under my prize crews.

COMMODORE: Oh. Well done, well done. Oh yes, yes, of course, well done.

JONES: And now sir, if you please, I would like the wages for my crew.

COMMODORE: Oh no, no, Congress hasn't given me a pound for wages.

JONES: Well then, you can advance some money on the cargoes we captured. The crew is pledged to receive one third value on all captured cargo.

COMMODORE: You're mistaken, sir. The government takes two-thirds, and I, naturally, receive most of the remainder.

JONES: I didn't notice your presence on board ship when cannons were firing, Commodore.

COMMODORE: I will be addressed as befits the Commodore of the Continental Fleet, Captain Jones!

JONES: What fleet? Those six sloops rotting in the harbor? When are you going to fit them out? When will they make to sea!

COMMODORE: I will make to sea when there's a ship in the fleet that won't sink as soon as she reaches open water!

JONES: And what did I sail on? A man o' war? Or a glorified fishing smack! Washington begs for guns, the soldiers die for food and everything sails unmolested into the enemy's lap!

COMMODORE: I will not be spoken to in this fashion!!

JONES: We can stop the war right there on the sea and nobody does anything about it!

SECRETARY: Excuse me, Commodore. A special messenger has just arrived from the Congress.

COMMODORE: Congress? I'll see him in the parlor. Wait, Mr. Jones.

(*Sound: door closing.*)

MESSENGER: I have been sent by the Congressional Naval Committee to deliver this command, sir. The fleet must make to sea at once regardless of difficulties. The situation is becoming a scandal. If this order is again ignored measures will be taken to insure execution. Signed, Naval Committee. . . .

COMMODORE: Thank you, thank you . . . Begone now. (*To himself.*) I can't take out those ships! . . . they'll fall to pieces . . . I don't know . . . (*calls*) . . . Mr. Jones! Mr. Jones!

JONES (*footsteps*): Yes sir.

COMMODORE: It's time the fleet got to sea. Definitely! Sail out as soon as you can find crews.

JONES: You mean I command the fleet?

COMMODORE: You will be responsible for anything that happens. Hurry now.

JONES: Thank you sir! Thank you, with all my heart!

(*Music up & down.*)

What do you mean, they deserted! Where's the crew! Where've they gone!

STACY: Most of the boys hired on to those privateers there at the end of the harbor. The shipowners offered them fifty percent of all cargo captured. They figure why should they sail with the navy and die fighting warships when they can loot merchantmen?

JONES: Ah!—these people, these blessed people!

STACY: You're offering blood and glory, sir; the merchants are payin' out in pound sterling.

JONES: Pound sterling, is it? Lower the boat, Stacy. We're bringing back a crew if we have to drag 'em on board by the hair!—pound sterling!

(*Music up & down.*)

MERCHANT: Get off the ship! This is my crew!

JONES: Get over the side, boys, there's hot lead in this pistol!

MERCHANT: I've got a right to hire crews for my vessels! I'll report you to Congress you bandit!

JONES: And what's the navy going to sail by, ghosts? You realize there's a war on!

MERCHANT: I'm not responsible for the navy! I've got a right to hire crews for my ships!

JONES: Over the side, boys, come on, come on . . . (*Grumbling as they go.*) . . . And as for you, sir, and your rights. I believe you hang an American flag over your household door; doubtless you're a fiery patriot at the dinner table. This country is bleeding to death and you know it, but so long as they don't bombard your Philadelphia harbor it's business-as-usual and the devil with liberty. Aye, you'd lick the heels of the tyrant if he'd let you keep your purse!

MERCHANT: I'll report to the Congress, you pirate!

JONES: And you'll find sympathy there . . . with a certain few. But you are not America, and neither are they . . . And until you are the navy will sail and the armies fight, and there'll be peace again when the despot's sword is knocked from his fist and not an hour before!—aye, though you bleed out all the red ledger ink in your veins!

(*Music up & down.*)

JACK: He was that sort, lordship. Month after month he roamed the seas with that boxwood fleet, clawing the wind, sheering in and dashing away like a terrier, until the British'd give a million pounds for the sight of his head in a basket!

Aye, they came to know Paul Jones, and at last Congress sent him to Portsmouth to take command of the finest ship in New England. What a day that was when he mounted the quarterdeck to present himself. . . .

(*Music up & down.*)

JONES: Captain Douglas? I'm Commander John Paul Jones.

DOUGLAS: So you're to take over, eh? Well, she's a fast one and a beauty, this ship.

JONES: Aye, a glance at her tells that. My papers, sir. I'd like to get to sea at once.

DOUGLAS: Hmmm . . . (*papers*) . . . I hear you're to meet Ben Franklin in Paris?

JONES: I shall have the honor of handing him the news of General Burgoyne's surrender. I can't wait to sail. . . .

DOUGLAS: I'm afraid you're going to wait.

JONES: My papers, sir . . . everything is in order. I take command.

DOUGLAS: There is no document here ordering me to give up my ship to anyone.

JONES: But you can infer that if I am to take command you must give it up!

DOUGLAS: I can't give a ship away on inference, sir. There is no document here. . . .

JONES: Surely you're not going to hold me up for a piece of paper! Franklin must have the news in Paris, I tell you!

DOUGLAS: And I must have that paper here in Portsmouth. I'm sorry. . . .

JONES: Sorry! And pray tell me how I'm to get back to Philadelphia without a shilling in my pocket! You'll delay me a month!

DOUGLAS: I cannot act without that paper.

JONES: Paper! Paper! The country is dying and they talk about paper! Bunglers, money-grubbers, politicians,—everyone afraid of the one next above him,—afraid for his skin, afraid for his pocket, but nobody fears for the fate of his country! I want a ship, I tell ya, a ship and a pox on the documents!

(*Music big up, then down.*)

FRANKLIN: So this is John Paul Jones! You know, I suppose, that all Paris is roaring with tales of your exploits at sea?

JONES: There's but one thing on my mind sir. All through the dark nights at sea I've dreamed of how I'd tell you this. . . .

FRANKLIN: Indeed. What is it?

JONES: General Burgoyne's army surrendered!

FRANKLIN: Excellent! Yes . . . hmm . . . even better now that I've heard it twice.

JONES: Heard it twice!

FRANKLIN: A French packet arrived from America a few hours ago. . . .

JONES (*crestfallen*): Oh. I'll be on my way, sir. There's work on board ship.

FRANKLIN: It is hard to tell you this, Captain Jones. But you've been relieved of your command.

JONES: . . . Relieved of my command! What have I done, what . . . ?

FRANKLIN: I am not the only representative of our country here in Paris. There are others, Heaven help us, and they have many friends to whom they owe favors. Your First Lieutenant, Mr. Simpson, is one of them. He will take command. You see, I am overruled.

JONES: My First Lieutenant, sir, is a drunken lout, he is utterly incapable of commanding a ship of war, he knows not starboard from a teacup,—the man, sir, is a treacherous fool!

FRANKLIN: And with those sentiments, Captain Paul, I take you for a friend, and a patriot. . . .

JONES: Aye, patriot. And I've a shipload of men waiting for wages eight months due. Shall I pay them with salutes?

FRANKLIN: They will all be paid . . . in time. . . .

JONES: Aye, in time. And I will have another ship . . . in time?

FRANKLIN: I'll do my best. Meanwhile make yourself at home in Paris. . . .

JONES: For how long, sir? Tell me the truth?

FRANKLIN: Negotiations take time, there are papers and documents to be gone through. . . .

JONES: Oh, papers, and documents again! If there were five honest patriots in Paris I could be sailing in a week!

FRANKLIN: Aye, but five honest patriots take a long time to find when there is little to gain and much to lose.

(*Music up & down quickly.*)

JONES: I've come again, Mr. Franklin. Is there any news?

FRANKLIN: There was a ship for sale in Marseilles last week. But we were overbid by a merchant in need of a privateer.

JONES: I see. I'll . . . I'll be back again. I beg you, sir, don't forget that I'm waiting. . . .

(*Music up quickly & down.*)

I'll lose my mind, Mr. Franklin, I can't bear this stagnation! I have a strategy that could wipe the seas clean of enemy ships! Give me five good vessels and the war is over!

FRANKLIN: I'm trying, Captain Paul. I've spoken to the King. . . .

JONES: Get me four then . . . four . . . give me ships and America is free!

FRANKLIN: There's a ship in Holland . . . give me another month. . . .

JONES: I'll not last the year without a ship! There's hundreds lying in the harbors and I'm eating out my heart on land!

FRANKLIN: Another month. I'm doing my best, Captain Paul.

(*Music up quickly & down.*)

Calm yourself, Captain . . . (*laughs*) . . . the ship is far from ready to sail. . . .

JONES: But it's a ship! A ship at last!

FRANKLIN: Plus a squadron of four which will follow you in command of French captains.

JONES: I must leave for Holland at once!

FRANKLIN: Remember, your vessel is not quite new. In fact . . . she's sixty years old.

JONES: *Sixty* years?

FRANKLIN: Aye, you'll have to look around for cannon and. . . .

JONES: Oh, she has no guns. . . .

FRANKLIN: And be careful to bargain when you buy your sails. . . .

JONES: She's not rigged then!

FRANKLIN: But she's large, very large. And when you get your crew. . . .

JONES: Ah . . . no crew.

FRANKLIN: Aye, but she's yours. And when you're fitted up, you'll sail with a squadron of four behind you . . . Commodore.

JONES: And that's enough. I'll be on the waves when the month is up.

FRANKLIN: Oh she'll need more than a month. Five I'd say.

JONES: One month, sir, not a day over. And her name will be, *The Bon Homme Richard* . . . Poor Richard in honor of your famous book.

FRANKLIN: Good. I wish her luck. But one thing more; these four French captains . . . ah, they will obey your commands at their own option.

JONES: You mean they won't obey me?

FRANKLIN: They're independent, but under your command. But I'm sure they'll feel the force of your character.

JONES (*laughs*): After this age of waiting, Mr. Franklin, there is enough force in my character to turn the Atlantic on her side!

FRANKLIN: Farewell then, Captain Paul. And Godspeed to the *Poor Richard!*

(*Music up then down.*)

(*Sound: ship sailing: A pen scratching within cabin.*)

JONES: "My Dearest Dorothea! I write this cruising along the Scottish coast. Dusk is falling fast. I pray this will be my last voyage and then home to you and the beginning of my life. We have done much damage to shipping here and raided coast, but insubordination among the French commanders becoming desperate; two of the squadron ships have disappeared, chasing merchantmen for loot, so only two remain behind me. But withal, you, my dear, are ever with me, and some day soon. . . .

LOOKOUT (*from distance*): SAIL HO TO PORT BOW!

(*Sound: few running steps: door swung open.*)

STACY: Man o' war off the port bow, Commodore!

JONES: Up we go, Mr. Stacy! How big is she? (*As they mount deck.*)

STACY: You'll see better through your glass, sir. There she rides around the circle of the land!

JONES: Oh, she's a big lady, Jack! If I see aright she's . . . yes, she's the flagship of the British Baltic Fleet!

STACY: Look, the squadron is running away! They're turning to the wind!

JONES: Let them go, the yellow dogs. . . .

STACY: But this warship's too big for us alone!

JONES: Mr. Jackson!—up with the gun ports! Beat to quarters, Mr. Stacy!

(*Sound: drumroll: running men: action noises.*)

(*Calling loud*): Sand the decks, Mr. Carrol and shake a leg to it! Haul down the lightsails, Anderson! Brightly boys, lay the boarding nets, lively to it, Mr. Barton . . . !

    (*Fade under drumroll.*)

      (*Music up & quickly down.*)

      (*Sound: quiet: only wash of sea on the hull.*)

(*Hushed*): Cleared for action, Mr. Stacy? She's closing to us.

STACY: Aye, sir, all cleared, all hands ready.

JONES: Oh, I like a smooth sea for a battle. And look at that moon!

STACY: Aye sir, a good moon, sir.

JONES: Quietly now. Hard starb'd.

STACY (*raises voice slightly, calls*): Hard starb'd.

SAILOR (*distant*): Hard starb'd, sir.

JONES: Hand topgallants aloft.

STACY (*as before*): Aloft there! Hand topgallants!

SAILOR (*aloft*): Hand topgallants, sir!

    (*Sound: pulleys: wash of sea on hull.*)

JONES: We're going to fight her in close, Jack. She's too big for us.

STACY: I could hit her with a stone right now.

VOICE OVER WATER: Ahoy! WHAT SHIP IS THAT!

JONES: Be ready, Jack. (*Calls.*) THE PRINCESS ROYAL! COME CLOSER WILL YOU? AND WHAT SHIP IS THAT?

VOICE OVER WATER: HIS MAJESTY'S SHIP *SERAPIS*! CAPTAIN RICHARD PEARSON! WHERE ARE YOU BOUND!

JONES (*calls*): COME CLOSER I CAN'T HEAR YOU!

VOICE OVER WATER: ANSWER DIRECTLY OR I SHALL FIRE!

JONES: Mr. Jackson, run up the flag! Mr. Stacy!

STACY: Aye, sir!

JONES: Fire!

STACY (*calling off*): Fire!

    (*Sound: broadsides to fade.*)

JACK (*excitedly*): Aye, lordship, and in short order the *Poor Richard*'s ancient big guns exploded right between decks, the hull was smashing up so you could drive a coach-and-four right through her beam. Captain Paul rammed the *Serapis* and lashed the two ships side by side so we could storm her decks. But they threw us back, and big fires started from stem to stern, and we were so close the *Serapis'* guns were stickin' right into our side and pounding us to splinters. All night we fought, dyin' by scores, throwin' spears, grenades, hatchets, and everything burning yellow under the moon. And suddenly up from below our carpenter comes a runnin'. . . .

(*Sound: cannon: battle.*)

CARPENTER: The hold's full of water! We're going under! Strike the flag, pull it down . . . !

JONES (*loud*): Let a man touch that flag rope and he's dead!

VOICE OVER WATER (*as everything quiets*): AHOY *RICHARD*! HAVE YOU SURRENDERED!

(*Sound: only the sea on the hulls.*)

AHOY *RICHARD*! HAVE YOU SURRENDERED!

JONES (*roar*): NEVER! I HAVE JUST BEGUN TO FIGHT!

(*Sound: cannonade.*)

(*Music up victorious, then changes into 18th century dance.*)
(*Sound: high class court chatter ad lib.*)

COUNTESS: Will they never come out? I never knew the King to keep anyone so long in conversation.

COUNT: Commodore Jones is going to score another victory I think when the ladies lay eyes upon him.

COUNTESS: I can't wait to see him! Is he very handsome?

COUNT: Amazingly so for a Scotsman.

COUNTESS: Is it true, Count, that Louis is going to knight the Commodore?

COUNT: I think His Majesty is so astounded he'll give him a province. Of all incredible things,—they sink the *Richard* right under his feet and he rides into Brest harbor, master of the enemy man o'war and flying the stars and stripes on her masthead!

COUNTESS: Hush!—here they come. The King is going to speak!

KING LOUIS: Monsieur John Paul Jones is yours now. And to you, the court of France, I say treat him as you would my son, for this is the new monarch! John Paul Jones, King of all the Seas!

(*Music up then down.*)
(*Sound: ad lib chatter.*)

FRANKLIN: Well, Commodore? How goes it with the idol of France?

JONES: Mr. Franklin! I've been looking all over for you! I must have money to pay my men. . . .

FRANKLIN: I hear the King is going to give you a sword of gold. . . .

JONES: Oh the people have been wonderful here! Wherever I go, crowds, parades!

FRANKLIN: Good, you deserve everything.

JONES: But my men, sir, their clothes are burned up, they go hungry . . . When can I expect money?

FRANKLIN: Now that the war is over, I think we have a good chance for some cash.

JONES: But can't you be more definite?

FRANKLIN: That reminds me, Commodore. The Russian ambassador called to ask whether you would like to go to Russia and reorganize Catherine's fleet for a war against the Turks. There'd be money in that.

JONES: Russia! I'm bound for America, Virginia, in fact . . . that is, once I pay off my crews. . . .

FRANKLIN: Virginia!—yes, of course . . . I must be doddering, here's a letter for you just came from the states.

JONES: A letter? Oh . . . it's from Dorothea . . . excuse me, will you? (*Tearing paper.*) "Dear John . . . I can hold them off no longer . . . father insists I marry Mr. Patrick Henry and . . . so I will . . ." (*Roars.*) Patrick Henry! She'll marry Patrick Henry! That dumpy, middle-aged, widower . . . !

(*Sound: court is shocked.*)

FRANKLIN: What's come over you? You're shaking. . . .

JONES: I beg your pardon. I've waited so long . . . I couldn't restrain. . . . Will you be good enough, Mr. Franklin, to tell the Ambassador of Russia that I am ready to serve Catherine at once. I'll leave tomorrow. Aye . . . tomorrow! Surely under so great a queen there is justice. Somewhere . . . somewhere it must be!

(*Music up & down.*)

(*A weaker voice*): You need only look upon my face, Your Majesty, to see how I have aged in this six-month service with your fleet.

CATHERINE: Your face proves nothing, Commodore. I have recalled you from the fleet because of my admirals' reports of your inefficiency.

JONES: But, Majesty, under my hand your fleet has won victory upon victory. . . .

CATHERINE: Despite you, it appears, Commodore Jones.

JONES: Aye . . . it appears. Very well then. It would do no good to tell you, I suppose, that your trusted admirals are so corrupt, so incompetent, and so jealous of my talents that they lie to you for fear of betraying their own bottomless ignorance of fleet warfare!

CATHERINE: For that, Commodore, you will leave Russia at once.

JONES: With, I pray, the money due me for my services?

CATHERINE: That, I am sure, will be forthcoming . . . in time.

JONES: Ah . . . in time.

CATHERINE: Yes, Commodore . . . in all . . . due . . . time. (*Music up & down.*)

LANDLADY (*weeping*): I've tried everything, Monsieur Jones, but the doctors won't come here to this poor house.

JONES: Don't cry, old woman. I doubt there'd be much use for doctors now. Hear me, please . . . I'm sorry I have still to pay you for my room. . . .

LANDLADY: Please don't mention that, Monsieur!
(*Sound: crowd sweeping by outside: shots.*)

JONES: They are still fighting in the streets?

LANDLADY: Paris is risen, everywhere people dying. God knows where it will end. But you, sir, I promise a funeral however poor it may be.

JONES: Aye, and poor let it be. For no better had my boys who died gasping in the waves, nor those brave ones who starve this very hour in twenty harbors of the world, those heroes without glory, the Jackys and the Bobs, the boys of Boston and the Nantucketeers who stand the watch in wait for the mail that will bring them their shilling wage. Weep, old woman, and pray this rushing mass of men that shatters kings and all their glittering decay, will cut a common grave for me, the bones of kings, and the monster of injustice that bleeds us all.

(*Music up: hold in b.g.*)

JACK: And there's where I found him, Lordship. Will you let me move him now?

CHIEF: Let me see. First we'll need a restraining order from court. . . .

JACK: Ah, the documents . . . !

CHIEF: Then the cemetery deed will have to be. . . .

JACK: And the deeds, Lordship!

CHIEF: An affidavit from you would have to be signed before the mayor . . . And he's not feeling well this week. . . .

JACK: Lay it to rest, Lordship. I see it all. Documents and papers, affidavits and deeds, and when it's all over I'll be back where I was before and a criminal record besides, no doubt. Forget it, Lordship, I'm off to sea where the wind stops for no relatives nor fears a document though it be signed, written, and recited by all the lawyers in Christendom. Let the stars remember Captain Paul, for the sea, I know, will not forget!

(*Music up to finish.*)

NARRATOR: And the fate of John Paul Jones lingered a long time to plague his memory. It took Congress twenty five years to finally send for his remains. And once on American soil they lay for a century before a fitting memorial was raised over them on the grounds of the Naval Academy at Annapolis. In time, Captain Paul, yes, all in due time.

BUFFALO BILL
DISREMEMBERS

CHARACTERS

CODY
ANNOUNCER
BAKER

Buffalo Bill Disremembers

Fine rain pouring steadily and distant thunder.

Music: Trumpet fanfare on bugle call . . .

CODY: Ladies and gentlemen!
> (*Crowd: applause and cheers of nine people . . .*)
>> (*All under rain.*)

Allow me to introduce the equestrian portion of the Wild West exhibition. First on our program, a mile race between a cowboy, a Mexican, and an Indian. You will please notice that these horses carry the heaviest trapping and that neither of the riders weighs less than 145 pounds!
> (*Music: bugle call. . . .*)
>> (*Gallop of three horses to fade . . .*)

ANNOUNCER: That's Buffalo Bill talking. His exact words. We know, because in the Library of Congress there are manuscripts that tell just what he used to say to the people who came to see his wild west show back in the beginning of the century. But there's also a lot of things we don't know about Bill Cody, so The National Broadcasting Company and the Library of Congress and I—we want to tell you a little about Buffalo Bill and if you've got any facts or stories to add to the subject send them in. But first, listen to Bill himself. He's just come into the tent. Outside the show goes on in the rain. (*Softly.*) The year 1910. He's nearly seventy years old now. His long white hair hangs wet upon his shoulders. . . .
> (*Rain on tent: outside the galloping, yipees, etc.*)

BAKER: Here, Bill, sit down . . . You look tired.

CODY: Oh, Baker, I'm an old man. . . .

BAKER: Go on, the rain's gettin' you. Rest, you got some time till the next act.

CODY (*sitting*): Ah . . . I'm an old, old man, Baker . . . Rain . . . When you get old it always rains . . . How many bought tickets today?

BAKER: Nine. . . .

CODY: Nine. Nine people to see Buffalo Bill's wild west show. Rain. Nine people in the rain. I guess I better lay down and die, Baker.

BAKER: The sun'll shine tomorrow, we'll have a big crowd again.

CODY: We ain't never goin' to have a big crowd, Baker. People don't want to see wild west anymore; want to go to those new movie shows, ride in aeroplanes. Wild west is gone and forgotten just like the buffalo . . . People don't remember anymore, don't remember. You know what bothers me? What bothers me is they wrote so many lies about me and I can't remember what happened anymore . . . I try to remember my life and everything's like a great big lie, a man likes to know what really happened and I can't remember the truth anymore. They even say there's a feller who's really Buffalo Bill and that I ain't. This feller Matthewson, his name is. I remember him. He claimed for a long time that he was Buffalo Bill and . . . I don't like to say it but sometimes I wonder. Was he Buffalo Bill? Or was I? Y'know in those days there was always a lot of Buffalo Ikes and Buffalo Als and a Buffalo Mike and Buffalo Joes, oh about twenty Joes, and ah . . . myself I didn't even know I was goin' to be it until that feller Ned Buntline, remember Ned Buntline, the writer? Yeh, he made me Buffalo Bill. . . . (I weren't more'n just grown up that time, laying under a wagon I was, yeh layin' under a wagon and he come out there to me) . . . he was a writer for a . . . for a . . . used to write sea stories and all kinds of thrillers and shockers and he come west for stories and he come over to the boss and he says he wanted stories and the boss said well there's a feller over there layin' under the wagon you might talk to him, and he woke me up and I give him a couple a stories. I don't know what they were . . . I suppose I made up a few, told him the truth a little, and he published them, yeh, like Deadly Eye and the Prairy Rover . . . dime novels ten cents a piece, kids liked them, and I read them books and I was real proud to know that I'd done all that. Some of it was true some of it weren't, and I thought well, after a while I'll write my own books, when I get myself a handwriting and I'll really tell the truth. But it didn't come somehow, that feller he wrote about 200 books before I could catch up with him. (And before I knew it I was a real big feller known all over, and the Duke Alexsis of Russia come out there to shoot buffalo, yeh,) that was the time when the buffalo was runnin' fifty miles wide and about three hundred miles long, you couldn't see a blade of grass, just thick, used to run the trains out they'd shoot them right down from the trains. Excursions ten dollars for four days you'd get out and shoot buffalo right outa the train window . . . killed them all off and then the Indians didn't have nothin' to eat . . . government liked that, yeh . . . got rid of the Indians that way. (I always try to remember—I always try to remember how things really happened and it's so hard, y'know?) I look back and all my friends are dead and I ask people what they remember about me, and they don't know either, they just keep saying I'm a great hero, but f'r instance I try to remember how did I get in the army . . . Y'know it says in the books they wrote about me that I'd been tryin' to get into the army since I was fourteen years old . . . and then when the war between the states started they say I changed my age and all just to get taken . . . you know the old story . . . but I don't know, I remember my mother, Oh, I always loved and adored my mother, loved her all my life; well, she said Billy don't go in the army, they'll kill ya in the war . . . well, I didn't want to get in the army 'cause my mother said they'd kill me . . . and I loved my mother, so I kinda wait a while and then she died and then I—well, my sister says the next day I came around with Wild Bill Hickock in a Union uniform, all blue and brand new with gold buttons on it, and we rode into the courtyard and he was on a horse and I was on a horse and there we were in the Union army . . . but I don't remember it that way . . . I remember that my mother died and then I led a dissolute and reckless life with gamblers and drunkards and bad characters generally. I was becoming a hard case and one day after I was kinda drinkin' a while I woke up to find myself a soldier in the Seventh Kansas . . . I don't remember how or when but there I was and I guess I couldn't get out so . . . I was in the army. But the time that I stood between savagery and civilization is when I was a kid, from fourteen to eighteen

when all the other kids were in the back yard . . . y'know
. . . hangin' around with their mothers and I was out
fightin' Indians. . . . Yah . . . killed hundreds of Indians
before I was old enough to shave . . . yah . . . killed
them by the thou . . . hundreds . . . killed them all . . .
that's what they say . . . that's what they say, I can't quite
remem . . . My father thought he was a great man, yah he
was killed for opposing slavery in bleeding Kansas . . . and
then sometimes they say he died of a cold . . . I don't
know . . . I guess he must have died of a cold and he was
stabbed . . . I don't know . . . I try to remember, but it's
hard . . . y'know, the nicest lady I ever did meet was
Queen Victoria . . . when we had the wild west show in
London that time, and the Shah of Persia was there and a
lotta kings . . . Annie Oakley was there with me then . . .
she shot a cigarette right outa Kaiser Willy's mouth . . .
but that was in Germany I think . . . but Victoria, she
leaned over to Annie and she says, you're a very, very clever
little girl . . . Queen Victoria of England, that's what she
said. . . . (What I would like to find out is if I was really
the Chief of Scouts of the United States Army or if I was just
a scout for the regiment . . . I think I was chief . . . all
the books say so, I guess I must have . . . But the best time
was when I became a spy against the Confederates, that's
right I was a spy, oh that was terrible work—riding through
the night with death always at my side . . . Eighteen years
of age, yes sir, I was a pretty good spy. You never knew one
minute to the next when you'd get a bullet in your back and
. . . why did the Adjutant General say I was a hospital orderly all through the war? I don't think that's true . . .
I . . . probably I was an orderly and a spy . . . oh, but I
do remember how I met Louisa . . . my wife . . . yeh, we
were ridin' up the street a lotta Union soldiers and a couple
of the boys were drinkin' a little I guess and up ahead I saw
a beautiful girl standing there and waiting for us to pass,
goin' to school she was with her books tucked neatly under
her arm . . . oh, she was pretty . . . how young she was.
And the Sergeant stopped in front of her and you know he
tried to kiss her. And she jumped away and I galloped up
and I took her in my arms and pulled her up to the saddle

and away we went, yes, yes, sir . . . that's how we . . .
I met Loui. . . . I don't know, her cousin said I met her
over at his house. I wonder . . . Well, I can tell you for
sure anyway how I actually became Buffalo Bill, I remember
that good . . . a couple a fellers around Kansas were con-
testing my title to be Buffalo Bill . . . see out there you
were Buffalo Bill if you could enforce it . . . and a man
who said you weren't and if he died and then you were . . .
so I . . . lotta fellers going out there killin' buffalo in those
days . . . they used to work for the Kansas Pacific . . .
Yeh . . . I was one of them . . . hunter . . . see the
railroad would push out into the desert . . . there was no
way of bringin' up food and keepin' it fresh but they were
buffalo nearabouts all the time, so they'd hire a hunter. Yeh
. . . five hundred dollars a month that's what I got, five
hundred a month. I'd go out there and shoot down buffalo
and bring 'em back fresh . . . twelve a day minimum . . .
keep the gang workin', keep them fed . . . killed four thousand two hundred and eighty head in eighteen months . . .
well, the biggest Buffalo Bill that was opposin' me was Billy
Comstock . . . he used to be a hunter too . . . well, we
bet five hundred I think, that I could kill more than him in a
day . . . more buffalo . . . we made the bet and a couple
of trainloads of people came out to watch . . . way out to
the plains and we found a herd and we rode into them . . .
(and I used to get my herds arunnin' in a circle and then I'd
stand aside and pick them off, but Billy he ran after his, ran
for miles and I only stayed in one place). . . . I killed sixty
nine against forty six for Billy that day . . . and my last cow
I chased till she was fifty yards . . . I ran her right up to
where the ladies were sitting . . . Oh, they were scared . . .
what a day that was . . . I ran right down there and the last
bull I dropped him ten yards from a lady's foot and he was
stone dead. And from that time on I was Buffalo Bill . . .
that's the truth. I remember that . . . once we used to
shoot buffalo because we had to eat them, we shot them
because we wanted the hides, there were millions of them,
millions and millions of them, they covered Texas right up
into Canada and we shot them by the ten thousand but after
a while it got to be a sport, y'know, people come out there

with guns and pistols and whatnot and just go run after them shootin them and leavin' them dead there. That was no good . . . I saw piles of bones higher than freight cars . . . that was no good because the Indians . . . the buffalo was the Indian's bread and they'd get mad and that's how we come to have Indian wars . . . I remember the Russian Dukes come out there and English Gentlemen and I used to guide them so they could hunt . . . thousand dollars a month . . . used to take them out there, yeh, and they'd drink champagne over a dead buffalo . . . I was real famous even that time, and then this Ned Buntline, the writer, he came around again and he said would I act in a play with him and he'd take me back to New York and we'd be on the stage . . . I'd be a show-player . . . Billy Comstock laughed, he said he'd never make a damn fool out of himself that way but I went, (I went because I wanted to tell people about the west . . . it was like a fairy land place in those days . . . and I wanted to tell them what a beautiful place it was, and I just wanted to go and make some money too . . . so we went out East) and I got on a horse on Fifth Avenue and I rode in my chaps and my big hat right there in New York with my long hair hanging to the shoulders . . . we used to cut our hair long those days because it was like a dare for the Indians to come on and try to scalp us . . . and wherever I'd go on my horse in New York would be big crowds, oh, it sure was a fine time, and when I said to Ned, well, how's about this play and Ned said well, we gotta go over to the producer's . . . and so we went over there, and the producer said, fine, boys, just fine, and everything's all set for the opening . . . theatres all booked, advertising is going out and everything, and he . . . where's the play? We got to start rehearsing the play right today, he wanted to see the play . . . Well, Ned said "didn't write the play yet, but we got about three days yet, plenty time" . . . So the producer said, "Git outa this office, you ain't never goin' to open on Monday at this rate, and it's all off," he said. . . . "Git outa the office." So Ned said, "Here's six hundred dollars and I'll hire the theatre myself," and we sit down that night in the hotel and Ned made a play for us . . . three acts . . . he wrote it all in about four hours and we had the bellhops copy down the parts and he asked me how long would it take you to memorize this, Bill, and I said, oh, about seven years, if I'm lucky . . . but I had it all by morning . . . and we opened and the curtain went up and I forgot every word and there we was on the stage and I couldn't talk and Ned he hadn't bothered to write himself a part figuring that I'd talk and he'd kinda fill in as we went along, so he turns to me and says, "How you doin', Bill?" And I said "I'm doin' all right" . . . And then he said . . . "Oh, where you been lately?" . . . And I told him where I was lately and then the Indians came on . . . They was supposed to come on in the second act but they come then so we had to shoot them dead and when they come on again the second act we had to shoot them dead again in the second act . . . I don't remember how many times we shot them same Indians that night but it was a big number of times . . . But the people they loved the show . . . that was a great hit . . . *Scouts of the Plains* was the name, eighteen seventy-one. I made a hundred and thirty-seven thousand dollars that year, and I was an actor . . . Gosh, Baker, people liked the West that time . . . that was a great time in the world. They come to see anything that had Buffalo Bill in it . . . not like today . . . when it always rains. And I'm an old man. . . .

(*Music: bugle fanfare. . . .*)

BAKER: I guess it's your turn again, Bill, you better get on out there.

CODY: Yah . . . yah . . . hold the stirrup, will ya? That's it . . . just give me a little shove there.

(*Horse shifting as it is mounted.*)

I be all right. There . . . ah . . . How do I look, Baker?

BAKER: Like the day you broke the record on the pony express.

CODY: Well, I hope we ain't lost none of our nine customers yet. Open the tent, Baker . . . How does my hair look?

BAKER: Oh, long and fine and gray, Billy, you got good hair.

CODY: I never did want to wear my hair long but after they took pictures of me I just couldn't cut it off or nobody'd think I was a real scout. That's what keeps troubling me.

BAKER: What, Bill, what's the matter?

CODY: Nothin' seems real. It's like I started play-acting, and I lived a whole life trying to find my way out of the theatre . . . Am I Bill Cody or Buffalo Bill? A cowboy or an actor? And when did I become which?

(*Music: bugle fanfare. . . .*)

Hang it all, every time I try to figure somethin' out . . . that bugle. . . .

BAKER: Better button up, Bill, you'll catch cold.

CODY: Buffalo Bill couldn't catch cold . . . Impossible . . . The country wouldn't stand for it . . . Out of my way, Baker, let's see what I can do to amuse the wet customers.

(*Horse walking . . . applause . . . rain pouring.*)

Thank you, thank you, ladies and gentlemen. "Next on the program, the riding of bucking ponies. There is an impression in the minds of many people that these horses are taught or trained to buck, or that they are compelled to do so by having foreign substances placed under their saddles. This is not the fact. Bucking is a natural trait of the animal." It is natural, these are simply wild ponies, unspoiled by civilization, untrammeled by men or machines, and anybody who says that foreign substances are placed under their saddles. . . .

(*Fade in rain.*)

(*Music: up to tag and finish.*)

ANNOUNCER: You have just heard the story of Buffalo Bill as it is found in the diaries and documents in the Library of Congress. There are many people living today who remember Buffalo Bill, people who saw his wild West show, people who lived beyond the Mississippi in the days when Bill Cody was young . . . Will you help Bill to complete his story? Write and tell us what you remember of this hero of the plains . . . The Library of Congress, Washington D.C., would like to hear what you've got to say about the man who made the West famous. *Buffalo Bill Disremembers* was written by Arthur Miller. Next week the Radio Research Project of the Library of Congress in cooperation with NBC will present *A Story in Early American Medicine* told in part by Thomas Jefferson.

(*Music: up to tag and out. . . .*)

THE BATTLE OF THE OVENS

CHARACTERS

KATEY
CHRIS
JERRY
ORDERLY
WASHINGTON
CAPTAIN
1ST SOLDIER
2ND SOLDIER
3RD SOLDIER
GEORGE
ALFRED
ROBERT
4TH SOLDIER
5TH SOLDIER
GREENE
ANNOUNCER
MALCOLM
SERGEANT
MAJOR
CASEY
TRUMAN
JONES
BACH

The Battle of the Ovens

Sound: in distance tramp of soldiers passing and faint beat of the regimental drums.

KATEY (*calling . . . off-mike*): Christopher? Chris? (*Approaching.*) Christopher . . . oh. Sitting by the open window again, you want to catch your death? Come to bed, it's after midnight.

CHRIS: I like to sit and watch the soldier boys marching off to war.

KATEY: Every night the same thing, and every morning you complain your back hurts. Come up to bed.

CHRIS: Katey . . . it's such a bad year to be an old man.

KATEY: It's a good year to be a dead man with your rheumatism. Come upstairs. . . .

CHRIS: I am not talking about rheumatism! Katey, I don't know what I shall do with you! You have no heart! Listen . . . you hear? . . . marching, young legs, young bodies marching, young voices calling commands . . . Washington says he need soldiers and they rise and go. . . . I feel like the whole world is being born these days . . . and look at me, sixty one years old, baking rolls in Philadelphia with such great things happening.

KATEY: Close the window. The draught is on your neck.

CHRIS: O, Katey, forget my neck! Every day I take from the drawer Mr. Jefferson's declaration, I read . . . "Certain unalienable rights, life, liberty and . . ." whatever he says there. Such words, they make me cry that I can't go out and help to make them come true! Oh why must a man be old when the time is so young! Ach . . . you will never understand.

KATEY: What more can you do, Chris? You sent Jerry, your best apprentice, to bake for the army. You're doing two men's work, you're. . . .

CHRIS: Jerry. Sometimes I feel like Jerry is my son that I sent off. After all, I taught him everything he knows about baking bread, didn't I? Maybe that makes him part of me, a little piece of me that is young and brave. . . . Only I was wondering if Jerry is drinking warm beer. If that boy drinks warm beer in the army he will disgrace me, I'll break his neck if he . . . !

KATEY: Christopher Ludwick, I am going to bed. Are you coming?

CHRIS: I can't sleep, Katey. Listen to the marching. . . .

KATEY: Ach . . . a person would think you were three days in the world.

(*Sound: footsteps away.*)

Marching, war, armies . . . at his age! Such craziness I never heard. . . . (*Fade.*)

(*Sound: distant marching.*)

CHRIS (*to himself*): To be thirty again . . . even forty . . . ach, this way is no good, no good at all this way. . . .

(*Sound: light knock on door.*)

Hey? At this hour?

(*Sound: light knock on door.*)

Coming!

(*Sound: door opening.*)

Jerry!

JERRY: Yeh, it's me. Let me in, heh?

CHRIS: Of course, come in, I'm so happy to see you, how are you! What are you (*sound: door closing*) doing back in Philadelphia?

JERRY: Oh, thought I'd drop in. Got a little business.

CHRIS: Fine. Tell me, did you do like I told you? You got a loaf of your bread to General Washington?

JERRY: Well, general's a pretty busy man, Mr. Ludwick.

CHRIS: I'm surprised at you, Jerry. I told you, the bread they bake for him is like a table top. He is not eating good. . . . Stand up straight, Jerry, and wipe that flour off your coat. General Washington will see you slumping around like this all untidy he will say to himself so this is the kind of people Christopher Ludwick employs in his bakery! Did you buy clean aprons with the money I gave you or did you buy warm beer?

JERRY: Look, Mr. Ludwick, I've got to get back to camp before dawn. I've got some business to talk about.

CHRIS: With me?

JERRY: I've a wagon load of flour outside. I'd like to sell it. Cheap, mind you. I could make a good price, mind you.

CHRIS (*softly*): How did you come by a wagon load of flour?

JERRY: Well, it's a funny situation. But only between you and me, mind you. The Congress allots a pound ration of flour per soldier, y'know. The boys don't know how to make bread so they give the flour to a comrade to bake. That's me. I'm baking for the regiment. And ah. . . .

CHRIS: Yes?

JERRY: Well the way it works is that I give them back a pound loaf for their pound of flour. Naturally, bread needs water and salt and leavening so that I always have some flour left over for myself.

CHRIS: You mean you are stealing flour from the army.

JERRY: Where's the stealing in it? I can't put a pound of flour in a pound loaf of bread can I? And no use throwin' away the extra, is there?

CHRIS: No, but you could make two loaves perhaps from the same pound. And I could break your neck, Jerry, too.

JERRY: Now just a minute, Mister Ludwick. . . .

CHRIS: Go with that flour and give it back to the government.

JERRY: I guess you don't know what's going on in the army, Mr. Ludwick.

CHRIS: I guess I know better than you what is going on. All these weeks I sit watching the boys go off to the war and I curse my bones for being so old, and the only thing that brightens my life is that I know I taught a man how to bake an honest loaf of bread and he is baking for the army. And now you come to sell me stolen flour! You common thief!

JERRY: Me and about five hundred others. All the bakers are doing it in every regiment.

CHRIS: You're lying . . . !

JERRY: Who's been in the army, you or me? I tell you there's a fortune in it. But you got to have capital. Now you, for instance. Ludwick, I could get you loads of flour, you buy it up, then sell it back to the government. At a fancy price too, mind you. In a month we can be rich . . . hey . . . let go my ear . . . hey!

CHRIS: You vandal! You are a disgrace to every honest baker in the world!

JERRY: That flour belongs to me . . . ! Let go my ear . . . !

CHRIS: Take it back this minute. I'll have you hanged! Now . . .
go.

JERRY: I guess you're just the same old fool. You don't even know
there's a war on. What's a war for except to make money?

CHRIS: Get out of this house! I'll show you what a war is for.
Old man or not I'll show all you pigs what this war is!
(*Music up and down.*)

KATEY: You will not send me to my grave, Christopher Ludwick, I will not allow you to kill me!

CHRIS: Katey, please, I don't know how to write. Sit down and
write the letter for me. . . .

KATEY: I'll do no such thing. A man of sixty years wanting to
join the army! Are you out of your mind? They'll laugh at
you!

CHRIS: Here's pen and ink. . . .

KATEY: Don't give it to *me*! What will become of us? The business will go to ruin. You work all your life and now you
want to throw everything away . . . what will happen to
our old age?

CHRIS: Our old age will come soon enough without talking
about it. Here, take the pen.

KATEY: Chris . . . what has got into you? You're an old man.
And your rheumatism. They'll make you sleep in the open,
what will become of your rheumatism?

CHRIS: If I must have rheumatism I would rather have it as a
free man than a slave. . . .

KATEY: It's not your place to be a soldier! How could you
shoot a gun?

CHRIS: Katey. Dear. If I cannot fight with a gun I can fight with
my own weapons . . . flour and salt. Even General Washington can't do that. And I have plenty to say to him. . . .

KATEY: Plenty to say! And who will listen to what you say?
You're nobody, a baker. . . .

CHRIS (*as* KATEY *snivels*): So? A baker is not allowed to love
liberty? Come . . . that's a good woman . . . write as follows. Dear General Washington . . . no. My Dear Excellency General Washington . . . no wait. Here . . . My
Dear Honorable Excellency General George Washington
Esquire; I am a baker. That is, of bread, not pastries. It is

scandalous how these knaves are stealing flour from the soldier boys. I know you are a busy man but if you would see
me a moment I could tell you what is going on in your army
. . . that is in the way of (*music sneak*) bread. Bread, my
dear General, is not to be trifled with. I will not stand for it.
If you would see me, perhaps next week, I would be happy to
join the army and knock some heads together. . . .

(*Music up and down.*)

Let me in there I tell you . . . !

ORDERLY: Don't take another step toward that door or I'll run
you through!

CHRIS: Out of my way you young snipper! Let me by!

ORDERLY: Now look here, gaffer, that's General Washington's
headquarters in there. . . .

CHRIS: Who do you think I came to see!

ORDERLY: There's also five other generals in there, and it's a
high-strategy conference, and I doubt that they invited you.

CHRIS: And what is higher strategy than bread? What can an
army do without bread?

ORDERLY: Put that rock down.

CHRIS: Out of my way or you'll be picking up your brains. . . .

ORDERLY: Don't touch that door you old . . . !

(*Door opening.*)

CHRIS: Ssssh! See that nobody disturbs us, young man.

(*Footsteps into conference, voices ad lib . . . voices hush as
footsteps halt.*)

I kindly beg your pardon, Gentlemen.

WASHINGTON: What are you doing in here?

CHRIS: General Washington, my name is Christopher Ludwick.
I am a baker . . . I kindly beg your pardon, sir . . . I am
a baker.

WASHINGTON: I'm afraid you're interrupting a. . . .

CHRIS: Your time is too valuable to waste, General. I have here
a loaf of my bread. Fresh. Will you be good enough to taste
a piece? Here, sir. Chew it good.

(*Generals: astonished chuckling.*)

WASHINGTON: Hmmmmm . . . very tasty. Did you bake this?

CHRIS: I baked it, sir, and I want to say . . . (*angering*) . . .
that if our soldier boys had such bread you would win the

war in a month. It's a scandal how they're stealing flour and I won't stand for it, I beg your pardon I'll break their necks for them . . . !

WASHINGTON: Here, here now. What do you propose to do? By the way, you wrote me a letter didn't you?

CHRIS: My wife, sir, but I told her what to say. (*Quaking with anger.*) I am a simple man. I speak only straight. I want you to let me be in the army to look after the baking. And if anybody starts with this nonsense about stealing flour, I'll smash them!

WASHINGTON: Aren't you a little over age for such a task?

CHRIS: Are you too old to be a general?

WASHINGTON: Hem. . . .

CHRIS: I have forty years' experience in baking. I know the trade from top to bottom. Let me take charge of bread. I know I am nobody but with bread I am somebody. Bread is my life.

WASHINGTON: I believe you, Mr. Ludwick. Tell me, do you honestly think you can straighten out the baking situation? We couldn't pay you very much, you know.

CHRIS: All I ask is a trial. The nonsense must go.

WASHINGTON: Of course, but. . . .

CHRIS (*at end of his patience*): If I beg your pardon, General Washington, don't you realize we are in a war?

WASHINGTON: Hm. I seem to have heard it mentioned. Mr. Ludwick, I'll give you a trial.

CHRIS: But I must have complete charge.

WASHINGTON: Agreed. I'll see to your commission tomorrow.

CHRIS: But one more thing, sir. I know bakers. Good men, but stubborn. A baker will never listen to advice from another baker. Except pastry men, of course, but they got no mind of their own anyway. . . .

WASHINGTON: Of course, of course. What's your point?

CHRIS: If I beg your pardon I would like to have a title.

WASHINGTON: Certainly. How would . . . Director of Baking do?

CHRIS: That's nice . . . as far as it goes. But it don't say nothing about the bakers. Bakers and baking is not the same horse. Better add on, Superintendent of Bakers.

WASHINGTON: *And* Director of Baking?(!)

CHRIS: If it wouldn't trouble you. I would enjoy to have the title, Superintendent of Bakers and Director of Baking.

WASHINGTON: Is that all?

CHRIS: Come to think of it, better add on . . . in the Grand Army of the United States.

WASHINGTON: Is that satisfactory to you gentlemen?

(*Ad lib agreement.*)

Mr. Ludwick, consider yourself Superintendent of Bakers and Director of Baking in the Grand Army of the United States.

CHRIS: General Washington . . . if I beg your pardon . . . I . . . we have won the war!

WASHINGTON: Let me say, sir, that with such spirits as yours I don't see how we can lose.

(*Music up and segue.*)

(*Tramp of body of soldiers along a road.*)

CAPTAIN: . . . Halt!

(*Tramping stops.*)

Fall out! (*Ad lib of men in the background.*)

CHRIS (*off*): All right, boys, line up here behind the wagon! Mr. Wilson will hand you your bread ration!

1ST SOLDIER: Phew, I'm tired down to my bones.

2ND SOLDIER: And a forty mile march tomorrow. They'll have to carry me. . . .

3RD SOLDIER (*off*): Hey, Ludwick, this ain't bread you're handing out, is it?

CHRIS: It's bread, it's bread. Eat, you're hungry.

3RD SOLDIER: Yeh, but not this hungry. Man, this stuff is no better than mud. Look at it, it's leakin'!

GEORGE: What, again!

ALFRED: I'm not goin' to eat any more of that mud!

ROBERT: Hey, Ludwick, I thought you were supposed to be a baker!

CHRIS: I'll hear no nonsense! Take your bread and go eat!

4TH SOLDIER: Look at it! You try eating it, Ludwick! We can't march with cement in our bellies!

CHRIS: What do you want! You don't give me no time to bake a decent loaf. You march, you stop, and quick you want bread. Bread needs time to rise, and where's the ovens? I'm baking on stones . . . !

5TH SOLDIER: Ah, go back to Philadelphia and. . . .

CHRIS: Don't you tell me where to go!

MEN: Boo! Back to Philadelphia! (*Catcalling.*)

CHRIS (*topping them*): Shut up, you stupids! I'll bake my bread and you eat it and don't tell me . . . !

GREENE: Ten . . . shun!

(*Quiet.*)

What is going on here?

CHRIS: They're complaining about the bread again, General Greene. I do my best, but I. . . .

GREENE: Come off that wagon, Ludwick, I want to speak to you. At ease, men. Wilson, continue giving out the bread. Ludwick, come this way.

(*Double footsteps away from grumbling of men.*)

Ludwick, I do believe you're a good baker and an honest man. The way you stopped the flour-stealing proves that.

CHRIS: I try, I try my best, but. . . .

GREENE: Tomorrow dawn we start a forty-mile march. The men must have decent bread. Now what can you do about getting it for them?

CHRIS: I have only one idea, General Greene, but perhaps you won't permit it. It is something that has never been done.

GREENE: What is it?

CHRIS: The army marches too fast to allow the bakers time to put bread together like it ought to be. So why can't you do this; give me directions where the army will head for. I leave now with my bakers, get there in good time ahead of you, set up real ovens in the woods, and by the time the soldiers reach there I have plenty of good bread waiting. . . .

GREENE: Bakers going ahead of the army! It's unheard of.

CHRIS: Until now. It's the only way you will have proper bread. Bread is a stubborn thing, it must grow in its own good time.

GREENE: But good heavens, man, you can't go alone into enemy territory. And your wagons won't carry many guards. . . .

CHRIS: I would like to take the chance.

GREENE: How about your bakers?

CHRIS: I will give them a raise in pay from my own pocket. And then I'll threaten them. They'll go.

GREENE: All right, Ludwick. I'll trace your course on a map

and give it to you. Leave immediately. But keep a sharp eye to the woods. They aren't friendly. You're positive you're ready to risk it.

CHRIS: Ready? Look, General. If day after day everybody tells you, you are a bad general, you would be willing to take a chance to prove you are a good one, wouldn't you?

GREENE: I dare say I would.

CHRIS: Well, I am a baker. Goodbye.

(*Music up and down.*)

ANNOUNCER: You are listening to an original radio play starring Jean Hersholt on the Cavalcade of America, sponsored by the Du Pont Company of Wilmington, Delaware. As our play continues we find Christopher and his small crew of bakers just finishing the erection of their ovens in a clearing in the forest. It is almost evening. They are about to prepare the dough for a great quantity of bread. Unknown to them an enemy patrol has been watching their activities for over an hour from the dark height of a hill close by.

BRITISH SERGEANT: All right, Malcolm, give the signal, we'll pounce on them now. Are you men ready?

MALCOLM: We've got them circled, but why not wait, Sergeant? Let them get a few loaves done. It's been a bloody long time since I've seen a decent piece of bread.

SERGEANT: No, they're liable to be at it all night. Better start at them now.

MALCOLM: As you say, sir.

(*Sound: shot . . . men running through brush . . . cries of attackers.*)

SERGEANT: Round 'em up there, come on you get over here. Keep your hands high . . . Anybody get away, Malcolm?

MALCOLM: All accounted for, sir.

SERGEANT: Now which of you is in command here?

CHRIS: I am.

SERGEANT: Who are you?

CHRIS: I am Christopher Ludwick, Superintendent of Bakers and Director of Baking in the Grand Army of the United States and we are going to win the war.

SERGEANT: Oho! Quite a boy, aren't you, Grandpa?

CHRIS: I am quite a boy, yes. What do you want with me?

SERGEANT: Malcolm, take all these men back to the C.O. I'll just want you, Grandpa. And Malcolm, report to headquarters that a large body of Americans are due here sometime soon. Probably General Greene's army.

MALCOLM: Bakers, fall in!

(*Grumbling . . . hubbub.*)

Forward, march! Left, left, left. . . . (*Fade.*)

SERGEANT: Now let's hear it, Grandpa. How many troops are coming this way? Well? Oh come now, save me the trouble of guessing from the amount of dough you've mixed. Eighty? Hundred? Two hundred?

CHRIS: A thousand . . . no, two thousand, I beg your pardon.

SERGEANT: Oh? Cannon?

CHRIS: Plenty cannon.

SERGEANT: Quite a system you've gotten up, haven't you. Regular ovens, bakers going ahead of the army . . . tell me, you bake a good loaf? You do, eh. Strictly in private, could you knock something together for me? Something tasty. For a lady. What do you say?

CHRIS: For a lady? I could make some for you too.

SERGEANT: That would be decent of you. Go ahead. I'll sit here and keep an eye on you if you don't mind.

CHRIS: Just make yourself comfortable, and I will bake you something that you will never forget.

SERGEANT (*laughs*): Oh, I daresay it won't be that good.

CHRIS (*laughs*): Oh, I daresay it will!

(*Music up and down.*)

(*Body of soldiers marching . . . few horses at a walk on a road.*)

MAJOR: General, there's something white moving in the trees . . . straight ahead, you see?

GREENE: It's a man, I think. He's running . . . waving at us. Hold up the troops, I think I recognize him. . . .

(*All sound stops but one man running toward us.*)

CHRIS (*breathless, approaching*): General! General Greene!

GREENE: What are you doing here, Ludwick. Your ovens aren't supposed to be anywhere near this vicinity.

CHRIS: They captured all the bakers. Don't go any further, they'll trap you!

GREENE: How did you escape?

CHRIS (*catching his breath*): Well . . . I made . . . a little dumpling for a gentleman and his lady. I guess it didn't agree with him.

GREENE (*laughing*): Ludwick, I do believe you'll come to no good end . . . I suppose they captured the bread too?

CHRIS: We didn't have time to get it ready, but you can't go that way. They're waiting for you.

GREENE: Nonsense, I've got to keep moving Southwest. I should have guessed it was a blunder letting bakers go ahead of the army. . . .

CHRIS: It was a wonderful idea, sir. But I have even a better idea now.

GREENE: I believe I've had about enough of your ideas, Ludwick.

CHRIS: I was thinking as I ran away, why not send out not just a few bakers but fifty or sixty with enough flour to make five, ten, fifteen thousand loaves, and. . . .

GREENE: Fifteen thousand loaves! Mr. Ludwick are you well?

CHRIS: I never felt so good in my whole life! Listen to my plan, I beg you, General. You send fifty bakers ahead with me. We take everything we need. And we bake . . . yes, we bake, and we bake, and we bake. . . .

(*Music up and down.*)

(*Sound: walking through brush.*)

SERGEANT: You'd better bend low, sir, we'll be in sight at the top here. Now. Look down there. You see? In the corner of the valley? Right beside the turn in the river?

MAJOR: By George! They must be expecting a whole army—fifty bakers if there's one! But isn't it peculiar that they've returned to almost the exact spot as before?

SERGEANT: I think it means, sir, that they've really got a major force coming this way. They must figure on overpowering our ambush. Notice, these bakers are very well guarded.

MAJOR: But what they didn't figure on is that we know how to count. Post a man here. Have him count the loaves as they come from the ovens. Each loaf is a soldier expected. We'll have two ready for every one of theirs. I'll contact headquarters. They must send us up another regiment!

(*Music up and down quickly.*)

(*Iron vessels clanking as they bake, fire crackling.*)

CHRIS: Hurry, hurry, get a move on there, Redhead! Come, pull this tray out, Casey!

CASEY: Pull it out! I just put it in! That bread's not hardly warm.

CHRIS: Out, out I said, Casey, and be quick about it. You there, your bread has been in long enough, pull it out and get that other tray into the oven!

CASEY: Well if this ain't the craziest war I ever heard of. Takin' bread out of an oven when it's still wet! Mr. Ludwick, nobody's goin' to eat this stuff.

CHRIS: It is not being made for anybody to eat.

CASEY: I know but . . . What is that you just said?

CHRIS: I said it is not being. . . .

TRUMAN (*off*): Hey! Look up there! Ludwick!

CHRIS: What's the matter now?

TRUMAN: Up there on the top of the hill!

JONES: Enemy soldiers! Look, they've gone now!

BACH: No, there's more looking down from the other side! They're all around us!

CASEY: Ludwick, I'm gittin' outa here!

CHRIS: Casey, you keep quiet!

CASEY: I'm not going to get my head blown off, I'm a baker not a soldier!

(*Bakers: uproar of agreement ad lib.*)

CHRIS: Wait a minute! Please, just a minute! Before you all go, I see it is time to explain myself.

CASEY: We ain't interested in any more of your explanations, Ludwick! First you come around turning us in for pocketing a little flour. Then you start draggin' us out into the woods without any proper guard and pullin' the bread out of the ovens when it's lumpy as clay and we standin' here like idiots now waiting to be picked off by the first bloomin' fool who's got an itchy shootin' finger—man I'm sick of your explanations! I'm going back to civilization and bloody the man as tries to stop me! I'm a baker, not a walkin' target!

CHRIS: You're winning the battle for Philadelphia, Casey.

CASEY: Don't go tellin' me what. . . . What's that you said I'm winnin'?

CHRIS: The enemy is watching us. They are undoubtedly counting the loaves and preparing a trap for our soldiers. I have just had a message from our patrols. The enemy are drawing off hundreds of troops to capture the whole American regiment coming this way. Well, there is no American regiment coming this way. Our troops are heading South where there will be no resistance left. We are tying up thousands of the enemy, we are soldiers with spoons and ladles, we must go on baking as though our ovens were cannon and our breadloafs bullets. Come, we will fight with our trade! Mr. Carson, will you put some more wood on that fire!

(*Sound of wood falling onto a fire.*)

Thank you,—Higby there, will you scrape down that tray!

(*Sound of scraping.*)

Back to your work, gentlemen . . . !

CASEY: Get movin', you thickheads, can't you hear what the man says? It's a battle we're fightin' just like he says! . . . aye, call it the battle of the ovens, and if this bread ain't fit for eatin' it's fit for throwin' so you'd best be doin' something useful before I lose me temper!

(*The noise of work—clanking, scraping, crackling fire, rises high.*)

CHRIS: Thank you, Casey, you're a good man.

CASEY: Every man's a good man when you give him a thing to do and his heart knows it's right for him to be doin' it.

CHRIS: Look how wonderful they work now. Bread-makers! I'm proud of them.

CASEY: I'll wager you'll be made a general for this job, Ludwick.

CHRIS: General! No, no. What would my customers in Philadelphia say?—who would have the nerve to come to a general and ask him for a dozen fresh rolls? No, general, I got to make a living when I get home.

(*Music up and down.*)

(*Footsteps on empty street . . . halt . . . door opening with tinkle of bell.*)

(*Calls.*) Katey? Ka. . . . Why are you sitting here in the shop all alone, so late at night?

KATEY: Hello, Chris. You came to see me?

CHRIS: The war is over, Katey. Didn't you hear? I hurried back.

KATEY: Yes, I heard, but I didn't believe . . . Oh, Chris, I'm so glad you've come back. The ovens are cold three months, the house is cold.

CHRIS: Where are the men, they should be working now.

KATEY: I couldn't pay them, I kept sending you so much money there was nothing to pay with. We have nothing left, Chris. I had to sell even the linen. Why did you go away?

CHRIS: I brought you something finer than all the linen in the world.

KATEY: What did you bring?

CHRIS: A new, free country! Smile to me, Katey. . . .

KATEY: How is your rheumatism?

CHRIS: Rheumatism! In a young country there is no place for rheumatism! Don't you realize I have just come from talking to George Washington?

KATEY: Really?

CHRIS: And you know what he told me? He says the bread I baked for him is the first bread he could eat that didn't catch in his teeth?

KATEY: Did he say anything about returning you the money you paid for the bakers' wages in the army?

CHRIS: No. But he said to give his best wishes to you.

KATEY (*alive*): *Me?*

CHRIS: Give my best wishes to Mrs. Ludwick, he said. She is a very good woman to wait for you so long.

KATEY: Me? General Washington said that about *me?*

CHRIS: You, Katey! Only you!

KATEY (*slight pause*): Well, I always said, Chris, that your place was in your army. After all, it's not every man understands the bakery business like you . . . what else did General Washington say?

CHRIS: He said I am a brave man. And that I shall be proud of myself. He said he could not have won the war unless men like me, the bakers and the shoemakers and all the people got so mad they could not rest until they won. And I told him, I said, General Washington, if I beg your pardon, you are perfectly right.

(*Music up and finish.*)

THUNDER FROM THE
MOUNTAINS

CHARACTERS

Announcer
Narrator
1st Ambassador
2nd Ambassador
3rd Ambassador
4th Ambassador
Juárez
Felipe
Don Manuel
Santa Anna
Father
Margarita
Louis
Bernal
Comonfort
José
Diego
Saligny
Soldier
Texan

Thunder from the Mountains

ANNOUNCER: Seventy-five years ago on June 19th as the light of dawn broke over the peak of Mount Popocatapetal, death by rifle fire was administered to Ferdinand Maximilian last Emperor of Mexico. With it came liberty to a nation. More than any other one man was responsible. He was Benito Juárez. It is his ever glorious story that we tell tonight, with the celebrated young actor of stage, screen and radio, Orson Welles, portraying the role of Juárez and narrating our program.

(*Music.*)

(*Music: flare then to background.*)

NARRATOR (*clipped, newsy*): On a morning in June, 1867, the Ambassadors of all the crown governments of the world filed into the Presidential Palace in Mexico City. Standing before the door of his office Mexican President Benito Juárez stolidly listens to the prepared speeches of the diplomats as they pass before him and shake his labor-toughened hand.

1ST AMBASSADOR: His Majesty, the King of Prussia, fervently desires that the President spare the life of His Highness Maximilian.

2ND AMBASSADOR: His Majesty, the Emperor of Austria urgently beseeches your Excellency to pardon His Highness Maximilian.

3RD AMBASSADOR: Her Majesty, the Queen of Spain (*over the above . . . but quietly fade under to B.G.*) prays that the President will show his mercy by pardoning the Archduke.

4TH AMBASSADOR: His Majesty, the King of Italy, particularly (*move off mike*) asks the President to spare the life of Maximilian. . . .

NARRATOR: As Benito Juárez listens to the pleas of the world's mightiest states, the royal courts of Europe wait at the telegraph for his answer. And Mexico also waits. Juárez stares through the window at the morning sun, motionless Indian, like a man remembering whole lifetimes . . . Now he turns, speaks.

(*Echo.*)

JUÁREZ: Honored Ambassadors, I will try to tell you why it is that Maximilian must surely die.

(*Music: swift, spanning vast distances.*)

NARRATOR (*excited, wondrous*):

Listener, there were two men who lived a century ago,
And it is a strange and marvelous thing,
But if they were to stand side by side before the sun
They would have cast two identical shadows!

(*Music: twists to a lower key, continues in B.G.—sound: pacing back and forth on creaking floor.*)

This Northern one you know.
You remember him in his long black coat,
His stove pipe hat, his craggy face.
This one is Lincoln, the farmer's son and now
A lawyer here in Salem Illinois, waiting
For the client's step across his porch.
Yes, you remember Lincoln!

(*Music: up suddenly, changed now to Mexican beat . . . to background.*)

Now travel your eye down the spine of our continent
Two thousand miles south of Salem, across the Rio Grande,
Across the high spikes of the Sierra Madre
This other lawyer lived, a century ago.

(*Sound: pacing on creaking porch.*)

This other Lincoln, this Indian man
With the narrow Indian eyes you do not remember.
But his craggy face, his stove pipe hat and long black coat
Make a familiar silhouette. This Mexican one is Juárez,
Benito Juárez pacing his office floor like Lincoln in the North,
Waiting for the client's step as Lincoln waits
In that same quiet year one century ago!

JUÁREZ: Let me understand, old man. You have been working this piece of land very long?

FELIPE: All my life, Señor. . . . They told me if I go to Juárez I will find justice. Where is justice, Juárez?

JUÁREZ: Before Justice must come the facts. Every year you pay one hundred measures of beans for the land. How many measures did you offer to pay your landlord this time?

FELIPE: The whole crop was thirty measures. That's what I

gave him. But it was not enough, he says. He must have my little grey donkey besides. He goes to the donkey and starts to lead him away. So little Pedro. . . .

JUÁREZ: Pedro is your son?

FELIPE: No, I found Pedro on the roadside last year. He's a little boy, God forgot to teach him how to speak. A little dumb boy. He was like a friend of that grey donkey! It is possible, Señor!

JUÁREZ: Yes, that is possible.

FELIPE: So when Don Manuel, my landlord, tried to take the donkey away, little Pedro would not let go of him. And he took out his whip, Señor, and he beat my Pedro, and he beat him again, and he beat him to the ground. Pedro cannot walk now. He cannot walk! Juárez, I have no money . . . is there justice in Mexico for a man without money!

JUÁREZ: . . . Come with me.

(*Sound: footsteps, door.*)

FELIPE: Juárez. (*Steps halt.*) Where?

JUÁREZ: To Don Manuel. There are laws in Mexico, Uncle.

(*Music: up & down.*)

(*Sound: walking in hall-like place toward ad lib laughter of two men.*)

DON MANUEL (*off mike*): An excellent story, Excellency, a very funny situation. . . .

(*Sound: footsteps halt as laughter and talk stops.*)

MANUEL: Who gave you permission to enter this house, Juan Felipe?

JUÁREZ: Juan Felipe is my client, Don Manuel. We have come to inform you, Don Manuel, that we are going to sue you for injuries done to the little boy, Pedro. . . .

MANUEL: He's a peasant, Juárez, get him out of here, he stinks! . . . .

SANTA ANNA: Juárez? So this is that Juárez! Do you recognize me, Señor Juárez?

JUÁREZ: I have seen you speak, Señor President Santa Anna.

SANTA ANNA: Ah ha. You like my speeches?

JUÁREZ: You always give a good performance, Excellency, considering that you do not charge admission.

SANTA ANNA: Juárez, a smart man like you, why do you keep giving these oxen such ideas? A peasant is made for working and dying, Don Manuel is not guilty of anything wrong, the man is a stupid peasant.

JUÁREZ: The laws of Mexico. . . .

SANTA ANNA (*reasonably*): The laws of Mexico have nothing to do with Mexico.

JUÁREZ: That remark does not amuse me, Señor President.

SANTA ANNA: Juárez, Juárez! A man like you! Stand by my side! Hold my hand! I will drown you in gold, take my advice, Juárez, take it, take it! I will make you a great, rich man!

JUÁREZ: Don Manuel. I will bring you to court.

SANTA ANNA: What makes you like this, Juárez? (*Steps halt.*) Why do you embarrass yourself for a stupid idiot peasant boy? Why?

JUÁREZ: You see my hands, Santa Anna . . . they are not a lawyer's but a peasant's hands. My face has been beaten, my lips have been split open, my spine has bent to the hoe. In school the Spanish gentlemen turned their backs on my Indian face as though it were the color of disease. I am not bitter, Señor President, I am ashamed for Mexico. It is not a Christian thing that seven eighths of the people should live like slaves where there are laws to prevent slavery, it is not a Christian thing, Excellency. The laws must be obeyed. Good day.

   (*Music: up and under.*)
      (*Sound: slow pacing on sidewalk outdoors.*)

NARRATOR:
   In Illinois that other Lincoln loved silently
   In those days, while this Southern one, wordless,
   Walked up and down in his stove pipe hat
   Before the house of Margarita,—courting—playing the bear,
   Pacing the sidewalk in his methodical way
   Until her door would open respectably and a voice would call,
   . . . You may come in now, good Señor. . . .

FATHER: Come away from the window, Margarita, it is not correct to peek at him when he is playing bear. It is not nice for a girl.

MARGARITA: How he must love me! Every night for six weeks! Not one night has he failed to appear.

FATHER: I think it's about time to let him into the house. Six weeks—that's quite a lot of walking up and down, and he such a busy man.

MARGARITA: Just let me watch him one minute more! How dignified he is! Say my new name father.

FATHER: Señora Margarita Juárez.

MARGARITA: Margarita Juárez! Yes . . . tonight it seems to sound so natural. It must be time now. Father . . . open the door, please?

(*Sound: going to door.*)

FATHER: Go upstairs now. When we've settled everything you may come down and speak to your future husband for a moment.

MARGARITA: Don't be long with him, Father!

(*Sound: she running off. Door opening on the footfalls outside.*)

FATHER (*clears his throat*): Señor Juárez?

(*Sound: outside footfalls halt on pavement.*)

JUÁREZ: Did you . . . did you call me Señor Maza?

FATHER: Yes. Would you be good enough to step into my house?

JUÁREZ: Ah . . . thank you, Señor. . . . I have always thought it a lovely house!

(*Music: up perhaps into a blend of Mexican and Battle Hymn.*)

NARRATOR:

Peering outward on the several states,
The taller one in Illinois saw the drums of war
Uncovering, and listened for the sound he feared. . . .

(*Music: twist of key.*)

And Juárez too, Governor Juárez now.
Feeling the ground tremble with a brewing civil war,
Walked quietly and listening among his Mexicans.
A strange Governor! No braided uniform or painted women
Running drunken through his palace halls,
He walked in places no Governor had ever walked before . . .
Searching, searching for that dangerous core of anger
That festered somewhere in the state.

(*Music: quick out.*)

LOUIS: Excellency, you will get dirty if you go down into the mine.

JUÁREZ: Oh, I have been dirty in my life. I have always wanted to see a silver mine . . . especially yours, Señor. Will you lead the way?

LOUIS: . . . Yes, Excellency.

(Sound: footsteps in cavernous place . . . coming toward sound of picks . . . chain rattle.)

To the right, Excellency, this way, please.

JUÁREZ: No, let us see them dig.

LOUIS: I beg your grace, turn here to the right. . . .

JUÁREZ *(all footsteps halt)*: Señor! Are these men chained?!

LOUIS: Excellency, I. . . .

JUÁREZ: By what law do you chain these men? Are they apes!

LOUIS: They . . . they are always running away.

JUÁREZ: Are you aware, Señor, that the law forbids this!

LOUIS: . . . I had heard of it, Excellency.

JUÁREZ: You had heard of it! You had heard of it! Break these chains. At once! And remember, friend, laws are made to be obeyed not to be "heard of"! Cut the chains. I will be back. Remember it!

SANTA ANNA: Schools! Now he is building schools for peasants! Did I tell him to build schools for peasants?

BERNAL: No, Señor President.

SANTA ANNA: No. Did I not warn him to stop sticking his nose into the silver mines, did I not warn him to stay away from the peasants and to stop stirring them up!

BERNAL: Si, Señor.

SANTA ANNA: Bernal, you will take a force of men; ride to his house and in my name, in the name of Santa Anna. . . . *(Fade.)*

ANNOUNCER: You are listening to Orson Welles, as Benito Juárez on the Cavalcade of America, presented by Du Pont. Exiled from Mexico, Juárez, penniless, lands in New Orleans. Many months later, a tall gentleman enters the top floor room of a shabby rooming house in New Orleans, and is talking with Benito Juárez.

COMONFORT: Juárez . . . it is time to go back, it is time to pull Santa Anna down!

JUÁREZ: No, Comonfort, the people elected him. He is president. Let them vote him out as they voted him in.

COMONFORT: Can you vote out a king, Juárez?

JUÁREZ: King! Is he mad? Is the beast mad too?

COMONFORT: He has made himself king of Mexico, Juárez. A new revolutionary army is forming on the West Coast. I've raised three shiploads of munitions. It is time to pull him down, Juárez!

JUÁREZ: Yes, now . . . now it is time. He is the rebel now, not we. When can we leave?

COMONFORT: I haven't enough passage money for you and your staff—but you will come, and General Montenegro, and. . . .

JUÁREZ: No. The others are military men. Let them go by boat. I will make my way.

COMONFORT: Without money? Without. . . .

JUÁREZ: I have my hands, and two good feet. . . . Toward Mexico, toward home, a good dog can always make his way.
  (*Music: up and under.*)

NARRATOR: Lincoln in Springfield, standing at the rail of the Washington-bound express, turned to the people who stood waiting in the rain; I leave now for the capital, he said, with a task before me greater than that which rested upon Washington. And they waved him silently on his way toward war. . . .
  (*Music: twist of key and beat.*)
  And the one called Juárez, with no farewells
  Gathered up his pennies and his long black coat
  And shipped across the shining Gulf to Panama;
  And facing the West he left all cities behind
  And walked alone across the curved and narrow finger
  That joins the continents, through jungles he walked
  Where parrots flew, and stood at last on the Pacific beach.
  And there he was hired into the galley of a ship
  And he sailed toward Western Mexico, where
  In a deep cut between big hills—
  In a greener Valley Forge, a ragged army waited to attack. . . .
  While Lincoln rode solemnly to the White House
  On that same dark day. . . .
  (*Music: out.*)

JOSÉ: Señor President Benito Juárez has landed in Mexico!

SANTA ANNA: Juárez! So. Exile, I see, was too merciful. We will ride against him, Señores! Tear him out of the hills. Juárez has come home to die.

(*Music: up and into war music.*)

NARRATOR:

The land is on fire! The sky burns!
The people lift up like lions,
Roaring their anger from the coast; from Mazatlan
And Atoyac, from the towns of the Spaniard
And the Indian towns! They came from Tehuantepec,
Durango and the river there, from the Bay of Banderas
The fishermen ran with salt on their lips
As once the fishermen of Marblehead came
In their boats to crash the Heights for Washington!
The sowers of corn and the makers of bread,
The black-eyed and the fair, the forest men
Whose backs were bent like the trees they cut—
They came, they came, sweetening with blood
The deserts of long dead centuries,
And they scrawled new names on Mexico's face!—
Díos y Libertad!—For God and Liberty!
And the stones rang like bells from Guadalajara
To the Gulf!

(*Sound: ad lib talking. Through it one man walking, halts.*)

DIEGO: "*President*" Juárez . . . that has a beautiful sound—President.

JUÁREZ: Diego! Where is my family? Are they here yet?

DIEGO: They will be here immediately, Excellency. You may enter the city at your pleasure now. The flags are flying, the people are dancing under the new archways. . . .

JUÁREZ: Eh? I do not believe we have met, Señor.

SALIGNY: Ambassador Saligny, your Excellency, of France. I have an urgent request.

JUÁREZ: Yes, Monsieur, what is your request?

SALIGNY: My Emperor asks Mexico's immediate payment of her debt to France. Twelve million dollars. Immediate payment, Excellency.

JUÁREZ: You know well enough, Monsieur, that Mexico cannot pay any debts for at least two years.

SALIGNY: In that case it is my duty to inform you that Emperor Napoleon's army under his Highness the Archduke Ferdinand Maximilian is at this moment landing on your coast. (*Pause.*)

May I have the honor of carrying your reply to his Highness?

JUÁREZ: You may have that honor. Yes, go to this Hapsburg, this military doll, this sudden Mexican Emperor, and tell him that though he has very cleverly arrived at a moment when the people are exhausted from civil war, he will be received with the same exquisite hatred as only the people of the Americas know how to brew for conquerors. Tell him, please, that if we have buried thousands upon thousands of our patriots this frightful year, the soil of Mexico is still broad enough and deep enough for one more grave.

(*Sound.*)

(*Music.*)

NARRATOR: At Gettysburg the taller one halted between battles and spoke his vision, that government of the people, by the people, and for the people shall not perish from the earth!

(*Sound: distant cannon intermittently.*)

COMONFORT: Juárez! Why do we fight him! Listen to me, they've got us with our backs against Texas, our bullets are almost gone, we'll all die . . . for what now!

JUÁREZ: Señores . . . all of you . . . hear me out. We could make peace with Maximilian. Yes—we could make peace. But not with these hills, not with this Mexican earth. I do not speak as Juárez, but as that unseeable thing through which the people govern themselves. I can no more surrender than the Rio Grande can turn into the Rhine.

MARGARITA (*off mike*): Benito! Thank heaven—Benito!

JUÁREZ: Margarita! Speak . . . what's happened to you?

MARGARITA: On the road here we were being followed. Juan Felipe dropped back to fire at them while we drove on. They leaped on him. They stood him to a tree . . . and shot him there. There was no reason. He was going with them!

JUÁREZ: Is it clear, Señores, that we cannot surrender? They are shooting prisoners.

COMONFORT: Neither can we fight, Juárez, not without ammunition. In ten days our stocks are gone!

SOLDIER: Excellency!

JUÁREZ: Yes, soldier.

SOLDIER: This man to see you. He says he comes from across the river.

JUÁREZ: You are from Texas?

TEXAN: Yes, sir. You Juárez, sir?

JUÁREZ: I am.

TEXAN: I just come over to let you boys know that we can't figure you out. Every night we been leaving a pile of rifles, powder and cartridges right out on the river bank on our side, and they ain't one bullet been taken yet. Don't you want the stuff?

JUÁREZ: It belongs to the United States Army, it. . . .

TEXAN: Between us, Mister, we kinda figure we can spare it.

JUÁREZ: I don't know how to thank you, Señor.

TEXAN: I guess Abe Lincoln ain't too happy about that foreign prince yellin' across the river at us the rest of our lives. Well . . . good night. . . .

JUÁREZ: God bless you, Señor, and Abraham Lincoln.

TEXAN (*off mike*): Thanks, sir . . . 'bye!

JUÁREZ: That was thirty million people talking, Señores! Mexico is not alone!

> (*Music: up high, then same as the very first music for the first scene.*)

NARRATOR: Mexico was not alone. And the time came when Juárez standing in the vaulted palace of the President paused a moment to look at each Ambassador pleading for the life of Maximilian and continued—

JUÁREZ (*again in the palace . . . speaking as though in a vaulted place*): . . . So it is not difficult to understand, honored Ambassadors, why Maximilian must die. Not for the sorrow he caused, nor the blood he spilled—that would call only for revenge, and the Mexican state does not stoop to vengeance. Why then must he die? Gentlemen I ask you a question. Why is it that the United States of America alone among all the great powers has not sent an ambassador to plead with me for Maximilian's life. Why do they not send a plea? Because they know that for a democratic state to pardon a would-be tyrant is to make mockery of that state and its whole people. Therefore, in the name of Mexican democracy, to her ever-lasting honor and the undying dignity of her people I command that the sentence of execution be carried out against the Archduke Ferdinand Maximilian, by a firing squad upon the Hill of Bells, at dawn.

(*Music: up to finish.*)

GLIDER DOCTOR

CHARACTERS

Narrator
1st Voice
2nd Voice
Dr. Hook
Billy
Colonel
Pilot
Al
Joe
Corporal
G.I.
Officer

Glider Doctor

(*Music: Very soprano, thin, moonlike.*)

NARRATOR: The moon was round as a barrel head that night; poured her icy light on the English coasts. On the choppy sea England floats like a great moored ship. Along the dark and hidden piersides from Plymouth to the Scottish coast, men stop in the dark to study the moon. In the flared bows of waiting cruisers, doctors lift up equipment for the hundredth inspection, like old women fussing in their shopping bags. Further inland where the concrete carpets of the airports have thrust through woodland, where King Arthur rode, doctors stow plasma in grossly shadowed bombers whose silent motors even now nose toward the wind. And nearby, squatted on the ground like headless ducks, there waits another kind of winged machine. But these are motorless. Silent. The dread and terror of all defending Armies. Gliders.

(*Music: Switch. Specific now. On scene. Immediate.*)
Hundreds of them. And hundreds more in the dark behind them. A push of wind wrinkles their fabric skin; box kites with wings, ugly ducklings of the air, square wings, pug noses, built to float on a sneeze.

(*Sound: Tractors, jeeps, noise of commands, shouts, all off mike.*)
Whole acres of them out this night. Crews swing up their blunt noses that open on hinges.

1ST VOICE: Make that safety hook fast. All right, Clem, roll her in.

(*Sound: Jeep engine.*)
Little right . . . OK, lash her down. Tighter than that, Harry!

NARRATOR: They hook the jeep's wheels to the floor, draw the body down so tight her springs flatten out. She mustn't bounce an inch when they hit the air.

2ND VOICE: Let's get behind her . . . come on!

(*Effort sound of four men.*)
NARRATOR: Into another glider goes an artillery piece, small

and deadly. Another one takes only men and machine guns, another. . . .

(*Music: Out.*)

DR. HOOK: Billy!

BILLY: Yes, sir!

DR. HOOK: I don't want you to put anything on top of those stretchers. Keep them clear. . . . (*Fade back and out.*) . . . What'd you do with the tourniquet cartons I had here . . . ?

(*Sound: Off-mike commands, questions, tractors, a few shouts.*)

NARRATOR: Yes, stretchers will soar into the sky this night, and tourniquets to stanch the blood that will surely flow before the morning comes again. Through the squat glider squadrons an officer comes on the trot, stops at the open nose of a machine whose loaders wear little red crosses pinned to their sleeves.

COLONEL (*a little breathless*): Hook! Where's Captain Hook!

HOOK (*coming in*): Right here, Colonel.

COLONEL: You should be loaded up by now.

HOOK: I am, I'm just checking supplies. How does it look, sir? Real thing this time?

COLONEL: Don't ask me, I don't know. It's a good moon for invasion, but . . . well, I guess you'll know when you get there.

PILOT: Time to take your places, Captain. We're going to button up in a minute.

HOOK: Right. Goodbye, Colonel.

COLONEL: Good luck. Oh, Pilot.

PILOT: Yes, sir.

COLONEL: Excuse me, I can't see your rank in the dark. . . .

PILOT (*laughs*): That's all right, sir.

COLONEL: You take care of Captain Hook and his men, see that they get down in one piece. He's a doctor, remember that every minute. If we're making the continent tonight we'll need doctors worse than water. Good luck to you.

PILOT: Thank you sir. All right, Doctor, in you go.

(*Music: Bass, portentious, motor-like.*)

NARRATOR: All right, Doctor, in you go. And your first-aid men unhook the overhead cables letting the nose fold down on her hinges, and the pilot takes his seat, and the hooks are hooked, and the safety straps are pulled up tight, and the dark settles inside this loaded box, and you wait. The radium dial on your wrist grins up at you like fate. On two benches along each flat wall of the glider your men settle down. There are no windows excepting through the nose. You can see nothing but the silhouette of the pilot's shoulders up ahead. You wait. . . .

(*Music: Out.*)

BILLY: Doc?

HOOK: Huh?

BILLY (*on mike. He is next to* HOOK): I heard a rumor before.

AL (*further away*): I heard that. . . .

BILLY: You're always telling him. Let me tell him one time, will you? (*Light laughter.*)

HOOK: What's it now, Bill?

BILLY: They say Eisenhower's been visiting all the paratroop outfits. Been at it all night, they say.

HOOK: Who told you that?

BILLY: It's all over the field.

AL: I think we're in tonight. Going for a big ride tonight.

JOE (*further away still*): You've been sayin' that since we left Carolina.

AL: Look at the moon, you jerk. They don't waste a moon like that on maneuvers.

BILLY (*on mike, therefore quieter, more intimate with* HOOK): They're hookin' us onto the cable, Doc.

HOOK: So I see.

BILLY: I hope it's a good cable.

HOOK: You're talking too much. (*Louder to all.*) Everybody got some gum?

AL: Yeh . . . OK . . . we're set . . .

(*Sound: Roar up, but muffled, of plane engines. Hold.*)

NARRATOR (*music in*): With a little jerk the glider starts to move. The talk dies. All eyes turn toward the pilot's slanted windshield. Ahead the moon illuminates the big blundering towplane. Out of her tail, as from a spider's, the tow line shudders as it drags the ugly duckling to the concrete runway. Now you're on it. Now the glider wheels roll smoothly, slowly. The glider seems to stiffen, the wings creak. The world takes a breath. Suddenly the first harbinger of flight grabs at your heart . . . Wind. Blasting wind. The glider weaves under you. You feel her tilt as her tail comes up. Now speed takes you by the back of the neck. Speed, more speed . . . a finger of wind taps the glider from above. She sits a little, then suddenly you notice the tow plane is in the air ahead, over the trees. Your pilot throws a lever. Your wheels detach and fall to the earth. You, doctor of medicine, man of peace, examiner of the delicate pulse, you are soaring through the dark night air, pulled irrevocably and beyond all further questioning, pulled toward. . . .

(*Music out.*)

(*Sound: Hold wind in BG.*)

HOOK: Pilot?

PILOT: Yes, Doc?

HOOK: Is that a wheat field out ahead down there? I don't remember seeing it before.

PILOT: You'll never see a wheat field as big as that, sir. That's the channel down there.

(*Music: A dreadful chord it dies.*)

(*Sound: Wind in stronger. Include motors very muffled.*)

BILLY: We're going over, heh, Doc?

HOOK: That's right. Not surprised are you?

BILLY: Aren't you?

HOOK: Sure. But we've been flying around over England every night, I didn't expect it'd be too long before we'd make the jump. Don't lean your knee against me. You're shaking.

BILLY: Sorry, sir.

(*Pause: Only the wind.*)

How long does it take to be a doctor?

HOOK: About seven years. Why, you got ambitions?

BILLY: Maybe. If I get home before I'm too old. I'm only nineteen now, though. Can a fella really work his way through?

HOOK: I did, partly.

BILLY: Parents helped you for the rest, heh?

HOOK: No, borrowed from an aunt. My parents are dead fifteen years now.

BILLY: What'd your wife say about you flyin' around in gliders? Raised sand, I bet, heh?

HOOK: I'm not married. You?

BILLY: Oh no, sir. I got prospects, but . . . Then you . . . you don't get any mail, then, heh?

HOOK: Oh sure. From the storage company . . . bills on my car . . . (*They laugh a little.*) No, I've got nobody. Actually, not a friend in the world outside the Army. Got my degree, interned, practiced three months, then into the Army.

BILLY: How was it? You get a kick out of studying?

HOOK: Oh sure. But I always wanted a day to come when I'd be out among people . . . doing something in the open air. Something with a little adventure connected with it.

BILLY: I guess you got it, all right. Plenty of open air up here.

HOOK: You scared, Billy? I mean really scared?

BILLY: . . . Not yet, but I'm gettin' there fast. You?

HOOK: I'm there. I've been there since I got into this outfit.

BILLY: Then why'd you pick gliders?

HOOK: A man sometimes likes to test himself. Do something he knows his whole nature rebels against. I always feared flying. I still do. When I go back to my books . . . if I come through this . . . I want to know I have the guts to do anything. A doctor ought to be sure of that.

BILLY: That's the funniest reason I ever heard for flyin' these boxes.

HOOK: Sing out when we're over France, will you, Pilot?

PILOT: Right over the coast now, sir. Plenty of company too. Can you see from back there?

HOOK: No, what's doing?

PILOT: Must be a thousand gliders in the air. I don't see any firing. Looks like we'll be the first to land. We'll be down in two minutes now.

(*Music: In.*)

NARRATOR: Two minutes. Two minutes of air left to shield you from the deadly forests below, the mined roads, the eyes of the enemy. Two sure minutes. After that . . . you can't think beyond those two minutes. In the dark your mind counts equipment, remembers the location of every suture, every thread of gauze, each mighty bottle of plasma . . . each unit of penicillin . . . riding under this moon with you. Your men no longer shift their feet. The air within the glider seems to settle in stillness. You ride the flexing of the wings as though they were attached to your shoulders. You wonder where you will land. God forbid a lake under you. God forbid an unbroken woods. Pray God for a flat piece of earth. You watch the towline which seems to extend from the pilot's chest. The line is still taut as a curved girder. To right and left beyond these fabric walls are other flying fabric walls, and within them men praying for your safety. You are the doctor. Their doctor. Their life. You are carrying their blood. You are carrying their dreams of tomorrow. You are carrying all their tomorrows. . . .

    (*Music: Out.*)

BILLY: There goes the line, Doctor!

HOOK: Take it easy.

PILOT: Ready for landing. Ready! We're free, hold on!

    (*Sound: Motor sound fades away. Only the shrill air-sound now.*)

      (*Music: A glider soaring through the air.*)

      (*Music: In.*)

NARRATOR: You hear only what a bird hears now. The moon tilts against the windshield, flashes across the pilot's shoulder and away. Nosing down now. Nosing toward Normandy. No more horizon now. Only black down there. Only black air. A dream is this way. Falling in a dream, tilting leftward in a dream, sighing downward toward the blackness, weaving against a thrust of air, pushed upward ten yards in the space of a second, down again twenty yards, bobbing in the empty air like a snowflake in a courtyard. Where will it end? When will it end? Where is the earth!

    (*Music: Out.*)

PILOT: LANDING! Hold it now!

    (*Sound: The whistle of wind. Sudden scraping. Silence.*)

HOOK: Let's get her open, come on.

    (*Sound: Clank of steel hooks. Pounding of feet on board floor of glider . . . Heavy breathing of men working.*)

Nice soft landing, Pilot. Thanks.

PILOT: Good wind, that's all.

HOOK: All right, boys, get that nose up. Keep it quiet now.

    (*Sound: Hinge squeek, panting of men.*)

  (*Hoarse whisper.*) Sergeant.

BILLY (*hoarse whisper*): Yes, sir.

HOOK: Pilot and I are going to move out and try to contact Battalion. Unload and have everything ready to move soon as we get back. Be quiet now.

BILLY: Right, sir.

HOOK: Well, let's go.

(*Sound: Walking.*)

Gosh, it's dark. Feels like a road, doesn't it?

PILOT: Yes, it's . . . hold it!

(*Sound: Walking stops.*)

Don't move! What are we on, a cliff here? Good . . . !

HOOK (*hushed*): It's a building! You landed on a roof!

PILOT: Sssh! Listen below. . . .

(*Ad lib: Voices . . . distant. They speak in German, an argument . . .*)

HOOK (*all hushed now*): Germans. Come away from the edge.

(*Sound: Few footsteps.*)

Sergeant . . . Billy.

BILLY: Huh? Yes, sir.

HOOK: We're on the roof of a building. . . .

(BILLY *utters.*)

Listen, all of you. There are Germans downstairs. They must be important potatoes to have a building like this to stay in. Where's the corporal of the riflemen?

CORPORAL: Right here, sir.

HOOK: I can't have medics carrying weapons. You understand that.

CORPORAL: Yes, sir.

HOOK: We've got to get off this building and make our way to the assembly area. Take your squad down into the building and win yourself the Congressional Medal. I'd try to capture them if possible. This looks like some kind of a command post, probably high officers.

CORPORAL: OK. We'll go down. I think that's the skylight over there, isn't it, sir?

HOOK: Looks like it. I'm sorry we have to stand and watch but that's the rules. Go to it, fellas.

(*Sound: Several tiptoed footsteps away.*)

Billy . . . attention, the rest of you. We'll follow down right behind them. Pick up as much equipment as you can carry, especially the plasma and those six drug cases. Once you're inside the building get out as quick as possible with the equipment. Stay close to me all the time. All right, load yourselves up.

(*Sound: Rifle fire rapid from below . . . hold.*)

PILOT: Doctor? I think you'd better try to rush through while things are still confused down there.

HOOK: Right. Follow me, boys. And for Pete's sake don't drop anything. Let's go.

(*Sound: Rifle fire closer, closer, finally on mike. Shouts. This is indoor fire and echoes like hell. Pick up running feet now. Focus on running feet and start fading the echo of rifles. Rifles now heard from outside. Major focus now on the running, which is on gravel.*)

(*Breathless, running: As loud as he dares.*) Billy, Sergeant!

BILLY: Right ahead of you, Doctor!

HOOK: Anybody get it?

BILLY: None of our gang. Those riflemen got it hot in there, though.

(*Sound: Running comes down to a walk.*)

HOOK: We'll have to send somebody back to them later. Pull over to the side here, men!

(*Sound: Gathering of men on gravel.*)

We've got one job now. Forget everything else. We've got to find the battalion. We're going to move due North as scheduled. Stay off this road and don't get lost, those woods ahead look pretty dense. Let's go.

(*Music: Into sound . . . and out.*)

(*Sound: Walking in brush.*)

NARRATOR: And now the forest moves in, into your heart, into the space behind your eyes. The forest is alive with the movement of trees. . . .

(*Sound: Crack of a twig . . . walking stops.*)

Or is it only trees?

(*Sound: Walking again.*)

(*Music: In.*)

Instinctively now, as though through ages of ancestry born for this, you seek your wounded; man of medicine, guardian of the living heart, climbing like water climbs, inevitably toward its own, its source. The night creeps toward your throat like a crooked hand. What eyes are watching you even now, waiting for your skull to cross the range of fire? Why do you not hide, wait for dawn, for safety? You are lost, a man can honorably get lost. Why, doctor, why do you move in this forest?

(*Music: Out.*)

(*Sound: Distant salvos of naval guns. Walking out . . . hold guns B.G.*)

BILLY: That sounds like the Navy, sir. They must be starting to take the beaches.

HOOK: Where's the Pilot?

PILOT: Here, sir.

HOOK: I don't understand. We landed with the rest of the battalion. Where are they?

PILOT: While we were perched on that roof they must have moved toward the objective.

HOOK: But there's no firing.

PILOT: We're in a woods, sir. Maybe down in a hollow at that. Be hard to hear rifles down here.

HOOK: The Germans must be tipped off by this time, though. You think they'd be combing the area for us.

PILOT: Yes, sir but. . . .

(*Sound: Sudden vicious rifle fire. Register hard. Crackles to silence . . . hold Naval guns in B.G.*)

BILLY: Straight ahead, sir. I saw the flashes.

HOOK: Let's go.

(*Sound: Distant rifles. Walking on mike.*)

Billy. No matter what happens we're not getting captured. You understand that?

BILLY: Yes, sir. But we might be walking right into the backs of the Germans now.

HOOK: We'll take all precautions, but we can't just stand still. Remember, I don't care if you have no weapons, you'll fight your way out with your fists if they try to grab you. Do you hear me?

BILLY: . . . Yes, sir.

HOOK: You understand, don't you, Billy? There'll be wounded men screaming for us all over this lot. I don't want to be behind German barbed wire when that happens. . . .

BILLY (*hesitates*): All right, sir. I only. . . .

(*Sound: Rifles closer. Walking comes to sudden halt.*)

HOOK: You heard it, didn't you?

BILLY (*whisper*): I did, yeh.

PILOT: What is it, Doctor?

HOOK: Up ahead there . . . somebody's moaning. Stay here. I'll take a look.

PILOT: Watch it. That's an old German trick. We may be behind their lines. They'll often trick you like that.

HOOK: Will they? Wait here! I'll see what he is and where we are.

(*Sound: Walking through brush.*)

(*Music: In.*)

NARRATOR (*quietly*): And why did you smile in the dark when the Pilot said it might be a trick? Because you knew it would be? Because you want a Nazi to strangle in the dark, perhaps the very one who tricked another doctor in another wood, a brother you had, a brother you loved? No relatives Dr. Hook. No, none anymore.

(*Music: Out.*)

(*Sound: Stop walking. Faint moan of a man.*)

Behind that mound now . . . he's there two yards away now.

(*Sound: Walking in.*)

Circle him now . . . as your brother forgot to . . . circle him, confuse him . . . now move in fast!

(*Sound: Quick rush in brush. Moan of man close in.*)

G.I.: Who's there! Who!

HOOK: Who . . . what are you . . . what?

G.I. (*weeping*): I'm dyin', that's what I am.

HOOK: Where are we? Are those our boys up there?

G.I.: Who else do you think could lay down a fire like that?

HOOK (*shouts. The first shout in many minutes. Triumphantly*): Billy! Billy! They're our boys! Bring up the stuff!

(*Music: Up thrilling down fast.*)

(*Sound: Spasmodic firing.*)

Hold his arm out stiff. There! Break out more sutures, Billy.

BILLY: There's no more after this box, sir. Seems to me you've sewed up the whole battalion the last three hours. Any news about the beachhead guys?

HOOK: Forget them. They'll be lucky to hold the beaches, let alone drive this far inland. Hold your hand still . . . Billy, what's the trouble?

BILLY: I'm just cold, is all. The boys got those new wounded under control very nice, sir. All the guys are very happy we came. I was afraid they'd be sore we got so lost. A doctor around makes some guys feel like they were wearing armor or something.

OFFICER: Doctor Hook. You can get these wounded ready for transport now.

HOOK: Transport! We're in German territory. Where can we go?

OFFICER: We've just intercepted a German runner. Our beachhead forces have broken through. They'll be spearheading right into us any minute now. They. . . .

(*Sound: Distant roar of men joining forces.*)

HOOK: They're here. They've broken through! Billy, look at our tanks!

(*Sound: Roar all about now. Plenty of yippees, cowboy yells . . .*)

Billy . . . Get up, what's got you? Why, you dope, you're wounded!

BILLY: They . . . they got me when we ran through the house, sir. I didn't want to get left behind.

HOOK (*shocked, angry*): Why didn't you tell me, you fool! Don't try to move.

BILLY: I'm awful sorry, sir. I didn't think it was so serious.

HOOK: It's not. Shut up now.

BILLY: I wanted to be with you, Sir . . . after all the training I . . . (*breathes in with pain*) . . . I wanted to see you work. All of a sudden I knew why I was alive . . . you think I could make any kind of a doctor, sir?

HOOK: I had no idea you wanted to be one.

BILLY: Neither did I . . . until tonight. You think I stand a chance?

HOOK: If you can keep your mouth shut and make believe this doesn't hurt.

COLONEL (*same as at the English take off*): Hook, is that you? . . . Oh, I beg your pardon. Here, I'll hold that.

HOOK: Thanks, Colonel. Hold tight now, Billy. . . .

(*Effort as though probing down into bone.*)

COLONEL: Good job, man. Good job. Lucky you've got some light to work by.

HOOK: It is dawn, isn't it. Billy, look at that sky . . . your first morning in France . . . look at it, Bill.

BILLY: Thanks, Doc.

COLONEL: What'd he say?

HOOK: He said . . . it was a very pretty dawn, sir. Will you hand me that gauze?

(*Music: In and under for . . .*)

NARRATOR: A very pretty dawn, yes, but the night would never end if you, Doctor and all our men of medicine did not move into battle at the very elbow of our fighting men. And there will be other dawns, Doctor . . . until the most beautiful dawn of all rises over the Armies of our nations on that saddest and happiest day of all; that first morning when we will stand, all together, all enemies of death, all the life-loving peoples of the world, clasping hands over the Berlin grave of the tyrant. And that will be the reddest, tallest, brightest dawn that ever woke a bird to singing on this earth. You will give us that dawn, Doctor!

MARE ISLAND AND BACK

CHARACTERS

Doctor Kessler
Henry
Logan
Luke
Major
Instructor

Mare Island and Back

KESSLER: Hear this! You blessed ones, you lucky ones sitting in your bedrooms with ten pink toenails to clip, and you in your kitchens opening a beer bottle with two living hands, hear this. And you especially who sit by the loudspeakers and smoke, having but recently learned how to open a pack of cigarettes with one hand . . . hear this.

(*Music: Punctuate in flow . . . Brief. Into background.*)

This is no tale designed to inspire you for twenty minutes and leave you staring through your tears at the trouser leg hanging empty from your hip. I have laced too many steel and leather forearms to your elbows to promise you'll play Chopin in ten easy lessons. But hear this and know what can be done, because this was done. This is Sam Logan's story, Captain Sam Logan, United States Marines.

(*Music: Drop down quickly into . . .*)

(*Sound: Strong fighter plane sound in air. Hold in background.*)

He was feeling good that morning. Plenty of sky over Guadalcanal and the smoke of the guns didn't come up this high. Might have been Florida below, it was so clean up here, and the clouds washed his wings as he banked left to circle the island. This was the life, this was the joy of it, this was Sam Logan's life, the beginning and the end of it. To wish for a cloud and be there, to yearn for higher air and climb it on the hot back of his engine. Levelling off now, he dipped a wing to the boys below to show them he was there with his big hand over them. And then he saw the sun, and saw the speck on it, and grinned like a boy; and the clouds moved under to make a floor that he could fight on. It came like a black stone, growing, sprouting wings now, firing now . . . The sun like a mirror shining in his eyes . . . something went past . . . he banked hard right, the strong right leg on the pedal. . . .

(*Sound: Machine gun burst. Engine clanks . . . Stops . . . Wind on the wings as he goes down.*)

The hatch opened hard with the wind sucking it. Horizon over his left ear now. The wind on his head like a hammer as

he stands on his seat and walks out and slides down the sky.
. . . ONE, two, three . . .

(*Sound: Wind sound suddenly finer as he falls without plane.*)

. . . four, Sam Logan gripped the steel handle at his chest.
Eight, nine. . . .

(*Sound: A whoosh as the chute opens.*)

His shoulders jerked and he grinned again; far below he saw
the sea between his legs like a great pillow. And then, then it
came.

(*Sound: Plane approaching.*)

Zero turning back, nosing up toward him, the sun flashing
like water on the prop. Angry, squirming upward like a
snake. . . . Sam Logan hung from his parachute and the
Japanese pilot, husbanding his Imperial cartridges, performed a successful but unnecessary amputation two thousand feet above the sea, and Sam Logan's right leg flew in a
high and bloody arc and followed him down, while the
Zero, propellor dripping, moved northward toward Japan.

(*Music: Stab.*)

(*Sound: Let the Zero fade away. Hold an instant of silence.*)

HENRY (*as though* LOGAN *had just told him the above story*):
Well . . . that's tough, but consider yourself lucky Logan.

LOGAN: Yeh, heh?

HENRY: Sure. Take little Henry. I wasn't even supposed to be
out here. I had too many independents. Wife and two kids.
Had it all figured I'm safe. All right, so I'm in. I figure, well,
I get myself in the band; no violins allowed. Quartermaster;
I ain't fat enough. Air Corps; too fat. Landing barges; just
right. We get back in the States, I'm gonna get up in the
morning, my kids tie my shoes, my wife puts on my hat, and
I go sell my apples. Toss you for the intersection of Forty-
second and Broadway, Logan. Or are *you* going to corner
the Mackintosh market?

LOGAN: That doctor said he'd put a hand on you, didn't he?

HENRY: You can't tie your shoes with a hook. What're you
going to do? You give it any thought?

LOGAN: I don't know. I went to see that doctor. What's his
name? Kessler?

LUKE (*southern*): He's nice, that doctor. But he can't grow you nothin' you can put a shoe on.

LOGAN: Well, at least we've only got one missing, Luke.

LUKE: Which just about puts me square flat behind the outhouse. Man, I heard the way you lost yours . . . that sure was. . . .

LOGAN: I didn't lose it, I gave it.

HENRY: Yeh, well whatever you did you ain't got it, bud. . . .

LOGAN: What'd you do, Luke, farmer?

LUKE: Yeh, that's all I ever did. And they ain't no corner to sell apples in Clay County.

LOGAN: I heard those artificial legs are pretty good the way they've got them down.

LUKE: Yeh, but I ain't pitchin' no artificial hay and I ain't plowin' no artificial ground. It was tough enough with two legs. I just hope to God they never let me out of this hospital, that's all I hope.

(*Sound: Footsteps approaching.*)

HENRY (*quietly*): Here's Doc Kessler, Logan.

KESSLER: Morning, boys. Hot in here, isn't it?

(*Sound: Window opening.*)

That's better. Some of that New Hebrides ozone. Why didn't you open the window next to your chair, Henry?

HENRY: I can't open that window. It needs two hands.

KESSLER: It'll open with one and a half. Try it.

(*Sound: Window slowly opening.* HENRY*'s effort.*)

Let's see it, Henry. . . .

HENRY: There it is . . . what there is of it.

KESSLER: . . . Looks nice.

HENRY: Yeh, pretty.

KESSLER: Could be worse, Henry.

HENRY: I know, every morning I thank God it wasn't my head.

KESSLER: What head? Henry, when you get back to the States they'll do a fancy operation on you. Fix you up with a hand that you can open and close just by thinking. You won't have to move your shoulders to operate it. Works right off your own muscles. Now all you've got to do is learn how to think.

HENRY: That's great, Doc.

KESSLER: Now look here. . . .

HENRY: I appreciate it, Doc, but you don't have to kid me. I'm a truck driver. Ten-ton Macks. How'm I gonna drive a truck with a tin hand?

KESSLER: You can do it with a tin hand but you can't with a tin brain.

HENRY: I appreciate it, Doctor, but I ain't kiddin' myself.

KESSLER: Okay, it's your funeral. Luke, take the cover off. Let me see the leg.

LUKE: It don't hurt anymore, hardly.

KESSLER: No reason why it should. Yeh, looks fine. Cover up. Tell me, boy, you've got the farm waiting for you back home, haven't you?

LUKE: I can't go back to that farm, sir. They can't afford to feed me.

KESSLER: Why, you tired of working?

LUKE: No, sir, but I can't. . . .

KESSLER: Talk to you about it later.

(*Sound: Two steps.*)

Let's see it Logan.

LOGAN: Feels peculiar.

KESSLER: Raise it.

LOGAN: Feels funny . . . How's it look?

KESSLER: Cover up. Move over, let me sit on your bed.

LOGAN: How am I doing. Is it healing sir?

KESSLER: Yeh, coming together in great shape. I've been wanting to talk to you, Logan. What are your plans?

LOGAN: Plans for what?

KESSLER: They'll fit you with an artificial leg back in the States. The thing I'm interested in is the kind of work you want to do. Maybe you can get started on it in the hospital, and by the time you're a civilian. . . .

LOGAN: Oh. Well, I'm going to fly, sir.

(*Pause.*)

KESSLER (*his pins knocked out*): You're going to fly.

LOGAN: That's right.

KESSLER: Well. That's a pretty damn nice way of taking it, Logan. I'm glad you feel that way.

LOGAN: How long will it take for me to get a leg?

KESSLER: Oh, a few months. You'll have plenty of time to get used to it, and then . . . I don't know, maybe a commercial line will give you a chance.

LOGAN: Oh, I'm not interested in commercial flying. I'm going back into combat.

KESSLER (*quietly*): I see . . . Did you . . . you ever know anybody with an artificial leg?

LOGAN: No, but . . . I know what you mean, sir, but it doesn't apply to me. I'll be able to walk, won't I?

KESSLER: Definitely.

LOGAN: Well if I can walk I can fly. And if I can fly I can fly combat.

KESSLER (*laughs*): Well, all right! I don't think it's ever been done but who knows, maybe nobody tried. I'll see you later, Logan. See you later, boys.

(*Sound: Walking away.*)

HENRY: Hey. Hey, Logan.

LOGAN: Heh?

HENRY: What's the matter with you, you hypnotized or something?

LUKE: He ain't hypnotized. He's just naturally crazy.

(*Music: Up and under.*)

KESSLER: That was Sam Logan. Of course he'd never fly, certainly not for the Navy combat. In the beginning I berated myself for not telling him the truth. And every day I made up my mind to tell him, but it kept getting harder and harder. I'd come into the ward and he'd be smiling up at me with that kid grin on his face. And whenever we'd talk. . . .

LOGAN (*off mike perspective*): You know, when I get a plane, Doc, I'm going to take you up and turn you over so many times you'll think you drank a gallon of high octane. (*Fade.*) I'll show you a power dive like you never saw in . . . (*Out.*)

KESSLER: And another time, when we were alone. . . .

LOGAN (*off-mike perspective*): I was just reading about these jet-propulsion jobs. Man, that's for me. . . . (*Fade.*) They'll never touch us in those babies. Seven hundred miles per . . . (*Out.*)

KESSLER: One day I went out to the field that was a few miles from the hospital. I knew a Major there. We were old friends.

(*Music: Out.*)

MAJOR: That's right, Captain, this is the kind of fighter he was flying.

KESSLER: I'd like to look in the cockpit.

MAJOR: Here, step right up. . . . There you are. Hoist in. What's up?

KESSLER: I just wanted to get the feel of these pedals. How far does this pedal go?

MAJOR: Go ahead, press it.

KESSLER: Uh huh. Major, I want your opinion. What would you say to a man flying one of these in combat . . . with one artificial leg. . . .

MAJOR: Impossible.

KESSLER: Wait a minute now. He's got the action of his knee. It's just from the knee down.

MAJOR: Couldn't do it. I doubt that he'll fly, and he'd certainly never make combat.

KESSLER: He's a remarkable kid, Major, he's all g——

MAJOR: Wouldn't help. I'm not a doctor, I'm a flyer. But I don't believe that a man is ever going to time the use of an artificial leg so that he could go into combat and come out alive. That leg's got to *respond*, Captain, a man's got to act on a split tail of a second. . . .

KESSLER: Is there any rule against it that you know of?

MAJOR: Well there isn't any rule against a blind man flying either, but we don't give them airplanes.

KESSLER: But there's no rule.

MAJOR: No, but it's just out of this world. I wouldn't let him kid himself, Captain, he's got all the flying medals he's ever going to get.

(*Music: Bridge.*)

HENRY: Heeyah, get your Mackintoshes, all red, all ripe, five a piece, help the veteran, heeyah! How's that, better, Logan?

LOGAN: Great. Henry, why don't you shut up?

HENRY: What do you mean? Doc Kessler says you would practice up on what you're going to be in life. I'm doin' my occupational therapy.

LOGAN: We're going back to the States today! Buck up old boy. Free ocean voyage.

HENRY: You know, Luke, I think his mother must've been thinking of a boy scout.

(*Sound: Footsteps coming closer.*)

LUKE: I sure hope they don't put me out of the hospital, that's all I hope.

LOGAN: Hello, Doctor, when are we leaving?

KESSLER: About an hour. Move away, will you boys? I want to talk to Logan. Go ahead, Henry, give Luke a push.

HENRY: Yeh, don't you think we make a great pair, Doc? He could carry the pencils and the tin cup and I push him.

KESSLER: You're breaking my heart. Get outa here. You're going to Mare Island Hospital, Logan, California.

LOGAN: Swell. I heard about that place.

KESSLER: I won't be with you, so I want to tell you a few things. First of all . . . I'm not sure that you'll ever fly again.

LOGAN: No, sir, I've got to fly. . . .

KESSLER: Wait a minute now. You see Luke and Henry here . . . they've made up their minds that they can't do anything. That's a bad attitude. Obviously. But it's just as bad for a man to think that he can do everything and. . . .

LOGAN: If I can't fly I might as well be dead.

KESSLER: Now you cut that out. . . .

LOGAN: No sir, that's the way I feel. I was just getting hot, I was just getting good.

KESSLER: Tell me this. Before you ever started to think about flying what were you interested in?

LOGAN: Nothing.

KESSLER: Oh come on now.

LOGAN: When I was six or seven years old my dad drove us out to the flying field. You know where they took you up for a dollar? Well when I saw one of those planes go up that's when I knew. And I never changed, not for five minutes.

KESSLER: Good enough. Now listen to me. Supposing I were God. God of the Navy and the Marines.

LOGAN (*laughs*): Would you have trouble.

KESSLER (*laughs*): You said it. But just supposing . . . supposing I had the power to put you in a plane and send you into combat. And you get in and take off. And after five minutes in the air you realize that you can't make it. You come down and. . . . (*Breaks off.*) You see what I mean? I want you to have something to fall back on, an ace in the hole.

LOGAN (*shaken*): I realize what you're saying, sir. . . .

KESSLER: I don't want you to think that it's completely out.

LOGAN: I know what you want me to think. I'd just like to tell you something, sir. You deal with hundreds of crippled men every week, and maybe after a while you begin to look at them as though they felt crippled.

KESSLER: What do you mean?

LOGAN: I sit here looking out this window, and I see the sky and I see the planes going over and I feel like Sam Logan that's all. The same way I ever felt when I saw planes flying. I look different but I feel the same. And I hope to God they're going to treat me in the States the way I feel and not the way I look.

KESSLER: You think I've treated you that way?

LOGAN: You've been all right, Doctor, but I still don't think you realize what a man can do if he's got to do it.

KESSLER: It's funny. Ever since I became a surgeon I've been trying to make patients understand just that.

LOGAN (*eagerly*): Then you . . . you believe that I can fly combat again. You do don't you?

KESSLER: Officially no. Medically no. But . . . (*Breaks off.*) Well I'm official and I'm a medic so . . . good luck to you Sam.

LOGAN: I'll be back and when I fly over here I'll buzz you at fifty feet!

KESSLER: Do that boy. Goodbye.

   (*Music: In and under for.*)

It doesn't happen this way very often. But it did this time. Sam Logan left the Hebrides with Henry and Luke and a little while later I followed; on the boat going home there were many boys with arms missing and legs. They were the normal the usual boy not so dedicated to any kind of life that they could not give it up without being destroyed. But Sam Logan. . . . I knew he was that rare man found among priests and artists and yes doctors, that man who knows he was born for one purpose only. And when I saw the lovely coast and the boys crowding the rail I caught the longing in their eyes and I remembered Sam Logan's eyes and as we docked I felt and I knew that I must either do something that was impossible for Logan was going to have to do it. And that's how it was when I sat with him and the boys in the warm Mare Island sun.

(*Music: Out.*)

LOGAN: Am I glad to see you, Doc. They've got me marked nuts around here.

KESSLER: Good judges of character. Let me see the leg.

LOGAN: I bumped into a Captain I knew in the Pacific and he says anytime I want I can come out to the field and he'll give me a plane to take up.

KESSLER: Don't say.

LOGAN: Yeh. I got Henry and Luke working for me too. Henry's —Here he comes now. Hey Henry come over here! There's Luke, come here!

HENRY: Hullo Doc. How's he doin'? (*Sotto.*) Hey Doc I was just talking' to a nurse. . . .

LUKE: Hullo Doc.

KESSLER: Pull up Luke.

HENRY: This nurse is got an uncle who worked in the Admiral's office. And she's goin' to tell him to put in a word for Sammy here to get a plane when he's ready.

LUKE: Only thing, she says you gotta put the okay on him first. When's he going to be ready to take off Doc?

KESSLER: What are you paying these fellows, Logan?

LOGAN: I promised to name my plane Henry and Luke.

HENRY: And when I get a Mack again I'm going to paint "Sammy" over the radiator.

KESSLER: When did you change your mind about truck driving?

HENRY: I didn't change my mind, I just figured if this jerk can fly an air-o-plane with one leg I can drive a truck with a tin hand anyhow. I mean, he ain't that good.

LUKE: They both crazy, Doc. Whyn't you tell 'em what's goin' on?

KESSLER: How about you, Luke? You make any arrangements at home?

LUKE: My old man keeps writing when I'm comin', but I dis-courage him. Man that eats and don't work, people ain't goin' to like him after a while and I ain't gonna get myself into none of that.

HENRY: How about it, Doc? We get another operation, don't we?

KESSLER: Here's the story. You've got a lot of work on your arm, Henry, and we'll start right away. There's just one more surgery for you, Sam, and another session for you, Luke. When I get you all fitted up, we'll start walking. Up and down stairs, climb some ladders, put you in a car, Henry, and start you driving. Maybe some horseback riding. So on. And while this is all going on, Sam, I want you to do some thinking about your future. I understand there's a lot of good jobs in the local aircraft plant. . . .

LOGAN: No, sir, I'm. . . .

KESSLER: I'll do the best job I know how to do, Sam, you'll be able to do anything you want to do in civilian life, and there'll be plenty of jobs in the Marines for you. . . .

LOGAN: Sharpening pencils, you mean. . . .

KESSLER: I mean there'll be plenty of jobs. Think about it.

LOGAN (*angering*): You didn't say this in the Hebrides.

KESSLER: I hoped you'd come to realize it yourself. I can only make you walk. I can't think for you, Sam, and you're not thinking.

HENRY: Oh no, he thinks all the time, Doc. . . .

LOGAN: They're working over Tokyo day and night, it'll be over soon. I didn't finish what I was suppose to do. I've got to finish. . . . I want to finish it!

KESSLER (*slight pause*): Don't you see how impossible it is? Even with bad teeth a man can't get into the air force, how in the world. . . .

LOGAN (*bursting out*): I don't care, I gotta do it!

HENRY (*quietly*): He's got very good teeth, Doc.

KESSLER (*slight pause*): I'll operate this afternoon. Be ready at four o'clock.

   (*Music: Up and under.*)

In time Sam Logan was walking, and so was Luke. And Henry was picking up magazines with his new hand. It's no good to put romance into this. It's not right to forget the sadness in this. But they *were* walking, and Henry was tying his shoes. In fact, he was going around tying everybody's shoes who would let him, and I noticed he forgot about the apple business. And then the thing happened. The thing that always happens. . . .

   (*Music: Out.*)

(*Sound: A man falling with the clatter of a cane.*)

HENRY: Hey, Sam, give me a hand here. Hey, Luke, come on, get up. . . .

LOGAN (*laughing*): Come on, buttertoes, get up. What're you, lazy again?

LUKE: I can't. I can't do it.

LOGAN: Oh, baloney. You're just lazy again. Up, up. . . .

HENRY: Sit him here. . . . That's it, sit down, Luke. What're you tryin' to pick up cigarette butts for?

LUKE (*heaving*): Cut it out. Let me alone.

LOGAN (*shaken*): Come on, Luke, we're going for a walk.

LUKE: I ain't walking no more. I'm stayin' here. I ain't gettin' up again. Let me alone.

LOGAN: We're going horseback riding next week. You gotta get in trim.

LUKE: I ain't gettin' in no trim. They ain't gonna make no damn fool outa me. I'm sittin' here and I'm goin' to sit here.

HENRY (*quietly as though close to* LUKE*'s ear*): You know what you're goin' to do? You'll go and disgrace Doc Kessler. Look at the nice work he did on you. You want to go an' disgrace the Doctor? Luke, open your eyes. Open your eyes and get on your feet. Sam . . . tell him . . . Sam. Where'd he go now?

(*Music: Bridge.*)

LOGAN: I saw you waving to me Doc, you want me?

KESSLER: I was planning on some horseback for you boys next week. You feel up to it today?

LOGAN: Well . . . yeh, sure.

KESSLER: You sound doubtful.

LOGAN: He just shook me up a little, that's all.

KESSLER: You sure now, because I want Luke to see you.

LOGAN: Oh, I'll be all right, Doc.

KESSLER: Then I'll see about some horses.

(*Music: Bridge.*)

(*Sound: Shifting of horses' hooves.*)

HENRY: Tally ho! Let me get on, Doc!

KESSLER: One at a time. All right, Sam, get up on this block.

LOGAN: Get that smile off your face, Luke.

LUKE (*off-mike*): Better hitch a basket under that horse, aviator.

KESSLER: Grab onto the pommel, Sam. Okay, now. Get up.

LOGAN (*effort*): Give me a little push, just a little push!

KESSLER: Do it yourself. Go on, go on. . . . There you are. All right, here are the reins. You got both feet in the stirrups?

LOGAN: I don't know, I can't feel. . . . Yeh, they're both in.

LUKE (*off mike*): What're you sweatin' about, Sam?

KESSLER: No remarks from the gallery. All right, Henry, let's see you now.

HENRY: Doc, you are lookin' at the man who won the 1936 Kentucky Stetson. That's a soft derby. Ha! Big joke. Which end do I climb?

KESSLER: Go ahead, you're doing all right. Up! There you are. Clamp your knees, now, there are no doors on this thing to hold you in. Open your hand. All right, take the reins. Pull now. Harder. Hurt you?

HENRY: Me! Ask the horse. I could pull his head off. How about a threesome, Luke?

KESSLER: Get up, boy, let's see what you learned on the farm.

LUKE (*off mike*): I think I'll just sit it out today, sir, if you don't mind.

KESSLER: Up to you. (*Intimately.*) You comfortable, Sam? Don't try anything you can't do. Tell me if you feel anything wrong in any way.

LOGAN: I'm . . . I'm fine. . . . I'm really all right. I just want to be sure I don't lose that right stirrup.

KESSLER: All right, around the circle now. Give him a kick.

LOGAN (*clucks*): Giddap. Come on!

LUKE (*off mike*): That horse is daid.

KESSLER: Give him your heel, Sam!

LOGAN: Come on! Giddap!

(*Sound: Horse starting to walk.*)

KESSLER: Get moving, Henry! Follow behind him!

HENRY (*off mike*): Giddap! Tally ho, boy, tally ho! Hey, Luke, looka me!

(*Sound: Hold the horse in background.*)

KESSLER (*on mike*): I want you to try it, Luke. Come on.

LUKE: Sam going to fly a plane?

KESSLER: What's that got to do with it?

SAM (*off mike*): Hey, Henry! I'm trotting!

LUKE: I'd like to know. Is he?

KESSLER: If he doesn't get scared he will.

HENRY (*off mike*): Tally ho, boy. Tally ho!

LUKE: No kiddin'.

KESSLER: You'll keep that under your hat.

LUKE: Why should he get scared?

 (*Sound: Plane overhead.*)

LOGAN (*off mike*): Doc! Hey, Doc! That's the same plane I was flying! (*Closer.*) Look at her tear! Look at her!

 (*Sound: For an instant just the plane passing over as they watch.*)

 (*Excited.*) Heading west, too. When am I going to do it, Doc?

LUKE: You want to get yourself killed? Sam, you crazy, you can't. . . .

LOGAN: Doc, please. Give me a chance, one chance. Get me into a training plane, anything. I'll tell you if I can't do it. I swear. I'll tell you.

KESSLER: All right, Sam. . . .

LOGAN: Doctor, you're not kidding now!

KESSLER: I have a light plastic leg I want to fit you with first. Then you'll get used to that and we'll see what we can do. I'm not guaranteeing the Navy is going to give you a plane, now.

LOGAN: But you'll tell them I can fly.

KESSLER: I can only tell them what I know, boy. I know that you want to fly, and I don't know any reason why you shouldn't. The rest is up to them. Get those horses going now.

HENRY: And when do I get a car to drive? This horse is got no gears to shift, you know.

KESSLER: I'll let you know when you're ready, Henry.

LOGAN (*off-mike*): Let's go, Susy, gaddap!

 (*Sound: Horses' hooves again.*)

KESSLER: What do you say, Luke?

LUKE: I . . . I'll wait, Doctor. I'll just wait.

 (*Music: Bridge.*)

  (*Sound: Plane engine idling.*)

INSTRUCTOR: He's all set, sir, sorry you can't come along.

KESSLER: I'd just like to stick my head in for a minute, Lieutenant.

INSTRUCTOR: Get right up on the wing, sir.

KESSLER: Thanks, I got it. It's all yours now, Sam. How's the leg feel?

LOGAN: Just like my own. Don't worry about anything, Doc, I'll be all right. And say, Doc?

KESSLER: Yeh?

LOGAN: I never thanked you for everything. I'd like to thank you.

KESSLER: One look at that puss of yours now is enough for me. Let's see you fly, Sam.

LOGAN: Step aside, Mister!

KESSLER: And remember, fly over the hospital. The boys will all be out watching for you!

LOGAN: I'll be there in five minutes! Make way!

(*Sound: Engine up. . . . Taking off and away . . . into . . .*)

(*Music: Into background . . .*)

KESSLER: I have three letters now. One is from New York. Part of it says, "I knew I'd get mixed up with apples one way or another. I'm delivering them from upstate in a ten-ton Mack. The hand steers fine; you were right . . . all I gotta do is think and it opens and closes. And I know how to think now. Any news from Sam the Flying Man. Henry." The second is from Clay County. "My Son Luke," it says, "is out hoeing now, so I'm taking this opportunity to say that he still feels embarrassed about the trouble he was to you, but is fine and works good. Keeps wondering about a boy name of Logan, and his mother and myself are wondering how he made out finally. Our thanks to you for Luke." And the third letter has an APO number. "Just a quick one," it says, "to let you know I am now Major Logan. Hope you're still at Mare Island when I get back because you're not getting out of that ride I promised you. Button up, Doc, I'm coming, and the way it looks out here, it'll be soon. P.S. I wrote your name on the leg. Just in case I start forgetting who put me back in the clouds." It's signed, Sam.

(*Music: Up to finish.*)

NOTES AND ESSAYS ON THE PLAYS

On Screenwriting and Language
(Almost Everybody Wins)

A FUNNY thing happens to screenplays on the way to the screen. It isn't simply that they get changed, subtly or otherwise, from their earlier incarnations, but that they become brittle. This is only true for the writer, of course. He misses the lines that were merely shadings of meaning and would probably hold things up in a movie, which, after all, has to *move*. But in the final version of *Everybody Wins*, compared to earlier drafts, surprisingly little of the basic material was altered, although I agreed to cut a few scenes and revise the ending. In general, what I think happened—and this is probably usual in moviemaking—is that suggestion through words became rather more blatant indication through images.

I hasten to add that this is not a gripe, if only because it is, in my view, a generic quality of the form. A description in words tends to inflate, expand, and inflame the imagination, so that in the end the thing or person described is amplified into a larger-than-life figment. But something photographed is lifted out of the imagination and becomes simply what it really is, or less. It is montage rather than the actual photograph itself that gives the impression of an imaginary world larger than life. Words, unable to imitate reality, must in their nature serve it up in metaphoric guise, but film gives us the appearance of reality directly.

If a telephone is photographed, isolated on a table, and the camera is left running, it becomes more and more what it is—a telephone in all its detail. Andy Warhol let the camera run on the Empire State Building for maybe an hour or more. I left before the "end" of this picture, so I'm not sure how long it lasted, but in the twenty minutes I watched, it never to my mind rose to metaphor, simply remaining what it was—the Empire State Building.

Things go differently on a stage. Set a phone on a table under a light and raise the curtain, and in complete silence, after a few minutes, something will accrete around it. Questions and anticipations will begin to emanate from it, we will begin to imagine

841

meanings in its isolation—in a word, the phone becomes an incipient metaphor. Possibly because we cannot see its detail as sharply as on film or because it is surrounded by a much greater space, it begins to animate, to take on suggestive possibilities, very nearly a kind of self-consciousness. Something of the same is true of words as opposed to images. The word is not and can't be any more than suggestive of an idea or sensation; it *is* nothing in itself.

There is always too much dialogue. And it's true, there is, for one thing because dialogue cannot be seen. The contradiction, I suppose, is that movies—most of them, anyway—require a writer's sense of form while inherently rejecting his word-love. And so the writer, accustomed to forming sentences on which all his effects rely, ends up with something truncated and not quite his own on paper; with luck, however, it is paradoxically more his own on the screen. For it turns out—if he is lucky with director and actors—that the meaning of his lost lines is actually visible in pictures. I think that the quality of the final work is rougher and cruder, more brutally telegraphic, than when it was action described in words. But again, the word made flesh may *be* more and suggest less. It is a very mysterious business, and by no means a simple question of better or worse, but of differences of aesthetic feeling, of timbre and tissue, that always accompany differences of form. One need only recall the innumerable fine novels that simply could not be made to work on the screen because the quality of their language was removed; their story-essence vanished when their language was discarded.

Among "real" writers—novelists, playwrights, poets—screenwriting, when it is not regarded as a cousin of engineering, is seen as an art on a par with clothing design; the product has no life of its own until it is occupied by the wearer. I am afraid that this, at least in my view, is truer than one would wish, but it is necessary to add that there have been many more significant films over the past twenty-five years than plays or, proportionately, even novels. Nevertheless, screenplays, especially the good ones that work, tend by the nature of the art to be self-effacing, vanishing, as it were, into the total impression of the film, this in contrast to the play, which in the Western tradition has been assimilated to literature as a respectable form apart from performance (something that was not yet the case as late as Elizabethan times, when playscripts were tossed to managers and actors without reaching print). Except among technicians, the screenplay has little or no existence unless filmed, and the few exceptions, like Pinter's unproduced work for the screen, are precisely that—isolated examples that illuminate the rule.

The screenplay is the first element in a collaborative art, but only an element for all that, and not, like a stage play, a thing in itself. It is a sort of libretto for camera, its energies moving outward to serve the other elements in the film and to organize them for a common purpose. The forces in and around the stage play, in contrast, move in the opposite direction, for it is the play that is to be served—by director, actors, designer, costumer. An opera libretto is likewise content not to be noticed by the public, even as the singers and conductor know that it is their vital support, without which the music would fail to fly out to the audience's ear.

The screenplay may do many things, but one thing it must do, and that is give meaning to the pictures. In this sense it is equivalent to the words in a cartoon balloon or the titles sometimes given photographs or paintings. These may orient us as to the time and place a photo was shot or a picture painted, but there can't be many photos or paintings made memorable by their labels and dates. Indeed, the vitality of a screenplay, indispensable as it is to the finished film, springs from the life-giving structure by which the order of the images—the film's most affecting element—is organized.

The very invisibility of the screenplay accounts for the screenwriter's anonymity before the audience and most critics. To be sure, he alone was there when the pages were blank, it was his godlike hand that gave form to dust, but his occasional smart or touching line of dialogue notwithstanding, it isn't really words that people come to hear or long remember; it is actors and their mannerisms, their noses and hair and tones of voice, that really matter to them. And ironically, the more authority the actor has in performing his role, the further from sight the screenwriter recedes; in effect, the actor has eaten him. Indeed, when this happens, the movie is successful, since the actor seems to have originated his lines.

Except for the money, when there is any, screenwriting is a rather thankless profession compared with other forms of writing. The film medium belongs essentially to the director, its attraction for the public will always be the actor, and there will never be a way around that. There cannot be a Eugene O'Neill of the movies. Every element and person in the enterprise exists to serve the director's central purpose, which is to make the actors seem believable.

This may be why the most persuasive film acting is as close to wordless as possible. For a long time the idea that Gary Cooper might be an actor was thought a joke, and the same for Clark Gable, John Wayne, and their numerous heroic-type contemporaries who were "merely" personalities rather than actors. A Spencer Tracy, on the other hand, was certainly an actor because he could speak so well. This mistaken judgment was historically determined by the fact that movies were originally offshoots of the stage, and stage acting was something for which these heroes were indeed unfit. Their way of speaking was either silly and boyish, as in Wayne's case, whiny, as with Gable too much of the time, or monotonous, as with Cooper. But the point, which was missed because it was so new, was that all these heroes could show attitudes and feelings—usually simple and fundamental ones like anger or sexual desire, indignation or aggression—much better with their mouths shut than open. And even "show" is too strong a word—it is more accurate to say that they were eminently attributable actors. The mute human, like an animal, keeps all his possibilities intact, gives us nothing to make us doubt his reality, while any speech is bound to narrow his plausibility dangerously. Thus, there is a peculiar pressure on words in film to contribute to silent communication rather than monopolizing communication as words do on the stage. Words must above all be utilizable, each one as unadorned a story-mover as possible. The director's first instinct when faced with a multi-sentence speech is to pick it apart with a question for each word: "Why do we need this?" Needless to say, confronted with such a question, no Shakespeare play would last more than an hour.

When an actor talks he is more vulnerable to disbelief than when he is simply standing there. The very purpose of words in movies is to justify the silences that are the picture's main business. It is silence that creates an infinity of potential meaning that words can only diminish. This, I think, is also why very good prose writers do not usually prosper as screenwriters. Faulkner, Fitzgerald, Tennessee Williams, and a long line of eminent others discovered that their brightest stylistic inventions were precisely what movies reject like excrescences. Language tends to get in the way of the images, and the brighter the language, the more it draws attention to itself, the more it interferes.

The real poetry of a film lies first in its structure of meaning, distinctly a function of the screenplay, and second in the expressiveness of its images, which are realized by the director but have their root if not more than that in the writer's work. Language, nevertheless, cannot be more than a servant to the images in the final impression.

Inevitably, especially if one is not accustomed to writing films, the question arises as to exactly why words are in such rivalry with the image as to be nearly self-indulgences. Even the wordy films that come to mind—Huston's *The Dead*, Capra's *Mr. Smith Goes to Washington*, Wilder's *Some Like It Hot* (a brilliantly and eminently *written* film by the late I. A. L. Diamond in collaboration with Wilder)—endure in memory not primarily for their lines but for the snap and marksmanship of their visual moods, their portraits of actors and settings, the things they have let us *see*, and the image-driven story. In the final analysis, dialogue exists at all in film in order to justify images and bridge them to sustain continuity. Dialogue is the musculature of the gestalt, the combination of images whose interactions create meaning. Altogether unlike the novel and even the play, film simply will not stand for writing that is basically commentary, however illuminating or beautiful or telling it may be. The closest one may safely verge on such adornment is in verbal wit, providing it is not convoluted, as it may be on the stage, but pithy and quickly understood. Otherwise, adornment and commentary are left to the director and his cinematographer, who indeed may elaborate through pleasurable explorations of things seen—locales, flesh, fingernails, eyes, all the wonders of the visible that film adores.

The reason or reasons for this image supremacy seem obvious: it is film's replication of dream, or more precisely, of our relationship to dreams. The film scene, even the apparently legato one, is always secretly in a hurry, much like its unacknowledged matrix, the dream scene, which flashes up in the sleeper and dies away in a matter of seconds. Dreams (if the reader's are anything like mine) are almost never verbal. Sometimes a single emblematic word, or perhaps two, may emerge in a dream scene as a clue (most likely ambiguous) to its intent, but everyone knows the dream in which people are avidly talking, with no words coming from their mouths, thus creating the image of talk rather than talk itself. We all know, too, the dream in which we are shouting a warning or a plea to others, with no sound issuing forth. Yet we know the meaning of what was being said or shouted. The meaning, in short, stems from the situation and not from the words we are trying to say about it. The dreamer is essentially deaf, and this suggests that film's origins, like those of dream, reach back to archaic stages of our evolution, to a period antedating our capacity to understand language, when we communicated in the primitive sign language of infancy. Long before he can understand words, the infant is obviously moved by what he sees, made frightened or happy or curious or anxious by purely visual stimuli. After a mere few months of life he has all the mental capacities required to direct movies or to paint pictures —everything, that is, except a grasp of the coherency of theme that brings relevance and meaning to what he is so pleasurably staring at.

For coherency's sake words—whether spoken or printed on the screen—are indeed necessary, however brief and minimal they may be, and this needs a screenwriter, someone capable of using words efficiently in order to make some sense of pleasure, or, to put it differently, in order to provide a social justification of sensuousness. But coherency in film remains distinctly secondary in importance to the enticing infantile riddle of sheer image itself.

The primitiveness of the image-story, growing as it does primarily from our very earliest months of life, tends to thin out the filmed tale in comparison to the word-driven one. This is admittedly debatable and may be a purely personal reaction brought on by too many years in the theatre, but it seems to me the brain needn't work hard before a film; it can coast along in neutral. And perhaps this absence of effort simply makes one's appreciation that much shallower, for dreaming and movie watching are essentially passive activities, something happening *to* us, rather than an active and willful participation in another's imaginary world, as is the case with reading or even watching stage plays built on words instead of pictures.

Before a play we are forced to do the chores of editing, of deciding what is more or less important, of shifting our attention from actor to actor on the stage. In reading any text we have to decide and sometimes puzzle out what the words themselves mean. At the movies we decide nothing, our treasured infantile inertia is barely nudged, for the editor, the director, the lighting, the orchestration, and the overwhelming size of the image itself hand us an unmistakable hierarchy of importance and lay before us the predigested results to wonder at and enjoy. In point of fact, a film is even more primitive than a dream if we consider how far more densely packed with ambiguity and insoluble mystery dreams are. But it is their dream-born primitiveness that accounts for the universal attraction of movies, and it is perhaps the passivity with which they are viewed that supplies the delights of release and escape for people everywhere. A movie is something being done to us, and this is very nice relative to the other forms, which by comparison are work.

So the screenwriter, charged as he is with creating and maintaining coherency in the film, stands in some contradiction to its real nature and fundamental sources of pleasure, which are incoherent, subconscious, sensuous. Indeed, it has long been standard procedure to disinvite screenwriters from the sets and locations of the films they have written (although not this one). They are like a guilty conscience arriving at the scene of a crime, necessary for upholding civilization but not really much fun. Their presence crowds the director, inhibits the actors. In the usual orgy of creative play that filmmaking is, with actors and director and cinematographer seeking to fabricate real feelings and marvelous accidents, the screenwriter—who started it all—represents the principle of good order without which all meaning is likely to escape the enterprise. Naturally, he is suspect.

But he has one final satisfaction. He may, if he so desires, contemplate the amazing fact that from his typewriter clicking away in his lonely room veritable armies of people have sprung forth—actors, makeup artists, food concessionaires, explosives teams, horse wranglers, plane pilots, chauffeurs, bankers, ushers, box office people, ad men and women, sign painters, costumers, hair designers, frogmen, attending physicians, dentists, nurses, truck drivers, mechanics, turbine experts, electricians, and people who know how to stretch shoes quickly or disguise a sudden pimple, plus their spouses and lovers. And all these regiments from the same typewriter ribbon and a few score sheets of paper with words on them. Magic.

Without in the least belittling screenwriting, I would say that it does not require one to write very well. The often agonizing stylistic effort that writing normally demands is obviated, if only because the work is not written to be read. So in this sense screenwriting is easier than other forms. On the other hand, the human relationships, the thematic coherency, and the story in a *good* screenplay are as tough to get right as they are in any other form. I must add my own (probably minority) view, however, that the screenplay requires much more of a shorthand approach to scene writing than the stage play or the novel. It wants things indicated, and as deftly as possible, rather than fleshed out in words, perhaps because the actor's image on the screen is so vast and omnipotent as to be overwhelming in its suggestive power. What in other forms must be written out or spoken may on the screen be achieved with a raised eyebrow, the movement of a mouth or a hand, or a mere mute stare. But the condensation of image demanded by screenwriting is reminiscent of poetry as opposed to the prose of the stage form. In all, then, writing screenplays has its own formidable challenges, not the least of which is the capacity to bear the pleasure and the pain of being a member of the orchestra—in the first section, perhaps, but a member nonetheless—rather than playwright-soloist or novelist-virtuoso. The good part is that if the screenwriter gets less of the credit than he deserves, he may also get less of the blame, so it evens out in the end, and that, one supposes, is fair enough.

Author's Note
(Almost Everybody Wins)

THE passage of time does wonders for a perspective on past labours. Over a decade ago I wrote this screenplay, later produced as *Everybody Wins*, with Debra Winger and Nick Nolte. It was based on a one-act play of mine called *Some Kind of Love Story*, performed at the Young Vic in a marvellously directed production by David Thacker, with Helen Mirren and Robert Peck.

Now, twelve years after writing this screenplay, it seems a shame that I helped change it from what I believe could have been a wonderfully ironic and funny film into a fairly interesting one. In the original script printed here, the woman, Angela, has a personality split into quite separate parts. Tom the detective, in trying to unearth whatever shreds of truth might be shuttling from one of her personalities to the other is driven half mad trying to figure out when she is fantasizing, when she is lying outright, and when she is being truthful—or more or less so. In the course of production Angela's character lost its various personas and her fantastic quality and she ended up merely a terrified woman who dares not reveal what she knows about a frightful murder.

For better or worse—I am still not sure which—the present script is built as much on language as on visualization, while the balance of the finished film leaned far more toward the pictorial. Naturally, I prefer this version for reasons both subjective and the other kind.

About Theatre Language
(The Last Yankee)

I

When I began writing plays in the late thirties, something called realism was the undisputed reigning style in the American commercial theatre—which was just about all the theatre there was in this country. The same was more or less the case in Britain. If not a mass art, theatre then could still be thought of at least as a popular one, although everyone knew—long before television—that something of its common appeal had gone out of it, and a lot of its twenties' glamour, too. One blamed the movies, which had stolen so much of the audience and thus theatre's old dominance as a cultural influence. Notwithstanding the obvious fact that the audience was predominantly middle class, we continued to imagine that we were making plays for people of many different educational and cultural levels, a representative variety of the city and even the country. If this was never really true, there was certainly no thought of appealing to a clique of college graduates or to academics and their standards. A *New York Times* critic like George S. Kaufman had both feet in show business and became the most popular writer of comedies of the period, while Brooks Atkinson may have had one eye on Aristotle but understood that his readers were Americans impatient with any theatrical enterprise that required either education or patience. Outside New York there were at least the remains of the twenties' touring wheel, theatres in many smaller cities regularly attended by quite ordinary citizens eager for last year's Broadway hits, albeit with replacement casts. In New York, with a ticket price of fifty-five cents to four dollars and forty cents, one somehow took for granted that a professor might be sitting next to a housewife, a priest beside a skilled worker or perhaps a grammar-school teacher, a small or large business executive beside a student. This conception of the demotic audience, accurate or not, influenced the writing of plays directed at the commonsensical experience of everyday people.

Missing were black or Asian or Hispanic faces, of course, but they were beyond the consciousness of the prevailing culture. As for production costs, even into the forties they were within reason; plays like *All My Sons* or *Death of a Salesman*, for example, cost between twenty and forty thousand to produce, a budget small enough to be raised by half a dozen modest contributors, who might lose all, with some embarrassment but reasonably little pain, or make a killing.

Radicals—people like myself, trying to convince ourselves that we were carrying on the age-old tradition of theatre as a civic art rather than a purely commercial one—were in a conflict; to attract even the fitful interest of a Broadway producer, and subsequently to engage the audience, we had to bow to realism, even if the poetic forms were what we really admired or at least wished to explore. An Expressionist like the German Ernst Toller, for example, would not have been read past his sixth page by a Broadway producer or, for that matter, one in London. Among the playwrights one thinks of as important, not one was—or is now—welcome in the commercial theatre. Not Chekhov, not Ibsen, not Hauptmann, not Pirandello, Strindberg, Turgenev—not even Shaw. To so much as think of performing a Beckett play like *Waiting for Godot* in the general proximity of Broadway a cast of movie stars and a short run are essential—Lincoln Center pulled it off in 1988—and things were probably a bit worse half a century ago. One need only read O'Neill's letters of complaint at the "showshop" of Broadway and the narrow compass of the American audience's imagination—or in Britain, Shaw's ridicule of his countrymen's provincialism—to understand the problem; for some mysterious reason the Anglo-Saxon culture regarded theatre as an entertainment first and last, an art of escape with none of the Continental or Russian interest in moral and philosophical opportunities or obligations. Very occasionally in America there was an *Adding Machine* by the young Elmer Rice, but such a breakout from conventional realism was rare enough to be brought up in conversation for years after, like a calf born with five legs. The English-language theatre was pridefully commercial, a profit-making enterprise which wed it to a form whose surfaces of familiar reality would be universally recognized. Captain Shotover's outcry, "I like to know where I am!"

could have been sewn to the flag of this theatre. Only musicals had the happy license to stretch reality, at least to some extent. But for straight plays, even satire was too strange to prosper; George Kaufman defined satire as what closes on Saturday night.

The point here is that what we think of as "straight realism" was tiresome half a century ago, indeed longer ago than that, but it was accepted by the audiences and almost all the reviewers as a reflection of life. Nonetheless it should be remembered that realism has reemerged at various moments to very capably express the essence of an era. At a time when "experimental" is all the virtue a play needs in order to gain serious consideration, it is not a bad idea to confess that an extraordinarily few such researches have achieved any kind of enduring life. It is not quite enough to know how to escape; one has also to think of arriving somewhere.

In the thirties, probably the single exception—at least that I was aware of—to realism's domination was the WPA's *Living Newspaper*, the one formal innovation of American theatre. An epic in more or less presentational form, written like movies by groups of writers, rather than individually, it dealt in an overtly exuberant spirit with social issues like public ownership of electrical power, labor unions, agriculture, and medicine, and was extremely popular. Significantly, the WPA was government-subsidized, and did not have to make a profit. Using unemployed actors, designers, technicians, a show could call upon large casts and elaborate scenery and production elements. And the ticket was low-priced. The WPA could send Orson Welles, for example, into Harlem storefronts with a big cast playing *Doctor Faustus*, charging a quarter a seat. But theatre-for-profit was hardly affected by what might be called this epic-populist approach—it was simply too expensive to produce.

I mention these mundane matters because they profoundly affect style in the theatre, which, like politics, is always the art of the possible.

There were at least a dozen playwrights regularly feeding the commercial theatre in the years before World War II, and all but perhaps Odets and Hellman would have pridefully declared that their sole purpose was to entertain. Those playwrights were sophisticated and no doubt knew all about the

Continental theatre tradition, and its aspiring to the philosophical condition, something like that of the Greeks or, in a
different way, the Elizabethans. The Theatre Guild, for one,
had been started in the twenties in part to bring that kind of
theatre to America, the theatre of Pirandello, Schnitzler, Ibsen,
and Strindberg.

In the thirties, one American styled himself a political revolutionary, and that was Clifford Odets. O'Neill, of course, had
been the aesthetic rebel but his socialism was private rather
than informing his plays, although *The Hairy Ape* is surely an
anticapitalist work. It was his formal experiments and tragic
mood that set him apart. O'Neill was a totally isolated phenomenon in the Broadway theatre as a maker and user of new
and old theatrical forms.

Odets, on the other hand, while describing himself as "a
man of the Left," was, with the possible exception of his first
play, *Waiting for Lefty*, no innovator where form was concerned. He attempted a poetic realism but it was still trying to
represent real people in actual social relationships. And this
was perhaps inevitable given his actor's temperament as well as
his Marxist commitment; he had the revolutionary's eye on
the great public, on the reconstitution of power once a failed
capitalism had been brought down—for such was the Marxist
and non-Marxist Left position on the proper moral obligation
of the artist. But by temperament he was a poet seeking words
that would lift him into a takeoff, regardless of his realist political commitments. O'Neill, on the other hand, was not the
revolutionary but the rebel with a despairing anarchism in his
heart. If he glimpsed any salvation, it was not to arrive in a
more benign reconstitution of political power but in the tragic
cleansing of the life-lie permanently ensconced in the human
condition. Since he took no responsibility in theory for a new
and better policy to take the place of the corrupted present
one, he was free to explore all sorts of theatrical means by
which to set forth the situation of the damned. Moreover, if
O'Neill wanted his plays to register, and he surely did, they
need not be popular to justify his having written them, for he
was hunting the sounding whale of ultimate meaning, and he
expected to suffer for it; oppositely, a critical or box-office failure for Odets meant rejection of a very personal kind, a spit in

the eye by an ungrateful, self-satisfied bourgeois society. A failed play for Odets was a denial of what he was owed, for he was chasing the public no differently from his bourgeois non-revolutionary contemporaries. O'Neill could say, and he did, that he was not interested in relations between men, but between Man and God. For America, in his view, was damned and if there were a few individuals who behaved justly and well it was not because they belonged to a particular social class or held a generous or unselfish political viewpoint, but by virtue of a grace whose source is beyond definition.

II

The realism of Broadway—and the Strand and the Boulevard theatre of France—was detested by the would-be poetic dramatists of my generation, just as it had always been since it came into vogue in the nineteenth century. What did this realism really come down to? A play representing real rather than symbolic or metaphysical persons and situations, its main virtue verisimilitude, with no revolutionary implications for society or even a symbolic statement of some general truth. Quite simply, conventional realism was conventional because it implicitly supported the conventions of society, but it could just as easily do something quite different, or so it seemed to me. Nevertheless, we thought it the perfect style for an unchallenging, simpleminded linear middle-class conformist view of life. What I found confusing at the time, however, was that not so very long before, the name "realism" had been applied to the revolutionary style of playwrights like Ibsen, Chekhov, and quite frequently Strindberg, writers whose whole thrust was in opposition to the bourgeois status quo and the hypocrisies on which it stood, or, in Chekhov's case, the futilities of the Czarist system.

My own first playwriting attempt was purely mimetic, a realistic play about my own family. It won me some prizes and productions, but, interestingly, I turned at once to a stylized treatment of life in a gigantic prison, modeled on Jackson State Penitentiary in Michigan—near Ann Arbor, where I was in school—the largest prison in the United States, which I had visited over weekends with a friend who was its lone psychologist. The theme of that play was that prisons existed to make desperate workingmen insane. There was a chorus of sane prisoners chanting from a high overpass above the stage, and a counter-chorus of the insane trying to draw the other into their ranks. It was inevitable that I had to confront the problem of dramatic language, for it was impossible to engage so vast a human disaster with speech born in a warm kitchen. I gradually came to wonder if the essential pressure toward poetic dramatic language—if not of stylization itself—came from the inclusion of society as a major element in the play's story or vision. Manifestly, prose realism was the language of the individual and of private life, poetry the language of man in crowds, in society. Put another way, prose is the language of family relations; it is the inclusion of the larger world beyond that naturally opens a play to the poetic.

But I wanted to succeed, I wanted to emerge and grip an audience. Minds might be illuminated by speeches thrown at them but it was by being moved that one was changed. And so the problem was that our audiences were trained, as it were, in a pawky realism and were turned off by stylistic novelty, by "art." How to find a style that would at one and the same time deeply engage an American audience, which insisted on a recognizable reality of characters, locales, and themes, while opening the stage to considerations of public morality and the mythic social fates—in short, the invisible?

Of course this was not my preoccupation alone. I doubt there was ever a time when there was so much discussion about form and style. T. S. Eliot was writing his verse plays, and Auden and Isherwood theirs; the poetic mimesis of Sean O'Casey was most popular; and W. B. Yeats's dialogue was studied if not very often produced. The impulse to poetry reached into the ex-newspaperman and realistic writer Maxwell Anderson, whose attempts to imitate Elizabethan prosody with contemporary characters and social themes were widely celebrated, as curios by some, as moving experiences by others.

To be just to Odets, it was he who challenged the Broadway theatre's addiction to verisimilitude by his idiosyncratic dialogue. And he was surely the first American playwright to be celebrated—and more wildly and lavishly than any other before him—for his writing style. For younger writers such as myself, Odets for a couple of years was the trailblazer; he was bringing the suffering of the Great Depression onto the Broadway stage and making audiences listen. If he had not solved the problem of a contemporary American style, he had dared to invent an often wildly stylized stage speech. But I suppose that since his characters lacked elegance or strangeness, were, in fact, the very exemplars of realistic theatre, Odets was called a realist— indeed, a kind of reporter of Jewish life in the Bronx. I may not have lived in the Bronx but the speech of Brooklyn Jews certainly bore no resemblance to that of Odets's characters.

> CARP [in *Golden Boy*]: I'm superdisgusted with you! . . .
> A man hits his wife and it's the first step to fascism!
> Look in the papers! On every side the clouds of war!
> . . . Ask yourself a pertinent remark; could a boy
> make a living playing this instrument [a violin] in our
> competitive civilization today?
> ROXY: I think I'll run across the street and pick up an
> eight-cylinder sandwich.

The audiences roared with delight at these inventions. It was as though Odets were trying to turn dialogue into jazz. And his devotees went to his plays especially to pick up his latest deliciously improbable remarks and repeat them to their friends. Had any Bronxite—or anyone else in the century—really exclaimed, "God's teeth, no!" "What exhaust pipe did he crawl out of?" Lorna: "I feel like I'm shot from a cannon."

Inevitably, in a theatre bounded by realism, this had to be mistakenly labeled as accurate reportage, news from the netherworld. But of course it was an invented diction of a kind never heard before on stage—or off, for that matter. Odets's fervent ambition was to burst the bounds of Broadway while remaining inside its embrace, and if as time went on his lines began to seem self-consciously labored, no longer springing from characters but manifestly from the author and his will-to-poeticize, he at a minimum had made language the identifying mark of a playwright in America, and that was something that hadn't happened before.

Admittedly, I did not look at his style with objectivity but for its potential usefulness in breaking through the constricted realism of our theatre then. Odets was tremendously exciting to young writers. I was troubled by a tendency in his plays toward overtheatricalized excess, however—lines sometimes brought laughter where there should have been outrage, or pity, or some deeper emotion than amusement—and at times the plots verged on the schematic. Odets often overrhapsodized at the climaxes when he should have been reaching back to ancillary material that was not there. He wrote terrific scenes, blazing speeches and confrontations which showed what theatre could be, but with the exception, perhaps, of *Awake and Sing* and the racy *Golden Boy* he never wrote a play that lifted inexorably to its climactic revelation.

I came out of the thirties unsure whether there could be a viable counterform to the realism around me. All I knew for sure was that a good play must move forward in its depths as rapidly as on its surfaces; word-poetry wasn't enough if there was a fractured poetry in the structure, the gradually revealed illuminating idea behind the whole thing. A real play was the discovery of the unity of its contradictions; the essential poetry was the synthesis of even the least of its parts to form a symbolic meaning. Of course the problem had much to do with language but more primary was how to penetrate my own feelings about myself and the time in which I lived. Ideally, a good play must show as sound an emotional proof of its thesis as a case at law shows factual proof, and you can't do that with words alone, lovely as they might be.

Odets's contribution, ironically, was not his realistic portrayal of society—his alleged aim—but his willingness to be artificial; he brought back artificiality, if you will, just as ten years later Tennessee Williams did with his birdsong from the magnolias. But Williams had an advantage—his language could be far more faithful to its sources in reality. Southern people did love to talk, and in the accents Williams captured (as in *The Glass Menagerie*):

> AMANDA: . . . But Laura is, thank heavens, not only pretty but also very domestic. I'm not at all. I never was a bit. I never could make a thing but angel-food

cake. Well, in the South we had so many servants.
Gone, gone, gone. All vestige of gracious living! Gone
completely! I wasn't prepared for what the future
brought me. All my gentlemen callers were sons of
planters and so of course I assumed that I would be
married to one and raise my family on a large piece of
land with plenty of servants. But man proposes—and
woman accepts the proposal!—To vary that old, old
saying a little bit—I married no planter! I married a
man who worked for the telephone company!—That
gallantly smiling gentleman over there! (*Points to husband's picture.*) A telephone man who—fell in love
with long distance! Now he travels and I don't even
know where! . . .

This too was called realism, and it probably was in the sense
that there were people who talked like this. But then how did
it differ from the conventional realistic play? Clearly, it was that
the very action of Williams's plays, certainly the best of them,
was working toward the building of symbolic meaning that
would embrace both the psychological development of his
characters and his personal specter of a menacing America
struggling with its own sexuality and the anomie born of its
dire materialism. In a word, Williams's style arose from his pain
and anxiety at being overwhelmed and defeated by a gross violence that underlay the American—one might say the whole
Western—ethos.

Their obsession with words notwithstanding, it was their need
to communicate their resistance to something death-dealing in
the culture that finally pressed Odets and Williams to address the
big public and made them playwrights rather than sequestered
poets. Stylistic invention without an implicit commitment of
some kind to a more humane vision of life is a boat without
rudder or cargo or destination—or worse, it is the occupation of
the dilettante. Odets, when he began, thought his egalitarian
Marxism would heal America and create its new community, but
that ideology devolved into a rote religion before the thirties had
even passed. Williams unfurled the banner of a forlorn but resisting heroism to the violence against the oddball, the poet, the
sexual dissident. But it may as well be admitted that in their

different ways both men in the end unwittingly collaborated with the monster they saw as trying to destroy them.

The plays these men wrote were shields raised against the many-arrowed darkness, but in the end there was little from outside to give them the spiritual support to complete their creative lives. Odets's best work ended with his rejection by Broadway and his move to Hollywood; Williams, likewise rejected, kept nevertheless to his trade, experimenting with forms and new methods that drew no encouragement from reviewers unable or unwilling to notice that the theatre culture had boxed in a writer of greatness who was struggling to find an audience in the passing crowd of a generation other than his own. At his strongest he had spoken for and to the center of society, in a style it could relate to, an enhanced, visionary realism. In the end a writer has no one to blame for his failings, not even himself, but the brutally dismissive glee of critics toward Williams's last plays simply laid more sticks on his burden. Toward the end he was still outside, scratching on the glass, as he had once put it, and it was the shadowed edges of life that drew him, the borderland where how things are said is everything, and everything has been said before.

The advent of the Absurd and of Beckett and his followers both obscured and illuminated the traditional elements of the discussion of theatre style. For O'Neill a good style was basically a question of the apt use of metaphor and argot. "God, if I could write like that!" he wrote to O'Casey, who, incidentally, would no doubt have labeled himself a realistic writer in the sense that he was giving his audiences the substance of their life conflicts. But like Williams, O'Casey came from a culture which loved talk and sucked on language like a sweet candy.

MRS. GROGAN: Oh, you've got a cold on you, Fluther.

FLUTHER: Oh, it's only a little one.

MRS. GROGAN: You'd want to be careful, all th' same. I knew a woman, a big lump of a woman, red-faced and round-bodied, a little awkward on her feet; you'd think, to look at her, she could put out her two arms an' lift a two-storied house on th' top of her head; got

a ticklin' in her throat, an' a little cough, an' th' next
mornin' she had a little catchin' in her chest, an' they
had just time to wet her lips with a little rum, an' off
she went.

(*Juno and the Paycock*)

Even in the most mundane of conversational exchanges
O'Casey sought, and as often as not found, the lift of poetry.
Indeed, that was the whole point—that the significantly poetic
sprang from the raw and real experience of ordinary people.
J. M. Synge, O'Casey's forerunner at the turn of the century,
had struck a similar chord; Synge was in a supremely conscious
revolt against the banality of most theatre language. As John
Gassner noted, in Ireland the popular imagination was still,
according to Synge, "fiery and magnificent, and tender; so that
those of us who wish to write start with a chance that is not
given to writers in places where the springtime of local life has
been forgotten, and the harvest is a memory only, and the
straw has been turned into bricks."

Synge rejected the then-dominant Ibsen and Zola for the
"joyless and pallid words" of their realism and as in *Riders to
the Sea*, when the women are lamenting the deaths of so many
of their men working the angry sea:

MAURYA: In the big world the old people do be leaving
things after them for their sons and children, but in
this place it is the young men do be leaving things behind for them that do be old.

As far as style is concerned, the Beckett difference, as it
might be called, was to introduce humble people—bums, in
fact, or social sufferers—with the plainest of language, but arranged so as to announce and develop pure theme. His could
be called a presentational thematic play, announcing what it
was about and never straying very far from what it was con-
ceived of to prove, or what his instinct had led him to confirm.
Beckett had parted with inferential playwriting, where speeches
inferred the author's thematic intentions while hewing to an
apparently autonomous story building to a revelatory climax

that united story and theme. In Beckett the story *was* the theme, inseparably so. Moreover, as will be shown in a moment, he interpreted the theme himself in his dialogue.

If—instead of the prewar poetic drama's requirement of an elevated tone or diction—the most common speech was now prized, it was not the speech of realistic plays. It was a speech skewed almost out of recognition by a surreal commitment to what at first had seemed to be the impotence of human hopes, and hence the futility of action itself. All but the flimsiest connections between speeches were eliminated, creating an atmosphere of sinister danger (in Pinter) or immanence (in Beckett). It was quite as though the emphatic absence of purpose in the characters had created a loss of syntax. It seems that in later years Beckett took pains to clarify this impression of human futility, emphasizing the struggle *against* inertia as his theme. In any case, however ridiculous so much of his dialogue exchanges are, the tenderness of feeling in his work is emphatically not that of the cynic or the hard ironist.

The dominating theme of *Godot* is stasis and the struggle to overcome humanity's endlessly repetitious paralysis before the need to act and change. We hear it plainly and stripped clean of plot or even incident.

ESTRAGON: Then adieu.
POZZO: Adieu.
VLADIMIR: Adieu.
POZZO: Adieu.
    Silence. No one moves.
VLADIMIR: Adieu.
POZZO: Adieu.
ESTRAGON: Adieu.
    Silence.
POZZO: And thank you.
VLADIMIR: Thank *you.*
POZZO: Not at all.
ESTRAGON: Yes yes.
POZZO: No no.
VLADIMIR: Yes yes.
ESTRAGON: No no.
    Silence.

POZZO: I don't seem to be able . . . (*long hesitation*)
. . . to depart.
ESTRAGON: Such is life.

This is a vaudeville at the edge of the cliff, but vaudeville anyway, so I may be forgiven for being reminded of Jimmy Durante's ditty—"Didja ever get the feelin' that you wanted to go? But still you had the feelin' that you wanted to stay?"

It is a language shorn of metaphor, simile, everything but its instructions, so to speak. The listener hears the theme like a nail drawn across a pane of glass.

So the struggle with what might be called reportorial realism, written "the way people talk," is at least as old as the century. As for myself, my own tendency has been to shift styles according to the nature of my subject. *All My Sons, The Crucible, A View from the Bridge, Death of a Salesman, The Price, The American Clock*, my earliest work, like *The Golden Years*, about the destruction of Mexico by the Spaniards, and the more recent plays, like *The Creation of the World, Some Kind of Love Story*, and *The Last Yankee*, differ very much in their language. This, in order to find speech that springs naturally out of the characters and their backgrounds rather than imposing a general style. If my approach to playwriting is partly literary, I hope it is well hidden. Leroy Hamilton is a native New England carpenter and speaks like one, and not like the New York working men and women in *A Memory of Two Mondays*, or Eddie Carbone, who comes out of a quite different culture.

So the embrace of something called realism is obviously very wide; it can span the distance between a Turgenev and a Becque, between Wedekind and your latest Broadway hit. The main thing I sought in *The Last Yankee* was to make real my sense of the life of such people, the kind of man swinging the hammer through a lifetime, the kind of woman waiting forever for her ship to come in. And second, my view of their present confusion and, if you will, decay and possible recovery. They are bedrock, aspiring not to greatness but to other gratifications—successful parenthood, decent children and a decent house and a decent car and an occasional nice evening with family or friends, and above all, of course, some financial security. Needless to say, they are people who can be inspired to great and noble sacrifice, but also to bitter hatreds. As the world goes I suppose they are the luckiest people, but some of them—a great many, in fact—have grown ill with what would once have been called a sickness of the soul.

And that is the subject of the play, its "matter." For depression is far from being merely a question of an individual's illness, although it appears as that, of course; it is at the same time, most especially in Patricia Hamilton's case, the grip on her of a success mythology which is both naïve and brutal, and which, to her misfortune, she has made her own. And opposing it, quite simply, is her husband Leroy's incredibly enduring love for her, for nature and the world.

A conventionally realistic play would no doubt have attempted to create a "just-like-life" effect, with the sickness gradually rising out of the normal routines of the family's life, and calling up our empathy by virtue of our instant identification with familiar reality. But while Patricia Hamilton, the carpenter's wife, is seen as an individual sufferer, the context of her illness is equally important because, for one thing, she knows, as do many such patients, that more Americans (and West Europeans) are in hospitals for depression than for any other ailment. In life, with such people, a high degree of objectification or distancing exists, and the style of the play had to reflect the fact that they commonly know a great deal about the social setting of the illness even as they are unable to tear themselves free of it. And this affects the play's style.

It opens by directly, even crudely, grasping the core of its central preoccupation—the moral and social myths feeding the disease; and we have a discussion of the hospital's enormous parking lot, a conversation bordering on the absurd. I would call this realism, but it is far from the tape-recorded kind. Frick, like Leroy Hamilton, has arrived for a visit with his wife, and after a moment's silence while the two strangers grope for a conversational opening . . .

> FRICK: Tremendous parking space down there. 'They need that for?
> LEROY: Well a lot of people visit on weekends. Fills up pretty much.

FRICK: Really? That whole area?
LEROY: Pretty much.
FRICK: 'Doubt that.

The play is made of such direct blows aimed at the thematic center; there is a vast parking space because crowds of stricken citizens converge on this place to visit mothers, fathers, brothers, and sisters. So that the two patients we may be about to meet are not at all unique. This is in accord with the vision of the play, which is intended to be both close up and wide, psychological and social, subjective and objective, and manifestly so. To be sure, there is a realistic tone to this exchange—people do indeed seem to talk this way—but an inch below is the thematic selectivity which drives the whole tale. Perhaps it needs to be said that this split vision has informed all the plays I have written. I have tried to make things seen in their social context and simultaneously felt as intimate testimony, and that requires a style, but one that draws as little attention to itself as possible, for I would wish a play to be absorbed rather than merely observed.

I have called this play a comedy, a comedy about a tragedy, and I am frankly not sure why. Possibly it is due to the absurdity of people constantly comparing themselves to others—something we all do to one degree or another, but in Patricia's case to the point of illness.

PATRICIA: There was something else you said. About standing on line.
LEROY: On line?
PATRICIA: That you'll always be at the head of the line because . . . *breaks off.*
LEROY: I'm the only one on it. . . . We're really all on a one-person line, Pat. I learned that in these years.

The play's language, then, has a surface of everyday realism, but its action is overtly stylized rather than "natural."

Finally, a conventionally realistic work about mental illness would be bound to drive to a reverberating climax. But repression is the cultural inheritance of these New Englanders and such theatricality would be a betrayal of *their* style of living and dying. Indeed, short of suicide, the illness, properly speaking, never ends in the sense of tying all the loose strings, nor should the play, which simply sets the boundaries of the possible. For the theme is hope rather than completion or achievement, and hope is tentative always.

A play about them should have a certain amplitude of sound, nothing greater or less, reflecting their tight yet often deeply felt culture. And in a play about them they should recognize themselves—and even possibly what drives them mad—just like the longshoremen who saw themselves in *A View from the Bridge* or the cops in *The Price* or the salespeople in *Death of a Salesman*. That would be a satisfactory realism as I saw it.

I suppose the form itself of *The Last Yankee* is as astringently direct and uncluttered as it is because these people are supremely the prey of the culture, if only because it is never far from the center of their minds—the latest film or TV show, the economy's ups and downs, and above all the endless advertising-encouraged self-comparisons with others who are more or less successful than they. This ritualistic preoccupation is at the play's dramatic core and, I felt, ought not be unclear or misted over, for it is from its grip they must be freed if they are ever to be free at all. Hence, the repeated references to ambition, to success and failure, to wealth and poverty, to economic survival, to the kind of car one drives and the suit one wears. In a word, the play could not be amorphously "realistic" if it was to reflect the obsessiveness of the characters in life. So if *The Last Yankee* is realism it is of this kind resulting from an intense selectivity, which in turn is derived from the way these people live and feel.

But obviously, to make such a strictly thematic play demands intense condensation and the syncopating of idea and feeling and language. More than one actor in my plays has told me that it is surprisingly difficult to memorize the dialogue. It sounds like real, almost like reported talk, when in fact it is intensely composed, compressed, "angled" into an inevitability that seems natural but isn't. For it is always necessary to employ the artificial in order to arrive at the real. So that the question I bring to a play is not whether its form and style are new or old, experimental or traditional, but first, whether it brings news, something truly felt by its author, something thought through to its conclusion and its significance; and second, whether its form is beautiful, or wasteful, whether it is aberrant for aberrancy's sake, full of surprises that discover little, and so on.

Something called Realism can land us further from common reality than the most fantastic caprice. But in the end, if stylization in theatre needs justification—and it does, of course—it is not in its novelty but in its enhancement of discovery of how life works in our time. How a thing is said is therefore only as important as what it is saying. The proof is the deep pile of experimental plays of two, three, five, ten years ago, which can be appreciated now only by the scholar-specialist, a pile, incidentally, no smaller than the one for so many realistic plays of the same era. So finding the truth is no easier now when we are totally free to use any stylistic means at hand than it was a century or half a century ago when a play had to be "real" to even be read, and had to make sense to sensible people.

Call it a question of personal taste rather than principle, but I think that in theatre work there is an optimum balance between two kinds of approaches. One is the traditional attempt to fill characters with acknowledged emotion, "as in life." The other is, in effect, to evacuate emotion from characters and merely refer to it rather than acting it out. Brecht, for one, tried to do this and failed, excepting in his most agitprop and forgettable plays. Actually, the strict containment not of emotion but of emotionalism is the hallmark of the Greek tragic plays, of Molière and Racine and the Japanese No plays, while Shakespeare, it seems to me, is the balance, the fusion of idea and feeling. In short, it is by no means the abstracting of emotion I dislike; on the contrary, it is the lack of it and the substitution for it of fashionably alienated ironies.

As I am not a critic and would not do anything to make any writer's life harder, I will desist from naming names, but there has been a plethora of plays in recent years whose claim to modernity is based on indicated rather than felt emotion, on the assumption, I suppose, that this *sec* quality intellectualizes a work and saves it from the banality associated with writing aimed at the audience's belly rather than at its head. The devil to be avoided is, of course, sentimentality—emotion unearned. But emotion can be earned, of course. Yet a play that is not camp and moves people is in danger of dismissal. (Unless it appears in old films, which we allow ourselves to be moved by if at the same instant we can protect our modernity by feeling superior to their time-bound naïveté.) But if the pun can be pardoned, man lives not by head alone, and the balance between the two modes, one aimed at the mind and one at the flesh, as it were, is what will interpret life more fully, rather than headline it with conceptualizations that too often simply clump about on the stilts of dry irony that time and the shifts of cultural politics will make thoroughly disposable. After all, at least part of the aim of a modern play must be to show what life now *feels like*.

Ultimately every assault on the human mystery falls back to the ground, changing little, but the flight of the arrow continues claiming our attention over more time when its direction is toward the castle rather than the wayward air.

Preface
(Mr. Peters' Connections)

A PLAY ought to explain—or not explain—itself, but a play with both living and dead characters interacting may justifiably ask for a word or two of explanation.

Mr. Peters is in that suspended state of consciousness which can come upon a man taking a nap, when the mind, still close to consciousness and self-awareness, is freed to roam from real memories to conjectures, from trivialities to tragic insights, from terror of death to glorying in one's being alive. The play, in short, is taking place inside Mr. Peters' mind, or at least on its threshold, from where it is still possible to glance back toward daylight life or forward into the misty depths.

Mr. Peters is, of course, alive. So is his wife, as well as Rose, who turns out to be their daughter, and Leonard, her boyfriend. Adele, the black bag lady, is neither dead nor alive, but simply Peters' construct, the to-him incomprehensible black presence on the dim borders of his city life.

Cathy-May is long dead, but the dead in memory do not quite die and often live more vividly than in life. Cathy-May's husband is Peters' conjecture as to what kind of man she might have married, given her nature as he knew it when they were lovers. And Calvin, a.k.a. Charley, who turns out to be Peters' brother, is also long dead, even if the competition between them is very much alive in Peters' mind along with its fraternal absurdities.

As for the set, it should look like whatever the reader or producer imagines as a space where the living and the dead may meet, the gray or blue or blazing red terrain of the sleeping mind where imagination runs free. Fragments of jazz and sheer-sound should also rise and fall. The stage may be ablaze with light at times or steeped in cavernous darkness at others. It may threaten or reassure, for the action of the play is the procession of Mr. Peters' moods, each of them summoning up the next, all of them strung upon the line of his anxiety, his fear, if you will, that he has not found the secret, the pulsing center of energy—what he calls the subject—that will make his life cohere.

CHRONOLOGY

NOTE ON THE TEXTS

NOTES

Chronology

1915   Born Arthur Asher Miller on October 17 in New York City, the second child of Isadore and Augusta ("Gussie") Barnett Miller. (Father emigrated at the age of six from Eastern Europe and joined his parents and six siblings in New York City, where his father, Shmuel, owned a clothing business on the Lower East Side. As a young man he established his own highly successful business, the Miltex Coat and Suit Company, in Manhattan's garment district. Mother was born in the United States to immigrant parents. Their first child, Kermit, was born three years before Miller.) Family lives in a sixth-floor apartment at 45 West 110th Street, with a view of Central Park.

1916–28   At age six Miller begins attending P.S. 24 on West 111th Street. Sister Joan is born in 1922. Miller celebrates his bar mitzvah in 1928.

1929   Stock market crash devastates family finances and threatens the solvency of Miltex. Family moves to Gravesend in Brooklyn, living in a small house at 1350 Third Street where Miller shares a bedroom with his recently widowed maternal grandfather. Attends James Madison High School on Bedford Avenue.

1930–32   Brother Kermit begins attending New York University in the fall of 1930, while Miller transfers to Abraham Lincoln High School on Ocean Parkway. Works for Miltex in the summer of 1931, carrying samples for salesmen as they make their rounds. In the fall Kermit quits NYU to work full-time for Miltex. Miller makes deliveries for a local bakery before school, then takes new job driving a delivery truck for an auto-supply store.

1933–34   Graduates high school in June 1933. After working at Miltex in the summer, he finds a job paying $15 a week as stock clerk at the Chadick-Delameter auto-parts warehouse at 10th Avenue and West 63rd Street in Manhattan. Reads *Crime and Punishment* during his commute from Brooklyn. Applies unsuccessfully to the University of Michigan twice. Enrolls in classes in history and chemistry at City College of New York's night school but stops

873

attending after two weeks. Writes to the University of Michigan and asks that his application be reconsidered and is accepted on a probationary basis provided he prove his ability to pay tuition, room, and board. Matriculates at University of Michigan in Ann Arbor in fall 1934. Rooms with fellow New Yorker Charles Bleich in a private home.

1935   Works as reporter on school newspaper, *The Michigan Daily*; does well enough in his courses that the university rescinds his probationary status and offers him a loan to help cover expenses. Hitchhikes home for summer break. In the fall lives in rooming house off campus. Takes creative writing course and continues to write for *Michigan Daily*, covering organizing efforts of the United Auto Workers and interviewing UAW leader Walter Reuther.

1936   Meets first-year student Mary Grace Slattery and becomes romantically involved with her. In six days writes his first play, *No Villain*, which wins $250 Hopwood Award from the university. Writes "In Memoriam," short story about a salesman; attempts to adapt it for the stage but abandons the effort. Miltex closes in the summer. Miller revises *No Villain* and submits new version, entitled *They Too Arise*, to a student playwriting contest sponsored by the Theatre Guild. Attends performance on Broadway of Ibsen's *A Doll's House* during his winter break and is deeply impressed.

1937   Enrolls in playwriting seminar with Professor Kenneth Rowe. Awarded $1,250 scholarship when *They Too Arise* wins Theatre Guild competition; the play is staged on campus and then in Detroit. Miller writes *Honors at Dawn*, which wins the Hopwood Award. Meets Norman Rosten, who has come to the university on a Theatre Guild scholarship to study with Kenneth Rowe. Interviews prisoners at nearby Jackson State Penitentiary and uses the material as the basis of play eventually entitled *The Great Disobedience*.

1938   Completes *The Great Disobedience* in March. Graduates from University of Michigan in June and returns to New York City, living in the family home in Brooklyn. Writes new version of *They Too Arise* entitled *The Grass Still Grows*, which after an enthusiastic response at the literary agency Leland Hayward and Company is sent to Broadway producers. Miller is hired by the Federal Theatre and Writers Project and moves into a studio apartment on

East 74th Street in Manhattan, but is then let go when the Project is forced to cut back.

1939   Writes tragedy about the Aztecs' encounter with Cortez called "The Montezuma Play," "The Children of the Sun," and ultimately *The Golden Years*. Collaborates with Norman Rosten on one-act play *Listen My Children* and *You're Next!*, satire of the House Committee on Un-American Activities, which had investigated the Federal Theatre Project. Radio play *William Ireland's Confession* is performed on CBS on October 19.

1940   Miller marries Mary Slattery in a Catholic ceremony in her hometown in Ohio on August 5. The couple return to New York and move into a Brooklyn Heights apartment. In September, Miller sails alone to South America on a two-week trip to research *The Half-Bridge*, a play set on a merchant ship.

1941   Starts writing novel "The Man Who Had All the Luck" and receives modest advance from Atlantic Monthly Press; when he submits a partial manuscript, it is rejected by the publisher. Travels alone to North Carolina and sketches out ideas and stories for plays; trip is sponsored by Library of Congress to collect dialect speech for the folk division.

1942–43 Begins working the night shift at the Brooklyn Navy Yard. Finishes "The Man Who Had All the Luck" and sends it to Doubleday, Doran, which rejects it. Writes radio plays that are aired on the NBC Dupont Cavalcade of America. Quits job at Brooklyn Navy Yard when he is hired to write *The Story of G.I. Joe*, film adaptation of Ernie Pyle's *Here Is Your War*.

1944   Interviews soldiers at army training camps for *The Story of G.I. Joe* but is fired before script is completed and receives no writing credit on the film; uses material in a book of reportage, *Situation Normal . . .* , published by Harper. Adapts "The Man Who Had All the Luck" into a play and an early version is included in anthology *Cross-Section: A Collection of New American Writing*. Daughter Jane born September 7. *The Man Who Had All the Luck*, directed by Joseph Fields, opens at the Forrest Theatre on November 23 to unfavorable reviews and closes after four performances.

1945   One-act play *That They May Win* is included in anthology *Best One-Act Plays of 1944*. Writes *Focus*, novel about anti-Semitism, which is published by Reynal & Hitchcock and becomes a commercial success.

1946   Completes play *All My Sons*. After Leland Hayward agency is bought out by MCA, Miller is assigned to Kay Brown, who will represent him for the next four decades. Harold Clurman, formerly of the Group Theatre, reads *All My Sons* and agrees to produce it, with Elia Kazan directing.

1947   After trial runs in New Haven and Boston, *All My Sons* opens on Broadway on January 29 and runs for 328 performances; book version is published by Reynal & Hitchcock. Miller buys house in Roxbury, Connecticut. Works for one week in a Queens factory assembling boxes as "a moral act of solidarity with those who had failed in life." *All My Sons* is named best new play of the 1946–47 season by the New York Drama Critics Circle; Miller and Kazan receive Antoinette Perry ("Tony") Awards for their work on the play. Son Robert is born on May 31. Moves in June to converted stable house at 31 Grace Court in Brooklyn Heights, living on upper floors and renting out two apartments in the building. Publishes essay in *The New York Times* arguing for a subsidized theater that "would lay upon all work and works the standards of art, and not primarily the standards of business men." Declines offer to write the screenplay for Alfred Hitchcock's *Rope*. Works on *Death of a Salesman*. Max Sorensen, leader of the Catholic War Veterans, denounces *All My Sons* as Communist "propaganda," and the War Department prevents it from being staged in American-occupied Germany. *All My Sons* is performed in the Netherlands and Poland.

1948   Miller travels to Europe for the first time, visiting Italy, Greece, and France. *Focus* is banned by the principal of DeWitt Clinton High School in New York on grounds that it is offensive to Roman Catholics. Film version of *All My Sons*, directed by Irving Reis and starring Edward G. Robinson and Burt Lancaster, is released. *All My Sons* is produced in London and is warmly received, with one critic calling it "the best serious play that America has sent us for some time." Miller completes *Death of a Salesman* and Kazan agrees to direct it. Revises play based on suggestions by Kazan, but does not use revised version after producer Kermit Bloomgarden expresses strong preference for original version.

1949   After successful trial run in Philadelphia, *Death of a Salesman* opens on Broadway on February 10 and runs for 742 performances. Miller publishes essay "Tragedy and the Common Man" in *The New York Times* in February and another essay about tragedy and *Death of a Salesman* in the *New York Herald-Tribune* the following month. Attends Cultural and Scientific Conference for World Peace in New York City, a gathering criticized by anti-Communist liberals who claim it is too sympathetic to communism, and chairs panel on the arts whose members include Dmitri Shostakovich, Aaron Copland, and Clifford Odets. *Death of a Salesman* is named best new play of the 1948–49 season by the New York Drama Critics Circle and is awarded Pulitzer Prize, Donaldson Award, and Antoinette Perry Award; London staging is met with an enthusiastic reception. Continues working on "The Hook," a screenplay about union corruption on the Brooklyn waterfront, and an adaptation of Ibsen's *An Enemy of the People*. *Death of a Salesman* is published in book form in America and England and becomes first play offered as a selection of the Book of the Month Club.

1950–51   *Death of a Salesman* tours the U.S. and is staged in Vienna, Copenhagen, Düsseldorf, and other European cities. Short story "It Takes a Thief," first published in *Collier's* three years earlier, is adapted for television and broadcast on NBC Cameo Theatre. Adaptation of *An Enemy of the People* opens on Broadway on December 28, 1950, and runs for 36 performances. Travels with Kazan to Los Angeles to seek studio backing for "The Hook." Meets actress Marilyn Monroe. Columbia Pictures expresses interest in "The Hook," but Miller withdraws screenplay after studio executive Harry Cohn asks him to revise script along anti-Communist lines. Writes to Monroe, and they begin corresponding. Buys house at 155 Willow Street in Brooklyn Heights and moves family there. Film of *Death of a Salesman*, directed by Laslo Benedek and starring Frederic March, is released.

1952   Miller's relations with Kazan deteriorate after Kazan testifies before the House Committee on Un-American Activities on April 10 and names associates he knows to be members of the Communist Party. Miller begins researching and writing play about seventeenth-century

Salem witch trials and works on it throughout the summer. Writes several pages of dialogue based on his job at
the auto-parts warehouse that will later be developed into
A Memory of Two Mondays.

1953–54   *The Crucible* opens on Broadway on January 22, 1953, to
mixed reviews and runs for 197 performances; it is also
staged in London, and in Paris in Marcel Aymé's French
adaptation, *Les Sorcières de Salem,* starring Yves Montand
and Simone Signoret. When he is invited to Brussels for
the Belgian premiere of the play, Miller's passport application is rejected by the State Department "under regula-
tions denying passports to people believed to be
supporting the Communist movement."

1955   Miller becomes romantically involved with Marilyn Monroe. Writes one-act version of *A View from the Bridge,*
drawing on Brooklyn waterfront research for "The Hook."
Works on screenplay for film about juvenile gangs in
Brooklyn to be made in cooperation with the city government. After a summer tryout on Cape Cod and trial
runs in New Haven and Boston, *A View from the Bridge:
Two One-Act Plays* (*Bridge* and *A Memory of Two Mondays*) opens on Broadway on September 29 and runs for
149 performances. Miller separates from wife in October
and moves into the Chelsea Hotel in Manhattan. City authorities cancel the gang film project after Miller is de-
nounced as "a veteran backer of Communist causes" by
the *New York World-Telegram.*

1956   Settles with wife on terms of divorce in February, and
then spends six weeks near Reno to establish residency for
a Nevada divorce. Works on a two-act version of *A View
from the Bridge* and the introduction to his *Collected
Plays.* Visits Los Angeles to see Monroe, who is filming
Bus Stop. Granted divorce in June. Receives honorary
Doctorate of Humane Letters from the University of
Michigan. Appears before House Committee on Un-
American Activities on June 21 in hearing ostensibly related to his passport application. In his testimony Miller
admits to having attended meetings with Communist
writers in 1947, but he refuses to identify others at these
meetings and denies ever having submitted himself to
"Communist discipline." Marries Marilyn Monroe in civil
ceremony in White Plains, New York, on June 29 and in
a Jewish ceremony in Katonah on July 1. Miller is cited
for contempt by Congress on July 10. Travels to England

with Monroe for honeymoon, where she films *The Prince and the Showgirl* with Laurence Olivier. Returns briefly to New York and writes short story "The Misfits, or Chicken Feed: The Last Frontier of the Quixotic Cowboy." Goes back to London for premiere in October of expanded *A View from the Bridge*, directed by Peter Brook. (Production is staged under the aegis of a private club after the censor refuses to license public performances because of the play's references to homosexuality.)

1957   Miller is convicted of contempt of Congress in federal district court in Washington, D.C., on May 31 after a six-day trial and is sentenced on July 19 to one-month suspended jail term and a $500 fine. Moves with Monroe from 2 Sutton Place to apartment on East 57th Street; also spends time at rented house in Amagansett, Long Island. Monroe has miscarriage in early August. *Arthur Miller's Collected Plays* published. *Les Sorcières de Salem*, film adaptation of *The Crucible* starring Yves Montand and Simone Signoret and with a screenplay by Jean-Paul Sartre, is released in France. *Death of a Salesman* is staged in Moscow. Miller begins adapting "The Misfits" into a screenplay intended as a vehicle for Monroe.

1958   Buys farm in Roxbury. Contacts Frank Lloyd Wright to design new house on the site but declines Wright's proposed plan and instead renovates existing eighteenth-century farmhouse; buys property adjoining the farm. Completes screenplay of *The Misfits*. Named a member of the National Institute of Arts and Letters. U.S. Court of Appeals for the District of Columbia overturns Miller's conviction for contempt of Congress in August. Miller writes essay "My Wife Marilyn" for *Life* magazine. Monroe suffers another miscarriage.

1959–60   Miller is awarded Gold Medal for Drama from the National Institute of Arts and Letters. Sends completed screenplay of *The Misfits* to John Huston, who agrees to direct the film. Travels with Monroe to Los Angeles, where she is filming *Let's Make Love*. Miller goes to Ireland to work with John Huston on *The Misfits*, but soon returns to California at Monroe's request. Works on rewrites of the *Let's Make Love* script. Monroe has an affair with co-star Yves Montand; Miller returns to Connecticut. They travel to Reno, Nevada, in July 1960 for location shooting for *The Misfits*. Miller meets Ingeborg (Inge) Morath, an Austrian-born photographer sent by the Magnum agency to document the production. In late August, Miller takes Monroe, who is in a fragile mental state and dependent on barbiturates, to Los Angeles to be hospitalized. Returns to New York and moves out of the 57th Street apartment; divorce plans are announced on November 11.

1961   Monroe is granted divorce in Juárez, Mexico, on January 24. Novelization of *The Misfits* by Miller is published shortly before the film is released on February 1. Mother dies on March 6. Miller discovers that *Death of a Salesman* has been filmed in the Soviet Union without his permission. *Uno Sguardo del Ponte*, opera of *A View from the Bridge* by Renzo Rossellini, premieres in Rome and is staged in several European cities; Robert Ward's opera of *The Crucible* is staged in the fall and wins a Pulitzer Prize the following year. Short story "I Don't Need You Anymore" is included in *Prize Stories 1961: The O. Henry Awards*. Filming begins in Brooklyn and Paris for screen version of *A View from the Bridge*, directed by Sidney Lumet with screenplay by Norman Rosten.

1962   One-hour television adaptation of *Focus* is broadcast on NBC. Film of *A View from the Bridge* released in the U.S. in late January. Miller marries Inge Morath in Connecticut on February 17 and the couple depart for honeymoon in Europe. New production of *The Crucible* with essayistic passages read from the stage is presented in Boston. Marilyn Monroe dies from an overdose of barbiturates on August 5. Miller works on *After the Fall*. Daughter Rebecca Augusta born September 15.

1963   As *After the Fall* is planned for production in the inaugural season of the Lincoln Center Repertory Theater, Miller works with director Elia Kazan for the first time since the early 1950s. Writes children's book *Jane's Blanket* for daughter Jane. Joins forty-seven other playwrights in refusing to allow their plays to be performed in South African theaters enforcing apartheid. *Death of a Salesman* staged as part of the inaugural season of the Guthrie Theater in Minneapolis.

1964   *After the Fall*, starring Jason Robards, premieres on January 23 and runs for 208 performances; among those attending the gala opening are Lady Bird Johnson, Adlai Stevenson, and Ralph Bunche. The play attracts controversy because of its presumed autobiographical elements, particularly concerning Miller's marriage to Monroe. Writes for the *New York Herald-Tribune* about trial in Frankfurt of former SS men who had served at Auschwitz. Returns home and completes draft of play *Incident at Vichy* in three weeks. Film rights for *After the Fall* bought by Carlo Ponti, Ira Steiner, and MGM; Miller works on script but then withdraws from the project because of differences with producers about the screenplay and casting. Makes cuts in *After the Fall* seven months into its run. Directed by Harold Clurman for the Lincoln Center Repertory Company, *Incident at Vichy* premieres on December 3 and runs for 32 performances.

1965   Miller travels to the Soviet Union and Poland. Elected president of PEN International at its annual conference and serves four years in the position. Participates in demonstrations against the Vietnam War and antiwar teach-in at the University of Michigan, and refuses invitation from President Johnson to attend signing of the federal Arts and Humanities Act because "the occasion is so darkened by the Vietnam tragedy that I could not join it with clear conscience" (will maintain his antiwar activism for the duration of the conflict).

1966–67   While in England for production of *Incident at Vichy*, Miller falls ill with hepatitis and is hospitalized. Television version of *Death of a Salesman* is broadcast on CBS on May 8, 1966, with Lee J. Cobb and Mildred Dunnock reprising their roles from the original Broadway production; adaptation of *An Enemy of the People* is broadcast by National Educational Television. Publishes story collection *I Don't Need You Anymore*. A son, Daniel Miller, is born. Miller travels to Abidjan, Ivory Coast, for PEN International conference in July 1967.

1968   *The Price* opens on Broadway on February 7 and runs for 429 performances. Harold Clurman publishes essay "The Merits of Mr. Miller" in *The New York Times* in response to negative assessment of Miller's career by critic Alfred Bermel. Campaigns for Democratic presidential candidate Eugene McCarthy and attends Democratic Party convention in Chicago as delegate from Roxbury. Travels to the Soviet Union and visits Czechoslovakia after Soviet invasion. *The Price* is staged in Tel Aviv.

1969   London production of *The Price* opens in March. Miller refuses to have his work published in Greece as a protest against the Greek military regime. One-act play *The Reason Why* filmed for television at Miller's Roxbury farm. Signs letter condemning the expulsion of Alexander Solzhenitsyn from the Soviet Writers' Union. *In Russia*, the first of several collaborative books with photographer Morath, is published.

1970–71   Miller receives Creative Arts Award from Brandeis University. Russian television production of *The Price* is canceled and Miller's works are banned in the Soviet Union. American television productions of *A Memory of Two Mondays* and *The Price* are broadcast in February 1971.

1972–74   Miller is a delegate to the Democratic National Convention in Miami. After trial run in Washington, *The Creation of the World and Other Business*, comic adaptation of the Book of Genesis, opens in New York on November 30, 1972, and closes after 20 performances. Miller serves as writer-in-residence at University of Michigan. Adapts *The Creation of the World and Other Business* into a musical, *Up from Paradise*, which he directs, and plays the onstage role of narrator in a production at the University of Michigan. Writes editorial of support for Soviet physicist Andrei Sakharov's six-day hunger strike in 1974 and criticizes the Nixon administration's silence about Sakharov and other dissidents as a "message . . . that the United States is a moral nullity." Becomes active supporter of Peter Reilly, a teenager from Canaan, Connecticut, who had been convicted of manslaughter in the killing of his mother; believing that Reilly had been coerced into confessing, Miller raises money for Reilly's legal fees and eventually hires a detective to investigate the case. Television version of *After the Fall*, starring Christopher Plummer, is broadcast on NBC on December 10, 1974.

1975–76   *Death of a Salesman*, starring George C. Scott, Teresa Wright, and Harvey Keitel, is revived on Broadway in June 1975 and runs for 71 performances. Persuades *The New York Times* to publish a series of articles about the Peter Reilly case. Appears before Senate subcommittee in November to advocate American pressure on governments that violate human rights and the freedom to publish, emphasizing the situation in Czechoslovakia. Peter Reilly is granted a new trial on March 26, 1976, and the charges against him are dismissed in November (he is fully exonerated in 1977).

1977   *The Archbishop's Ceiling* has world premiere on April 23 at
the Kennedy Center in Washington; the play's scheduled
New York run is canceled by its producers. *Up from Paradise* is also staged at the Kennedy Center. *In the Country*, a collaboration with Inge Morath, is published.

1978   Miller's version of *An Enemy of the People* is filmed, directed by George Schaefer and starring Steve McQueen,
but film never receives wide release. Miller speaks in front
of Soviet mission in New York protesting the trials of
dissidents Alexander Ginzburg and Anatoli Shcharansky.
Visits China with Morath in November. *The Theatre Essays
of Arthur Miller* is published. Hour-long comedy *Fame* is
broadcast on NBC on November 30.

1979   *Chinese Encounters*, in collaboration with Morath, is published. *The Price* is revived in New York in a successful
off-Broadway run, then moves to Broadway; it is also
staged at the Spoleto Festival USA in Charleston. Miller
accepts offer to write television adaptation of *Playing for
Time*, a memoir by Fania Fénelon, who had been forced
to play in an orchestra of female prisoners at Auschwitz,
and defends controversial casting of Vanessa Redgrave, a
supporter of the Palestine Liberation Organization, in the
lead role. *Arthur Miller on Home Ground*, documentary
by Harry Rasky, is released in November.

1980   Version of *The American Clock* premieres at the Spoleto
USA festival. After Miller extensively revises the play, the
London production by the National Theatre receives
Olivier Award for the season's best new play, but the
Broadway production, with his sister Joan playing Rose
Baum, closes after 12 performances in November. *Playing
for Time* is broadcast on CBS on September 30.

1981   Attends inauguration of French president François Mitterrand. Second volume of *Collected Plays* is published.
First New York performance of *Up from Paradise* is staged
at the Whitney Museum. Two-act version of *A View from
the Bridge* is revived at the Long Wharf Theater in New
Haven.

1982   Monologue *I Think About You a Great Deal*, written as a
tribute to imprisoned Czech playwright Václav Havel,
whom Miller had met in the 1960s, is performed at the
International Theatre Festival in Avignon, France. Program of two one-act plays, *Elegy for a Lady* and *Some
Kind of Love Story*, runs for six weeks at the Long Wharf.

1983   First Broadway production of the two-act *A View from the Bridge* opens on February 3 and runs for 149 performances. Miller agrees to direct a production of *Death of a Salesman* in Beijing and visits China with Morath from March to May; while they are away, a fire at their Roxbury house destroys many of his papers and possessions.

1984   Receives honorary doctorate from the University of Hartford. Broadway revival of *Death of a Salesman* starring Dustin Hoffman is well received and runs for 185 performances. *Salesman in Beijing*, with photographs by Inge Morath, is published in June. *After the Fall* is revived in New York in October. Miller threatens legal action against avant-garde troupe The Wooster Group for performing a segment of *The Crucible* without permission in their production *L.S.D.*; the troupe closes the play. Receives Kennedy Center Honors for lifetime achievement in the arts.

1985   Under the aegis of PEN, travels with British playwright Harold Pinter to Istanbul for five days in March to conduct inquiries into human-rights abuses and censorship in Turkey. Film of *Death of a Salesman*, starring Dustin Hoffman and directed by Volker Schlöndorff, is screened at the Venice Film Festival in September and is broadcast on CBS; *Private Conversations*, Christian Blackwood's documentary about the making of the film, is shown at the New York Film Festival. *The Archbishop's Ceiling* premieres in England. Miller visits the U.S.S.R. to meet with Soviet writers.

1986   Stage adaptation of *Playing for Time* premieres at theater festival in Edinburgh. Miller travels to the U.S.S.R. in October for a conference in Kyrgyzstan and meets Soviet leader Mikhail Gorbachev at the Kremlin.

1987–88   *All My Sons* is broadcast on the Public Broadcasting System's American Playhouse. *Danger: Memory!*, program of the one-act plays *Clara* and *I Can't Remember Anything*, opens at Lincoln Center in New York. London revival of the two-act *A View from the Bridge* runs for six months. *The Golden Years* is broadcast by the BBC as a radio play. Autobiography *Timebends* is published. *The American Clock* is revived for a run at the Williamstown Theatre Festival.

1989   Miller's original screenplay *Everybody Wins* enters production, directed by Karel Reisz and starring Nick Nolte and

Debra Winger. Arthur Miller Centre for American Studies is established at the University of East Anglia, under the directorship of Christopher Bigsby. *The Crucible* is revived at the Long Wharf in New Haven.

1990   *Everybody Wins* is released. Miller travels to Prague for Czech productions of *The Archbishop's Ceiling* and *The Crucible*. *The Archbishop's Ceiling* is performed for the first time in New York. *After the Fall* is revived in London at the Royal National Theatre. Miller travels to South Africa to interview Nelson Mandela for the BBC.

1991   *Clara* is broadcast on the Arts & Entertainment network. *The Ride Down Mt. Morgan* premieres in London in the fall. *The Crucible* is staged in New York as the inaugural offering of the National Actors Theater.

1992   *The Price* is revived on Broadway and runs for 46 performances. One-act version of *The Last Yankee* staged in East Hampton, N.Y. Miller works on "Gellburg," play that will eventually be staged as *Broken Glass*. Directs production of *Death of a Salesman* in Stockholm.

1993   Full-length version of *The Last Yankee* premieres in New York and a production is mounted in London. *The American Clock* is broadcast on the TNT network. Miller receives National Medal of Arts.

1994   *Broken Glass* premieres at the Long Wharf in New Haven in March, starring Ron Silver (soon replaced by David Dukes), Amy Irving, and Ron Rifkin, with Miller revising the play during the production in preparation for its April 24 opening on Broadway; play earns Tony Award nomination for best play, and runs for 73 performances. Miller continues to work on the play for its London staging, and once again wins an Olivier Award for best new play of the season. With Peter Reilly, becomes involved in the case of Richard Lapointe, a mentally disabled Connecticut man sentenced to life imprisonment after confessing to the rape and murder of an 88-year-old woman. Oxford University names Miller to a one-year appointment as Professor of Contemporary Theatre.

1995   One-act *The Ryan Interview* is staged in May in New York. Film version of *The Crucible*, with screenplay by Miller, directed by Nicholas Hytner, and starring Daniel Day-Lewis and Winona Ryder, begins shooting; son Robert is one of the producers. PEN American Center organizes tribute to Miller on the occasion of his 80th birthday. *Homely Girl: A Life*, a novella, is published by Viking.

1996　　*The Ride Down Mt. Morgan* has its American premiere at the Williamstown Theatre Festival. *Broken Glass* is broadcast on PBS's Masterpiece Theater on October 20, directed by David Thacker; Thacker's revival of *Death of a Salesman* is mounted at the Royal National Theatre. Film version of *The Crucible* is released in November, and Miller's screenplay is published by Penguin.

1997　　Screenplay of *The Crucible* receives Academy Award nomination. Roundabout Theater Company revives *All My Sons* in New York, in a production that soon moves to Broadway. Signature Theater Company in New York begins season-long Miller retrospective, staging revivals of *The Last Yankee* and *The American Clock*.

1998　　Miller receives Berlin Prize fellowship by the American Academy in Berlin. *Mr. Peters' Connections* premieres as part of the Signature Theater's retrospective. Revised version of *The Ride Down Mt. Morgan*, starring Patrick Stewart, is staged in New York at the Public Theater.

1999　　*Death of a Salesman*, starring Brian Dennehy and Elizabeth Franz, is revived on Broadway, runs for 274 performances, and wins four Tony Awards; Miller also receives a lifetime achievement award. William Bolcom's opera of *A View from the Bridge*, with libretto by Miller and Arnold Weinstein, is performed by the Lyric Opera of Chicago in October. *The Price* is revived on Broadway in November and runs for 128 performances.

2000　　*The Ride Down Mt. Morgan* is staged on Broadway, with Patrick Stewart reprising his role in the Public Theater production, and runs for 121 performances. In Los Angeles, *The Man Who Had All the Luck* has its first American staging since 1944. *Mr. Peters' Connections* premieres in London, where the National Theatre revives *All My Sons*. *Echoes Down the Corridor: Collected Essays 1944–2001* is published.

2001　　Miller's one-act *Untitled* is performed as a prelude to a staging of Havel's *Vanek Plays* in New York. *On Politics and the Art of Acting*, originally a National Endowment for the Humanities lecture, is published. Film adaptation of *Focus*, directed by Neil Slavin and starring William H. Macy and Laura Dern, is released in the fall. At National

Book Awards ceremony in November Miller receives Medal for Distinguished Contribution to American Literature.

2002   Inge Morath dies of lymphoma on January 30. *The Crucible* is revived on Broadway in a production starring Liam Neeson and Laura Linney that runs for 101 performances; *The Man Who Had All the Luck* is also revived on Broadway for 62 performances. Miller meets painter Agnes Barley, who later becomes his companion. *Resurrection Blues* premieres in August at the Guthrie Theater. Bolcom's *A View from the Bridge* is performed at the Metropolitan Opera in New York. Gail Levin's documentary *Making "The Misfits"* is broadcast on PBS in October.

2003   Miller completes *Finishing the Picture*. Brother Kermit dies on October 17.

2004   *After the Fall* is revived on Broadway and runs for 53 performances. *Finishing the Picture* has world premiere at the Goodman Theater in Chicago.

2005   Arthur Miller dies of congestive heart failure in Roxbury on February 10 and is buried in the Roxbury Center Cemetery.

Note on the Texts

This volume contains all of Arthur Miller's plays first performed between 1987 and 2004, and a screenplay first produced in 1990. Companion volumes previously published in The Library of America series, *Collected Plays 1944–1961* and *Collected Plays 1964–1982*, gather Miller's earlier works. The plays are presented in order of their first public performance, though in one case (*Almost Everybody Wins*) the version presented here, reflecting Miller's final preference, is not the version initially performed, and in another (*The Golden Years*) the play was written decades before its premiere. Two "Early Plays" and six "Radio Plays," all of them written between 1939 and 1945, follow the collected plays of 1987–2004. A section of four short notes and essays on the plays concludes the volume.

Miller usually completed numerous drafts of his plays before arriving at a version he considered worthy of the stage. He tended to make further revisions in the course of early readings, rehearsals, and out-of-town previews, and sometimes after opening night. In some cases he made extensive changes after a play's initial performance run was finished. In the present volume, the texts of Miller's plays have been taken from the first editions Miller prepared for general readers after his plays premiered, except where he subsequently favored an alternate version, or where the plays remained unpublished. The text of Miller's screenplay *Almost Everybody Wins* has been taken from the first published edition of his original script, rather than from the revised script ultimately produced in 1989 and published in 1990 as *Everybody Wins*. None of the "Early Plays" and "Radio Plays" included in the present volume is known to have been previously published; texts have been taken from Miller's original typescripts, which are now among his papers at the Harry Ransom Center, University of Texas at Austin. Sources from which Miller's notes and essays on his plays have been taken are listed below.

I Can't Remember Anything and *Clara*. In his memoir *Timebends: A Life* (1987), Miller suggests that *I Can't Remember Anything* was inspired by his Roxbury, Connecticut, neighbors Alexander and Louisa Calder; it was a work in which he tried "to express [his] love for them both." Along with *Clara*, the play premiered at Lincoln Center on February 8, 1987, as part of a double bill titled *Danger: Memory!* Both plays were staged again in London the next year; Miller had not revised either. The texts of *I Can't Remember Anything* and *Clara* in the present volume have been taken from *Danger: Memory!*, published by Grove Press in New York in 1986.

The Golden Years. Miller was unable to find a theater willing to produce *The Golden Years*, originally written from 1939 to 1941, and he left the play unpublished. Over four decades later, Christopher Bigsby rediscovered the play among Miller's papers at the Ransom Center and suggested it to the BBC as a possible radio drama. Miller himself revisited his early script and made some modest revisions, cutting what he called "some purple passages"; the play premiered on BBC Radio 3 on November 6, 1987. The text of *The Golden Years* in the present volume has been taken from *Plays: Four* (London: Methuen Drama, 1994).

Almost Everybody Wins. Miller's screenplay *Almost Everybody Wins* grew out of his one-act stage play *Some Kind of Love Story*, produced in 1982. Originally written in 1983 and 1984, the screenplay was substantially revised in the course of production in 1989. The film premiered as *Everybody Wins* on January 19, 1990, with Karel Reisz directing and Debra Winger and Nick Nolte in the lead roles. Miller had a hand in some but not all of the changes made to his initial script and later expressed a preference for the earlier version. He wrote (introducing *Almost Everybody Wins* when he included in the 1995 Methuen edition of his plays), "it seems a shame that I helped change it from what I believe could have been a wonderfully ironic and funny film into a fairly interesting one." A text of the screenplay ultimately filmed, titled *Everybody Wins*, was published by Grove Weidenfeld in New York in 1990. The text printed here, from *Plays: Five* (London: Methuen Drama, 1995), is that of Miller's unrevised original screenplay.

The Ride Down Mt. Morgan. Though *The Crucible* had recently been revived to considerable acclaim on Broadway, Miller felt that *The Ride Down Mt. Morgan* would be more favorably received in London than in New York, and it saw its first public performance at the Wyndham Theatre on October 23, 1991. Miller made some modest revisions to the play for subsequent productions at the Williamstown Theatre Festival in 1996 and at the Public Theatre in 1998; it also had a run of 121 performances at the Ambassador Theatre on Broadway in 2000. The text of *The Ride Down Mt. Morgan* in the present volume has been taken from the Penguin edition of 1991.

The Last Yankee. Miller first presented an early, one-act version of *The Last Yankee* in June 1991 at the Ensemble Studio Theatre, off Broadway, as part of the theater's annual Marathon of One-Act Plays; it ran for fourteen performances. He later expanded the play into two acts, its final form; it premiered in New York at the City Center Stage on January 5, 1993, and in London at the Young Vic on January 26. The text of *The Last Yankee* in the present volume has been taken from *The Last Yankee* (New York: Penguin, 1994).

Broken Glass. After previews at the Long Wharf in New Haven, *Broken Glass* opened at the Booth Theatre on Broadway on April 28, 1994, and ran for 73 performances. Miller had considered a number of alternate titles for the play ("Gellburg's Time," "Gellburg's Year," "The Gellburg Time," "Gellburg," "The Glass Years," "Years of Glass," "The Glass Time," "The Age of Glass," "The Glass Age"), and revised it (adding a short scene and altering the ending) for its London premiere three months later. The text in the present volume has been taken from the first edition, published by Penguin in New York in 1994.

The Ryan Interview, or How It Was Around Here. First performed at the Ensemble Studio Theatre in New York on May 3, 1995, as part of its 18th annual festival of one-act plays, *The Ryan Interview* was published in *EST Marathon '95: The Complete One-Act Plays* (Lyme, NH: Smith and Kraus, 1995), from which the text in the present volume has been taken.

Mr. Peters' Connections. Begun in 1995, *Mr. Peters' Connections* was titled "The Powder Room" and "The Subject" at various early stages in its development; the final title was suggested by Garry Hynes, who directed the play's opening run in New York. (It premiered on April 28, 1998, with Peter Falk in the title role.) Miller did not alter the play for its subsequent performance in London, at the Almeida Theatre, in 2000. The text of *Mr. Peters' Connections* in the present volume has been taken from the Penguin edition of 1999.

Resurrection Blues premiered at the Guthrie Theater in Minneapolis on August 9, 2002, and was first published in book form by Penguin in New York in 2006. The text in the present volume has been taken from the Penguin edition.

Finishing the Picture. The last play on which Miller worked during his lifetime, *Finishing the Picture* opened at the Goodman Theatre in Chicago on October 5, 2004, and was first published posthumously in *Plays: Six* (London: Methuen Drama, 2009). The text in the present volume has been taken from the Methuen edition.

Early Plays and Radio Plays. None of the early stage and radio plays included here is known to have been published before. Texts have been taken from Miller's original typescripts at the Harry Ransom Center. In the case of both stage plays and some of the radio plays, more than one version are present among these papers; the last dated of the available versions has been selected. Some features of the typescript texts have silently been emended. Titles of works and the names of vessels have been printed in italics; the length of dashes and ellipses and the capitalization of character names have been regularized; where speaking parts have been attributed with the name of an actor rather than the name of the character represented, the character name has been substituted.

Notes and Essays on the Plays. The list below indicates the sources from which Miller's notes and essays on his plays have been taken:

On Screenwriting and Language: *Everybody Wins* (New York: Grove Weidenfeld, 1990), v–xiv.

Author's Note [on *Almost Everybody Wins*]: *Plays: Five* (London: Methuen Drama, 1995), 135.

About Theatre Language: *The Last Yankee* (New York: Penguin, 1994), 75–98.

Preface [to *Mr. Peters' Connections*]: *Mr. Peters' Connections* (New York: Penguin, 1999), vii–viii.

This volume presents the texts of the original printings and typescripts chosen for inclusion here, but it does not attempt to reproduce nontextual features of their typographic layout. The texts are reprinted without change, except for the emendations to typescripts described above and the correction of typographical errors. Spelling, punctuation, and capitalization are often expressive features, and they are not altered, even when inconsistent or irregular. The following is a list of typographical errors, cited by page and line number: 51.2, designed.; 51.6, ancestors!; 51.8, bless.; 51.11, shot; 52.12, Huitzilpochtli; 52.14, Quauhopc; 53.4, *Tenochtitlan,*; 57.2, gods (*To*; 60.22, Quetzalcuatl; 66.3, *days*; 66.18 (and *passim*), SOLIDERS; 67.8. Jesus sake;; 70.20, now.; 70.35, *indian*; 71.19, twelve-years-old.; 72.25 (and *passim*), señor; 76.11, so, (*he does so*); 76.30, left (; 79.22, (XICO-TENNA.; 80.29, (*laying*; 81.1–2, *resists.* Believe; 81.19, QUETZACOATL; 81.20, HUITZILPOCHTLI,; 83.26, HUITZILPOCHTLI; 87.13, Lord; 87.36, splended; 88.6, mangificent; 96.7, Pedro to; 97.19, Señores at; 98.5, Medillin,; 98.13, sea; 103.8, *table looks*; 104.24, Its; 106.33, *with a*; 107.36–37, two's and three's; 115.36, *floor and*; 122.13, Alvardo!; 142.21, postive,; 158.24, Watcha; 162.15, trying'; 162.28, *with the*; 165.32, means; 167.6, *embarrased*; 170.14, *sunrise in*; 175.3, CALLAGAHAN.; 180.32, time time!; 182.17, *quanties*; 186.27, *statute*; 196.7, MARK'S; 228.12, THEODORA; 233.11, *at the her*; 273.25, this; 291.10, LEROY: 293.4, talk.; 301.3, *tone . . .*) I; 303.34, family; 304.12, LEROY:; 305.10, *fury:*; 308.7, it better; 309.26, callling; 314.28, JOHN:; 344.8 and 10, SYLVIA:; 359.9, everthig; 360.27, world it's; 370.18, Yes, And; 370.25, *indicting*; 373.19, anymore.; 389.18–19, occasion that's; 391.1, while; 391.8, decent.; 397.6, being'; 404.30, yes,; 413.10, Misha Ellman; 413.11 and 12, Misha; 415.12, *sonno*; 439.24, jaquaranda; 447.30, to about?; 493.39, it's; 499.11, *leave*; 503.3, PHILLIP; 523.7–8,

Rosselini,; 523.8, Kurasawa; 546.29, Benhardt; 548.13, musn't; 550.13, going be; 565.13, Any; 568.23, exczema.; 570.5, *when latter's*; 571.13 (and *passim*), Forsythe; 575.26, weltanschaung; 583.22 (and *passim*), interne; 597.35, [speaker omitted]; 606.4, Bus; 607.25, *envelopes*; 607.25, get; 609.4, cases,; 610.2, theirs; 611.4, bawled; 616.12, ARN:; 618.19, want ask; 621.9, Boy,; 628.15, *preceeding*; 632.30, consumation; 632.31, consumated.; 639.25, speciman,; 641.40, England, comes; 642.4, LOUISE:; 644.4, Florida.; 650.12, I'll might; 653.26, *hsi his*; 661.10, *capstain*; 661.23, or razor; 662.1, or too,; 667.9, nice a blade; 668.4, nicht war?; 668.5, is stark.; 668.6, is der; 670.37, it's *daminga*, 675.28–29, Johanesburg. . . .; 672.29, *as does*; 676.13, but-in; 676.33– 34, getting'; 680.4, sportsman; 680.9, Soisant; 687.22, life; 687.35, *Bankok*; 689.5, Hongkong; 689.30, got think!; 694.5, *who's*; 696.8, aint; 696.15, What' it's; 696.35, it's; 670.37, it's *daminga*,; 700.12, *Exit*,; 701.1, cam; 701.34, I wan,; 702.7, your; 707.5, *look*; 707.8, syre; 709.4, me; 710.7, guage; 712.21, when dies.; 718.1, grossfater,; 718.9, you; 719.27, [speaker omitted]:; 721.10, *Takes on*,; 724.9 and 23, *lense*; 727.33, tempermental; 731.1, there's hand; 735.15, *sparing*; 737.17 and 22, SHEP:; 737.35, *knees unscrews*; 738.15 (and *passim*), ropend; 741.34, caliber; 744.39, we lost; 753.24 (and *passim*), SARGEANT or SARG.; 755.5, But your; 766.34, Jack's and the Bob's; 771.7, equestrian; 771.11, weigh; 772.8, aeroplanes Wild; 772.20 and 21, Ike's / Al's / Joe's; 774.7, though; 774.38, Sargeant; 776.15, laughed he; 781.33, sometime; 783.12, men you; 787.8, Superintendant; 789.11, COLLYER:; 789.37, Directors; 791.2, gentlemen; 792.33, you; 793.6, enemy we; 794.20, wagers; 794.28, is not; 794.31, am brave; 798.35 (and *passim*), Senor; 799.12, be beat my; 799.18, (*Stops*; 800.21, eights; 802.23, noise; 802.32, pennyless; 802.38, His is; 803.38, merceful.; 804.32, Emporer; 805.5, Has; 805.32, The; 806.26, Maximillian; 806.29, honor; 811.34, and inch; 813.6, sillouhette; 813.6, shoulder's; 813.35, windshild; 814.13, Doc; 817.11, *arguement*; 818.8, of of; 820.10, *quietely*; 821.39, isn't is.; 825.31, growning; 826.3, *wound*; 826.9, then then; 826.27, independants; 826.39, What's is his; 827.14, LUKW:; 829.11, knoes,; 830.14, makde; 830.15, all g; 832.15, Doctor but; 832.21, no But; 832.30, followed on; 832.35, doctors that; 833.8, He'll; 833.13, Luke come; 833.14, Doc How's; 835.12, gettin; 835.40, pummel,; 837.3, kiddin.; 838.12, boy's; 855.18, verisimiltude; 860.29, conficts.; 866.37, order arrive; 868.11, *alike.*

Notes

In the notes below, the reference numbers denote page and line of this volume (the line count includes chapter headings but not blank lines). No note is made for material included in standard desk reference works. For further information on Arthur Miller, see Susan C. W. Abbotson, *Critical Companion to Arthur Miller: A Literary Reference to His Life and Work* (New York: Facts on File, 2007); S. K. Bhatia, *Arthur Miller: Social Drama as Tragedy* (London: Heinemann, 1985); Christopher Bigsby, *Arthur Miller: 1915–1962* (Cambridge: Harvard University Press, 2009) and *Arthur Miller: 1962–2005* (London: Weidenfeld & Nicolson, 2011); Christopher Bigsby, ed., *The Cambridge Companion to Arthur Miller* (Cambridge: Cambridge University Press, 1997); Robert W. Corrigan, ed., *Arthur Miller: A Collection of Critical Essays* (Englewood, NJ: Prentice Hall, 1969); Mel Gussow, *Conversations with Arthur Miller* (London: Nick Hern Books, 2002); Alice Griffin, *Understanding Arthur Miller* (Columbia, SC: University of South Carolina Press, 1996); Robert A. Martin, *Arthur Miller: New Perspectives* (Englewood, NJ: Prentice Hall, 1982); Arthur Miller, *Timebends: A Life* (New York: Grove, 1987); Benjamin Nelson, *Arthur Miller: Portrait of a Playwright* (New York: McKay, 1970); Matthew C. Roudané, ed., *Conversations with Arthur Miller* (Jackson, MS: University Press of Mississippi, 1987); Dennis Welland, *Miller: The Playwright* (London: Methuen, 1979).

I CAN'T REMEMBER ANYTHING

Original cast:

Leo	Mason Adams
Leonora	Geraldine Fitzgerald

Director: Gregory Mosher. Producer: Bernard Gersten. Set: Michael Merritt. Premiered at Lincoln Center, New York, on February 8, 1987 (with *Clara*, as part of the double bill *Danger: Memory!*).

CLARA

Original cast:

Clara Knoll	Karron Graves
Albert Knoll	Kenneth McMillan
Detective Lieutenant Fine	James Tolkan
Tierney	Victor Argo

Director: Gregory Mosher. Producer: Bernard Gersten. Set: Michael
Merritt. Premiered at Lincoln Center, New York, on February 8, 1987
(with *I Can't Remember Anything*, as part of the double bill *Danger:
Memory!*).

45.6   "*Shenandoah.*"] Nineteenth-century American folk song.

THE GOLDEN YEARS

Original leading cast:

Montezuma	Ronald Pickup
Guatemotzin	Kim Wall
Cuitlahua	John Samson
Cagama	Brian Hewlett
Judge	Norman Jones
Tecuichpo	Victoria Carling
Fr. Olmedo	Norman Bird
Cortez	John Shrapnel
Marina	Hannah Gordon
Alvarado	John Hollis
Quauhopoca	Norman Jones

Director: Martin Jenkins. Music: Christos Pittas. Premiered on BBC
Radio 3 on November 6, 1987.

51.1–18   What if the glory . . . *Yeats*] From Yeats's poems "Meditations in
Time of Civil War," "The Tower," and "On a Picture of a Black Centaur by
Edmund Dulac," all published in his collection *The Tower* (1928).

104.38   arquebussiers] Soldiers armed with harquebuses (portable firearms).

ALMOST EVERYBODY WINS

Original cast (Everybody Wins, 1990):

Angela Crispini	Debra Winger
Tom O'Toole	Nick Nolte
Jerry	Will Patton
Connie	Judith Ivey
Amy	Kathleen Wilhoite
Judge Harry Murdoch	Jack Warden
Charley Haggerty	Frank Converse
Felix	Frank Military
Father Mancini	Steven Skybell
Jean	Mary Louise Wilson
Bellanca	Mert Hatfield
Sonny	Peter Appel
Montana	Sean Weil
Defense Attorney	Timothy D. Wright

Judge	Elizabeth Ann Klein
Reporter	James Parisi
Driver	R. M. Haley
Judge #2	T. M. Nelson George

Director: Karel Reisz. Producer: Jeremy Thomas. Music: Mark Isham. Additional music: Leon Redbone. Editor: John Bloom. Production designer: Peter Larkin. Director of photography: Ian Baker. Executive producers: Linda Yellen, Terry Glinwood. Co-producer: Ezra Swerdlow. Premiered on January 19, 1990.

152.35   biography of Joan Crawford] Christina Crawford's *Mommie Dearest*, first published in 1978, controversially depicted her mother as a violent, abusive alcoholic.

THE RIDE DOWN MT. MORGAN

Original cast:

Lyman Felt	Tom Conti
Theo Felt	Gemma Jones
Leah Felt	Clare Higgins
Bessie	Deirdre Strath
Father	Harry Landis
Nurse Logan	Marsha Hunt
Tom Wilson	Manning Redwood

Director: Michael Blakemore. Producer: Robert Fox. Set: Tanya McCallin. Music: Barrington Pheloung. Premiered at the Wyndham Theatre, London, on October 23, 1991.

206.19   Earl Hines] Hines (1903–1983) was a jazz pianist and bandleader.

206.21   "I'm just . . . breeze . . ."] From "Breezin' Along with the Breeze," a popular song (1926) written by Haven Gillespie (1888–1975), Seymour Simons (1896–1949), and Richard Whiting (1891–1938).

236.10–11   Billie Holiday . . . died] Holiday (1915–1959), the widely influential jazz singer, died at forty-four of the effects of drug and alcohol abuse.

238.2–3   "oysterygods and the visigods . . ."] See Book I, Chapter I, of *Finnegans Wake* (1939), by James Joyce (1882–1941): "oystrygods gaggin fishygods."

241.23   segadina goulash] A central European pork and sauerkraut stew.

265.35–37   God's handwriting . . . Emerson.] In an essay on the National Gallery published in *Politics for the People* on May 6, 1848, Charles Kingsley (1819–1875), under the pseudonym "Parson Lot," wrote: "*Never lose an opportunity of seeing anything beautiful.* Beauty is God's hand-writing—a way-side sacrament, welcome it in every fair face, every fair sky, every fair flower, and thank for it *Him*, the fountain of all loveliness, and drink it in, simply and

earnestly, with all your eyes; it is a charmed draft, a cup of blessing." These
sentences have sometimes been misattributed to Emerson.

THE LAST YANKEE

Original cast:

Leroy Hamilton	John Heard
John Frick	Tom Aldredge
Patricia Hamilton	Frances Conroy
Karen Frick	Rose Gregorio
Unnamed patient	Charlotte Maier

Director: John Tillinger. Producer: Manhattan Theatre Club. Set:
John Lee Beatty. Premiered at the Manhattan Theatre Club, New
York, on January 21, 1993.

BROKEN GLASS

Original cast:

Phillip Gellburg	Ron Rifkin
Sylvia Gellburg	Amy Irving
Dr. Harry Hyman	David Dukes
Margaret Hyman	Frances Conroy
Harriet	Lauren Klein
Stanton Case	George N. Martin

Director: John Tillinger. Producers: Robert Whitehead, Roger L. Stevens, Lars Schmidt, Spring Sirkin, Terri Childs, and Timothy Childs in
association with Herb Albert. Music: William Bolcom. Set: Santo Lo-
quasto. Premiered at the Long Wharf Theatre, New Haven, on March 1,
1994, and moved to the Booth Theatre, New York, on April 24, 1994.

325.33   *mishugas*] *Meshugas* (Yiddish): craziness, idiotic behavior or ideas.

351.7   *Anthony Adverse*] Novel (1933) by William Hervey Allen (1889–1949),
filmed in 1936.

THE RYAN INTERVIEW, OR HOW IT WAS AROUND HERE

Original cast:

Reporter	Julie Lauren
Ryan	Mason Adams

Director: Curt Dempster. Assistant director: Anna Basoli. Premiered
at the Ensemble Studio Theatre, New York, on May 3, 1995.

MR. PETERS' CONNECTIONS

Original cast:

Calvin	Jeff Weiss
Harry Peters	Peter Falk

Adele	Erica Bradshaw
Cathy-May	Kris Carr
Larry	Daniel Oreskes
Leonard	Alan Mozes
Rose	Tari Signor
Charlotte	Anne Jackson

Director: Garry Hynes. Producer: Signature Theatre. Set: Francis O'Connor. Premiered at the Signature Theatre, New York, on April 28, 1998.

401.22–23   "September Song,"] Popular song (1938) composed by Kurt Weill (1900–1950) with lyrics by Maxwell Anderson (1888–1959).

409.31   "Just One of Those Things"] Popular song (1935) by Cole Porter (1891–1964).

413.6   "I've got a crush on you, sweetie-pie . . ."] From the song "I've Got a Crush on You" (1928), composed by George Gershwin (1898–1937) with lyrics by Ira Gershwin (1896–1983).

413.12   Mischa Auer . . . Odessa] Auer (1905–1967), the grandson of Hungarian violinist Leopold Auer (1845–1930), was born in St. Petersburg and was principally known as a comic actor in Hollywood films.

415.12   *Certo; non sono sordo?*] Italian: *Sure; I'm not deaf?*

423.36   *"If You Knew Suzie"*] Popular song (1925) written by Buddy DeSylva (1895–1950) and Joseph Meyer (1894–1987).

RESURRECTION BLUES

Original cast:

General Felix Barriaux	John Bedford Lloyd
Henri Schultz	Jeff Weiss
Emily Shapiro	Laila Robins
Skip L. Cheeseboro	David Chandler
Phil	Peter Thoemke
Sarah	Laura Esping
Police Captain	Emil Herrera
Jeanine	Wendy vanden Heuvel
Stanley	Bruce Bohne

Director: David Esbjornson. Producer: Guthrie Theater. Set: Christine Jones. Premiered at the Guthrie Theater, Minneapolis, on August 3, 2002.

FINISHING THE PICTURE

Original cast:

| Edna | Frances Fisher |

Ochsner	Stacy Keach
Kitty	Heather Prete
Derek	Harris Yulin
Flora	Linda Lavin
Case	Scott Glenn
Paul	Matthew Modine
Jerome	Stephen Lang

Director: Robert Falls. Producer: David Richenthal. Set: Thomas Lynch. Premiered at the Goodman Theatre, Chicago, on September 21, 2004.

515.22   Billy the Bomb Martinez] An apparently invented boxer.

THE GRASS STILL GROWS

Original cast: Not known to have been performed.

576.15   Flat on his face like Max Schmeling.] Joe Louis famously defeated Schmeling (1905–2005) for the title of world heavyweight champion on June 22, 1938.

587.26   Clara Bow] American film actress (1905–1965).

620.18   R. H. Macy] Rowland Hussey Macy Sr. (1822–1877), founder of the Macy's department store chain.

638.14–15   *"My Bonnie Came Over the Ocean."*] See "My Bonnie Lies over the Ocean," a Scottish folk song.

638.31   *onion watch*] A large, thick pocket watch.

639.17   Mr. Ickes] Harold L. Ickes (1874–1952), U.S. Secretary of the Interior from 1933 to 1946.

THE HALF-BRIDGE

Original cast: Not known to have been performed.

665.25–28   'The Ship of State . . . *won*."] See Walt Whitman's poem "O Captain! My Captain!" (1865).

695.6   Non comp a mentis tempus fugit] An amalgam of two Latin phrases, *non compos mentis* (not of sound mind) and *tempus fugit* (time flies).

701.32   junker] Young Lord (a German honorific).

706.23   Horace Greeley] Greeley (1811–1872) edited the *New York Tribune* and, in 1872, ran for president.

718.1   grossvater] German: grandfather.

745.26   warum nein] German: why no.

745.31   nicht leben] German: not live.

CAPTAIN PAUL

Original cast:

Announcer	Clayton Collyer
John Paul Jones	Claude Rains
Others	Betty Garde
	Frank Readick
	Kenny Delmar
	Horace Braham
	Ann Starrett
	Karl Swenson
	Jeanette Nolan
	John McIntire

Produced and directed by Homer Fickett. Music by Donald Voorhees. Adapted from *Captain Paul* (1941) by Edward Ellsberg. Premiered on October 27, 1941, in the "Cavalcade of America" series. The text of Miller's last extant typescript of *Captain Paul*, dated September 15, 1941, and printed here, differs substantially from the play as broadcast on October 27. John Driscoll was credited as a co-writer of the broadcast version.

BUFFALO BILL DISREMEMBERS

Original cast: Not known.

Premiered on October 12, 1941, in the series "Hidden History" on the Blue Network of NBC radio. The series was part of the Library of Congress Radio Research Project, funded by the Rockefeller Foundation.

THE BATTLE OF THE OVENS

Original cast:

Christoper Ludwick	Jean Hersholt
Announcer	Clayton Collyer

Produced and directed by Homer Fickett. Music by Donald Voorhees. Premiered on June 12, 1942, in the "Cavalcade of America" series.

THUNDER FROM THE MOUNTAINS

Original cast:

Announcer	Clayton Collyer
Narrator	Orson Welles
1st Ambassador	Ted Jewett
2nd Ambassador	Karl Swenson
3rd Ambassador	Al Shirley
4th Ambassador	Paul Stewart

Juárez	Orson Welles
Felipe	Frank Readick
Don Manuel	Stephen Schnabel
Santa Anna	Ed Jerome
Father	Karl Swenson
Margarita	Arlene Francis
Louis	Ken Delmar
Bernal	Ted Jewett
Comonfort	Paul Stewart
Jose	Stephen Schnabel
Diego	Ken Delmar
Saligny	Karl Swenson
Soldier	Al Shirley
Texan	Will Geer

Produced and directed by Homer Fickett. Music by Donald Voorhees. Adapted from the biography *Juárez, Hero of Mexico* (1942) by Nina Brown Baker. Premiered on September 28, 1942, in the "Cavalcade of America" series. An earlier or working title was "Juarez."

797.27   *B.G.*] Background.

807.4   *finish.*)] At the end of the drama, Collyer introduced "the star of our play," who spoke as follows: "Good evening, this is Orson Welles. It was a great privilege to play Benito Juárez for you this evening. A few weeks ago in Mexico I attended a great celebration in his honor. There were many speakers. The last of these speakers was a humble citizen of the Mexican Republic. He was also a very old man. I will never forget what he said. 'I am 87 years old,' he told us. 'I'm 87 years old, and I have the honor to be one of those who shot and killed the Emperor Ferdinand Maximillian.'"

GLIDER DOCTOR

Original cast:

Narrator	Raymond Massey

Produced and directed by Dee Englebach. Music by Leith Stevens. Premiered on June 20, 1944, on the Columbia Broadcasting System, in the series "The Doctor Fights." The program was followed by an informal address by Major General Norman T. Kirk, Surgeon General of the Army.

MARE ISLAND AND BACK

Original cast:

Doctor Kessler	Robert Montgomery
Henry	Alan Hewitt
Logan	Elliott Lewis
Instructor	Peter Leeds

Produced and directed by Dee Englebach. Music by Leith Stevens. Premiered on June 19, 1945, on the Columbia Broadcasting System, in the series "The Doctor Fights."

NOTES AND ESSAYS ON THE PLAYS

852.40 Captain Shotover's . . . where I am!"] Possibly a confusion of Captain Shotover's line in Act 2 of Shaw's *Heartbreak House* (1919)—"I can't remember what I really am"—with Johnny Tarleton's in Shaw's *Misalliance* (1910), "I confess I like to know where I am."

855.32–33 My own first playwriting . . . prizes] Miller won a Hopwood Award from the University of Michigan for his first play, *No Villain* (1935). He subsequently rewrote the play as *They Too Arise* (1936) and later as *The Grass Still Grows* (1939).

855.34–856.3 I turned at once . . . insane.] Miller's visits to his friend Sid Moscowitz, a psychologist at Jackson Penitentiary, inspired his play *The Great Disobedience* (1938).

857.26–27 "God's teeth . . . cannon."] See Odets's *Golden Boy* (1937).

860.26 "God, . . . O'Casey] O'Neill praised O'Casey's *Within the Gates* in a letter of December 15, 1933: "I wish to God I could write like that!"

861.12–18 As John Gassner . . . into bricks."] Gassner, introducing Synge in the anthology *A Treasury of the Theatre* (1951), quotes from Synge's 1907 preface to *The Playboy of the Western World*.

*This book is set in 10 point ITC Galliard Pro, a
face designed for digital composition by Matthew Carter
and based on the sixteenth-century face Granjon. The paper
is acid-free lightweight opaque and meets the requirements
for permanence of the American National Standards Institute.
The binding material is Brillianta, a woven rayon cloth made
by Van Heek–Scholco Textielfabrieken, Holland.
Composition by Dedicated Book Services. Printing and
binding by Edwards Brothers Malloy, Ann Arbor.
Designed by Bruce Campbell.*